Brown & Marriott's
ADR Principles and Practice

Fourth Edition

Brown & Marriott's ADR Principles and Practice

Fourth Edition

Dr Shirley A. Shipman LLB(Hons), BCL (Oxon), M Phil(Oxon), D Phil(Oxon)
Principal Lecturer in Law, Oxford Brookes University

Benjamin D. Waters MA(Ed)
Solicitor, Senior Lecturer in Law, Canterbury Christ Church University

William Wood QC
Brick Court Chambers, London

Consultant Editor

Henry J. Brown
Solicitor, England and Wales

SWEET & MAXWELL

Published in 2019 by Thomson Reuters, trading as Sweet & Maxwell. Thomson Reuters is registered in England & Wales, Company No.1679046. Registered Office and address for service: 5 Canada Square, Canary Wharf, London, E14 5AQ.

For further information on our products and services, visit *http://www.sweetandmaxwell.co.uk*.

Typeset by Letterpart Limited, Caterham on the Hill, Surrey, CR3 5XL.

Printed and bound by CPI Group (UK) Ltd, Croydon, CR0 4YY.

No natural forests were destroyed to make this product: only farmed timber was used and replanted.

A CIP catalogue record of this book is available from the British Library.

EU material in this publication is acknowledged as © European Union, 1998–2019. Only EU legislation published in the electronic version of the Official Journal of the European Union is deemed authentic.

ISBN: 978-0-414-07185-8

Thomson Reuters, the Thomson Reuters Logo and Sweet & Maxwell ® are trademarks of Thomson Reuters.

Crown copyright material is reproduced with the permission of the Controller of HMSO and the Queen's Printer for Scotland.

All rights reserved. No part of this publication may be reproduced, or transmitted in any form, or by any means, or stored in any retrieval system of any nature, without prior written permission, except for permitted fair dealing under the Copyright, Designs and Patents Act 1988, or in accordance with the terms of a licence issued by the Copyright Licensing Agency in respect of photocopying and/or reprographic reproduction. Application for permission for other use of copyright material, including permission to reproduce extracts in other published works should be made to the publishers. Full acknowledgement of the author, publisher and source must be given.

© 2019 H. J. Brown, S. Shipman, B. Waters & W. Wood QC

In memory of the late Arthur Marriott QC

Foreword

When Frank Sander, Professor Emeritus of Harvard University, coined the phrase "alternative dispute resolution" in his seminal lecture, *The Varieties of Dispute Processing*, at the Pound Conference in St Paul, Minnesota in April 1976, he had in mind the alternatives to litigation as a process for resolving disputes. When he spoke of *"the deadening drag of status quo-ism"* he was referring to the reluctance of both users and practitioners to recognise and take advantage of the alternative processes of ADR because they, the users and practitioners, were, and, alas, to some extent still are, immersed in the only dispute resolution process they knew, namely litigation. His concern—*plus ca change!*—about congested court lists, the heaping of pressure on the judiciary, delays and burgeoning costs caused him to propose entry to a multi-door courtroom where cases were appropriately directed to arbitration, early neutral evaluation, mediation or negotiation. Four decades later, Lord Dyson MR was able to write in his foreword to *The Jackson ADR Handbook*, *"ADR is now a well-established part of every lawyer's practice. ... The effective promotion of ADR is unquestionably in the public interest."* ADR can now justly be seen to be litigation's invaluable twin. As Lord Neuberger of Abbotsbury explains:

> "Promoting and facilitating the use of ADR for those cases where it will be of genuine advantage to the parties, because of, for instance, its informality, the flexibility of its processes and the availability of remedies not available to the litigation process, is of benefit not only to those litigants but also to the justice system. It is of benefit because it ensures that only those cases which truly call for, truly require, formal adjudication utilise the limited resources available to the justice system."

Leading the way in educating users, lawyers, judges and even the government and, of course, the mediators themselves is this towering work, now in its fourth edition. It is a privilege to have been invited to write this foreword.

No one can sensibly doubt today that mediation is a vital tool in the administration of justice. Commercial arbitration in the City of London has won world-wide acclaim and is flourishing. After a slow start, Family practitioners are beginning to see the merits of Family arbitration, especially where the parties wish for privacy. Forms of early neutral evaluation have their place in the Technology and Construction Court with its adjudication process and in the Family Courts with their Financial Dispute Resolution hearings. The biannual review conducted by CEDR confirms the growing use and value of civil mediation. Family justice had to acknowledge the benefits of early use of Mediation Information and Assessment Meetings (MIAMs). In the Employment

FOREWORD

Tribunals the success of Early Conciliation has been startling in reducing the workload for that Tribunal. In the Tribunal system generally more and more specialist mediation schemes are being promoted, for example for Special Education Needs. The NHS Litigation Authority has made huge savings in costs by promoting the early use of mediation in clinical negligence cases. The possibilities for Restorative Justice to reduce the prison population, and more importantly, to reduce the rate of recidivism are gradually beginning to dawn. What not so long ago might have been regarded as an esoteric aberration is now accepted in our law schools as a proper and necessary subject in its own right. A good start with the young is being made by introducing peer group mediation in our schools. Thus the landscape for the use of mediation continues to widen.

What more needs to be done? All departments of government can be reminded of the "Mediation Pledge" given by the Lord Chancellor, Lord Irvine of Lairg. Self-interest should prompt overworked, stressed trial judges to be more robust in staying cases in their list for the parties to pursue mediation. The Court of Appeal should gird its loins and review *Halsey v Milton Keynes General NHS Trust* [2004] 1 WLR 3002 and express whole-hearted support for the enlightened views of Briggs LJ, as he then was, in *PGF II SA v OMFS Co 1 Ltd* [2013] EWCA Civ 12 in preference to the Hazel Gennish views of Patten LJ in *Gore v Naheed* [2017] EWCA Civ 369. Some lawyers still need to be persuaded that the client who can live with a compromise of his claim may be a happier client than one who has been fed with the myth that he had a humdinging certain winner only to find him losing everything and paying his hated opponent's costs to boot. Warring neighbours should be told that one cannot be at peace with oneself whilst one is at war with one's enemies. All disputants should be reminded of the saintly Nelson Mandela's advice that if one wants to make peace with one's enemy, one must talk to the enemy because once you begin to talk to your enemy, you can become a partner with your enemy and as partners you can find the solution which works best for the partnership.

What more can mediators do for themselves? Perhaps they should embrace the desirability of some mediation for mediators, all too many of whom cling onto control of their little patch with all the fervour of the neighbours from hell who threaten a boundary action for the encroachment of an inch. What hope is there for the world of mediation before it can so organise itself as to be in a position to claim to be a profession with a proper governing body, some effective, if light, regulation and an enforceable disciplinary code? How can it be a profession without a single body at its head to speak for and on behalf of ALL forms of mediation? When will we have a Mediation Council as the umbrella organisation under which Civil Mediation, Family Mediation, Restorative Justice and the fragment organisations offering their valuable community and workplace mediation can all find shelter and speak with one voice?

This invaluable work shows the way. It covers all forms of ADR. It encouragingly points out that each form of ADR can learn something from the other and that strides are being made across the board to emphasise that more unites the different branches than divides them. Lessons can be learnt from every page. The ADR community must give thanks to the authors and the consulting editor for this book no self-respecting mediator can be without. The work's authority is self-evident. Two eminent mediation academics, Ben Waters and

FOREWORD

Shirley Shipman, and a vastly experienced practitioner, Bill Wood QC, together with the doyen of the mediation world, Henry Brown, ensure Premier League status for the fourth edition of *ADR: Principles and Practice*. I unreservedly commend this book to you.

Sir Alan Ward
Chairman of the Civil Mediation Council
June 2018

Preface

In the foreword to the first edition of this book Sir Thomas Bingham, then Master of the Rolls, wrote that we in Britain have been late starters to the field of ADR. He observed that the book drew liberally on the experiences of other countries from which we in the UK have over the years learnt so much. The preface to the first edition, however, mentioned the scepticism with which ADR as an American import had been treated in some circles. With the arrival of the fourth edition of this book, we can justifiably claim that ADR has come a long way in the intervening twenty-five years. It continues to learn from other jurisdictions and evolve, but it is true to say that ADR in the UK has, in its various forms, gained traction and become more accepted as part of the mainstream of dispute resolution. Processes such as arbitration, mediation, adjudication and ombudsman are undoubtedly becoming more widely used as a replacement for (not simply an adjunct to) the formal litigation processes. The "A" in ADR can now arguably be signified as "appropriate" rather than "alternative" in terms of dispute resolution process choice. Although reference is made to other jurisdictions throughout this book, the overseas influence is less evident in the new edition and is perhaps indicative of the distinctive identity which ADR has created for itself in the UK.

Since the first edition, the UK has witnessed three major civil justice reviews, two reviews of legal education and a detailed review of ADR by a Working Group of the Civil Justice Council. Not to mention the legislation (including the Access to Justice Act 1999 and the Legal Aid Sentencing and Punishment of Offenders Act 2012 (LASPO)), which has in various ways had a profound impact on attitudes and approaches to dispute resolution generally. Access to justice in terms of achieving dispute resolution for civil and family disputes has been compromised by government policy over the past decade. Prior to publication of this book's third edition, Lord Justice Jackson's Report: *Review of Civil Litigation Costs*, published in 2009, included a review of case management procedures with regard to litigation costs and funding. Jackson consulted widely and compared the costs regime in England and Wales with those of other jurisdictions. Many of his recommendations have been realised through primary legislation and, in particular, Pt 2 of LASPO which abolished the Legal Services Commission and replaced it with a Legal Aid Agency now administered by the Ministry of Justice. As a result, legal aid has been further restricted and controversially withdrawn from areas such as private family law. The only circumstances in which a party involved in a relationship or marriage breakdown might be eligible for legal aid assistance now is where issues of domestic violence or abuse exist. Public funding does however currently remain available

PREFACE

for family mediation. Nevertheless, the scope of legal aid has been greatly narrowed, to the extent that few areas remain eligible for civil legal aid support.

Emphasising ADR's importance within the dispute resolution continuum, a whole chapter of Lord Justice Jackson's report was reserved for ADR and its utility in the resolution of civil disputes in the UK. This included the recommendation that a serious campaign to ensure that all litigation lawyers and judges are properly informed about the benefits which ADR can bring and that the public and small businesses should be alerted to the benefits of ADR. Whilst perhaps there is growing ADR awareness in the UK, it is arguable that Jackson's vision in this regard remains to be fulfilled. The recommendation that an authoritative handbook should be prepared, explaining clearly and concisely what ADR is and giving details of all reputable providers of mediation, has however been adopted and the *Jackson ADR Handbook*, by Blake, Browne and Sime, first published in 2013, is a definitive practical guide to the use and operation of ADR, with a particular focus on mediation.

Mandatory mediation continues to be debated, but no significant changes have been made in that regard. There have, however, been important changes in the area of private family law in relation to dispute resolution. The Mediation Information and Assessment Meeting (MIAM) was initially introduced as being an expectation for parties in marriage or relationship breakdown seeking a court order (to deal with the financial and/or children arrangements) to meet with a trained family mediator, first to learn about mediation, and secondly to see if they are suitable for it. Since April 2014 this has become a requirement. In the area of employment law, updated Tribunal Rules introduced by secondary legislation set out a new duty for the Employment Tribunal to encourage the use of ADR, including ACAS conciliation, mediation and judicial mediation.

Extension of the MIAM principle to the county courts has been under consideration by the Ministry of Justice, by making mediation a mandatory requirement in small claims disputes, with a widened jurisdiction from £5,000 to £10,000 or perhaps £15,000 but this has not materialised. However, we do acknowledge that HMCTS has expanded and centralised its Small Claims Mediation Service. All cases with a dispute value of up to £10,000 are now automatically referred to mediation, without judicial intervention, where all parties request it.

This fourth edition also covers various other developments since the previous edition was published. These include the following:

- Case law, practice models and organisational and regulatory structures in various fields, particularly civil-commercial and family mediation practice, have developed over the last seven years, and ADR processes have become more integrated into the judicial process. For example, in the family field there has been greater recognition of the value of meeting parties separately and confidentially as well as jointly, where appropriate.
- Information Communication Technology (ICT), other technology and online processes have all developed since publication of the third edition, which has had an impact on dispute resolution processes. Chapter 20 on ODR (Online Dispute Resolution) has been substantially updated and amplified to take account of these changes.

PREFACE

- Lord Briggs' Interim and Final reports on his Civil Courts Structure Review set out his vision for an online court in which ADR is prompted and encouraged from the outset and, in the middle stage Tier 2, a Case Officer guides the parties in making appropriate ADR choices. The Money Claims Online system currently being developed and trialled is the first step towards the implementation of that approach.
- The Final Report of the Civil Justice Council's ADR working group is awaited but its work and its interim report have already generated significant discussion over compulsion and the current measures for the encouragement of ADR.
- The new Ch.18 reflects the fact that Ombudsman referrals (both in the public and private sectors) have increased significantly, making this probably the most-used ADR process in the UK. Its range and usage in a number of different fields have extended and it has also benefited from the development and integration of ADR schemes.
- The UK's Brexit decision will inevitably impact on dispute resolution processes, for example with regard to EU Directives. While the details of this cannot yet be anticipated, some preliminary consideration is given to this in Ch.22, Future Directions.
- In Ch.22 we acknowledge that ADR is becoming increasingly integrated into legal education and training in the UK and many other countries, and this edition has attempted to produce a more rigorous academic approach to the way it is presented, making it useful to academic institutions while at the same time maintaining its practical and pragmatic approach considered so valuable to practitioners. Important changes to solicitors' education and training are about to occur with the introduction of the Solicitors Qualification Examination. This is important for this book as the proposed syllabus, if implemented in its current form, includes aspects of dispute resolution, which will be a legal education requirement for the first time.

We should explain our new authorship of this fourth edition. Following the death of Arthur Marriott in 2015 and Henry Brown's retirement from mediation practice, Henry and the publishers asked us to take over as co-authors on the basis that Henry would act as the Consulting Editor. We were happy to undertake this collaboration and we are indebted to Henry for coordinating the editing in a consultancy capacity and for facilitating this transition so smoothly. Henry is also thanked for a greater contribution than perhaps originally anticipated and particularly for his contribution to the re-writing of significant areas of this fourth edition.

There are many people we should like to acknowledge for their help and support with this fourth edition. The publishing team at Sweet & Maxwell have been most helpful, and our special thanks go to Sohini Banerjee for her constructive help and support, also to Katherine Brewer and Skye O'Neill and the rest of the editorial team. A number of people have made valuable and much appreciated contributions to this edition, including Lisa Parkinson, Cressida Burnett, Angela Lake-Carroll and Elizabeth Rivers. Our thanks go to all of them. We are also most grateful to Sir Alan Ward for his foreword to this edition. Sir

PREFACE

Alan himself has made a huge contribution to the development of ADR in the UK and continues to be a strong supporter of the process and its development.

Finally, we join with Henry Brown in paying tribute to the late Arthur Marriott, co-author of the first three editions of this book, whose contribution to ADR was enormous. He will be particularly remembered for his significant role in the development and reform of English arbitration law as Chairman of a private group whose work led to the passing of the Arbitration Act 1996. A Deputy High Court Judge for England and Wales, a Recorder and President of Mental Health Review Tribunals, his legal role and significance were marked by his appointment as one of the two first solicitors ever to have been appointed as Queen's Counsel. He will be much missed and warmly remembered.

Ben Waters, Shirley Shipman and Bill Wood QC

TABLE OF CONTENTS

	PAGE
Foreword	vii
Preface	xi
Table of Cases	xxxi
Table of Statutes	xxxvii
Table of Treaties and Conventions	xxxix
Table of Arbitration and Practice Rules	xli
Table of Rules of Court	xliii
Table of Codes, Protocols and Guidance Notes	xlv

	PARA
1. Analysing ADR	
Introduction	1–001
"Alternative"	1–006
"Dispute"	1–013
Distinguishing dispute and conflict: the paradox	1–022
Submerged issues in disputes	1–028
Why only disputes anyway?	1–031
"Resolution"	1–032
Dispute resolution or settlement?	1–034
Dispute management or other intervention	1–039
Dispute resolution: transformation	1–042
Conflict resolution and other interventions	1–047
ADR reconstituted	1–052
2. An Overview of the ADR Landscape	
Introduction	2–001
Litigation and negotiation: the ADR symbiosis	2–010
The spectrum of processes from consensual to adjudicatory	2–014
Outline of the processes	2–016
Litigation	2–017
Private judging	2–018
Administrative or statutory tribunals	2–019
Arbitration	2–020
Court-annexed arbitration	2–021
Expert determination	2–022
Adjudication	2–023
Dispute Board	2–024
Ombudsman	2–025

CONTENTS

    Arb-Med 2–026
    Med-Arb 2–027
    Evaluation/Early neutral evaluation (ENE) 2–028
    Neutral fact-finding expert 2–029
    Mini-trial (Executive Tribunal) 2–030
    Negotiation (through representatives) 2–031
    Collaborative practice 2–032
    Mediation (involving evaluative element) 2–033
    Mediation (purely facilitative) 2–034
    Conciliation 2–035
    Negotiation (by parties personally) 2–036
Standard or bespoke processes 2–037
    Using the standard models and designing bespoke processes 2–042
Some further considerations for the development of ADR 2–046

3. ADR Philosophies and Motivation: Common Values and Differences
A broad church 3–001
Shared values and motivation 3–004
    The principle of negotiated agreement 3–006
    Facilitating resolution 3–012
    Personal empowerment and self-determination 3–015
    Creative and flexible decision-making 3–020
    Potential for healing and relationship preservation 3–026
    Maintaining ethical values 3–030
    Providing a confidential and secure environment 3–034
    Attributes, skills and sensitivity 3–036
    Seeking a beneficial outcome 3–039
    Overcoming the cost and delays of litigation 3–041
Differences of practice and philosophy 3–043
    Different fields of activity 3–044
    Different models of practice 3–045
    Evaluative or facilitative mediation 3–048
    Settlement-geared or problem-solving mediation 3–050
    Transformative and related approaches 3–052
    Other models and schools of thought 3–054
    Intervention and directiveness 3–055
Defining the processes 3–058
The momentum towards ADR 3–062
Conclusion 3–068

4. Negotiation
Negotiation—the primary tool 4–001
Theories of negotiation 4–003
An interest-based problem-solving approach
    Getting to Yes 4–004
    Underlying needs 4–011
    Creating value 4–012

Principled rejection 4–016
Designing creative solutions 4–020
Competitive theory 4–021
The "essential tension" between interest-based and competitive
approaches 4–026
Other theories and models 4–028
Some practical aspects of negotiation 4–033
    Whether or not to negotiate 4–034
    Preparation and set-up 4–037
    Zone of Possible Agreement and the negotiation dance 4–040
    Opening the negotiations 4–043
    Responses to proposals 4–047
    Continuing the negotiations 4–051
Skills, Strategies and Style 4–056
Power, Culture and Gender
    Power 4–059
Culture, gender and values 4–065
    Gender 4–067
    Values 4–071
Perceptions and psychology 4–072
Good Faith in Negotiation
    Theoretical Principles 4–076
    Legal Principles 4–077
    Good faith in ADR 4–078
    Duty to perform in good faith? 4–081
        Good faith in the ADR context 4–086
The neutral negotiation role 4–090

5. ADR and the Courts
Introduction 5–001
Rules, practice directions and protocols 5–002
    Civil Procedure Rules (CPR) 5–003
    Family Procedure Rules 2010 (FPR) 5–006
    Pre-action protocols 5–009
    Family pre-application protocol 5–012
Courts adopting ADR processes 5–013
    Court Settlement Process and ENE: The Technology and
    Construction Court 5–014
    Financial Dispute Resolution (FDR) 5–019
    The Small Claims Mediation Service 5–021
    Judges as mediators 5–024
        Issues around judges as mediators 5–028
Court-attached mediation by independent mediators 5–032
    County Court mediation schemes 5–034
    The Exeter small claims scheme 5–036
    The Court of Appeal mediation scheme (CAMS) 5–039
    Mediation Information and Assessment Meetings (MIAMs)
        Family proceedings 5–043

CONTENTS

Civil proceedings 5–046
Courts directing or recommending ADR processes 5–048
Courts imposing sanctions where ADR is not attempted........................ 5–061
Courts acting as a gateway to ADR (The Multi-Door Courthouse) 5–067
Mandatory ADR and human rights: the Article 6 argument..................... 5–072
Court-annexed arbitration 5–077
   Non-binding court-annexed arbitration... 5–079
   Adapting court-annexed arbitration principles 5–084
Court-attached ADR in some other jurisdictions 5–086
   United States 5–087
   Canada 5–089
   Australia 5–090
   Germany 5–092
   Denmark 5–095
   Japan 5–096
   China 5–099
   Singapore 5–100
   India 5–102
Conclusions 5–104

6. Arbitration

Introduction 6–001
The International Structure 6–007
The Arbitration Act of 1996 (England, Wales and Northern
Ireland) 6–011
The essential features of arbitration
   Agreement between the parties to arbitrate 6–014
   Appointment and impartiality of arbitrator 6–020
   Jurisdictional seat of the arbitration... 6–026
   Procedural freedom 6–028
   A binding award 6–035
   Costs 6–040
Amiable Composition and Ex Aequo et Bono Arbitration 6–045
Arbitration-related settlement 6–048
Arbitration of some particular kinds of disputes
   International investment disputes: ICSID 6–052
   Consumer disputes 6–058
   Family law arbitration 6–061

7. Contractual Adjudication and Other Adjudicatory Processes

Introduction 7–001
Contractual adjudication 7–002
   Common threads 7–003
   Statutory provision 7–004
   Outline of the adjudication process 7–008
   Adjudication in context... 7–012
Dispute Boards 7–014
   The Dispute Board concept... 7–017

CONTENTS

Examples of Dispute Boards..7–024
Expert determination...7–025
   Areas of application 7–027
   Procedural outline and discretion 7–031
   Finality of determination..7–036
   Distinguishing expert determination from single joint experts............7–043
   Distinguishing expert determination from arbitration 7–046
Administrative or statutory tribunals 7–051
   A range of administrative tribunals 7–056
Private judging...7–059

8. Mediation—General Principles
What is mediation—and who decides? 8–001
   What is "real" mediation?..8–009
   Conciliation and mediation 8–012
The principles of mediation 8–020
   The use of a mediator 8–021
   Impartiality or neutrality..8–027
   Facilitation..8–033
   Party self-determination 8–038
   Secure environment: Confidentiality and evidential privilege..............8–044
   Authority derived from the parties 8–047
   Consensual decision-making..8–048
   Dispute or conflict resolution or management as the objective............8–050
   Accommodating the conflict dynamic: containing escalation 8–054
   Empowerment of the parties 8–059

9. Mediation—Practice Overview
Different models: the strands of practice...9–001
   Rights-based or interest-based mediation 9–004
   Pure facilitation or an evaluative component.....................................9–009
   Settlement-geared process...9–012
   Therapeutic mediation process 9–014
   Transformative mediation 9–016
   Other models 9–020
The stages of mediation 9–024
   Pre-mediation: 9–029
   During mediation: 9–030
   Post-mediation:...9–031
Pre-mediation: Considering mediation, assessing suitability and
obtaining commitment 9–032
   Providing information: 9–033
   Considerations affecting the decision to mediate................................9–034
   Assessing suitability...9–037
   Obtaining commitment—the contract to mediate 9–039
   When does the mediation start?...9–044

CONTENTS

During the Mediation: Stage 1: Preliminary communications and preparation 9–048
    Preliminary communications 9–049
    Preliminary meeting 9–052
    Preparation 9–056
Stage 2: Commencement, establishing the issues and setting the agenda 9–057
    The issues as presented 9–059
    Underlying issues: the "iceberg" factor 9–063
    The mediator's working principles 9–066
Stage 3: Information gathering 9–068
    Displaying information: the flip-chart 9–069
    How much information is enough? 9–070
Stage 4: Conducting substantive negotiations 9–072
    Managing the process 9–073
    Facilitation 9–075
    Holding joint or separate meetings (caucuses) 9–077
    Generating and developing options 9–078
    Brainstorming 9–080
    Building trust and understanding 9–083
    Using communication and other skills 9–085
    Testing perceptions, positions and proposals 9–087
    Sensitivity to the expression of emotions 9–091
    Evaluation 9–094
Stage 5: Dealing with impasse 9–095
    The mediator's role and assumptions 9–098
    Blocks caused by terminology or symbolism 9–099
    Differences of perception: fairness, values and other aspects 9–103
    Emotional blocks 9–105
    Conflicting legal or technical advice 9–108
    Helping parties to assess risk 9–110
    Other strategies 9–113
Stage 6: Concluding mediation and recording the outcome 9–116
Addressing post-mediation issues 9–119
Multi-party disputes 9–120
    Some practical points for multi-party mediation 9–123
Outline of different fields of mediation activity 9–127

10. Civil and Commercial Mediation

What is covered in the field of civil and commercial mediation? 10–001
Development of civil-commercial mediation in the UK
    Private sector civil-commercial mediation bodies 10–005
    Low cost and publicly funded mediation 10–009
    Specialist civil and commercial mediators 10–011
    The Civil Mediation Council 10–014
Lawyers and rights in civil and commercial mediation 10–015
The stages of civil and commercial mediation 10–020

CONTENTS

Pre-Mediation: Considering mediation, assessing suitability and
obtaining commitment 10–022
    Raising public and professional awareness 10–023
    ADR pledges and contract clauses 10–025
    Judicial encouragement and orders 10–031
    Preliminary meetings 10–032
    Assessing suitability 10–034
    Providing information 10–037
    Trade and other associations 10–043
    Agreement to mediate 10–044
Stage 1: Preliminary communications and preparation
    Preliminary communications or meeting 10–049
    Establishing the venue 10–062
    Facilities at the venue 10–067
    Legal representation 10–069
    Authority of corporate representatives 10–071
Stage 2: Commencement, establishing the issues and setting the
agenda 10–073
    Opening the mediation session 10–075
    Establishing the issues: oral presentations 10–077
    Setting the agenda 10–080
Stage 3: Information gathering 10–083
    The written case summaries 10–086
    The bundles of documents 10–091
    Establishing underlying views and concerns 10–095
    Other information required 10–098
    Acquiring specialist information 10–099
Stage 4: Conducting substantive negotiations 10–100
    The first separate meetings 10–104
    Initiating discussions and negotiations 10–107
    Option development and reality testing 10–110
    Shuttle mediation 10–115
    Working with parties' lawyers and other professionals 10–118
    Arranging a series of meetings 10–123
    Dealing with emotions: the myth of rationality in civil and
    commercial disputes 10–127
    Other permutations of meetings and ways of working 10–135
    Using facilitation and communication skills 10–136
    Adopting an evaluative mode 10–139
Stage 5: Dealing with impasse 10–142
    Addressing risk perception 10–143
    BATNA and WATNA 10–152
    Examining underlying issues 10–154
    Exploring creative options 10–156
    Symbolism 10–158
    Brackets 10–160
    Adjournment for non-binding third-party evaluation of an
    issue 10–162

Making non-binding settlement proposals..................................10–164
Other strategies..10–169
Preparing for adjudication..10–173
Adjournment and "after-care"..10–175
Stage 6: Concluding mediation and recording the outcome 10–176
Addressing post-mediation issues.......................................10–184
Deal mediation 10–188

11. Divorce and Other Family Mediation
Introduction...11–001
Overview of family mediation in the UK
    Brief history...11–004
    Mediation and conciliation through the courts 11–012
    Financial Dispute Resolution (FDR).................................11–015
    The Family Mediation Council (FMC).............................11–017
    Family Mediation Standards Board (FMSB)....................11–019
    Mediation Information and Assessment Meetings (MIAMs)............11–020
Counselling/psychotherapy...11–022
Sole or anchor mediation and co-mediation 11–028
Lawyers and rights in family mediation 11–031
    Lawyers as mediators 11–038
Including children and young people in mediation and dispute
resolution processes...11–040
Issues around mediating with domestic violence or abuse
    Abuse between the couple..11–050
    Child abuse 11–058
Professional consultancy or supervision 11–061
Mediating unmarried cohabiting couples.............................11–065
Family issues other than separation and divorce 11–067
The stages of family mediation...11–069
Pre-Mediation: Considering mediation, assessing suitability and
obtaining commitment..11–070
    Intake sessions and MIAMs...11–074
    Preliminary meeting with lawyers 11–077
    The Agreement to Mediate..11–079
During the Mediation: Stage 1: Preliminary communications and
preparation 11–081
Stage 2: Commencing the mediation, establishing the issues and
setting the agenda..11–087
Stage 3: Information gathering..11–097
Stage 4: Conducting substantive negotiations 11–105
    Option development 11–106
    Providing information...11–110
    Using communication skills 11–113
    Dealing with the expression of emotions.......................11–114
    Managing the process 11–118
    Helping with reality testing 11–120
    Facilitating negotiations and decision-making................11–122

CONTENTS

Children's issues and parenting plans 11–126
Separate meetings (caucuses): using the "hybrid" model 11–128
Stage 5: Dealing with impasse 11–131
Pausing and reflecting 11–132
Allow the parties to absorb the progress 11–133
Addressing underlying fears and concerns 11–134
Addressing unresolved emotional blocks... 11–136
Dealing with cyclical patterns of behaviour 11–139
Considering perceptions of fairness 11–140
Recognising the power of words and symbolism............................... 11–142
Short term experiments and reviews... 11–145
Managing differences of legal perception.. 11–146
Using draft summaries.. 11–147
Risk assessment (BATNA/WATNA) 11–149
Separate meetings (caucuses)... 11–153
Family arbitration 11–154
Preparing for adjudication 11–155
Stage 6: Concluding mediation and recording the outcome
Concluding the mediation 11–156
Preparing summaries and memoranda 11–160
Concluding formalities 11–166
Addressing post-mediation issues 11–169

12. Neighbourhood and Community Mediation and Restorative Justice

Introduction to Neighbourhood and Community Mediation................. 12–001
Neighbour disputes.. 12–007
Noise problems... 12–008
Verbal abuse or harassment... 12–009
Children's behaviour 12–010
Pets and other animals 12–011
Boundary issues 12–012
Eyesores and other environmental issues 12–013
Parking and other neighbour issues... 12–014
Mediation of social conflicts and inter-group disputes 12–015
Mediation in schools and peer mediation... 12–016
Elder mediation 12–023
Gang mediation 12–024
UK gang mediation developments.. 12–027
Other community mediation 12–032
Community mediation services... 12–033
The mediation process in community disputes 12–037
Pre-Mediation: Considering mediation, assessing suitability and
obtaining commitment 12–040
During the mediation: Stage 1: Preliminary communications and
preparation.. 12–045
Stage 2: Commencement establishing the issues and setting the
agenda... 12–049

Stage 3: Information gathering 12–056
Stage 4: Conducting substantive negotiations 12–058
Stage 5: Dealing with impasse...12–063
Stage 6: Concluding mediation and recording the outcome 12–066
Addressing post-mediation issues..12–069
General observations 12–070
Introductory overview of restorative justice..12–074
Restorative justice 12–080
    Restorative justice: the rationale..12–083
    Victim-offender programmes 12–088
    Restorative cautioning..12–091
    Restorative justice for young offenders...12–093
    Kinds of offences dealt with by restorative justice
    programmes 12–095
Restorative practices 12–102
    Family Group Conferencing and youth restorative justice 12–103
    Circles...12–108
    Restorative practice in schools 12–109

13. Workplace and Employment Dispute Resolution
Brief UK historical background...13–001
Acas...13–005
Processes and terminology...13–007
    Conciliation 13–008
    Mediation..13–012
    Arbitration 13–014
    Employment and workplace issues distinguished 13–015
Rationale for ADR in employment and workplace disputes.................13–017
Conciliation practice and procedure 13–022
    Individual conciliation 13–023
    Collective conciliation 13–028
    Settlement (Compromise) agreements...13–032
Mediation practice..13–034
Stage 1: Preliminary communications and preparation.........................13–038
Stage 2: Commencement, establishing the issues and setting the
agenda...13–042
Stage 3: Information gathering 13–044
Stage 4: Conducting substantive negotiations 13–047
Stage 5: Dealing with impasse...13–052
Stage 6: Concluding mediation and recording the outcome 13–058
Post-Mediation 13–060
Collective mediation 13–062
Employment arbitration 13–064

CONTENTS

14. Mediator Attributes, Skills and Roles
Introduction 14–001
The concept of the construct 14–007
    Foundational knowledge
        Theoretical understanding 14–008
        Practical skills 14–009
        Ethical awareness 14–011
    Desirable attributes 14–019
        Sound judgment 14–020
        Sensitivity and empathy 14–023
    Leadership traits or style 14–031
        Creativity 14–033
        Flexibility 14–036
        Balance 14–039
Mediation skills 14–042
    Listening 14–043
    Observing non-verbal communications 14–046
    Helping parties to hear 14–049
    Questioning 14–052
    Summarising 14–055
    Acknowledging 14–057
    Mutualising 14–061
    Using language effectively and reframing 14–064
    Use of metaphor 14–069
    Normalising 14–073
    Managing conflict and the expression of emotions 14–075
    Lateral thinking 14–083
    Understanding triangulation and avoiding alliances 14–085
    Encouraging a problem-solving mode 14–092
    Being silent 14–095
    Constructive facilitation 14–098
The mediator's roles and functions 14–102
    The mediator as manager of the process 14–103
    The mediator as information gatherer 14–105
    The mediator as facilitator 14–106
    The mediator as reality tester and evaluator 14–107
    The mediator as host 14–112
    The mediator as scribe 14–117
    The mediator as settlement supervisor 14–118
Mediator Training 14–119

15. Confidentiality and Privilege
Introduction 15–001
Confidentiality
    General principles 15–012
    Confidentiality in ADR 15–022
        Confidentiality of matters dealt with in the process 15–023
        Confidentiality of separate meetings or caucuses 15–032

CONTENTS

Some general principles where confidentiality is not applicable...15–036
Privilege...15–037
   Professional privilege...15–048
   Without prejudice..15–053
   Reconciliation..15–068
   Mediation about children...15–072
   Part 36 of the Civil Procedure Rules: Without prejudice save as to costs..15–075
   Employment conciliation provision, family court practice..........15–076
Court excluding confidentiality and privilege....................................15–079
   The court stipulates for mediation and wishes to know what happened...15–080
   Allegations are made of fraud, misrepresentation, economic duress or undue influence...15–088
   The court wishes to determine whether an agreement was concluded...15–094
   Where there is an allegation of negligence...............................15–097
   Where the court wishes to interpret an agreement....................15–103
Proceeds of Crime Act 2002...15–106
Contracting for confidentiality and privilege....................................15–114
Privilege and confidentiality under the EU Directive.......................15–118
A mediation privilege?...15–123
   The mediator's position...15–138
   Clarification and reform..15–142

16. Ethics, Values, Fairness and Power

Introduction..16–001
Rules of underlying professional bodies...16–010
   The Law Society of England and Wales and the Solicitors Regulation Authority
      General provisions..16–012
      Specific mediation provisions..16–017
      The Law Society's Mediation Panels..................................16–019
   The Bar..16–020
ADR Ethics and Codes of Practice...16–021
The practitioner's values, attitudes and beliefs
   The concept of neutrality...16–026
   Personal values, attitudes and beliefs..16–028
      Attitude to conflict...16–030
      Rationality-emotionality..16–032
      Values, beliefs and assumptions..16–036
Fairness
   Fairness of process or fairness of outcome................................16–039
   What constitutes fairness?
      The parties' views guiding fairness.....................................16–044
      Legal principles guiding fairness...16–046
      Workability guiding fairness...16–048

CONTENTS

Legal representation guiding fairness 16–049
Other fairness considerations 16–050
Manifest unfairness 16–051
Conflicts of interest 16–052
Regulating conflicts of interest and perceived conflicts 16–054
The wider net covering conflicts and perceived conflicts 16–057
Absolute and relative bars to mediating by reason of conflicts
and perceived conflicts 16–060
Absolute bar to mediating 16–062
Qualified bar to mediating 16–065
Conflicts or perceived conflicts arising or identified after
mediation has started 16–067
Changing roles after the conclusion of mediation 16–069
Ethics of Confidentiality 16–071
Ethics of confidentiality in ADR generally 16–072
Ethics of confidentiality in private meetings 16–079
Disclosure of information from separate meeting into joint
meeting 16–081
Agreement to maintain confidentiality of separate meetings 16–085
Separate meetings with special rules 16–090
Power imbalances
Forms of power 16–093
Power imbalances: the mediator's role 16–099
Should a mediator try to redress a power imbalance? 16–101
What steps could a mediator take to redress power
imbalances? 16–109
Mediator cautions 16–117
When mediation is inappropriate 16–118
When mediation needs to proceed with caution or reservation 16–119
Conclusion 16–121

17. Lawyers' Role Representing Parties in Mediation
Introduction 17–001
Differences between civil-commercial and family mediation 17–004
Specialist mediation advocacy 17–007
Deciding on the mediation forum 17–009
Is the dispute suitable for mediation? 17–010
What kind of mediation is required? 17–018
Does the mediator need to be an expert? 17–020
Commercial and civil disputes 17–022
Family issues 17–025
Engaging the other party in mediation 17–030
Understanding the mediation process 17–032
The Pre-Mediation Phase 17–034
Preliminary meetings 17–035
Selecting a mediator 17–037
The agreement to mediate 17–040

CONTENTS

The Substantive Mediation Phase
    Preliminary meetings and communications 17–041
    Dealing with the documentation
        Civil-commercial disputes 17–043
        Family issues 17–048
    Preparation
        Civil-commercial cases 17–050
        Family cases 17–053
    The substantive meeting 17–055
        Presentation of the case in civil commercial mediation 17–057
        Presentations in family mediation 17–061
    Providing information 17–063
    Negotiating and communicating during the mediation 17–064
    Strategies 17–069
    The lawyer's role during substantive family mediation 17–071
    Drafting and formalising 17–075
    Vetting family mediation proposals 17–080
The Post-Mediation Phase 17–085

18. Ombudsman
The ombudsman concept 18–001
    The ombudsman's role and function 18–004
    The range of ombudsman institutions 18–007
How the ombudsman operates
    Ombudsman procedures 18–012
    Remedies 18–021
Online and communication ombudsmen and adjudicators 18–023
EU Directive on Consumer ADR: Implications for ombudsmen 18–030
Ombudsman developments, challenges and criticisms 18–035
Complaints adjudication 18–041

19. Non-Binding Evaluative ADR and Hybrid Processes
Introduction to non-binding evaluation 19–001
Reasons for evaluating 19–005
What constitutes neutral evaluation? 19–011
Some considerations relevant to neutral non-binding evaluation 19–018
Evaluation in mediation 19–019
    No idea of the parameters 19–022
    Deadlocked by differing outcome perceptions 19–025
    Opposition to evaluation in mediation 19–029
The mini-trial (Executive Tribunal)
    The mini-trial concept 19–032
    The mini-trial procedure
        Appointment of neutral adviser 19–037
        Preparation 19–040
        The conduct of the mini-trial 19–042
        The neutral adviser's role 19–043
        The settlement negotiations 19–047

CONTENTS

    Kinds of cases suitable for mini-trial 19–050
    Timing of mini-trial usage 19–053
    General observations about mini-trials 19–055
The summary jury trial 19–059
Early Neutral Evaluation, Case Evaluation, Financial Dispute
Resolution and the Court Settlement Process
    Outline of neutral evaluation 19–062
    ENE through the courts 19–066
    Neutral evaluation procedure 19–071
    General observations about evaluation 19–072
    Financial dispute resolution 19–076
    Court Settlement Process 19–079
Hybrid processes 19–080
Med-arb (mediation-arbitration)
    Outline and issues for consideration 19–082
    Meeting the concerns 19–088
Arb-med (arbitration-mediation) 19–094
Some further observations about med-arb and arb-med 19–101
Neutral fact-finding expert 19–103

20. Online Dispute Resolution
Introduction 20–001
Disputes arising online 20–005
"Real world" disputes dealt with by ODR 20–012
    Double-blind bidding 20–015
    Visual blind bidding 20–016
    Online arbitration 20–017
    Supporting traditional ADR 20–019
Other usages of ICT in dispute resolution 20–022
Regulation or harmonisation of ODR 20–024
Some practical ODR issues
    Confidentiality 20–032
    Enforcement 20–034
    Law and jurisdiction 20–038
ODR and the courts
    Money Claims Online 20–040

21. Jurisdiction, Forum and Law
ADR jurisdiction 21–001
Authority arising from statute 21–002
Authority arising from agreement 21–005
Contract clause stipulating for ADR 21–007
    Arbitration clause 21–012
    Clause for non-adjudicatory ADR 21–014
ADR agreement after dispute has arisen 21–020
Enforceability of ADR clauses in contracts 21–025
ADR Forum 21–039
Applicable Law 21–043

CONTENTS

22. Future Directions
ADR 25 years on...22–001
Brexit..22–005
Regulation 22–013
Education and academic developments 22–016
Review of civil justice and ADR.......................................22–022
Compulsion: where are we?...22–025
Black Swans and the GDPR 22–027
The Way Forward...22–032

Appendices
I. Drafting, Documents and Precedents A1–001
II. Court-Related Documents and Directives...................A2–001

                                                PAGE
Glossary...487
Bibliography..497

Index 519

TABLE OF CASES

AB v British Coal Corp [2004] EWHC 1372 (QB) 2–004
Aegis Blaze, The [1986] 1 Lloyd's Rep. 203 CA (Civ Div) 15–050
Aird v Prime Meridian Ltd [2006] EWCA Civ 1866; [2007] C.P. Rep. 18; [2007] B.L.R. 105; 111
    Con. L.R. 209; (2007) 104(2) L.S.G. 31; (2007) 151 S.J.L.B. 60 15–065
Al-Khatib v Masry [2004] EWCA Civ 1353; [2005] 1 F.L.R. 381; [2004] 3 F.C.R. 573 5–057
Alfred Crompton Amusement Machines Ltd v Customs and Excise Commissioners (No.2) [1972] 2
    Q.B. 102; [1972] 2 W.L.R. 835; [1972] 2 All E.R. 353; (1972) 116 S.J. 198 CA (Civ
    Div) 15–049
Ali Shipping Corp v Shipyard Trogir [1999] 1 W.L.R. 314; [1998] 2 All E.R. 136; [1998] 1 Lloyd's
    Rep. 643; [1998] C.L.C. 566 CA (Civ Div) 15–027, 15–029
Allco Steel (Queensland) Pty Ltd v Torres Strait Gold Pty Ltd Unreported March 12, 1990
    Queensland Sup CT 15–029
Anufrijeva v Southwark LBC; R. (on the application of M) v Secretary of State for the Home
    Department; R. (on the application of N) v Secretary of State for the Home Department; sub
    nom R. (on the application of Anufrijeva) v Southwark LBC [2003] EWCA Civ 1406; [2004]
    Q.B. 1124; [2004] 2 W.L.R. 603; [2004] 1 All E.R. 833; [2004] 1 F.L.R. 8; [2003] 3 F.C.R. 673;
    [2004] H.R.L.R. 1; [2004] U.K.H.R.R. 1; 15 B.H.R.C. 526; [2004] H.L.R. 22; [2004] B.L.G.R.
    184; (2003) 6 C.C.L. Rep. 415; [2004] Fam. Law 12; (2003) 100(44) L.S.G. 30 2–006
Associated Provincial Picture Houses Ltd v Wednesbury Corp [1948] 1 K.B. 223; [1947] 2 All E.R.
    680; (1947) 63 T.L.R. 623; (1948) 112 J.P. 55; 45 L.G.R. 635; [1948] L.J.R. 190; (1947) 177
    L.T. 641; (1948) 92 S.J. 26 18–037
Attorney General v Observer Ltd [1990] 1 A.C. 109; [1988] 3 W.L.R. 776; [1988] 3 All E.R. 545;
    [1989] 2 F.S.R. 181; (1988) 85(42) L.S.G. 45; (1988) 138 N.L.J. Rep. 296; (1988) 132 S.J. 1496
    HL 15–014
Avonwick Holdings Ltd v Webinvest Ltd [2014] EWCA Civ 1436 15–062
Balfour Beatty Construction Northern Ltd v Modus Corovest (Blackpool) Ltd [2008] EWHC 3029
    (TCC) 21–035, 21–036
Barker v Johnson [1999] EWCA Civ 1088 CA 5–055
Beaufort Developments (NI) Ltd v Gilbert-Ash (NI) Ltd [1999] 1 A.C. 266; [1998] 2 W.L.R. 860;
    [1998] 2 All E.R. 778; [1998] N.I. 144; [1998] C.L.C. 830; 88 B.L.R. 1; 59 Con. L.R. 66;
    (1998) 14 Const. L.J. 280; [1998] E.G. 85 (C.S.); (1998) 95(24) L.S.G. 33; (1998) 95(31)
    L.S.G. 34; (1998) 148 N.L.J. 869; (1998) 142 S.J.L.B. 172; [1998] N.P.C. 93; [1998] N.P.C. 91
    HL (NI) 21–032
Bernhard Schulte GmbH & Co KG v Nile Holdings Ltd [2004] EWHC 977 (Comm); [2004] 2
    Lloyd's Rep. 35 7–040
Bilta (UK) Ltd (In Liquidation) v Nazir [2010] EWHC 1086 (Ch); [2010] Bus. L.R. 1634; [2010] 2
    Lloyd's Rep. 29 21–029
Birse Construction Ltd v St David Ltd (No.1) [2000] B.L.R. 57; 70 Con. L.R. 10 CA (Civ
    Div) 21–027
Blunt v Park Lane Hotel Ltd [1942] 2 K.B. 253 CA 15–046
Bolkiah v KPMG [1999] 2 A.C. 222; [1999] 2 W.L.R. 215; [1999] 1 All E.R. 517; [1999] 1
    B.C.L.C. 1; [1999] C.L.C. 175; [1999] P.N.L.R. 220; (1999) 149 N.L.J. 16; (1999) 143 S.J.L.B.
    35 HL 16–057
Bowman v Fels [2005] EWCA Civ 226; [2005] 1 W.L.R. 3083; [2005] 4 All E.R. 609; [2005] 2 Cr.
    App. R. 19; [2005] 2 C.M.L.R. 23; [2005] 2 F.L.R. 247; [2005] W.T.L.R. 481; [2005] Fam. Law
    546; (2005) 102(18) L.S.G. 24; (2005) 155 N.L.J. 413; (2005) 149 S.J.L.B. 357; [2005] N.P.C.
    36 15–110
Brown v GIO Insurance Ltd [1998] C.L.C. 650; [1998] Lloyd's Rep. I.R. 201; (1998) 95(9) L.S.G.
    29 CA (Civ Div) 7–042
Brown v Rice [2007] EWHC 625 (Ch); [2007] B.P.I.R. 305; [2008] F.S.R. 3; (2008) 24 Const. L.J.
    238; [2007] C.I.L.L. 2467 .... 9–027, 9–044, 15–065, 15–094
Burchell v Bullard [2005] EWCA Civ 358; [2005] C.P. Rep. 36; [2005] B.L.R. 330; [2005] 3 Costs
    L.R. 507; (2005) 155 N.L.J. 593 5–058
Burchell v March, 58 U.S. 344, 349 (1855) 6–029
C (A Minor) (Care Proceedings: Disclosure), Re [1996] 2 F.L.R. 123; [1996] Fam. Law 603 Fam
    Div 15–074

TABLE OF CASES

Cable & Wireless Plc v IBM United Kingdom Ltd; sub nom Cable & Wireless Plc v IBM UK Ltd [2002] EWHC 2059 (Comm); [2002] 2 All E.R. (Comm) 1041; [2002] C.L.C. 1319; [2003] B.L.R. 89; [2002] Masons C.L.R. 58; (2002) 152 N.L.J. 1652 . . . . 4–080, 21–033
Calderbank v Calderbank [1976] Fam. 93; [1975] 3 W.L.R. 586; [1975] 3 All E.R. 333; (1975) 5 Fam. Law 190; (1975) 119 S.J. 490 CA (Civ Div) 15–058
Campbell v Mirror Group Newspapers Ltd [2004] UKHL 22; [2004] 2 A.C. 457; [2004] 2 W.L.R. 1232; [2004] 2 All E.R. 995; [2004] E.M.L.R. 15; [2004] H.R.L.R. 24; [2004] U.K.H.R.R. 648; 16 B.H.R.C. 500; (2004) 101(21) L.S.G. 36; (2004) 154 N.L.J. 733; (2004) 148 S.J.L.B. 572 15–018
Carleton (Earl of Malmesbury) v Strutt & Parker (A Partnership) [2008] EWHC 424 (QB); 118 Con. L.R. 68; [2008] 5 Costs L.R. 736; (2008) 105(15) L.S.G. 24; (2008) 158 N.L.J. 480; (2008) 152(14) S.J.L.B. 29 15–084
Central London Property Trust Ltd v High Trees House Ltd [1947] K.B. 130; [1956] 1 All E.R. 256 (Note); 62 T.L.R. 557; [1947] L.J.R. 77; 175 L.T. 333 4–084
Chalbury McCouat International Ltd v PG Foils Ltd [2010] EWHC 2050 (TCC); [2011] 1 All E.R. (Comm) 435; [2011] 1 Lloyd's Rep. 23; [2010] 2 C.L.C. 181; [2010] B.L.R. 593 6–027
Coco v AN Clark (Engineers) Ltd [1968] F.S.R. 415; [1969] R.P.C. 41 Ch D 15–014
Cofely Ltd v Bingham [2016] EWHC 240 (Comm); [2016] 2 All E.R. (Comm) 129; [2016] B.L.R. 187; 164 Con. L.R. 39; [2016] C.I.L.L. 3801 6–025
Colarusso v Petersen 61 Wash. App. 767; 812 P. 2d 862 (1991) 5–079
Courtney & Fairbairn Ltd v Tolaini Brothers (Hotels) Ltd [1975] 1 W.L.R. 297; [1975] 1 All E.R. 716; 2 B.L.R. 97; (1974) 119 S.J. 134 CA (Civ Div) 21–030
Couwenbergh v Valkova [2004] EWCA Civ 676; [2004] C.P. Rep. 38; [2004] W.T.L.R. 937; (2004) 148 S.J.L.B. 694 5–065
CTB v News Group Newspapers Ltd [2011] EWHC 1232 (QB) 15–020
Cumbria Waste Management Ltd v Baines Wilson (A Firm) [2008] EWHC 786 (QB); [2008] B.L.R. 330 15–098
Cutts v Head [1984] Ch. 290; [1984] 2 W.L.R. 349; [1984] 1 All E.R. 597; (1984) 81 L.S.G. 509; (1984) 128 S.J. 117 CA (Civ Div) 3–008, 15–054, 15–125
D (Minors) (Conciliation: Disclosure of Information), Re [1993] Fam. 231; [1993] 2 W.L.R. 721; [1993] 2 All E.R. 693; [1993] 1 F.L.R. 932; [1993] 1 F.C.R. 877; [1993] Fam. Law 410; (1993) 143 N.L.J. 438 CA (Civ Div) . . . . 5–019, 15–072, 15–073, 15–125—15–127
D v National Society for the Prevention of Cruelty to Children (NSPCC) [1978] A.C. 171; [1977] 2 W.L.R. 201; [1977] 1 All E.R. 589; 76 L.G.R. 5; (1977) 121 S.J. 119 HL 15–044, 15–045, 15–068, 15–127
DB v DLJ. See J v B (Challenge to Arbitral Award)
Deweer v Belgium (A/35) [1980] E.C.C. 169; (1979–80) 2 E.H.R.R. 439 5–072
Director General of Fair Trading v Proprietary Association of Great Britain; sub nom Medicaments and Related Classes of Goods (No.2), Re [2001] 1 W.L.R. 700; [2001] U.K.C.L.R. 550; [2001] I.C.R. 564; [2001] H.R.L.R. 17; [2001] U.K.H.R.R. 429; (2001) 3 L.G.L.R. 32; (2001) 98(7) L.S.G. 40; (2001) 151 N.L.J. 17; (2001) 145 S.J.L.B. 29 CA (Civ Div) 7–038
Douglas v Hello! Ltd (No.1) 2001] Q.B. 967; [2001] 2 W.L.R. 992; [2001] 2 All E.R. 289; [2001] E.M.L.R. 9; [2001] 1 F.L.R. 982; [2002] 1 F.C.R. 289; [2001] H.R.L.R. 26; [2001] U.K.H.R.R. 223; 9 B.H.R.C. 543; [2001] F.S.R. 40 15–018
Egan v Motor Services (Bath) Ltd [2007] EWCA Civ 1002; [2008] 1 W.L.R. 1589; [2008] 1 All E.R. 1156; [2008] 1 F.L.R. 1294; [2008] Fam. Law 317; (2007) 151 S.J.L.B. 1364 5–060
Ellerine Bros Pty Ltd v Klinger [1982] 1 W.L.R. 1375; [1982] 2 All E.R. 737; (1982) 79 L.S.G. 987; (1982) 126 S.J. 592 CA (Civ Div) 1–016
Emirates Trading Agency LLC v Prime Mineral Exports Private Ltd [2014] EWHC 2104 (Comm); [2015] 1 W.L.R. 1145; [2014] 2 Lloyd's Rep. 457; [2014] 2 C.L.C. 1; (2014) 164(7615) N.L.J. 19 6–017
Emmott v Michael Wilson & Partners Ltd. See Michael Wilson & Partners Ltd v Emmott
Essex CC v Premier Recycling Ltd [2006] EWHC 3594 (TCC); [2007] B.L.R. 233 6–038
Esso Australia Resources Ltd v Plowman (Minister for Energy and Minerals) (1995) 128 A.L.R. 391 . . . . 15–026, 15–028
Exfin Shipping (India) Ltd Mumbai v Tolani Shipping Co Ltd Mumbai [2006] EWHC 1090 (Comm); [2006] 2 All E.R. (Comm) 938; [2006] 2 Lloyd's Rep. 389 1–019
Farm Assist Ltd (In Liquidation) v Secretary of State for the Environment, Food and Rural Affairs [2009] EWHC 1102 (TCC); [2009] B.L.R. 399; 125 Con. L.R. 154 . . . 9–041, 15–089, 15–116, 15–127
Fraser v Evans [1969] 1 Q.B. 349; [1968] 3 W.L.R. 1172; [1969] 1 All E.R. 8; (1968) 112 S.J. 805 CA (Civ Div) 15–014, 15–036

TABLE OF CASES

Gartside v Outram (1857) 26 L.J. Ch. 113 15–036
Grant v Downs [1976] H.C.A. 63; (1976) 135 C.L.R. 674 15–048
Grant v South Western and County Properties Ltd [1975] Ch. 185; [1974] 3 W.L.R. 221; [1974] 2
    All E.R. 465; (1974) 118 S.J. 548 Ch D 15–069
Great Atlantic Insurance Co v Home Insurance Co [1981] 1 W.L.R. 529; [1981] 2 All E.R. 485;
    [1981] 2 Lloyd's Rep. 138; (1981) 125 S.J. 203 CA (Civ Div) 15–051
Guinness Peat Properties Ltd v Fitzroy Robinson Partnership [1987] 1 W.L.R. 1027; [1987] 2 All
    E.R. 716; 38 B.L.R. 57; (1987) 84 L.S.G. 1882; (1987) 137 N.L.J. 452; (1987) 131 S.J. 807 CA
    (Civ Div) 15–052
Halki Shipping Corp v Sopex Oils Ltd (The Halki) [1998] 1 W.L.R. 726; [1998] 2 All E.R. 23;
    [1998] 1 Lloyd's Rep. 465; [1998] C.L.C. 583; (1998) 142 S.J.L.B. 44; [1998] N.P.C. 4 CA (Civ
    Div) 1–018
Halsey v Milton Keynes General NHS Trust [2004] EWCA Civ 576; [2004] 1 W.L.R. 3002; [2004]
    4 All E.R. 920; [2004] C.P. Rep. 34; [2004] 3 Costs L.R. 393; (2005) 81 B.M.L.R. 108; (2004)
    101(22) L.S.G. 31; (2004) 154 N.L.J. 769; (2004) 148 S.J.L.B. 629 .... 5–061, 5–065, 5–072,
    5–076, 9–037,
    14–001, 16–016, 17–012
Hariz & Haque Solicitors v Legal Ombudsman & Tahira Quereshi. *See* R. (on the application of
    Hafiz & Haque Solicitors) v Legal Ombudsman
Hayter v Nelson & Home Insurance Co [1990] 2 Lloyd's Rep. 265; 23 Con. L.R. 88 QBD
    (Comm) 1–015
Henley v Henley (Bligh cited) [1955] P. 202; [1955] 2 W.L.R. 851; [1955] 1 All E.R. 590 (Note);
    (1955) 119 J.P. 215; (1955) 99 S.J. 260 PDA 15–071
Holloway v Chancery Mead Ltd [2007] EWHC 2495 (TCC); [2008] 1 All E.R. (Comm) 653; 117
    Con. L.R. 30 21–034
Homepace Ltd v Sita South East Ltd [2008] EWCA Civ 1; [2008] T.C.L.R. 4; [2008] 1 P. & C.R.
    24; [2008] N.P.C. 2 7–041
IDA Ltd v University of Southampton [2006] EWCA Civ 145; [2006] R.P.C. 21; (2006) 29(5) I.P.D.
    29038 5–059
J v B (Challenge to Arbitral Award); sub nom DB v DLJ; J v B (Family Law Arbitration: Award)
    [2016] EWHC 324 (Fam); [2016] 1 W.L.R. 3319; [2016] 2 F.L.R. 1308; [2016] 3 F.C.R. 117;
    [2016] Fam. Law 562 6–065
Jones v Sherwood Computer Services Plc [1992] 1 W.L.R. 277; [1992] 2 All E.R. 170; [1989] E.G.
    172 (C.S.) CA (Civ Div) 7–042
MacDonald Estates Plc v National Car Parks Ltd [2009] CSIH 79A; 2010 S.C. 250; 2010 S.L.T.
    36 7–048
McKennitt v Ash [2006] EWCA Civ 1714; [2008] Q.B. 73; [2007] 3 W.L.R. 194; [2007] E.M.L.R.
    4; (2007) 151 S.J.L.B. 27 15–019
Macob Civil Engineering Ltd v Morrison Construction Ltd [1999] C.L.C. 739; [1999] B.L.R. 93;
    (1999) 1 T.C.L.R. 113; 64 Con. L.R. 1; [1999] 3 E.G.L.R. 7; [1999] 37 E.G. 173; (1999) 15
    Const. L.J. 300; (1999) 96(10) L.S.G. 28 QBD (TCC) 7–008
Macro v Thompson (No.3) [1997] 2 B.C.L.C. 36 Ch D 7–039
McTaggart v McTaggart [1949] P. 94; [1948] 2 All E.R. 754; 64 T.L.R. 558; 46 L.G.R. 527; [1949]
    L.J.R. 82; (1948) 92 S.J. 617 CA 15–070, 15–124
Medicaments and Related Classes of Goods (No.2), Re. *See* Director General of Fair Trading v
    Proprietary Association of Great Britain
Mercury Communications Ltd v Director General of Telecommunications [1996] 1 W.L.R. 48;
    [1996] 1 All E.R. 575; [1995] C.L.C. 266; [1998] Masons C.L.R. Rep. 39 HL ... 7–036, 7–042
Michael Wilson & Partners Ltd v Emmott; sub nom. Emmott v Michael Wilson & Partners Ltd
    [2008] EWCA Civ 184; [2008] Bus. L.R. 1361; [2008] 2 All E.R. (Comm) 193; [2008] 1
    Lloyd's Rep. 616; [2008] C.P. Rep. 26; [2008] B.L.R. 515 CA (Civ Div) 15–029
Mole v Mole [1951] P. 21; [1950] 2 All E.R. 328; 66 T.L.R. (Pt. 2) 129; 48 L.G.R. 439; (1950) 94
    S.J. 518 CA 15–069, 15–070
Muller v Linsley & Mortimer [1996] P.N.L.R. 74; (1995) 92(3) L.S.G. 38; (1995) 139 S.J.L.B. 43
    CA (Civ Div) 15–100, 15–101
Mustad v Dosen; sub nom. O Mustad & Son v S Allcock & Co [1964] 1 W.L.R. 109 (Note); [1963]
    3 All E.R. 416; [1963] R.P.C. 41 HL 15–016
Myerson v Myerson [2009] EWCA Civ 282; [2010] 1 W.L.R. 114; [2009] 2 F.L.R. 147; [2009] 2
    F.C.R. 1; [2009] Fam. Law 564; (2009) 106(15) L.S.G. 16; (2009) 153(13) S.J.L.B.
    28 15–078
Nikko Hotels (UK) Ltd v MEPC Plc [1991] 2 E.G.L.R. 103; [1991] 28 E.G. 86 Ch D 7–038,
    7–042

TABLE OF CASES

Nokia Corp v InterDigital Technology Corp [2004] EWHC 2920 (Pat); (2005) 28(5) I.P.D. 28039 21–028
Northern RHA v Derek Crouch Construction Co Ltd [1984] Q.B. 644; [1984] 2 W.L.R. 676; [1984] 2 All E.R. 175; 26 B.L.R. 1; [1986] C.I.L.L. 244; (1984) 128 S.J. 279 CA (Civ Div) 21–031, 21–032
Oceanbulk Shipping & Trading SA v TMT Asia Ltd [2010] UKSC 44; [2011] 1 A.C. 662; [2010] 3 W.L.R. 1424; [2010] 4 All E.R. 1011; [2011] 1 All E.R. (Comm) 1; [2011] 1 Lloyd's Rep. 96; [2010] 2 C.L.C. 686; [2011] B.L.R. 1; 133 Con. L.R. 62; [2011] 1 Costs L.R. 122; [2010] C.I.L.L. 2943 . . . . 15–064, 15–103, 15–104
Ofulue v Bossert [2009] UKHL 16; [2009] 1 A.C. 990; [2009] 2 W.L.R. 749; [2009] 3 All E.R. 93; [2010] 1 F.L.R. 475; [2009] 2 P. & C.R. 17; [2009] 2 E.G.L.R. 97; [2009] Fam. Law 1042; [2009] 11 E.G. 119 (C.S.); (2009) 106(12) L.S.G. 15; (2009) 153(11) S.J.L.B. 29; [2009] N.P.C. 40 15–062
Owen Pell Ltd v Bindi (London) Ltd [2008] EWHC 1420 (TCC); [2008] B.L.R. 436; (2009) 25 Const. L.J. 168; [2008] C.I.L.L. 2605 7–037
Pais v Pais [1971] P. 119; [1970] 3 W.L.R. 830; [1970] 3 All E.R. 491; (1970) 114 S.J. 72 15–071
Philips Electronique Grand Public SA v British Sky Broadcasting Ltd [1995] E.M.L.R. 472 CA (Civ Div) 4–081
Porter v Magill [2001] UKHL 67; [2002] 2 A.C. 357; [2002] 2 W.L.R. 37; [2002] 1 All E.R. 465; [2002] H.R.L.R. 16; [2002] H.L.R. 16; [2002] B.L.G.R. 51; (2001) 151 N.L.J. 1886; [2001] N.P.C. 184 . . . . 6–025, 7–039
Pozzi v Eli Lilley & Co, Times, 3 December 1986 15–051
Practice Direction (Fam Div: Ancillary Relief Procedure) [2000] 1 W.L.R. 1480; [2000] 3 All E.R. 379; [2000] 1 F.L.R. 997; [2000] 2 F.C.R. 216 15–078
Practice Direction (Fam Div: Family Proceedings: Financial Dispute Resolution) [1997] 1 W.L.R. 1069; [1997] 3 All E.R. 768; [1997] 2 F.L.R. 304; [1997] 3 F.C.R. 476 5–019
Practice Statement (Comm Ct: Alternative Dispute Resolution); sub nom. Practice Note (Comm Ct: Alternative Dispute Resolution) [1994] 1 W.L.R. 14; [1994] 1 All E.R. 34; [1994] C.L.C. 11 5–049
Practice Statement (Commercial Cases: Alternative Dispute Resolution) (No.2); sub nom. Practice Note (Comm Ct: Alternative Dispute Resolution) [1996] 1 W.L.R. 1024; [1996] 3 All E.R. 383; [1996] C.L.C. 1042; (1996) 93(23) L.S.G. 36 5–049
Property Alliance Group Ltd v Royal Bank of Scotland Plc [2015] EWHC 1557 (Ch); [2016] 1 W.L.R. 361; [2015] 2 B.C.L.C. 401 . . . . 15–062, 15–064
R. (on the application of Cart) v Upper Tribunal [2011] UKSC 28; [2011] 3 W.L.R. 107; [2011] P.T.S.R. 1053; [2011] 4 All E.R. 127; [2011] S.T.C. 1659; [2011] S.T.I. 1943; (2011) 161 N.L.J. 916; (2011) 155(25) S.J.L.B. 35 7–053
R. (on the application of Cowl) v Plymouth City Council; sub nom Cowl (Practice Note), Re; Cowl v Plymouth City Council [2001] EWCA Civ 1935; [2002] 1 W.L.R. 803; [2002] C.P. Rep. 18; [2002] 5 C.C.L. Rep. 42; [2002] A.C.D. 11; [2002] Fam. Law 265; (2002) 99(8) L.S.G. 35; (2002) 146 S.J.L.B. 27 . . . . 2–005, 5–056
R. (on the application of Crawford) v Legal Ombudsman [2014] EWHC 182 (Admin); [2014] 4 Costs L.O. 560; [2014] A.C.D. 100 18–037
R. (on the application of Hafiz & Haque Solicitors) v Legal Ombudsman [2014] EWHC 1539 (Admin) 18–038
R. (on the application of Rosemarine) v Office for Legal Complaints [2014] EWHC 601 (Admin) 18–038
R. v Lewes Justices Ex p. Secretary of State for the Home Department. *See* Rogers v Secretary of State for the Home Department
Reed Executive Plc v Reed Business Information Ltd (Costs: Alternative Dispute Resolution) [2004] EWCA Civ 887; [2004] 1 W.L.R. 3026; [2004] 4 All E.R. 942; [2005] C.P. Rep. 4; [2004] 4 Costs L.R. 662; [2005] F.S.R. 3; (2004) 27(7) I.P.D. 27067; (2004) 148 S.J.L.B. 881 15–095
Rogers v Secretary of State for the Home Department; sub nom R. v Lewes Justices Ex p. Secretary of State for the Home Department [1973] A.C. 388; [1972] 3 W.L.R. 279; [1972] 2 All E.R. 1057; (1972) 116 S.J. 696 HL 15–043, 15–045
Rotenberg v Sucafina SA; sub nom. Sucafina SA v Rotenberg [2012] EWCA Civ 637; [2012] 2 All E.R. (Comm) 952; [2013] Bus. L.R. 158; [2012] 2 Lloyd's Rep. 54; [2012] 2 C.L.C. 20 6–039

TABLE OF CASES

Rush & Tompkins Ltd v Greater London Council [1988] 2 W.L.R. 533; [1988] 1 All E.R. 549; 40 B.L.R. 53; (1988) 138 N.L.J. Rep. 22; (1988) 132 S.J. 265 CA (Civ Div) 15–056, 15–058, 15–059
RWE Npower Plc v Alstom Power Ltd [2010] EWHC 3061 (TCC); 133 Con. L.R. 155 7–007
S v K Ltd Fed Sup Ct of Switzerland ICC Arbitration Tribunal in Zürich, ATF/BGE 116 II 639 6–035
S v S (Arbitral Award: Approval) [2014] EWHC 7 (Fam); [2014] 1 W.L.R. 2299; [2014] 1 F.L.R. 1257; [2014] 2 F.C.R. 484; [2014] Fam. Law 448; (2014) 158(3) S.J.L.B. 37 6–064
Saltman Engineering Co v Campbell Engineering Co (1948) [1963] 3 All E.R. 413 (Note); (1948) 65 R.P.C. 203 CA 15–015
Santa Fe International Corp v Napier Shipping SA (No.1), 1985 S.L.T. 430 OH 15–047
Scott v Avery (1856) 10 E.R. 1121; (1856) 5 H.L. Cas. 811 HL 21–012
Sierra Fishing Co v Farran [2015] EWHC 140 (Comm); [2015] 1 All E.R. (Comm) 560; [2015] 1 Lloyd's Rep. 514 . . . . 6–022, 6–025
Slade-Powell v Slade-Powell (1964) 108 S.J. 1033 15–071
Spiliada Maritime Corp v Cansulex Ltd (The Spiliada) [1987] A.C. 460; [1986] 3 W.L.R. 972; [1986] 3 All E.R. 843; [1987] 1 Lloyd's Rep. 1; [1987] E.C.C. 168; [1987] 1 F.T.L.R. 103; (1987) 84 L.S.G. 113; (1986) 136 N.L.J. 1137; (1986) 130 S.J. 925 HL 21–041
Sucafina SA v Rotenberg. See Rotenberg v Sucafina SA; sub nom. Sucafina SA v Rotenberg
Sulamerica Cia Nacional de Seguros SA v Enesa Engenharia SA[2012] EWCA Civ 638; [2013] 1 W.L.R. 102; [2012] 2 All E.R. (Comm) 795; [2012] 1 Lloyd's Rep. 671; [2012] 2 C.L.C. 216; [2012] Lloyd's Rep. I.R. 405 21–037
Sun Life Assurance Co of Canada v CX Reinsurance Co Ltd (formerly CNA Reinsurance Co Ltd) [2003] EWCA Civ 283; [2004] Lloyd's Rep. I.R. 58 21–027
Swain Mason v Mills & Reeve [2012] EWCA Civ 498; [2012] S.T.C. 1760; [2012] 4 Costs L.O. 511; [2012] W.T.L.R. 1827; [2012] S.T.I. 1511 5–066
Teekay Tankers Ltd v STX Offshore and Shipbuilding Co Ltd [2017] EWHC 253 (Comm); [2018] 1 All E.R. (Comm) 279; [2017] 1 Lloyd's Rep. 387 15–029
Thames Valley Power Ltd v Total Gas & Power Ltd [2005] EWHC 2208 (Comm); [2006] 1 Lloyd's Rep. 441; (2006) 22 Const. L.J. 591 1–020
Theodoropoulas v Theodoropoulas [1964] P. 311; [1963] 3 W.L.R. 354; [1963] 2 All E.R. 772; (1963) 107 S.J. 632 Assizes (Winchester) 15–071
Three Rivers DC v Bank of England (Disclosure) (No.4) [2004] EWCA Civ 218; [2004] Q.B. 916; [2004] 2 W.L.R. 1065; [2004] 3 All E.R. 168; (2004) 101(11) L.S.G. 36; (2004) 154 N.L.J. 382; (2004) 148 S.J.L.B. 297 15–048
Tiedel v Northwestern Michigan College 865 F. 2d 88 (6th Cir. 1988) 5–079
Tomlin v Standard Telephones & Cables Ltd [1969] 1 W.L.R. 1378; [1969] 3 All E.R. 201; [1969] 1 Lloyd's Rep. 309; (1969) 113 S.J. 641 CA (Civ Div) 15–056
Tubeworkers v Tilbury Construction (1985) 30 B.L.R. 67; (1985) 1 Const. L.J. 385; [1985] C.I.L.L. 187 CA (Civ Div) 21–031
Unilever Plc v Procter & Gamble Co [1999] 1 W.L.R. 1630; [1999] 2 All E.R. 691; [1999] F.S.R. 849; (1999) 22(5) I.P.D. 22042; (1999) 149 N.L.J. 370 Ch D (Patents Ct) 15–061, 15–063
Vestergaard Frandsen S/A (now called MVF3 APS) v Bestnet Europe Ltd [2013] UKSC 31; [2013] 1 W.L.R. 1556; [2013] 4 All E.R. 781; [2013] I.C.R. 981; [2013] I.R.L.R. 654; [2013] E.M.L.R. 24; [2013] R.P.C. 33; (2013) 157(21) S.J.L.B. 31 15–014
W v Egdell [1990] Ch. 359; [1990] 2 W.L.R. 471; [1990] 1 All E.R. 835; (1990) 87(12) L.S.G. 41; (1990) 134 S.J. 286 CA (Civ Div) 15–036
Walford v Miles [1992] 2 A.C. 128; [1992] 2 W.L.R. 174; [1992] 1 All E.R. 453; (1992) 64 P. & C.R. 166; [1992] 1 E.G.L.R. 207; [1992] 11 E.G. 115; [1992] N.P.C. 4 HL 4–079, 4–080, 4–086, 4–088, 21–030
Walker v Wilsher (1889) L.R. 23 Q.B.D. 335 CA 15–056, 15–057
White (Pamela) v White (Martin) [2001] 1 A.C. 596; [2000] 3 W.L.R. 1571; [2001] 1 All E.R. 1; [2000] 2 F.L.R. 981; [2000] 3 F.C.R. 555; [2001] Fam. Law 12; (2000) 97(43) L.S.G. 38; (2000) 150 N.L.J. 1716; (2000) 144 S.J.L.B. 266; [2000] N.P.C. 111 11–125

TABLE OF STATUTES

United Kingdom
- 1898 Criminal Evidence Act
  (c.36) 15–046
- 1967 Parliamentary Commissioner Act
  (c.13) 18–006
- 1968 Civil Evidence Act (c.64)
  s.14 15–046
- 1972 Criminal Justice Act (c.71) 12–090
- 1975 Arbitration Act (c.3) 1–015, 1–018
  s.1 1–015
  Employment Protection Act
  (c.71) 13–005
- 1984 Telecommunications Act
  (c.12) 21–004
  Police and Criminal Evidence Act (c.60)
  s.80 15–040
- 1989 Children Act (c.41)
  s.8 11–065
  s.98(2) 15–074
  Sch.1 11–065
- 1990 Law Reform (Miscellaneous Provisions) (Scotland) Act (c.40)
  Sch.7 6–011
  Courts and Legal Services Act
  (c.41) 18–007
- 1991 Water Industry Act (c.60) 21–004
- 1995 Civil Evidence (Family Mediation) (Scotland) Act (c.6) 15–006
- 1996 Employment Tribunals Act (c.17)
  s.18(7) 15–076
  Arbitration Act (c.23) ... 1–018, 1–021, 2–021, 2–023, 6–008, 6–011, 6–012, 6–013, 6–021, 6–027, 6–028, 6–030, 6–036, 6–037, 6–041, 6–065, 7–006, 7–058, 15–140, 21–002, 21–004, 21–013, 21–044
  s.1 6–010
  (b) 1–018
  s.2(4) 6–027
  s.9 1–018
  (1) 21–026
  ss.15—22 6–021
  s.16 6–021
  s.24(1)(a) 6–021
  s.30 6–034
  s.31 6–034
  s.32 6–034
  s.33 6–030
  s.34 6–030
  s.42 7–006
  ss.46—58 6–036
  s.58 6–036
  ss.59—65 6–041
  s.67 21–004
  s.68 21–004
  s.69 21–004
  (1) 6–037, 6–038
  (2)—(8) 6–037
  (3)(d) 6–038
  s.70 6–037
  s.71 6–037
  s.73 6–034
  Family Law Act (c.27) 11–008
  Trusts of Land and Appointment of Trustees Act (c.47) 11–065
  Housing Grants, Construction and Regeneration Act (c.53) 1–021, 2–007, 7–004, 7–005, 7–007, 21–002
  s.108 7–008
- 1997 Civil Procedure Act (c.12) 3–008, 21–001
- 1998 Employment Rights (Dispute Resolution) Act (c.8) 14–007, 14–014
  s.8 14–014
  Data Protection Act (c.29)
  Pt IV 22–030
  Sch.7 22–030
  Human Rights Act (c.42). 2–006, 15–017
- 1999 Access to Justice Act (c.22) ... 11–008, 22–032
- 2000 Criminal Justice and Court Services Act (c.43) 11–012
- 2002 Justice (Northern Ireland) Act
  (c.26) 12–094
  Proceeds of Crime Act (c.29) .. 15–011, 15–036, 15–106
  s.328 .... 15–106, 15–110
- 2004 Civil Partnership Act (c.33) 11–009, 15–006
- 2006 Family Law (Scotland) Act (asp 2) 15–006
- 2007 Tribunals, Courts and Enforcement Act
  (c.15) 7–054
  Legal Services Act (c.29) 18–007
  s.12(4) 22–030
- 2008 Employment Act (c.24) 13–004
- 2014 Children and Families Act
  (c.6) 22–025
  s.10 2–002
  (1) 5–001
- 2018 Data Protection Act (c.12) 22–029

Australia
- 2010 Commercial Arbitration Act (NSW)
  No.61 19–091
  s.27D(4) 19–091
  (7) 19–091

TABLE OF STATUTES

Austria
1895 Code of Civil Procedure
    s.594(1) 6–035

Canada
2002 Code of Civil Procedure (c.7) ... 5–089

China
1991 Law of Civil Procedure 5–099
    Ch.VIII 5–099

Germany
1998 Code of Civil Procedure
    (Zivilprozessordnung) . 4–082, 5–092
    art.278 5–092
2004 Unfair Competition Act
    s.3a 20–030
2012 Mediation Act
    (Mediationsgesetz) 5–094

India
1908 Code of Civil Procedure
    s.89 5–103
1987 Legal Services Authorities Act
    s.4 5–102
1996 Arbitration and Conciliation
    Act 5–102

Ireland
2017 Mediation Act (c.27) 15–008
    s.10 15–008

    s.17 15–009

Japan
1951 Civil Conciliation Act 5–097
2004 Act on Promotion of Use of Alternative
    Dispute Resolution (Act No.151 of
    2004) 5–097

Switzerland
1907 Civil Code 4–082
1987 Federal Private International Law
    Act 6–035
    s.192 6–035

United States of America
General Laws of the Commonwealth of
    Massachusetts
    s.23C 15–024
1975 Federal Rules of Evidence 19–104
1998 Alternative Disputes Resolution
    Act 5–087
    s.651 5–087
2000 Revised Uniform Arbitration
    Act 6–061
2001 Uniform Mediation Act .. 2–002, 3–033,
    15–007, 15–009,
    21–002

TABLE OF TREATIES AND CONVENTIONS

1950 European Convention on Human Rights and Fundamental Freedoms 15–018
    art.6 ... 5–064, 5–072, 5–073, 5–076, 10–046
    art.8 ..... 15–017, 15–019, 15–020, 15–036
    art.10 ..... 15–017, 15–019, 15–036

1957 EC Treaty (Treaty Establishing the European Community)
    art.65 22–011
    (a), (b) and (c) 22–011

1958 Convention on the Recognition and Enforcement of Foreign Arbitral Awards (New York Convention) . 6–007, 22–012, 20–035

1989 United Nations Convention on the Rights of the Child 11–040
    art.12 11–040

TABLE OF ARBITRATION AND PRACTICE RULES

1976	Rules of Conciliation and Arbitration (UNCITRAL, revised 2010) 6–008, 6–023, 21–013		2004	Model Family Law Arbitration Act (AAML) 6–061
	art.9 6–023		2012	Rules of Arbitration (ICC) 6–035, 6–041, 21–013
	art.12(1) 6–023			art.28 6–015
	art.27 7–050			art.38.4 6–041
1980	Conciliation Rules (UNCITRAL) 8–013		2014	Rules of Arbitration (London Court of International Arbitration)
1985	Model Law on International Commercial Arbitration (UNCITRAL, revised 2002, 2006) ... 6–008, 6–011, 6–023			art.28 6–041
			2015	Expert Rules (ICC) 7–050
			2018	Arbitration Rules (Family Law Arbitration Children Scheme)
	art.5 6–015			
	art.9 6–015			art.17 6–063
	art.28.3 6–045			
2001	ADR Rules (ICC) 8–018			
2002	Model Law on International Commercial Conciliation (UNCITRAL) 15–007, 15–009			
	art.10 15–007			

TABLE OF RULES OF COURT

1965	Rules of the Supreme Court (SI 1965/1776) 2–010		r.44.3 .... 5–005, 22–018	
			r.44.5 22–018	
1991	Family Proceedings Rules (SI 1991/1247) 5–019	1999	Family Proceedings (Amendment No.2) Rules (SI 1999/3491) 5–019	
	r.2.75(1) 5–019	2009	Practice Direction – Pre-Action Conduct para.8.1 5–011	
1998	Civil Procedure Rules (SI 1998/3132) ... 2–010, 3–008, 5–001, 5–003, 5–006, 5–057, 7–044, 10–093, 15–061, 15–075, 21–001, 22–018	2010	Family Procedure Rules (SI 2010/2955) .... 5–006, 9–038 Pt 3 ... 5–006, 5–008, 5–013, 5–043 r.3.1 .... 5–007 r.3.2 5–007	
	Pt 1 .... 5–003, A3–004		r.3.3 5–007	
	r.1 5–003		Practice Direction 3A . 5–008, 5–012, 5–043, 9–038, 11–011	
	r.1.1(1) 5–003			
	(2) 5–003		Practice Direction 12B	
	r.1.2(c) 1–011		para.5.11 15–077	
	r.1.4 22–018		r.35.3 15–119	
	(2)(e) 5–003		r.35.4 15–119	
	Pt 3 19–067	2011	Civil Procedure (Amendment) Rules (SI 2011/88) 15–121, 19–100	
	r.3.1(2)(f) 21–025			
	(m) 19–067		Sch.2 s.III r.78.24 19–100	
	PD 7E 20–040		r.78.26 15–121	
	r.11 21–029	2013	Employment Tribunals (Constitution and Rules of Procedure) Regulations (SI 2013/1237) 22–025	
	Pt 26 5–004			
	r.26.4 ...... 5–004, 21–025, 22–018			
	PD 29 22–018	2015	Practice Direction: Pre-Action Conduct and Protocols	
	Pt 35 7–044			
	r.35.8 19–103		para.4 1–011	
	Pt 36 15–075		para.8 1–011	
	r.36.13 15–075		para.9 1–011	
	Pt 44 5–005		para.10 1–011	

TABLE OF CODES, PROTOCOLS AND GUIDANCE NOTES

1983 Code of Practice and Guidance (Family Mediation Council) 11–005
1994 Model Standards of Practice (Association for Conflict Resolution) 11–064
   Standard XIIIB 11–064
1998 Principle III(x) attached to the Council of Europe's Recommendation No.R (98) 1 on Family Mediation 11–037
1999 Code of Practice for Family Mediation (Law Society of England and Wales) para.5.7.2 17–074
   Code of Practice (Internet Services Providers' Association) 18–029
   para.8.2. 18–029
2004 Guidelines on Conflicts of Interest in International Arbitration (International Bar Association) 6–024
   para.6. 6–024
2005 Model Standards of Conduct for Mediators (American Bar Association) . . . 3–033, 8–028, 8–041
2006 Renewable Energy Consumer Code (RECC) 18–036
2007 Code of Conduct (Solicitors Regulation Authority) 3–068
   Code of Practice for Family Mediation (Law Society of England and Wales) 11–007, 16–018
   para.5.10 19–024
2008 National Mediator Standards (Australia) 5–090
2009 Code of Conduct for Civil and Commercial Mediators (Law Society of England and Wales) 8–007, 8–027, 10–019
   Guidance Note No.1, Mediation Confidentiality (Civil Mediation Council, 8 July 2009) 15–116
2010 Code of Conduct (General Council of the Bar) 16–020
   para.301 16–020
   Guidance on the obligations of mediators under the Proceeds of Crime Act 2002 (Civil Mediation Council, 15 October 2010) 15–111, 15–113

Office for Criminal Justice Reform, A Revised Code of Practice for Conditional Cautions (Adults) (Stationery Office: London, 2010 para.7.7 12–092
Technology and Construction Court Guide . . 5–014, 5–015, 5–051, 7–044, 19–066, 19–079
   para.7.5.1 5–014
   para.7.6.1 . . . . 5–014, 7–015
   s.13 7–044
2011 Code of Conduct (Solicitors Regulation Authority) 3–070, 16–012
   para.2.02(1)(b) 3–068, 22–018
2012 Guide to Good Practice under the Hague Child Abduction Convention—Mediation 11–068
2013 ACAS Code of Practice 4: "Settlement Agreements (under section 111A of the Employment Rights Act 1996)" (July 2013) 13–033
2014 Guidance for the instruction of experts in civil claims (Civil Justice Council, August 2014) 19–103
2015 Family Law Protocol (Law Society of England and Wales) 5–010
   s.III 5–010
2016 Chancery Guide 5–053, 19–068, 19–069, 19–070, 19–077, 19–078
   para.18.7 19–068
   para.18.8 19–068
   para.18.16 19–077
   para.18.18 19–077
   Code of Practice for Family Mediators (Family Mediation Council, September 2016) . . . 11–049, 11–059
   para 5.5.3 11–059
   para 5.7.2 11–042
   para 6.15 11–091
2017 Admiralty and Commercial Courts Guide 5–049, 5–052

CHAPTER 1

Analysing ADR

INTRODUCTION

The resolution of disputes has varied widely across families, communities, nations, and internationally, since time immemorial. Mechanisms have included procedural means (such as the rolling of dice); the battle of the fittest (for example, pistols at dawn or war between nations); negotiation; mediation; and adjudication by a third-party (such as a tribal leader or a court judge). For some time state-administered court-adjudication[1] has been the prime means of dispute resolution across nations that adhere to rule of law principles. However, over the last 40 years or so,[2] there has been a fresh impetus to make use of alternative procedures as a counter to problems within legal systems (such as delay and expense), and in their own right, as a means to provide individuals and corporations with choice, flexibility, confidentiality, and autonomy in the resolution of their disputes.[3] Hence, in many jurisdictions, courts and government agencies have supported and promoted the use of alternative dispute resolution; mediation and conflict resolution organisations have been established; Bar Associations and Law Societies have embraced Alternative Dispute Resolution (ADR) principles; practitioners from a wide range of professional disciplines, including law, mental health and many others have trained in its use; and there is a flourishing body of academic and practitioner literature debating its theory, practice and principles.

1–001

The term ADR encompasses a wide range of processes broadly falling within two categories, determined by the way in which the dispute is resolved: *adjudicative* and *agreement-based* or *consensual*. In adjudicative procedures, such as arbitration, a third-party independent reaches a decision (which may be binding (e.g. arbitration) or may be a recommendation (e.g. Ombudsperson)) whereas, in agreement-based processes, the parties have the opportunity to reach an agreed outcome assisted by an impartial third party.

1–002

The range of ADR procedures may be viewed as a spectrum of processes, set apart from court proceedings, each of which may be utilised to bring resolution to parties engaged in a dispute, where arbitration sits at one end of the spectrum and

1–003

---

[1] Albeit that a significant majority of cases settle before they reach the courts.
[2] It is widely considered that the address of Professor Frank Sander at the Pound Conference 1976 led to the mainstreaming of ADR into the dispute resolution landscape in democratic nations.
[3] Prior to this, the ADR idea was "viewed as nothing more than a hobbyhorse for a few offbeat scholars": Harry Davies, "Alternative Dispute Resolution: Panacea or Anathema" (1985–1986) 99 *Harvard Law Review* 668.

mediation at the other.[4] Moreover, ADR procedures may be blended in different permutations into hybrid processes tailored to meet the needs of each individual dispute and situation, such as Med-Arb and Arb-Med, where parties agree to use an adjudicatory method if agreement is not reached through an agreement-based process, or they may opt to use an agreement-based process for some aspects and reserve others for adjudication. Mediation[5] has over recent years become the most widely used non-adjudicatory process whilst arbitration clauses are frequently found in commercial and construction contracts. It should be noted, however, that since a significant aim of the processes is to ensure greater party control of the type of process, rules for resolution, third-party intervention in their dispute, and so on, individual processes may vary considerably.

1–004 However, ADR has not been universally adopted for varying reasons. Individuals may lack sufficient knowledge about the range of possible approaches to dispute resolution[6]; legal advisors and courts may promote ADR but individuals may be committed to court-based resolution to vindicate their rights, to seek greater recompense or to gain publicity[7]; and, additionally, a case may be considered unsuitable for mediation (e.g. where a legal precedent is required or where an individual has been bullied or abused by another party).[8] However, even in such cases, the use of ADR may be advocated.[9]

1–005 In order to understand the complexities of ADR processes, it is instructive to analyse each of the three elements of ADR: "alternative", "dispute" and "resolution". In doing so, it is important to bear in mind that ADR is a generic and broad concept, covering a wide range of activities and embracing significant differences of philosophy, practice and approach in the dispute resolution field.

"ALTERNATIVE"

1–006 There is no universally accepted phraseology for dispute resolution procedures.

---

[4] Dispute resolution procedures may be formulated to include litigation, where court-based adjudication sits at one end of the spectrum and mediation at the other. Susskind prefers to categorise dispute resolution into two groups: those which are attached to the court or engage the supervision of the court and those which are not. In this formulation mediation may be sited on both sides of the formulation: L.E. Susskind, "Consensus Building and ADR: Why They are Not the Same Thing" in M.L. Moffatt & R.C. Bordone, *The Handbook of Dispute Resolution* (San Francisco: Jossey Bass, 2005) pp.358, 359–360.

[5] In certain jurisdictions, mediation may be termed as "conciliation" whereas in other contexts conciliation has a different meaning. See Ch.2, para.2-036 and fn.22 and Ch.8, paras 8-012 to 8-019, and in the employment context, Ch.13, paras 13-008 to 13-013.

[6] I. Pereira, C. Perry, H. Greevy and H. Shrimpton, "The Varying Paths to Justice" (Ipsos Mori Research Institute, Ministry of Justice Analytical Research Series 2015).

[7] See e.g. S. Shipman, "Court Approaches to ADR" (2006) C.J.Q. 181, 192; and see J. Wade, "Don't Waste My Time on Negotiation and Mediation: *This Dispute Needs a Judge*", *Conflict Resolution Quarterly*, Vol.18, Issue 3, 259–280, Spring, 2001; and Ch.5 ADR & the Courts.

[8] See Ch.16, para.16-118 for a list of some circumstances where mediation would be inappropriate.

[9] For example, National Human Rights Institutions may make use of ADR, such as mediation or conciliation, to resolve individual complaints of human rights violations: Paris Principles adopted by the United Nations General Council Resolution 48/134 1993. See F.E.A. Sander and S.B. Goldberg, "Fitting the Forum to the Fuss: A User-Friendly Guide to Selecting an ADR Procedure" (1994) 10 Neg. J. 49, 66; or (2005–2006) 7 Cardozo J. Conflict Resol. 83.

"ALTERNATIVE"

The term "alternative" has attracted criticism. One concern is that it may have negative social capital since its use in other contexts denotes separation from mainstream, accepted social activities and norms (such as alternative medicine, alternative lifestyle, and so on). Indeed, in recognition of this, and in view of changing public perceptions, "alternative" medical treatments may now be referred to as "complementary".

1–007

A linked concern is that the use of "alternative" in relation to mediation and other ADR processes, may suggest that these are subservient to litigation. This view pertains to the idea that ADR provides "second class justice", which notion may be predicated on the notion that ADR has been viewed as a way of dealing with cases that are less deserving of court resources and, hence, public money.[10] Thus the use of the term "alternative" dispute resolution is not unproblematic.

1–008

Following this line of thought, commentators and dispute resolution organisations have adopted other terminology and acronyms. Internationally, one of the most popular appears to be "appropriate dispute resolution".[11] Commentators appear to agree that the use of the word "appropriate" represents accurately the dispute resolution landscape since it encompasses a full range of possible DR options, including mediation, ombudspersons and litigation.[12]

1–009

Others, such as CEDR,[13] prefer to use the term "effective". This has the merit of providing positive imagery but does not have widespread recognition. Outside of CEDR, its use may be confusing since the acronym EDR may be used to refer variously to "effective", "employment", "environmental", "extra-judicial" and "electronic" dispute resolution.

1–010

Since the turn of the century the civil justice system has encouraged "proportionate" dispute resolution (PDR)[14] and this terminology is increasingly used.[15] Again, this conveys valid imagery in terms of reflecting that processes can be designed and used that are balanced, fair and in proportion to the nature of the dispute.

1–011

However, these terms are each sufficiently broad to encompass court litigation within the range of possible procedures. Hence, in the context of this work, the term "alternative" is adopted to differentiate between judicial decision-making in formal court proceedings and other forms of dispute resolution conducted and/or facilitated by independent third parties (irrespective of whether such processes

1–012

---

[10] For example S.B. Goldberg, E.D. Green and F.E.A. Sander "ADR Problems and Prospects: Looking to the Future" (1986) 69 *Judicature* 291, 293.

[11] Examples include: CADRE (Center for Appropriate Dispute Resolution) which, in the context of special education in the US, encourages the use of mediation and other facilitative processes in disputes between parents and schools; and the Appropriate Dispute Resolution Centre in Pretoria, South Africa.

[12] See C. Menkel-Meadow, "The History and Development of 'A'DR" (Volkerrechtsblog 20 July 2016), at: *http://voelkerrechtsblog.org/the-history-and-development-of-a-dr-alternativeappropriate-dispute-resolution/* [accessed March 2018].

[13] Centre for Effective Dispute Resolution, London, UK, which describes itself as the "largest conflict management and resolution consultancy in the world", at: *https://www cedr com/about_us/* [accessed April 2018].

[14] Civil Procedure Rules 1998 r.1.2(c); Practice Direction Pre-Action Conduct and Protocols paras 4, 8–10.

[15] Ministry of Justice references include: "Housing: Proportionate Dispute Resolution" Cm.7377 Law Commission No.309 May 2008.

are conducted pursuant to a court order or other form of court encouragement). "Alternative" also distinguishes these processes from conventional bilateral negotiation.[16]

"DISPUTE"

1–013 By definition, ADR deals with disputes. However, whilst the term generally denotes disagreement, it can be used in a variety of contexts. It may be used to describe debate or academic argument, for example: "this point has been much disputed". It can be used to represent challenge: "I dispute that". In the context of ADR, it may reflect a legal disagreement, such as neighbours who are "in dispute" about the boundary of their properties.

1–014 The English courts have, on a number of occasions, considered the ambit and meaning of the word in the context of contractual arbitration clauses. Successive Arbitrations Acts have obliged courts to stay proceedings where contracting parties have agreed to refer disputes to arbitration. Hence, in these cases, the exercise of the court's power to stay proceedings has turned on whether there is a dispute. The court decisions have been significant since, if it is decided that no dispute exists, the party who wishes to enforce any aspect of the contract may do so through the courts; but if the court finds that a dispute exists then the specified ADR process must be followed.

1–015 Under the Arbitration Act 1975,[17] the courts had resisted attempts to narrow the meaning of the word to apply only where a claim could be resisted on either the facts or the law. In *Hayter v Nelson*,[18] the parties had contracted to refer any differences that arose under the agreement to arbitration. The court considered that the word "differences" was sufficiently broad to encompass "disputes" and, therefore, had jurisdiction to exercise its power to stay proceedings under the Act. In doing so, it expressed the view that the ordinary meaning of "disputes" and "differences" should be given to these words in arbitration clauses. Hence it must stay proceedings even in situations where the court would otherwise have granted summary judgment.

1–016 In keeping with a wide definition, the courts have held that "dispute" encompasses silence in response to a request for action required under the contract. Hence, in *Ellerine Bros Pty Ltd v Klinger*,[19] there was a provision for disputes to be referred to arbitration. The defendant failed to account as required under the agreement but did not assert that a dispute existed until after a writ had been issued seeking an accounting and payment. The Court of Appeal held that "silence does not mean consent" and that:

---

[16] Negotiation is fundamental to virtually all forms of agreement-based or consensual ADR processes, so an understanding of it and its theories and principles is essential to undertaking and managing these processes effectively. See Ch.4 Negotiation.

[17] The Arbitration Act 1975 s.1 provides that the court "*shall* make an order staying the proceedings" unless it is "satisfied that the arbitration agreement is null and void, inoperative or incapable of being performed or that there is in fact *not any dispute* between the parties in regard to the matter agreed to be referred".

[18] [1990] 2 Lloyd's Rep. 265; *The Times*, 29 March 1990 QBD.

[19] [1982] 1 W.L.R. 1375 CA (Civ Div).

"DISPUTE"

"the fact that the plaintiffs make certain claims which, if disputed, would be referable to arbitration and the fact that the defendant then does nothing—he does not admit the claim, he merely continues a policy of masterly inactivity—does not mean that there is no dispute. There is a dispute until the defendant admits that a sum is due and payable."[20]

These decisions give rise to a potential problem. It was relatively easy, quick and inexpensive to issue proceedings in the court for a debt or to obtain summary judgment. Having to go to arbitration, appoint an arbitrator or arbitrators and get an award is likely to be both time-consuming and expensive.

1–017

In *Halki Shipping Corp v Sopex Oils Ltd*,[21] the Court of Appeal again considered the ambit of the term "dispute", this time under the Arbitration Act 1996 provision which concerns when the court must stay proceedings in the context of arbitration clauses.[22] Under the Arbitration Act 1975 courts could refuse to grant a stay of proceedings where there was "not in fact any dispute between the parties". However, s.1(b) of the Arbitration Act 1996 sets out a core principle: that "parties should be free to agree how their disputes are resolved". Hence, if a dispute exists the courts must grant a stay of proceedings unless satisfied that the arbitration agreement is null and void, inoperative or incapable of being performed.[23] In this case, which has been extensively followed, the Court of Appeal held that, in essence, if a valid arbitration clause exists, the court has very restricted and limited scope to consider the nature or effect of any dispute, and should stay any proceedings brought in the courts so that the matter can be dealt with in the agreed forum.

1–018

This principle was applied subsequently in a case in which it was argued that there was no "dispute" between the parties since the defendant admitted liability, agreed the amount of the claim, and acknowledged that payment had not been made. The question was whether failure to make payment admittedly due constituted a "dispute". The judge, Langley J, held that such refusal was a "dispute" on the basis that if one party required payment and the other refused to pay, they were in dispute: there was no difference between a refusal to admit a claim and a refusal to pay it.[24]

1–019

The courts have interpreted "dispute" in a similar way in the context of decisions relating to other forms of ADR. In *Thames Valley Power Ltd v Total Gas & Power Ltd*,[25] the contract provided for expert determination of any dispute or disagreement. The judge had to decide whether there was a "dispute or disagreement" between the parties, who could not agree as to whether a force majeure notice could be served, a matter which the judge considered was ill-founded. Hence, having regard to this view and to other factors that militated against a stay, he declined to grant a stay. Whilst he considered that the words "dispute or disagreement" should be accorded their ordinary meaning (in line with the arbitration cases), the court's power to order a stay of proceedings in this case was discretionary.

1–020

---

[20] *Ellerine Bros Pty Ltd v Klinger* [1982] 1 W.L.R. 1375 CA (Civ Div), per Templeman LJ at 1383.
[21] [1998] 1 W.L.R. 726; [1998] 1 Lloyd's Rep 465 CA (Civ Div).
[22] Arbitration Act 1996 s.9.
[23] Arbitration Act 1996 s.9.
[24] *Exfin Shipping (India) Ltd Mumbai v Tolani Shipping Co Ltd Mumbai* [2006] EWHC 1090 (Comm).
[25] [2005] EWHC 2208; [2006] 1 Lloyd's Rep. 441.

1–021　These cases suggest that the courts afford a generous interpretation of the word where parties have agreed to refer their disputes to ADR, even when this may lead to greater expense and delay for the parties. This accords with the principle, adopted by the Arbitration Act 1996, that parties should be free to choose their preferred method of dispute resolution. However, this approach may be limited where a court has discretion to refuse to grant a stay of proceedings.[26]

Distinguishing dispute and conflict: the paradox[27]

1–022　Whilst the courts have adopted a broad interpretation of "dispute" to include any difference between parties, whether or not articulated, it is important in the context of ADR to distinguish between disputes and conflict. Generally, "conflict" is used to denote a serious dispute or protracted and complex disagreement whereas disputes are disagreements which are amenable to resolution through third-party decision or party agreement (which may be facilitated). However, this distinction is not straightforward since the terms may be used interchangeably and, additionally, may be paradoxical: on the one hand, "conflict" may be viewed as a generic term, with "dispute" as a class or kind of conflict which manifests itself in distinct, justiciable issues. On the other hand, disputes are likely to involve some element of conflict within them, for example, where parties are in high conflict about the subject-matter of a dispute. Hence disputes may be found within conflicts, and conflicts may be found within disputes.

1–023　The essence of conflict is often associated with something negative and destructive.[28] It is defined as "a state of opposition or hostilities", "a fight or struggle" or "the clashing of opposed principles".[29] It has also been variously described as "a manifestation of differences working against one another"[30]; "disagreements between two or more parties which cause tension for the

---

[26] The issue of what amounts to a dispute also attracted a high incidence of litigation in the context of adjudication under the Housing Grants, Construction and Regeneration Act 1996. Under that Act disputes are referred to an adjudicator for interim decision pending final resolution of disputes through agreement or arbitration. See: I. Ndekugri and V. Russell "Disputing the existence of a dispute as a strategy for avoiding construction adjudication" (2006) 13(4) *Engineering, Construction and Architectural Management* 380; A. Reid & R.C.T. Ellis "Common sense applied to the definition of a dispute" (2007) 25(3/4) *Structural Survey* 239. In the context of housing disputes, subsequent recommendations arising from a Law Commission consultation suggest that in the context of housing disputes greater use should be make of dispute resolution procedures such as mediation and ombudspersons: "Housing: Proportionate Dispute Resolution" Cm.7377 Law Commission No.309 May 2008.

[27] Such disputes may revolve around intensely emotional issues, such as child custody, employment disputes, where parties have strong emotional attachment to the outcome. See, for example: C.A. Coates et al "Parenting Coordination for High Conflict Families" (2003) 41 *Family Court Review* 1.

[28] See Bernard Mayer, *The Dynamics of Conflict: A Guide to Engagement and Intervention*, 2nd edn (San Francisco: Jossey-Bass, 2012), pp.1–33, for his views on the sources of conflict.

[29] Oxford English Dictionary Online (at: *https//en.oxforddictionaries.com/definition/conflict* [accessed 10 May 2018]).

[30] John Crawley, *Constructive Conflict Management: Managing to Make a Difference* (London: Nicholas Brealey Publishing, 1992/1995), pp.10/11.

individuals concerned"[31]; or "a disagreement through which the parties involved perceive a threat to their needs, interests or concerns".[32]

Uncontained conflict may manifest itself in verbal and behavioural disagreements and ultimately in some cases in violence; and in the case of international conflict, war. However, conflict is an integral part of human behaviour, and may be utilised positively to bring about change.[33] Decision-making frequently involves an element of conflict; exchanges of ideas involve conflict; the democratic process is built on the basis of the normalcy of a conflict of ideas and interests.

Various management writers point out that conflict is a fact of life in organisations, though destructive handling of it does not need to be.[34] Other writers make similar points on a more general basis.[35]

Hence, conflict may have a healthy and positive function. It is when it becomes dysfunctional that problems arise. When parties or groups become irreconcilable and the natural mechanisms for managing and resolving conflict, for example by discussion and negotiation, are inadequate or go awry, then the conflict may become potentially damaging and other processes may be needed.

If conflict is more generalised as a clash of opposed principles or a manifestation of differences and may include differing viewpoints and attitudes, disputes—as will be seen from the above outline of case law—are much more specific and involve disagreement over issues capable of resolution by negotiation, mediation or third-party adjudication.[36]

On this definition, the nature of a practitioner's approach is likely to be different for a dispute that can be resolved than for an inter-personal or

---

[31] Vibeke Vindeløv, *Mediation: a non-model* (Copenhagen: DJØF Publishing, 2007), p.42.

[32] See Harry Webne-Behrman, *The Practice of Facilitation: Managing Group Process and Solving Problems* (New York: Quorum Books, 1998).

[33] Andrew Floyer Acland, *A Sudden Outbreak of Common Sense: Managing Conflict Through Mediation* (London: Random House Business Books, 1990), p.69 suggests that "the purpose of conflict is related to change ... all conflict is about the attempt to achieve or resist change". In Thomas F. Crum and John Denver, *The Magic of Conflict: Turning a life of Work into a Work of Art* (Touchstone, New York 1987), Thomas F. Crum says that conflict is "the interference patterns of energies caused by differences, that provides the motivation and opportunity for change". Conflict, he says, is not a contest, and resolving conflict is rarely about who is right, but about the acknowledgment and appreciation of differences.

[34] For example, David Lax and James Sebenius, *The Manager as Negotiator: Bargaining for Co-operation and Competitive Gain* (New York: The Free Press, 1986); and D. M. Kolb and J. M. Bartunek, *Hidden Conflict in Organisations* (USA: Sage Publications, 1992). D. Whetten, K. Cameron and M. Woods in *Effective Conflict Management*, (Pearson Education, 1996) say that "conflict is the life-blood of vibrant, progressive, stimulating organisations. It sparks creativity, stimulates innovation and encourages personal improvement."

[35] Susan Stewart says that "the evidence of history suggests that conflict is more characteristic of human behaviour than is harmony." *Conflict Resolution: A Foundation Guide* (Hampshire: Waterside Press, 1998), p.9. In *Mediating Dangerously: The Frontiers of Conflict Resolution* (San Francisco: Jossey-Bass, 2001), Kenneth Cloke says that conflicts contain information "essential for our growth, learning, intimacy and change."

[36] In a family context—but the principle may be extended to other fields—Marian Roberts describes disputes as "specific, identifiable issues which divide parties", distinguishable from the "wider conflict" associated with family breakdown: see *Mediation in Family Disputes*, 3rd edn (Hampshire: Ashgate Publishing, 2008).

Submerged issues in disputes

1-028 There is not uncommonly an "iceberg" factor in disputes, in which only part is initially apparent, but where much lurks below the surface. This may for example be the case with regard to disagreements involving parties who have or had some form of relationship with one another, which may have degenerated over a period of time. So, for example, in a partnership dispute the issue that has surfaced may not necessarily be the whole or the real problem, which may be more complex, involving underlying differences. There may be hidden agendas in other business or personal relationships, of which the parties themselves may not necessarily be fully conscious. However, this is by no means limited to personal or relationship disputes. Hidden agendas, emotional factors, personality differences, issues of principle, perceptions of fairness and justice, strategic considerations and symbolic significance can be—and commonly are—underlying factors in all kinds of disagreements that may affect the level of conflict and disguise the actual issues in dispute. These issues may make dispute resolution a more complex task than may initially be apparent.

1-029 The existence of submerged issues further blurs the distinction between conflict and dispute, since the underlying issues may well aggravate the conflict between the parties but may not be directly relevant to the actual dispute. By way of example, brothers may be in dispute about their respective rights to the allocation of new shares in a family business, and they may enter mediation to try to resolve this. There may however be deep underlying issues and resentments going back to childhood about how the one has always treated the other, feelings about how their parents may have differentiated between them, and how one is perceived as having taken advantage of family members' goodwill and many other personal issues and antagonisms. The main issue of the shares is the presenting dispute, but it is just one manifestation of underlying conflict between them. It is important for the ADR facilitator to be clear whether his role is to help them resolve the dispute about the shares or to help them resolve the deeper underlying conflict between them. The issue is whether the facilitator's role in this matter is one of dispute resolution, or of conflict resolution. This is not a rhetorical question: it addresses the facilitator's fundamental role and function and has to be agreed between the parties at the outset.

1-030 The intensity of the conflict level in a dispute can range between very low (as for example where there are no personality, emotional or other submerged issues, and the parties have a simple, basic disagreement which they want to resolve) and very high (as where there are serious personality problems coupled with intense emotional factors and other submerged issues, and the dispute carries significant outcome implications for the parties).

---

[37] See the next section under "Resolution" for the different approaches to conflict and dispute and for addressing enduring conflicts.

"RESOLUTION"

Why only disputes anyway?

Although the primary use of ADR is in relation to disputes, and perhaps conflict, the process of engaging a third-party neutral to facilitate or arbitrate an agreed outcome does not have to be limited only to addressing issues where parties are in dispute. Concepts such as "deal mediation", for example, are very properly part of the ADR umbrella. This is a form of mediation in which, rather than working with a dispute, a mediator assists parties who are setting up a deal to do so, particularly in relation to complex negotiations, and to overcome blockages.[38] Similarly, project mediation is a process that helps construction industry teams to communicate more effectively, work more collaboratively and avoid issues turning into conflictual disputes by addressing them at an early stage. The machinery for project mediation is generally built into the contract, and indeed it may be included in any procurement documents.[39]

1–031

"RESOLUTION"

ADR by definition refers to the "resolution" of disputes, which in the context of agreement-based forms of ADR may be understood to equate with settlement and, for adjudicative forms, relates to third-party decision-making to resolve the dispute. However, since ADR may be used at varying stages of a dispute, at times, dispute management may be appropriate rather than resolution. Additionally, the parties and/or the facilitator may have broader aspirations for the ADR process and may, for example, adopt a "transformative" approach to dealing with disputes.[40] Hence the concept of resolution needs to be further considered.

1–032

If there is a distinction between conflict and dispute, however interrelated these concepts may be, then there are surely differences in the way conflicts and disputes can be addressed. Additionally since the term ADR encompasses a broad range of processes, options include third-party decision-making, settlement, prevention, management, transformation, analysis and intervention.

1–033

Dispute resolution or settlement?

In the context of agreement-based ADR, successful "resolution" of the dispute is likely to result in an agreement between the parties to settle the issues under consideration and will, therefore, comprise processes that facilitate settlement.

1–034

However, settlement of the issues in the presenting dispute may leave underlying conflict unresolved. Hence a broader understanding of the term "resolution" may suggest that it should be used only when all issues, presenting

1–035

---

[38] See L. Michael Hager and Robert Pritchard "Deal Mediation: How ADR Techniques Can Help Achieve Durable Agreements in the Global Markets" (1999) *ICSID Foreign Investment Law Journal* 1 and Scott R. Peppet, "Contract Formation in Imperfect Markets: Should We Use Mediators in Deals?" (2004) 19 Ohio S.L.J.

[39] See for example Danny McFadden "Big Projects, Big Disputes—Bring in the Mediators" at *https://www.cedr.com/blog/big-projects-big-disputes-bring-in-the-mediators/*.

[40] See "Dispute resolution: transformation" below and Chs 3 and 9.

1-036 and underlying, have been resolved, and that the term "settlement" is more appropriate to where parties have reached agreement on the issues of the presenting dispute.

1-036 This goes to the essence of the distinction between conflict and dispute. If a practitioner is required to help parties reach agreement to settle a dispute that has no other or underlying conflict, then "settlement" and "resolution" would have the same meaning. If however the practitioner is required to help parties resolve a state of conflict that exists between them, and the dispute is merely one of the ways that the conflict manifests itself, then settlement of the dispute does not of itself necessarily resolve the wider conflict: here "settlement" may not be the same as "resolution" at all. On this principle, if any dispute has underlying conflict that is not resolved by a settlement, then even if the practitioner is only required to deal with the presenting dispute, the term "resolution" would arguably be inappropriate.

1-037 This raises the question as to what the ADR practitioner's proper role is: settlement of the presenting dispute or resolution of the underlying conflict, or both, or something else? The answer lies in the contract that the parties and the practitioner enter into with one another, and the informed decision that parties make as to their requirements. It is obvious that if parties choose mediation, it would not be right to provide psychotherapy, arbitration or any other process that is not mediation. Similarly, if parties seek help in resolving (and the word is used advisedly here) a particular dispute or issue, and they contract for that, then if the dispute is settled, the practitioner's contract is fulfilled even if an underlying conflict remains. If the parties wish the practitioner to help them with their underlying conflict, that would be a different contract—a proper one to address if so required.

1-038 However, in fact, working towards the settlement of a dispute may well provide the opportunity for addressing underlying conflict, and it is not uncommon that reconciliation may take place as the process unfolds. Practitioners would generally regard this as positive and desirable; but the explicit (and necessarily implicit) terms of the contract would have to decide whether this was the primary objective of the process, or an added bonus to an otherwise fulfilled contract.[41]

Dispute management or other intervention

1-039 Not all dispute intervention necessarily requires an ADR practitioner to help parties to resolve a dispute. Indeed, Mayer regards the terminology of "dispute resolution" as limiting, since it implies that resolution is necessarily the practitioner's objective, whereas there are times and situations where resolution is neither possible nor appropriate, yet where the neutral's role may be relevant and helpful.[42] Certainly, there are other roles that may assist parties which do not involve the practitioner in achievement of actual resolution or settlement.

---

[41] The issue of reconciliation and healing as part of an ADR process is addressed in Ch.3, paras 3-025 to 3-029. See also "transformation" below.
[42] Bernard Mayer, *Staying with Conflict—A Strategic Approach to Ongoing Disputes* (San Francisco: Jossey-Bass, 2009).

Parties may, for example, wish to have a neutral person facilitate certain aspects of a dispute, leaving resolution to be dealt with in a different way or forum or at a different time; or they may want the neutral to help manage aspects of an ongoing process. One form of Early Neutral Evaluation (ENE) is an example of such a role, where the evaluator works alongside the parties and their lawyers in guiding them through various stages of litigation, expressing informal and non-binding views on process and/or the merits and being available as needed to smooth the path of the litigation and help create conditions in which settlement can be effectively considered.[43]

Hence the word "resolution" in ADR should not be viewed in too rigid or limiting a way, as an ADR practitioner's role may quite properly comprise something that enhances the resolution process but does not itself engage with the actual resolution as such of the dispute.

Dispute resolution: transformation

In the context of agreement-based processes, there are primarily two ways of viewing transformation in dispute resolution. The first is the transformation of a dispute from an adversarial process into a problem-solving exercise and from a rights-based approach into one that includes an interest-based approach, and the reframing of issues so that they can be effectively addressed and resolved. This transformation of the dispute is what agreement-based ADR may aspire to achieve; but the usage of the term "transformation" is not usual in this context.

More commonly, however, the term refers to the ideological concept of *transformative mediation*.[44] Underpinning this approach are the twin concepts of "empowerment" and "recognition" (rather than problem-solving): the aspiration is that the mediation process has the potential not only to settle disputes but to transform people's lives by increasing their efficacy within conflict and helping them to gain greater acceptance of the person with whom they are in dispute. Hence, it is not the dispute that is transformed but the person.

For a mediator who adheres to a transformative approach, even if the matter is not settled and even if the parties remain unreconciled with one another, mediation is successful if it brings about party recognition and empowerment: settlement is a bonus if it occurs.[45]

While transformative mediation has its supporters, especially but not only in inter-personal issues, the process and matters for resolution are set by the contract agreed between the parties and the third-party facilitator. If the parties make an informed decision at the outset of the process that they seek empowerment and recognition irrespective as to whether or not the dispute is settled, then transformative mediation would be the right approach. If however their primary aspiration is to settle their dispute as far as possible, and if they are not seeking

---

[43] As to Early Neutral Evaluation, see Ch.19. Evaluation as a form of dispute management, which takes different shapes, clearly has potential to be further developed; and the neutral's role could in some circumstances be converted to that of mediator at some stage if required.

[44] For the origins and discussion of this ideology see: R.A. Baruch Bush and J.P. Folger, *The Promise of Mediation: the Transformative Approach to Conflict* (Jossey-Bass San Francisco 1994). See Chs 3 and 9 for further discussion about transformative mediation.

[45] Foreword to Baruch Bush and Folger, *The Promise of Mediation: The Transformative Approach to Conflict* (1994), by the consulting editor, Jeffrey Z. Rubin.

transformation (albeit that they might, if asked, be willing to accept it as a bonus), then the facilitator's task is to help them settle the dispute.

1–046 It is arguable that parties may not necessarily appreciate the transformative possibilities of the mediation process and may, therefore, agree to an issues-based approach. Conversely, parties choosing the transformative approach need to appreciate that settlement of the dispute is not the primary objective. The particular ideology or approach of the facilitator, and/or professional advice offered to the parties, is likely to be influential in determining the parameters of the process and its resolution. It is important that, in any case, the particular process, its objectives and possibilities, are fully explained in order in order to ensure that parties make informed choices.

Conflict resolution and other interventions

1–047 As indicated previously, conflict resolution is not necessarily the same as dispute resolution. A wide range of practitioners from all walks of life may specialise in conflict resolution. This may include, for example, family therapists and/or counsellors in relation to family conflict, or management consultants in relation to organisational conflict. These would not ordinarily be the professionals one might engage—in those capacities in any event—to help with specific dispute resolution.

1–048 As the name indicates, conflict resolution involves attempts to move people away from their conflict into positive outcomes. This may be achieved through the use of a variety of strategies and processes including, for example, mediation, facilitated dialogue, third-party consultation, collaborative problem-solving or consensus-building.[46]

1–049 There are further roles for neutral practitioners who choose to work in the field of conflict. One possibility is *conflict prevention*,[47] a process that is particularly relevant in the international field to prevent disagreements from escalating into violence and war. This is applicable, also, to conflict in the community, workplace, families and many other situations. Conflict prevention may involve a range of strategies such as changing one's communication style, responses and behaviour; developing systems and rules for anticipating and de-escalating conflict; and establishing consensus-building approaches. This is not the same as *conflict avoidance*, which espouses strategies, consciously or unconsciously, to sidestep having to address the conflict.[48]

---

[46] For detailed discussion about the theories and practice of conflict resolution and prevention see: O. Ramsbotham, T. Woodhouse and H. Miall, *Contemporary Conflict Resolution*, 4th edn (Polity Press, 2016); P.T. Coleman, M. Deutsch and E.C. Marcus, *The Handbook of Conflict Resolution: Theory and Practice*, 3rd edn (San Francisco: Jossey Bass, 2014); J. Berkovitch, V. Kremenyuk and I.W. Zartman *Sage Handbook of Conflict Resolution* (Sage Publications Ltd, 2008).

[47] This term was adopted by UN Secretary-General Dag Hammarskjold in the 1950s and has gained political currency due to the humanitarian and other costs involved in international conflict. See, for example the United Nations Development Programme on Democratic Governance and Peacebuilding: *http://www.undp.org/content/undp/en/home/democratic-governance-and-peacebuilding.html*.

[48] A number of professional bodies (including the International Chamber of Commerce, the Royal Institute of Chartered Surveyors and the Royal Institute of British Architects), in the construction and engineering industries have joined together to introduce measures designed to avoid conflict in an effort to combat the financial costs of disputes. In one example, they have introduced a Conflict Avoidance Pledge to encourage and equip signatories to work towards the avoidance of conflict.

Conflict prevention may be different, also, from *conflict transformation*, in which the aim is to transform conflict into a peaceful outcome, particularly but not necessarily at the societal, national and international level.[49] This approach focuses on the context and relationship between the actors and looks for ways to bring about collective healing, reconciliation, restoration and building of long term goals.[50]

1–050

Another way of addressing conflict is through *conflict management*, which is relevant where it is not practicable to seek to resolve conflict immediately, but where management of it over time may be appropriate. This may apply, for example, to intractable or enduring conflict,[51] which is deadlocked and not amenable to resolution. Such conflicts may, for example, embody profound differences of values that may not be able to be reconciled, such as the conflict between the pro-abortion and the pro-life lobbies, who may not be able to resolve their differences, but who may need to be able to live together in a common society; or the conflict between parents who have fundamentally different views about bringing up their children but who need to find a way to co-exist and to function effectively.[52]

1–051

ADR RECONSTITUTED

The message from an analysis of the three component parts of ADR is that a strict and comprehensive definition for the processes encompassed within the term ADR is elusive. The processes may be adjudicative or agreement-based, and though they may be prescribed to an extent by legislation (as under the Arbitration Acts), they are shaped by the requirements and wishes of the parties, and may be influenced by the ideologies and approaches of the third-party facilitator. Hence, rather than restrict the scope of ADR processes, we may be flexible and creative and adopt a wide range of possibilities under its umbrella.

1–052

---

[49] For example, the organisation Search for Common Ground describes itself as working "to transform the way the world deals with conflict—away from adversarial approaches and towards collaborative problem solving (working through) local partners to find culturally appropriate means to strengthen societies" capacity to deal with conflicts constructively: to understand the differences and act on the commonalities."

[50] John Paul Lederach has written extensively on this subject, for example *Preparing for Peace: Conflict Transformation Across Cultures* (New York: Syracuse University Press, 1996); and *The Moral Imagination: The Art and Soul of Building Peace* (USA: Oxford University Press, 2005).

[51] Mayer prefers to focus on such conflicts as being "enduring", "ongoing" or "long-term" rather than "intractable" because the latter term, in his view, suggests that there is no hope of working effectively to deal with the conflict. Bernard Mayer, *Staying with Conflict—A Strategic Approach to Ongoing Disputes*, see fn.42.

[52] A useful overview of "intractable" conflicts, their characteristics and approaches to addressing is provided at: P.T. Coleman, "Intractable Conflict" in P.T. Coleman, M. Deutsch and E.C. Marcus, *The Handbook of Conflict Resolution: Theory and Practice* p.708—see fn.46.

CHAPTER 2

An Overview of the ADR Landscape

INTRODUCTION

Third-party facilitation of disputes has gone on since people first established communities, in the earliest societies around the world.¹ 2–001

In its present manifestation, ADR has assumed a range of forms and processes. Over the last two or three decades, there have been a number of developments: 2–002

- Mediation has become the predominant non-adjudicatory process in England and Wales and has to a greater or lesser extent been integrated into the dispute resolution mainstream.² In the early days of ADR, there was a sense that dispute resolution could be creative and flexible, combining different elements in various permutations to create a wide range of hybrid, bespoke processes to be adapted to the needs of each individual situation and dispute.
- Whereas arbitration is regulated by statute in the UK and elsewhere, mediation does not have statutory authority; but various forms of regulation are in place or being developed.³ Standard-setting bodies have been established that provide directly or indirectly for mediator accreditation and practice in the civil-commercial, family and other fields.
- Mediation organisations and groups have been established internationally, nationally and regionally, dealing with civil, commercial, workplace, family, community and a wide range of other issues. Many also offer training and accreditation of mediators. These stand alongside arbitration

---

¹ S. Roberts in *Order and Dispute: An Introduction to Legal Anthropology* (Harmondsworth: Penguin Books, 1979) traces the way that simpler, non-State societies organised their systems for maintaining order and resolving disputes using a range of strategies including informal mediation and the use of neutral umpires. And Derek Roebuck has challenged "the assumption that mediation—even as we now know it and even as court-ordered—is a modern invention of lawyers when it is the most natural form of dispute resolution in the world". See Derek Roebuck's chapter: "The myth of modern mediation" in *Disputes and Differences: Comparisons in Law, Language and History* (Oxford: Holo Books, The Arbitration Press, 2010)—originally appearing in (2007) 73 *Arbitration* 105.

² This is certainly the case with family mediation where there is now a requirement under the provisions of the Children and Families Act 2014, s.10 of which requires a person to attend a family mediation information and assessment meeting before making a relevant family application. Whilst there is no equivalent statutory provision for general civil matters, threaded through the CPR are examples of efforts to encourage litigants to pursue ADR and more often than not when pursued, the process choice is mediation.

³ By way of example the USA have adopted the Uniform Mediation Act 2001, modified and updated in 2003.

- institutions, many of which also offer mediation and other processes. Many law firms and barristers' chambers have also established specialist dispute resolution groups.
- ADR processes have been incorporated into judicial procedures, court rules and protocols and are now expected to be considered and wherever practicable used before or alongside litigation. Court judgments and rulings periodically refer to or promote ADR processes.[4]
- Many institutions, organisations, commercial bodies and businesses now offer some form of facilitated dispute resolution process to address complaints, claims and disagreements.
- The teaching of ADR processes has become widespread in universities and law schools[5] and research and specialist writing have analysed, informed and supported practice.[6]
- Among the many other contexts for impartial third-party facilitation, the role of mediation in helping to resolve international conflict, for example in Northern Ireland, should not be overlooked.

2–003 The value of having a skilled impartial facilitator to assist parties in dispute to reach a resolution as an alternative to litigation has been widely recognised; and although mediation is the primary vehicle through which this is done, there are other various ways to do so. See Goldberg and Sander for their views on dispute resolution process choice.[7]

2–004 For example, a Claims Handling Agreement to administratively coordinate a significant number of coal miners' claims for damages arising from their respiratory illnesses was created as a form of ADR measure. When reviewed by the court, the judge considered it to be "a fair and workable scheme for disposing of many thousands of cases by administrative means". The judge expressed the view that:

> "consistent with the duty of the Court to deal with cases brought before it in ways which are just and proportionate it should do what it can to encourage parties only to litigate what cannot be reasonably disposed of by other means, whether those be by way of arbitration, mediation, administrative scheme or howsoever".[8]

2–005 In another example, a council had closed down a residential care home for the elderly and a number of residents sought a judicial review of the council's decision-making procedures. In appeal proceedings, Lord Woolf took the view that the applicants should have taken up the council's offer to set up a complaints review panel, which was perceived as a form of ADR—"steps to resolve the dispute without the involvement of the court." Lord Woolf stated:

> "Particularly in the case of such disputes, both sides must by now be acutely conscious of the contribution alternative dispute resolution could make to resolving disputes in a manner that both met the needs of the parties and the public, and saved

---

[4] See Ch.5.
[5] Particularly in the USA and Canada and to an extent university law schools in the UK as well.
[6] This is the case in the USA, but not nearly to the same extent in the UK.
[7] Frank E. A. Sander and Stephen B. Goldberg, "Fitting the Forum to the Fuss: A User-Friendly Guide to Selecting an ADR Procedure" (1994) 10.1 *Negotiation Journal* 49–68.
[8] Per Sir Michael Turner in *AB v British Coal Corp* [2004] EWHC 1372 at [52] and [109].

INTRODUCTION

time, expense and stress. Today, sufficient should be known about Alternative Dispute Resolution to make the failure to adopt it, in particular when public money was involved, indefensible."[9]

In another public law case involving a damages claim under the Human Rights Act, the court decided that the Parliamentary Commissioner and the Local Government Ombudsman were included within the ambit of ADR for the purposes of public law proceedings.[10] The judge expressed the view that:

2–006

> "if there is a legitimate claim for other relief, permission should if appropriate be limited to that relief and consideration given to deferring permission for the damages claim, adjourning or staying that claim until use has been made of ADR, whether by a reference to a mediator or an ombudsman or otherwise"

The construction industry has also found creative ways to avoid court litigation, where the practice of incorporating dispute resolution machinery into contracts for major projects is well established. Its use of adjudication is now underpinned by statute in the UK[11] and the creation of Dispute Boards is increasingly common even beyond the construction industry. In these processes, an adjudicator or a Dispute Board is established with the power to adjudicate (or, in the case of a Board, alternatively to make non-binding recommendations), which in either event become binding if neither party challenges them within a prescribed period, commonly 30 days, by referring them for further determination, usually by arbitration. These forms of ADR allow parties to continue work on the project notwithstanding the existence of the dispute, and provide for interim resolution by a person or group with knowledge, skill and understanding of the project.[12]

2–007

Although mediation has taken centre stage, the concept of creating hybrid ADR processes remains as relevant as ever and should be an essential part of every dispute practitioner's repertoire. This may involve combining different non-adjudicative processes with one another, or perhaps even just different models of the same process.[13] Alternatively, it may involve combining a consensual process such as mediation with an adjudicatory one, such as arbitration: hence the processes of med-arb and arb-med, or adjourning a mediation so that parties can jointly obtain a non-binding opinion on a sticking issue from an agreed expert and bring it back to the adjourned session for consideration.

2–008

---

[9] *R. (on the application of Cowl) v Plymouth City Council* [2001] EWCA Civ 1935; [2002] 1 W.L.R. 803 at [1] and [25].
[10] Per Lord Woolf CJ, in *Anufrijeva v Southwark LBC* [2003] EWCA Civ 1406 at [81]. The role of the Ombudsman in the resolution of disputes is considered in further detail in Ch.18.
[11] In the UK, the Housing Grants, Construction and Regeneration Act 1996 provided for mandatory adjudication in the construction and engineering industry.
[12] For further detailed discussion on the process of Dispute Boards in the construction industry, see Cyril Chern, *Chern on Dispute Boards* (CRC Press, 2015).
[13] For example, family mediators in the UK—and elsewhere—have tended to follow a mediation model in which, among other things, parties meet jointly with the mediator throughout the process and the mediator does not maintain any confidences; whereas in a commercial model, separate confidential meetings are standard. These models have been in a process of careful and appropriate integration in family mediation practice.

2–009   These ADR processes will be more fully examined in this book, but meanwhile, it may be helpful to have an overview of dispute resolution processes.

LITIGATION AND NEGOTIATION: THE ADR SYMBIOSIS

2–010   ADR refers to the alternatives to litigation, so it may be helpful, in order to place ADR processes in context, to outline briefly the key elements of the litigation process.

Litigation refers, of course, to a civil court action brought by a claimant against a defendant based on legal principles, asserting some right or legal entitlement. Formal procedures for the conduct of litigation may involve a number of stages including setting out the details of the dispute (in "pleadings" or "statements of case"), disclosure of relevant documents ("discovery"), pre-trial hearings before judicial officers dealing with any preliminary issues and preparing for the eventual trial, perhaps the preliminary exchange of evidence ("witness statements") and in some cases the joining of other parties to the action. If the case does not settle, the litigation process is concluded by a trial and a substantive judgment ("the court order").[14]

2–011   Litigation is State provided and supported: the courts are maintained for anyone to use, judges and court officials are paid by the State,[15] court orders can generally be appealed to a State-provided higher court, and once final, can be enforced by following procedural rules. In the ADR context, if one sees all dispute resolution processes as comprising a continuum, with the most rigid, adjudicatory processes at one end and the most flexible, consensual processes at the other, litigation would comprise the rigid, adjudicatory marker at one end of the line.

2–012   If litigation is at one end of the dispute resolution spectrum, bilateral negotiation (by parties personally) is at the other end, being the most flexible and consensual way of resolving disputes.[16] Negotiation is fundamental to all consensual ADR processes, and forms an inherent part of them, but on its own it is not generally regarded as an ADR process: the general view is that consensual ADR provides some additional process that enhances or supports negotiation, most usually some form of impartial third-party facilitation.[17]

2–013   ADR has a symbiotic relationship with litigation and negotiation, in that it depends on both for its vital functions, certainly as far as any consensual processes are concerned. Self-evidently the facilitated negotiation processes that comprise ADR could not exist in the absence of negotiation. ADR's synergic

---

[14] In England and Wales the Civil Procedure Rules which came into force on 26 April 1999, replaced the Rules of the Supreme Court, and provide procedural guidance for conducting litigation in the Court of Appeal, High Court and County Court for all civil claims.

[15] Though parties may be required to pay court fees for various procedures.

[16] Negotiation is further dealt with at Ch.4.

[17] A view is occasionally heard that bilateral negotiation without any supplementary facilitation is itself a form of ADR. Given the general and flexible nature of ADR, there is no definitive or purist view on this, nor indeed is there any need for one. Because of its inherent role in consensual dispute resolution, this work gives attention to negotiation as a separate process and it really does not matter whether or not it is defined formally as ADR.

relationship with litigation is, however, sometimes less acknowledged, as some proponents of consensual procedures promote these over litigation: the stark fact is that mediation would not be effective in most cases without the backstop of litigation or some form of adjudication. Mediation and other ADR processes take place "in the shadow of the law"[18]: if parties cannot resolve their dispute in a consensual ADR process, they are free to have it adjudicated, by a court if no other adjudicatory procedure is agreed or prescribed. Without some such machinery, any processes that relied purely on parties reaching agreement would be hopelessly deficient in the face of parties declining to agree, for good reason or not.

THE SPECTRUM OF PROCESSES FROM CONSENSUAL TO ADJUDICATORY

The spectrum of processes with litigation at the one end—adjudication with rigid procedures and minimal party control—and negotiation at the other end—consensual with flexible procedures and maximum party decision-making control—is sometimes referred to as the dispute resolution continuum. Between the adjudicatory and the negotiation ends of this continuum, hybrid ADR processes incorporate elements of negotiation, facilitation and adjudication, binding or non-binding, in different permutations. The greater the individual party's control, power and authority and the more flexible the process, the more consensual they may be regarded; the less their control, power and authority, and the greater the third-party decision-maker's power and the more rigid the procedures, the more adjudicatory they may be viewed. 2–014

Of course, individual power, control and authority are not necessarily objectives that disputants seek, but simply comprise one way of comparing processes. For many people, retaining power, control and authority are important and indeed provide a strong rationale for using ADR. For others, they are of little consequence: they seek an effective resolution of their dispute, through the assertion of their rights, by seeing "justice done" accordingly to the law, rather than a desire that their dispute be merely resolved efficiently and/or effectively. 2–015

OUTLINE OF THE PROCESSES

It should be noted that these processes will be considered in more detail elsewhere in this book. But by way of brief overview, the following summarises each process, with particular reference to the issue of third-party authority and control versus party control and the rigidity or flexibility of process.[19] The role of the law in all of these processes is important as it is in itself an arbiter between the parties and acts as a constraint on the third-party neutral. 2–016

---

[18] See R. H. Mnookin and L. Kornhauser "Bargaining in the Shadow of the Law: The Case of Divorce" (1979) 88 Yale. L. J. 950.
[19] See L. Steffek and H. Unberath, *Regulating Dispute Resolution: ADR and Access to Justice at the Crossroad* (Oxford: Hart 2014), for more detailed accounts of these processes.

AN OVERVIEW OF THE ADR LANDSCAPE

Adjudicatory: third-party responsibility

Litigation

Private judging

Administrative or statutory tribunals

Arbitration

Expert determination

Adjudication

Dispute Board

Court-annexed arbitration

Ombudsman

Arb-med; med-arb

Evaluation (early neutral evaluation)

Neutral fact-finding expert

Mini-trial (Executive Tribunal)

Negotiation (through representatives)

Collaborative practice

Mediation (involving evaluative element)

Mediation (purely facilitative)

Negotiation (by parties personally)

Consensual: parties' own responsibility

Litigation

The neutral is a judge, master or other official appointed by the Court to make a binding determination, and in some jurisdictions, also a jury.

2–017

Parties have least control. Third-party neutral has most power and makes binding determinations on procedure and substance. Procedural rules are strictly prescribed. The parties do however retain the choice to commence litigation or respond to it.

Private judging

Where this procedure has been adopted, the Court refers the case to a referee privately chosen by the parties to decide some or all of the issues, or to establish any facts.

2–018

Similar to litigation, but parties can choose (and must pay for) the neutral and can agree to simplify and speed up procedures.

Administrative or statutory tribunals

Binding adjudication based on statutory requirements, such as establishing rent levels, compensation awards or social security benefits through tribunals and appeal tribunals.

2–019

Procedures tend to be more informal.

Arbitration

A process, in England and Wales and elsewhere regulated by statute,[20] in which a neutral, privately chosen by the disputants or by a body agreed by them, makes a binding determination. Procedural rules may be ad hoc or set by arbitral organisation. Various sub-categories of arbitration have been developed.

2–020

Similar to litigation, but parties can agree choice of arbitrator, choice of legal rules and/or norms which should form the basis for the judgment and the procedure can be tailored to meet their needs. The arbitrator makes a binding, enforceable award.

Court-annexed arbitration

Available in some jurisdictions: the arbitration is initially non-binding, but may become binding if neither party appeals. In other jurisdictions, arbitration through the court is immediately binding. Where the award is not initially binding but may become so, this is similar to the principles of adjudication. Where it is binding right away, it is the same as arbitration.

2–021

---

[20] The Arbitration Act 1996.

Expert determination

2–022 Parties appoint an expert, who is not an arbitrator and is not subject to the 1996 Arbitration Act, to consider issues and make a binding decision or appraisal (which is not an arbitral award) without necessarily having to conduct an enquiry following adjudicatory rules.

Procedures accord with contractual instructions given by parties to the third-party expert.

Adjudication

2–023 Mainly used in construction and engineering industry: an informal process in which an adjudicator is appointed to deal with disputes as they arise.

The adjudicator has authority to make decisions using informal procedures, which are binding unless and until either party challenges them by going to arbitration or litigation.

Dispute Board

2–024 Set up at the start of a contract, in the construction industry and increasingly other industries,[21] to deal with disputes as they arise, either by making recommendations or decisions. Very similar to adjudication, but commonly three neutrals on Board rather than just one.

Ombudsman

2–025 An independent and impartial neutral third-party who deals with public complaints against maladministration. Also used in certain sectors such as legal services and insurance. Can investigate, criticise and publicise, and sometimes can award compensation.

Degree of party control depends on terms of reference of individual ombudsman. Usually power is in the hands of the neutral third-party. Sometimes a compensation award allows one party freedom to choose acceptance or not.

Arb-Med

2–026 Parties have an arbitration and the arbitrator seals the award, then they mediate the dispute, aiming to avoid unsealing the award. Another usage is to enter into and immediately adjourn arbitration, then mediate with a view to having agreement made a consent award.

Unlike med-arb, the arbitration procedure is held first—and the sealed award is used as a prompt to settlement. The other usage is mediation in all respects, but with an ability to turn the settlement into an award; and if not settled, the arbitration leg revives and takes effect.

---

[21] Notably the financial services industry, shipping, engineering and the oil and gas industries. For further details see The Dispute Board Federation at *http://www.dbfederation.org/* [accessed 10 May 2018].

Med-Arb

The impartial third-party neutral acts as mediator, and if the parties cannot agree, becomes an arbitrator to make a binding determination. There are variations giving parties rights to opt out of this process in some versions.

2–027

As for mediation during the first stage; but if parties are bound to the arbitration phase then the next stage may be viewed as for arbitration. In some versions different people may act in each capacity.

Evaluation/Early neutral evaluation (ENE)

An independent and impartial third-party neutral chosen by the parties makes an evaluation of the case based on legal norms, usually its merits or some aspect, which is not binding on the parties but helps them in their decision-making. An evaluator may also help parties narrow and define issues and promote efforts to settle.

2–028

This falls into the category of non-binding evaluative processes. Power remains with the parties, but the third-party neutral can influence them by evaluating.

Neutral fact-finding expert

A neutral expert is appointed by the parties to investigate issues of fact, technicality or law, who produces a report, helps towards settlement, and if agreed, a report may be used in court or arbitration. The third-party neutral may also be given a mediation role.

2–029

If the third-party neutral's role is to produce a report that all parties agree in advance to accept, this gives the neutral great power. If, more commonly, the report is non-binding, then it still has authority.

Mini-trial (Executive Tribunal)

Lawyers for the parties present their cases to a panel comprising the parties and an impartial third-party neutral. The neutral helps clarify the issues and evaluate the merits, and may also mediate after presentations and evaluation. No binding determination is made, but the process helps the parties evaluate realistically.

2–030

In the US, the presentation may be to a mock jury, which makes a mock, non-binding determination: the Summary Jury Trial.

Negotiation (through representatives)

No third-party neutral is involved. Representatives of each party negotiate with one another. Parties retain power to agree terms.

2–031

Parties retain control over outcome but little control over process and content, which is in hands of representatives.

Collaborative practice

2-032 Parties each appoint lawyer under contract to deal with issues by negotiation without contested proceedings and to stand down from further acting if contested action becomes necessary. Structured framework for process that includes parties in direct negotiations supported by lawyers. This is most commonly used for divorce and relationship breakdown disputes.

Parties retain control over outcome, supported by lawyers who are also active in negotiations in structured meetings.

Mediation (involving evaluative element)

2-033 An impartial third-party neutral who has no authority to make any decisions, uses skills to assist parties to negotiate settlement terms and arrive at their own resolution. The neutral may express some view on merits of issues (how and to what extent this is done may vary widely).

The parties have some influence over process and full control over decision-making. The evaluative aspect is non-binding and may help parties reassess their positions.

Mediation (purely facilitative)

2-034 As for evaluative mediation save that the impartial third-party neutral does not express a view in any way or challenge parties' perceptions.

Parties have influence over process, retain decision-making power, and are not directly influenced by the third-party neutral.

Conciliation

2-035 This is broadly the same as mediation, but there is some variation of understanding as to how it differs or indeed whether or not it is different. Some regard it as more proactive and evaluative than mediation, others take an opposite view and see it as very informal and exploratory with no evaluation possible. There is no consistency of usage. In this book no distinction is made between mediation and conciliation.[22]

Negotiation (by parties personally)

2-036 No impartial third-party neutral is involved. Parties negotiate directly with one another.

Parties have total control over process, content and outcome. Maximum power.

---

[22] It should be noted however that some international instruments (e.g. the United Nations where National Human Rights Institutions and their complaint handling roles are concerned) distinguish between conciliation and mediation where the third-party neutral ensures that settlements are in accordance with some external factor (such as the legal merits and/or the public interest).

STANDARD OR BESPOKE PROCESSES

It is an interesting phenomenon that innovative processes that challenge established procedures resist further innovation once they become the norm. Perhaps this is the systemic equivalent of homeostasis, the principle whereby living beings and organisms regulate their internal environment so as to function at a stable, constant level, despite changes in the environment. This can be a healthy force, preventing inappropriate changes from taking place. It can also be a reflection of stubborn resistance to change. 2–037

As mediation has become entrenched, so have some of the attitudes towards maintaining standard models of working. In the UK for example there are fixed expectations that the parties will exchange case summaries and documents and will then meet on an assigned "mediation day" when a broadly standard procedure will be followed. In family cases, the anticipation has been that couples will meet jointly with mediators without lawyers present and will have periodical joint sessions over a period of weeks or months, again following a standard format (though this has changed to some extent with the introduction of a "hybrid" model combining elements of the commercial model). 2–038

This preference for consistency is not surprising, given especially that when mediation was in its early stages, it was necessary to show that the process was a solid and viable alternative to litigation with procedural certainty and consistency. And in many ways these expectations are positive: there are advantages in having an established and known format and procedure. 2–039

But the disadvantage is that "one size fits all" is not always the best course for some individual cases, which may benefit from a more personalised and bespoke process. Indeed, some will be found to be quite inappropriate for the standard models, and sometimes practitioners may ironically be faced with resistance to considering other ways of working. 2–040

It may be helpful to consider the ways in which the standard models can be used to embody a creative approach, and the ways in which bespoke hybrid processes can be created. 2–041

Using the standard models and designing bespoke processes

Both arbitration and mediation have inherent scope within their frameworks for variation, flexibility and creativity: procedures can be adapted to suit the needs of each case. There is generally a wide discretion as to the conduct of each process.[23] 2–042

In mediation, a preliminary meeting at which the parties or their lawyers meet the mediator to identify the issues on an initial basis and discuss process is generally beneficial, where this is logistically and practically possible, and economically viable. It enables the mediator to assess whether a standard or bespoke process is needed. Where a bespoke process is required, it can be designed with the parties or lawyers. Where the standard procedure is required—as may be likely in most cases—the preliminary meeting can serve the 2–043

---

[23] This assumes that the mediator is using a model that gives him or her management responsibility, perhaps subject to consultation.

2–044 purpose of planning for the substantive meeting, arranging practicalities and enhancing the prospect of a successful outcome.[24]

Where a preliminary meeting is impracticable to arrange, the neutral may deal with matters on the phone. Further options are available and are likely to be increasingly used as communication resources and technology develop: for example virtual meetings, telepresence video-telephony and teleconferencing, secure email and encrypted document transactions all facilitate communication.

2–045 Procedures can be entirely novel and specific to the needs of the situation, as for example was established with the Claims Handling Agreement outlined above. What is needed is an understanding of available processes and a creative willingness on the part of all concerned to design a specific procedure that meets the needs of the situation. This is in the best traditions of ADR.

SOME FURTHER CONSIDERATIONS FOR THE DEVELOPMENT OF ADR

2–046 In January 2016 a decision was taken by the Civil Justice Council (CJC) to establish a Working Party "to review the ways in which ADR is at present encouraged and positioned within the civil justice system in England and Wales." That group produced its Interim Report on the future role of ADR in civil justice in October 2017, inviting submissions for its final report.[25]

2–047 That report reviewed the landscape of ADR provision in England and Wales and current measures for the encouragement of ADR and considered whether there was a need for measures stronger than pure persuasion to promote the use of ADR. It considered three different forms of possible compulsion. These were:

- a requirement that the parties in all cases (or in all cases of a particular type or subject-matter) engage in or attempt ADR as pre-condition of access to the court, with the claimant unable to issue proceedings until evidence of the appropriate efforts is produced;
- a requirement that the parties have in all cases (or all cases of a particular type or subject-matter) engaged in or attempted ADR at some later stage such as the Case Management hearing;
- a power in the court to require unwilling parties in a particular case to engage in ADR on an ad hoc basis in the course of case management.[26]

2–048 The working group expressed the interim view that the Court should promote the use of ADR "more actively at and around the allocation and directions stage". A minority of the group would go further and introduce ADR either as a condition of access to the Court or later as a condition of progress beyond the Court's case management conference.

---

[24] This is dealt with in Chs 8 and 9.
[25] See: *https://www.judiciary.gov.uk/publications/cjc-invite-submissions-on-the-future-role-of-adr-in-civil-justice/* [accessed 10 May 2018]. At the time of publication of this work, the Final Report is still awaited.
[26] See para.8.3 of the Interim Report.

SOME FURTHER CONSIDERATIONS FOR THE DEVELOPMENT OF ADR

The working group also gave positive consideration to the opportunities that digital access to the courts might give for online dispute resolution (ODR) resources to be used. In this regard, and generally, it referred to Lord Justice Briggs' Final Report on the Civil Courts Structure Review which he presented in July 2016.[27] In that Report Lord Briggs referred to ADR generally, and mediation and conciliation in particular.[28] He favoured the development of an Online Court and concluded that "The materials accessible to court users by engaging with the Online Court should emphasise that litigation should be regarded as a last resort, after using all available means of pre-issue ADR".[29]

2–049

---

[27] See *https://www.judiciary.gov.uk/wp-content/uploads/2016/07/civil-courts-structure-review-final-report-jul-16-final-1.pdf* [accessed 10 May 2018].
[28] For example, in the section "Civil/ADR" at paras 2.16–2.28 and at 6.71–6.74 and 11.22–11.28.
[29] See his specific recommendations at para.12.15, sub-para.11, also at sub-para.2 with reference to mediation and sub-paras 5–26 with reference to the Online Court.

CHAPTER 3

ADR Philosophies and Motivation: Common Values and Differences

A BROAD CHURCH

Unlike litigation, which has the single object of providing procedures to decide disputes based on the principles of law and rights, and in some very limited circumstances equity, there is no single philosophy underpinning or motivating ADR.[1] Rather, a number of different ideas, rationales and considerations have influenced its development, some overlapping and some inimical to the others.

3–001

Particular beliefs can share fundamental principles and convictions and yet can have internal divisions, where aspects of those philosophies conflict. Differing religious beliefs exist within the various branches of Christianity, Islam and Judaism. The political spectrum comprises diverse sub-groups, which despite a common underlying belief, have fundamentally different views on some detailed issue of principle.

3–002

In some ways, and not entirely without irony as introduced in Ch.2, ADR replicates some of these systems, in that although fundamental principles are shared by all the models and groups of practice, there are also some differences of *Weltanschauung,* or world view, within its proponents and practitioners. This "broad church" of models and beliefs enriches the whole and brings variety, vibrancy and a range of choices to the practice of ADR. This appreciation is relevant to understanding the variations of philosophy, attitudes and practice within the various ADR practices.

3–003

SHARED VALUES AND MOTIVATION

Within adjudicatory forms of ADR the shared motivation is to provide processes that are fair and effective and which provide a considered and just outcome more speedily and at a lower cost than litigating through the courts. All involve a privately appointed impartial person considering the relevant facts and making a decision as to which party is right and how that finding is to be incorporated into

3–004

---

[1] Note, however, the development of motivating influences in England and Wales such as the Mediation Information and Assessment Meeting requirement for private family matters and the encouragement of parties to use the services of ACAS, judicial or other mediation, or other means of resolving their employment related disputes by agreement, both underpinned by statutory provision and considered in more detail elsewhere in this book.

3-005 Similarly, within consensual ADR processes, the principles that are shared are more significant and fundamental than any differences of view and practice. The shared values and motivation in this context include the following:

The principle of negotiated agreement

3-006 A fundamental principle shared by all proponents of consensual ADR is the proposition that, with limited and specific exceptions, for example where matters of public policy need to be publicly heard and decided or where urgent injunctive relief is needed and is unlikely to be obtained by agreement, the parties have much more control over the outcome and can reduce cost, delay and risk if they choose to resolve their differences by a negotiated agreement that is acceptable to them, rather than through contentious proceedings. Invariably there is likely to be an element of compromise, but there is also scope for more creative and mutually beneficial provisions in an agreed outcome.

3-007 Negotiation underpins the mediation process and as pointed out by Roebuck, who has traced the use of settlement facilitation historically, even adjudicative processes have historically been incorporated into negotiated mediation agreements:

> "Everywhere in the Ancient Greek world, including Ptolemaic Egypt, arbitration was normal and in arbitration the mediation element was primary. However formal the procedure, mediation was attempted first and a mediated settlement was preferred, so that even an adjudication might, where possible, be incorporated in an agreement."[2]

3-008 There is a clearly established public policy in England and Wales "that parties should be encouraged so far as possible to settle their disputes without resort to litigation".[3] This approach has been incorporated into civil procedure of England and Wales and is an underpinning principle of the Civil Procedure Rules (CPR).[4] As processes that assist parties with their negotiations towards dispute settlement, non-adjudicatory ADR including in particular mediation fully supports this public policy.

3-009 It should be said that there is a view among some academics that a mediated compromise solution to a dispute may be undesirable. One of the primary concerns is that mediation places compromise ahead of legal justice. Fiss for instance takes the view that:

> "a capitulation to the conditions of mass society and should be neither encouraged nor praised parties might settle while leaving justice undone."[5]

---

[2] Derek Roebuck, "The myth of modern mediation" (2007) 73(1) *Arbitration: the Journal of the Chartered Institute of Arbitrators* 1.
[3] Per Oliver LJ in *Cutts v Head* [1984] Ch. 290; [1984] 2 W.L.R. 349.
[4] See Civil Procedure Act 1997 which introduced the CPR, which in turn place an emphasis on litigation avoidance and the promotion and use of ADR where possible.
[5] O. Fiss, "Against Settlement" (1984) 93 Yale L.J. 1073, 1075, 1085.

These views have engendered considerable debate, both for and against, and are to some extent mirrored in the views of Genn, who in 2008 claimed that "mediation is not about just settlement, it is just about settlement".[6]

3–010

There is however a substantial consensus among dispute resolution practitioners that an agreement between parties resolving[7] their issues in a way that both find acceptable is preferable to continued conflict culminating in judicial determination. Many such agreements are achieved by direct negotiation between the parties or more usually their representatives. Where that cannot be achieved, consensual ADR processes provide mechanisms for parties in dispute to work towards reaching a negotiated agreement. This view is widely shared by academics and writers on this subject.[8]

3–011

Facilitating resolution

If disputing parties cannot resolve their differences through bilateral negotiation, either by themselves or through legal representation, they may require a third-party intervener to facilitate their negotiations. This principle applies equally to a wide range of disputes and conflict situations, from neighbours who cannot agree about their boundary fence, to corporations with major transnational disputes who are locked into seemingly intractable litigation.

3–012

The facilitator's role is then to help achieve whatever change is appropriate in the circumstances, according to the needs and wishes of the parties and to help break the impasse.

De Bono, who coined the term "lateral thinking"[9] is clear that a third-party role is critical because parties in conflict are:

3–013

> "bogged down in the argument mode of thinking the third party is not an addition or an aid but an integral part of the process"[10]

As will be extensively explored in this work, the impartial role of the ADR practitioner, and particularly the mediator, covers a range of skills and activities that parties and, where represented their legal advisors, find difficult or impossible to achieve on their own.

3–014

---

[6] Hazel Genn, "What is Civil Justice For? Reform, ADR, and Access to Justice" (2013) 24(1) *Yale Journal of Law and the Humanities* 397, 411; See also M. Galanter, "Justice in Many Rooms: Courts, Private Ordering, and Indigenous Law" (1981) 19 *Journal of Legal Pluralism* 1, 17; Symposium Issue "Against Settlement: Twenty-Five Years Later" (2009) 78 *Fordham Law Review* 1117, 1117–1280; S. Shipman, "Compulsory Mediation: the Elephant in the Room" (2011) 30 C.J.Q. 163, 180–184.

[7] Resolution of disputes may be achieved, but resolving underlying conflict may not always be possible. Bernard Mayer writes that in certain kinds of enduring conflict, immediate resolution may not be practicable or even desirable, and the practitioner may need to help them live with the continuing conflict: B. Mayer, *Staying with Conflict: A Strategic Approach to Ongoing Disputes* (San Francisco: Jossey-Bass, 2009).

[8] Examples from the array of works supporting this view include the classic R. Fisher and W. Ury, *Getting to Yes: Negotiating Agreement Without Giving In* (New York: Penguin, 1981); H. Raiffa, The Art & Science of Negotiation (Massachusetts: Harvard University Press, 1982); E. De Bono, *Conflicts: A Better Way to Resolve Them* (London: Penguin Books, 1986); and R. Mnookin, *Bargaining with the devil: When to negotiate and when to fight* (New York: Simon & Schuster, 2011).

[9] See E. De Bono, *The Use of Lateral Thinking,* (London: Jonathan Cape, 1967).

[10] De Bono, *Conflicts: A Better Way to Resolve Them,* pp.124–125 at fn.8.

Personal empowerment and self-determination

3–015 One of the common motivations of ADR practitioners who favour non-adjudicatory models is to remove decision-making from a third-party neutral, such as a judge or arbitrator, and to place it firmly in the hands of the disputants themselves.[11]

3–016 In mediation and other non-adjudicatory ADR processes, the parties generally have a central role with lawyers sometimes having a supporting function. In corporate disputes, executives responsible for business decisions re-take responsibility for making decisions about resolving the dispute. In disputes of a more personal nature, including for example separation and divorce matters, the aim of the process is to involve the parties themselves in dealing directly with the issues and take responsibility for working through them.

3–017 At one level, therefore, the process empowers both or all the parties. At another level, it can also empower individual parties. Power may come in complex and often unclear packages[12] and processes and the way they are managed may help to redress power imbalances between the parties. For example, where one party controls relevant information that the other does not have, this may be shared[13]; or if one person's negotiating style is more powerful than the other, process rules and management may rebalance this.[14]

3–018 However, there are obviously limits to this: some imbalances may well remain as they would in the litigation system. There is also the question as to how far it is the ADR practitioner's role to seek to vary the power dynamic between the parties. Certainly, this may be desirable insofar as it may be necessary to ensure that the process is fairly conducted; but there is a view that some relationships that have to be continued after the end of the ADR process, such as those between employers and employees, should leave their power dynamic undisturbed by the process and that it is not the neutral's function to empower either party at the

---

[11] Self-determination suggests ownership. Self-determination and ownership may lead to empowerment but not necessarily. A person may decide to give all power away to resolve a dispute—either through dispute weariness, through reflection on the impact of the decision on third parties (e.g. children in a divorce—see T. Grillo, "The Mediation Alternative: Process Dangers for Women" (1991) 100(6) Yale L.J. 1545, 1563 (fn.73). Empowerment includes awareness that one has choices and the will and emotional readiness to exercise these.

[12] Power issues are more fully dealt with in Ch.16.

[13] It should be noted that there are disclosure rules in litigation which force parties to disclose evidence which is available to one and not the other. While similar rules apply in relation to financial issues in family mediation in the UK, this is not the case in civil-commercial mediation, where such disclosure is voluntary. In this regard, see Ch.9 at paras 9–070 and 9–071 under the sub-heading "How much information is enough?"

[14] There are also process rules in litigation that seek to redress an inequality of power between parties, which can be helpful, though they cannot necessarily address fundamental aspects such as inequality of ability to fund the litigation, individual vulnerabilities or limitations or helping parties with a better understanding of their options. In consensual ADR processes, codes of conduct generally place the onus on the facilitator to manage power inequality (or suggest that the facilitator should be excused from involvement in the proceedings if the inequality is such that the process cannot be conducted fairly or the neutrality of the facilitator is likely to be compromised in attempting to redress this). See Ch.4 Negotiation for further discussion on negotiating power.

expense of the other. The question for the neutral is how to prevent the dispute resolution process from being corrupted by an abuse of power.[15]

Although empowerment may well be one of the motivations for the development of ADR, many parties may choose to participate in an ADR process in order to settle a dispute, without necessarily seeking personal empowerment. In that event, they may well be more than willing for their lawyers to take a leading role, but with the parties having the ultimate decision-making power regarding settlement.

3–019

Creative and flexible decision-making

Litigation is limited both in the kind of factors that the court can take into account in arriving at its determination and in the range of decisions that it can make.

3–020

Litigation is rights-based, in that the function of the courts is to establish factually where rights lie, to identify and interpret precisely what those rights are, and to resolve any conflicts of fact, technicality and law. Judgments are then based on those interpretations and findings. In England and Wales, the Courts of Equity (the Chancery Division) can have some regard to certain principles of equity and fairness in a limited range of circumstances, for example in trust law. However, legal and sometimes equitable principles underlie all disputes in litigation.

3–021

Arbitration, too, is rights-based though in some circumstances the arbitrator may be given discretion to have regard to principles of equity and fairness in reaching a decision.[16] The parties can however determine which law or set of norms governs the arbitration procedure (albeit often at the contracting stage).

3–022

A particular advantage of mediation and some other non-adjudicatory ADR processes is that they are not limited to consideration of parties' rights and the applicable law. Parties can have regard to a wide range of considerations[17] when reaching a consensual agreement. These may, for example, include:

3–023

- legal rights and principles (whether they refer to these and which ones);
- principles of fairness and equity (whether they refer to these and which ones);
- mutual interests and needs;
- commercial considerations, such as the preservation or enhancement of a working relationship, or personal considerations, such as the preservation of personal or family relationships, and in either case allowing for better understanding, forgiveness, dignity, mutuality of respect and privacy;

---

[15] For further discussion of this see the commentary on power elsewhere in this book, notably in Ch.4 Negotiation and Chs 8–17 dealing with mediation.

[16] See Amiable Composition in Ch.6. That, however, is a civil law concept, rarely used in common law systems, though common law arbitrators, while relying on the law, may in practice take principles of equity and fairness into account when making their awards.

[17] See J. R. Sternlight, C. J. Menkel-Meadow, L. Porter Love and A. Kupfer Schneider, *Dispute Resolution: Beyond the Adversarial Model*, (New York: Aspen Press 2010), pp.266–390, for some other views on the considerations which may indicate that mediation and/or some other non-adjudicatory ADR processes may be desirable for a particular dispute.

- risk assessment, having regard to the uncertainties of litigation as well as the personal circumstances of the parties in relation to their willingness to run such risks;
- the cost factor inherent in legal action and the ability and willingness of parties to incur such costs[18];
- a wide range of other considerations which may for example include timing needs, avoidance of the stress of litigation for themselves and/or families, employees, colleagues and others or possible damage to reputation, credibility or authority if unsuccessful.

An ADR practitioner may help the parties, individually or jointly as appropriate, to take these considerations into account and to find an acceptable balance. Lawyers too should be considering these factors.

3–024 Terms of settlement may reflect this range of considerations, and may allow for more flexible and creative outcomes. Factors that can be provided for which are simply not available to a court may for example include:

- provision for any agreed payment to be made over time or providing value in some alternative way;
- agreeing conditional terms that depend on future events;
- rewriting a contract to amend terms found to be unacceptable;
- providing an acknowledgment, apology, explanation, public statement or credit;
- providing personal undertakings, individual or mutual, to do things or to refrain from doing things;
- arranging for third parties, for example trustees or others not party to the dispute, to provide payments, guarantees, indemnities or other support;
- making arrangements to a degree of detail and with a level of sensitivity to each person concerned that no court would be able to order.

3–025 De Bono has created the concept of a "design idiom"—a designed and creative outcome to a conflict situation.[19] This requires a third-party intervenor, who uses expertise to help the parties to achieve this designed outcome as part of a "design team".

Potential for healing and relationship preservation

3–026 Although ADR is widely used for issues where there is no relationship between parties, the common experience is that where personal and business relationships exist between disputing parties, ADR processes preserve or enhance them, where they might otherwise be damaged by the adversarial process.[20]

---

[18] It should be noted that in some circumstances mediation may be more costly, for example if it does not resolve the issues and the parties have to bear their own costs of the process and still have to proceed to litigation.

[19] See fn.10.

[20] See generally Ch.10 in R. H. Mnookin, S. R. Peppett and A. S. Tulumello, *Beyond Winning: Negotiating to Create Value in Deals and Disputes* (Boston: Harvard University Press, 2004); and Ch.10 by B. Patten, in M. L. Moffitt and R. C. Bordone, *The Handbook of Dispute Resolution* (San Francisco: Jossey-Bass 2005).

Disputes between siblings, parents and children, friends who are also business or professional partners, couples who have become alienated but who have to continue co-parenting—these are just a few examples of conflict within relationships that have broken down, that litigation does nothing to heal. Other kinds of relationship breakdown can also cause rifts in circumstances where people may need or want to continue together: business or professional partners who fall out, shareholders or co-directors of companies who have fundamental disagreements, employers and employees, co-workers, neighbours: disputes between all of these can only be exacerbated by pursuing litigation.

3–027

And then there are other working relationships that have become contentious: negligence allegations between doctors who were once perceived as caring and patients who trusted them or between lawyers and their clients.

When parties are helped to understand one another's positions and encouraged to respond appropriately and when they communicate respectfully and thoughtfully, conditions exist for a shift in disputants' attitudes towards one another which can preserve or restore good relationships. When adversarial roles are assumed, which includes claiming that the other is wrong and blameworthy, or when the relationship breakdown is exacerbated, it can be very hard for relationships to survive.

3–028

Although relationship preservation may be a common goal, ADR practitioners can have differing emphases. For some, it may be a primary aspiration and in the absence of reaching a settlement on all issues may be regarded as incompletely successful. For others, settlement of the dispute is the primary goal and relationship preservation would be a bonus if achieved. In many cases, these concepts are entwined: resolving the dispute may be the first step towards relationship restoration, which may take place over time.

3–029

Maintaining ethical values

Whereas litigation commonly takes place within the full glare of public gaze, mediation and other non-adjudicatory ADR processes are ordinarily conducted in private. In some models, widely used, the mediator has confidential separate meetings with each party without the other party knowing what was discussed.

3–030

This makes it very difficult for any outside agency to assess whether the process was fairly conducted. Parties may have been placed under undue pressure to agree to proposed terms, or something irregular might have been said or done that could have had an adverse effect on the outcome. Because of the confidential nature of many of these processes, ADR practitioners are very properly unwilling to discuss with the courts or any other outside agency what took place within the process.[21]

3–031

ADR practitioners and organisations are aware of these constraints, which they safeguard in the interests of maintaining the integrity of the process which may depend largely on confidentiality and trust. In these circumstances, they should be conscious of the need to conduct themselves and the process in a fair

3–032

---

[21] Confidentiality and evidential privilege are touched on below, and are more fully addressed in Ch.15. The courts are not without power to intervene where there are allegations of any irregularity that might warrant such intervention.

and ethically proper manner, albeit that different ADR systems, bodies and individuals may vary on the views that they take as to what is ethically proper.

3–033 The way in which ethical conduct is manifested in mediation and other ADR processes is a product of a number of different and interlocking factors, which may include:

- a written Code of Practice or other guiding document specifying the ethical and practical conduct expected of third-party facilitators;
- a written Agreement to Mediate or to conduct any other process, which a third-party neutral will enter into with the parties, regulating practicalities and behaviour;
- overarching professional rules or guidelines that may apply to the conduct of mediation in any country, territory or field of activity, as specified by regional authorities such as the EU, regulatory bodies or funding bodies such as the Legal Aid Agency in England and Wales[22];
- professional rules for the practice of ADR, as specified by any other professional body to which the facilitator may belong, for example the Law Society or Bar and in the US the American Bar Association's Model Standards of Conduct for Mediators;
- ethical guidelines provided by any training bodies;
- ethical discussions on a continuing basis in professional journals, at conferences and seminars;
- cultural expectations, constraints and guidelines which may arise from religion; community; family; trade, business or professional practice and organisations; or other relevant source;
- individual ethical codes and belief systems.

Providing a confidential and secure environment

3–034 All ADR process models will generally regard confidentiality as critical—unless the parties do not want it, for example where they are conducting a facilitated public enquiry or consultation.[23] This retains privacy for the parties about matters which may be personal to them and which do not need to be matters of public knowledge. It also allows greater freedom to consider ways of resolving issues without publicity.

3–035 All ADR process models also generally agree that the process environment should be secure, both in terms of physical and evidential security. Physical security is perhaps obvious: if parties are very hostile, there should be separate reception facilities for them and special care should be taken in managing the

---

[22] The USA for instance has the Uniform Mediation Act 2003 (UMA) which seems to be one of the primary pieces of consolidating legislation present in westernised jurisdictions concerning mediation regulation.

[23] In certain situations there may be a public interest dimension to the subject-matter and outcomes of agreement-based processes. In such situations confidentiality may be maintained by the aggregation and/or anonymising of mediation stories. This may enable public education, action to be taken to ensure public bodies change behaviour and processes, or may provide examples of the types of outcomes possible. An example is the Conciliation Register maintained by the Australian Human Rights Commission: at *https://www.humanrights.gov.au/complaints/conciliation-register* [accessed 10 May 2018].

process and the way in which they leave it. Support should be available if needed. Evidential security is provided by agreeing rules that preclude settlement discussions from being brought before the court, in particular the "without prejudice" rule, which applies in common law jurisdictions.[24] The existence of an overriding privilege, which varies from one country to another, is more fully addressed in Ch.15.

Attributes, skills and sensitivity

The attributes and skills that ADR practitioners are likely to need to perform their functions effectively are addressed in Ch.14 and broadly speaking include personal and professional attributes that enhance the process, and a range of communication and other skills that facilitate dialogue and process momentum. 3–036

While some people may naturally have some of these skills, most can be learned; and ADR practitioners will ordinarily have undertaken professional training to learn and practise these skills and how to use them appropriately.[25] There are now bodies in many countries that prescribe training, skills and practice criteria for practitioners: the public may have some assurances as to levels of competence where practitioners belong to such bodies and have met the qualification criteria. 3–037

Most ADR practitioners will also agree that a further common requirement for facilitative practice is sensitivity to the needs of parties and an ability to gain their confidence and to work effectively with them. This has little to do with models of practice, but is rather a reflection of the personality and individual qualities of the neutral. 3–038

Seeking a beneficial outcome

All practitioners want a good outcome for the parties and virtually all would agree that this would include resolution of the dispute and agreement on mutually acceptable settlement terms. For many practitioners, if this was the contract with the parties—whether explicit or implicit—that would be a completely successful outcome. For others, it would only be successful if other requirements were also met: for example, resolution of underlying issues, healing or closure, in some cases personal transformation. 3–039

A good outcome where litigation is pending might also include costs savings, avoidance of delay, absence of publicity, elimination of the risks, stresses and anxieties inherent in litigation and the relief of finality. Terms that meet mutual needs and interests, that enhance or preserve personal or working relationships, that allow people to close a chapter and move on with their lives—these may all be classified as good outcomes. 3–040

---

[24] This is addressed in Ch.15.
[25] Training requirements vary widely across jurisdictions and institutions. The desirable attributes may vary, also, according to the ideology of the facilitator. These aspects will be discussed in Ch.14.

Overcoming the cost and delays of litigation

3–041 ADR is also widely motivated by the fact that it is said to reduce the costs and delays of litigation. Litigation tends to be expensive and generally also involves delays of varying degrees. There has been an increasing consumer resistance to the costs, delays and risk of litigation which has contributed to the search for alternatives.[26]

3–042 The cost-savings element of ADR is based on the assumption that it will be effective. The costs of running a mediation will invariably be much lower than a full-scale trial; and the costs savings can be considerable. If, however, the ADR process does not resolve the issues and the parties have to proceed to adjudication, then the cost of the ADR will have to be aggregated with the costs of trial.[27] Nevertheless, there is often some value added by virtue of the ADR process, such as helping to gather information and clarify or narrow issues; and ADR discussions that do not produce an immediate resolution sometimes provide the basis for a later settlement.

DIFFERENCES OF PRACTICE AND PHILOSOPHY[28]

3–043 Differences of philosophy and approach are difficult to identify because models of practice and individual beliefs and approaches are very diverse. An attempt will nevertheless be made to indicate some broad differences of approach to ADR philosophy and practice:

Different fields of activity

3–044 ADR takes place in different fields of activity, each of which tends to have its own practice and culture. The fields include couples and family; civil and commercial; neighbourhood and community; employment and workplace; consumer claims; restorative justice; and environmental issues.[29] In each field, certain ways of working and certain cultural assumptions are fairly entrenched, and the overlap of processes between fields may therefore not be as great as might be expected.

Different models of practice

3–045 Writers, academics and some ADR practitioners distinguish between different models of practice, and while some of these distinctions are valid, others are questionable, especially as models and philosophical approaches do not always

---

[26] See R. Jackson, "*Review of civil litigation costs: final report.*" Office of the Judiciary of England and Wales (2009), available at: *https://www.judiciary.gov.uk/wp-content/uploads/JCO/Documents/Reports/jackson-final-report-140110.pdf* [accessed 10 May 2018].

[27] This may be particularly relevant in the case of small claims, where costs of an ADR process or of litigation may be disproportionate and/or where mediation settlements are low and where parties have to pay their own costs.

[28] The issues in this section are presented in brief outline and are further elaborated elsewhere in the book.

[29] Several of these fields of ADR activity will be considered in more detail elsewhere in the book.

DIFFERENCES OF PRACTICE AND PHILOSOPHY

follow predictable patterns. The distinctions have become blurred, as models have learned and borrowed from one another.

However, while there has been some cross-over of elements from one process model into another, there has also been an overriding tendency to keep process models substantially separate. Practitioners tend to favour particular process models, based no doubt on which one they trained in and are familiar with, which in turn may be a reflection of the field of activity and culture within which they primarily work. 3–046

Some attempts have been made in England and Wales to integrate aspects of the civil-commercial and the family process models to enhance both fields. This has been well if tentatively received. 3–047

Some specific differences of model and philosophy will be separately addressed below.

Evaluative or facilitative mediation

It is a seductive proposition to distinguish between a "facilitative" approach, which suggests that the mediator merely facilitates and does not express a view in any way and an "evaluative" approach, which suggests that the mediator's main thrust is to make an evaluation of the merits. 3–048

The term "evaluative mediation" is really a misnomer and its juxtaposition with "facilitative mediation" creates what in most cases is a false dichotomy. In fact all mediation is facilitative and there is a wide spectrum of evaluation, starting at one end with little or no evaluation, through at the other end to a mediator being willing to express a view on the merits. In between there are varying levels of evaluation, different shades of grey: selective questioning, "reality testing" and raised eyebrows are classic examples. It seems that most mediators fall somewhere between these two ends of the spectrum, and that "evaluative mediation", which has become pejorative in some eyes, is not a helpful term, unless qualified by an explanation as to where in the evaluative continuum a mediator is placed. 3–049

Settlement-geared or problem-solving mediation

One aspirational approach to mediation and ADR practice is to be settlement-geared and cost-saving which may go hand in hand with a negotiating bargaining style, seeking to trade issues in a search of "a deal". For some ADR practitioners, this does not reflect the spirit of ADR and the problem-solving approach that often seeks a "win-win" outcome, with the impartial exploration and understanding of underlying issues. 3–050

This distinction may have some validity, but is also questionable. Undoubtedly, some disputes require a bargaining approach and some require a problem-solving approach. Mediators with sensitivity will deal with each according to its needs. And many may involve a mixture of both approaches. Lax and Sebenius point out that although negotiation can be conducted in such a way 3–051

COMMON VALUES AND DIFFERENCES

as to create joint gains for both parties, "an essential tension in negotiation exists between co-operative moves to create value and competitive moves to claim it".[30]

Transformative and related approaches

3–052 There is a view that considers the problem-solving approach to be inadequate, in that it neglects a critical element of the process, namely the transformative potential of the process. This aspires to facilitate party transformation through the adoption by the mediator of an approach that helps to empower the parties and give them a greater sense of their own efficacy. Based on the work of Folger and Bush,[31] the transformative model of mediation, having as its key aspirations empowerment and recognition, has acquired a committed following, though there are also those who believe that seeking transformation is only appropriate if the parties have knowingly elected for this.

3–053 Cloke promotes another approach that aims for "personal and organisational transformation" and talks of "the quality of energy that is released in resolution, transformation and forgiveness".[32]

Other models and schools of thought

3–054 Other models of mediation reflect different schools of thought about the process, its aims and practice approach. While they are practised in some places, they are not widely known or used in the UK. They include:

- The narrative model is based on a story-telling metaphor, working with people in better understanding and reconstructing their "stories" rather than simply adopting an interest-based problem-solving approach.[33]
- Another school of thought sees mediation and other ADR processes through the lens of a communications perspective. They see conflict as a "socially created and communicatively managed reality occurring within a socio-historical context that both affects meaning and behaviour and is affected by it".[34]
- The therapeutic model of mediation, often undertaken by mediators with a background profession in counselling or therapy, is based on the

---

[30] D. Lax and J. Sebenius, *The Manager as Negotiator: Bargaining for Co-operation and Competitive Gain* (New York: The Free Press, 1986), p.33. In their later work, *3-D Negotiation: Powerful Tools to Change the Game in Your Most Important Deals* (Boston: Harvard Business School Press, 2006), Lax and Sebenius reaffirm this tension in a section entitled "The 'Negotiator's Dilemma': Productively managing the Creating/Claiming Tension" (p.131). This is further addressed in Ch.4 below.
[31] Robert A. Baruch Bush and Joseph P. Folger, *The Promise of Mediation: The Transformative Approach to Conflict* (San Francisco: Jossey-Bass, 1994).
[32] Kenneth Cloke, *Mediating Dangerously: The Frontiers of Conflict Resolution* (San Francisco: Jossey-Bass, 2001), p.xi–xii.
[33] See, for example, J. Winslade & G.D. Monk, *Narrative Mediation: A New Approach to Conflict Resolution* (San Francisco: Jossey-Bass, 2000).
[34] Joseph P. Folger and Tricia S. Jones, *New Directions in Mediation: Communication Research and Perspectives* (California: Sage Publications, 1994), p.ix.

assumption that parties cannot engage in effective communication and problem-solving until unresolved emotional and relational issues are addressed.[35]

Intervention and directiveness

In adjudicatory processes such as arbitration, the impartial third party necessarily has an interventionist role; but in England and Wales mediation training aims to establish minimal intervention and directiveness. This supports individual empowerment and self-determination.

3–055

Most mediators, irrespective of process model or approach, are likely to support the proposition that they should not be unduly directive or interventionist. However, there are different views about what level of directiveness and intervention is appropriate. Indeed, like evaluation, there is a continuum in this regard.

3–056

The injunction against excessive intervention and directiveness is entirely justified; but this should not be confused with effective management of the process, where the mediator may need to give directions and to intervene as necessary (though in some models, such as the transformative one, the mediator's management role is rather more minimal). There may be circumstances demanding intervention or directiveness, for example to ensure that the process is conducted fairly, effectively and non-abusively.[36] A blanket and undiscriminating injunction against directiveness and intervention is unhelpful.[37]

3–057

DEFINING THE PROCESSES

Defining such a broad range of dispute resolution processes as introduced by the spectrum of processes from consensual to adjudicatory in Ch.2 is challenging. Attempts will be made to do so in subsequent chapters. For instance in relation to mediation,[38] the question has been asked: "What is real mediation and who decides?" This is relevant to ask, where one finds some people holding themselves out as the arbiters of what constitutes proper practice and what does not.

3–058

As there is no universally accepted definition of mediation, we are left with seeking a consensus among ADR practitioners as to what constitutes acceptable practice and what does not. Yet even that cannot be authoritative in a field that provides such a wide range of activities, fields of work, models and approaches in a wide range of countries and cultures.

3–059

---

[35] Waldman offers an interesting early view of the facilitative-evaluative debate through the lens of therapeutic justice: E. Waldman "The Evaluative-Facilitative Debate in Mediation: Applying the Lens of Therapeutic Jurisprudence" (1998) 82 *Marquette Law Review* 155.
[36] This may be particularly the case in agreement-based processes which inherently involve an imbalance of power, such as National Human Rights Institutions which conduct mediation or conciliation processes to resolve individual human rights complaints.
[37] Process management as applicable to various forms of ADR will be discussed in greater detail in other relevant chapters in this book.
[38] See generally L. Steffek and H. Unberath, *Regulating Dispute Resolution: ADR and Access to Justice at the Crossroad* (Oxford: Hart 2014).

3–060 Addressing this issue in 2009, Larry Gaughan, who co-founded the US Academy of Family Mediators, sought an end to a "fundamentalist" approach to mediation.[39] Referring to mediation's rich history and its variety of successful approaches, he pointed out that:

> "the more different kinds of skills and knowledge a mediator has, the more likely it is that he or she can apply a model that will get the job done properly, i.e., get a signed agreement that is both fair and workable."

Gaughan cautioned mediators who only had training and experience with one model of mediation not to tell mediators who used other models successfully that they had to limit the scope of their practice.

3–061 The test of a successful and acceptable non-adjudicatory process, including mediation, should be threefold. Does it facilitate parties voluntarily shifting from entrenched positions? Is it ethical? Is it workable?

THE MOMENTUM TOWARDS ADR

3–062 Since the first edition of this work there has been a continuing momentum towards the use of mediation and other ADR processes in a wide range of activities. In that time, legal practitioners and other professionals, judges and the courts, the UK Ministry of Justice and other government departments, as well as the media and the general public, have developed an increasing awareness about it.

3–063 There are now pre-action protocols regulating parties' conduct before court action is commenced, which aim to facilitate settlement without the need to launch proceedings, all of which encourage the consideration of ADR.[40]

3–064 As set out in Ch.5, the courts of England and Wales support and encourage ADR in many ways and will impose costs sanctions against a party who fails to attempt to resolve a dispute by using mediation or some other ADR process when it is appropriate to do so, on the basis of criteria that have been established.

3–065 The principles and ethos of ADR have also permeated the legal profession, and although there are still lawyers who resist its use the general trend in the profession is towards the concept of "dispute resolution" rather than litigation.

3–066 Many ADR organisations now exist, including specialist mediation bodies and thousands of mediators have been trained in the UK and throughout the world in a wide range of fields.

3–067 This is an international trend. The US has largely led the way, but Australia and Canada have also been influential, as well as many other countries, including a number in Europe, where the EU has supported mediation and issued Directives promoting and regulating its use, both for cross-border disputes and, on an optional basis, domestically. The momentum continues, both nationally and internationally.[41]

---

[39] See Larry Gaughan, "Models", in *Family Mediation News* (Newsletter of the Family Section of the Association for Conflict Resolution), Fall 2009.
[40] See Ch.5 for further information about the protocols.
[41] See the Report from the Commission to the European Parliament, the Council and the European Economic and Social Committee on the application of Directive 2008/52/EC of the European

CONCLUSION

ADR processes can stand in their own right as alternatives to adjudication; or they can complement the court's procedures. Lawyers need to be aware of the occasions when litigation, arbitration, mediation or any other ADR process has its appropriate value and to advise accordingly.[42]

3–068

While acknowledging the difficulty in achieving any one agreed ADR philosophy, the following might perhaps embody much of the essence of ADR:

3–069

> "ADR complements litigation and other adjudicatory forms, providing processes which can either stand in their own right or be used as an adjunct to adjudication. This enables legal practitioners to select procedures (adjudicatory or consensual) appropriate to individual disputes. ADR gives parties more power and greater control over resolving the issues between them, encourages problem-solving approaches, and provides for more effective settlements covering substance and nuance. It also tends to enhance co-operation and can be conducive to the preservation of relationships. Effective impartial third party intercession can help to overcome blockages towards reaching a settlement, and by expediting and facilitating resolution the costs, delays, risks and uncertainties of litigation can be avoided. Sometimes it can help to heal or provide the conditions for healing underlying conflicts between parties. ADR processes, like adjudicatory procedures, have advantages and disadvantages which make them suitable for some cases but not for others."[43]

Parliament and of the Council on certain aspects of mediation in civil and commercial matters, 26.8.2016, available at: *http://ec.europa.eu/justice/civil/files/act_part1_adopted_en.pdf* [accessed 10 May 2018].

[42] Solicitors' Code of Conduct includes under r.2.02 (1)(b), the requirement to give the client a clear explanation of the issues involved and the options available. The obligation is further clarified under Guidance Note 15 to r.2.02 (1)(b), which states that when considering the options available to the client, if the matter relates to a dispute between the client and a third party, the solicitor should discuss whether mediation or some other ADR procedure may be more appropriate than litigation, arbitration or other formal processes. See generally Code of Conduct 2007, available at *http://www.sra.org.uk/documents/code/rule-2-client-relations.pdf* [accessed 10 May 2018].

[43] Refer to Ch.2 and the spectrum of processes from consensual to adjudicatory for consideration of process suitability.

CHAPTER 4

Negotiation

NEGOTIATION—THE PRIMARY TOOL

Negotiation has been described as "the process we use to satisfy our needs when someone else controls what we want."[1] **4–001**

Everyone learns to negotiate from the earliest age. Children learn to recognise when "no" means "maybe", when they can trade favours with their parents and (sometimes) when something is genuinely non-negotiable. They may explore strategies including making persistent demands, promising something in the future to gain something more immediate, showing their distress when they do not get what they want and understanding when concessions have to be made to achieve their wishes.

As time passes, negotiation becomes more refined. By adulthood we will probably have negotiated many different kinds of agreements and we will have developed our own individual styles for trying to persuade others to give us what we want or need. People may bargain with ease or be uncomfortable with haggling; they may adopt a pleading manner or a browbeating style; they may avoid situations which involve confronting others in resolving differences; or they may use the threat of withdrawal as a strategy. This will to some extent reflect individual personalities, although learned negotiation skills will enhance and augment natural inclinations. **4–002**

Awareness of the theories and principles of negotiation and conscious practice will enable practitioners to employ these effectively and appropriately and to help others to do so.

THEORIES OF NEGOTIATION

Theories of negotiation may be classified in a variety of ways. One important distinction lies between the interest-based, problem-solving or co-operative approach and the competitive approach.[2] These two predominant approaches will be discussed, as well as overlapping areas between them. Additionally other theories will be mentioned briefly. **4–003**

---

[1] Robert Maddux, *Successful Negotiation*, 2nd edn (London: Kogan Page, 1999), p.5. According to Maddux, negotiation normally occurs "because one has something the other wants and is willing to bargain to get it."

[2] See Jeffrey Z. Rubin and Bert R. Brown, *The Social Psychology of Bargaining and Negotiation* (New York: Elsevier, 2013) (categorising negotiators as "co-operative versus individualistic versus competitive"); Gerald R. Williams, *Legal Negotiation and Settlement* 18–40 (1983) (studying

AN INTEREST-BASED PROBLEM-SOLVING APPROACH

Getting to Yes

4-004 The interest-based problem-solving approach to negotiation is particularly helpful to consensus-based ADR practices. Also called "integrative" negotiation (because of the potential for parties' interests to be integrated in ways that enhance the creation of joint value), interest-based negotiation focuses on the interests of the disputants, which may include their needs, wishes, concerns and fears. It aims to find a resolution of the issues that meets all such interests and needs in a mutually beneficial way. The process of interest-based negotiation involves joint problem-solving, expanding options and aiming for mutual benefit.

4-005 Fisher and Ury in their seminal work, *Getting to Yes*, developed their particular form of principled, problem-solving negotiation and identified certain key negotiation principles[3]:

- concentrate on parties' respective interests rather than taking and defending positions;
- adopt a problem-solving approach instead of allowing personality differences to side-track the negotiation;
- before making decisions, generate as many options as possible particularly those creating mutual benefit;
- establish objective and fair criteria for a resolution, rather than the judgment of either party.

4-006 Fisher and Ury describe how these principles can be achieved in practice through the concept of BATNA (Best Alternative to a Negotiated Agreement), which identifies to each party what the best outcome would be if the issues were not settled by negotiation.[4]

4-007 Alternatively, Haynes refers to WATNA (Worst Alternative to a Negotiated Agreement), which is the worst potential outcome if the issues are not settled by negotiation.[5] Negotiators need to be aware of their own and the other side's best and worst alternatives to a negotiated settlement, and by focusing on these are better able to make decisions as to whether or not to settle and on what terms.

4-008 The following demonstrates a creative example of undertaking a BATNA and WATNA exercise. In a passing off action between media companies, the defendant denied passing off but was willing in mediation to consider changing a competing brand name, albeit that there would be tens of thousands of pounds of expenses in doing so. The claimant calculated that its BATNA would be an injunction to stop use of the competing name; but this would involve over a year's delay and an irrecoverable cost element of over £35,000. Its WATNA

---

negotiator behaviour and categorising negotiators as "cooperative" or "competitive" types) in Russell Korobkin, "A Positive Theory of Legal Negotiation", 88 Geo. L.J. 1789 (1999–2000).

[3] See Roger Fisher and William Ury, *Getting to Yes: Negotiating Agreement Without Giving In* (New York: Penguin, 1981), Ch.2.

[4] D. Lax and J. Sebenius, Harvard colleagues of Fisher and Ury, prefer the term "no-deal option" to BATNA. See their book *3-D Negotiation: Powerful Tools to Change the Game in Your Most Important Deals* (Boston: Harvard Business School Press, 2006), pp.23 and 256.

[5] John Haynes and Gretchen Haynes, *Mediating Divorce* (San Francisco: Jossey-Bass, 1989), p.11.

would see the case lost, with heavy costs of its own and liability for the other party's costs. The claimant accordingly agreed to contribute £30,000 to the defendant's expenses of voluntarily changing the brand name, which led to a settlement. The claimant got the best result it would have had at trial, with certainty, more quickly and at a slightly lower cost.

Galanter points out[6] that as "transaction barriers", such as legal costs, increase, so there is a greater range of possible settlements from which parties can choose rather than proceed to adjudication.

White criticised the *Getting to Yes* principles as being naive in the face of tough and unprincipled negotiators on the basis that the authors seem to assume that a clever negotiator can make any negotiation into problem solving and thus completely avoid the difficult distribution type situations which can arise in negotiations.[7] Fisher however argued that to treat the distributional issue as a shared problem was a better approach than to treat it as a contest of will in which a more deceptive, more stubborn, and less rational negotiator would tend to fare better, and that even win/lose bargaining could profit from the kind of analysis suggested in *Getting to Yes*.[8] There is no doubt that the *Getting to Yes* principles were ground-breaking in negotiation theory and practice, evidenced by the value still placed on them decades after initial publication. 4–009

Fisher and Brown, for example,[9] further developed the original principles to deal with disagreements within relationships and to consider ways to nurture and maintain relationships. Ury, in later work, dealt with the subject of negotiating with people who do not use a principled, interest-based approach[10] and more recently, in 2015,[11] continued the principled negotiation theme, but focused on the need to first negotiate with ourselves before attempting to achieve our negotiating goals. 4–010

Underlying needs

An important theme of interest-based negotiation concerns underlying needs. This theme suggests that the negotiator looks beyond stated aspirations and attempts to assess underlying needs or preferences. Distinguishing between needs and wants can allow many opportunities for arriving at creative solutions in all fields of activity.[12] 4–011

---

[6] See M. Galanter, "The Quality of Settlements" (1988) *Journal of Dispute Resolution* 82.
[7] E.g. see James J. White, Essay Review: "The Pros and Cons of Getting to Yes" (1984) 34 *Journal of Legal Education* 115.
[8] White p.121 (see fn.7); and see also Roger Fisher, "Negotiating Power" in (1983) 27 *American Behavioural Science*; and in J. Murray, A. S. Rau and E. Sherman, *The Processes of Dispute Resolution: The Role of Lawyers*, 2nd edn (USA: Foundation Press, 1989), pp.99–100.
[9] Roger Fisher and Scott Brown, *Getting Together: Building a Relationship that Gets to Yes* (New York: Penguin (Non-Classics), 1989).
[10] William Ury, *Getting Past No: Negotiating with Difficult People* (London: Random House, 1992).
[11] William Ury, *Getting to Yes with Yourself: and Other Worthy Opponents* (London: Harper Thorsons, 2015).
[12] Andrew Acland, *A Sudden Outbreak of Common Sense: Managing Conflict Through Mediation* (London: Random House Business Books, 1990) recommends mediators to discover the interests behind positions, and the needs behind interests.

Creating value

4-012   A further approach adopts the view that it is possible to create value within the context of interest-based negotiation by taking advantage of differences. For example, it may be possible to construct a settlement that accommodates the different aspirations and priorities of the parties.

4-013   Behind the notion that it is possible to create joint gains, is the idea that a co-operative, problem-solving model, with pooled information, a flexible and creative approach and an appreciation of one another's interests and concerns, will enable parties to arrive at an outcome which enhances the position of all parties, rather than having one party as a "winner" and another as a "loser".

4-014   The following real life example illustrates this approach. Shareholders in a fast-food company with a number of branches found it impossible to continue working together. They split into two groups, each of which wanted to buy out the other. Neither would sell to the other, and each threatened court action. Their impasse left them at loggerheads. In a problem-solving negotiation they examined ways of dividing the company and arrived at a solution whereby each group took over the branches in an agreed area, with an appropriate cash adjustment. They agreed to operate independently but would liaise on activities that could benefit all branches, such as some joint publicity and occasional bulk purchasing to achieve advantageous buying prices.

4-015   As observed by Lax and Sebenius,[13] there would ultimately be a tension between the creation of joint gains and the division of the resources. In the above example, there was also hard bargaining about the allocation and valuation of the branches and the size of the cash adjustment. Nevertheless, this approach to problem-solving negotiation allowed greater opportunities for positive and mutually beneficial outcomes than a purely "value claiming" approach.

Principled rejection

4-016   Ury has identified, also, how important it is that parties are able to reject unacceptable requests or demands in an effective way that does not entrench conflict, but rather supports principled negotiation.[14]

The thrust of what Ury describes as a "positive No", is that negotiators need to reflect on any underlying positive aspect of their reason for rejecting a particular demand and to maintain this at the forefront of their thinking and response. Negotiators need to prepare for the negotiation by rooting their approach in the positive principle and values, crystallising their positive intention and what they are aiming to achieve. Preparation also includes having a "Plan B"—what will be done in the event that agreement cannot be reached: this adds power to a negotiating position and removes dependence on gaining agreement.

4-017   The "No" should be thoughtfully and positively presented but remain firm about the commitment to address the underlying concerns. This avoids personal blaming, presents facts objectively, uses language with care, gives due respect to

---

[13] See below under "The essential tension between interest-based and competitive approaches".
[14] Ury, *The Power of a Positive No: How to say No and Still Get to Yes* (2007). This work sets out both a theoretical underpinning as well as practical strategies that enable negotiators to reject inappropriate demands or behaviour but at the same time to maintain a positive approach.

the other negotiator and where appropriate invokes common principles or shared interests. The clear rejection can then flow from that commitment and respect. Ideally, this should be accompanied by alternative options, appropriate qualifications or constructive requests.

Any reaction to rejection should be listened to with respect and with acknowledgement of the other person's viewpoint, without concession of one's own position and without over-reaction. Patience and consistency are needed. If there is an impasse, it may be necessary to explain the consequences of not reaching agreement, but care should be taken to ensure that this is not perceived as a threat. At this point, Plan B may have to be invoked, and cooperation withdrawn. 4–018

If underlying interests and needs cannot be met, then it may not be appropriate to enter an agreement at all.

However, there may still be ways to achieve an agreement. Ury suggests building a "golden bridge" for the other to cross towards resolution: reaching out to the other party, exploring their unmet needs and interests, helping them to save face, finding ways for them to present an outcome satisfactorily to their constituents, and rebuilding confidence—these may all help to bridge the differences. The secret, Ury suggests, is the integration of "Yes" and "No": the ability to stand firm on what one needs without damage to valuable agreements and prized relationships. 4–019

Designing creative solutions

Another proponent of a problem-solving approach is Edward De Bono, the originator of the term "lateral thinking", which he describes as being concerned with restructuring fixed concept patterns (insight) and creating new ones (creativity). De Bono believes that the traditional methods used to resolve conflicts and disputes are primitive, inadequate and destructive, and that a fundamental shift in approach is needed. Hence he advocates the adoption of techniques that facilitate the creative design of solutions to problems. His work,[15] which analyses modes of thinking and the way the mind works, suggests that disputants themselves are worst-placed to resolve their own issues since they are caught up in a "tension of hostility" and take positions that do not allow them to communicate with or trust one another easily and, hence, are inimical to the design of solutions. The conclusion that either representation in negotiations or assistance, perhaps from a third-party neutral, can be drawn from De Bono's views on this. De Bono suggests that the use of lateral thinking and the adoption of a creative, problem-solving, approach to the design of solutions, encourages the generation of alternative solutions to issues, large and small.[16] 4–020

---

[15] Edward De Bono, *Conflicts: A Better Way to Resolve Them* (Penguin Books Limited, 1985).
[16] An example of creative problem-solving provided by De Bono is illustrated in an exercise in "lateral thinking" called the *Tale of Two Pebbles* or *The Black Pebble*.

COMPETITIVE THEORY

4-021   The competitive approach to negotiation is sometimes called "positional", "distributive" or "distributional" bargaining, in that there are seen to be limited resources for distribution and the more that one party achieves, the less there will be for the other. In this approach negotiation is a form of contest in which there will be a winner and a loser, and that in order to be the winner, the negotiator needs to be tough, powerful and skilful in maximising his own or his principal's self-interest, irrespective of the overall effect on others.[17] This approach is sometimes linked to "power-based" negotiation (determining who is more powerful).

4-022   Competitive negotiators may consider any gesture of goodwill as a mistake because there is no certainty that such a gesture will be reciprocated and because it may be construed as a display of weakness and, hence, may produce an even tougher response from the opposing negotiator. Toughness involves opening high, making few concessions, and being untroubled by the prospect of an impasse.[18]

4-023   Murray, Rau and Sherman[19] have analysed the risks of adopting strategies favoured by competitive theory. These strategies tend towards a hostile and confrontational approach and response, focusing on manipulation and threat rather than on trying to understand the issues sufficiently to find a mutually acceptable solution. This means that joint gains cannot be identified, communications are distorted and tension, mistrust, anger and frustration may result. It is not uncommon that the brinkmanship inherent in the competitive approach and the concern not to be outdone by opponents results in deadlock and a breakdown of negotiations, with consequent delays, stress and additional costs of all kinds. This form of negotiation may be viewed as antithetical to some proponents of ADR, but it is an approach that is commonly used in one form or another and needs to be understood and accommodated.

4-024   The question that inevitably arises is how a negotiator who adopts a problem-solving approach can cope with one who adopts the competitive approach. Ury has suggested various practical techniques, such as recognising and responding appropriately to tactics used by the other side, making acknowledgments without conceding, using questions skilfully, reframing tactics, exposing tricks and helping the other side to save face.[20]

4-025   Should these or any other problem-solving strategies not be fruitful, an appropriate response can be chosen: examining the best and worst alternatives, maintaining a principled position, trying to seek mutual gains through a problem-solving approach and resisting all attempts to bully, threaten and cajole,

---

[17] See J. S. Murray, "Understanding Competing Theories of Negotiation" (1986) 2 *Negotiation Journal* 179.

[18] See Gavin Kennedy, *Everything is Negotiable: How to Negotiate and Win*, 3rd edn (Arrow Books Limited, 1997). (See also 4th edn, 2008). In a personal email to this book's consultant editor, Gavin Kennedy added: "I would not recommend aggressive behaviour; more firmness of trading than fighting talk."

[19] J. S. Murray, A. S. Rau and E. F. Sherman, *Processes of Dispute Resolution: The Role of Lawyers* (New York: Foundation Press, 1989), pp.78–80; (and 3rd edn, 2002).

[20] See Ury, *Getting Past No: Negotiating with Difficult People* (fn.10).

even if this may lead to an impasse. A problem-solving negotiator does not have to be weak, but can maintain a strong, principled approach in the face of the toughest negotiator.

THE "ESSENTIAL TENSION" BETWEEN INTEREST-BASED AND COMPETITIVE APPROACHES

Lax and Sebenius[21] have adopted a balanced position between the competitive and interest-based approaches. They view these two perceptions of the bargaining process as being a distinction between "value creators" and "value claimers". Value creators are those who consider that the negotiators should be sufficiently co-operative and resourceful to ensure that their agreement produces more positive results for each party than if they had not reached an agreement. Value claimers believe that negotiation involves hard bargaining to ensure that negotiators, or the people they represent, obtain the most favourable terms, thereby "winning" as against the other party who thus necessarily "loses". Lax and Sebenius consider that both kinds of process are present in negotiation, and that there is an "essential tension" between the creation of value and the division of it. Their understanding and synthesis of problem-solving and competitive approaches has resulted in a particularly useful model of negotiation. 4–026

Thompson also views the apparent dichotomy between the two approaches as a false choice and argues that a skilled negotiator does not have to choose between being tough or being nice but, instead, must be able to function both co-operatively and competitively, sometimes simultaneously.[22] 4–027

OTHER THEORIES AND MODELS

Interest-based negotiation is sometimes contrasted with rights-based negotiation, in which the negotiators are primarily concerned with the law and the likely outcome in the event of a court trial. While in practice negotiators may have regard to rights as an element in negotiation, in many cases this is unlikely to be the only consideration, and parties may well consider other factors, including commercial and personal ones. It is arguable that pedagogic practice in law schools continues to focus on a "rights-based" model of justice at the expense of considering either the existence or the value of interest-based negotiation.[23] 4–028

Another model of negotiation, with a socio-anthropological base, is described by Gulliver. This comprises various phases which cover: the search for an appropriate arena for the resolution of the dispute, defining the issues and asserting differences, then narrowing these through the bargaining process, eventually "ritualising" the outcome.[24] 4–029

---

[21] See Murray, Rau and Sherman, *Processes of Dispute Resolution: The Role of Lawyers* (fn.19).
[22] Leigh L. Thompson, *The Truth About Negotiations,* 2nd edn (Pearson, 2013).
[23] See B. Waters, "The Importance of Teaching Dispute Resolution in a Twenty-First-Century Law School" (2017) 51(2) *The Law Teacher* 227–246.
[24] See P. H. Gulliver, *Disputes and Negotiations: A Cross-Cultural Perspective* (Academic Press, 1979).

4-030 Murray, Rau and Sherman[25] refer to further methodology: "Game Theory" which is in fact a method of analysis used to establish the optimum settlement strategy to be adopted in any particular case. In essence, it involves a "tit for tat" approach allowing for parties to negotiate co-operatively as long as both or all do so, but changes to a competitive and retaliatory approach as soon as anyone defects from a co-operative mode.

4-031 Brams and Taylor have devised complex processes to create fair divisions, whether of goods or preferred positions, on a set of issues in negotiations.[26] Their approach involves three elements. The first is to set forth explicit criteria, or properties, that characterise different notions of fairness. The second is to provide systematic procedures, or algorithms, for obtaining a fair division. The third is to illustrate these algorithms with applications to real-life situations. This approach brings together work drawn from different disciplines and includes philosophical questions of fairness and justice, economists' issues of the requirements of a fair scheme, and mathematical concepts.

4-032 The methods and theories discussed in this chapter do not present an exhaustive or comprehensive chronicle but rather serve to indicate the range of possible approaches.

SOME PRACTICAL ASPECTS OF NEGOTIATION

4-033 While it is not feasible to address the practicalities of negotiation in any comprehensive way, some aspects will be briefly mentioned.

Whether or not to negotiate

4-034 A fundamental question may arise at the outset as to whether or not one should be negotiating at all. Sometimes the "other side" may be perceived as untrustworthy, malevolent, dishonest or even evil. Should the issues rather be resolved in another forum, for example through litigation—or in an international context, through direct confrontation?

4-035 Mnookin has addressed this dilemma in *Bargaining with the Devil: When to Negotiate, When to Fight*.[27] In assessing real life situations—including Churchill who chose to fight rather than negotiate, and Nelson Mandela who chose to negotiate when others were fighting, in both cases correctly judged—Mnookin has provided helpful guidance for negotiations where this issue arises. In the former, the decision not to negotiate was influenced by Churchill's personal moral beliefs and gut feelings; and Mandela's decision to negotiate with the South African government was linked to the management of three tensions. The first of these being what is going on *across the table* with your adversary and what is happening *behind the table* with your constituents. The second relates to the tension between pragmatism and principle, or a clash between "rational" and

---

[25] See Murray, Rau and Sherman (fn.19, p.89); see also R. Axelrod, *The Evolution of Co-operation* (New York: Basic Books 1984; Revised edn, 2006).

[26] Steven J. Brams and Alan D. Taylor, *Fair Division: From Cake-Cutting to Dispute Resolution* (New York: Cambridge University Press, 1996).

[27] Robert Mnookin, *Bargaining with the Devil: When to Negotiate, When to Fight* (New York: Simon & Schuster, 2010).

"intuitive" thinking. The third tension relates to the contest between empathy and assertiveness, the former requiring good listening skills to demonstrate an understanding of the interests, needs and perspectives of your adversary and the latter, the ability to state clearly and confidently the interests and perspectives of one's own side.

In essence, Mnookin's conclusion is that there are situations where one should properly decline to negotiate but that more often than not negotiation may well be appropriate and productive in cases where the initial reaction might be to regard the other as "the devil"—too untrustworthy or dishonest to contemplate negotiating with.

4–036

Preparation and set-up

All practitioners and writers agree that preparation is fundamental to effective negotiation. For example, Fisher and Shapiro refer to the three lessons a lawyer had learned on one of Fisher's negotiation workshops: Prepare. Prepare. Prepare.[28] Preparation includes reflection on purpose and goals; considering the present and future potential of the relationship with the other party; thinking about each party's interests and how far these are compatible; listing and prioritising options; reflecting on one's BATNA; being emotionally prepared; and having a clear idea of intended process.

4–037

Lax and Sebenius have referred to three dimensions of negotiation[29]: *tactics*; *deal design*; and *set-up*. These aspects include: ensuring that the right parties and their decision-makers are involved; identifying potential blockers; researching and understanding all interests; avoiding psychological misconceptions; considering the no-deal options on all sides and the Zone of Possible Agreement (see below); ensuring that the other party understands that one is not compelled to agree at any cost; and preparing the correct process and sequence of steps to be taken.

4–038

In the design stage, Lax and Sebenius suggest negotiators consider how to create value by looking behind stated positions and understanding all the interests involved, thinking imaginatively how to create greater value all round, and dovetailing differences.

4–039

Zone of Possible Agreement and the negotiation dance

Howard Raiffa[30] has emphasised the need: to undertake detailed assessments of the risks of litigating, to analyse the parties' positions and prospects of success, and to examine the criteria for settlement on each side. He deals with the concept of "zones of agreement" (also called the "bargaining zones" or the Zones of Possible Agreement (ZOPA)) which denote the parameters of the range of

4–040

---

[28] Roger Fisher and David Shapiro, *Building Agreement: Using Emotions as You Negotiate* (London: Random House Business Books, 2007), p.169.

[29] See Lax and Sebenius, *3-D Negotiation: Powerful Tools to Change the Game in Your Most Important Deal* (fn.4).

[30] Howard Raiffa, *The Art & Science of Negotiation* (Massachusetts: Harvard University Press, 1982).

4-041 possible terms of settlement within which a particular dispute may be resolved, given the aspirations of each party, and any other factors relevant to settlement.[31]

4-041 Raiffa refers to "the negotiation dance" or the fluctuating pattern of concessions and reassessment of perceptions and aspirations that takes place during negotiations. The concept of a negotiation dance has been put forward by other writers, for example Adair and Brett, who see it as the way in which co-operative and competitive behaviours wax and wane during the stages of the negotiation process.[32]

4-042 Indeed Thompson has presented an image of ZOPA as a dance floor on which the negotiators dance, each trying to lead the other to the point beyond which they will not go—what Raiffa calls their reservation point (RP), sometimes viewed as a "bottom line".[33] To illustrate the "bargaining zone" or ZOPA between a buyer and a seller, if the buyer's RP is higher than the seller's, the distance between the two points is called the "bargaining zone".[34]

Opening the negotiations

4-043 Korobkin makes the point that good negotiators do as much (or more) "asking" as they do "telling".[35] Hence, negotiation time should be spent on asking the other party questions in order to gain information. This enables the parties to establish the RPs and the bargaining zone.

4-044 Many negotiators prefer to allow the other side to make the opening offer rather than do so themselves. This avoids the potential risk of offering more than was expected and also gives an indication of the opponent's thinking first. This enables them to respond appropriately and enter into a negotiation process.

4-045 Thompson considers that this approach may well be correct where a negotiator does not know as much about the other side as they know about him; but considers that in other circumstances it will be advantageous to make the first offer.[36] Thompson's assertion is that, although conventional wisdom suggests that one should not open first, the indications from research and literature are that it always benefits a party to make the opening proposal.

4-046 The reason for this lies in the principle of anchoring.[37] This describes a cognitive bias that occurs when individuals place undue weight on one piece of information, event or suggestion that has been placed before them. A significant body of research suggests that when an anchor is introduced, eventual agreements tend to be guided towards the anchor.[38] Whoever makes the first proposal establishes the anchor.

---

[31] Where a zone of possible agreement exists, it will be found in the overlap between the bottom end of what a claimant will ultimately accept and the top end of what a respondent will ultimately offer.
[32] Wendi L. Adair and Jeanne M. Brett, "The Negotiation Dance: Time, Culture, and Behavioral Sequences in Negotiation" (2005) 16(1) *Organization Science*.
[33] See Thompson, *The Truth about Negotiations* (fn.22).
[34] Korobkin, *A Positive Theory of Legal Negotiation* (fn.2 at 1792).
[35] Korobkin, *A Positive Theory of Legal Negotiation* (fn.2 at 1804).
[36] See Thompson, *The Truth about Negotiations* (fn.22).
[37] See Thompson, *The Truth about Negotiations* (fn.22).
[38] See Lax and Sebenius, *3-D Negotiation: Powerful Tools to Change the Game in Your Most Important Deals*, (fn.4).

Responses to proposals

The following are some of the matters to be considered in responding to proposals. 4–047

Where an extreme and unrealistic demand is made, clearly the response must reflect its unacceptability. Two further points need to be borne in mind. First, there may be an impasse at some future stage that could lead to the suggestion, either explicit or implicit, that matters be resolved by splitting the difference (the midpoint rule). However, this may not have regard to the fact that one side may have started with an extreme position while the other started moderately, nor to the fact that one side may have made significant concessions in negotiations while the other has made smaller ones. Alternatively, some negotiators might respond to an extreme demand by making an equally extreme response. Hence, if a moderated response is made, this should be borne in mind if, subsequently, splitting the difference is proposed. Secondly, a response needs to undermine the anchoring effect of the initial proposal.

It is not easy to undermine the power of the initial anchor, which has a continuing effect even where people are aware of its influence. One possibility is to change the frame of reference in the response to the initial proposal. Lax and Sebenius give an example of this: in negotiations for the acquisition of a software company, the initial (anchoring) offer was based on a price/earnings ratio. In response, the required price was based on a different valuation method—a discounted cash flow analysis. This effectively unfroze the initial anchor.[39] 4–048

Another way to overcome the initial anchor is to set out one's own proposals—supported as far as possible with data and facts. This can be further enhanced by writing down the responding proposals: it seems that putting proposals in writing, whether initially or in response, helps to entrench an anchoring effect. 4–049

Opening offers are not commonly accepted, as there is an expectation that the negotiation dance will take place. This is often built into the level of opening offer and response. If an opening offer is accepted, it may raise the question whether the proposal was too generous and lead to possible attempts to backtrack. 4–050

Continuing the negotiations

Some factors in this regard will be briefly mentioned. 4–051

Where there are a number of related issues it is generally advisable to negotiate them on a parallel basis rather than sequentially. This widens the range of possibilities for prioritising and trade-offs. If some of the issues are resolved, it is better to "park" them subject to addressing the others, rather than to regard them as finally settled: it is not at all uncommon to have to revert to resolved issues and bring them into the reckoning during negotiation of the remaining issues. Ultimately, comprehensive terms will need to be formulated that pick up all the different elements.

---

[39] Lax and Sebenius *3-D Negotiation: Powerful Tools to Change the Game in Your Most Important Deal* (fn.4, pp.194–196).

Negotiators should be aware of some of the emotional and psychological factors at play in negotiations and which affect people generally.[40]

4–052 Appropriate questioning and discussions are likely to take place during negotiations about: the issues, the effects of proposals, and express and underlying interests and concerns. Information can be released and exchanged that will help to provide insights both ways and to establish rapport between the negotiators, which can also be helpful.

4–053 The more parties are able to progress their negotiations, usually the greater the momentum there is to complete the remaining aspects: there is more to lose by letting a potential agreement slip the closer one gets to resolution.

4–054 Negotiators should also be aware of the power of symbolism that can disrupt settlements as they appear to be reaching conclusion. Sometimes symbolic issues need to be resolved by symbolic solutions. The power of words and physical things which are used to represent deeper meanings for negotiators may have a profound effect on how they function and make decisions. A word or image is symbolic. Symbolism may emerge in many contentious situations, should be taken seriously and where necessary negotiators should attempt to reach solutions that recognise the power (albeit sometimes disproportionate) that each party has invested in the issue. So, for example, apparently trivial issues may sometimes arise at the end of a successful negotiation, with the potential to disrupt agreement. This may symbolically represent to each party who was right and who was wrong, so each holds out for their position to be adopted. Solutions may need to respect the symbolic power attached to them by both parties and may often need to be creative and multi-layered.

4–055 Symbolic solutions may be illustrated by the significance placed on acknowledgments and apologies, for example in negligence cases, and the importance that may be placed on forms of restitution where the primary objective is not necessarily just the recovery of money—though symbolic acts may need to complement and not necessarily replace financial compensation. In some cases, symbolic restitution may for example be achieved by an agreed payment to a party's nominated charity or the wording of an agreed public statement.

SKILLS, STRATEGIES AND STYLE

4–056 Negotiation skills refer to the adeptness of the negotiator and include techniques and methods for dealing with situations as they arise; these may be learned or intuitive. Strategies refer more specifically to the actual approaches and tactics that a negotiator may employ in order to achieve the required end. Style refers to the way in which a negotiator presents himself or herself, and generally depends upon individual personality and attributes such as personal authority, humour, flair and demeanour.

---

[40] See the section "Perceptions and Psychology" below. See also Henry Brown, Neil Dawson and Brenda McHugh's *Psychology, Emotion and Intuition in Work Relationships: The Head, Heart and Gut Professional* (Routledge, 2018).

SKILLS, STRATEGIES AND STYLE

As pointed out by Murray, Rau and Sherman,[41] the terms strategy, theory and style are often confused and used interchangeably, whereas their differences are important; and there is not necessarily a relationship between them. A negotiator may well use an informal, relaxed style, follow an approach which falls, in theory, squarely into the competitive camp, and adopt a strategy which may be to make slight concessions in order to gain far more substantial advantages.

4–057

Individual strategy will be affected by a number of factors, including the following:

4–058

- The negotiating model followed by the negotiator: a competitive approach will give rise to a different strategy from a problem-solving approach:
  — If both (or all) adopt a co-operative approach, then the strategy is likely to be relatively open and creative, seeking joint gains and the most effective outcome for all. If the approach is competitive, the strategy is likely to include withholding information and lack of co-operation, manipulating and manoeuvring, scoring points, and seeking ways to achieve a better result than the opponent.
  — If, however, one negotiator adopts a competitive approach while the other is co-operative, the co-operative negotiator will need to adapt his or her strategy to accommodate this situation. This may require changing to a competitive mode or declining to negotiate. However a better response tends to involve maintenance of a strong, principled approach which is tough in substance but which keeps the possibilities for co-operation open, and continues to seek outcomes which work for both parties.[42]
- The relative power bases of the parties: this is dealt with below.
- The culture within which the negotiator is operating and the values of the negotiators and their principals.
- The aims, aspirations and underlying needs of the principals and the emotional factors underlying the issues.
- The personalities and psychological make-up of the negotiators, the extent of their mandate and authority, their own private agendas, the skills which each uses, and the perceptions which each has of the personalities and aspirations of the other side.

---

[41] Murray, Rau and Sherman, *Processes of Dispute Resolution: The Role of Lawyers* (fn.19).
[42] See the discussion above, and see also Ch.18 of J. H. Wilkinson, *Donovan Leisure Newton and Irvine ADR Practice Book* (New York: Wiley Law Publications, 1990) entitled "Effective Negotiation" by Gerald R. Williams.

POWER, CULTURE AND GENDER

Power[43]

4–059　Power may exist in different forms including: the relationship between the parties, hierarchical structure and patterns of behaviour; relative economic and financial circumstances; status and authority; relative prospects of successfully litigating the issues; greater access to information; or the power to harm the other side or damage their interests.

4–060　Power may also, however, be less obvious, and could for example reside in a morally strong (even if legally doubtful) position; the ability to withhold co-operation; the ability to inflict damage on another through damaging oneself (as where a debtor goes into bankruptcy). There is even the power of irrationality—the possibility that someone will act unpredictably and irrationally with uncertain effects and consequences.

4–061　Although power may be real, it may also be blurred by the perceptions which parties have of their own power and the power of the other side, neither of which may necessarily be accurate. Power is not a static concept and may change, for example where relationships change or where one side's vulnerability to adverse publicity may lessen, which in turn may weaken the other side's power base.

4–062　In negotiation, parties may use their power directly, in the form of an actual or implied threat, or indirectly merely by allowing the reality of the respective power bases to be understood. Where power vests wholly or substantially in one party, others may capitulate, or may decide to withdraw from the negotiations. Some may try to work out the best outcome achievable, recognising the other's power.

4–063　However, it is unusual for all the power to be on one side and none on the other. More commonly, even if one side may appear to be more powerful than the other, there may be balancing forces and consequences flowing from the exercise of power which make it necessary for power to be used with some circumspection.

4–064　A negotiator will need to understand the realities of his or her own power, strengths and weaknesses as well as those of the other side, and will be guided by these in formulating a strategy for the conduct of the negotiations. To redress the power imbalance a negotiator might want to think about being accompanied and supported by another person, possibly a legal advisor, at the negotiation.

---

[43] An appreciation of power issues is crucial to effective negotiation and all processes involving negotiation. See Murray, Rau and Sherman, *Processes of Dispute Resolution: The Role of Lawyers* (1989), pp.212–220; S. Goldberg, E. Green and F. Sander, *Dispute Resolution* (Boston: Little, Brown, 1985), pp.24–33; G. Chornenki's chapter "Mediating Commercial Disputes: Exchanging 'Power over' for 'Power with'" in J. Macfarlane, *Rethinking Disputes: the Mediation Alternative* (London: Cavendish Publishing, 1997); De Bono, *Conflicts: A Better Way to Resolve Them* (London: Penguin Books, 1986), pp.148–152; L. Parkinson, *Family Mediation*, 3rd edn (Bristol: Jordan Publishing, 2014), Ch.11.

CULTURE, GENDER AND VALUES

These factors may affect negotiation. 4–065
Culture may relate to a number of different aspects, for example:

- there is the culture of the country within which the parties are operating;
- there will be cultural differences where negotiations are carried out across countries;
- local cultural differences or religious or other ethical factors may influence negotiations[44];
- there may be a culture in the industry or field of work in which the dispute arises.

In an increasingly complex and diverse world, an effective negotiator will need to appreciate the influence of cultural diversity on the course and outcome of any negotiations and to translate such understanding into a practical strategy.

Much has been written about cultural diversity in negotiation and mediation.[45] 4–066
Certainly, flexibility and a non-judgmental approach are required, and an ability to obtain the acceptance of the parties in the process; the negotiator needs to be alive to the assumptions being made by the parties and their respective perceptions of fairness; and an avoidance of stereotypical responses is essential.

Gender

Gender in relation both to the parties and to their negotiators may influence 4–067
negotiations.

Some common images and perceptions of men and women as negotiators reflect the gender stereotypes of society. For example, men are perceived as tougher and more competitive, women as more concerned and co-operative. These stereotypes have been under challenge, and one interpretation of some of the studies on the subject would suggest that these perceptions of gender differences may be a factor of power and status differentials rather than an effect of gender distinctions.[46]

---

[44] Rack has highlighted this in relation to mediations conducted between Latino and white parties. Latino culture embues a strong notion of fairness which means that Latino bargaining begins with a fair offer. This opens the parties to disadvantageous negotiation: C Rack, *Latino Anglo Bargaining: Culture, Structure and Choice in Court Mediation* (New York & London: Routledge, 2006).

[45] See, for example, Michelle LeBaron's excellent article: "Culture-Based Negotiation Styles" in G. Burgess and H. Burgess (eds), *Beyond Intractability. Conflict Research Consortium* (U. of Colorado, 2003). Also available at: *http://www.beyondintractability.org/essay/culture-negotiation* [accessed 11 May 2018]; John Paul Lederach, *Preparing for Peace: Conflict Transformation Across Cultures* (New York: Syracuse University Press, 1996); Michele J. Gelfand and Jeanne M. Brett (eds), *The Handbook of Negotiation and Culture* (California: Stanford University Press, 2004); and some negotiation stories across cultures in Guy Olivier Faure, *How People Negotiate: Resolving Disputes in Different Cultures (Advances in Group Decision and Negotiation)* (The Netherlands: Springer (formerly Kluwer Academic Publishers), 2003).

[46] Carol Watson in SPIDR "Beyond Borders" 1991 Proceedings, 19th Annual Conference, *An Examination of the Impact of Gender and Power on Managers' Negotiation Behaviour and Outcomes: Implications for ADR Practitioners*.

4-068 Nevertheless, the fact may remain that for whatever sociological, personal or other reasons, the different sexes may sometimes have real differences of power in the negotiating forum. This can be particularly relevant in family and domestic disputes, where patterns of behaviour between a man and a woman may result in disparities of power and influence.[47]

4-069 A study of the methodology of conversation analysis, with mediators from a psycho-social background, concluded that women are neither generically advantaged nor disadvantaged by the process of mediation, although certain aspects of it may seem to have a more masculine character, which for some may pre-suppose that this may potentially disadvantage women in general. Mediators themselves were treated as gender-neutral, except occasionally in the context of hostile interactional moves.[48]

4-070 Babcock and Laschever's thesis is that women need to negotiate more and that the enhancement of negotiating performance is essential for women. However, this does not translate into an assessment of the relative negotiating effectiveness of the sexes—though it may indicate that women are less likely than men to enter into negotiation following an initial offer.

Values

4-071 *Values* are concerned with individual ideals and principles. The values which parties and their negotiators hold is likely to influence negotiations to a certain extent. A party who has deep religious or ethical convictions may well take a different approach than a party who takes a robust competitive approach to life and to negotiations. Strongly held views and convictions about the subject of the dispute may also make a party less likely to bargain than a give-and-take approach to the matter. Sometimes it may be necessary to examine whether the issues are intractably bound up with principles, in which event negotiation might be very difficult, or whether they can be separated from the principles so as to leave the principles intact but the issues negotiable.

PERCEPTIONS AND PSYCHOLOGY

4-072 *Perceptions* may have a fundamental effect on the attitudes of negotiating parties. These may or may not have any basis in reality, but their mere existence has its own effect. The concept of reality-testing, which is one of the functions of third-party intervention, is to help people review their perceptions against the facts.[49] During the course of bilateral negotiations, a similar reality-testing role may need to be performed by the negotiators.

4-073 *Psychological and emotional factors* may also influence negotiations. Negotiators should be aware of the extent to which individual personality traits

---

[47] See Ch.16: Ethics and values, fairness and power, also Ch.11 "Issues around mediating with domestic violence and abuse". Lisa Parkinson addresses the issue of gender issues in *Family Mediation*, 3rd edn, Family Law, (Bristol: Jordan Publishing, 2014).

[48] See R. Dingwall, D. Greatbatch and L. Ruggerone "Gender and Interaction in Divorce Mediation" (1998) 15(4) *Mediation Quarterly* 277.

[49] For further explanations of reality testing, see Chs 10, 11 and 19.

affect negotiations. Murray, Rau and Sherman[50] highlight that this involves combinations of variables such as self-esteem, personal drive, risk-taking propensities, aggressiveness, tolerance for ambiguity and confrontation, and ethical flexibility.

Parties may also use psychological factors and ploys in the way they negotiate. Strategies are to some extent based on a judgment as to how the other side will react to a given offer, response or movement. This necessitates some ability to understand the other side and their own motivations and aspirations, and to have some insights into their psychology.[51]

4–074

Additionally, parties may have strong feelings about the issues or about the people with whom they are in dispute, whether this relates to personal and family issues or civil and commercial disputes.[52] Negotiators may need to seek ways in which these can be expressed without damaging the negotiating process. Fisher and Shapiro suggest that such strong negative emotions may be dealt with by being prepared, which they consider involves: taking one's emotional temperature, and having an emergency plan in order to soothe strong negative emotions, to diagnose the triggers of one's emotions and to act with a clear purpose in mind.[53]

4–075

GOOD FAITH IN NEGOTIATION

Theoretical Principles

Within common law jurisdictions, there are no fixed rules to suggest that negotiations should be entered into or conducted in good faith. Expectations about maintaining ethical standards are the closest in application and this will be dealt with in the context of mediation elsewhere in the book.[54] Goldberg et al make the point that within legal negotiations, the question is not whether a negotiator may mislead an opponent, but on what subjects and by what means. They go on to claim that it is difficult to obtain general agreement on ethical standards for answering such questions and equally difficult, in view of privacy in which most negotiations are conducted, to enforce agreed-upon standards.[55]

4–076

---

[50] In *Processes of Dispute Resolution: The Role of Lawyers* (1989), p.221, Murray, Rau and Sherman offer some valuable insights into the negotiating and litigation styles of lawyers, and how some may tend to make assumptions and unwittingly practise self-deception, which can sometimes result in their predicting their clients' prospects of success more favourably than warranted.
[51] Lax and Sebenius, *The Manager as Negotiator: Bargaining for Co-operation and Competitive Gain* (1986), p.86. See also Henry Brown, Neil Dawson and Brenda McHugh's *Psychology, Emotion and Intuition in Work Relationships: The Head, Heart and Gut Professional* (Routledge, 2018).
[52] See "The myth of rationality in civil and commercial disputes" in Ch.10.
[53] Roger Fisher and Daniel Shapiro, *Building Agreement: Using Emotions as you Negotiate* (London, Random House, 2007), p.168.
[54] See Ch.16 for more detailed discussion on ethical standards when engaging in mediation.
[55] Stephen B. Goldberg, Frank E. Sander, Nancy H. Rogers and Sarah R. Cole, *Dispute Resolution: Negotiation, Mediation and Other Processes* (Aspen: Wolters Kluwer Law & Business, 2014). See also James White, "Machiavelli and the Bar: Ethical Limitations on Lying in Negotiation" (1980) Am. B. Found. Research J. 926, 926-935,938, on the difficulty of proposing acceptable rules concerning truthfulness in negotiation, also available in Goldberg et al, at pp.70–71.

Legal Principles

4–077 In the context of dispute resolution through the process of negotiation, in the UK there is no specific legal duty to negotiate in good faith and overall. Consequently, the concept of liability for a failure to enter into pre-contract negotiations in good faith remains relatively undeveloped in the English legal system. The situation is slightly more developed on the Continent however.

Good faith in ADR

4–078 A further issue to consider is whether parties owe a duty to negotiate in good faith with one another. In this regard, a fundamental difference of approach appears between the common law systems (which includes the UK, the US, and most Commonwealth countries), and the civil law systems (such as France, Germany, Switzerland and other European countries). Civil law systems are traditionally readier than common law systems to impose pre-contractual liability upon parties for a failure to negotiate and transact in good faith. Indeed, in civil law systems there is an overriding principle of good faith in the formation and performance of contracts. Common law systems, on the other hand, have traditionally been reluctant to impose a duty of good faith on negotiating parties, save where a specific fiduciary relationship exists.

4–079 In England and Wales good faith and fair dealing have so far played a limited role in English contract law. In fact, the House of Lords, in *Walford v Miles*, has gone so far as to say that:

> "the concept of a duty to carry on negotiations in good faith is inherently repugnant to the adversarial position of the parties when involved in negotiations. Each party to the negotiations is entitled to pursue his (or her) own interest, so long as he avoids making misrepresentations. To advance that interest he must be entitled, if he thinks it appropriate, to threaten to withdraw from further negotiations or to withdraw in fact, in the hope that the opposite party may seek to reopen the negotiations by offering him improved terms."[56]

4–080 Even though there have not been any subsequent UK decisions since *Walford and Miles* (which was made in an adversarial and not private or consensual context)[57] specifically concerning the good faith issue within the context of ADR (see below), the "good faith" principle considered in that case has been revisited. For example in *Cable & Wireless Plc v IBM United Kingdom Ltd*,[58] court proceedings were stayed to enable ADR to be pursued, in accordance with the agreement between the parties.

Duty to perform in good faith?

4–081 No such duty has been imported into English law, but the remarks of Sir Thomas Bingham MR (as he then was) in the case of *Philips Electronique Grand Public SA v British Sky Broadcasting Ltd* are significant. He said:

---

[56] Lord Ackner in *Walford v Miles* [1992] 2 A.C. 128; [1992] 2 W.L.R. 174 HL at 181.
[57] See below: "Good faith in the ADR context".
[58] [2002] EWHC 2059 (Comm).

"For the avoidance of doubt, we would add that we would were it material, imply a term that B Sky B should act with good faith in the performance of this contract. But it is not material".[59]

In civil law systems there are express statutory requirements of good faith and fair dealing such as are found in the Swiss and German codes and there is also the concept of *culpa in contrahendo* which does not have a statutory foundation. Courts and commentators have developed this notion by way of analogy to individual statutory provisions. According to this doctrine, the mere initiation of negotiations creates a pre-contractual relationship as a matter of law which imposes on the negotiating parties a reciprocal duty of care. 4–082

The following case, in which the German court granted a *culpa in contrahendo* claim, illustrates the doctrine. The owner of an apartment and a prospective tenant were negotiating a lease agreement. The owner gave the tenant the impression that the agreement would definitely be executed. On the strength of that, the prospective tenant terminated his current lease. Later, the owner refused without reasonable cause to rent the apartment. The court held the owner was liable for the prospective tenant's damages. 4–083

Under English law, remedies in a similar case might be found by applying doctrines of misrepresentation or promissory estoppel.[60] 4–084

Under both German and French law, there is a duty not to break off negotiations without reasonable cause if one party has led the other party to expect that the contract will be concluded in any event and if there is no reason to withdraw. 4–085

Good faith in the ADR context

The decision of *Walford v Miles*, in which the concept of good faith was described as "inherently repugnant" to the adversarial position of parties in negotiation, was made in the adversarial context.[61] However, the concept of a contract negotiation has been described as: 4–086

> "a battle of wits where each tries to manoeuvre the other into an unfavourable position, alone found in common law countries, seems deeply unattractive in the late twentieth century."[62]

ADR processes are designed to function not only in a co-operative environment but also within an adversarial context. Consequently, they may be 4–087

---

[59] *Philips Electronique Grand Public SA v British Sky Broadcasting Ltd* [1995] E.M.L.R. 472 CA (Civ Div).

[60] Promissory estoppel is an equitable doctrine which prevents a party from going back on a promise which was not supported by consideration and is illustrated by the leading case of *Central London Property Trust Ltd v High Trees Ltd* [1947] K.B. 130.

[61] Lord Ackner in *Walford v Miles* [1992] 2 A.C. 128; [1992] 2 W.L.R. 174 HL at 181. The distinction about the context is that if parties are negotiating the settlement of a dispute where there is a case pending and the negotiations are "adversarial", Lord Ackner's comments can be understood; but if the parties have agreed to go into mediation and have chosen a "problem-solving" or interest-based context, and have agreed to negotiate in good faith in that context, then it is questionable as to whether Lord Ackner was right to refer to good faith being repugnant to their positions.

[62] Richard B Mawrey QC, "Good faith" *The Commercial Lawyer*, July/August 1995.

used whether parties are negotiating in a hostile adversarial mode or a co-operative problem-solving mode. However, most consensual ADR processes would be enhanced by an obligation on participants to negotiate in good faith. This should not imply a duty on parties to act against their best interests, but rather a duty to conduct negotiations in a proper and constructive manner. There would also seem to be a distinction between two different good faith aspects. The one concept imports good faith principles into the process, by attempting in good faith to arrive at a settlement agreement, even if the negotiations are conducted with individual self-interest. This at least would be required. The other concept would import principles of good faith into the substance of the negotiations.

4–088 The question arises as to whether *Walford v Miles* would have been decided in the same way if it had arisen in the context of a consensual ADR process. The distinction would be that parties would have chosen a non-adversarial context for their negotiations. In such event, it would be arguable that any good faith provision in their contract should be respected and enforced. Of course, even in a non-adversarial, consensual process, parties in dispute retain separate interests. Each still aims to negotiate the outcome most favourable to him or herself, even if this may be arrived at through a principled and problem-solving approach. Hence there could well be a counter-argument that parties remain engaged in a process that respects their separate interests even where they have chosen a non-adversarial forum to try to resolve the dispute.

4–089 Any changes to the principles enunciated by Lord Ackner may well have to be introduced and implemented as part of a legislative programme, though judicial decisions could lead the way for this.

THE NEUTRAL NEGOTIATION ROLE

4–090 The principles of negotiation outlined in this chapter apply in relation to bilateral or multilateral negotiations. They are not specifically geared to implementation through a neutral role. They are, however, also relevant to a neutral who needs to understand the issues outlined in this chapter and in particular to appreciate the theories, practice, benefits and shortcomings of problem-solving negotiation. An ADR neutral will need to draw on his or her own negotiating experience and skills to assist the parties with their negotiations. This should be done in a neutral and ethical way, without bias towards either party and without unduly influencing the parties in any way which is not expressly or implicitly envisaged and agreed by the ground-rules for the process.

4–091 Some ADR practitioners may initially be uncertain how to convert their negotiating experience and skills into a neutral role. When conducting separate meetings, do they negotiate with each side as if representing the other? Or do they hold back because they are in a privileged position and have some idea where the respective strengths and weaknesses lie? This uncertainty may have a paralysing effect and it is vital for an ADR practitioner to be comfortable in the neutral role of facilitating the parties' negotiations without becoming the champion of either.

4–092 An impartial ADR practitioner has various roles and functions, which include managing the process as well as facilitating the negotiations which may involve

THE NEUTRAL NEGOTIATION ROLE

the use of various strategies and skills.[63] The practitioner can help the parties to move away from conflict and into a creative and constructive frame of mind, to implement the agenda, to communicate effectively, to generate and explore options and to re-examine their perceptions through reality testing. In these and many other ways, the practitioner helps them to engage in constructive dialogue and negotiations. Ultimately, it is the parties who negotiate with one another: the practitioner simply acts as a skilled facilitator of those negotiations, and neither an agent for either, nor a quasi-principal.

---

[63] See Ch.14.

CHAPTER 5

ADR and the Courts

INTRODUCTION

Although ADR represents a range of alternatives to the court-based litigation system, it has also increasingly permeated and intersected that system in a number of significant ways, including the following:

5–001

- *Rules, practice directions and protocols:* The Civil Procedure Rules in England and Wales (CPR) contain various rules and practice directions relevant to ADR. In addition, a number of pre-action protocols have been established under the CPR, which specify certain preliminary steps to be taken before commencing proceedings, which include reference to ADR. In the family field, there have been major developments in relation to ADR including mandatory consideration of mediation.[1]
- *Courts adopting ADR processes:* There are a number of court procedures in which the principles of ADR are employed by judges or other court officials to cut through the full trial process in order to arrive at a speedy, informal outcome.[2]
- *Court-attached mediation by independent mediators:* Court-attached schemes exist and have been piloted to provide third-party mediation for litigants through independent mediators.
- *Courts directing or recommending ADR processes to the parties:* Cases may be adjourned for parties to enter into mediation or some other form of ADR outside the court system. This may be ordered, or the court may simply adjourn with the proposal that the parties do so. The courts have also used judgments and other platforms to recommend the use of these processes.
- *Courts imposing sanctions where ADR is not attempted:* As indicated below and in Ch.17, there has been a line of cases in the UK in which the courts have imposed sanctions for a failure by a party to mediate or enter into ADR in circumstances where it was considered reasonable that they should do so.

---

[1] Introduced under s.10(1) of the Children and Families Act 2014, attending a Mediation Information Assessment Meeting (MIAM) is a requirement for a person before making certain kinds of private family related applications to obtain a court order.

[2] See for example: Solving disputes in the county courts: creating a simpler, quicker and more proportionate system A consultation on reforming civil justice in England and Wales—the Government Response at: *https://consult.justice.gov.uk/digital-communications/county_court_disputes/results/solving-disputes-in-cc-response.pdf* [accessed 11 May 2018].

- *Courts in some jurisdictions acting as a gateway to ADR (The Multi-Door Courthouse):* There is a concept of the court administration serving as the entry point to whatever kind of dispute resolution process may be appropriate—whether litigation through the courts or some alternative form of dispute resolution. This may be adopted in its entirety or perhaps only in some partial way.

Each of these will be considered together with other aspects of court-related ADR in the UK and elsewhere.

RULES, PRACTICE DIRECTIONS AND PROTOCOLS

5–002 The Courts of England and Wales have introduced and promoted ADR through a number of rules, practice directions and pre-action protocols.

Civil Procedure Rules (CPR)

5–003 A number of CPR provisions touch directly or indirectly on ADR, including the following:

Part 1—Rule 1: The overriding objective of the Rules is set out in r.1.1(1), namely "enabling the court to deal with cases justly", which in turn is achieved through the methods stipulated in r.1.1(2) which includes ensuring that parties are on an equal footing, saving expense, and dealing with cases proportionately, expeditiously and fairly. To this end, part of the Court's duty of active case management arising under r.1.4(2)(e) is:

> "encouraging the parties to use an alternative dispute resolution procedure if the court considers that appropriate and facilitating the use of such procedure".

5–004 *Part 26—Rule 26.4:* This provides that a party may, when filing an allocation questionnaire, ask for the proceedings to be stayed while the parties try to settle the case by ADR or other means; and allows courts to stay cases to enable parties to try using ADR.

5–005 *Part 44—Rule 44.3:* This outlines the court's discretion as to the award of costs, and contains provisions regarding parties' conduct that can be taken into account, which includes the extent to which parties followed pre-action protocols, as further mentioned below.

Family Procedure Rules 2010 (FPR)

5–006 The FPR have a broadly similar overriding objective as the CPR, with an additional welfare consideration. Part 3 of the FPR deals specifically with ADR in family matters.

5–007 Rule 3.1 refers to the court's powers to encourage the parties to use ADR and to facilitate its use. Rule 3.2 provides that the court "must consider, at every stage in proceedings, whether alternative dispute resolution is appropriate". Rule 3.3

allows the court to adjourn proceedings to enable the parties to obtain information and advice about ADR, or to enable it to take place.

As amplified below, an important Practice Direction (3A) supplementing Pt 3 of the FPR has been issued that significantly extends the court's relationship with mediation by making it essential for divorcing couples to attend a mandatory meeting to consider mediation before being able to make an application to the court in relation to financial or children issues.

5–008

Pre-action protocols

Lord Woolf introduced the concept of pre-action protocols in 1996 as part of his *Access to Justice* Report. Their aims are to enable parties to settle their issues without launching proceedings, by encouraging them to exchange information about the issues, and to consider using a form of ADR. The protocols describe the conduct the court will normally expect of the prospective parties prior to the start of proceedings. Courts making costs orders in any subsequent proceedings will have regard to the extent to which parties have complied with the protocols, or they may impose other sanctions such as staying the proceedings until the necessary steps have been taken.

5–009

Protocols have been established in relation to a range of specific kinds of actions, including for example personal injury, clinical negligence, defamation, construction and engineering, judicial review and professional negligence. A family law protocol has also been published. There has been relatively little support for a "one-size-fits-all" protocol; but s.III sets out principles governing the conduct of parties in cases not subject to a pre-action protocol.

5–010

A fundamental principle running through all the protocols is the clear support for the use of ADR. Paragraph 8.1 of the Practice Direction stipulates that:

5–011

> "Starting proceedings should usually be a step of last resort, and proceedings should not normally be started when a settlement is still actively being explored. Although ADR is not compulsory, the parties should consider whether some form of ADR procedure might enable them to settle the matter without starting proceedings. The court may require evidence that the parties considered some form of ADR."

Particular forms of ADR suggested are mediation, early neutral evaluation and arbitration.

Family pre-application protocol

Practice Direction (3A) supplementing Pt 3 of the FPR makes it essential for parties, with certain limited exceptions, to attend a mandatory meeting to consider mediation before making an application to the court in relation to various financial or children issues. This is not mandatory mediation, but mandatory pre-application consideration of mediation.

5–012

These meetings to consider mediation, called Mediation Information and Assessment Meetings (or MIAMs) are further considered below.

COURTS ADOPTING ADR PROCESSES

5–013 Although many courts and judges have traditionally encouraged settlement, ADR has had some influence on the way in which this is done, with formal structures created in which judges suspend their usual judicial role and assume a more facilitative function, or in which other court officials are employed to mediate or to support ADR or quasi-ADR processes. Some of these court-attached processes will be briefly considered.

Court Settlement Process and ENE: The Technology and Construction Court

5–014 The Technology and Construction Court (TCC) in its official Guide,[3] and in its day to day practice, encourages ADR and the informal resolution of disputes. This is built into its pre-action protocol, its Case Management Conference and its procedures, which include provision for an ADR order to be made, with proceedings stayed while ADR is undertaken. The primary ADR procedures envisaged by the court—though parties are not limited to these—are mediation and Early Neutral Evaluation (ENE). The Guide provides (at 7.5.1) that:

> "In an appropriate case, and with the consent of all parties, a TCC judge may provide an early neutral evaluation either in respect of the full case or of particular issues arising within it. Unless the parties otherwise agree the ENE will be produced in writing and will set out conclusions and brief reasons. Such an ENE will not, save with the agreement of the parties, be binding on the parties."

If the judge assigned to the case undertakes the ENE, he or she will not take any further part in the proceedings, unless the parties agree otherwise.

5–015 The TCC also provides an innovative ADR procedure, the Court Settlement Process described (at 7.6.1) as a form of mediation carried out by TCC judges in appropriate cases and where all parties consent. The draft order for this process, contained in the Guide, outlines its procedure, which is generally decided by the parties together with the Settlement Judge. The Guide includes the following procedure for the process:

> "Unless the Parties otherwise agree, during the Court Settlement Conference the Settlement Judge may communicate with the Parties together or with any Party separately, including private meetings at which the Settlement Judge may express views on the disputes. Each Party shall cooperate with the Settlement Judge. A Party may request a private meeting with the Settlement Judge at any time during the Court Settlement Conference. The Parties shall give full assistance to enable the Court Settlement Conference to proceed and be concluded within the time stipulated by the Settlement Judge."

5–016 If the parties do not reach a settlement during the process, they may request a non-binding assessment from the Settlement Judge:

---

[3] Technology and Construction Court Guide, 3rd Revision (March 2014) available at *https://www.gov.uk/government/uploads/system/uploads/attachment_data/file/448256/technology-and-construction-court-guide.pdf* [accessed 11 May 2018].

"setting out his views on such matters as the Parties shall request, which may include, for instance, his views on the disputes, his views on prospects of success on individual issues, the likely outcome of the case and what would be an appropriate settlement. Such assessment shall be confidential to the parties and may not be used or referred to in any subsequent proceedings."

This may be considered to be an evaluative form of mediation, with the evaluative element at the further end of the evaluation spectrum and undertaken by a neutral whose views are likely to be highly persuasive, given that he or she would have been the judge deciding the case at the trial. Of course, the whole process is confidential and privileged, and the Settlement Judge takes no further part in the case, and may not be called as a witness in any subsequent proceedings. The Settlement Judge is also given the same immunity from suit as he or she would have had if acting in a judicial capacity.

5–017

According to research on the TCC conducted by King's College London[4]:

5–018

"an internal report by Akenhead J, summarised in the TCC's 2008 Annual Report, suggests a slow take-up at the start but a high settlement rate (78%) in those cases which have been through the CSP".

The 2014 Annual Report of the Technology and Construction Court reported that ADR has continued to play a large role in resolving technology and construction disputes, with many cases being resolved by means of ADR.

Financial Dispute Resolution (FDR)[5]

In this scheme, a District Judge meets the parties and their lawyers with a view to helping move them towards the settlement of financial issues arising on divorce. This FDR hearing is evidentially privileged, to allow the parties and their lawyers freedom to discuss the matter freely and to negotiate settlement terms.[6] The judge dealing with the FDR does not hear the case if the parties do not settle: it is appointed to another judge. In this evidentially privileged environment, the judge is provided with information about offers, responses and counter-offers made to date, albeit that these have been made on a without prejudice, evidentially privileged basis, and can comment on the proposed terms, without hearing any evidence. The judge can also, if appropriate, indicate his or her views on the issues and what judgment he might give if he or she were to be hearing the case. Parties and lawyers are invited to consider these privately, and may return to the District Judge for further discussion and guidance from time to time after their private meetings.

5–019

---

[4] Nicholas Gould, Claire King and Philip Britton, *Mediating Construction Disputes: An Evaluation of Existing Practice* (London: King's College, Centre of Construction Law and Dispute Resolution, 2010).
[5] Family Proceedings Rules 1991, amended by Family Proceedings (Amendment No.2) Rules 1999.
[6] *Practice Direction (Fam Div: Family Proceedings: Financial Dispute Resolution)* [1997] 1 W.L.R. 1069; [1997] 3 All E.R. 768, stipulates that "the FDR appointment is part of the conciliation process and should be so regarded by the courts and the parties". It refers to r.2.75(1) and to *Re D (minors)* and concludes that, with specified exceptions, "evidence of anything said or of any admissions made in the course of an FDR appointment will not be admissible in evidence".

5-020 The FDR meeting is conducted as an evaluative ADR process, albeit with a higher level of evaluation than in many other ADR forms. As with other non-binding neutral evaluative processes, the evaluation is intended to help the parties and their lawyers to address settlement realistically.

This procedure is reported to be working very successfully, though it can be stressful and some parties may prefer the mediation alternative.

The Small Claims Mediation Service

5-021 As outlined in the next section, the mediation of small claims by independent mediators, referred by the court, has been undertaken with reasonably significant success in a few courts for some years. There has, however, been a development with the establishment of a Small Claims Mediation Service, which initially employed in-house mediators to undertake the mediation of small claims by telephone (or occasionally face-to-face) as a free service.

5-022 The scheme was originally established to deal with claims of under £5,000 where proceedings have been started and if the parties agree to mediate, the service will contact them. The average time from allocation to mediation is around five weeks, and the average time for a mediation session is about one hour. In a keynote speech to the Civil Mediation Council in May 2014, Lord Faulks, then Minister of State for Justice, reported that HMCTS had expanded and centralised its Small Claims Mediation Service. All cases with a dispute value of up to £10,000 are now automatically referred to mediation, without judicial intervention, where all parties request it. He claimed that this service is now considering over 10,000 referrals a year, helping people settle disputes earlier in the proceedings, and so far saving over 9,400 hours of judicial hearing time. On average 64 per cent of cases referred to the service settle. He claimed that results of a recent survey reveal that 95 per cent of Small Claims Mediation Service users would use the service again.[7]

5-023 According to Lord Justice Briggs, statistics kept by the originator of the scheme in the Hampshire, Dorset, Wiltshire area suggest that 25 per cent of the entire small claims track list is disposed of due to non-attendance, 50 per cent at the conciliation hearing, and a significant proportion of the remaining 25 per cent settles before trial, due (anecdotally) to progress towards settlement achieved at the conciliation hearing.[8]

Judges as mediators

5-024 Apart from the processes outlined above in which judges and court officers have mediatory functions, there are many jurisdictions in which the judges serve as mediators in an ordinary mediation process. For example, in Quebec, the justice

---

[7] See Lord Faulks, keynote speech at the Civil Mediation Conference, 22 May 2014 available at: *https://www.gov.uk/government/speeches/mediation-and-government* [accessed 11 May 2018].

[8] Lord Justice Briggs, *Civil Courts Structure Review: Final Report*, July 2016 available at: *https://www.judiciary.gov.uk/wp-content/uploads/2016/07/civil-courts-structure-review-final-report-jul-16-final-1.pdf* [accessed 11 May 2018].

system integrates adjudication and mediation in all areas of law. "It is a unified and hybrid system of justice, unique in the world in its longevity and its comprehensiveness."[9]

Quebec is not, however, unique in the use of judges as mediators. So, for example, this has been widely adopted in some Scandinavian countries. Germany has a tradition of judges helping to deal with cases consensually as well as adjudicating, and there are now a significant number of court-based mediation projects. Judges also act as mediators in Australia.

5–025

In Europe, the organisation GEMME—the European Association of Judges for Mediation—is a body with national sections whose members are judges working to support the development and implementation of mediation in a coordinated manner.

5–026

These are just examples of judicial interest and involvement in mediation. In addition, there is also an increasing trend of judges becoming private mediators after their retirement from the Bench, and making significant contributions to ADR in that capacity.

5–027

Issues around judges as mediators

Although the fact that judges are supporting and recommending mediation and other ADR processes is widely welcomed, there are concerns about judges themselves mediating in their judicial capacities, though there are also positive aspects to this development.

5–028

The arguments against judges mediating include the following:

5–029

- Mediation is not a proper exercise of the judicial function. Judges make determinations based on fair trial and the principles of natural justice. Sir Laurence Street, former Chief Justice of New South Wales and after retirement an eminent mediator, said that:

    "A court that makes available a judge or a registrar to conduct a true mediation is forsaking a fundamental precept upon which public confidence in the integrity and impartiality of the court system is founded. Private access to a representative of a court, by one party, in which the dispute is discussed and views are expressed in the absence of the other party, is a repudiation of basic principles of natural justice and absence of hidden influence that the community rightly expects and demands that the courts observe."[10]

- The mediation role is a very different one from the judicial one, requiring a different skills set and an entirely different way of exercising personal authority. Judges are used to being directive and making evaluations, neither of which is necessarily appropriate in mediation mode.
- Mediation by judges threatens public confidence in the court:

---

[9] Louise Otis and Eric H. Reiter, "Mediation by Judges: A New Phenomenon in the Transformation of Justice" (2006) 6 *Pepperdine Dispute Resolution Law Journal* 351.

[10] Sir Laurence Street, "Mediation and the Judicial Institution" (1997) 71 *Australian Law Journal* 794.

> "Allowing judges to mediate cases can cause mischief to the point of seriously compromising both the impartiality and neutrality of the court and its appearance of impartiality and neutrality, thus undermining the public respect that is the foundation of its very existence."[11]

- Being a good judge does not automatically translate into being a good mediator. There is no recognised method of assessing judges' qualification and ability to mediate, as there is in conventional mediation training programmes, nor is there any follow-up regime of continuing professional development (CPD).
- Confidentiality is vitally important in those models that involve separate and private meetings. Even if the judge who mediates will not try the case if it does not settle, there may be a risk of another judge in the same court becoming aware of what was said—or a perception in the parties' minds that this might happen.

5–030 On the other hand, the arguments in favour of judicial mediation include the following:

- ADR has become part of the mainstream of dispute resolution, and courts and judges need to adapt to this reality.
- Judges would train and undergo the same rigorous preparation for mediation as private mediators undertake. There is ample experience that judges, lawyers and others accustomed to being directive in their usual professional roles and exercising authority can learn to work in another way required by the mediation process.
- Judges are used to being impartial and are:

> "well-suited for the role of mediator for several reasons, relating both to the perceptions of the parties and to the specific skills possessed by judges. Of particular importance is the perception of the judicial office as one of impartiality and independence, which confers on judges a degree of moral authority,"

the exercise of which is "extremely delicate".[12]

- Judges would maintain confidentiality of the process, and if the matter were not settled in judicial mediation, a different judge would have conduct of the case.
- The judge-mediator is well able to help parties "reality test" effectively, though there is a view that judge-mediators should not express any view on the merits.
- Judicial mediation can also be more cost-effective than private mediation, as there would not be a mediator's fee to pay—making access to mediation more affordable for those in the court system.

---

[11] Alan Limbury, "'Why judges shouldn't be mediators' and 'mandatory mediation'—an Australian perspective" (Summer 2006) 11(1) *The Expert & Dispute Resolver*.
[12] Otis and Reiter, "Mediation by Judges: A New Phenomenon in the Transformation of Justice" (fn.9).

It does seem that judicial mediation alongside the option of private independent mediation offers the public a valuable range of options. 5–031

COURT-ATTACHED MEDIATION BY INDEPENDENT MEDIATORS

The term "court-attached" mediation (sometimes also referred to as "court-annexed", "court-related" or "court-linked" mediation) is used to describe the process in which the court incorporates mediation as part of its procedural system and/or makes the arrangements for the appointment of the mediator, and/or provides its premises for the mediation. 5–032

In some forms of court-attached mediation, a judge or court official will serve as the neutral. These have been considered in the previous section. In other forms of court-attached mediation, the mediator appointed is not a judge or court officer, but an independent third party, commonly on a court-approved panel. This form of court-linked process is considered in this section. 5–033

County Court mediation schemes

A number of pilot schemes have been established over the years in which selected County Courts in England and Wales referred cases to independent mediators. None of these have continued in operation, having been replaced in 2007 by the National Mediation Helpline, which itself has been replaced by an online directory hosted by the Ministry of Justice.[13] 5–034

Examples of pilot County Court schemes, now discontinued, include *The Birmingham Civil Justice Centre* which provided for litigants to be introduced to a professionally qualified mediator to conduct a three hour mediation at a modest fee; *The Leeds Combined Court Centre* pilot scheme, with mediators appointed on a rota basis and remunerated on a set scale of fees; and *The Central London County Court* mediation scheme, which was the first and main one to operate in England, having run as a pilot scheme from 1996 to 1998 and then as a permanent part of the court until 2006. The choice whether or not to use the scheme was voluntary, save for a trial of an Automatic Referral to Mediation Scheme (ARMS) in which selected cases were referred to mediation, with an opt-out provision, where considered justifiable. The scheme was evaluated in 1998 and again in 2007 by Professor Dame Hazel Genn.[14] 5–035

---

[13] The online directory can be accessed at *http://civilmediation.justice.gov.uk/* [accessed 11 May 2018].

[14] For the 1998 research, see: *http://webarchive.nationalarchives.gov.uk/+/http://www.dca.gov.uk/research/1998/598esfr.htm* [accessed 11 May 2018]. For the 2007 research, see *https://www.researchgate.net/publication/32894907_Twisting_arms_court_referred_and_court_linked_mediation_under_judicial_pressure* which, as the title suggests, inter alia expresses concern at judicial pressure to mediate. See also fn.31 below.

The Exeter small claims scheme[15]

5–036 In the Exeter scheme solicitor-mediators worked on a voluntary basis to provide free 30-minute mediation appointments (initially only 20 minutes) to litigants referred by the district judges.

5–037 The tight time frame meant that complex cases could not be undertaken. Each party was given about two minutes to explain their case, and the focus was then on settlement. Mediators also had limited time to prepare: they were required to read six files in about 40 minutes, on the mediation day. They thus only had a loose understanding of the issues, and limited time to explain their role to the parties. Although individual styles varied, mediators needed to be more directive in order to meet the required time-frame. The judge was immediately available to make an order to reflect the settlement terms, which was helpful in itself, and also to give additional authority to the mediator and the process.

5–038 A research report on the Exeter scheme[16] reflected that 70 per cent of the cases referred to mediation settled before trial—58 per cent in the mediation and 12 per cent either before or afterwards.

The Court of Appeal mediation scheme (CAMS)

5–039 Where a court has made a judgment or award and an appeal is made to the Court of Appeal, parties may use the mediation scheme provided by the Court of Appeal, which dates back to 1996, using independent mediators, to try to resolve their issues. Both or all parties need to agree to do so as the scheme is entirely voluntary.

5–040 Civil and commercial cases are administered by CEDR Solve, the service arm of the Centre for Effective Dispute Resolution. CEDR Solve will then arrange for the appointment of a mediator from a panel of independent mediators, unconnected with the court, and the process will take place on a confidential and evidentially privileged basis.

5–041 Where an appeal referred to CAMS is exceptionally complex or substantial, and the parties are able to fund mediation at commercial rates, CEDR Solve may suggest that a commercial mediation outside CAMS be arranged. Or if both parties are litigants in person and mediation through CEDR Solve may not be possible, LawWorks Mediation (a charity with lawyer volunteers offering support where public funding is not available) may be able to provide a mediator free of cost to the parties as well as pro bono assistance.

5–042 Family cases are administered and monitored by the Civil Appeals Office, which appoints a mediator from a panel of one of the specified family mediation providers authorised from time to time, including the Law Society.

---

[15] This scheme was set up on the initiative of local solicitor Jeremy Ferguson together with District Judge Jill Wainwright.
[16] Research Report by Dr Sue Prince, *Court-based Mediation: A preliminary analysis of the small claims mediation scheme at Exeter County Court* (Civil Justice Council, 2004).

Mediation Information and Assessment Meetings (MIAMs)

Family proceedings

Reference has been made to Practice Direction (3A), supplementing Pt 3 of the Family Procedure Rules, which applies where a person is considering applying for an order in relevant family proceedings (most proceedings relating to children or matrimonial finance, with specified exceptions such as emergency or enforcement proceedings), and under which it is mandatory to attend a meeting to consider mediation. The court will wish to know whether this has been complied with.

5–043

There are certain limited exceptions, for example where either party is bankrupt; where there has been an allegation of domestic violence against a party resulting in a police investigation or the issuing of civil proceedings for the protection of any party within the last 12 months; where an urgent application needs to be made that involves potential risk of harm or hardship; where there are specified difficulties in getting a mediator; or where a mediator considers that a preliminary meeting would not be suitable.

5–044

MIAMs are conducted by currently practising family mediators who comply with prescribed requirements, which include membership of an organisation belonging to the Family Mediation Council, complying with training, supervision/consultancy and continuing professional development criteria, and being specifically qualified to undertake MIAMs. This may either involve having been accepted to deal with public funding preliminary meetings or undertaking a specific MIAMs training workshop.

5–045

Civil proceedings

In 2012 The Ministry of Justice published the response to its consultation process, which included the question as to whether a procedure similar to the family MIAM might be introduced on a mandatory basis for civil claims of up to £100,000 and, if so, what form of process should be specified. Fifty-eight per cent of respondents disagreed with the proposal, with 42 per cent of respondents, mainly from the mediation provider sector, suggesting that compulsory mediation information sessions would be helpful to parties in court. Overall, respondents generally agreed that it would be useful for parties to have information to enable them to engage in mediation or other forms of alternative dispute resolution, and that information as to mediation could be sent to each party as a matter of course during the pre-trial process. They are, however, concerned that an additional compulsory stage might result in further unnecessary costs and delays being incurred as part of the civil justice process.[17]

5–046

There are no firm plans to introduce a MIAM for civil cases. However if this were to be introduced, questions arise as to who will conduct these meetings, what qualifications might be prescribed for them, and what exemptions might apply.

5–047

---

[17] See the Government Response to the consultation on reforming civil justice in England and Wales at fn.2.

COURTS DIRECTING OR RECOMMENDING ADR PROCESSES

5–048 Another way in which ADR intersects with the court system arises when judges direct parties to try mediation or some other ADR process in appropriate cases.

5–049 *The Commercial Court:* English Commercial Court judges have been making orders directing parties to try using ADR in appropriate cases since 1993, bolstered by two Practice Directions, one in 1994 and one in 1996.[18] The relevant court guide[19] states that:

> "While emphasising its primary role as a forum for deciding commercial cases, the Commercial Court encourages parties to consider the use of ADR (such as, but not confined to, mediation and conciliation) as an alternative means of resolving disputes or particular issues.... The commercial judges will in appropriate cases invite the parties to consider whether their dispute, or particular issues in it, could be resolved through ADR.... The judge may, if he considers it appropriate, adjourn the case for a specified period of time to encourage and enable the parties to use ADR.... The judge may further consider in an appropriate case making an ADR order...."

5–050 A report on ADR in the Commercial Court was produced in 2002 by Professor Hazel Genn[20] who analysed the outcome of ADR orders and found that the success rate was around 50 per cent, with the majority of those that did not settle during the ADR stage settling afterwards and only a very small proportion proceeding to trial. Some solicitors expressed concerns and scepticism but in the majority of cases an ADR order was not seen to have a negative impact on negotiations, and experiences of ADR, when it was successful, were "overwhelmingly positive". When ADR was not successful, there was—unsurprisingly—a lower level of satisfaction, and concern about increased costs, the time spent on the failed ADR, and the problem of putting pressure on an unwilling opponent to come to the negotiating table.

5–051 *The Technology and Construction Court* (TCC) has also taken a robust position in supporting ADR. In addition to its Court Settlement Process its official Guide provides as follows[21]:

> "The court will provide encouragement to the parties to use alternative dispute resolution ('ADR') and will, whenever appropriate, facilitate the use of such a procedure.... at the first CMC [Case Management Conference], the court will want to be addressed on the parties' views as to the likely efficacy of ADR, the appropriate timing of ADR, and the advantages and disadvantages of a short stay of proceedings to allow ADR to take place.... the court may order a short stay to facilitate ADR at that stage. Alternatively, the court may simply encourage the parties to seek ADR...."

---

[18] Practice Note (Commercial Court: Alternative Dispute Resolution) Cresswell J [1994] 1 All E.R. 34; Practice Statement: Alternative Dispute Resolution, 7 June 1996, Waller J.
[19] Ministry of Justice, *The Admiralty & Commercial Courts Guide* (2014, updated March 2016).
[20] Professor Hazel Genn, *Court-based ADR Initiatives for Non-Family Civil Disputes: The Commercial Court and the Court of Appeal* (London: Lord Chancellor's Department, 2002).
[21] Technology and Construction Court Guide, 2nd edn, 3rd Revision March 2014.

COURTS DIRECTING OR RECOMMENDING ADR PROCESSES

The Guide indicates that mediation is most likely to be the appropriate process. The court expects parties to comply with any ADR procedure selected, and may impose a cost sanction if there is a failure to do so, though the confidentiality of the process is expressed as being something that will need to be preserved.

5–052

The Chancery Division of the High Court also supports ADR in its official Guide,[22] which provides:

5–053

> "The settlement of disputes without a trial, by means of Alternative Dispute Resolution ('ADR') can help litigants (a) to save costs, (b) to achieve settlement of their disputes while preserving their existing commercial relationships and market reputation and provide litigants with a wider range of solutions than those offered by the determination of the issues in the claim.... The court will readily grant a stay at an early stage of the claim to accommodate mediation or any other form of ADR if the parties are agreed that there should be a stay...."

These are examples of the court's encouragement of ADR and willingness to give directions and make orders for ADR; but many other courts similarly support and encourage the use of ADR, and mediation in particular. There are many reported cases in which mediation or other ADR has been promoted, in addition to those where the court actually imposed sanctions for a failure to mediate, including for example:

5–054

Barker v Johnson [1999] EWCA Civ 1088: This was a bitterly contested neighbour case, in which Ward LJ said:

5–055

> "I would urge these parties to seek the help of this court's ADR service in order to explore whether a compromise would not only enable this litigation to be killed off sooner rather than later, but that some sense of compromise might bring a greater sense of happiness and peace in the respective homes of neighbours."

R. (on the application of Cowl) v Plymouth City Council [2001] EWCA Civ 1935; [2002] 1 W.L.R. 803 Lord Woolf said:

5–056

> "Particularly in the case of such disputes, both sides must by now be acutely conscious of the contribution alternative dispute resolution could make to resolving disputes in a manner that both met the needs of the parties and the public, and saved time, expense and stress Today, sufficient should be known about Alternative Dispute Resolution to make the failure to adopt it, in particular when public money was involved, indefensible."

Al-Khatib v Masry [2004] EWCA Civ 1353; [2005] 1 F.L.R. 381: This was a family case involving children and Sharia law, which was settled by mediation organised by the Court of Appeal, in which Thorpe LJ said:

5–057

> "From the point of view of the Court of Appeal it supports our conviction that there is no case, however conflicted, which is not potentially open to successful mediation, even if mediation has not been attempted or has failed during the trial process."

---

[22] Chancery Guide, February 2016.

5-058   *Burchell v Bullard* [2005] EWCA Civ 358: A building dispute in which Ward LJ, said:

> "The parties cannot ignore a proper request to mediate simply because it was made before the claim was issued. With court fees escalating it may be folly to do so. I draw attention, moreover, to para 5.4 of the pre-action protocol for construction and engineering disputes, which I doubt was at the forefront of the parties' minds, it should preferably apprise the parties to consider at a pre action meeting whether some form of alternative dispute resolution procedure would be more suitable than litigation. These defendants have escaped the imposition of a costs action in this case but defendants in a like position in the future can expect little sympathy if they blithely battle on regardless of the alternatives."

5-059   *IDA Ltd v University of Southampton* [2006] EWCA Civ 145: Jacob LJ said:

> "This sort of dispute is particularly apt for early mediation. Such mediation could well go beyond conventional mediation (where the mediator facilitates a consensual agreement). I have in mind the process called 'medarb' where a 'mediator' trusted by both sides is given the authority to decide the terms of a binding settlement agreement."

5-060   *Egan v Motor Services (Bath) Ltd* [2007] EWCA Civ 1002; [2008] 1 W.L.R. 1589: Ward LJ said:

> "This case cries out for mediation' should be the advice given to both [parties] Mediation can do more for the parties than negotiation Mediation is a perfectly proper adjunct to litigation. The skills are now well developed. The results are astonishingly good. Try it more often."

COURTS IMPOSING SANCTIONS WHERE ADR IS NOT ATTEMPTED

5-061   The policy of the courts in relation to the imposition of costs sanctions for a failure to mediate or use any other ADR process is set out in Ch.10. As mentioned there, the leading case on this is *Halsey*[23] in which the Court of Appeal set out guidelines for deciding whether costs sanctions should apply in the event of a refusal to mediate.

5-062   In his judgment, Lord Justice Dyson said:

> "The value and importance of ADR have been established within a remarkably short time. All members of the legal profession who conduct litigation should now routinely consider with their clients whether their disputes are suitable for ADR."

5-063   Indeed, no mediator would consider that mediation was appropriate in all circumstances and the issuing of guidance, adopted from the Law Society's submissions to the Court of Appeal, helps clarify when it is or is not reasonable to expect parties to undertake ADR.

---

[23] *Halsey v Milton Keynes General NHS Trust* [2004] EWCA (Civ) 576; [2004] 1 W.L.R. 3002. For further discussion and background, see Ch.17.

COURTS IMPOSING SANCTIONS WHERE ADR IS NOT ATTEMPTED

Two elements of the judgment may need further consideration, as raised by Lightman J in a speech on the subject.[24] The first is the issue of art.6 of the European Convention on Human Rights, which is dealt with further below; and the other is the question as to where the onus of establishing reasonableness or otherwise should fall. In this regard, Lightman J expressed the view, which the authors of this work would support, that it was wrong and unreasonable to place the burden of proof of reasonableness on the party who wished to mediate. He considered that this needed to be guided by three factors: access to justice,

5–064

> "the commonsense proposition that the party who has decided not to proceed to mediation and knows the reasons for his decision should be required to give, explain and justify his decision";

and the duty of the court to encourage the use of mediation. In his view, all these factors pointed in the opposite direction to that taken by the Court of Appeal.

The *Halsey* principles have been followed in a number of cases since they were formulated. In *Couwenbergh v Valkova*[25] the Court of Appeal reaffirmed the relevance of *Halsey*, notwithstanding serious allegations of fraud (negating any suggestion that it is not possible to mediate where there are allegations of fraud). Wall LJ was critical of the Legal Services Commission, who had funded the action but declined to participate in mediation, indeed were said to have obstructed it, saying that the court:

5–065

> "could not contain our criticism of the authorities for such an intransigent view. When costs do finally have to be allocated, we hope these observations will be borne in mind when the court comes to apply the guidelines in *Halsey v Milton Keynes General NHS Trust* [2004] EWCA (Civ) 576 on how to deal with failures to mediate despite the encouragement to do so."[26]

But consider *Swain Mason v Mills & Reeve*[27] where in having regard to the Halsey guidelines, the Court of Appeal took the view that a parties' refusal to mediate was in the circumstances of the case justified and in exercising the court's discretion on costs, held that having not acted unreasonably in refusing mediation, on that basis the successful party should not be penalised in costs. Each case must therefore be considered on its individual merits and with judicial consideration of the Halsey guidelines. What this case illustrates is that refusal to mediate, despite judicial encouragement to participate, may in some circumstances be justified and considered reasonable. Nevertheless declining an invitation to mediate remains a high-risk strategy, as an unreasonable refusal may result in the court imposing punitive costs sanctions.

5–066

---

[24] Speech given at the London law firm, S.J. Berwin, on 28 June 2007.
[25] [2004] EWCA Civ 676.
[26] *Couwenbergh v Valkova* [2004] EWCA Civ 676 at [55].
[27] [2012] EWCA Civ 498.

COURTS ACTING AS A GATEWAY TO ADR (THE MULTI-DOOR COURTHOUSE)

5-067 The concept of the multi-door courthouse was originated in 1976 by Professor Frank E. A. Sander, Professor of Law at Harvard University. He considered certain criteria to be important for determining the effectiveness of a dispute resolution system, namely:

> "cost, speed, accuracy, credibility (to the public and the parties), and workability. In some cases, but not in all, predictability may also be important."[28]

5-068 Sander identified two questions as important, namely the significant characteristics of various alternative dispute resolution mechanisms, and how these characteristics could be utilised so that some rational criteria could be developed for allocating various types of disputes to different dispute resolution processes. He outlined a spectrum of processes, on a decreasing scale of external involvement, with adjudication at the one end and "avoidance" at the minimum involvement end (an approach he described as "clearly undesirable").

5-069 Sander's analysis led him to recommend:

> "a flexible and diverse panoply of dispute resolution processes, with particular types of cases being assigned to differing processes (or combinations of processes) ... one might envision by the year 2000 not simply a court house but a Dispute Resolution Centre, where the grievant would first be channelled through a screening clerk who would then direct him to the process (or sequence of processes) most appropriate to his type of case."

An initial enquiry to the court would be dealt with by an intake officer, who would aim to give an individual and specialised answer to each inquirer.

5-070 The Multi-Door Courthouse was implemented in several US courts, but although it was tested in many states, few of these went on to implement it. Nevertheless, the Multi-Door Courthouse may well have had a role in encouraging the exploration of new dispute resolution concepts, and may well have influenced the way in which the courts have supported ADR, albeit not in the structured way envisaged by Sander. The idea of courts being able to serve as an initial point of contact not just to litigation but to other appropriate forms of dispute resolution is an excellent one, and remains a valid aspiration.

5-071 Indeed, the concept continues to serve as an inspiration to court systems in some parts of the world. In Nigeria, the Lagos Multi-Door Courthouse is the first court-connected ADR Centre in Africa offering mediation, conciliation, arbitration and early neutral evaluation with its main focus on the enhancement of justice, facilitated by online case processing and scheduling. Changes to the Lagos Court's civil procedure rules in 2012 made it mandatory for lawyers and litigants to embrace the multi-door ADR system. Singapore, too, has a multi-door courthouse for its subordinate courts.

---

[28] See the Pound Conference report, cited as 70 Federal Rules Decisions, (FRD) 79 at p.113.

MANDATORY ADR AND HUMAN RIGHTS: THE ARTICLE 6 ARGUMENT

One of the issues that arises in the context of incorporating ADR as part of the court system is whether requiring parties to participate in an ADR process might infringe their rights under art.6 of the European Convention of Human Rights, which provides inter alia that:

5–072

> "In the determination of his civil rights and obligations or of any criminal charge against him, everyone is entitled to a fair and public hearing within a reasonable time by an independent and impartial tribunal established by law."

The contention is clearly set out in the *Halsey* judgment, in which Dyson LJ says:

> "It seems to us that to oblige truly unwilling parties to refer their disputes to mediation would be to impose an unacceptable obstruction on their right of access to the court. The court in Strasbourg has said in relation to article 6 of the European Convention on Human Rights that the right of access to a court may be waived, for example by means of an arbitration agreement, but such waiver should be subjected to 'particularly careful review' to ensure that the claimant is not subject to 'constraint': see *Deweer v Belgium* (1980) 2 EHRR 439, para 49. If that is the approach of the ECtHR to an *agreement* to arbitrate, it seems to us likely that *compulsion* of ADR would be regarded as an unacceptable constraint on the right of access to the court and, therefore, a violation of article 6."[29]

There are many reasons to believe that the Court of Appeal were mistaken in their view that compulsory mediation would infringe art.6. First, by way of background, it should be said that the Law Society, whose submissions as an Interested Party were adopted by the Court of Appeal in formulating their criteria, did not submit the proposition that compulsory mediation would be an infringement of art.6, and indeed that was not a view that they had expressed. Secondly, the court itself was not dogmatic about the proposition, Dyson LJ going on to say:

5–073

> "Even if (contrary to our view) the court does have jurisdiction to order unwilling parties to refer their disputes to mediation, we find it difficult to conceive of circumstances in which it would be appropriate to exercise it."

The fundamental point is that nobody is deprived of their right to a fair trial by virtue of being required to enter into mediation or any other consensual ADR process any more than if they were required to attend a hearing for directions as a procedural step in the process. Requiring parties to negotiate with one another on the basis that they can continue to trial if they are unable to agree simply cannot be regarded as depriving them of a "fair and public hearing within a reasonable time".

5–074

Perhaps Lightman J may be quoted to sum up the position[30]:

5–075

---

[29] *Halsey v Milton Keynes General NHS Trust* [2004] EWCA (Civ) 576 at [9].
[30] Speech given at the London law firm, S.J. Berwin, on 28 June 2007.

> "(1) The court appears to have been unfamiliar with the mediation process and to have confused an order for mediation with an order for arbitration or some other order which places a permanent stay on proceedings. An order for mediation does not interfere with the right to a trial: at most it merely imposes a short delay to afford an opportunity for settlement and indeed the order for mediation may not even do that, for the order for mediation may require or allow the parties to proceed with preparation for trial; and (2) the Court of Appeal appears to have been unaware that the practice of ordering parties to proceed to mediation regardless of their wishes is prevalent elsewhere throughout the Commonwealth, the USA and the world at large, and indeed at home in matrimonial property disputes in the Family Division"

5–076　A similar point is made by Professor Hazel Genn and others in their evaluation review of the mediation programmes at the Central London County Court.[31] They say:

> "It is arguable whether, in fact, a direction to attempt mediation prior to a hearing would infringe Article 6. Referral to mediation is a procedural step along the way to a court hearing if the case does not settle at mediation. It does not exclude access to the courts and to require parties to attend a three-hour low-cost mediation session does not order them to compromise their claim. Having attended the mediation meeting, the parties are free to terminate and leave at any point and to continue with the litigation."

It is to be hoped that the argument about the effect of mandatory mediation as part of a court process in relation to art.6 will be more fully presented and argued in the future, rather than the somewhat spontaneous way it arose in *Halsey*.[32]

COURT-ANNEXED ARBITRATION

5–077　In order to avoid confusion we should distinguish between two different kinds of arbitration through the courts:

- In England and elsewhere, a binding arbitration may be effected by a commercial court judge; or the county court may order that a small claims dispute be dealt with by binding arbitration by a district judge or a third party, with the force of a court order.
- These conventional binding forms of arbitration by the court may be useful and valuable, but in this book they are not included in the terms "court-annexed arbitration" or "court-ordered arbitration", and will not be further addressed in this chapter.
- In a different procedure, used in the US and elsewhere, but not in England, the court orders a case to be dealt with by arbitration by a third party, whose

---

[31] See Genn et al at fn.14.
[32] There is an argument that the position may be more nuanced than outlined above. Case law from the European Court of Human Rights suggests that, in certain circumstances, there could be an issue with the right of access to courts. See the article by Shirley Shipman, "Compulsory Mediation: the Elephant in the Room" (2011) 30 C.J.Q. 163. See also the forthcoming article by Lorna McGregor, Rachel Murray and Shirley Shipman in *Human Rights Quarterly* 2019, "Should National Human Rights Institutions Institutionalise Dispute Resolution?"

finding is initially non-binding. Either party may require a re-hearing by a judge, but if neither does so the award becomes a binding court order. However, if the case is re-heard by a judge, and the judge's decision does not result in a better award to the person who applied for the re-hearing, sanctions may apply to that party (where they are constitutionally allowed). It is this process that is called "court-annexed arbitration" (the term which for convenience this book will henceforth use) or "court-ordered arbitration".

Although court-annexed arbitration is not available in England, it has become established in a number of other jurisdictions as an effective way of dealing with disputes without having to embark on full-scale litigation. 5–078

Non-binding court-annexed arbitration

Non-binding court-annexed arbitration has been viewed as successfully achieving two goals: 5–079

> "... [providing] prompt, relatively inexpensive, fair and less formal resolution of a great many civil cases; and [preserving] at the same time the procedural and substantive rights of citizens involved in law suits."[33]

Court-annexed arbitration might be less effective if a significant proportion of disputants chose to have a re-hearing. Applications without merit for a re-hearing need to be discouraged, while preserving an effective right to do so. One such sanction in the US is a costs award against the applicant for a re-hearing who does not improve his position at a trial. This has been held to be invalid in Michigan by reason of being outside the trial court's rule-making authority[34]; but the Washington and Florida ADR statutes make specific provision for this, and Washington state's intermediate appellate court has upheld such provisions.[35]

The court-annexed arbitration procedure can also facilitate settlements because, after the non-binding arbitration, realistic settlement discussions can and do take place, which necessarily have regard to the non-binding award made by the arbitrator and the fact that the losing party may wish to seek a re-hearing. 5–080

The level of jurisdiction and the nature of subject-matter appropriate to court-annexed arbitration is generally fixed by the relevant statute or rules: this process tends to be used for lower levels of dispute and not for cases involving more substantial sums. 5–081

The hearings tend to be informal, brief and summary, and rules of evidence may be relaxed. The arbitrator will usually make an immediate decision. Unless otherwise agreed, any re-hearing of the case would ordinarily (but not necessarily) be fresh and without reference to the arbitration evidence. 5–082

The results of a number of studies indicate that most litigants are satisfied with this process and that it achieves a high rate of success. A study of one American 5–083

---

[33] First US National Conference Report, 1985.
[34] *Tiedel v Northwestern Michigan College*, 865 F. 2nd 88 (6th Cir. 1988).
[35] *Colarusso v Petersen,* 61 Wash. App. 767; 812 P. 2nd 862 (1991).

programme found that the concern of some critics that this might deliver "second class" justice was not supported, and that the average citizen's notion of "fairness" did not require:

> "the judicial robes, formal procedures, or the various components of due process that are the hallmark of trial. But his notion of fairness is not simply cheap, quick dispute resolution. Rather, the average individual seems to believe that a 'fair' dispute resolution procedure is one that provides an opportunity for a hearing of the facts of the case before a neutral third party adjudicator. Our data suggests that ability to appeal the arbitration award contributes to individuals' perceptions that the process is fair"[36]

Adapting court-annexed arbitration principles

5-084 An informal alternative to the introduction of the court-linked process of court-annexed arbitration as described above, has been suggested in England. This process has been named "concilio-arbitration" by its proponent, Rowland Williams.[37] The suggested procedure is for a concilio-arbitrator to examine the case informally, consider the evidence, hear the parties' representations and make a non-binding award. If both parties accept the award, it becomes binding. If one party does not accept then the case proceeds to litigation; and if the party who refuses to accept the award does not achieve a significantly better result at the trial, there is a costs penalty.

5-085 It will be apparent that court-annexed arbitration differs from ordinary arbitration by virtue of the fact that it is not binding in the first instance, and that disputants do not lose their right to have the matter heard by the court. Also, the awards, once accepted, become as effective as orders of the court. These differences appear to make them more acceptable to the public than traditional binding arbitration.

COURT-ATTACHED ADR IN SOME OTHER JURISDICTIONS

5-086 In this context, court-attached ADR means that the ADR process is available, and may be mandated, as part of the litigation process. The programme may be an integral part of the organisation of the court, it may be separate from the court and litigation process, or the connection between the court and the ADR programme may fall between these two poles.

---

[36] J. Adler, D. Hensler and C. Nelson, "Simple Justice: How Litigants Fare in the Pittsburgh Court Arbitration Program" in J. S. Murray, A. S. Rau and E. F. Sherman, *Processes of Dispute Resolution: The Role of Lawyers* (New York: Foundation Press, 1989), pp.629–637.

[37] Rowland Williams, "Concilio-Arbitration: A New Proposal for the Quick and Inexpensive Resolution of Disputes" *Law Society's Gazette,* 23 November 1983. See also Rowland Williams, "Concilio-Arbitration: the Service Commences" *Law Society's Gazette,* 28 May 1986.

COURT-ATTACHED ADR IN SOME OTHER JURISDICTIONS

United States

5-087 The use of ADR in US courts goes back to the mid-1970s but this was strongly reinforced by The Alternative Disputes Resolution Act of 1998[38] which required each federal district court to authorise the use of ADR in all civil cases and to establish its own ADR programme. It also required the district courts to establish procedures for making neutrals available, to adopt local rules regarding confidentiality, compensation, and conflict of interest and to appoint a judge or staff person to administer the programme.

5-088 Many court-attached or court-annexed ADR programmes tend to be administered by ADR Coordinators, who are responsible to oversee the programme, and who will generally arrange the appointment of a settlement officer or provide information about approved settlement officers so that the parties can make their own selection. The parties then usually contact their settlement officer directly and the court's involvement is suspended pending the outcome of the mediation. ADR Coordinators ensure that appointed settlement officers have been properly trained and accredited, and that they maintain proper standards of practice.

Canada

5-089 In Quebec, parties have an option to engage a private mediator, or mediation may be conducted by a judge in a settlement conference, which is free. A Code of Civil Procedure,[39] effective from 2003, includes provisions relating to the settlement conference. The principle is established that the judge, appointed by the Chief Justice, has the function of a conciliator or mediator.[40]

Australia

5-090 Court-related schemes are well established in Australia. In the Federal Court, a judge will consider at an early stage of a case whether ADR, including mediation, is likely to assist, and may order the parties to attend mediation even if they do not agree to it.[41] Ordinarily the mediator will be a Registrar of the Federal Court, who has been duly accredited under the Australian National Mediator Standards, though parties can engage a private mediator at their own expense.

5-091 In New South Wales, an ADR Directorate was established in the NSW Attorney General's Department to coordinate, manage and drive ADR policy, and to support a number of published proposals for the development of ADR.

Voluntary and mandatory court-related mediation schemes are also in operation at the state and local levels.

---

[38] Public Law 105-315 codified at 28 U.S.C., ss.651 et seq.
[39] Bill 54, An Act to reform the Code of Civil Procedure (CCP), 2002 c. 7.
[40] Najda Marie Alexander, *Global Trends in Mediation,* 2nd edn (London: Kluwer Law International, 2006).
[41] See the Federal Court's website: *http://www.fedcourt.gov.au/services/ADR.*

Germany

5-092 Germany has a long record of judicial intervention in the settlement process, and has more recently developed a mandatory regime for judicial mediation. A number of administrative courts offer mediation by judges, pursuant to the German Code of Civil Procedure, under which judges order mediation hearings unless these would be inappropriate.[42]

5-093 Until the turn of the 21st Century, interest in non-adversarial ADR methods was modest in Germany, with mediation rarely used, and limited to the fields of divorce and environmental disputes. In 2000, conciliation was introduced for small claims; and from 2003, a pilot programme for voluntary mediation was introduced in several courts, undertaken by judge-mediators. The success rate of this court-related mediation was 79 per cent.[43]

5-094 The Mediation Act (Mediationsgesetz) 2012 was the first legislation to regulate mediation services in Germany. Exceeding the requirements of the European Directive, the Act incorporates incentives in the official procedural codes. For example, the court may suggest mediation and if the parties decline this option, the Court may suspend the proceedings.

Denmark

5-095 In Denmark, mediation projects have been piloted since the turn of the 21st Century. Court linked mediation is now widely available in Danish District Courts. Mediation can also be used in the Maritime and Commercial Court. A mediator can be a judge or an officer of the court in question who is designated to serve as a mediator, or a lawyer who has been approved by the Court Administration to serve as a mediator in the High Court district concerned. Mediation is also used in family proceedings, including children's issues, and in a wide range of civil and commercial disputes.

Japan

5-096 ADR processes in Japan are governed by the ADR Promotion Law,[44] which came into force in 2007, and which applies both to domestic and international disputes.

5-097 However, there are particular provisions for court-linked ADR procedures, contained in the Civil Conciliation Act 1951. Under this Act, any party can apply to the court for conciliation, or the court may order conciliation if it thinks that a case is suitable. Any conciliation or mediation undertaken by the court is confidential; and the court retains the power to decide whether a settlement proposed to be agreed by the parties is acceptable to the court. If an agreement is reached in court-annexed mediation, it will be registered at the court and may be enforced as a court judgment.

---

[42] Article 278 of the Code—the Zivilprozessordnung.

[43] Professor, Dr Renate Dendorfer, "One Continent: Many Methods: Mediation in Germany: Structure, Status Quo and Special Issues" (Paper to the 2011 Conference of the Chartered Institute of Arbitrators, European Branch, Paris). Available at: *http://docplayer.net/48518922-One-continent-many-methods-mediation-in-germany-structure-status-quo-and-special-issues-ciarb-chartered-institute-for-arbitrators-european-branch.html* [accessed 11 May 2018].

[44] The Act on Promotion of Use of Alternative Dispute Resolution, Act No.151 of 2004.

Both Government and courts are supportive of ADR in Japan, and the courts have recommended conciliation in many cases. Referrals to court-annexed conciliation have numbered around a half a million a year.

5–098

China

China's Civil Procedure Law[45] gives the courts discretion to attempt mediation in relation to cases before them. Article 85 provides:

5–099

> "The people's court shall, in handling civil cases, distinguish between right and wrong and conduct conciliation under the principle of voluntariness of the parties and on the basis of evident facts."

Conciliation is conducted locally, where the court is located, either by a single judge or a collegial panel. If foreign parties are involved, they will be required to have Chinese legal representation for the process. Any agreement reached will have the same effect as a court judgment, but without any right of appeal.

Singapore[46]

Court Dispute Resolution (CDR) has been available in the Subordinate Courts in Singapore since 1994 at the Primary Dispute Resolution Centre and is used in most cases going through those courts. CDR processes primarily involve Settlement Conferences, which are conducted as an integral part of the civil justice process, presided over by a District Judge who assumes the role of settlement judge. They also involve mediation, early neutral evaluation, and binding and non-binding evaluation.

5–100

CDR is a highly evaluative form of mediation, with settlement judges being proactive in their interventions and guidance to the parties. It is "rights-based" and the merits of the dispute are actively discussed and debated. Model Standards of Practice for Court Mediators of the Subordinate Courts refers to a Code of Ethics for Settlement Judges. These include aspects concerning training and qualification, impartiality, confidentiality, informed consent and other relevant matters.

5–101

India

ADR is covered in India by the Arbitration and Conciliation Act 1996, as amended in 2015, supplemented by s.4 of the Legal Services Authorities Act 1987, which provides for the establishment of people's courts—Lok Adalats. These courts may deal with a dispute if the parties agree, if one party applies for referral, or if the court dealing with the dispute refers the matter to a Lok Adalat. The principles guiding the Lok Adalat are conciliation and compromise, based on

5–102

---

[45] Law of Civil Procedure of the People's Republic of China, 1991. Chapter VIII deals with conciliation.
[46] With acknowledgment to Michael Hwang SC of Singapore for his contribution to the Asia section. See: Michael Hwang, Loong Seng Onn & Yeo Chuan Tat, "ADR in East Asia" in J. C. Goldsmith et al (eds), *ADR in Business: Practice and Issues across Countries and Cultures* (USA: Kluwer Law International, 2006).

justice, fairness and equity. The neutrals are commonly retired judges, and their awards are regarded as civil court decrees.

5–103   An alternative route lies under s.89 of the Code of Civil Procedure, which provides that if a court considers that elements of a settlement exist that may be acceptable to the parties, it is to formulate terms of settlement and give them to the parties for their observations. After receiving their observations, the court may reformulate the terms of a possible settlement and refer these for arbitration, conciliation, judicial settlement including settlement through Lok Adalat or mediation. However, referral to arbitration or judicial settlement requires the written consent of all parties.

CONCLUSIONS

5–104   Clearly, establishing proper court-annexed ADR programmes requires a substantial degree of innovative administration. The programmes cannot work satisfactorily without the wholehearted commitment of judges and practitioners.

5–105   There are also indications that some litigants and lawyers expect in court-annexed schemes a measure of helpful but not coercive evaluation. Parties are aware that if ADR fails in court-annexed mediation, the case will go back to the judge. For those requiring it, there is a case for providing some guidance about the merits of the issues.

5–106   It is also clear (unsurprisingly) that the quality of the ADR process is closely related to the quality of the mediator. It is essential to have mediators who are well-trained and of high quality. This in turn raises questions as to training, accreditation and control. If court-annexed ADR schemes are to work then the allocation of resources by both Government and the private sector is required. Government must be prepared to devote part of the expenditure on the court system to providing for the administration of court-annexed ADR. Initially there may need to be a significant contribution from the private sector.

5–107   As most informed commentators recognise, introducing ADR in the court system raises difficult constitutional and ethical questions. The constitutional right of access to the courts is central to the workings of a democratic and pluralist society. It is therefore essential that if ADR schemes are to be mandatory as part of the court system, safeguards exist against abuse. This means that the court has a role to play in developing systems which, even if mandatory, fit easily within adjudicatory processes. It also means that courts must insist on high standards of training, ethics and competence on the part of mediators to whom cases are going to be referred.

5–108   It is in our view false to judge the efficacy of court-related ADR only by applying economic yardsticks and establishing savings in time and cost. These do have a place, for example, in evaluating changes which may become necessary in existing systems or in deciding to which of a range of ADR methods resources should be applied. But the issue of court-annexed ADR transcends statistical analysis. Civilised society must be vitally concerned to ensure access to civil justice, by which is meant that citizens are able to take their legitimate complaints and grievances to the courts for fair, skilled and impartial resolution. We need to seek new ways of resolving civil disputes, but to do so respecting traditional and

CONCLUSIONS

essential values of justice, fairness and equality before the law. The objectives of a court-based system must be to settle cases and, failing settlement, to ensure that cases are properly adjudicated in a manner appropriate and proportionate to the issues and amounts at stake.

Finally, the value of court-related mediation does not only lie in the saving of costs and of court time, as important as these considerations may be. Mediation also provides a route to empowering people to find creative ways of resolving their issues themselves, on terms that they decide, taking personal control and responsibility allowing them to move forward constructively without the stress and anxiety (let alone the risk and cost) of a trial. These factors all need to be weighed in the balance in valuing court-based alternatives to litigation.

5–109

CHAPTER 6

Arbitration

INTRODUCTION

Arbitration is widely used for international and domestic disputes, cross-border commercial disputes, contractual disputes, employment rights disputes[1] and many other kinds of issues including consumer disputes and disputes arising in connection with international investment and trade agreements. As indicated below, it is also available for the resolution of certain kinds of family issues. 6–001

Arbitration is a private form of adjudication outside the court system, in which the parties can select the arbitrator or arbitral panel, and in which the procedures are intended to be less formal and more flexible than those of the court. That is sometimes the case, particularly in consumer disputes, but, as considered below, this is not always achieved in practice, especially in large and complex disputes. 6–002

The arbitrator is required to observe due process (or natural justice) and to make a binding determination in the form of an enforceable award. Unlike a court's decision, there is generally no appeal against the award, though some consumer organisations may allow limited forms of appeal. Under some circumstances, issues of law can be reserved to the courts, which also have a supervisory power, for example where there are allegations of irregularity. 6–003

The procedure for arbitration is generally set out in the rules of the relevant arbitral organisation under whose auspices the process is to be conducted. While some procedures may be simplified, for example by way of documents-only arbitration in some consumer disputes, the process in larger disputes, domestic and international, tends to follow similar lines once the arbitrator has been appointed. This is likely to follow the broad approach of the courts, albeit more informally, including for example the making of claim submissions and responses, the provision of relevant documents, the exchange of statements of evidence, a hearing with parties legally represented, and the making of an award. 6–004

In both the first and second editions of this work in 1993 and 1999 respectively, there was a chapter on arbitration and other adjudication, but the authors took the view that arbitration was to be distinguished from ADR. The principal distinction was (and remains) that while both arbitration and other ADR processes involve a choice by parties to enter into them, arbitration results in a legally binding and enforceable award, whereas consensual ADR processes may or may not result in an agreement. "Alternative" in ADR was initially construed as alternative to litigation or to any form of third-party determination. 6–005

---

[1] These are dealt with in Ch.13.

6–006　However, the consensus for some time has been that ADR is to be construed as an alternative to litigation and that arbitration is in the mainstream of ADR methods and procedures. That view was adopted in the third edition of this work and continues to reflect the position of the current authors.

THE INTERNATIONAL STRUCTURE

6–007　The structure of international commercial arbitration is firmly established. At the core of the international system is the New York Convention of 1958.[2] This convention has been ratified by over 150 states. It provides for the recognition and enforcement of arbitration agreements and resulting awards. The convention provides a means for, in effect, domesticating an international arbitration award in over 150 nations. The convention mandates recognition of an award, without a review of the merits, unless the party challenging enforcement can show incapacity or invalidity of the arbitration clause, lack of notice, want of jurisdiction, improper composition of the tribunal or that the award is not final; or where enforcement of the award would contravene public policy.

6–008　The whole system of international arbitration is underpinned by the convention, which taken together with the UNCITRAL Model Law of 1985,[3] and the UNCITRAL Rules of Conciliation and Arbitration,[4] establishes an international system not only for the recognition and enforcement of arbitration agreements and awards, but also for the conduct of arbitration. The UNCITRAL Rules are also widely used for ad hoc arbitrations, i.e. arbitration without an institution (and many institutions will administer arbitrations pursuant to the UNCITRAL Rules). The UNCITRAL Rules have influenced heavily the conduct of arbitration, both ad hoc and institutional. So too, has the Model Law, widely adopted as the template or benchmark for states seeking to enact legislation for international commercial arbitration and even domestic arbitration as well. Many jurisdictions have done so, such as India, Germany, Austria, Singapore, Malaysia and even England and Wales. Although the 1996 Arbitration Act[5] in England does not reproduce the Model Law verbatim, the language and structure closely follow the composition and principles of the Model Law.

6–009　The international structure is supported also by an increasing number of arbitral institutions, both regional and local. Currently, the foremost global arbitral institution is the Paris-based International Chamber of Commerce which was established in 1920 after the First World War.

6–010　A vital part of the system is that many jurisdictions, indeed all the leading ones, have executed arbitration statutes, which fully support the process. Arbitration is a derogation from state sovereignty. The state recognises and supports and will enforce agreements to arbitrate and resulting awards.

---

[2] The Convention on the Recognition and Enforcement of Foreign Arbitral Awards, done at New York, 10 June 1958 (the "New York Convention"). See *http://www.newyorkconvention.org/* [accessed 15 May 2018].

[3] The United Nations Commission on International Trade Law: 1985—UNCITRAL Model Law on International Commercial Arbitration, with amendments as adopted in 2006 (the "Model Law").

[4] Adopted by UNCITRAL on 28 April 1976 and revised in 2010. For more information visit, *www.uncitral.org* [accessed 15 May 2018] (the UNCITRAL Rules).

[5] Text available at *http://www.legislation.gov.uk/ukpga/1996/23/contents* [accessed 15 May 2018].

Legislation has given considerable party autonomy in jurisdiction and procedural matters and state courts will intervene, for example, to restrain a party from litigating if there is a valid agreement to arbitrate. What the state requires in return, certainly in England, Wales and Northern Ireland, is that arbitration is conducted in the words of s.1 of the 1996 Act,[6] which provides as follows:

> "(a) the object of arbitration is to obtain the fair resolution of disputes by an impartial tribunal without unnecessary delay or expense;
> (b) the parties should be free to agree how their disputes are resolved, subject only to such safeguards as are necessary in the public interest;
> (c) in matters governed by this Part the court should not intervene except as provided by this Part."

THE ARBITRATION ACT OF 1996 (ENGLAND, WALES AND NORTHERN IRELAND)

The 1996 Arbitration Act fundamentally affected arbitration in the territories it covered, namely England, Wales and Northern Ireland. Scotland adopted different rules governing arbitration, based on the UNCITRAL Model Law.[7]

6–011

Arthur Marriott, subsequently to become one of the UK's two first solicitor Queens Counsel, was a principal proponent of the reform of English legislation governing arbitration, which resulted in the passage of the 1996 Act, and chaired the Private Group engaged in the preparation of the 1996 statute.[8] Marriott was a very strong supporter of the arbitration process and one of its foremost proponents and practitioners, but he recognised after some time that the Act had not produced all the changes that the process potentially offered. The 3rd edition of this book in 2011 which he co-authored reflected the following:

6–012

> "(It) is now clear from experience with the 1996 Act in England that it has not resulted in radical change in the procedures of arbitration, both domestic and international. Neither arbitrators nor counsel have used the great freedom given to them to devise more cost effective systems to reduce delay and cost. Arbitration in England is now very expensive, on a par with litigation in the commercial and technology courts."

Marriott was not being critical of the arbitration process, which he championed, but was rather encouraging greater use of the procedural freedom allowed by the Act.[9]

While the 1996 Act significantly developed the practice of arbitration in the jurisdiction covered by it, there are also aspects that have been regarded as

6–013

---

[6] See *http://www.legislation.gov.uk/ukpga/1996/23/part/I* [accessed 15 May 2018].
[7] See: Sch.7 to the Law Reform (Miscellaneous Provisions) (Scotland) Act 1990.
[8] See the article by B. Harris, "The Arbitration Act 1996—10 Years On: Preliminary Observations of a Major Survey of Users' Views" (2006) at *https://www.biicl.org/files/2126_the_arbitration_act_1996_10_years_on.pdf* [accessed 15 May 2018] and the Tribute following Marriott's death in 2015 by the International Council for Commercial Arbitration (ICCA) at *http://www.arbitration-icca.org/news/2015/137/tribute-to-arthur-leslie-marriott-qc-1943-2015.html* [accessed 15 May 2018]. Marriott was also co-author of the 4th edition of *Bernstein's Handbook of Arbitration and Dispute Resolution Practice* (Sweet & Maxwell, 2003).
[9] See the sub-heading below: Procedural Freedom.

shortcomings, including in particular the absence of any proceedings akin to summary judgment in the courts, to address claims that might be considered to be without merit. Consequently, at the end of 2017 the Law Commission indicated that it would consider proposals for possible reform of the Act.[10] It identified the use of a statutory summary judgment style procedure as one potential reform, and the design of an arbitration system appropriate for trust disputes as another. The latter aspect will include for example considering issues regarding compliance with human rights law, the possible interests of the tax authorities in the outcome of arbitration proceedings, and whether any change in the law should extend to all types of trust (including charitable trusts).

THE ESSENTIAL FEATURES OF ARBITRATION

Agreement between the parties to arbitrate

6-014   The arbitral process rests on agreement between the parties. There can be no arbitration proper without an arbitration agreement, and there can be no arbitration initiated by, or conducted against, a person who is not a party to the arbitration agreement. Developed arbitration law admits the validity of arbitration agreements and enforces them, which means that the ordinary courts may not (in principle) hear a dispute which is to be referred to arbitration and will stay proceedings to enable the arbitral process to function.

6-015   As a general rule, the courts have limited jurisdiction when the parties have entered into a valid arbitration agreement.[11] First, the courts have jurisdiction to grant interim relief of various kinds, for example, to preserve the subject-matter of the dispute,[12] secondly, they have jurisdiction in order to support the arbitral process where it breaks down, such as in the appointment of arbitrators (supportive function); thirdly, they have jurisdiction in order to ensure that basic standards of justice are upheld (the supervisory function); and fourthly, they have jurisdiction to enforce the award.

6-016   The agreement to refer any disputes to arbitration may be incorporated into a contract so as to provide in advance for this process to apply rather than litigation

---

[10] See The Law Commission: Thirteenth Programme of Law Reform, No.377 (December 2017) paras 4.52–4.58 at *https://www.lawcom.gov.uk/project/13th-programme-of-law-reform/* [accessed 15 May 2018].

[11] This idea is reflected in art.5 UNCITRAL Model Law 1985: "In matters governed by this Law, no court shall intervene except where so provided in this Law". For a discussion of the relationship between courts and the arbitral tribunal when parties have entered into a valid arbitration agreement see B. Goldman, *The Complementary Roles of Judges and Arbitrators in Ensuring that International Commercial Arbitration is Effective, in 60 Years of ICC Arbitration—A Look at the Future* (Paris: ICC Publication No.412, 1984), p.257; M. Rubino-Sammartano, *International Arbitration Law* (London: Kluwer Law and Taxation Publishers, 1990), pp.229–250.

[12] See, e.g. art.9 UNCITRAL Model Law 1985: "It is not incompatible with an arbitration agreement for a party to request, before or during arbitral proceedings, from a court an interim measure of protection and for a court to grant such measure". See also art.28 of the ICC 2012 Rules of Arbitration regarding "Conservatory and Interim Measures".

through the courts.[13] The relevant contractual provision may incorporate some consensual process to be attempted before arbitration, such as negotiation and/or mediation.[14]

Alternatively, an agreement to arbitrate can be entered into on an ad hoc basis when a dispute arises or appears imminent.

The agreement to arbitrate needs to be clear and unambiguous. There have been many cases where a party has challenged the validity of such a provision, seeking to have the dispute resolved in the courts instead. So, for example, in *Emirates Trading Agency LLC v Prime Mineral Exports Private Ltd*[15] the relevant contract clause provided that any dispute should be resolved by arbitration under the rules of the International Chamber of Commerce. It also provided that:

6–017

> "...the Parties shall first seek to resolve the dispute or claim by friendly discussion. Any party may notify the other Party of its desire to enter into consultation to resolve a dispute or claim. If no solution can be arrived at in between the Parties for a continuous period of 4 (four) weeks then the nondefaulting party can invoke the arbitration clause and refer the disputes to arbitration."

In seeking to avoid arbitration, it was argued in the Commercial Court that the provision quoted above constituted a condition precedent to be satisfied before the arbitrators would have jurisdiction to hear and determine the claim and that as there had not been four weeks of continuous consultations, the arbitral tribunal lacked jurisdiction. Apart from a dispute as to whether there had been such consultations, the response was that the suggested condition precedent was unenforceable, because it was a mere agreement to negotiate.

6–018

After analysing the facts and the relevant case law, the judge, Mr Justice Teare, concluded that he was "not bound by authority to hold that a dispute resolution clause in an existing and enforceable contract which requires the parties to seek to resolve a dispute by friendly discussions in good faith and within a limited period of time before the dispute may be referred to arbitration is unenforceable." He decided that such an agreement was indeed enforceable and that as a matter of fact friendly discussions did continue for over four weeks and that the condition precedent was satisfied and the arbitrators had jurisdiction to decide the dispute. This case, among others, illustrates the need for unambiguous drafting of clauses providing for arbitration.

6–019

Appointment and impartiality of arbitrator

The contractual provision for arbitration may stipulate the arbitrator or the panel of arbitrators by name, or may require arbitrators to be chosen and appointed by the parties; or alternatively it is common to stipulate an arbitral organisation which, or whose President or nominated officer may, nominate the arbitrator or panel.

6–020

---

[13] For a specimen of an arbitration clause (short form) see Appendix I, Document 7, para.A1-041.
[14] For a specimen of such a combined clause see Appendix I, Document 8, para.A1-042.
[15] [2014] EWHC 2104 (Comm).

6–021 The Arbitration Act 1996 contains detailed provisions for the appointment of arbitrators.[16] It stipulates that "The parties are free to agree on the procedure for appointing the arbitrator or arbitrators, including the procedure for appointing any chairman or umpire" and makes provision for appointment where there is no such agreement.[17]

6–022 Arbitrator impartiality is fundamental to the process. The 1996 Act provides that a party may apply to the court to remove an arbitrator on the ground that "circumstances exist that give rise to justifiable doubts as to his impartiality".[18] An example of a successful application based on a lack of impartiality is the case of *Sierra Fishing v Farran*[19] in which the Commercial Court removed an arbitrator who the judge decided had lost the necessary objectivity to determine the merits of the dispute.

6–023 Similar provisions for arbitrator impartiality exist in the rules of all other arbitral institutions, including for example UNCITRAL, which provides in its 1976 Arbitration Rules that "When a person is approached in connection with his or her possible appointment as an arbitrator, he or she shall disclose any circumstances likely to give rise to justifiable doubts as to his or her impartiality or independence."[20] This is incorporated into the UNCITRAL Model Law on International Commercial Arbitration 1985 as amended in 2006.[21]

6–024 The concepts of impartiality and independence are of course closely aligned to the proposition that the arbitrator should not have any conflict of interest in relation to the dispute, the parties or in any other way.[22] Conflicts or the perception of these may exist in different ways, including for example the obvious case where the arbitrator has a significant financial or personal interest in one of the parties, or the outcome of the case, or where the arbitrator has "within the past three years, served as counsel against one of the parties, or an affiliate of one of the parties, in an unrelated matter."[23]

6–025 In the *Sierra Fishing* case, the court had regard to the test of bias articulated by Lord Hope in *Porter v Magill*[24] namely whether a "fair-minded and informed observer, having considered the facts, would conclude that there was a real

---

[16] 1996 Act ss.15–22.
[17] 1996 Act s.16.
[18] 1996 Act s.24(1)(a).
[19] [2015] EWHC 140.
[20] 1976 Rules art.9.
[21] UNCITRAL Model Law 1985 with amendments adopted in 2006 art.12(1).
[22] For an analysis of this subject, see for example the paper by Luke Parsons QC "Independence, Impartiality and Conflicts of Interest in Arbitration" given at the 2nd IPBA (The Inter-Pacific Bar Association) Asia-PAC Arbitration Day, Kuala Lumpur in September 2016 at *http://www.quadrantchambers.com/images/uploads/documents/Luke_Parsons_QC_-_IPBA_paper.pdf* [accessed 15 May 2018].
[23] The International Bar Association has published its "IBA Guidelines on Conflicts of Interest in International Arbitration" adopted in 2014, which have been widely accepted within the international arbitration community. However, they are strictly for guidance only and will not necessarily be applicable in all cases. Paragraph 6 of the Guidelines makes it clear that they "are not legal provisions and do not override any applicable national law or arbitral rules chosen by the parties". Among other things, they grade different kinds of conflicts of interest into a non-waivable Red List, a waivable Red List, an Orange List and a Green List. The examples cited in para.6-024 are respectively from the red and the orange lists. The Guidelines are available for download at: *www.ibanet.org/Publications/publications_IBA_guides_and_free_materials.aspx* [accessed 15 May 2018].
[24] [2002] 2 A.C. 357.

possibility that the tribunal was biased". The court also referred to the *Sierra Fishing* case, among others, in *Cofely Ltd v Anthony Bingham and Knowles Ltd*,[25] in which Hamblen J found a real possibility of apparent bias, and in deciding to remove the arbitrator stated that: "Where there is actual or apparent bias there is also substantial injustice and there is no need for this to be additionally proved."

Jurisdictional seat of the arbitration

Whereas the venue of an arbitration is the location where the arbitration meetings are to be conducted, the jurisdictional seat identifies the law governing the arbitration procedure and the court in the jurisdiction that has the power to consider relevant legal issues arising in the arbitration such as the removal of the arbitrator or the nullifying of an award. The venue and the seat are not necessarily the same. Nor is the law that is applicable to the arbitration procedure necessarily the same as the law governing the substantive contract containing a clause for arbitration.

6–026

The Arbitration Act 1996 gives the court the power to support the arbitral process if the seat has not been designated or determined if by reason of a "connection with England and Wales or Northern Ireland the court is satisfied that it is appropriate to do so".[26] It has been held that where English law is applicable to the dispute, this provides a sufficient connection.[27]

6–027

Procedural freedom

The policy expressed in the 1996 Arbitration Act recognising party autonomy by allowing arbitrators and parties procedural freedom is in accord with international practice in the developed arbitral jurisdictions. It is a feature of modern commercial arbitration practice in developed systems that the parties may organise their proceedings as they like and, for example, may choose an adversarial or inquisitorial procedure, or a mixture of the two.[28]

6–028

The freedom of the parties to organise their procedure is constrained by basic principles of fairness referred to in different legal systems by different terms of art, but very similar in intention, for example natural justice, due process, *principe du contradictoire*, *rechtliches Gehör* and *droit d'être entendu*. In the continental European systems as well as in the US legal system, such fundamental rules apply to arbitration because the arbitrators are perceived to be performing a judicial function.[29]

6–029

By the 1996 English Act, any residual doubts as to arbitrators' powers to control the procedure were swept away. Sections 33 and 34 make it clear that the

6–030

---

[25] [2016] EWHC 240 (Comm).
[26] 1996 Act s.2(4).
[27] Per Ramsey J. in *Chalbury McCouat International Ltd v P.G. Foils Ltd* [2010] EWHC 2050 (TCC).
[28] This is a far more significant feature of arbitration than the freedom which the parties have to choose the proper law, for parties have this equally, whether in arbitration or before the court.
[29] M. de Boisséson, *Le droit français de l'arbitrage* (Paris: Joly 1990), p.180: "l'arbitre est un véritable juge"; *Burchell v March*, 58 U.S. 344, 349 (1855): "arbitrators are judges chosen by the parties".

6–031 Broadly, the arbitration process follows litigation in providing for the exchange of statements of claim, defence and perhaps counterclaim, case management and the holding of a substantive hearing where evidence is led, including experts where appropriate, witnesses may be cross-examined and cases argued. However, the aim is to streamline the process and to save time and costs, without prejudicing a fair trial. One of the ways this is done is by limiting the paperwork and eliminating the full discovery procedure, which can be very extensive and time-consuming in court proceedings. Another is by allowing relaxation from the strict rules of evidence.

yardsticks of economy, expedition and fairness must be observed and the specific powers under s.34 of the Arbitration Act give the arbitrators a full panoply of procedural power.

6–032 Where parties agree to institutional arbitration—appointing an arbitral institute such as the LCIA (London Court of International Arbitration) or the ICC (International Chamber of Commerce) to administer the arbitration—that organisation will have established procedures and rules for the process, which parties will ordinarily adopt. Inherently this is likely to offer less flexibility of process for the parties than if they designed the procedures themselves. The institutions do, however, have the benefit of extensive experience in working within their own rules and procedures and applying them effectively.

6–033 While arbitration can offer more flexible and informal procedures, with the savings in time and cost that this can provide, a corresponding disadvantage can arise where either party fails to comply with any agreed procedure or timetable and the arbitrator does not have, or declines to exercise, power to enforce such procedures or timetable. Another procedural disadvantage (as mentioned in para.6–014) is the inability to provide any remedy akin to summary judgment for cases without merit.

6–034 The arbitrators' powers may include the power of the arbitral tribunal to rule on its own substantive jurisdiction, including the validity of the arbitration agreement, whether the arbitral tribunal is properly constituted and what matters have been submitted to arbitration in accordance with the arbitration agreement.[30]

This is known as *kompetenz-kompetenz*, which is an arbitral tribunal's ability to rule on the question of whether it has jurisdiction. This principle is well established in international arbitration.

A binding award

6–035 It is a principal feature of commercial arbitration that the award should be binding.[31] It may or may not be final. In some jurisdictions it is possible to challenge an award, if there are defects in it. In other jurisdictions, such as

---

[30] 1996 Act s.30. Provision for objections to the substantive jurisdiction of a tribunal is contained in s.31. There is also provision in s.32 (read with s.73 about the loss of the right to object) for the court, on the application of any party, to determine any question as to the substantive jurisdiction of the tribunal.

[31] Usually, arbitration is a one-tier procedure. Some national legal systems and rules of international arbitration institutions (such as GAFTA—the Grain and Free Trade Association), however, allow the parties to provide contractually for a full appeal to a second arbitral instance. See, e.g. 594(1) of the Austrian Code of Civil Procedure.

Switzerland[32] the parties are generally at liberty to agree to exclude the control of the courts over an award made in the country. But there is no trend to such exclusion agreements.

The English Arbitration Act 1996 provides that unless otherwise agreed by the parties, and subject to the right to challenge the award by any available arbitral process of appeal or review or in accordance with the part of the Act dealing with awards, "an award made by the tribunal pursuant to an arbitration agreement is final and binding both on the parties and on any persons claiming through or under them."[33]

6–036

The Act further provides that unless otherwise agreed, a party to arbitral proceedings may appeal to the court on a question of law arising out of an award made in the proceedings.[34] The provisions applicable to such appeal are further set out in the Act.[35]

6–037

The question arose in *Essex County Council v Premier Recycling Ltd*[36] as to whether a term in an arbitration agreement that the arbitrator should make a "final and binding decision" would constitute an agreement under s.69(1) of the Act to exclude an appeal to the court on a point of law. The court decided that these words in themselves did not amount to such an agreement, but that in the exercise of its discretion to grant permission to appeal under s.69(3)(d) of the Act, they carried "great weight"—sufficient in the circumstances of that case to refuse permission to appeal.

6–038

And in *Sucafina SA v Rotenberg*[37] the Court of Appeal considered whether a final award made by an arbitral appeal board and described as "appeal interim award" was indeed final and binding. The award was made subject to its being published, which in turn was subject to payment within a prescribed period of certain fees and expenses of the Coffee Trade Federation (through which the arbitration was conducted). These were not paid in the prescribed period—so was the award interim and conditional or was it final and binding? The Court of Appeal took the view that an award is either final and binding or it is not. An award intended to be final and binding could not be rendered nugatory because a fee for a subsequent award was not paid.

6–039

---

[32] The Federal Private International Law Act 1987 s.192, permits the parties to exclude proceedings to set aside an award, provided both parties are domiciled, or have their habitual residence, registered office or branch office in Switzerland. The Federal Supreme Court has decided in *S v K Ltd* and ICC Arbitration Tribunal in Zürich, ATF/BGE 116 II 639, that an exclusion agreement must be evidenced by and made in express terms and that words to the effect that the award shall be binding and subject to no appeal are insufficient; a reference to the ICC Rules of Arbitration will therefore not operate as an exclusion agreement under Swiss law. For further discussion see M. E. Schneider & P. M. Patocchi, "The New Swiss Law on International Arbitration" (1989) 55 *Arbitration* 268, 279; Lalive, "The New Swiss Law on International Arbitration" (1988) 4(2) *Arbitration International* 18.
[33] 1996 Act s.58. The part of the Act dealing with awards runs from ss.46–58.
[34] 1996 Act s.69(1).
[35] 1996 Act ss.69(2)–(8), 70 and 71.
[36] *Essex County Council v Premier Recycling Ltd* [2006] EWHC 3594.
[37] [2012] EWCA Civ 637.

Costs

6–040 There is no doubt that the cost of international commercial arbitration has increased. The reasons are many and complex touching as they do upon the funding of dispute resolution, the role of institutions, the expectation of the parties, the role of lawyers from different jurisdictions and backgrounds and the prevalent economic model of legal practice.

6–041 Many statutes and rules may provide for the award of costs in arbitrations. The English Arbitration Act has a comprehensive regime based on the premise of the successful party should recover his costs.[38] The London Court of International Arbitration (LCIA) Rules, for example, take their cue from this and provide in art.28 as follows[39]:

> "28.2 The Arbitral Tribunal shall specify by an award the amount of the Arbitration Costs determined by the LCIA Court. The Arbitral Tribunal shall decide the proportions in which the parties shall bear such Arbitration Costs (in the absence of a final settlement of the parties' dispute regarding liability for such costs)....
> 28.3 The Arbitral Tribunal shall also have the power to decide by an award that all or part of the legal or other expenses incurred by a party (the 'Legal Costs') be paid by another party. The Arbitral Tribunal shall decide the amount of such Legal Costs on such reasonable basis as it thinks appropriate. The Arbitral Tribunal shall not be required to apply the rates or procedures for assessing such costs practised by any state court or other legal authority."

The ICC Arbitration Rules 2012 provide that:

> "The final award shall fix the costs of the arbitration and decide which of the parties shall bear them or in what proportion they shall be borne by the parties".[40]

6–042 It has increasingly been the practice for arbitrators to award costs to a successful party, although there is sometimes difficulty in deciding upon success. A successful party may have raised two jurisdiction arguments, lost both, and then lost on all the merits arguments bar one. He wins the case. Alternatively a party may have claimed damages on more than one issue and for more than one amount, yet received only a small award having lost, for example, on all important questions of loss of profits or consequential losses by virtue of a ruling against him on the meaning of relevant contractual clauses. How then should costs be apportioned? A robust common sense approach is usually taken. While the party with the award in its favour will get costs, they may be reduced to reflect that he lost on a number of issues.

6–043 In order to contain the costs of arbitration, two basic steps need to be taken. The one is to encourage settlement at all stages of the process. The other is to harness new technology. Much work has been done for example on the problems of email disclosure in litigation in the US. Email and telepresence systems may be employed to save costs and speed up mediation and arbitration.

---

[38] 1996 Act ss.59–65.
[39] LCIA Arbitration Rules (2014). See *http://www.lcia.org/Dispute_Resolution_Services/lcia-arbitration-rules-2014* [accessed 15 May 2018].
[40] 2012 Rules art.38.4. See: *https://iccwbo.org/dispute-resolution-services/arbitration/rules-of-arbitration/* [accessed 15 May 2018].

The broad objective is twofold, first to improve radically the procedures for domestic arbitration in particular; and secondly, to provide a system for international arbitration to make the resolution of disputes less protracted and costly. So far few arbitral institutions have responded effectively to technological change. There needs to be real institutional reform if arbitration is to respond properly to contemporary challenges.

6–044

AMIABLE COMPOSITION AND EX AEQUO ET BONO ARBITRATION

These concepts have found expression in arts 28.3 of the UNCITRAL Model Law as follows:

6–045

> "The arbitral tribunal shall decide *ex aequo et bono* or as *amiable compositeur* only if the parties have expressly authorized it to do so."

These forms of arbitration refer to decision-making by reference to general notions of fairness and equity, rather than by application of strict rules of law. It requires all parties to agree to this approach. *Amiable composition* is a civil law concept, rarely used in international law if statistical and anecdotal evidence is anything to go by.

When parties consent to resolve their disputes by seeking solutions perhaps outside the strict legal interpretation of their rights, they are more likely to do so by mediation rather than importing *amiable composition* into the arbitral process. It is commonplace in long-term joint ventures, for example, where it is important to preserve relationships and perhaps cope with unexpected problems to have staged or staggered dispute provisions. These envisage negotiation at different levels within the joint venture. Mediation can be a precursor to arbitration or going to the courts. It is through dispute resolution provisions of this kind that problems are more generally addressed rather than by *amiable composition*.

6–046

Certainly in the modern world, *amiable composition* appears to have been ignored and other ways of achieving the resolution of disputes have been found.

6–047

ARBITRATION-RELATED SETTLEMENT

There is little statistical evidence to inform us how many arbitrations settle before an award. Anecdotal evidence suggests that many cases do settle, sometimes after the final hearings and submissions, but before the award itself.

6–048

There is in principle no objection to experienced arbitrators trying to assist the parties to settle their differences. This can be done directly or indirectly. Thus, by skilful use of procedure and procedural orders arbitrators can encourage parties to come to grips with the issues in the case at an early and informed stage.

6–049

For example, in a dispute involving a long and complex joint venture for research purposes with a view to producing chemical or pharmaceutical products, discussing how the joint venture can be brought to an end with the least possible

6–050

6–051 damage and indeed the salvaging of valuable work may be what the parties really need and may be acceptable to them and cause them to discuss a reasonable settlement.

It is not beyond the wit or imagination of informed arbitrators to help parties to settle all or part of their differences if the parties really want to. The arbitrator has the opportunity and arguably a duty to promote settlement and if that fails the primary duty is then to render a binding and enforceable award.

ARBITRATION OF SOME PARTICULAR KINDS OF DISPUTES

International investment disputes: ICSID

6–052 ICSID (The International Centre for Settlement of Investment Disputes) describes itself as the world's leading institution devoted to international investment dispute settlement.[41] Its dispute resolution processes are designed to take account of the special characteristics of international investment disputes and the parties involved and to balance the different interests.

6–053 A major aspect of ICSID's dispute resolution activity relates to Bilateral Investment Treaties (BITs), which are agreements between two countries regarding the promotion and protection of investments made by investors from one another's countries in each other's territory. Functioning under the auspices of the World Bank, it deals with disputes between a state and a foreign investor.

6–054 ICSID has come under some criticism over the years, including in previous editions of this book, which included adverse comment about the workings of its appellate annulment procedure and the difficulty of registering a claim with ICSID and in particular the length of time for the publication of awards in ICSID cases.

6–055 The 3rd edition of this book suggested that the principal problem appeared to be that ICSID has been under-resourced, both in personnel and in its financing. As a consequence it has not been able to keep pace with the demands made upon it. Others have referred to high legal costs, lack of transparency by arbitration panels and the absence of an appeals process.[42]

6–056 We observed in the 3rd edition that it had become increasingly clear that the system of BITs involving as it does different treaty provisions required by different States, had not operated as well as a single treaty or series of regional treaties might have done and that it was possible that more regional groupings and treaties would develop. There did though now appear to be an element of consistency in the approaches taken by different tribunals under BITs to various issues of international law. In the first decade of this century, the use of BIT

---

[41] See *https://icsid.worldbank.org/en/Pages/about/default.aspx* [accessed 15 May 2018].
[42] See for example the paper by K. Grant, "The ICSID Under Siege: UNASUR and the Rise of a Hybrid Regime for International Investment Arbitration" (2015) Osgoode Legal Studies Research Paper Series Paper 108: *http://digitalcommons.osgoode.yorku.ca/olsrps/108* [accessed 15 May 2018]; and the article by L.E. Trakman, "The ICSID Under Siege" 45 Cornell Int'l L.J. 603 (2012) at *http://www.lawschool.cornell.edu/research/ILJ/upload/Trakman-final.pdf* [accessed 15 May 2018] which evaluates the criticisms levelled at the ICSID with reference to certain specific respects including perceived bias and ways of achieving greater transparency.

arbitration expanded considerably and there was every reason to believe that it would continue to do so, as both investors and host Governments sought adequate protection for inward investment. However, the view persisted that the delays and expense of the ICSID system needed to be addressed if it was truly to protect both the small investor and the host state.

In 2017 ICSID listed 16 topics to be canvassed by way of review. These include the issue of disclosure of third-party funding, the possible introduction of a code of conduct for arbitrators and procedural aspects such as consolidation, the annulment mechanism, the preliminary objections process and expanded transparency provisions to publish awards as soon as possible. An objective of the review is to improve time and cost effectiveness while maintaining due process and balance. 6–057

Consumer disputes

As observed in the introduction, arbitration is commonly used for consumer disputes. A number of industries or businesses impose a term in their contracts that import an arbitration provision into the relationship. The arbitration procedure is usually prescribed. 6–058

One such example is the arbitration scheme adopted by travel agents in relation to holiday bookings: the ABTA arbitration scheme.[43] The ABTA scheme allows for appeals to an Appeals Procedure Arbitrator through the ABTA Arbitration Scheme Appeals Procedure, subject to strict time limits. 6–059

An Independent Consumer Arbitration Service (ICAS) is administered by IDRS, the International Dispute Resolution Centre, a subsidiary of CEDR, the Centre for Effective Dispute Resolution. Among the schemes administered by CEDR or IDRS are CISAS (the Communications and Internet Services Adjudication Scheme), the Glass and Glazing Federation (FENSA), the Postal Redress Service and schemes for various other trade bodies.[44] 6–060

Family law arbitration

The arbitration of family issues has been adopted in various jurisdictions outside the UK, including for example Ontario,[45] Queensland (for property disputes) and in various US states including North Carolina, Colorado, Connecticut and Michigan. The American Academy of Matrimonial Lawyers has published a Model Family Law Arbitration Act,[46] based on and adapted from the Revised Uniform Arbitration Act. 6–061

In 2012 arbitration was introduced to England and Wales as a way of resolving financial and property disputes in the context of couples and families under a scheme established by the Institute of Family Law Arbitrators (IFLA), a body formed jointly by the Chartered Institute of Arbitrators, the Family Law Bar 6–062

---

[43] See *https://abta.com/holiday-help-and-complaints/abtas-adr-scheme* [accessed 15 May 2018].
[44] For further particulars, see *https://www.cedr.com/idrs/* [accessed 15 May 2018].
[45] See *http://www.attorneygeneral.jus.gov.on.ca/english/family/arbitration/* [accessed 15 May 2018].
[46] See *http://www.aaml.org/library/publications/21215/model-family-law-arbitration-act* [accessed 15 May 2018].

Association, Resolution and the Centre for Child and Family Law Reform.[47] The rules applicable to financial or property disputes with a family background, called the "Family Law Arbitration Financial Scheme" are available online.[48]

6–063 Initially the scheme did not arbitrate issues concerning children, but it was extended to cover such issues in 2016, called The Family Law Arbitration Children Scheme. Under this scheme, disputes concerning the exercise of parental responsibility and other private law issues about the welfare of children may be resolved by arbitration. The rules applicable to such children's issues are similarly available online from the IFLA. In addition to all the usual procedural rules for the arbitration, there are special rules designed to ensure the safety and welfare of children.[49]

6–064 In the matter of *S v S* an application for the approval of a consent order giving effect to an arbitral award was referred to the President of the Family Division, Sir James Munby, who felt that it was appropriate to provide guidance about the proper approach of the court to such applications.[50] In approving the order, the judge expressed the view that an arbitral award under the IFLA Scheme or something similar would obviously need to be checked, but that the judge's role would be simple. The judge would "not need to play the detective unless something leaps off the page to indicate that something has gone so seriously wrong in the arbitral process as fundamentally to vitiate the arbitral award".[51] Following this case, in November 2015 the President issued practice guidance on arbitration in the Family Court.[52]

6–065 In another matter before the Family Division of the High Court, *DB v DLJ*,[53] the wife sought to vitiate an arbitral award because of an alleged mistake about the true value of a property allocated to her, or on the basis that that events occurring since the award invalidated the finding made by the arbitrator as to the value of that property. In analysing the facts and the law and rejecting the wife's claim and making an order in the terms of the award, Mostyn J set out the scope for challenging a commercial award governed exclusively by the 1996 Act. He concluded that if following an arbitral award evidence emerged that would, if the award had been in an order of the court, entitle the court to set aside its order on the grounds of mistake or supervening event, then the court would be entitled to refuse to incorporate the arbitral award in its order and instead to make a different order reflecting the new evidence. Outside those heads of correction, challenge or appeal within the 1996 Act he considered those to be the only realistically available grounds of resistance to an incorporating order. The judge also commented that the award was "thorough, conscientious and clear" and its quality was "a testament to the merit of opting for arbitration".

---

[47] For a description of the scheme, see Sir Peter Singer's articles "Arbitration in Family Financial Proceedings: the IFLA Scheme": Pt 1 [2012] Fam Law 1353, and Pt 2 [2012] Fam Law 1496.
[48] 5th edn, 2016—See: *www.ifla.org.uk* [accessed 15 May 2018].
[49] Safeguarding measures are contained in art.17 and in the Form ARB1CS and Safeguarding Questionnaire which parties are required to complete. These measures include full and complete disclosure of all relevant matters, as identified in art.17.
[50] *S v S* [2014] EWHC 7 (Fam).
[51] *S v S* [2014] EWHC 7 (Fam) at [21].
[52] See: https://www.familylaw.co.uk/system/froala_assets/documents/341/Arbitration_in_the_Family_Court.pdf [accessed 15 May 2018].
[53] [2016] EWHC 324 (Fam).

ARBITRATION OF SOME PARTICULAR KINDS OF DISPUTES

Clearly, arbitration in the family context has become part of the mainstream of family practice. **6–066**

CHAPTER 7

Contractual Adjudication and Other Adjudicatory Processes

INTRODUCTION

Although arbitration is the main form of adjudicatory ADR, there are various other third-party decision-making processes outside litigation, including:

7–001

- contractual adjudication;
- dispute Boards;
- expert determination;
- administrative or statutory tribunals;
- in some jurisdictions, private judging.

These will each be considered in this chapter.

CONTRACTUAL ADJUDICATION

Contractual adjudication (sometimes called "interim" or "fast-track" adjudication) is frequently used to resolve certain types of commercial disputes, particularly within the construction industry, and indeed may be the primary dispute resolution machinery in this field in the UK. The term "adjudication" in this context refers to a specific process, rather than its general meaning. It is a way of allowing contracts to run smoothly without being interrupted or held up by disputes, by providing a speedy interim decision that is binding on the parties, but allows any party dissatisfied with the decision to have the issues reheard and determined in arbitration or litigation; but pending doing so, the decision remains binding.

7–002

Common threads

An adjudicator's terms of reference and authority will be contained in the relevant contract. There is no standard basis, but a number of common threads usually exist:

7–003

- the adjudicator will usually be a third-party neutral who, unlike the engineer or architect, will not have any personal involvement in the contract;

- the adjudication takes place as soon as possible after the dispute has arisen rather than waiting until completion of the works;
- the procedure is likely to be more summary and informal than arbitration, with the adjudicator making such enquiries and accepting such submissions as he may consider appropriate;
- the adjudication has a binding quality, insofar as the parties are bound by it unless and until there is a subsequent arbitration award, court judgment or agreement between the parties varying the adjudication;
- the right is commonly reserved for either party to refer the matter to arbitration (or to litigation if this is envisaged under the contract) notwithstanding that an adjudication has been made; consequently the adjudicator's decision has the interim quality to it noted above;
- it should be the overall aim of any construction dispute scheme to achieve resolution of disputes by or very shortly after the end of a contract.

Statutory provision

7–004 Adjudication in the construction industry found statutory expression in England in the Housing Grants, Construction and Regeneration Act 1996 (also called the Construction Act 1996).

7–005 The Act made it mandatory to include adjudication in construction contracts entered into after 1 May 1998.[1] It was amended by the Reform of the Housing Grants, Construction and Regeneration Act 1996 ("HGCRA") as a result of the Local Democracy, Economic Development and Construction Act 2009, which came into effect in 2011.

7–006 This statutory scheme is cross-related to the Arbitration Act 1996 in that if an adjudicator has made a decision, a party can apply to the court under s.42 of the Arbitration Act 1996 for a Court Order to enforce it.

7–007 In a case before the Technical and Construction Court, *RWE Npower Plc v Alstom Power Ltd*,[2] the parties had adopted adjudication as a method of dispute resolution and incorporated the Scheme for Construction Contracts 1998 into their contract. However, the contract had not been a "construction contract" under the Construction Act 1996 as it did not relate to "construction operations". It was accordingly held to be unenforceable. This case illustrates the need for care to be exercised when preparing bespoke construction and engineering contracts.

Outline of the adjudication process[3]

7–008 Section 108 of HGCRA 1996 requires construction contracts to include procedural stipulations enabling the parties to a contract to give notice of intention to refer a dispute to an adjudicator, with a timetable, so that the

---

[1] See also the statutory instrument containing the Scheme for Construction Contracts (England and Wales) Regulations 1998 *(SI 1998/649)*. This Scheme (and the equivalent Scheme for Construction Contracts (Scotland) Regulations 1998 (SI1998/687) has been amended by The Scheme for Construction Contracts (England) Regulations 2011, The Scheme for Construction Contracts (Wales) Regulations 2011 and The Scheme for Construction Contracts (Scotland) Regulations 2011.
[2] [2010] EWHC 3061 (TCC).
[3] In 2010 the Adjudication Society and the Chartered Institute of Arbitrators set up a joint working group to produce adjudication Guidelines for adjudicators, parties and representatives. These

adjudicator can be appointed and the dispute referred within seven days of the notice. The adjudicator is required to reach a decision within 28 days of the referral, plus any agreed extension. The adjudicator has wide powers to take the initiative to ascertain the facts and law related to the dispute: he is given "a fair and free hand" in deciding how to conduct the adjudication. He must act impartially, but can choose his own procedure whether adversarial or inquisitorial.[4]

7–009 Proceedings are commenced under the Act by submitting a written notice of adjudication to the other party with an outline of the dispute and the redress sought and a nomination of an impartial adjudicator or nominating body, unless this has been agreed. A referral notice containing details of the dispute, with relevant documents in support, is then sent to the adjudicator and the other party. The receiving party is then required to respond, and may counterclaim if appropriate—or may challenge the appointment.

7–010 The adjudicator may seek further information or documents and may decide to have a site visit and/or a hearing, which would generally be informal, or may decide the matter on the basis of the documents submitted. Lawyers may be involved, but not necessarily, depending on the issues and the amount involved. Some cases adjudicated may be very substantial, and lawyers are likely to be instructed.

7–011 The adjudicator will make a decision and may award interest, and costs if the contractual provision allows for this. The decision can, if necessary, be enforced, usually in the Technology and Construction Court. Although enforceable, it remains possible to take the dispute to court or to arbitration, whichever applies under the contract. That would be a new hearing, which would be started de novo.

Adjudication in context

7–012 Adjudication plays a significant role in construction cases providing a form of summary judgment obtained rapidly and to be complied with unless clearly given in breach of natural justice. In that sense adjudication does resemble a form of fast track arbitration or litigation. It is best used as part of a comprehensive process that provides for the parties to try to resolve their problems by direct negotiation between those on all sides charged with the management of the contract. Failing that, there should be some form of mediation and then adjudication, subject to the ultimate safeguard that the adjudicator's decision can be reviewed by an arbitrator in due course.

7–013 The interim nature of the adjudication, its contractual basis, the informality of the procedure including the adjudicator's ability to make a decision without hearing the parties, and the provision for an arbitration award or court judgment to supersede the decision combine to distinguish the process from arbitration and remove it from the statutory regime applicable to arbitration.

Guidelines and updates are available online from the Adjudication Society (*www.adjudication.org* [accessed 15 May 2018]) or the Chartered Institute of Arbitrators (*www.ciarb.org* [accessed 15 May 2018]).

[4] Per Mr Justice Dyson, as he then was, in *Macob Civil Engineering Ltd v Morrison Construction Ltd* [1999] C.L.C. 739; [1999] B.L.R. 93 QBD.

DISPUTE BOARDS[5]

7–014 The Dispute Board is a form of adjudication established by contract, which originated in the US, and which enhances the adjudicatory process by adding to it a layer of on-site involvement from the start of a project that makes it part of the project administration and brings dispute avoidance and the management of differences into the equation.

7–015 Initially conceived in the construction industry for major infrastructure projects, with some of the same motivations as adjudication, Dispute Boards are now used in a wider range of industries including information technology, insurance contracts and financial and other services. The aim is to provide a mechanism particularly in large and complex projects for disputes to be "nipped in the bud", communications to be facilitated and early resolution informally achieved; and ultimately, for a dispute resolution device to be available "that is considered fair and economic and one which will maximise the likelihood of due performance of the contract".[6]

7–016 Disputes in substantial construction and other projects can be very costly and time-consuming, and Dispute Boards are considered to be an economic, fair and efficient way of addressing potential issues when they arise, rather than having lengthy, complex and costly litigation or arbitration afterwards. Although much of the Board's work is informal, it can move into formal mode and make recommendations and/or decisions, as outlined below.

The Dispute Board concept

7–017 The Dispute Board is also known as a Dispute Review Board, a Dispute Resolution Board and sometimes as a Dispute Adjudication Board or a Dispute Avoidance Panel.

7–018 Various organisations have adapted and harmonised project contracts to include provision for a Dispute Board as an inherent part of the project.[7] The Board will commonly comprise three members, one of whom might be nominated by each party, with an independent Chair, who might be appointed by the parties or by the initial two members; or the Chairman may be jointly

---

[5] The authors are grateful to Peter Chapman for his contribution to this section and for permission to draw on his article "Dispute Boards on major infrastructure projects" (June 2011) *Proceedings of the Institution of Civil Engineers (ICE) Management, Procurement and Law* 162, February 2009 Issue MP1.

[6] Chapman, "Dispute Boards on major infrastructure projects". See fn.5.

[7] The Geneva based Dispute Board Federation promotes the use of adjudication and of Dispute Boards as a means of dispute resolution and dispute avoidance (*http://www.dbfederation.org/* [accessed 15 May 2018]). The US based Dispute Resolution Board Foundation (DRBF) "provides assistance with the worldwide application of the DB method" (*http://www.drb.org/* [accessed 15 May 2018]). The International Federation of Consulting Engineers (FIDIC) (*http://www.fidic.org/* [accessed 15 May 2018]) has standard forms of Dispute Board contracts, and has worked with the World Bank to harmonise international provisions. The International Chamber of Commerce (ICC) launched its own Dispute Board procedure in 2014 and the Royal Institution of Chartered Surveyors (RICS), among many other organisations that support the contractual establishment of Dispute Boards, maintains a register of accredited Dispute Board Members.

nominated first, and assist the parties in selecting the other members. There may be more than three members, and in smaller projects the Board may comprise a single member.

7–019 The Board is established at the start of the contract and functions throughout the lifetime of the project.[8] It should visit the site early on, become conversant with the technical aspects, meet relevant personnel, and maintain periodical contact and engagement. In this way, it can help to maintain communications with and between different elements of the project, can influence attitudes and behaviour and can address any difficulties as they arise.

7–020 In its informal capacity, the Board can use its expertise, understanding of the project and relationships to provide a forum for the discussion of difficult or contentious matters, and if required, to help devise practical solutions consistent with the needs of the contract. If a Board does make suggestions, it should obviously do so in a way that is consistent with any formal adjudicatory functions it may have, and should not make injudicious statements or pre-judge contentious issues.

7–021 In its formal capacity, the Board may function in a number of different ways, the two most common being either making a non-binding recommendation, or making an interim binding decision that can be overridden by a later determination.

7–022 *Non-binding recommendations:* As there are no binding outcomes, the hearings are shorter, simpler and less costly. Parties retain the right to have the issues resolved in arbitration or through the courts, but in practice, these recommendations often help the parties resolve any dispute rather than having to go through a longer and costlier adjudicatory process. There are said to be two main reasons why they are effective:

> "First that if the DB recommendation is admissible in later proceedings (as it often is), the parties know that an arbitrator or judge will be greatly influenced by a decision (on the facts) given by a panel of experienced, impartial construction experts who were familiar with the project during its construction. In this way the parties are likely to accept the recommendation—'warts and all'. Second, there are the swings and the roundabouts. Indeed it is unlikely that over the course of a large project the DB will always find in favour of the same party. It is, however, probable that each party will be pleased with certain decisions and if they expect the other party to honour the favourable decisions, they would be obliged to accept those which are less than favourable."[9]

7–023 *Interim binding decisions:* Under this option, the Board makes an interim determination that must be implemented immediately, and may be enforced by legal process (subject to various legal and jurisdictional questions) albeit that a party who does not accept it has the right, similar to that in adjudication, to refer the issue on to arbitration or the courts, depending on the contract terms. This option, as Chapman observes, "has teeth" and tends to be adopted in FIDIC contracts; but it also tends to be lengthier and costlier than the recommendation option, and of course decision-making is taken away from the parties.

---

[8] A Board can be established on an ad hoc basis to deal with a specific dispute, but this rather defeats the dispute avoidance aspect of the process.
[9] Chapman, "Dispute Boards on major infrastructure projects". See fn.5.

Examples of Dispute Boards

7–024　Dispute Boards have been established in a number of projects, including for example:

- Dispute Boards are now used by the World Bank and all international development banks.
- The Channel Tunnel project had a Dispute Resolution Board; and the Channel Tunnel Rail Link project envisaged two panels: a technical panel comprising engineers for decisions on construction-related disputes and a finance panel for decisions on disputes concerning financial provisions.
- The Docklands Light Railway extension to Lewisham established technical and financial panels (each of three people). However, the presence of the panels and their informal processes resulted in there being only one (post-completion) dispute arising and submitted to them.
- The Hong Kong International Airport had six disputes referred to its Dispute Board, only one of which went on to arbitration, where the Board's decision was upheld.
- An Independent Dispute Avoidance Panel was established to help avoid disputes during the project to deliver the venues and infrastructure for the London 2012 Olympic and Paralympic Games. Alongside it, an adjudication panel was also set up to adjudicate any issues that the Dispute Avoidance Panel could not resolve.
- The new Panama Canal has established a standing Dispute Adjudication Board under its FIDIC "Silver Book" contract.[10]

EXPERT DETERMINATION

7–025　"Expert determination has existed in the shadows for well over two centuries, rubbing shoulders uneasily with the law of arbitration and certification. Like some forms of commodity arbitration it seems to owe its survival to the simple fact that it works and is found commercially useful—A and B agree to abide by the decision of C. The system is infinitely flexible: there need not be a dispute, no writing is necessary and any form of procedure can be adopted".[11]

7–026　As a simple, informal, cost-effective, confidential and final form of dispute resolution, expert determination has become increasingly used. Its principles are straightforward and regulated entirely by contractual agreement: either in the dispute resolution provisions of a contract or on an ad hoc basis when a dispute arises, the parties agree on an independent expert whom they both or all trust to examine and consider the issue(s) to which the determination relates. Subject to such contractual appointment, he decides how to conduct the process and he makes a determination that is final and binding on everyone.

---

[10] FIDIC "Silver Book" contracts relate to turnkey projects.
[11] Professor John Uff QC's Foreword to Kendall's, *Expert Determination*, 2nd edn (London: Sweet & Maxwell, 1996). See also *Kendall on Expert Determination* by C. Freedman and J. Farrell, 5th edn (London: Sweet & Maxwell, 2014).

EXPERT DETERMINATION

Areas of application

Expert determination has long been used in relation to property issues such as the valuation of properties and the determination of rents. It is also used to establish share valuations, profit and/or turnover for the sale and purchase of companies and in relation to the activities of joint ventures including price completion. These are perhaps the kinds of areas with which the process is most commonly associated. 7–027

It is however also used in other industries, such as the oil and gas industry for the determination and re-determination of interests in oil and gas fields and the determination and implementation of contractual price review provisions. It is also used in the construction and engineering industries, for example, where payment under the contract is subject to the satisfactory completion of works or part works: commonly the certifying authority might be the engineer or architect, but in some contracts it is an independent expert. The Institution of Chemical Engineers (IChemE),[12] which has prepared a suite of standard term contracts for expert determination, suggests that subjects might include objecting to a variation order, whether a completion certificate or final certificate should have been issued, the cost and time implications of suspension orders and the amounts payable following termination. 7–028

The process of expert determination is adaptable to many other fields of activity, for example, whether IT products or services match the specifications, or in relation to disputes about long term commodities supply contracts, or boundary disputes; also in areas as diverse as broadcasting, energy and natural resources, banking and finance. 7–029

Given the extremely wide powers and procedural and substantive discretion of the expert and the finality of his decision, it is prudent to ensure that his contractual appointment relates to a specific aspect appropriate to the expert's field of expertise, and not to disputes generally. 7–030

Procedural outline and discretion

The expert appointed in the contract is required to carry out the specified determination in accordance with the contract; but subject to this, has complete freedom to decide on the procedure to be followed and what matters are to be taken into account in arriving at a decision. While this can make the process simple and cost-effective, it also removes options for appealing or challenging the determination or the way that it was arrived at. 7–031

The process may be regulated by the expert determination rules of the organisation through which the expert is appointed or whose rules are adopted, if applicable, for example the Academy of Experts or the Institution of Chemical Engineers. Ordinarily, the process will start, once the appointment is made, by the parties providing the expert and one another with written details of the dispute and submissions, including any counter-claims, together with copies of any relevant documents. 7–032

In some cases, the expert may arrange a preliminary meeting with the parties to discuss the documents and to clarify the issues in dispute, perhaps also to 7–033

---

[12] See *http://www.icheme.org/* [accessed 15 May 2018].

7-034   There is no obligation of natural justice in the expert determination process. This means that the expert is not required to give each party an opportunity to be heard and to respond to the other. Experts can choose to deal with the matter on a documents only basis or if they think it would be helpful, can arrange a meeting or formal hearing, or may conduct a technical examination. They can make their own investigations without any reference to the parties, adopting an inquisitorial approach.

consider the proposed process. The expert may also ask for further information, documents or evidence as he or she may consider appropriate.

7-035   Meetings can be held in person, or through telephone conference calls, video conferences, web conferences or virtual meetings. Where parties have engaged their own experts, the expert responsible for the determination may meet with the parties' experts to see whether the issues can be narrowed, with total discretion over the process and how to manage such meetings.

Finality of determination

7-036   The expert's decision has a final and binding quality, irrespective of the procedure followed, with very limited possibilities for challenging it. By and large, only fraud or an excess of jurisdiction will cause the expert's decision to be set aside. In the latter respect, the House of Lords said[13]:

> "if [the expert] makes a determination on the basis of an incorrect interpretation, he does not do what he was asked to do".

But the fact that a party does not agree with the decision or feels that the expert did not have regard to the correct principles, or made an error, will not be sufficient to enable a successful challenge to be mounted; and there is no appeal.

7-037   The case of *Owen Pell Ltd v Bindi (London) Ltd*[14] illustrates the principle of expert discretion. This was a dispute about a building extension which the parties agreed to have determined by an independent expert appointed by the Royal Institution of Chartered Surveyors. The expert made a determination which one party did not accept, and in the subsequent litigation the dissatisfied party contended that:

> "(a)   the expert failed to conduct himself in accordance with the principles of natural justice; or
> (b)   the expert conducted himself in such a way as either was biased or gave the appearance of bias; or
> (c)   in conducting himself and/or reaching his conclusions, the expert was guilty of gross or obvious error and/or was perverse in his conclusions."

7-038   Kirkham J reviewed the relevant case law on the subject, including:

---

[13] *Mercury Communications Ltd v Director General of Telecommunications* [1996] 1 W.L.R. 48; [1996] 1 All E.R. 575 HL.
[14] [2008] EWHC 1420 (TCC); [2008] B.L.R. 436.

EXPERT DETERMINATION

Nikko Hotels (UK) Ltd v MEPC Plc[15]: a mistake by an expert will not render the determination invalid, provided that he has answered the question which was put to him; and
Re Medicaments and Related Classes of Goods (No.2)[16]: distinguishing between "actual bias" and "apparent bias".

In *Porter v Magill*[17] the House of Lords laid down the test for apparent bias: 7–039

> "whether the fair-minded and informed observer, having considered the facts, would conclude that there was a real possibility that the tribunal was biased";

Macro v Thompson (No.3)[18]:

> "When the court is considering a decision reached by an expert valuer who is not an arbitrator performing a quasi-judicial function, it is actual partiality, rather than the appearance of partiality, that is the crucial test".

In *Bernhard Schulte GmbH & Co KG v Nile Holdings Ltd*[19]: there is no requirement for the rules of natural justice or due process to be followed in an expert determination in order for that determination to be valid and binding between the parties. While actual partiality on the part of an expert would invalidate his determination, apparent or unconscious bias does not have this effect. 7–040

Homepace Ltd v Sita South East Ltd[20]: the binding effect of an expert determination depends on the terms of the contract under which the determination is made, both as to what it is that the expert has to decide, and as to how far his decision is binding on the parties. 7–041

> "The first question is what the agreement has entrusted to the expert. The second is whether that is what he has decided. If so, the third is whether it can be shown that he has made a mistake which vitiates his decision."

In summary, Kirkham J remarked that it was: 7–042

> "not open to the court to set aside or to refuse to enforce the decision by reason of errors in the determination, whether gross, obvious or perverse. [The expert's] determination is binding and thus enforceable even if it is wrong."

She also confirmed by her judgment that actual rather than apparent bias was necessary to challenge an expert's decision—bias that she did not find on the facts of that case. Several other leading cases reinforce the binding nature of the expert's determination.[21]

---

[15] [1991] 2 E.G.L.R. 103; [1991] 28 E.G. 86 (Ch).
[16] [2001] 1 W.L.R. 700; [2001] U.K.C.L.R. 550 CA (Civ Div).
[17] [2001] UKHL 67; [2002] 2 A.C. 357.
[18] [1997] 2 B.C.L.C. 36 (Ch).
[19] [2004] EWHC 977 (Comm); [2004] Lloyd's Rep. 352.
[20] [2008] EWCA Civ 1; [2008] T.C.L.R. 4.
[21] For example, *Jones v Sherwood Computer Services Plc* [1992] 1 W.L.R. 277 CA (Civ Div); *Nikko Hotels (UK) Ltd v MEPC Plc* [1991] 2 E.G.L.R. 103; [1991] 28 E.G. 86 (Ch); *Mercury*

Distinguishing expert determination from single joint experts

7–043   In cases where expert opinions are needed to help the court address differences between the parties on technical or other specialised issues, the usual procedure was, and still largely remains, that each party has an expert to provide evidence to the court of their competing views. However, as part of the attempt to reform the court rules and to keep costs contained, provision has been made for parties to agree a single joint expert, who provides an opinion that guides the court, albeit that it is not binding or determinative.

7–044   The Civil Procedure Rules in fact make provision for single joint experts to be appointed and for the court to make an order that the evidence on any particular issue(s) be given by a single joint expert agreed by the parties, or if necessary selected by the court, or appointed in whatever manner the court may direct.[22] A number of pre-action protocols make provision for the appointment of experts including single joint experts. The Civil Justice Council has published guidance for experts in civil claims.[23] The TCC Guide deals with expert witnesses including single joint experts.[24]

7–045   Expert determination needs to be distinguished from this concept of a single joint expert. Although both cover similar ground in seeking to limit the appointment of experts to one, expert determination allows the expert to make a binding determination, whereas the appointment of a single joint expert under the rules is designed to limit costs and leaves the decision-making authority with the court or tribunal to whom the single expert is expressing his opinion.

Distinguishing expert determination from arbitration

7–046   It is important to note that expert determination is different from arbitration: a common formula in expert determination clauses or contracts is that the expert is appointed to act "as an expert and not as an arbitrator".

7–047   Some of the key differences between expert determination and arbitration are:

- expert determination is not subject to the rules and statutory regime of arbitration and the Arbitration Act is commonly excluded in terms;
- expert determination is not a judicial or quasi-judicial process, nor is it judicial in character, and may be conducted according to the expert's discretion;
- the expert makes a final determination, and the right to challenge it is more limited than in arbitration; and there is no power, as in arbitration, to state a case to the court on a point of law;
- the principles of natural justice do not apply, as they do in arbitration;
- an arbitration award has an enforcement regime that is internationally recognised, which does not apply in relation to expert determination.

Communications Ltd v Director General of Telecommunications [1996] 1 W.L.R. 48; [1996] 1 All E.R. 575 HL; *Brown v GIO Insurance Ltd* [1998] C.L.C. 650; [1998] Lloyds Rep. I.R. 201.

[22] CPR Pt 35: Experts and assessors.

[23] See the Courts and Tribunals Judiciary website: *https://www.judiciary.gov.uk/related-offices-and-bodies/advisory-bodies/cjc/working-parties/guidance-instruction-experts-give-evidence-civil-claims-2012/* [accessed 15 May 2018].

[24] Technology and Construction Court Guide, 2nd edn, 3rd Revision (March 2014) s.13.

ADMINISTRATIVE OR STATUTORY TRIBUNALS

The Scottish Court of Session considered this distinction in the case of *MacDonald Estates Plc v National Car Parks Ltd*,[25] which was an appeal on a judicial review application concerning the question whether the contractual appointment of an expert actually constituted an "agreement to refer to arbitration", which would have brought the process within the provisions of the arbitration regime. It was argued that Scots law did not recognise a distinction between arbitration and expert determination; but the court expressed the view that "Scottish legal terminology and practice have not stood still", and that:

7–048

> "understanding of the nature of arbitration and of its legal consequences has also developed ... the legal incidents of arbitration may not meet the needs of the parties in all the situations in which commercial disputes arise, [and] other forms of alternative dispute resolution have developed, such as mediation, conciliation, early neutral evaluation, adjudication and expert determination. Expert determination, in particular, can be broadly distinguished from arbitration in not being judicial in character."

The court observed that the distinction between the expert role and that of the arbitrator (arbiter) had become well understood in commercial practice, and that if the intention of the parties was to refer a case to expert determination rather than arbitration, the law would give effect to that intention.

7–049

Other jurisdictions recognise this distinction between arbitrator and expert, for example, Switzerland, France[26] and Germany[27]; and the distinction between arbitrators and experts is also recognised in international arbitration rules[28] and rules of arbitration institutions.[29]

7–050

ADMINISTRATIVE OR STATUTORY TRIBUNALS

The history of tribunals in the UK goes back to the early 20th century, when the adjudication of disputes by administrative agencies was first introduced. The Franks Report of 1957 reviewed the tribunal system as it then was, and made a number of procedural recommendations, based on the principles of openness, fairness and impartiality, also independence and an appropriate level of informality.

7–051

There were a number of reasons for the development of the use of administrative tribunals by statute, which included having an informal, cost-effective system of dealing with issues arising in specialist administrative areas by engaging people with relevant knowledge and experience to make necessary decisions, rather than generalist judges in courts that would increasingly be unable to cope with the volume of cases involved.

7–052

---

[25] [2009] CSIH 79A.
[26] M. de Boisséson, *Le droit français de l'arbitrage* (Paris: Joly 1990), pp.181 et seq.
[27] See, e.g. Schlosser, *Das Recht der internationalen privaten Schiedsgerichtsbarkeit Rz 20*, 2nd edn (1989); K.H. Schwab, *Schiedsgerichtsbarkeit*, 3rd edn (1979), pp.6 et seq.
[28] See, e.g. art.27 UNCITRAL Arbitration Rules.
[29] See the ICC Expert Rules (2015).

CONTRACTUAL AND OTHER ADJUDICATION PROCESSES

7–053 UK law on tribunals was significantly affected by major legislation in 2007, described as follows in *R. (on the application of Cart) v Upper Tribunal*[30]:

> "The edifice of administrative and adjudicative tribunals created by the Tribunals, Courts and Enforcement Act 2007 (TCEA) is a landmark in the development of the United Kingdom's organic constitution. For the first time, a single structure has been created within which a huge variety of existing tribunals is gathered."

7–054 The judgments of the Divisional Court and the Court of Appeal contain a comprehensive summary of the law relating to tribunals,[31] and conclude that TCEA 2007 considerably narrows the scope for judicial review of Tribunal decisions:

> "The new tribunal structure, while not an analogue of the High Court, is something greater than the sum of its parts. It represents a newly coherent and comprehensive edifice designed, among other things, to complete the long process of divorcing administrative justice from departmental policy, to ensure the application across the board of proper standards of adjudication, and to provide for the correction of legal error within rather than outside the system..."

7–055 As to the broad process of tribunals, although they tend perhaps to be more inquisitorial than adversarial, there is no consistency, and the Senior President is required to explore innovative ways of determining disputes. Procedures vary within different tiers of tribunal activity, and between individual tribunals.

A range of administrative tribunals

7–056 The Tribunal system is currently based on two tiers: a First-tier Tribunal and an Upper Tribunal, both of which are split into Chambers. The Upper Tribunal primarily, but not exclusively, reviews and decides appeals arising from the First-tier Tribunal.

7–057 By way of example, the following are some of the tribunals that function in the UK:

- Employment Tribunals hear employment claims including unfair dismissal, redundancy payments and discrimination, also wage and other payment claims;
- the Employment Appeal Tribunal hears appeals from Employment Tribunals;
- the first-tier immigration tribunal (Immigration and Asylum Chamber) is an independent Tribunal dealing with appeals against decisions made by the Home Secretary and his or her officials in immigration, asylum and nationality matters;
- the Upper Tribunal (Immigration and Asylum Chamber) deals with appeals against decisions made by the Immigration and Asylum Chamber;

---

[30] *R. (on the application of Cart) v Upper Tribunal* [2010] EWCA Civ 859; [2011] Q.B. 120; appeal from the Divisional Court, reported at [2009] EWHC 3052 (Admin); [2010] 2 W.L.R. 1012.

[31] A detailed exposition and analysis of the new law is also contained in Sir Robert Carnwath (Senior President of the Tribunals), "Tribunal justice—a new start" [2009] 1 *Public Law* 48.

- the Copyright Tribunal decides disputes about the terms and conditions of licences offered by, or licensing schemes operated by, collective licensing bodies in the copyright and related rights area;
- the Valuation Tribunal hears appeals concerning council tax, non-domestic rates and land drainage rates in England and Wales.

This is just a sample cross-section of the UK's tribunals. HM Courts and Tribunals Service was created in 2011 bringing together HM Courts Service and the Tribunals Service into one integrated agency providing support for the administration of justice in courts and tribunals.[32] There is also the Administrative Justice and Tribunals Council which: 7–058

> "keeps under review the administrative justice system as a whole with a view to making it accessible, fair and efficient seek(ing) to ensure that the relationships between the courts, tribunals, ombudsmen and alternative dispute resolution providers satisfactorily reflect the needs of users".

PRIVATE JUDGING

Where parties need a third-party decision, and wish to retain the backing of the court (for example because they need a formal court order) and they wish to preserve the right of appeal (not available in arbitration), they have another option in those jurisdictions that have adopted it, in the form of private judging. By consent and with the approval of the court, which makes an appropriate appointing order, the parties select, appoint and pay for a private decision-maker, who may well be a retired judge or lawyer and/or have special expertise, and who hears the case and issues a binding, enforceable and appealable judgment, as a judge would in the ordinary course. The private judge ordinarily has all the usual judicial powers, except the contempt power. 7–059

The parties and the judge may agree on their own procedure, which may be simplified and expedited, subject to the overriding supervision of the appointing court. Legal principles and judicial authorities and precedents as well as the standard of proof are the same as they would be if litigating through the court, and the decision is subject to appeal in the ordinary course. The judgment is enforceable in the same way as a judgment of the court. 7–060

Special legislation is needed to introduce and govern private judging in any territory. It has been provided for in the statutes of approximately half of the US. In California, where the practice is most widely used, it has been available for about a century. The process is not available in the UK, and there are no indications that it might be introduced, though "private final appeals" were at one time being conducted in a small number of cases using retired Law Lords and other retired judges, with parties agreeing to give their decisions binding effect; but that was not on the strict "private judging" basis as outlined above. 7–061

---

[32] For further information about the UK's tribunals see: *https://www.gov.uk/government/organisations/hm-courts-and-tribunals-service/about#our-tribunals* [accessed 15 May 2018]; and also see: *https://www.judiciary.gov.uk/about-the-judiciary/the-justice-system/jurisdictions/tribunal-jurisdiction/* [accessed 15 May 2018].

CHAPTER 8

Mediation—General Principles

WHAT IS MEDIATION—AND WHO DECIDES?

Two children have a playground fight and a friend urges them to "break it up", encouraging them to "make friends" again. Or a teacher intercedes and helps them to "sort it out". Both of these constitute fundamental mediation: all the rest is gloss.

8–001

As Roberts has observed, in most societies, even for early nomadic hunters, "meeting and talking" has been used to resolve some disputes; and in stateless societies, with no central authority to make or enforce third party decisions, mediators would have been used "actively coaxing parties towards a settlement".[1] Gulliver described the mediator as "a facilitator and adviser but not a decision maker"[2] and has outlined how disputes might involve groups of kinsmen with third parties called in to perform a mediatory function.[3] In relation to current mediation practice, Gulliver has pointed out that:

8–002

> "contrary to some idealistic and ethnocentric assumptions, there is no such thing as *the* role of *the* mediator. The range is wide, both of the statuses of mediators (who they are and why they are so acting) and of the roles they play (the strategies they choose or are forced to adopt)...He may be rather passive... (he) may chair the talking sessions... he may work at clarifying issues, demands and offers and suggesting appropriate norms and their application; he may, from the first or later, make creative suggestions for outcomes... he may consult and advise parties in caucus or in joint sessions. At the extreme of mediation, he may press his own evaluations of the situation and his opinions as to effective outcomes".[4]

This sums up the position. Mediation involves a wide range of practice and practitioners, using a wide range of strategies, from passive to highly directive and evaluative. It differs from arbitration in that the role of the neutral third party in arbitration is to consider the issues and then to make a decision which

8–003

---

[1] S. Roberts, *Order and Dispute: an Introduction to Legal Anthropology* (London: Penguin, 1979), p.26. See also Derek Roebuck, *Disputes and Differences; Comparisons in Law, Language and History*, Pt 3, *The Myth Of Modern Mediation* (Oxford: Holo Books, 2010), outlining the use of mediation in the ancient world to AD 500 and then through the subsequent centuries.
[2] P.H. Gulliver, "Arbitration and mediation" in Adam Kuper, and Jessica Kuper, *The Social Science Encyclopedia*, (Abingdon: Routledge, 1985). Gulliver, an anthropologist, specialised in processes of dispute management and decision-making in traditional African societies.
[3] P.H. Gulliver, *Disputes and Negotiations: a Cross-Cultural Perspective* (New York: Academic Press, 1979).
[4] Gulliver, fn.2.

8–004 Even where the mediator expresses a view about the merits of the dispute, which may happen in some but not other models of mediation, this would only be a non-binding opinion to help parties with their decision-making, and in no circumstances would a mediator have the power to impose this view on the parties. Indeed, any such power would be contrary to the spirit of mediation, which is inherently consensual.

It is against this background, that some definitions of mediation are considered.

8–005 In previous editions of this work mediation has been described as:

> "a facilitative process in which disputing parties engage the assistance of an impartial third party, the mediator, who helps them to try to arrive at an agreed resolution of their dispute. The mediator has no authority to make any decisions that are binding on them, but uses certain procedures, techniques and skills to help them to negotiate an agreed resolution of their dispute without adjudication."

This definition continues to be applicable.

8–006 Mediation has been defined:

> "in a broad and general sense to include all forms of decision-making in which the parties are assisted by someone external to the conflict, the mediator, who cannot make binding decisions for them, but assists their decision-making in various ways. It can be contrasted with those forms of dispute resolution in which the external person is the formal decision-maker for the parties, such as arbitration, adjudication, expert determination and court proceedings".[5]

8–007 The Law Society of England and Wales has adopted a more detailed definition of civil-commercial mediation, namely:

> "Civil and commercial mediation is a process in which:
> 1.1 two or more parties in dispute
> 1.2 whether or not they are legally represented
> 1.3 and at any time, whether or not there are or have been legal proceedings
> 1.4 agree to the appointment of a neutral third party (the mediator)
> 1.5 who is impartial
> 1.6 who has no authority to make any decisions with regard to their issues
> 1.7 which may relate to all or any part of a dispute of a civil or commercial nature
> 1.8 but who helps them reach their own decisions
> 1.9 by negotiation
> 1.10 without adjudication."[6]

8–008 Clearly, the underlying elements of mediation are consistently reflected in these different definitions. Nor do these definitions limit the way in which

---

[5] L. Boulle and M. Nesic, *Mediator Skills and Techniques: Triangle of Influence* (Haywards Heath: Bloomsbury Professional, 2010).
[6] The Law Society Code of Practice for Civil and Commercial Mediation (Last updated November 2011) under its Civil & Commercial Mediation Accreditation Scheme.

mediation may be practised: as indicated by Gulliver,[7] the range of strategies that mediators may adopt is wide, and indeed the models and approaches that they may use and the philosophies that they may follow are many and varied, reflecting the richness of the process.

What is "real" mediation?

Despite this broad range of possible mediation activity, voices are sometimes heard to the effect that some or other mediation model or approach "is not mediation" or "is not real mediation". Gray,[8] in relation to an issue about evaluation in mediation asked: "What is 'real' mediation and who decides?" Her underlying question was whether an evaluative form of mediation could still properly be termed "mediation". Her concern was whether we could definitively state what constituted "real" mediation and what didn't; and even if a definition could be agreed, "how do we measure whether something fits that definition? And if 'experts' are to decide, who will be the experts?" 8–009

There is, of course, no central authority deciding on informal dispute resolution processes and their definitions. Much of their vibrancy and value arises from the fact that they have developed spontaneously and creatively in response to the rigidities and limitations of formal court systems, and are continuing to develop. 8–010

Gray considers that it would be: 8–011

> "better to consider mediation as a continuum from facilitative to evaluative, with a variety of styles of practice, a number of approaches, and a wide assortment of contexts in which it is practised".

That is a view to which the authors of this book readily subscribe.

Conciliation and mediation

There is universal acceptance that conciliation has broadly the same attributes as mediation, involving the use of an impartial third person to help disputing parties to resolve their differences. However, there seems to be some variation of understanding as to what each concept involves, and whether or not there is any difference between them. There is no national or international clarity or consistency of usage of these terms. 8–012

Conciliation is sometimes described as a process in which the neutral, the conciliator, is more proactive and evaluative than in mediation, and in some views, may propose terms of settlement where the parties do not reach these themselves. For example, the Conciliation Rules of UNCITRAL, the United Nations Commission on International Trade Law, provide that: 8–013

---

[7] Gulliver, fn.3.
[8] Ericka B. Gray, "What is 'Real' Mediation?" (1996) 15(2) *AFM Mediation News*.

> "The conciliator may, at any stage of the conciliation proceedings, make proposals for a settlement of the dispute. Such proposals need not be in writing and need not be accompanied by a statement of the reasons therefor."[9]

8–014   Conciliation has been described as:

> "... an informal process for settling disputes through direct negotiations. A conciliator contacts the parties directly, usually by telephone, to attempt to encourage a negotiated settlement between them. The conciliator allows the parties to reach their own resolution to a dispute, although the conciliator has the power to recommend (but not impose) a particular solution in the event that the parties are unable to reach one themselves. Any settlement reached through conciliation will become binding as a contractual agreement once both parties sign a copy of it."[10]

8–015   On the other hand, sometimes the opposite view is taken, with mediation rather than conciliation being evaluative. For example, ACAS—the UK's non-governmental Advisory, Conciliation and Arbitration Service, largely funded by the Department for Business Innovation & Skills to deal with employment relationships—says that conciliation will be explanatory and will:

> "help you to understand how the other side views the case, and explore with you how it might be resolved without a hearing; and tell you about any proposals the other side has for a settlement"

but the conciliator:

> "will not make a judgement on the case, or the likely outcome of a hearing or advise you whether to accept any proposals for settlement or not".[11]

8–016   The term "conciliation" is also used to describe processes involving the informal resolution of complaints, for example in the UK's National Health Service[12]; and to describe a court-based process in helping parties settle issues about children.[13]

8–017   Distinctions between mediation and conciliation generally arise because of differing conceptions as to what mediation entails. It can only be considered more evaluative than mediation if one takes the view that mediation is a purely facilitative process. If however mediation is seen as comprising a broad range of activity, including a spectrum from purely facilitative to evaluative, then this distinction loses its significance.

8–018   There seems little doubt that the term "mediation" is now generally regarded as a generic term and that "conciliation" is relatively declining in use. The

---

[9] Adopted in 1980, the UNCITRAL Conciliation Rules are expressed as providing "a comprehensive set of procedural rules upon which parties may agree for the conduct of conciliation proceedings arising out of their commercial relationship."

[10] The Centre for Effective Dispute Resolution: *https://www.cedr.com/idrs/documents/170823112849-conciliation-guidance-notes-for-consumers.pdf.*

[11] See *http://www.acas.org.uk/index.aspx?articleid=2011* [accessed 15 May 2018].

[12] Following Department of Health guidance, many Primary Care Trusts offer conciliation to address complaints.

[13] See Imogen Clout, *"The Which?" Guide to Divorce: The Essential Practical Guide to the Legal and Financial Arrangements for Divorce* (London: Which? Books, 2005), p.81.

National Family Conciliation Council changed its name in 1993 to National Family Mediation. The International Chamber of Commerce used to offer conciliation, but now offers ADR instead.[14]

8–019 In this book, the term "mediation" is treated as synonymous with "conciliation". There does not seem to be any sound reason to maintain a distinction, given that mediation covers a wide range of practice, styles and approaches, and includes the whole spectrum between purely facilitative and wholly evaluative.[15]

THE PRINCIPLES OF MEDIATION

8–020 Some common threads run through all different forms of mediation. These should be viewed broadly rather than prescriptively, given the wide range of activity and philosophies that mediation encompasses. The most widely accepted principles are set out below.

The use of a mediator

8–021 It is fundamental to mediation that there is a third-party mediator involved in the process who assists the parties in dealing with the issues that they face. The mediator does not have to be present with the parties all the time, but may for example arrange for them to liaise with one another directly at some point or may set up other mechanisms without being present; but if there is no mediator in the process it is not mediation.

8–022 There are a number of reasons why a third party's involvement is so helpful. For a start, the presence of a third party creates a dynamic that does not exist when only the parties themselves or their representatives undertake direct negotiation. De Bono, who created the concept of "lateral thinking", says[16] that:

> "In any dispute the two opposing parties are logically incapable of designing a way out. There is a fundamental need for a third party role."

De Bono describes this role as converting the two-party dispute "into a three-dimensional exploration leading to the design of an outcome."[17]

8–023 This concept of helping parties to design an outcome reflects the creative element of the third-party role. According to de Bono this "design idiom" generally develops as the mediator gets to understand the needs, interests, positions and priorities of the parties and is able to help synthesise these into acceptable terms.[18]

8–024 Even without this creative element, the mediator brings a different dynamic to the dispute. Parties explain and discuss their positions and views to an objective

---

[14] The ICC ADR Rules "offer a framework for the amicable settlement of commercial disputes with the assistance of a neutral. They were launched in 2001 to replace the 1988 Rules of Conciliation."
[15] Issues concerning the use of evaluation in mediation are addressed in Ch.8 and non-binding ADR in Ch.19.
[16] Edward de Bono, *Conflicts: A Better Way to Resolve Them* (Harmondsworth: Penguin 1986).
[17] De Bono, fn.16.
[18] De Bono, fn.16.

8–025 person, usually one who is encouraging a problem-solving mode and "testing reality"; and commonly this may assist a process of review and re-evaluation, of movement and shift, and of adopting a more realistic view of the deadlocked position. Of course, this does not always happen, and parties can sometimes remain entrenched notwithstanding whatever the mediator's may do efforts to bring about some re-evaluation and movement.

8–025 While the mere intercession of a third party brings this dynamic, mediation offers more than just another person in the room. Professional mediators bring communication and conflict resolution skills into the arena, as well as their personal attributes such as understanding, judgement, patience, creativity and sometimes authority.

8–026 Because negotiation is such a fundamental component of mediation and of most other non-adjudicatory dispute resolution processes, and because some dispute resolution organisations refer to negotiation as part of the resources that they offer, there is sometimes a view that negotiation stands on its own as an ADR process. The value of bilateral negotiation without a third party intermediary is beyond question,[19] but it is not by itself mediation or an ADR process.

Impartiality or neutrality

8–027 It is fundamental to the integrity of the mediation process that the mediator should conduct it in an even-handed and impartial manner. In the sense of not favouring either party over the other, that is indeed the position. The Law Society of England and Wales for example, specifies in its Code of Conduct for civil and commercial mediators:

> "The impartiality of the mediator is a fundamental principle of mediation. Impartiality means that (1) the mediator does not have any significant personal interest in the outcome of the mediation; and (2) the mediator will conduct the process fairly and even-handedly, and will not favour any party over another."

8–028 The Model Standards of Conduct for Mediators[20] adopted in 2005 by the American Arbitration Association, the American Bar Association and the Association for Conflict Resolution describes impartiality as "freedom from favoritism, bias or prejudice".

8–029 However, the situation is perhaps not entirely black or white: a mediator can be linked in some way to a party and can nevertheless still conduct the mediation. Gulliver points out that the mediator may often be a structural intermediary:

> "the common kinsman or neighbour, co-member of their group, member of an allied group—who has legitimate concern for both the dispute and the disputants to whom he is linked."[21]

---

[19] De Bono, fn.16, and see Ch.4.
[20] Available at: *https://www.mediate.com/articles/model_standards_of_conflict.cfm* [accessed 15 May 2018].
[21] Gulliver, fn.3.

If parties make an informed choice to engage a mediator who has links to either party, does that mean the process is not mediation? Clearly not, though there may be practical questions as to whether the mediator can be fully trusted and wholly effective; and there may be ethical constraints against such an appointment.[22] 8–030

The mediator should not have an interest in the outcome of the mediation. However, here again Gulliver argues that every mediator brings interests, values, norms and ideas of his own, which will have some influence on his role in the mediation.[23] This brings into focus the distinction that is sometimes drawn between "impartiality" and "neutrality". There is a view that mediator neutrality (as distinct from impartiality) implies that the mediator will not bring his or her personal values into the process.[24] As this may be difficult if not impossible to achieve, some consider that "neutrality" should not be offered unless the word "neutral" is used specifically in relation to outcome rather than process.[25] 8–031

Generally, the concept of neutrality is given its everyday usage, i.e. "not helping or supporting either of two opposing sides, especially states at war or in dispute". It is in this sense that neutrality is usually mentioned in an ADR context, and the noun "neutral" refers to a third party fulfilling the mediator role of impartiality and even-handedness.[26] 8–032

Facilitation

Facilitation is an integral and primary aspect of mediation. All mediation involves some element of such facilitation, which is enhanced by the mediator's communication, negotiation and other skills. The mediator does not, however, negotiate with the parties, but rather assists them to negotiate with one another. 8–033

Facilitation can take many forms. Traditionally it involves helping parties with their communications and negotiations, helping them sort out misunderstandings and misconceptions, and supporting a problem-solving rather than a competitive approach.[27] 8–034

If facilitation helps people towards better understanding and arriving at a good decision, there seems to be no reason why it should not include helping them towards a better understanding of the issues, a better perception of the merits of 8–035

---

[22] Parties can agree to engage a mediator whose connection with either or both parties is known or disclosed provided that this is not precluded by the mediator's Code of Practice. For further comments on conflicts of interest and other ethical considerations, see Ch.16.
[23] Gulliver, fn.3.
[24] See Lisa Parkinson, *Family Mediation* (London: Sweet & Maxwell, 1997), p.491. In the 2nd edition of her book (Family Law, 2011) she points out that mediators "cannot be neutral in the sense of having no influence, because their personal and professional values and experience inevitably have some influence in the mediation process", p.20.
[25] See Principles III (i) and (ii) of the Council of Europe's Recommendation No. R (98) 1 on Family Mediation (1998) which provide that the mediator is "impartial between the parties" and "neutral as to the outcome".
[26] See Oxford English Dictionary Definition.
[27] There is though a view that even within a problem-solving, interest-based approach, parties are still likely to seek to maximise their own separate interests: there is an "essential tension" between value creating and value claiming see D. Lax and J. Sebenius, *The Manager as Negotiator: Bargaining for Co-operation and Competitive Gain* (New York: The Free Press, 1986); reinforced in their later work D. Lax and J. Sebenius, *3-D Negotiation: Powerful Tools to Change the Game in Your Most Important Deals* (Boston: Harvard Business School Press, 2006).

8-036 the dispute and a realistic view of the available options. Indeed, many mediators and organisations consider it to be entirely appropriate to test, question and challenge factual, legal or technical perceptions as part of facilitative party decision-making.[28]

8-036 To what extent it is appropriate for mediators to carry out this facilitative function of helping parties obtain a better understanding of the issues and a better perception of the merits is a moot point. The more effectively and authoritatively a mediator may do this, the more this may constitute "evaluation" which for many mediators is not an acceptable way of working. The distinctions between facilitation and evaluation require reflection and review that has often been missing from any discussion about this subject: they are dealt with more fully elsewhere in this book.[29]

8-037 Facilitation is also referred to as an ADR process in its own right, involving a third-party neutral, the facilitator, carrying out a role very similar to that of the mediator in mediation, in the context commonly of helping groups or organisations work more effectively together, either generally or in relation to specific projects.

Party self-determination

8-038 The essence of mediation is that it is non-adjudicatory and helps parties to make their own decisions. If the third party makes a binding determination of the issues, the process is not mediation. And if, for example, parties jointly ask a mediator to decide the issues on a binding basis, as in med-arb, and the mediator agrees to do so, the process changes from mediation to one of the adjudicatory forms such as arbitration.

8-039 This should though be distinguished from the situation in which the mediator is asked by the parties to make a non-binding settlement recommendation, which is part of the mediation procedure of some organisations and individual mediators. Such a recommendation allows the parties the freedom to accept or reject it, and consequently does not diminish their self-determination. There is a misperception among some practitioners that this transforms the process into an adjudicatory or quasi-adjudicatory form: that is certainly not the case. Whether it is an appropriate, wise or effective thing to do depends on the circumstances, but doing so does not change the character of the process.

8-040 Parties may be advised and assisted by their lawyers and perhaps other professionals in the process. This does not detract from the parties' role as the ultimate arbiters of how the matters should be resolved or from their self-determinative function.

8-041 If, however, a party is coerced into making a decision, that would generally undermine the principle of self-determination: negotiation should not be a

---

[28] This is generally described as "reality-testing".
[29] See Ch.19. In the 1st edition the authors of this work adopted the commonly-held perception of mediation as being either facilitative or evaluative, albeit not in later editions. That perception, which continues to be widely held today, has arguably had an insidious effect on training and practice as it has diverted productive discussion about what kind of evaluation is useful in mediation, with the result that many mediators have surreptitiously used their own versions of evaluation in what is (simplistically) said to be a purely facilitative process.

coercive process.[30] Mediators may sometimes encourage parties towards settlement—if done appropriately this is a standard element of the process—but if they try to coerce a party into settling, or become so directive that their actions amount to coercion, that would undermine the principle of party self-determination and would not be acceptable mediator conduct.

8–042 This unacceptable form of mediator coercion within the mediation process should be distinguished from two other kinds of pressure. The one is pressure from another party or from personal circumstances that may compel a party to settle the dispute. This is probably inherent in most if not all disputes and in all fora. The risks, costs and delays of litigation, potentially damaging financial implications and the possibility of adverse publicity or other negative consequences are all factors that may impel a party towards settlement whether or not done within mediation, and are not peculiar to the mediation process. If, however, such pressure is improperly coercive, and for example amounts to undue duress, then the possibility may exist for any resulting settlement terms to be set aside.

8–043 The other distinguishable form of coercion is compulsion to enter into mediation, whether under Court Rules or judicial or other pressure. This may compel a party to try out the mediation process and forum, but cannot compel him to enter into any settlement and does not impinge on his self-determination within the process.

Secure environment: Confidentiality and evidential privilege

8–044 Although mediation may take place in very difficult and challenging circumstances, including perhaps in war zones and on the streets,[31] the process in relation to civil-commercial, family, neighbourhood, employment and all other kinds of disputes and issues should take place in conditions that are conducive to discussion, negotiation and the exploration of settlement options and possibilities.

8–045 This applies to the physical arrangements, to the ambience that is created by the mediator, and to the ground rules regulating the process.[32] Parties need to be able to negotiate freely, without fear, threat or harassment.[33]

8–046 Providing a secure environment also includes the arrangements for confidentiality and evidential privilege. Unless otherwise agreed, or very exceptionally, for example if mediation is agreed to take place in a public forum when addressing an issue of public policy, parties will be entitled to expect that their issues and deliberations will be dealt with confidentially in mediation. This principle of confidentiality is built into virtually all agreements and Codes of mediation organisations and practitioners. Similarly, parties will generally agree

---

[30] The Model Standards of Conduct for Mediators adopted in 2005 by the American Arbitration Association, the American Bar Association and the Association for Conflict Resolution reflects self-determination as the first standard and says: "A mediator shall conduct a mediation based on the principle of party self-determination. Self-determination is the act of coming to a voluntary, uncoerced decision in which each party makes free and informed choices as to process and outcome."

[31] Mediating conflicts between gangs can be a hazardous activity taking place wherever necessary including "on the streets". For further information about gang mediation see Ch.12.

[32] See for example the suggestions for protecting vulnerable parties where mediation takes place in the context of potential domestic violence, at Ch.11.

[33] Though in mediation as in other processes, the threat of litigation or other lawful action that underlies negotiations may be very powerful.

that their deliberations may not be used as evidence in any court proceedings and here again virtually all mediation organisations and practitioners provide for their process to be conducted "without prejudice" or otherwise privileged from being used in evidence.[34]

Authority derived from the parties

8–047　The mediator has no power or authority other than that given by the parties expressly or implicitly.[35] If any party decides to withdraw power and authority from the mediator, that ends the mediation. If mediation is part of a court-annexed procedure, and the parties are compelled by the court to enter into it, they should nevertheless have the freedom to decide to end it with or without a resolution.

Consensual decision-making

8–048　The only binding outcome in mediation is one on which all the parties agree. No decision can be imposed on them, and no decision by some parties in a multi-party dispute can bind those who do not agree—even if the agreeing parties constitute a substantial majority. This does not preclude some parties, in appropriate circumstances, reaching agreement between themselves and the dispute continuing between those who do not agree, or some parties forming alliances to negotiate with others.

8–049　If the parties are unable to reach agreement on the resolution of their dispute, they will be free to have their issues dealt with in some other forum, usually adjudicatory. It is not uncommon in these circumstances for the dispute later to be resolved by agreement on terms flowing from those discussed in the mediation.

Dispute or conflict resolution or management as the objective

8–050　In the first edition of this book, mediation was expressed as having a "settlement objective". That remains substantially true for many cases, especially in the civil-commercial field. Indeed, based on the research findings of Genn,[36] parties and their solicitors indicated that "the primary motivation for agreeing to mediate was the desire to end the litigation as quickly and cheaply as possible".

8–051　In the second edition of this work, it was observed that some mediators did not see "settlement" as the objective, but also where appropriate addressing and

---

[34] Confidentiality and privilege are addressed in Ch.15.
[35] See Bernard Mayer, "The Dynamics of Power in Mediation and Negotiation" (1987) 16 *Mediation Quarterly* 75, dealing with the sources of a mediator's power. These sources include the structure and credibility of the process, the mediator's personal authority and qualities, substantive and process expertise, procedural control, and the value of his or her neutrality and independence in helping to achieve a resolution.
[36] Professor Hazel Genn, *Evaluation Report of the Central London County Court Pilot Mediation Scheme* (London: Lord Chancellor's Department, 1998), para.7.7.3; available at: *http://www.cnmd.ac.uk/laws/judicial-institute/files/Central_London_County_Court_Mediation_Scheme.pdf* [accessed 15 May 2018].

resolving the underlying conflict causing the dispute. From the third edition onwards, "resolution" with its wider context has been adopted, which embraces both concepts.

While dispute resolution, incorporating settlement, remains a valid objective, the net is cast more widely. The objective of mediation may extend beyond the resolution of conflict and disputes, and this needs to be reflected. Mayer refers to conflict that may not be amenable to resolution, for some time in any event. Sometimes people may be in conflict that cannot be resolved, and mediation may be required to help them live with that conflict rather than actually resolve it. Mediation will not for example resolve the differences between those who oppose abortion and those who support it, but it may enable the two groups to co-exist without either attacking the other. Nor will it necessarily resolve fundamental value differences that divorcing parents may have about the bringing up of their children, but it may provide a machinery for these differences to be held without adversely affecting the children. Enduring conflicts or ongoing disputes may be deep-rooted and may reflect fundamental value differences that people have to accept will continue—and the role of mediation may be simply to help them find a *modus vivendi* that enables them to do so: what may be described as staying with and managing rather than resolving the conflict.[37]

8–052

Mediation is also used in ways that are not necessarily dispute settlement or resolution. Indeed, helping a couple re-arrange their family structure on divorce does not necessarily fall within that ambit, though commonly it does include elements of dispute resolution. Deal mediation, or assisted deal-making, is another area in which parties are not concerned with settling disputes or resolving conflict, but rather gaining assistance in constructing a mutually favourable contract instead of simply negotiating it bilaterally. Brown refers to "the value of using mediators to cut deals" on the basis that parties negotiating a new contract can do so "more effectively if a neutral person is engaged to manage the process on the parties' collective behalf".[38]

8–053

Accommodating the conflict dynamic: containing escalation

Conflict and dispute tend to have their own broadly predictable dynamic and momentum. Various writers and practitioners have observed that conflicts tend to pass through a series of phases, though it is also clear that no one model can adequately cover the wide range of conflictual situations that can arise in any sphere of life. While conflict models may be helpful to give a broad framework for guidance, they cannot possibly provide a definitive structure.

8–054

One such model is Friedrich Glasl's Nine-Stage Model of Conflict Escalation,[39] which describes the nine stages as:

8–055

---

[37] See Bernard Mayer, *Staying with Conflict: A Strategic Approach to Ongoing Disputes* (San Francisco: Jossey-Bass, 2009).
[38] John Seely Brown, the former Chief Scientist of Xerox Corporation, International Mediation Institute at: *http://www.imimediation.org/deal-mediation* [accessed 15 May 2018]. This subject is also further dealt with in Ch.10.
[39] Contained in his book Friedrich Glasl's, *Konfliktmanagement. Ein Handbuch für Führungskräfte, Beraterinnen und Berater* (Bern: Paul Haupt Verlag, 1997) and in his English language work, *Confronting Conflict: A First-aid Kit for Handling Conflict* (Gloucester: Hawthorn Press, 1999).

1. *Hardening* in which differences about an issue become crystallised and fixed.
2. *Debates and polemics* involving forceful verbal confrontations.
3. *Actions not words* with parties promoting their own interests and blocking the other.
4. *Images and coalitions*—negative stereotypes prevail with veiled hostility and an attempt to enlist support from others.
5. *Loss of face* of the other, who is now seen in a new, transformed mode as having lost morality and entitlement to trust, with negative values and motives imputed to them.
6. *Strategies of threats* now follow, increasingly firm and unequivocal and leading to ultimata, aiming to force concessions.
7. *Limited destructive blows* with corresponding retaliation and an abandonment of any real or effective communication.
8. *Fragmentation of the enemy* with destructive attacks.
9. *Together into the abyss* as the need to destroy the other dominates even at the cost of one's own self-preservation.

8–056 Other models include reference to a possible latent period, during which the conflict exists but is undeveloped, contained or suppressed, and which eventually becomes a manifest conflict, with all the uncertainties and difficulties that this brings in its wake; and a stalemate period during which both parties may suffer but neither can shift the other.[40]

8–057 The common thread among conflict theorists is that conflict has a tendency to harden and escalate at some stage, and this is certainly the experience of practitioners dealing with the realities of conflict and disputes. Ultimately, it is into this scenario that mediation may enter, and its role in all cases is to accommodate itself to the stage that has been reached and to contain any further inappropriate escalation.[41] Insofar as the mediation is geared to attempts to resolve or manage the conflict or dispute, containment is an obvious goal irrespective of the stage at which the mediation process starts.

8–058 In practical terms, the mediation process tends to encourage a problem-solving approach (albeit that this is not always practicable), to facilitate communications and to allow feelings to be expressed in a respectful forum. Consequently, mediation generally has the effect of containing escalation. This in turn means that parties in disagreement who have a relationship with one another, whether business, family or personal, are generally more likely to sustain that relationship, or to vary or end it in a more co-operative way in mediation than through the adversarial process.

Glasl's model is comprehensively covered by Thomas Jordan, "Glasl's Nine-Stage Model of Conflict Escalation", available online at *http://www.mediate.com/articles/jordan.cfm* [accessed 15 May 2018].

[40] See generally Bernard Mayer, *The Dynamics of Conflict: A Guide to Engagement and Intervention*, 2nd edn (Jossey-Bass, 2012), Ch.1, pp.1–33, by way of a theory example.

[41] There are some cases, involving enduring conflict, in which a mediation process may not necessarily be geared to containing the conflict, but to helping parties develop multiple sources of power for sustaining the conflict in a more effective way. This is a theme developed by Mayer in *Staying with Conflict—A Strategic Approach to Ongoing Disputes* (San Francisco: John Wiley & Sons 2009).

THE PRINCIPLES OF MEDIATION

Empowerment of the parties

The question of empowerment of parties in dispute arises in two ways. At one level, it relates to the relative power of the parties as between themselves. At another level, it concerns the relationship between the parties on the one hand and their lawyers and the legal system on the other. 　　8–059

As between the parties themselves, it is inevitable that there may be some power differences and imbalances. As mentioned elsewhere in this book,[42] the mediator can and should help to redress imbalances insofar as they may affect the mediation process, for example, by allowing each to be properly heard, by checking that they can each obtain necessary advice and information, by preventing any abusive or manipulative behaviour and by maintaining an even-handed approach to each. In some cases, particularly in family and inter-personal issues, the dynamic of the process, the way in which communications can be improved, and the attention given to power imbalances in the process can all have an empowering effect on an individual party. However, if one party has greater financial resource than the other, or is better able to undertake litigation than the other, or has better support, these will be inherent in any process and cannot be addressed in the mediation. 　　8–060

At the other level, mediation enhances the power of the parties in dealing with their dispute. In the traditional court system, the decision-making power is in the hands of the judge, and the way the process is conducted is generally in the hands of the parties' lawyers, who are of course bound by court procedures and conventions. The parties in dispute may feel like third party observers in a process that makes what may be profound decisions for them.[43] 　　8–061

Empowerment in this context means the increase in the parties' ability to make their own decisions as to the outcome of their dispute, and the corresponding reduction of their dependence on third parties including professional advisers and judges. This arises in mediation because the parties are directly involved in the process and retain control over whether they wish to settle and on what terms. 　　8–062

Empowerment is an important part of mediation, and to some mediators, an essential one.[44] This is true in the sense that parties will always have control over the outcome. For some parties, this control is a fundamental issue, for others it may be peripheral as their primary objective may be to find a pragmatic way to end litigation or a practical way to sort out their family and domestic arrangements. 　　8–063

---

[42] The question of power and its imbalances is dealt with in Ch.16.
[43] Linda Singer, a Washington D.C. lawyer, mediator and arbitrator, puts this succinctly: "Court or administrative action displaces litigants' power over their own disputes. The legal process distorts reality; not only are speed and economy affected, but the real issues in dispute and the treatment of disputants by the professional dispute resolvers escape our control as well. Even top corporate managers feel as if their business problems take on a legal life of their own once they are turned over to the lawyers and courts", see L. Singer, "The Quiet Revolution in Dispute Settlement" in (1989) 7(2) *Mediation Quarterly*.
[44] See for example Paul Wahrhaftig, "Nonprofessional Conflict Resolution" in J.E. Palenski and H.M. Launer, *Mediation Contexts and Challenges* (Springfield: C C Thomas, 1986) referring to mediation as the attempt by "everyday people to wrestle back control" over their issues. And see R.B. Bush and J. Folger, *The Promise of Mediation: Responding to Conflict Through Empowerment and Recognition* (San Francisco: Joey-Bass, 1994).

CHAPTER 9

Mediation—Practice Overview

DIFFERENT MODELS: THE STRANDS OF PRACTICE

Describing mediation practice is not straightforward because although there are shared principles—as outlined in the previous chapter—the process may vary considerably between different fields of activity, models of practice, cultures, philosophies and ideologies, ways of working and styles, approaches and roles adopted by individual practitioners. There is a wide range of activity under the generic heading of "mediation process". This is a reflection of the richness and diversity of mediation practice, but it does make the description and classification of practice more complex.

9–001

By way of overview, mediation practice will be considered having regard to the broad models and approaches in use, then to an analytical breakdown of mediation practice into a series of notional stages. Practice in different fields of activity is then developed in separate chapters.

9–002

Models of practice tend often to blur and overlap, with shades of grey within each approach, so categorisation in this way can be misleading; but if seen together with other aspects, it can, like the pieces of a jigsaw puzzle, help to provide the bigger picture. With these reservations in mind, the following is a broad outline of mediation models and approaches.

9–003

Rights-based or interest-based mediation

The concept of a rights-based mediation is that the parties aim to achieve an outcome by negotiation that as closely as practicable corresponds to the outcome that they might expect to achieve in the court process. The concept of an interest-based mediation is that the parties focus on their respective interests, rather than their rights, and seek an outcome that best meets those interests.

9–004

Following an interest-based process was largely motivated by Fisher and Ury[1] who distinguish between the positions that people take and their interests, which these authors describe as "the silent movers behind the hubbub of positions"—the factors that in effect cause you to take your positions. Lax and Sebenius define interests as "whatever you care about that is potentially at stake in the negotiation".[2] Interest-based negotiation looks at shared interests and value

9–005

---

[1] Roger Fisher and William Ury, *Getting to Yes: Negotiating Agreement Without Giving In* (New York: Penguin 1981).

[2] This theoretical approach is taken by Fisher and Ury's Harvard colleagues David Lax and James Sebenius, in *3-D Negotiation: Powerful Tools to Change the Game in Your Most Important Deals* (Boston: Harvard Business School Press, 2006).

MEDIATION—PRACTICE OVERVIEW

creation, as opposed to a more competitive negotiation approach that looks at value claiming, which is commonly at the core of a rights based approach.[3]

9–006 In practice, a rights-based approach process is likely to give more attention to the parties' respective legal positions, may allow more time for the presentation of legal argument and may allow the parties' lawyers a greater negotiation role. In an interest-based approach, the mediator is less likely to focus on legal issues and the process will be geared towards an exploration of the parties' needs and interests and helping them engage in a process of mutual problem-solving.

9–007 In most cases, even if a party is motivated by asserting his rights, other considerations of an interest-based nature are inevitably likely to be taken into account; and even if a party has an interest-based approach, it is unlikely that he will be totally oblivious to the respective rights position and the way that a court or adjudicator might deal with the matter.

9–008 The position is well addressed by Lax and Sebenius[4] who argue that "there is an essential tension between cooperative moves to create value and competitive moves to claim it."[5] In essence, even if someone is negotiating in an interest-based mode, there is still likely to be an objective of achieving the best available outcome—maximum value. Lax and Sebenius refer to the need to balance these competing tensions.

Pure facilitation or an evaluative component

9–009 Although the first edition of this work distinguished between facilitative and evaluative mediation, the authors do not wish to perpetuate this division, which can be argued as being a false dichotomy. In fact all mediation is facilitative, since that is an integral aspect of the process, with parties for example being assisted in communicating and negotiating effectively. Onto that fundamental base, many practitioners graft elements of probing, questioning, "reality-testing", challenging perceptions, eyebrow-raising and other strategies designed to facilitate parties assessing their positions more realistically—another facilitative function, particularly where parties are having regard to their perceived rights as a factor in arriving at a resolution.

9–010 In this spectrum of facilitating a better understanding of their positions, which starts at one end with minimal evaluation such as challenging perceptions and reality testing, and continues through making private non-binding and indirect hints and observations, to expressing a view on the merits at the other end, the question arises as to where it is proper for a mediator to "draw the line". At what point does this evaluation become inappropriate? These are proper questions of strategy and propriety, but to suggest that evaluation within mediation is an alternative to facilitation, rather than a supplementary way of working, is arguably a misunderstanding.[6]

9–011 There is a view that working exclusively in a facilitative mode without introducing any kind of challenge to a party's perceptions and understandings, or

---

[3] For a more detailed discussion about negotiation approaches, see Ch.4.
[4] See Lax & Sebenius, fn.2.
[5] See Lax & Sebenius, fn.2, p.33.
[6] For a fuller discussion about forms of non-binding evaluation, see Ch.19.

any other evaluation, is a "pure" form of mediation. That view makes a number of assumptions about the nature of mediation and its objectives that require further debate.

Settlement-geared process

This approach sees settlement as an objective and the negotiation process as a route to achieving it. It does not view mediation as a relationship-enhancing or healing process, though it may have this indirect consequence, but simply as a method of achieving settlement. 9–012

This objective may be achieved by using a rights-based or a problem-solving interest-based approach and by incorporating any other model or approach with the mediator possibly incorporating any level of evaluation into the process. A settlement-geared mediator may concentrate on trade-offs and bargaining and seek practical ways of resolving impasse, as well as developing creative problem-solving solutions where possible. 9–013

Therapeutic mediation process

The mediation process can also be seen as having the capacity to address unresolved emotional issues, to help communication and understanding between parties, and consequently to have some healing function. Those who tend towards the therapeutic approach are more likely to favour problem-solving rather than competitive negotiation. They would be more responsive to the expression of emotions; they would examine interests and needs rather than rights; and they are more comfortable with uncertainty and a slower pace in the conviction that the parties themselves have the competence to work things out for themselves eventually, given appropriate help and sometimes greater directiveness.[7] 9–014

The therapeutic approach may well be helpful for inter-personal issues, including for example working with parents in conflict about their children, or conflict within families and groups, or between neighbours and others who require an ongoing relationship, focusing on better understandings, reduction of conflict and improved communications rather than the settlement of legal issues. 9–015

However, perhaps not surprisingly, this approach may be less well suited to civil court disputes and the expectations of parties as found in research undertaken by Genn.[8]

---

[7] For a detailed work on therapeutic mediation in the family context, see for example Howard H. Irving and Michael Benjamin, *Therapeutic Family Mediation: Helping Families Resolve Conflict* (USA: Sage Publications, 2002).
[8] Professor Hazel Genn, *Evaluation Report of the Central London County Court Pilot Mediation Scheme No.5/98* (London: Lord Chancellor's Department, July 1998), paras 6.3.1, 6.3.2 and 7.6.3.

Transformative mediation

9–016   The transformative view was primarily developed by Bush and Folger, whose proposition is that mediators may help people to change by achieving greater personal efficacy and empowerment while allowing for respect and recognition of the other party.[9]

9–017   Bush and Folger are critical of the problem-solving approach, which they consider to be unduly directive in its aim of settling the immediate dispute rather than enabling the parties to define the issues themselves and arriving at their own solutions. The transformative approach goes deeper, and has the capacity to change not only how people behave in a particular conflict, but also in their future life. In Bush and Folger's own words "they learn how to draw on those positive capacities in dealing with life's problems and in relating to others".[10]

9–018   The twin goals of empowerment and recognition are fundamental to the transformative model: the settlement of the dispute is not viewed as a primary goal. By empowerment, Bush and Folger mean helping parties to find their own strength to explore goals, resources and options and make their own decisions. By recognition they mean giving due consideration and recognition to the views of the other party to the conflict: "the evocation in individuals of acknowledgment and empathy for the situation and problems of others".[11]

9–019   Transformative mediation practitioners are likely to have a different approach and procedure from those using other models, and would eschew the problem-solving model. They would also challenge the proposition that, whereas the parties control outcome, the mediator controls the process: mediators should not exercise such control. Bush and Folger identify ten hallmarks of transformative practice.[12] These include articulating the principles of empowerment and recognition at the outset, adopting a responsive rather than a directive approach, particularly towards emotions and past events, patiently exploring uncertainty and ambiguity, and optimistically supporting the parties' ability to arrive at their own resolution.[13]

Other models

9–020   Other mediation models include for example the *narrative model*, which is based on the proposition that conflict arises from the stories and descriptions that people have constructed, both personal and from within a socio-cultural context,

---

[9] Robert A. Baruch Bush and Joseph P. Folger, *The Promise of Mediation: Responding to Conflict Through Empowerment and Recognition* (San Francisco: Jossey-Bass, 1994).

[10] See the Preface in Bush and Folger, *The Promise of Mediation: Responding to Conflict Through Empowerment and Recognition*, fn.9.

[11] Bush & Folger, *The Promise of Mediation: Responding to Conflict Through Empowerment and Recognition*, fn.9, p.2.

[12] Robert A. Baruch Bush and Joseph P. Folger, "Transformative Mediation and Third-Party Intervention: Ten Hallmarks of a Transformative Approach to Practice" (1996) 13(4) *Mediation Quarterly* 263.

[13] For more information about the transformative model and practice, see the Institute for the Study of Conflict Transformation Inc at *http://www.transformativemediation.org/* [accessed 15 May 2018]; and Joseph P. Folger, Robert A. Baruch Bush and Dorothy J. Della Noce, *Transformative Mediation: A Sourcebook—Resources for Conflict Intervention Practitioners and Programs* (New York: Association for Conflict Resolution and the Institute for the Study of Conflict Transformation, 2010).

and that the mediator's function is to hear those stories, analyse them with the parties, uncover assumptions and biases, and help the parties move away from their narratives into new understandings, respect and collaboration. These understandings are not based on problem-solving or interest-based principles, but rather on "... helping mediators and their clients make sense of the complex social contexts that shape conflicts."[14]

The *humanistic model* of mediation is geared towards the healing of relationships and according to Umbreit it:

9–021

> "parallels a humanistic style of psychotherapy or teaching which emphasizes the importance of the relationship between the therapist and client and embraces a strong belief in each person's capacity for growth, change, and transformation".[15]

The model aims to help parties find inner peace.

Hybrid models of mediation involve drawing on elements of more than one model, and different ways of working. There seems to be an increasing trend towards adopting hybrid models in various fields of activity, so that the distinctions outlined above may sometimes blur—though the transformative model does tend to remain purist in its approach.

9–022

Vindeløv has adopted the concept of a *mediation non-model*, which she characterises as being eclectic, "because it allows for inspiration to be drawn from all the best known mediation models" and applies elements of them as appropriate in practice. Vindeløv is rather more concerned with the mediator's values and assumptions that are integrated into his or her practice.[16]

9–023

THE STAGES OF MEDIATION

Breaking the mediation process down into a series of stages is a helpful way of gaining an overview, though it should be emphasised that these will not necessarily follow the same sequence or be present in every case, and the stages may well overlap and blur in practice. It is simply a device to help provide a useful framework for the process and practitioners are cautioned against viewing stages and practices as a rigid norm that has to be observed.

9–024

These stages can be formulated in different ways. For example, The Law Society of England and Wales envisages ten stages in its schedule of competencies for mediators.[17] Acland identifies nine stages, from preparation, designing the mediation process and bringing the parties together through to formulating and formalising the proposals.[18] Parkinson refers to a 12-stage

9–025

---

[14] John Winslade and Gerald D. Monk, *Narrative Mediation: A New Approach to Conflict Resolution* (San Francisco: Jossey-Bass, 2000), p.xi (Preface).
[15] Mark S. Umbreit, "Humanistic Mediation: A Transformative Journey of Peacemaking" (1997) 14(3) *Conflict Resolution Quarterly* 201.
[16] Vibeke Vindeløv, *Mediation: A Non-Model* (Copenhagen: DJÒF Publishing, 2007).
[17] Helpfully divided by the Law Society into three phases: Before mediation, during the substantive mediation and the end of mediation and afterwards.
[18] Andrew Acland, *A Sudden Outbreak of Common Sense: Managing Conflict through Mediation* (London: Random House Business Books, 1990).

process for family mediation.[19] Gulliver has adopted a staged process for cross-cultural negotiation from an anthropological perspective.[20]

9–026 However a staged process does not work for every model of practice, and in particular it is not fully compatible with the transformative model which may prefer a non-sequential paradigm that focuses on whatever emerges for the parties (an "emergent-focus" model).[21]

9–027 For the purpose of this work the pre-mediation and post-mediation activities will not be considered as part of the mediation process, so that there should be no risk of blurring the boundaries of when mediation might start and end. It has become clear that those boundaries might well be important.[22]

9–028 The following framework provides a structural overview:

Pre-mediation:

9–029 Considering mediation, assessing suitability and obtaining commitment.

During mediation:

9–030
1. Preliminary communications and preparation.
2. Establishing the issues and setting the agenda.
3. Information gathering.
4. Conducting substantive negotiations.
5. Dealing with impasse.
6. Concluding mediation and recording the outcome.

Post-mediation:

9–031 Addressing post-mediation issues.

PRE-MEDIATION: CONSIDERING MEDIATION, ASSESSING SUITABILITY AND OBTAINING COMMITMENT

9–032 This initial stage, before mediation commences, may involve informing parties about the mediation process, dealing with queries, where appropriate checking that mediation is suitable and obtaining a commitment to the process.

---

[19] Lisa Parkinson, *Family Mediation*, 3rd edn (Bristol: Jordan Publishing, 2014).
[20] Philip Gulliver, *Disputes and Negotiations: a Cross-Cultural Perspective* (Academic Press, 1979).
[21] See the article by James R. Antes, Donna Turner Hudson, Erling O. Jorgensen and Janet Kelly Moen, "Is a Stage Model of Mediation Necessary?" (1999) 16(3) *Mediation Quarterly*.
[22] See *Brown v Rice* [2007] EWHC 625 (Ch), where one of the issues was whether a term of the Agreement to Mediate was or was not in force, which in turn depended at least in part on whether the parties were "in mediation" at the time certain proposals were made. See also below: When does the mediation start?

Providing information:

Information about the mediation process is increasingly available, including as follows: 9–033

- Lawyers are being encouraged by the courts to refer cases to mediation where appropriate and many firms promote it actively.[23]
- Mediation and other dispute resolution organisations and groups provide information on their websites and commonly through newsletters, information sheets, practice updates and other resources
- Individual mediators may provide relevant information and material on their websites, electronically, through the post and/or by phone. This may outline procedures, give estimates of time and cost, provide a biography indicating their qualifications and experience, and generally address standard questions.
- A preliminary pre-mediation meeting or "intake session" with the parties and/or their lawyers can serve a number of functions: the mediator can provide process information and answer questions and can assess suitability of the case and parties for mediation, and the parties can decide whether or not they want to mediate and whether they wish to appoint the mediator to do so. This would not form part of the mediation process, as the parties have not yet committed to it or signed a mediation contract; but they should agree on confidentiality and that this preliminary process is evidentially privileged.

Considerations affecting the decision to mediate

There may be other considerations affecting a decision whether or not to mediate. These may include commitments that the parties may have given at some earlier stage, for example a contractual provision when entering into a commercial relationship that any disputes would be dealt with in a prescribed way, such as mediation and/or arbitration.[24] 9–034

Both government and the courts are keen for parties to seek ways of resolving their disputes through negotiation and ADR processes before using the courts, and this is reflected in various ways, including for example, costs sanctions for a failure to do so where appropriate. For all family disputes there is a requirement for the parties to attend an intake meeting before making certain kinds of applications to obtain a court order.[25] Pre-action protocols regulating matters to be dealt with before commencing proceedings generally provide for ADR to be considered.[26] 9–035

These matters and other relevant considerations are addressed in the context of the different fields of activity dealt with in the chapters relating to those activities. 9–036

---

[23] For further information about courts' increasing encouragement of mediation, see Ch.5.
[24] See "ADR pledges and contract clauses" in Ch.10.
[25] See fn.28 below; and see Ch.11 for further consideration of this.
[26] See Ch.5.

Assessing suitability

9–037 Mediation is likely to be appropriate whenever parties wish and have the legal capacity to settle their differences, however far apart they may be in their thinking.[27] There are however some circumstances in which mediation would be inappropriate, for example if a party does not have legal capacity to enter into an agreement, or if the issue affects status or constitutional rights, or if it is essential to have a precedent or injunctive relief, or where either party is likely to abuse the process, or where a party is unable to negotiate freely.

9–038 In the family field in England and Wales, a preliminary Mediation Information and Assessment Meeting (known by its acronym MIAM) is mandatory in certain circumstances unless specified exemptions apply before parties may make certain kinds of application to the court. One of its primary functions is to assess the suitability of mediation for the dispute.[28] This process also involves screening parties to ensure that there is no threat of violence or abuse that might adversely affect participation or outcome.

Obtaining commitment—the contract to mediate

9–039 Parties or their lawyers may jointly decide to mediate or to explore the possibility of doing so. Where an enquiry is made by only one party, ADR organisations and practitioners may assist that party as necessary to gain the agreement to mediate of any other party, for example by providing material to send on to the other party. Some mediators or organisations will agree to approach the other party themselves, outlining their services, enclosing material and enquiring if the party would be interested in mediation.

9–040 A pre-mediation meeting can be useful as a way to provide information and to engage both parties in the process. It can provide an opportunity for them to work with each other and with the mediator, and can lead into the substantive mediation process, for example by dealing with some of the procedural practicalities in anticipation of any substantive meeting(s). This is further addressed in the chapters on individual fields of activity.

9–041 Mediation voluntarily entered into involves some form of contract, explicit or implicit, regulating the relationship between the mediator and the parties. Ordinarily, and particularly for civil, commercial and family mediation, parties will be required to enter into a written agreement to mediate before the mediation starts. Of course parties may orally agree with a third party to act informally as a mediator. It is, however, good practice to have a written agreement that records the terms and ground rules of the process and avoids any possible misunderstanding later about the basis on which the mediation was undertaken, and this is

---

[27] The English Court of Appeal, adopting submissions made by the Law Society of England and Wales, provided in the case of *Halsey v Milton Keynes General NHS Trust* [2004] EWCA (Civ) 576; [2004] 1 W.L.R. 3002 a list of guidelines as to when parties might face costs sanctions for failing to mediate. This list—outlined in Ch.10 and Ch.17— indicate the factors relevant to suitability to mediate in civil and commercial cases.

[28] Practice Direction 3A (Pre-application protocol for mediation information and assessment)—supplementing the Family Procedure Rules 2010, came into force on 6 April 2011 and was updated in January 2018.

commonly required by the relevant Code of Practice. Some terms may be important, especially if parties do not reach agreement and any issue arises about what took place in the mediation.[29]

The agreement may explicitly or implicitly provide that the mediation will take place under the rules or provisions of a particular Code of Practice to which the mediator and/or the organisation subscribes.[30] It will usually record matters such as confidentiality, privilege, payment of fees and other practical aspects. It can outline the ground rules of the mediation. Parties may in some instances be required to commit themselves to dealing with one another in good faith in the mediation, though different systems of law place different weight on good faith commitments.[31]

9–042

All parties signing the agreement at the start of the initial mediation meeting, having approved it in advance, has a symbolic significance, committing the parties to the search for a resolution.

9–043

When does the mediation start?

In some situations it may well be essential to know whether parties are "in mediation" and whether the terms, express or implied, of an Agreement to Mediate are in force. For example, a dispute resolution clause in a contract may provide for parties to be free to pursue litigation or arbitration if the matter is not resolved within a specified period from the start of the mediation. Or if a party makes a statement or concession believing it to be protected as to confidentiality and evidential privilege, it may be critically important if the terms of the agreement are not applicable. In *Brown v Rice & Patel*[32] a term of the Agreement to Mediate was that "any settlement reached in the mediation" would not be binding until reduced to writing and entered into. In that case, one of the questions was whether the parties were still "in the mediation" at the time that certain alleged proposals were made.

9–044

In practice, the start of the mediation is often blurred. Parties or their lawyers might meet the mediator on a preliminary basis to assess suitability and consider initial matters, and may move on seamlessly to the substantive part of the process. Or initial communications on the phone, electronically or by mail may take place before any initial meeting with a mediator, when certain things may be said that could later be in issue and need to be examined.

9–045

One of the UK's major bodies refers in its standard terms to the "mediation" as being the actual day on which the substantive meeting takes place and by implication does not include preliminary or subsequent communications.

9–046

---

[29] There are a number of cases in point on this for example *Farm Assist Limited (In liquidation) v Secretary of State for the Environment, Food and Rural Affairs* [2009] EWHC 1102 TCC; [2009] B.L.R. 399.
[30] See Ch.16 dealing with codes of practice.
[31] As to the requirement to negotiate in good faith, see Ch.4. An example of an Agreement to Mediate in the family context can be found in Appendix I, Document 10 at para.A1-044; and reference to an agreement in the civil-commercial context can be found at para.A1-043.
[32] See *Brown v Rice* [2007] EWHC 625 (Ch), where one of the issues was whether a term of the Agreement to Mediate was or was not in force, which in turn depended at least in part on whether the parties were "in mediation" at the time certain proposals were made.

9-047 The mediation may actually begin before the initial substantive meeting, or more rarely after the start of that meeting.[33] Clearly, the signing of an Agreement to Mediate, or implicitly accepting its terms, would be a possible point of starting the process, as may the appointment of a mediator—and sometimes these are done simultaneously. Ultimately, the question might be, what was the intention of the parties, as indicated by them and by their actions?

DURING THE MEDIATION: STAGE 1: PRELIMINARY COMMUNICATIONS AND PREPARATION

9-048 Having agreed to mediate, the parties are likely to have some preliminary communications with the mediator or with the organisation arranging the mediation. This may be by telephone, electronically, by mail or personally.

Preliminary communications

9-049 Preliminary communications may cover a range of subjects, which may vary according to the field of activity concerned and individual needs, but which may broadly include the following:

- Addressing procedural matters such as arranging the venue and timetable for the initial or substantive mediation meeting, identifying what documents and information are required and within what time frame, and perhaps arranging to obtain an indication or summary of the parties' respective cases and contentions.
- In one model, particularly in civil and commercial disputes, a single block of time is generally allotted, which may vary between a few hours and a few days or more. In another model, mainly in relation to couples' issues, shorter meetings—often 1 and a half hours each—may take place over weeks or months.
- Establishing who will attend the mediation, including legal representatives. All necessary parties should attend the mediation: the whole process can be frustrated if a party whose agreement to a settlement is essential to make it effective is missing.
- Representatives of corporate or institutional parties need to have authority to negotiate and reach agreement. If authority is limited or conditional, this fact needs to be known and may need to be recorded. Where parties are indemnified by their insurers, they should arrange with the insurers to honour any agreement reached by them, perhaps within specified parameters; or alternatively the insurers might send a representative to the

---

[33] In one case at the start of the joint meeting the mediator asked the parties and their lawyers to sign the Agreement to Mediate, which had been approved electronically beforehand. Before they did so, an initial issue arose about the true identity of one of the participants and the process was abruptly terminated. Various potential questions might have arisen as to the status of the meeting, whether confidentiality and privilege applied, and whether mediation costs were payable. In the event, these did not become live issues; but they illustrate the possible relevance of the question as to whether or not the mediation had started. This also illustrates the need to obtain a firm commitment to the terms of the agreement before attending a meeting.

mediation.³⁴ In a multi-party dispute, the mediator will generally want to ensure that all parties attend whose agreement is essential for an effective resolution.³⁵

- Consideration can be given to the way in which legal issues, either specific or general, will be addressed so that there are no inappropriate expectations. There may, for example, be short presentations by the lawyers so that each side can have a better idea of the other's contentions, especially as in many cases negotiations will take place "in the shadow of the law" inasmuch as parties know that they will be able to have the issues adjudicated upon if they do not resolve them in mediation.³⁶
- Consideration can be given to steps that might be taken before an initial substantive meeting so as to enhance the prospects of resolving issues at that meeting. For example, accountants might be asked to prepare certain accounts, or experts might be asked to liaise and produce a note specifying areas of agreement and disagreement, or preliminary drafts of required documents might be created.³⁷

These early communications set the process up effectively, introduce the mediator to the parties or their lawyers and start the process of establishing a working relationship, rapport and trust; and may also give the mediator an initial picture of the issues. 9–050

These preliminary communications may be conducted with each party separately, but where practicable they may be carried out by a preliminary meeting with the parties or their lawyers. 9–051

Preliminary meeting

The preliminary mediation meeting may be distinguished from the pre-mediation intake meeting in that the intake meeting is intended to help parties decide whether or not to enter into mediation whereas the preliminary mediation meeting is held once parties have entered the process and as a step in it. 9–052

There may sometimes be a blurring of the two kinds of initial meetings in practice. A mediator may, for example, meet parties or lawyers to help them assess whether or not mediation is appropriate. If they are satisfied and wish to go ahead, they can immediately sign the Agreement to Mediate and convert the meeting into a preliminary meeting and start addressing procedural matters or sometimes even substantive issues. 9–053

Where it is practicable to hold a preliminary meeting, all the preliminary communications outlined above can be dealt with at one time, rather than the mediator doing so through a series of phone calls and emails. Not only is this efficient, but it affords the parties and the mediator an opportunity to start 9–054

---

[34] As to the relationship between insurance interests and compromise, see D. Foskett, *The Law and Practice of Compromise*, 7th revised edn (London: Sweet & Maxwell, 2010); and *Foskett on Compromise*, 8th edn 2015.

[35] Sometimes though the mediation can take place on a more limited basis with some parties missing. See "Multi-party disputes" below.

[36] A concept based on the article by R. H. Mnookin and L. Kornhauser, "Bargaining in the Shadow of the Law, The Case of Divorce" (1979) 88 Y.L.J. 950.

[37] See fn.2: Lax and Sebenius emphasise the importance of set-up in preparing for negotiations.

9–055 working together and perhaps to touch on some of the issues that will need to be addressed, facilitating preparation for the substantive meeting. It may also stimulate dialogue about ways of considering the issues, and allow the parties to explore steps that they might take before the substantive meeting to narrow the issues—something that cannot be done where the preliminary communications are conducted through a series of separate exchanges.

It is of course not always practicable to hold a preliminary meeting, and mediators and parties will be guided by pragmatic considerations of cost and proportionality particularly where parties and lawyers are based some distance apart. However, with the improvement and development of technologies such as Skype, video conferencing, telepresence video telephony and virtual meetings, travelling to meetings may well not be such a necessity or inhibition to preliminary meetings.[38]

Preparation

9–056 After dealing with preliminary matters, the mediator generally needs to prepare for the substantive meeting(s). This may include the following:

- *Establishing a venue:* If practicable this should be neutral though the premises of the lawyer for either party may in some cases be acceptable. There needs to be a room in which the parties and the mediator can meet jointly; and in those models which involve separate meetings, also separate (soundproof or well apart) rooms for each party. The joint meeting room can double as a room for one party.
- *Reception arrangements:* These should ideally be planned to provide that the parties are not kept waiting together in the same waiting room if there is a high level of animosity or tension between them.
- *Seating arrangements:* This should be arranged with care. Where practicable it should avoid the parties facing one another in a way that could feel confrontational.[39]
- *Hosting arrangements:* One of the mediator's roles is that of host.[40] The mediator needs to ensure that there are adequate facilities, refreshments and meals for the parties, as well as resources such as wi-fi if practicable, flip charts, printers, photocopiers and anything else that may be needed to enable the process to function efficiently.
- *Reading and research:* The mediator will read any material submitted by the parties. Some mediators also undertake research into the issues, for example concerning legal or technical aspects, others prefer to be educated by the parties into the issues as the mediation progresses.
- *Coaching:* Some mediators find it helpful to provide informal coaching to the parties and/or their lawyers as to how to make best use of the process, on the phone or by providing information sheets. Lawyers may be encouraged to adopt an explanatory rather than combative approach in

---

[38] For more information about the use of technological developments in relation to dispute resolution processes, see Ch.20.
[39] See the comments about seating arrangements in Ch.10, para.10-070.
[40] See Ch.14 for mediator roles including that of host.

- *Other practical preparation:* There may be other matters that can usefully be prepared in advance. The mediator may suggest that arrangements be made for experts to be contactable by the parties as needed during the process, or may arrange for after-hours facilities to be available where it is contemplated that the mediation could run beyond the anticipated time. All preparation will depend on the needs of each individual matter.

STAGE 2: COMMENCEMENT, ESTABLISHING THE ISSUES AND SETTING THE AGENDA

In most models and fields, the mediator will welcome the parties, make some form of opening statement outlining the process and any relevant ground-rules, and facilitate getting the proceedings under way. In some models, the parties or their lawyers may make a formal opening statement, in others this is not required or considered appropriate. This stage commonly tends to be conducted by way of joint meeting, though not necessarily. This joint meeting may be an opportunity to explore matters of common concern before separating into private meetings, in those models where parties separate for negotiations. 9–057

One of the mediator's initial tasks is to establish the issues for resolution and to establish an agenda for the process. This may be done formally, with the agenda agreed and recorded, or informally and even implicitly, with the mediator merely maintaining a personal note that is not specifically shared with the parties. 9–058

This stage may be viewed from three perspectives:

1. The issues as presented

In a more formal and structured process the parties provide an initial written summary of the issues and their positions, amplified by oral presentations, whereas in more informal processes the issues are outlined orally in the course of discussion. 9–059

Once the mediator and the parties have an indication of the issues in dispute, the issues may be crystallised into a formal written agenda, which can be varied as the mediation progresses and aspects are addressed and new issues emerge. Having these presented in a visual format, for example on a flipchart, can be helpful to the parties and the mediator in maintaining focus and prioritising issues. 9–060

Parties do not necessarily share the same view as to what the issues are, particularly in family, couples' and inter-personal disputes. The mediator may need to find a neutral problem-definition that will satisfy both or all parties. 9–061

An agenda should ordinarily be a flexible tool, guiding the progress of the mediation. Where mediation takes place over a series of meetings, it may be advisable for the mediator to check the agenda at each meeting to ensure that new or other issues do not need to be addressed, or the prioritisation of issues re-organised. 9–062

2. Underlying issues: the "iceberg" factor

9–063   In many cases, the presenting issues may be "the tip of the iceberg" and other issues, often underlying, emerge. A commercial dispute between two corporations may well turn out to reveal underlying issues of competition, lack of trust, anger at past dealings and other deep-seated negative attitudes existing between the management of the respective companies. A boundary dispute between neighbours may conceal underlying issues about individual autonomy, lifestyle choices and mutuality of respect. A clinical negligence damages claim may be as much about getting an explanation, apology and accountability as receiving compensation.

9–064   Sometimes the parties are aware of the underlying issues and quickly bring them into the open. Sometimes, however, they take time to surface, either because the parties do not want to express them directly, or perhaps because they are unaware of their existence or are not conscious of their effect on the dispute.

9–065   Mediators should be sensitive to the possibility of underlying issues emerging, and should watch for them through remarks and body language, and gently—or if necessary robustly—probe where appropriate. Some commercial mediators are encouraged to take time at the outset, usually in the initial confidential session with each party, to explore all issues, including those that may underlie the dispute as presented. A common experience is that underlying issues if left unaddressed can subvert the resolution of the main issues.[41] It is a matter for the judgment of the mediator to consider whether, how and at what stage to bring any underlying issues into the open, having regard to confidentiality, party preferences and the efficacy of the process.

3. The mediator's working principles

9–066   Clearly the agenda is that of the parties and not the mediator's. A rather more subtle and difficult question is how to ensure that the parties understand and approve of the underlying approach and working principles used by the mediator, which may constitute a different basis from the parties' expectations, given especially the different models and approaches outlined above.

9–067   As observed by Brown in relation to the conduct of mediation undertaken by dispute resolution organisations, "… it would be helpful to the creation of confidence to have a note that briefly sets out the process and the individual mediator's approach to material aspects particularly evaluation. (How this is done will need some discussion and coordination between organisations and mediators)."[42]

Mediators should be explicit about the process that they offer to the parties, so that the parties can make an informed choice as to what they want.

---

[41] See fn.18 where Acland suggests in *A Sudden Outbreak of Common Sense*, that the more that comes out at this early stage, the fewer the new issues that will emerge later when agreement may be approaching.

[42] Henry Brown, "Creating Confidence in Mediators and the Process: An Exploration of the Issues" (2010) Chartered Institute of Arbitrators Symposium 2010.

STAGE 3: INFORMATION GATHERING

The way in which information is gathered may vary. In civil and commercial disputes, where the substantive mediation meeting commonly takes place over one block of time, relevant documents are ordinarily required to be with the mediator before the substantive mediation begins. Where, however, the mediation takes place over a number of sessions, as in a family model, information may be received throughout the process, supplemented as required.

9–068

Information may be of different kinds and come from different sources:

- Facts about the parties and the issues, and each party's views and submissions, may be obtained from an initial referral form or from written statements furnished by the parties.
- Copies of relevant documents may be submitted by the parties.
- Oral comments may be made by each party at the initial joint meeting and/or in separate meetings with the mediator and will of course continue informally throughout the process.
- Technical, legal and other expert opinions, valuations and other specialised data can be introduced into the mediation through the respective lawyers, experts and professional advisers, or the parties may obtain such information and opinions from neutral sources.
- Witnesses of fact are not involved as such in the mediation process, though this has been suggested[43] and is sometimes done in the mini-trial, which may be viewed as a structured form of evaluative mediation.[44]
- The mediator's observations during the mediation may also provide useful insights.[45] The dynamic between the parties, their attitudes and underlying concerns all comprise part of the broader picture. Indirect and sometimes quite subtle clues—tone of voice, a remark, a nod, a smile, a gesture of disapproval or irritation, a shift of the eyes, signs of distress—these may all help the mediator to gain insights into the motivations, concerns and aspirations of the parties.

Displaying information: the flip-chart[46]

Some of the data gathered during the mediation will be noted and retained by the mediator, some will need to be shared and perhaps more prominently displayed for the mutual benefit of the parties and the mediator. In the latter regard, a flip-chart is an invaluable aid to the displaying of information, and also serves other functions:

9–069

- It can be seen by all parties and keeps information and issues in focus.

---

[43] Peter Lovenheim and Lisa Guerin, *Mediate Don't Litigate* (California: Nolo, 2004), p.94 say that a mediator may suggest that witnesses of fact should be called. However, this is rarely if ever done.
[44] See Ch.19 on neutral evaluative processes.
[45] See Ch.14 and in particular the section on communication skills such as listening, observing non-verbal communications and questioning.
[46] Electronic digital "flip charts" exist which can replicate material from laptop to screen. The principles outlined here apply to any such method of displaying information.

- Data can be reverted to as matters develop. For example, financial data in family mediation may be recorded and amended from time to time as supplementary data is received and information becomes clearer.
- The overt sharing of information can be an empowering process.
- Some facts are more graphic when they appear on a chart, and can have an impact on the parties without having to be orally articulated.
- Listing options and recording brainstorming ideas visually helps to create a positive sense of seeking problem-solving approaches to the dispute.[47]
- It can be used to distract parties from negative exchanges.

How much information is enough?

9-070 There can be no standard answer to this question: much invariably depends on the nature of the issues. As a general proposition there needs to be sufficient information for the parties and the mediator to understand and address the issues: there is no need to replicate the document disclosure process or further particularisation in litigation. Disputes can be and are resolved at any stage, very often before the start of any legal action and commonly before the exchange of document disclosure or witness statements, so clearly these are not essential to settlement.

9-071 This principle does not, however, apply to couples' mediation in jurisdictions like England and Wales where issues on divorce require full and frank disclosure of all, and not just selective, financial information. The mediation process accommodates this by requiring the same level of disclosure in divorce mediation as would be provided in contested proceedings.

STAGE 4: CONDUCTING SUBSTANTIVE NEGOTIATIONS

9-072 In this stage the mediator helps the parties to communicate with one another, either directly in joint session, or indirectly by means of separate meetings ("caucuses"), explores and narrows options, and generally facilitates the parties' negotiations with a view to narrowing their differences and helping them eventually to resolve their issues. Approaches and strategies relevant to this phase of the mediation include the following:

Managing the process[48]

9-073 In most models, the parties are responsible for decision-making in relation to the substantive outcome whereas the mediator is the manager of the process and responsible for making the administrative arrangements for the mediation, organising the facilities, chairing the meeting and the process, and maintaining an orderly, secure and constructive working environment in which the parties can negotiate effectively.

---

[47] The corollary is that the deletion of an option may inhibit parties from re-opening a deleted option if on subsequent reflection it may become relevant. Consequently, in narrowing options, it is better to focus on preferred options without physically deleting those initially expressed to be unsuitable.

[48] For further details of the mediator's management role, see Ch.14.

STAGE 4: CONDUCTING SUBSTANTIVE NEGOTIATIONS

The mediator derives authority from the parties and should not be autocratic, riding roughshod over their views and wishes. This does not, however, mean that the mediator should not, after due consultation where appropriate, make necessary management decisions.

9–074

Facilitation

The primary and fundamental role of the mediator is to facilitate the parties' negotiations with one another. Mediators may try to help parties to use an interest-based problem-solving approach in their negotiations though that will not always be possible or practicable: parties commonly adopt a competitive approach, and in the mediation process may move to a mixture of this and problem-solving.[49]

9–075

The mediator will also try to facilitate communications between the parties. This may be particularly important where they have a continuing relationship such as parenting or partnership. Usually this can better be achieved through joint rather than separate meetings.

9–076

Holding joint or separate meetings (caucuses)

A mediator may meet the parties together, separately, or both. Practice tends to vary in different fields of activity, but some factors are relevant in all kinds of disputes:

9–077

- Conducting mediation exclusively through joint meetings demands substantial mediator skill and care. Parties cannot speak privately to the mediator, so the mediator must continually be alert to the parties' stresses, power imbalances and negotiating inequalities. Separate meetings demand different kinds of skill and care. Mediators are subject to competing party pressures and greater risks of triangulation, and need to exercise great judgment and care in carrying proposals and communications between the parties.
- The mediator needs to make it clear whether discussions in the separate meetings will be shared with all parties, or whether separate confidences will be maintained, save as the mediator is authorised to disclose, which is more usual. In joint sessions there are no secrets between parties and the mediator, whereas separate meetings inherently involve private communications between each party and the mediator, especially where the mediator promises each party confidentiality. This places the mediator in a powerful position as the keeper of separate secrets. Some mediators do not favour being placed in this position and prefer not to undertake separate meetings.
- The mediator will ordinarily encourage each party in the separate meetings to disclose their aspirations, interests, needs and concerns and to indicate broadly what nature of settlement terms would be acceptable. The mediator

---

[49] Theories of negotiation are outlined in Ch.4. See also fn.2 and Lax and Sebenius's observations about the essential tension between interest-based approaches and an individual's aims to achieve the best available outcome for himself.

may try to establish any hidden agendas of each party, going behind their stated positions and aspirations to seek information to help them devise options that will meet all needs.

- Separate meetings are commonly conducted on a shuttle basis. The mediator moves between the parties, narrowing and helping resolve the issues between them.
- By their nature separate meetings may reinforce detachment, which may be inappropriate where the process is trying to heal relationship rifts, unless they are used with a view to re-establishing a joint process. Parties may feel isolated and be anxious about what is being said to the mediator by the other during the separate meeting. Having some support and a task such as considering some aspect or making specified enquiries while the mediator is engaged with the other party can be helpful.
- Separate meetings take longer than joint meetings and require ample time to be effective.

Generating and developing options

9–078   Parties in dispute cannot always see their options clearly, often focusing on one specific outcome instead of viewing matters more widely. Developing options is an intrinsic part of the problem-solving approach and a significant part of the mediator's role is to help the parties to generate and consider their options, and to develop them into viable courses of action.

9–079   Options may be suggested by the parties or the mediator. Sometimes the mediator may suggest ways in which other people in disagreement have dealt with similar situations, or may indicate different approaches that courts have taken. There should be no inhibition on the mediator adding ideas, as long as these are expressed in a way that does not cause them to be perceived as "the mediator's recommendations". As parties examine and work through their options, narrowing or eliminating some and widening others, their ability to work together in finding a solution is likely to increase.

Brainstorming[50]

9–080   Brainstorming involves the mediator encouraging the parties to put forward as many ideas and options as possible as they come to mind without inhibiting their flow by considering them individually or rejecting any at that stage, even if they may seem unworkable.

9–081   The mediator may need to manage the brainstorming session firmly and creatively, helping parties to build on and develop options as they arise and deterring parties from examining them while they are being generated.

9–082   As options are being generated they are recorded and prioritised later. When subsequently considering options, it is not a good idea to eliminate any notwithstanding that some may be unacceptable. It is not uncommon that options

---

[50] See Edward de Bono, *Lateral Thinking: An Introduction* (London: Vermilion, 2014) in which he suggests that the three principal elements of brainstorming are putting forward ideas to stimulate others; suspending judgment, so that no idea is thought to be to be too ridiculous to put forward; and a relatively formal setting.

STAGE 4: CONDUCTING SUBSTANTIVE NEGOTIATIONS

initially considered to be unacceptable later come back into focus as possibilities, perhaps by way of permutation with other ideas.

Building trust and understanding

People in conflict may find it difficult to trust one another, especially where they are or have been in a personal or business relationship that has deteriorated. The mediator can normalise the lack of trust by pointing out that this commonly happens where relationships break down, and can try to help to improve the trust of the parties in one another, where appropriate. The parties now have an opportunity to explore ways of restoring that trust. 9–083

This is not a naive exhortation to "trust one another". It is rather a process of providing the parties with opportunities to demonstrate their sincerity and credibility. This could, for example, take place where possible solutions are tested for short periods before they are applied on a longer-term basis. The mediator can also help the parties to understand one another more clearly by presenting their perceptions in a way that the other can comprehend and by correcting distortions or misunderstandings. Of course, many disputes are resolved pragmatically without trust or understanding; but these factors are helpful in the process of resolving issues consensually. It is also particularly important where the parties are hoping to re-establish working or personal relationships. 9–084

Using communication and other skills[51]

The mediator uses various skills at all stages of the proceedings, but especially during this negotiating phase. These include listening, observing body language, helping parties to hear and understand what others are saying, summarising accurately and appropriately, giving appropriate acknowledgment and where appropriate mutualising concerns and interests. It may where necessary involve reframing what they have said so that it may be better understood in its context. The effective use of questions is also a considerable mediator skill. 9–085

The mediator's skills constitute a critically important ingredient in mediation. While some people may have many of the required attributes and skills to enable them to mediate effectively, mediators invariably need to train in order to make the transition from their occupation of origin to mediator. 9–086

Testing perceptions, positions and proposals

People in dispute may develop their own "view of the world" based on their understanding of the facts and issues. Prospects of success, perceptions of the other party's position and the acceptability of proposals are all assessed on the basis of those views and understandings. 9–087

The mediator may need to "reality test" parties about these matters by checking that parties appreciate their implications and consequences by asking appropriate questions ("What if ?") which compel the party to reflect on the position more carefully, or by making appropriate observations which do not damage the mediator's impartiality. 9–088

---

[51] The skills used by mediators are set out more fully in Ch.14.

9-089 Lawyers, while giving realistic assessments, will generally do so within the context of supporting the client. Lawyers appreciate that their clients wish them to be partisan on their behalf and to champion their cause. This often makes it difficult to express views that contradict the client's views and expectations. Even when told the true position and risk, people do not always accept and act on that advice. It is against this background that mediators may "test reality". The mediator's challenges may not be welcomed, but this may be an essential exercise if the mediator is to have an effective function in helping the parties to move towards a realistic settlement.

9-090 The mediator of course brings a subjective element into this process of reality-testing.[52] What one person considers reasonable and proper another may believe to be unreasonable and improper. Consequently, this exercise must be undertaken with sensitivity and judgement.

Sensitivity to the expression of emotions

9-091 People in conflict will often have strong feelings about the position. They may be distressed, angry, frustrated, apprehensive or disappointed, or they may experience other emotions, without even necessarily being consciously aware of them. Mediators need to be sensitive to these feelings and to be able to respond appropriately without crossing the boundary into counselling or therapy. They can recognise and acknowledge the feelings and help a party nevertheless to deal with the substantive issues in the mediation.

9-092 This can be necessary. Submerged anger can sabotage attempts to reach an agreed resolution, as the anger manifests itself in a disguised form, such as destructive comments or an unwillingness to co-operate with the other party or the process. Other emotions may block progress towards resolution in the short term, apart from any adverse long-term implications.

9-093 The mediator can maintain a balance, providing a safe environment for emotions to surface and accepting the normalcy of that, but ensuring that it does not destabilise the process. The mediator will generally try to bring the parties back to the task of dispute resolution as quickly and gently as practicable. Mediation is not a counselling or therapy process (though it can in some cases, especially inter-personal, have a therapeutic effect).

Evaluation

9-094 In some models of mediation, a mediator may, in addition to the usual facilitative role, also adopt an element of evaluation of the issues, or may be required to assist in the formulation and development of settlement terms. This is dealt with in Ch.19.

---

[52] Reality-testing, even by asking questions, constitutes a form of evaluation: see Ch.19.

STAGE 5: DEALING WITH IMPASSE

Mediation procedures provide a framework within which the parties can generate momentum towards resolution. An impasse arises when negotiations grind to a halt, momentum stops and the mediation seems set to terminate. In this event, some strategies may help the parties back into negotiation. Although this may occur at any stage of the process, it will be treated here for convenience as a separate stage of mediation.

9–095

An impasse strategy is not something that aims to settle all issues but rather a course of action that helps to get parties back into negotiation. These will be considered more specifically in relation to different fields of activity. Meanwhile the following are some generic strategies that can be applied to all kinds of mediation:

9–096

First, it can help to consider the cause of the impasse, which may arise from any one or a combination of the following factors:

9–097

- the mediator's role and assumptions: this will be further considered below;
- an external cause over which the parties have no direct control—in which case pragmatic alternatives and perhaps short-term by-passes may need to be explored;
- a transactional issue, in which proposed terms are unacceptable because they do not meet the needs of the parties—needing creative strategies to explore alternative terms;
- an internal cause arising from emotional issues, differing values or a sense of unfairness—needing a sensitive approach to address this underlying cause.

The following strategies may be appropriate in all kinds of mediation:

The mediator's role and assumptions

The mediator may be perpetuating the problem by perhaps being stuck in one approach or by unwittingly supporting one party or position. Self-reflection might reveal that the mediator is unconsciously following a line that is not acceptable, and from which everyone including the mediator should be stepping back. Or the mediator may unconsciously be making inappropriate assumptions or may be triangulated with one of the parties causing a block in the dynamic of constructive facilitation.

9–098

Bringing this into the mediator's awareness and taking some deliberate step to redress the position can change the dynamic and help the process to shift forward again.

Blocks caused by terminology or symbolism

Where the impasse arises because of terminology or a symbol, it can help to remove the focus from the words or symbols in question, and to examine the underlying needs and concerns giving rise to the impasse.

9–099

9–100 This is sometimes called the "ginger jar factor" arising from a case in which a complex divorce settlement broke down over the question of who would get a ginger jar, which was a gift from someone who, the other party felt, would not have approved of the behaviour of the person now claiming it. The jar represented symbolically who was right and who was wrong, and also symbolised the ending of the relationship. To resolve this, a creative and symbolic solution was needed, involving both parties giving the jar to a child of the family.

9–101 This symbolic aspect can arise in all kinds of situations, not just family. An example arose in relation to claims brought against the Alder Hey Children's Hospital, in which the organs of hundreds of children and non-viable babies were retained following post-mortems without the knowledge or consent of the next-of-kin. Some 1,200 claimants brought litigation against the hospital, and the dispute was dealt with, and resolved, by way of mediation. Ian Cohen, lead solicitor for the claimant legal team, subsequently wrote:

> "It is quite clear that, had the defendants only offered a financial remedy, the litigation would not have concluded. The offer of seven non-financial remedies, including a press conference, letters of apology and a plaque being erected at the hospital, were without question the key to the parents accepting the offer of settlement."[53]

9–102 Parties may adopt strong positions about something which does not appear to have any significant economic value or other importance, causing an impasse. To overcome impasses based on symbols it may be necessary to identify the issues underlying the symbolism. Sometimes creative solutions can then be found with the benefit of these insights.

Differences of perception: fairness, values and other aspects

9–103 Where there are differences of view about fairness, it can help to explore what this means to each party. What aspect of the proposals is not fair? What needs to happen to make it fair? Exploring different perceptions of fairness may not be conclusive, but it allows each side to obtain a better understanding of the other's sense of fairness, and to confront one notion of fairness with another equally strongly held one.

9–104 Perceptions can also differ in other respects, such as with regard to motives, values and aspirations. The mediator can help parties by identifying and normalising differences of perception, explaining that they are quite common and refusing to be drawn into accepting either side's views. Rather, the mediator can seek ways of clarifying the factual position and reframing the differences.[54]

---

[53] Ian Cohen, "Apology accepted" *The Lawyer*, 7 April 2003.
[54] For reframing, see Ch.14.

STAGE 5: DEALING WITH IMPASSE

Emotional blocks

An impasse may arise because of strong emotions. It is not only family or other inter-personal disputes that give rise to strongly felt emotions. Contrary to a popular perception, there is often a high degree of emotional intensity in civil and commercial disputes.[55]

9–105

In such event, the mediator may need to allow the emotional issues to surface, rather than allowing them to fester, even if they cannot be resolved.[56] In appropriate circumstances the mediator may wish to discuss with the parties the possibility of their seeking other professional help such as counselling, especially where the emotional blocks run deep.

9–106

Where the representatives of corporate parties cannot move forward because of their emotional involvement with the issues, the mediator may consider suggesting that different people take over or augment the party's representation. This may, however, not always be possible or appropriate; and in any event would need to be handled with tact and discretion.

9–107

Conflicting legal or technical advice

In most models, the mediator would not express a view on the respective merits when faced with parties who are deadlocked because they have received conflicting advice from their respective lawyers or technical advisers. The mediator can, however, reality-test with each, being careful not to impose his or her views indirectly through the form of questioning. It can also help to have the lawyers outline their positions to one another and to the parties and mediator at a meeting, not necessarily to persuade the other, but to allow a forum for each to hear the other's argument, and maybe to realise that there are sustainable arguments on both sides. The risk of a court accepting the other's case can be made more manifest.

9–108

Where the deadlocked issue is capable of some form of third-party adjudication, one option may be for the parties to refer it to an appropriate third party for a non-binding opinion while the mediation is pending. Where the sticking point is a legal one, the mediator could, for example, assist the parties to formulate an agreed form of instructions to solicitors or counsel, whose opinion would be helpful but not binding. That opinion could then be brought into the mediation as a discussion document to help move matters forward.[57]

9–109

---

[55] Roger Fisher, co-author of the classic *Getting to Yes*, and Daniel Shapiro have written a helpful book addressing the effect of emotions on negotiations—*Building Agreement: Using Emotions as You Negotiate* (London: Random House Business Books, 2007).

[56] Christopher Moore refers to a Circle of Conflict, with value, relationship and data conflicts including strong emotions and misperceptions that need to be addressed before people can engage in effective negotiations about interests. Christopher Moore, *The Mediation Process: Practical Strategies for Resolving Conflict*, 4th edn (San Francisco: Jossey-Bass, 2014).

[57] Such an opinion would have to be sensitively drafted with an awareness that it will be used in a negotiating process.

Helping parties to assess risk

9–110 Some mediators tend to encourage parties in rather general terms to consider the risks of proceeding to trial, drawing attention to the uncertainties of doing so. While this may be a sensible reminder, it is questionable whether this is likely to have any significant impact and it certainly does not amount to effective reality testing or risk assessment.

9–111 Where parties are deadlocked, it can be more helpful to assist them to undertake a risk analysis, particularly if this can be done on a considered and systematic basis. This does not involve the mediator evaluating the outcome—though in some models it might—but rather providing a framework for the parties to make their own assessments and helping them to identify the factors that they might usefully consider.

9–112 There are different ways of doing this, including providing a formal risk analysis framework, or more informally drawing their attention to their BATNA (Best Alternative to a Negotiated Agreement) and WATNA (Worst Alternative to a Negotiated Agreement). These strategies will be more fully considered in reviewing practice in each field of activity.[58]

Other strategies

9–113 The impasse strategies outlined above are by no means comprehensive, but are merely examples of the kinds of strategies that a mediator might wish to consider. Many other options exist, some of which will be further considered in examining specific fields of activity. These may include the obvious options of splitting the difference, deferring stuck issues while tackling others or taking time out.[59]

9–114 Sometimes there is no easy answer for the parties, and they are faced with a stark choice either to settle or to litigate. "Just do it!" may be the watchword from their advisers.

9–115 Deciding to terminate the mediation because impasse cannot be resolved and offering to explore whether mediation can help narrow the issues in litigation may serve as an impasse strategy itself and a stimulus to finding a way to resolve the impasse. Parties should however not regard it as a failure if they need a third-party decision: that is an ultimate remedy that may be appropriate where people cannot agree on the proper outcome themselves.

STAGE 6: CONCLUDING MEDIATION AND RECORDING THE OUTCOME

9–116 Mediation may terminate in a number of circumstances. All the issues may have been resolved or the parties may have resolved some issues and decided to take the others into a different forum such as arbitration or litigation; or may resolve

---

[58] See Ch.4 and the references to BATNA and WATNA: (best and worst alternatives) in the section "An interest-based problem-solving approach".

[59] See for example John Wade's 16 options for overcoming deadlock in his chapter "Crossing the Last Gap" in Andrea Kupfer Schneider and Christopher Honeyman, *The Negotiator's Fieldbook: The Desk Reference for the Experienced Negotiator* (Washington DC: American Bar Association, 2006).

the remaining issues themselves or through lawyers. Alternatively, the mediator may decide that it is inappropriate to continue with the mediation because there is no reasonable prospect of resolution or because the relevant Code of Conduct requires this.

Where settlement terms have been agreed, procedures vary in different fields of activity and models. In civil-commercial mediation, the parties would usually sign a binding agreement before concluding the session. In the family field, the proposed terms may be non-binding pending the parties obtaining legal advice and the respective lawyers preparing the final form of agreement or court order. In such cases, it is common for the mediator to prepare a non-binding and off-the-record summary of the proposals that would be acceptable to both parties, commonly in the form of a Memorandum of Understanding.   9–117

Where the mediation ends without settlement terms being agreed, there are no specific formalities. Some mediators conscientiously persevere in assisting the parties to reach agreement despite the imminence of ending the process, for example by suggesting concluding communications or strategies, which are dealt with in the chapters about different fields of activity. Others bring the process to an immediate end.   9–118

ADDRESSING POST-MEDIATION ISSUES

In most cases, the termination of the mediation and the recording of the settlement terms will signal the end of the mediator's role. However, it is possible for the mediator, or the ADR organisation that arranged the mediation, to have a post-mediation function, for example: 9–119

- *Stakeholder:* The parties may wish the mediator or the ADR organisation to act as a stakeholder in relation to funds to be released on agreed terms (though this is rare), or to hold documents in escrow pending the implementation of the settlement.
- *Continuing mediator:* The parties may agree that if any issues should arise in the course of executing their settlement obligations, these will be referred to mediation for further discussion. Or where there is a continuing relationship between the parties (whether working or personal, as in parenting), the parties may agree that if any new problems arise in the future, they will revert to mediation.
- *Adjudicator:* The parties may appoint the mediator to act as an arbitrator, expert or adjudicator in relation to any issues that may in the future arise in relation to the fulfilment of the settlement terms. This should be distinguished from med-arb, where all the initial issues are dealt with by arbitration if mediation does not resolve them. In this case, the initial issues are resolved in the mediation, but any new aspects of the agreed terms may be dealt with by informal adjudication.
- *Settlement supervisor:* Although in practice this is unusual, the parties may wish the mediator to supervise the implementation of the settlement terms.

MULTI-PARTY DISPUTES

9–120　Any early concerns about mediating multi-party disputes have been wholly dispelled by the success achieved with them in practice in a variety of fields including especially the construction industry. David Richbell, who has mediated a large number of multi-party cases, has written about his experience and way of working with them, and concludes that, although they are very demanding "most do settle".[60] There are many other examples: in one case, claims of mismanagement of an investment portfolio of a pension scheme were mediated. The respondents included the pension trustees, company directors, legal advisors, bankers, investment advisors and insurance underwriters. All were represented in the mediation, in a complex negotiation involving seven different parties, resulting in an agreed settlement.

9–121　Randall W. Wulff writes of having taken part as a mediator or as an advocate in many multi-party disputes, one involving 28 parties and their respective counsel, and another necessitating the hire of a hotel banquet room and suites to accommodate some 60 participating client representatives and witnesses.[61] Gerald S. Clay writes from his personal experience that neither the degree of complexity of a case nor a multiplicity of parties are any hindrance to mediation.[62]

9–122　Public law disputes and environmental issues generally involve multiple parties, and mediation is used for dealing with many of these.[63] Professor Lawrence Susskind considers that:

> "the mediation of multi-party, multi-issue disputes at the local level, such as battles over the design and location of public facilities, the setting of policy priorities (like how to spend public funds), and the specification of health and safety standards (like acceptable levels of risk) can be particularly effective."[64]

Some practical points for multi-party mediation

9–123　The following practical suggestions are based on the experience of multi-party mediation in the civil-commercial field in the UK:

- Multi-party mediation requires significantly more planning than two-party mediation. There is a consensus among practitioners who undertake

---

[60] Chris Newmark and Anthony Monaghan, *Butterworth's Mediators on Mediation: Leading Mediator Perspectives on the Practice of Commercial Mediation* (Haywards Heath: Bloomsbury Professional (formerly Tottel Publishing), 2005), Ch.13 (Mediating multi-party disputes).

[61] See Randall W. Wulff, "A Mediation Primer" in J. H. Wilkinson, *Donovan Leisure Newton and Irvine ADR Practice Book* (New York: Wiley Law Publications, 1990), p.114.

[62] Wilkinson, *Donovan Leisure Newton and Irvine ADR Practice Book*, 1990, Ch.9 (Counselling clients on mediation).

[63] See, e.g. S. Murray, A. S. Rau and E. F. Sherman, *Processes of Dispute Resolution: The Role of Lawyers* (New York: Foundation Press, 1989), pp.329–336 (Public law disputes).

[64] Professor Lawrence Susskind, "Multi-Party Public Policy Mediation: A Separate Breed" (Fall 1997) *Dispute Resolution Magazine* (ABA Section of Dispute Resolution).

- multi-party work that preparation is key, and that time needs to be spent with the parties in designing a suitable process.[65]
- It is helpful and in some cases essential to have a preliminary meeting with the parties and their lawyers.[66] In addition, separate meetings with each may also be useful. These allow the mediator to obtain information about each party's position, and to start building rapport. It also helps to identify parties whose interests may coincide and who may decide to join one another for the purpose of mediation discussions.
- Co-mediation is commonly indicated for multi-party disputes. If a sole mediator is initially appointed, these preliminary exchanges allow the mediator to assess whether a co-mediator is needed.
- The simultaneous exchange of written statements by the parties can be difficult to arrange and implement. It may be advisable to have them all sent (with copies if required) to the mediator, who can dispatch them simultaneously to the parties when all are received.
- Parties can be asked to send draft statements to the mediator on a confidential and interim basis, in advance of their final versions. This can be especially helpful where time constraints exist. This allows the mediator to consider the position and if appropriate to seek clarification or particularisation.
- The time between separate meetings is invariably longer in multi-party disputes. If this is explained to parties in advance, they will be more prepared for the delays between separate meetings and less likely to be troubled by them. The mediator may suggest that they bring work files, reading matter or anything else to occupy themselves between meetings. Richbell refers to this "idle time" and suggests that the parties' lawyers have responsibility for keeping everyone in their team engaged and active, preferably with useful activities such as risk analysis, brainstorming and considering possible solutions.[67]
- The opening oral presentations will be important to each party, and sufficient time needs to be allowed for them; but to avoid these taking too long, time limits should be agreed, appropriate to the complexity of the issues. The sequence of presentations also needs to be considered, and where practicable, agreed.
- The joint meeting may continue for as long as the mediators consider this to be helpful. Richbell finds these valuable and points out that it is also an efficient use of time, since everyone is engaged. This is an opportunity to seek common ground insofar as it may exist and to identify and prioritise areas of disagreement.

---

[65] See Lax and Sebenius fn.2, in which they emphasise the need to set matters up properly in all negotiation situations, and this applies especially in multi-party disputes. This includes ensuring that the right people are brought to the table and the process thoughtfully designed. Michael T. Lesnick and John R. Ehrmann in their article "Selected Strategies for Managing Multiparty Disputes" (1987) 16 *Mediation Quarterly* suggest a number of strategies for dealing with multi-party disputes, including designing the process structure, establishing an agenda and in suitable cases establishing an advisory committee to address preliminary issues.
[66] See "Preliminary meeting" above.
[67] See fn.60.

- Once separate meetings are set up, co-mediators must decide whether they should conduct their meetings together or split up. If time permits, they may wish to be together for the initial meeting in the mediation with each party, but then separate for subsequent meetings.
- The mediator needs to have a separate room as a base for managing the discussions. This is particularly important for co-mediators, who may also wish to have a flip chart for keeping a record of their meetings as well as the issues and possible solutions as they develop. This can also help to tell one where the other is at any time.
- If long delays between meetings are expected once the process is under way, the mediator may wish to release parties from waiting, by agreeing a time to return or being available on short notice. Some mediators prepare outline timetable schedules so that parties or their lawyers can actually leave the meeting and return when needed, with flexibility: mobile phones can be useful here.
- Mediators will be alert to possible changes during the process, as parties identify their interests and may find alliances with others. In some cases, this may involve physically moving groups together with one another, either generally or for specific discussions.
- Personal meetings can be supplemented by telephone or Skype discussions with parties who are unable to attend in person or who are not immediately available.

9–124 Wilkinson suggests that the key to using ADR in disputes involving multiple parties is to get the process going with those who are willing to participate, and others may join in later. Even if they do not, those parties participating in the ADR process may be able to arrive at resolutions helpful to their mutual interests.[68] While this view has been shown to be workable in practice, it does call for some note of caution in that a mediation or other ADR process which proceeds without all the essential parties being involved runs the risk of being abortive. If the missing parties are not crucial to the outcome or if the participating parties can identify areas in which limited agreement would be helpful to them, then there is no reason why the process should not proceed without full participation.

9–125 One strategy for complex and prolonged multi-party disputes might be for the mediators from time to time to prepare interim summaries of the position as it develops, which clarify the extent of agreement reached and the range of issues still outstanding. This would, of course, need to have careful regard to such duty of confidentiality as may exist in relation to the respective parties. The agenda can be reviewed from time to time in the light of any such interim summaries and reports.

9–126 If agreement is reached, all parties will need to review and comment on any draft document and to execute it when it is in its final approved form. In some cases, separate agreements between different parties may be required, rather than one document embodying all settlement terms. Procedures for obtaining court

---

[68] J.H. Wilkinson, *Donovan Leisure Newton and Irvine ADR Practice Book* (John Wiley & Sons, 1990) pp.22–23.

OUTLINE OF DIFFERENT FIELDS OF MEDIATION ACTIVITY

orders where necessary, for implementing the agreement and for dealing with any residual issues should they arise may also need to be considered.

OUTLINE OF DIFFERENT FIELDS OF MEDIATION ACTIVITY

Mediation can take place in any environment, whether between sovereign states or in the school playground. This book will however be limited to the use of mediation in relation to disputes arising in the following fields of activity: **9–127**

- civil and commercial;
- family issues particularly couples issues arising on separation and divorce;
- workplace and employment;
- neighbourhood, community mediation and Restorative Justice;
- online dispute resolution (issues arising from, or addressed via, Web usage).

Each field has its own culture and practice in dealing with disputes in the traditional way and these differences have at least to some extent been imported into mediation practice, though general mediation principles will overlap all fields of activity. **9–128**

CHAPTER 10

Civil and Commercial Mediation

WHAT IS COVERED IN THE FIELD OF CIVIL AND COMMERCIAL MEDIATION?

Distinguishing different fields of activity is necessary and useful for a number of reasons. In each sphere there are different cultures, laws, procedures, expectations and judicial approaches, so it is not surprising that mediation processes, models and approaches should differ, albeit that there may be some increasing cross-over. As a consequence, training programmes similarly vary between the fields of activity.[1] Most mediation organisations make these distinctions, with practitioners in each field joining organisations specific to their areas of work. Similarly, court directions and practice, European directives and statutory and quasi-statutory provisions differentiate, for example between civil-commercial and family mediation. 10–001

With some qualifications, the category of civil and commercial mediation relates to all kinds of disputes that might be dealt with in the civil and commercial courts. The qualifications concern areas of overlap with other fields of mediation activity. So, while this kind of mediation would ordinarily exclude couples' issues on separation and divorce, other kinds of family disputes could come within the ambit of civil and commercial mediation, including for example, family business disputes, property or other civil disputes between siblings or between parent and child, or contentious issues concerning the administration of trusts involving family members. 10–002

Another potential overlap relates to some community or neighbour disputes which are capable of being litigated in the civil courts. Similarly, workplace disputes fall into their own category, but some may overlap and be regarded as civil-commercial. There is no strict demarcation, nor a need for one. 10–003

A very wide range of cases fall into the civil and commercial field. They include all kinds of issues arising under contract or tort. It is impossible to list these comprehensively, but they would cover all contractual and general business and property disputes, claims for negligence and breach of duty and personal injury cases, partnership disagreements, shareholder and other company disputes and claims for maladministration of estates or trusts. Specialist areas such as libel, intellectual property and passing off, disputes in the construction industry, 10–004

---

[1] There are generic training courses, but people undertaking them may also undertake follow-up specialist training in particular areas of work.

shipping and aviation disputes, commodity disputes, banking, insurance and other financial disputes, computer software and other information technology disputes would all be included.

DEVELOPMENT OF CIVIL-COMMERCIAL MEDIATION IN THE UK

Private sector civil-commercial mediation bodies

10–005 Two organisations, the ADR Group and CEDR (the Centre for Effective Dispute Resolution), effectively led the way for civil and commercial mediation in the UK around the late 1980s. Both followed a similar model, adapted from US practice, in which broadly speaking a block of time is fixed for the process, commonly a day, but more or less as needed, at which each party outlines their case in a joint session, followed by a series of separate, confidential meetings undertaken by the mediator "shuttling" between the parties in separate rooms, carrying thoughts, ideas and proposals and endeavouring to craft an acceptable resolution, with other permutations of meetings as required.

10–006 A number of other organisations have also joined the field of mediation provision, including the Academy of Experts; the Chartered Institute of Arbitrators, which extended its activities from arbitration and adjudication to include mediation; ADR Chambers; ADR-ODR International; and the RICS (The Royal Institution of Chartered Surveyors). In addition, mediation groups and panels of mediators were established, including Independent Mediators; In Place of Strife; PIM Senior Mediators (originally the Panel of Independent Mediators); Clerksroom (mediation chambers); and Core Solutions in Scotland. Mediation panels were also set up by the London Court of International Arbitration, London Maritime Arbitrators' Association, the MMTA (Minor Metals Trade Association) and others.

10–007 The Law Society of England and Wales has established a specialist panel of civil and commercial mediators and the Bar Council has an ADR Committee to guide and assist barrister mediators. A number of law firms and barristers' chambers have set up specialist mediation sections and some practitioners from different backgrounds have established mediation practices and groups.

10–008 Regional groupings include the Association of Midlands Mediators, the Association of Northern Mediators, the Association of Cambridge Mediators, the Association of South West Mediators, Middlesex & Thames Valley Mediators, Oxford Mediation, and Solent and Wessex Civil Mediation.

Low cost and publicly funded mediation

10–009 Unlike the family and community fields, where some mediation organisations concentrate on the public sector and others on the private sector (though not exclusively in either case), there are no civil and commercial mediation bodies that focus primarily on publicly funded or low cost services, although the pro bono lawyers' group, LawWorks, supported by the Law Society, has in the past had a mediation arm offering this service on a pro bono basis.[2]

However, there are a number of options for low cost and publicly funded civil mediation, which include the following:

10–010

- Initially a National Mediation Helpline was established for civil court users, with a sliding scale of low cost services and referral to LawWorks where appropriate. This was replaced by a website[3] which offers advice about mediation and links to a panel of approved mediators.
- Following a successful pilot scheme, HMCTS provides a Small Claims Mediation Service on a free and confidential basis for court users who are involved in defended small claims cases. This process is usually carried out by telephone, though where necessary, face-to-face meetings can be arranged. Mediation appointments generally occupy about an hour in total. Anecdotally, it appears that demand from parties who wish to use the small claims mediation service regularly outstrips supply. There has been some criticism of the number of small claims mediators who have been available in recent years as well as a suggestion that the system of arranging appointments is somewhat inflexible.[4]
- Some mediation organisations offer low cost options. For example, CEDR Solve has a Personal Injury Unit that covers not only substantial cases, but also time-limited lower cost mediations for lower value cases and telephone mediation where a full mediation may not be necessary or justifiable. It also offers a process called eValuate, which is a paper neutral evaluation service helping the parties towards finding a solution.
- While public funding (legal aid) is available for family mediation, civil mediation may be funded as a disbursement under certain forms of public funding, namely Legal Help, Legal Representation or Support Funding.[5]
- Private sector mediation organisations and individual mediators may be willing to provide low-cost or pro bono services by special arrangement.

Specialist civil and commercial mediators

Within the field of civil and commercial mediation, there are a number of specialist sectors, including for example clinical negligence and personal injury; the construction industry; banking; the insurance industry; shipping and aviation; property law; intellectual property; information technology; and indeed, in all the fields of law in which lawyers may specialise. Some mediators are seen and wish to be seen as being specialists in particular areas.

10–011

The question arises as to the relevance or otherwise of a mediator having substantive specialist expertise in the subject matter of the dispute. The conventional answer is that it is more important for the mediator to be skilled in

10–012

---

[2] See the LawWorks website at *http://www.lawworks.org.uk/* [accessed 16 May 2018].
[3] See: *http://civilmediation.justice.gov.uk/* which provides a link to mediation services.
[4] Lord Justice Briggs, Civil Courts Structure Review: Final Report, July 2016 paras 2.14 and 2.15, available at: *https://www.judiciary.gov.uk/wp-content/uploads/2016/07/civil-courts-structure-review-final-report-jul-16-final-1.pdf* [accessed 16 May 2018].
[5] Eligibility for legal aid can be checked online at *https://www.gov.uk/civil-legal-advice* [accessed 16 May 2018].

the mediation process than to be knowledgeable about the substance of the dispute. That distinction is otiose where parties should be able to have both: a skilled mediator who also has substantive knowledge of the issues in dispute.

10–013 In practice, although there are excellent generalist mediators who are well able to undertake specialist cases, and although many people will instruct a well-regarded and trusted generalist mediator for a specialist dispute, there does seem to be a tendency for parties to appoint mediators with expertise in the subject-matter of the dispute. So in a construction dispute, parties might prefer a mediator who is a lawyer with construction law expertise, or an engineer or surveyor; and in a dispute involving complex accounting, they might prefer an accountant or business-based mediator. There are a number of reasons for this. First, there is a sense that the mediator will understand the issues and the parties' needs without requiring a lengthy explanation. Secondly, experts carry some implicit authority, and many people prefer a mediator who has the authority to help move everyone towards a resolution. Thirdly, there is a perception that a specialist mediator will be better able to ask the right questions and to "test reality" effectively. Fourthly, insofar as there may be some spectrum of evaluation, and insofar as a mediator may find it helpful and appropriate to challenge stuck perceptions, a mediator with substance expertise may be preferred to a generalist. On the other hand, some parties may want a fresh and creative view from someone unconnected with their industry; and in many cases, the issues do not necessarily turn on the specialist topic.

The Civil Mediation Council

10–014 Over the years, the Civil Mediation Council (CMC), which was established in 2003, has become an increasingly accepted umbrella body for civil, commercial and workplace mediation in the UK. Its objectives include primarily the promotion and a wider understanding and use of mediation, acting as a voice for civil, commercial and workplace mediators, and encouraging good practice in the interests of mediators and users. In this last mentioned role, it accredits mediation providers who satisfy them as to their standards of practice. It has from the outset accredited mediation providers. It has recently begun to publish a register of individual mediators and mediation training bodies. It is a matter of some controversy as to whether this is properly to be regarded as regulation of the profession or not.

The membership of the CMC comprises both individuals and mediation organisations, both of whom are represented on its Board.

LAWYERS AND RIGHTS IN CIVIL AND COMMERCIAL MEDIATION

10–015 It is widely accepted that rights significantly influence parties in civil and commercial mediation. This is because they mediate "in the shadow of the law",[6] in the sense that they could rely on their respective rights if they chose to resolve

---

[6] A concept based on Robert Mnookin and Lewis Kornhauser, "Bargaining in the Shadow of the Law, The Case of Divorce" (1979) 88 Y.L.J. 950.

the matter in court or any other adjudicatory forum. Having said this, there are costs and risks in litigating, and many factors apart from rights, such as continuing relationships, may influence the parties in seeking a solution. This is, after all, why they choose the mediation forum. They will have regard to rights and to the possible outcomes of potential or actual litigation, but not necessarily as an exclusive consideration.

10–016
The significance attached to legal rights is at least in part reflected by the extent to which parties tend to be represented by their lawyers in civil and commercial mediation. The majority of mediations undertaken through mediation organisations take place with legal representatives in attendance.

10–017
Commercial and civil mediations may be conducted without lawyers attending, though they may have advised parties outside the process. This is especially the case with disputes having a personal element such as inheritance and partnership disputes. It is also the case in small claims disputes and those where it is uneconomic for a lawyer to attend—though in all these cases parties are still likely to have regard to their legal rights, as they perceive them.

10–018
Mediators tend to be drawn from a wide range of background disciplines. This reflects the fact that law does not dominate civil and commercial mediation. Not surprisingly, solicitors and barristers almost certainly constitute the largest group based on background disciplines. The Law Society has recognised the part that solicitors play in dispute resolution generally and mediation in particular, and has developed a Code of Practice and training standards for solicitors who undertake civil and commercial mediation.[7]

10–019
A distinction exists between mediation that is purely facilitative and mediation that may contain an element of evaluation of the respective rights of the parties. Some civil and commercial mediators, in common with their colleagues from other fields, will only mediate on a facilitative basis. They will decline to offer any element of evaluation. Others may be willing, if appropriate, to introduce some element of non-binding evaluation if the facilitative approach proves to be insufficient.[8]

THE STAGES OF CIVIL AND COMMERCIAL MEDIATION

10–020
The stages set out below follow the outline contained in Ch.9. It must be emphasised that these are not intended to provide a rigid structure, but rather a notional framework to facilitate consideration of the process. Within this broad framework, there may be considerable flexibility and huge variations of practice.

10–021
As stated in Ch.9, the pre-mediation and post-mediation stages do not take place within the mediation process but outside it. They are nevertheless included here as they form an important part of understanding and providing a context for the process.

---

[7] The Solicitors Regulation Authority (SRA) regulates solicitors in all aspects of their practices, including mediation. Solicitor mediators must comply with the Code and regulations of any mediation organisation to which they belong, but this does not avoid the necessity for them also to comply with SRA and Law Society requirements.

[8] See Ch.19 for discussion about evaluative mediation.

PRE-MEDIATION: CONSIDERING MEDIATION, ASSESSING SUITABILITY AND OBTAINING COMMITMENT

10–022 The impetus for considering the use of civil or commercial mediation may come from a number of different sources, including:

- lawyers representing clients in dispute may be considering the process and may or may not have agreed with the other party that mediation is the best way forward;
- individuals or corporations in dispute may be considering mediation as a suitable way to deal with their issues.
- the court may adjourn a pending case so that the parties may try to mediate the issues, or there may be court rules, directions or procedures requiring this to be done or sanctions for failing to do so;
- pre-action protocols consistently require due consideration to be given to the use of mediation or other ADR processes;
- parties may have given a commitment to consider ADR or may have entered into a contract containing a dispute resolution clause providing for mediation as a part of the resolution procedure;
- some industries and trade associations have dispute resolution mechanisms that include mediation.

Mediators need to be able to provide information about the mediation process and about their own services and qualifications, and to respond appropriately to enquiries arising from these sources and any others.

The following may help to amplify these considerations:

Raising public and professional awareness

10–023 Commercial ADR organisations have been active in raising public awareness of the availability, practice and potential value of using ADR for civil and commercial disputes. The CMC has also been instrumental in engaging government in discussions about promoting the use and development of mediation; and government itself is supportive of the process.

Individual mediators have written articles, given talks and promoted mediation, and some have established effective groups and websites that explain and promote mediation.

10–024 Both the Law Society of England and Wales and the Bar Council have incorporated mediation into their structures, and few solicitors or barristers can legitimately claim not to be aware of the availability and benefits of the mediation process, especially as there have been many cases in which the use of mediation and other ADR mechanisms has been referred to with approval, as well as others imposing potential costs sanctions for a failure to consider the use of ADR where it is appropriate.[9]

---

[9] For a review of relevant case law on cost sanctions, see Ch.5.

ADR pledges and contract clauses

It is sensible and pragmatic for people entering into commercial relationships to address the question of how they will address disagreements should these arise. Among other things, this means that disputes may be "nipped in the bud" before they turn into full-blown cases taken through the courts or some other adjudicatory mechanism.

10–025

It also means that neither party may be perceived as suggesting mediation or some other ADR process out of weakness. This used to be a concern in the earlier stages of mediation development, but this has become much less the case as the mediation process has become more widespread, supported and expected by the courts, and generally accepted. Referring to ADR processes, a Ministry of Justice Consultation Paper says that:

10–026

> "of all these processes, mediation and arbitration are most common and are well established and sit parallel to the legal and judicial framework in England and Wales."[10]

Nevertheless, having a prescribed and pre-agreed process does help provide the route to a negotiated outcome.

The concept of making a pledge to consider and use ADR was developed by the US institute CPR (The International Institute for Conflict Prevention and Resolution, originally the Center for Public Resources) which has a number of different pledges: a Corporate Pledge to explore the use of ADR for business disputes, a Law Firm Pledge to ensure that members of the firm are knowledgeable about ADR and to discuss its use, and Industry Specific Pledges. This has been extended worldwide, in conjunction with ADR organisations in other countries, including CEDR in the UK.[11]

10–027

In the UK, the then Lord Chancellor, Lord Irvine in 2001 committed government departments and agencies to using ADR processes in suitable cases whenever the other side to litigation agreed to it.[12]

10–028

Dispute resolution clauses in contracts may take various forms. They may for example provide for mediation, or for arbitration, or for mediation to be followed by arbitration if the dispute is not settled in the mediation phase. They may provide for a specified organisation to appoint the mediator or arbitrator in the event that the parties are unable to agree on one.[13]

10–029

There is a question as to whether an agreement to mediate would be upheld by the court. In the past, agreements to negotiate have not generally been regarded as enforceable; but there has been a line of cases on this subject providing guidance as to the criteria for the enforceability of ADR clauses in contracts.[14]

10–030

---

[10] Ministry of Justice, Consultation Paper CP6/2011, *Solving disputes in the county courts: creating a simpler, quicker and more proportionate system—A consultation on reforming civil justice in England and Wales* (MoJ, March 2011), Cm.8045.
[11] See *https://www.cpradr.org/resource-center/adr-pledges* [accessed 16 May 2018].
[12] In a speech at the CMC conference in May 2011, the Minister of Justice, Jonathan Djanogly, said that since the inception of the government's ADR Pledge, the state had saved an estimated £360 million, and that he wanted to extend the benefits beyond central government to businesses and local government.
[13] See "Contract clause stipulating for ADR" in Ch.21, paras 21-007 to 21-019.
[14] See Ch.21, paras 21-025 to 21-038.

Judicial encouragement and orders

10–031 Over the years judges have encouraged parties to mediate or use other ADR procedures. There has also been a line of cases in which the courts have specifically referred to the need to use mediation or other forms of ADR, or have indeed recommended or directed the parties to attempt to do so.[15]

Preliminary meetings

10–032 A preliminary meeting with the mediator may sometimes be a good way to assist parties in deciding whether or not to engage in mediation. The mediator would meet with the parties or their lawyers and might discuss process and ground rules, and any queries can then be dealt with. It also affords the parties or lawyers an opportunity to assess whether or not they wish to appoint that mediator, and for the mediator to assess whether or not the matter is suitable for mediation.

This procedure is partly useful as a step in the pre-mediation process, and may be partly seen as an element of the mediator's marketing. Some lawyers may meet with a number of mediators before deciding whom to appoint.

10–033 This meeting would not yet ordinarily be covered by an Agreement to Mediate, so if substantive matters may be discussed, the confidential and "without prejudice" nature of the meeting should be made clear. This is particularly important if the parties or lawyers decide during the meeting that they wish to go ahead with the mediation, and convert the meeting into an initial discussion about actual process and arrangements. The opportunity can then be used to enter into an Agreement to Mediate, agree a timetable, agenda (if required), arrange for the submission of statements and documents and generally deal with venue, representation and any other practical matters.

Assessing suitability

10–034 While the issue of assessing suitability for mediation may be significant in some other fields such as family, restorative justice and neighbour disputes, it is less likely to be critical in commercial disputes and in most civil cases, on the principle that if it is capable of being discussed, negotiated and settled bilaterally as between the parties or their lawyers, then it is likely to be suitable for mediation.

10–035 However, there may nevertheless be individual circumstances that make a civil or commercial dispute inappropriate for mediation or other ADR processes. This would be more likely to relate to the parties rather than to the subject-matter of the dispute, since most substantive matters can be addressed in mediation. If a party lacks the capacity to negotiate and make decisions, whether through disability, addiction or any other reason that cannot be overcome through having an authorised representative or other support, or if for example it is clear that power imbalances are so great that mediation could not be effectively conducted, then mediation would not be appropriate.

10–036 The opportunities for assessing suitability before mediation commences are limited. A preliminary and minimal assessment would necessarily be done on the

---

[15] See for example Ch.5, paras 5-054 to 5-066.

basis of limited information. If anything obvious suggests itself at that stage, the mediator or case manager dealing with preliminary matters would need to raise further questions as appropriate; but in practice, this issue is more likely to emerge during the substantive process rather than in advance.

Providing information

Preliminary enquiries about mediation may be made through a number of different sources, including an ADR organisation or panel, or directly to the mediator.

10–037

The following is quoted from Henry Brown's paper published by the Chartered Institute of Arbitrators for their 3rd Mediation Symposium 2010[16]:

10–038

> "The civil-commercial model with which we are all familiar is an excellent way of working, and one which we can promote with confidence. However, we should not be satisfied with a 'one size fits all' approach nor should we expect parties and their lawyers to do so. Some people will want a purely facilitative and non-directive mediator, others may want and need a mediator who will help them firmly forward and nudge them (or their opponents) back on course if they are clearly following mistaken paths: this can be done in a way that facilitates their own decision-making and does not press them into any course favoured by the mediator, and hence would be perfectly proper for mediation."

There has not been any way of knowing in advance what approach a mediator takes. The International Mediation Institute (IMI) classifies mediators as "facilitative" or "evaluative" but in view of the range of activities that are perceived to fall within each category, and the extent of misperception as to what each involves, these categorisations, although potentially helpful, do not really add to a proper understanding of an individual approach.[17] Large firms of solicitors with extensive experience of mediation and litigation will have useful records about mediation and mediators' particular styles and approaches.

10–039

Organisations and individual mediators need to be able to provide enquirers with information that helps to clarify the process generally, the individual mediator's qualifications and experience, and where appropriate, the mediator's approach. ADR organisations generally have case managers to deal with enquiries. This may be done on the telephone, by email or by correspondence. They may need to explain how mediation or other ADR forms work, generally or for a specific case, and may assist in putting forward names of suitable mediators for consideration. Where appropriate, and by arrangement with an inquiring party, they may engage the other party or parties to see whether ADR can be agreed upon.

10–040

Mediators approached individually rather than through ADR organisations will similarly need to provide relevant information. There is a potential difficulty, in that a mediator approached by only one party may be perceived as that party's choice, and for this reason, be unacceptable. In this respect, ADR organisations or

10–041

---

[16] Henry Brown, "Creating Confidence in Mediators and the Process: An Exploration of the Issues" (2010) Chartered Institute of Arbitrators Symposium 2010.

[17] For further discussion about the distinctions between facilitative and evaluative mediation, see Ch.19.

mediation consortia have an advantage over individual practitioners, because their neutrality cannot generally be called into question.

10–042 Information may be provided in a number of ways:

- Perhaps the most used resource is the web with increasingly informative websites and links between related topics, people and organisations. ADR organisations typically may have details on their websites of their services, training (where applicable), panels of members, news and articles, specialist aspects, fees, terms and conditions and marketing information. Individual mediators' websites tend to vary between basic information through to highly sophisticated sites incorporating personal information about qualifications, testimonials, experience, articles and writing as well as information about process, relevant law and links.
- In response to individual enquiries, mediators may provide personal biographies, marketing information, details of availability and sometimes a draft Agreement to Mediate.
- Personal communications, on the phone or occasionally face to face, can be very helpful in enabling the mediator to address specific questions and situations rather than doing so on a generalised basis. It is also an initial step in establishing rapport that can be invaluable in the mediation process itself.
- Preliminary meetings, as outlined above, provide an opportunity for both or all parties or their lawyers to meet the mediator, address common questions, discuss and clarify procedures and allow the parties, without commitment, to decide whether they wish to go ahead with the mediation and the appointment of that mediator.

Trade and other associations

10–043 Trade associations with a code of practice that has been approved by the Office of Fair Trading must provide low-cost mediation. These include for example the motor trade, estate agents, debt management companies, car repair and servicing firms, the direct selling industry and home furnishing businesses. Professional associations that specifically provide mediation as a resource for the resolution of disputes include GAFTA (the Grain and Feed Trade Association), MMTA (the Minor Metals Trade Association) and OFGEM (the Office of the Gas and Electricity Markets). These are just examples, and the list of bodies providing for mediation is long and growing.

Agreement to mediate

10–044 Civil or commercial disputes can only be dealt with by way of mediation if the parties agree to use this process, either in general terms at the time that an original contract containing a dispute resolution clause was entered into or in specific terms after a dispute has arisen. All mediation organisations and individual mediators are likely to require this agreement to be explicitly recorded and signed by or on behalf of the parties.

STAGE 1: PRELIMINARY COMMUNICATIONS AND PREPARATION

Where mediation is undertaken as a consequence of court rules or procedures requiring it to be considered or tried, the need for an agreement to mediate remains: the terms and basis of the process need to be agreed and recorded. This may well be different from any form of mandatory court-attached process, which might in such event be regulated by court rules and implicitly or explicitly adopted. **10–045**

Parties may contract to try mediation and if this fails to resolve the dispute, to refer it to arbitration, either retaining as arbitrator the same person who acted as mediator, or appointing someone else. In any event, the right to proceed to adjudication if the mediation is unsuccessful will invariably be reserved, implicitly or explicitly.[18] **10–046**

The parties should agree to the procedural rules that will apply to the mediation. This would cover matters such as legal privilege and keeping discussions off the record, confidentiality, whether a written agreement is needed to create binding obligations, and other such matters. Mediation organisations and individual mediators are likely to have standard terms of agreement embodying these matters. It is good practice for that agreement to be based on the Code of Practice to which the mediator or organisation works, and to incorporate the Code by reference or by attaching it. **10–047**

Almost invariably, the mediator will be a party to the agreement to mediate or will be identified in it.

There are no particular rules as to how or when the agreement should be executed. A common practice is to send a draft to the parties when they are considering mediation, and to inform them that the document will need to be signed before the substantive mediation starts. They may be invited to raise any queries or to propose any amendments in advance of the meeting, so that these can be considered and dealt with. Any proposed amendments would have to be acceptable to the mediator and the other party. Once the terms are agreed in advance, the document can be signed at the start of the mediation meeting. This can be a positive symbolic act to launch the process. However, it is essential to have the terms agreed before meeting so that the proceedings are covered right from the outset, even if the act of signature takes place at the meeting as a symbolic act. **10–048**

STAGE 1: PRELIMINARY COMMUNICATIONS AND PREPARATION

Preliminary communications or meeting

Having engaged the parties in the mediation forum and agreed on the contract to mediate and the ground-rules, a number of preliminary communications may be necessary before the substantive mediation commences. **10–049**

---

[18] For a discussion about med-arb, see Ch.19. For a consideration of the implications of mediation on the right to a fair trial, for example under art.6 of the European Convention on Human Rights, see Ch.5 under the heading "Mandatory ADR and human rights: the Article 6 argument" at paras 5-072 to 5-076.

10–050 If the dispute is particularly complex or substantial, the mediator may wish to have a preliminary meeting with the parties, or more likely with their legal representatives, to discuss a framework for the process and the furnishing of information.[19] These are distinct from "beauty parade" meetings, which may be held before the parties have even agreed to the use of mediation and certainly before they decide who to use as a mediator. At that preliminary meeting, a timetable can be agreed for the furnishing of documents and information, and in effect, "directions" for the mediation can be agreed. These may for example providing bundles of documents, who will attend the mediation, the nature of authority they will have, and whether each party will make an oral presentation and if so for how long and on what basis. This is a good opportunity to discuss and clarify the ground-rules, including principles of confidentiality and privilege. The parties may wish to discuss the extent to which the mediator may be evaluative, and whether and how rights arguments will be addressed.

10–051 There may also be ways in which preparation for the substantive meeting can be enhanced, for example, parties may agree that accountants or other experts will meet before the substantive meeting and try to narrow specified issues; or disagreements about applicable legal principles can be narrowed and perhaps agreed in part for the purpose of mediation. Anything that will help the substantive meeting to run more smoothly may be considered.

10–052 Lax and Sebenius, in their work *3D Negotiations*, refer to three dimensions of deal strategy, one of which is to set up the right negotiation.[20] In commercial mediation, more attention may need to be given to the setting up of the mediation to ensure not only that the right parties attend and that the substantive meeting "hits the ground running", but also that the mediator helps the parties consider their own and one another's interests, and to prepare appropriately for the substantive mediation meeting. A preliminary meeting allows each party or their lawyers an initial opportunity to meet the other in a mediation context, and to have a constructive look at how the substantive mediation day might take place.

10–053 However, preliminary meetings tend to be the exception rather than the norm. The practice has developed of dealing with administrative preparation on the telephone, usually sequentially or occasionally by conference call, and by email or other communications.

10–054 The mediator is likely to require relevant information and documents in advance of the substantive mediation meeting. Commonly the documents will comprise a written statement of case from each party and a bundle of copy documents and correspondence relevant to the issues, which may include copy statements of case and other documents filed in the proceedings.[21] If the statements, documents or information appear to be incomplete, or if supplementary information is needed, the mediator can ask for amplification prior to the meeting. The mediator may prefer to do this during the mediation, but in such event, the required documents may not be readily available, and delay or frustration could result.

---

[19] Philip Naughton QC, "Mega mediation—a case history" [1996] A.D.R.L.J. 215, considers that in a substantial and complex mediation "a pre-mediation meeting is invaluable".

[20] D. Lax and J. Sebenius, *3-D Negotiation: Powerful Tools to Change the Game in Your Most Important Deals*, (Boston: Harvard Business School Press, 2006). See Ch.4 on negotiation.

[21] For details, see below under "Information gathering".

STAGE 1: PRELIMINARY COMMUNICATIONS AND PREPARATION

If there are technical issues in the case, and if experts have been engaged on both sides, the parties may wish the mediator to see the experts' reports. In some cases, valuation reports, accounts, illustrations, photographs or any other existing data may need to be produced in relation to specific issues. 10–055

Practical arrangements for the meeting will be made. The usual procedure is to allot a period of time for a substantive meeting, appropriate to the issues. This may vary between a few hours and a number of days.[22] A balance needs to be struck between allowing sufficient time to mediate effectively and not allotting more time than is necessary and economic. The aim is usually to conclude the mediation within the allotted time; but sometimes an adjournment may be necessary and beneficial, for example where further information is essential to the outcome, or some interim action is needed, or ideas or proposals need to be developed. 10–056

However, as observed above, this "one size fits all" approach is not ideal for all cases, and a more thoughtful, bespoke process may sometimes be beneficial. There are cases where it is impracticable or inappropriate to try to resolve everything in one single meeting, and where a series of meetings is likely to be necessary; or cases involving high conflict where small steps over time may be necessary; or cases where longstanding commercial, professional or personal relationships are under strain or have broken down, which may not necessarily be amenable to resolution in one session. In such event, the initial meeting may deal with certain aspects and it may be agreed that subsequent meetings will deal with other aspects. 10–057

The main point about this approach is that it moves away from the automatic assumption that every case will be dealt with in the same way, that one block of time is appropriate and should be fixed for every dispute, and that if the matter is not resolved at the end of that block of time, the mediation has in some way failed. If parties know at the outset that there will be more than one meeting, expectations and attitudes are likely to be more realistic, which in turn allows for the process to be conducted in an environment that may feel less stressful—which in many situations may be more desirable and effective. 10–058

The automatic fixed period meeting assumption and set-up has been reinforced by the fact that mediation organisations cannot easily assess the needs of parties, and case managers cannot make the necessary enquiries and assessments that might emerge from a carefully conducted preliminary meeting. Lawyers representing parties have developed an expectation that this is how civil and commercial mediation must necessarily be conducted. Consequently fixing a block of time has become a default mechanism. This may well continue to be the case for the majority of civil and commercial disputes; but some alternative must be allowed for those matters that do not fit into this mould. This is further considered below.[23] 10–059

The mediator may need to discuss other practical matters with the parties, together or separately. These may for example include guidance about the case summaries and the oral presentations at a joint meeting; discussing timing and 10–060

---

[22] In court schemes, three hours is commonly allowed for the mediation, though in small claims mediation, the usual time frame is about an hour. In private mediation, it is more usual to set aside a day or so for the mediation, sometimes two days, and occasionally but rarely up to about a week.
[23] See under Stage 4, "Arranging a series of meetings".

checking availability to continue after hours if the matter is not resolved within the allotted time. Some mediators will continue into the night if required and appropriate, others would not be prepared to do so; mediators may wish to check that parties have arrangements with third parties or experts, tax advisers, or specialist consultants, to be able to contact them during the mediation or after hours, if needed. Where parties are attending without lawyers, particularly if they will be on their own, it is often prudent to prepare them for the fact that they may be sitting on their own for periods of time, while the mediator is engaged with the other, so they may be well advised to bring material to occupy themselves during the waiting periods.

10–061   These considerations militate in favour of a preliminary meeting, as it may not be practicable to address them in phone conversations. Preliminary meetings may not be viable or economic especially where parties and lawyers are based far apart, in separate cities or perhaps in different countries. However, with increasingly available technological resources such as video conference facilities, internet voice and video resources, and the possibilities for virtual meetings, it should be possible for some of these logistical difficulties to be overcome.

Establishing the venue

10–062   The mediator or case manager where appropriate will ordinarily arrange the venue for the substantive meeting, in consultation with the parties. The venue will usually be neutral, such as the mediator's premises or hired rooms. The offices of one of the lawyers acting for a party may sometimes be used, provided that the mediator and all parties are agreeable.

10–063   Where there are two parties, or two groups of parties, three rooms should ordinarily be arranged: one for each party and one as a joint meeting room, which the mediator will use as his or her own, and which may also be used for special meetings, for example if the mediator wants to meet the lawyers or anyone else separately while the parties remain in their rooms. However, if this is impracticable, a minimum of two separate rooms may suffice.

10–064   In the latter event one room should be large enough to accommodate all the parties and their representatives as well as the mediator for joint sessions: it will be occupied by one party between joint sessions. The other room will be the base for the other party. An additional room is needed for each additional party or group of parties.

10–065   Parties' rooms should not be immediately adjoining one another, unless this is unavoidable and they are adequately soundproofed. It can be very inhibiting for parties to think that their confidential discussions might possibly be overheard.

10–066   The seating arrangements will be for the mediator to decide. To facilitate direct communication, the mediator may sometimes choose to have the parties, rather than their lawyers, seated nearest to him or her. Conventional wisdom dictates that hostile parties should not sit facing one another during the joint session. That creates unnecessary tensions. Seating arrangements will depend on the logistics of the situation, numbers of participants and available resources. Possibilities include having the mediator on one side of the table, and the parties and lawyers all on the other side (though this is a bit formal). Another option may

STAGE 1: PRELIMINARY COMMUNICATIONS AND PREPARATION

be to have each opposing group on either side of the table, but to have parties sitting diagonally opposite one another rather than directly opposite.

Facilities at the venue

The mediator needs to ensure that there are adequate facilities at the venue to support the process as necessary. This might include, for example, flipcharts or other presentational material, photocopying and printing facilities, and any other resources that may be needed in specific cases such as projectors or scanning and electronic communication facilities. 10–067

The venue may need to be available after hours, in case the mediation should run on after regular business hours as it sometimes does. It should be able to provide meals as required—or the facilities for these to be delivered in—and refreshments during the day, so that the mediator can carry out the necessary function of hosting the proceedings. 10–068

Legal representation

Whether parties are legally represented in mediation will usually depend on the nature, substance and complexity of the issues, financial resources, and their preferences. In most commercial disputes, it is likely that parties will be legally represented, sometimes by teams of lawyers including, in substantial disputes, senior counsel. In smaller disputes or cases of a personal nature, such as partnership disagreements or family business disputes, legal representatives might not necessarily attend. They might though advise their clients, and if required attend at a later stage of the process, for example at an adjourned meeting.[24] 10–069

Where they participate in the mediation, lawyers can have different kinds of roles. They might be actively involved, including making the presentation and leading the negotiations. Alternatively, they might attend in support of their clients, and allow the latter to deal primarily with the case. Much will depend on the individual client, the lawyer and their relationship. Some lawyers find it difficult to take a subsidiary role, but that may well be what is required. That is a matter for the party; but the mediator can help to influence this where appropriate, for example, by where he or she seats the lawyer in the joint session and by directing questions to the party rather than necessarily through the lawyer. 10–070

Authority of corporate representatives

The mediator needs to check in advance of any substantive meeting that all corporate parties have someone present with full authority to conclude a settlement at the meeting and to sign any necessary settlement documents. Individual parties attending in person will obviously be able to do so for themselves, but if they do not attend and are instead represented by a third party, that person will need to have the necessary authority to enter into a settlement agreement. This is essential to avoid the frustration and loss of goodwill that 10–071

---

[24] See Ch.17 for the role of the parties' lawyers in representing their clients in ADR procedures.

generally arises if parties work through the mediation, arrive at an agreed resolution and then find that one party does not have the authority to sign an agreement.

10–072 To anticipate this, many forms of Agreement to Mediate stipulate that the parties' representatives have the necessary authority to agree and sign settlement terms. There is an element of aspiration in relation to these clauses. In many cases organisations will send representatives who are given limited authority, to agree terms subject to certain limitations, rather than an open authority to agree anything in their discretion. In fact it is unlikely that a representative of a bank, an insurance company or any large corporate body will attend with a complete discretion either to accept no payment on a claim or as defendant to pay 100 per cent of the other side's claim together with interest and costs. This can make negotiations more difficult, as the representative may decline to shift in circumstances where it would seem sensible and appropriate to do so—and the reason may be that the proposal lies outside his or her authority. Hence it is generally helpful, where practicable, for the mediator to arrange for the representative to be able to get additional authority if possible.

STAGE 2: COMMENCEMENT, ESTABLISHING THE ISSUES AND SETTING THE AGENDA

10–073 The mediator will ordinarily welcome the parties when they arrive for the substantive meeting, and show them to the separate rooms that they will each occupy during the mediation, where they will await the start of the process.

10–074 Some mediators take the opportunity to speak to each party in their separate rooms, putting them at ease, perhaps offering them tea or coffee, and outlining briefly the plan for the day and checking on any aspects, such as how they will make their oral presentations.

At the pre-arranged time the mediator will call the parties together and start the process.

Opening the mediation session

10–075 There is no set way to open a mediation session, which will commonly (but not invariably) be an initial joint meeting. The following is an example of how this might be conducted:

- The mediator would welcome the parties to the mediation.
- There might be brief introductions round the table.
- The next step might be to sign and exchange the Agreement to Mediate, which would have been approved in advance. The mediator may wish to draw attention to key terms, such as the without prejudice nature of the process, the rules relating to confidentiality and any other particular terms. Each party will usually receive a signed copy of the Agreement with one also being retained by the mediator.
- The mediator might then outline the intended procedure for the mediation. The mediator explains that each party or their lawyer will be asked to make

STAGE 2: COMMENCEMENT, ISSUES AND AGENDA

a presentation. They should expect that, having been forewarned to prepare for it. The mediator will explain that after the presentations and any discussion in joint session, the joint meeting will end and that the mediator will then meet the parties privately in their separate rooms. The mediator will outline (either at this stage or more usually after the presentations) how these separate, private meetings will be held, and what the confidentiality rules are.

- The length and style of this opening stage will be a matter for the mediator's judgment. It will depend on the mediator's personality and style, the nature of the issues, the parties' requirements and their previous experience, if any, and the mediator's sense as to the pace and detail needed at this stage.
- The mediator can now turn to the substantive mediation.

The mediator should try from the outset to be an effective manager of the process, a sensitive judge of the requirements of the parties and a competent facilitator; but ultimately, mediators can do no more than be themselves, albeit armed with the skills, techniques and strategies that they have learned. 10–076

Establishing the issues: oral presentations

The mediator establishes the issues between the parties in a number of ways. First, each party will submit a case summary outlining the issues and their comments on them. Secondly, the bundle of documents will usually clarify and amplify the issues. Thirdly, the parties will in many cases make an oral presentation to the mediator further clarifying their position and the issues as they see them.[25] 10–077

The following may be noted with regard to the parties' oral presentations: 10–078

- The presentation can be made by the parties or by their lawyers. A personal presentation by a party can sometimes be more effective and powerful than a formal statement by the lawyer, because it can explain a person's views and feelings in a very personal way. Even if the lawyer presents the case, the mediator may ask the party personally whether he or she would like to add anything: the parties should be told in advance that this will happen, so that they can prepare appropriately.
- The method of presentation is a matter for each presenter. It usually highlights relevant matters which may already have been mentioned in the written submissions. Other devices may also be used: for example, flipcharts, projectors, videos, maps, plans, photographs can be used or referred to, though this is rarely done.
- The length of the presentations will depend on the complexity of the issues. In many cases five or 10 minutes may be sufficient for each presentation, especially where these are informal and the issues straightforward. Lengthy presentations may be counter-productive and should be avoided as far as possible. A 20-minute presentation on each side will generally be the most that can usefully be made.

---

[25] See also the section below on information gathering.

- In preliminary discussion with the parties' lawyers, when explaining what is required, the mediator can give guidance and, if appropriate, can indicate that the presentation should be explanatory rather than combative. In some cases, the mediator may suggest that the presenters not only outline their case, but also indicate in general terms what they hope the mediation might achieve (though obviously not so as to compromise their position).
- It is not usual to have further responses to the presentations, though there is no reason why a mediator should not allow the parties to reply briefly in appropriate cases. In any event, they will be able to comment further in the separate meetings with the mediator.
- Some clarifying questions may be allowed if the mediator thinks that they would be helpful. If the mediator is doubtful about their value, questions should be deferred until they can be raised in the separate sessions.
- In some circumstances, presentations might not be appropriate, for example where they would inflame an already hostile situation and nothing would be added, or where there are severe time constraints, or where a party's sensitivities are so raw that presentations would just cause distress without serving any positive purpose.[26]

10–079 Parties may have a need for their "day in court" and being heard, which can to some extent be met by putting their case to a neutral third party, even if that person has no power to make any determination. In any event, the parties are bound to want the mediator to understand their point of view, and will want to ensure that the case is forcefully and clearly put.

The mediator needs to manage the presentations even-handedly and empathetically, and also firmly and fairly, not allowing interruptions.

Setting the agenda

10–080 Having established the issues, the mediator will need to construct an agenda. That may be done formally and explicitly, in discussion with the parties; or it may be implicit from the issues that have been raised. Where the issues are complex, and especially if the parties have each brought different issues, the mediator may need to identify and prioritise these.

10–081 As observed in Ch.9, the presenting facts sometimes conceal underlying issues that emerge as the mediation develops. For example, in a shareholders' dispute about a family business, arguments about company administration may disguise questions about parents' intentions and influence and unspoken issues of sibling rivalry and which child the parents had preferred.

10–082 A mediator will not necessarily be able to address the underlying issues in a mediation, but it may be necessary to understand them in order to help with the presenting issues. Underlying issues do not only exist in family disputes, but commonly also in other relationship disputes such as partnerships, shareholder disagreements, professional negligence claims and other working and personal relationships. In fact, they are likely also to be found in many other civil and

---

[26] For example, where a claim against a health authority related to a traumatic death, a presentation of the allegations and the defence would have caused renewed and pointless distress. A short and general opening presentation by each lawyer was sufficient in those circumstances.

commercial issues: commonly, what you see is not necessarily what you get. Some sensitive and skilled probing in private may elicit nuggets of relevant information that may help the mediator to address some of the real issues between the parties and help them reach a satisfactory resolution.

STAGE 3: INFORMATION GATHERING

Unlike family mediation, where information may be gathered over time, the usual practice in civil and commercial mediation is for the mediator to receive as much information as possible before embarking on a substantive meeting with the parties. 10–083

A mediator may acquire information in a number of different ways: 10–084

- an initial indication of the dispute and the issues may be obtained in discussions with the parties or their lawyers when they are considering mediation;
- when setting up the arrangements for the mediation or at a preliminary meeting, the nature of the dispute, the issues and the differences between the parties are likely to emerge;
- one of the main sources of substantive information will be a written summary of each party's case and submissions that is delivered to the mediator and the other party or parties prior to the substantive meeting;
- this summary will usually be supported by a bundle of copy documents relevant to the dispute, which may be amplified by further documents during the mediation;
- commonly the parties and/or their lawyers will make an oral presentation in joint meeting of their position and views;
- in appropriate cases, the mediator may have private meetings with each party and will elicit their underlying views, concerns, interests and needs;
- as the mediation progresses, further information may come to light as a result of disclosures made privately or jointly, questions raised by the parties or the mediator, data provided by experts or other third parties and through other developments;
- throughout the process the mediator gleans additional information by observation of non-verbal cues and clues: body language, tone, and changes in dynamics and attitudes.

A number of specific considerations arise in relation to this process of information gathering: 10–085

The written case summaries

As part of the preparation for the substantive mediation meeting, each party is ordinarily required to provide the mediator and the other party with a written summary of his case. 10–086

There is no prescribed way of writing these case summaries, which vary in style, content and approach. Some are quite legalistic, others are more personally 10–087 and informally drafted. Some combination, maintaining informality while ensuring that all aspects, personal, legal, factual and technical are all covered, can be effective. The purpose of the summary is to outline the position as the parties each see it, explaining their position, sometimes by reference to the law, facts and/or technical and expert implications. Inevitably the summaries are likely to be contentious, since they reflect the different sides of a dispute; but bearing in mind that they are intended to lead into negotiations, the mediator might find it useful to remind parties that they should be explanatory rather than combative.

10–088 The mediator may also guide the parties as to the required length of the summaries. Much depends on the complexity of the issues. Rather than make rigid rules that are not observed (or are observed by only one party) some flexibility on this instruction may be preferable, for example:

> "I am not specifying what length the summary should be, but for your guidance, I would expect something in the region of perhaps 10–20 pages or so."

10–089 Summaries do not follow the litigation model of one party claiming and other responding and perhaps counter-claiming. It is more common for them each to reflect the position as they see it, independently of one another. So the usual practice is to have the summaries delivered to one another and to the mediator on the same day. It can be arranged for the parties to deliver the summaries to the mediator, who circulates them simultaneously.

10–090 Some organisations and mediators also allow supplementary summaries to be furnished to the mediator, and not to any other party, "for the mediator's eyes only". These presage the separate confidential meetings that the mediator will have with each party, and allow a party to provide some advance confidential information to the mediator that they do not wish the other party to share. These insights can be helpful, but are more commonly provided in the separate meetings rather than in the advance material.

The bundles of documents

10–091 At the same time as delivering case summaries, parties usually also provide the mediator and one another with a bundle of documents relevant to the dispute. Unlike the position in litigation, it is not necessary for this to comprise a comprehensive batch of all documents that might be relevant to the dispute, but will rather just contain those selected documents that the parties consider necessary or helpful for the purpose of the mediation.

10–092 Parties may sometimes select those documents that they think would be most helpful to explain and support their view of the case, hence each produces their own bundle. Wherever practicable, it will help if the parties can agree on one common bundle of documents. If they can agree on most documents, but if there are any that one party feels inappropriate to include, it may be possible to overcome this by having an agreed bundle that excludes the contentious items, which can either be provided by one party separately, or appended to the agreed bundle marked "Not agreed".

10–093 If the case has already been commenced in the courts or by way of arbitration, the bundle commonly, but not necessarily, includes copy statements of case

STAGE 3: INFORMATION GATHERING

(pleadings), affidavits, orders, witness statements and other documents. If these are extensive, the parties may agree to select relevant extracts.[27]

If the mediator thinks that any material documents are missing, for example, where replies are sent to letters but the letters themselves are missing, it would be sensible to seek the documents before the start of the mediation meeting. Once the meeting is under way, it may not always be possible to obtain further documents without an adjournment.

Establishing underlying views and concerns

Where time permits, it is very helpful for the mediator's first confidential separate meeting with each party to be largely devoted to getting a better understanding of the party's views, interests, needs and concerns, including the status of past negotiations and any underlying concerns, rather than embarking immediately on the process of negotiations and carrying messages, views and proposals from one party to the other.

It would be helpful if each party gave their true aspirations to the mediator, who could use that private knowledge to help them "design" settlement terms.[28] In practice, it seldom works that way because although some parties may disclose their true positions and aspirations to the mediator, most are reluctant to do so right away. That may be because they are not ready to move to what they may perceive as their worst outcomes right at the start, even though the mediator has undertaken to maintain that confidentially. They may, whether in hope or as a matter of strategy, prefer to hold as closely as they can to their public positions.

Consequently, the mediator would not expect to establish the true negotiating positions of the parties at that initial meeting, nor would that be the aim. The objective is a broader one of gaining more general insights, perceptions and understandings of each party's position. Moving towards achieving each party's aspirations may be a slow process that develops during the mediation, especially as trust develops and a negotiating pattern emerges. In any event, aspirations and positions tend to shift as negotiations develop, new perspectives emerge, differences and gaps narrow and solutions are formulated.

Other information required

Other information that the mediator will need to establish may include the following:

- The status of any pending litigation or arbitration: if proceedings are pending, the mediator should be informed of this, including whether any material court orders have been made, or hearings are due to take place. There is no reason why mediation should not take place parallel with pending proceedings. Indeed, the existence of a hearing date can act as a

---

[27] To those not steeped in the culture of litigation, court pleadings and particulars were seen as opaque documents written in an obscure legal style that obfuscated rather than clarified the issues. Under revised Civil Procedure Rules, "pleadings" became "statements of case" and should be simpler, more factual and less technical. That is a very welcome reform.

[28] See de Bono's concept of third-party design in Ch.3, para.3-025, and his "design idiom" at fn.30 below.

spur to negotiations. Sometimes though, if more time is needed or the parties prefer to lift the threat (and defer the cost) of a hearing, it may be preferable to adjourn proceedings either generally or to a fixed date while the mediation takes place.
- The status of prior settlement negotiations: while some parties may include in their case summary the current status of settlement negotiations, or may reflect their proposals, that does not commonly happen. Consequently, the mediator needs to establish the position in order to place any negotiations in the mediation into a context of past negotiations.
- The relationship between the parties: this will usually be clear from the submissions and documents. What can be more difficult, however, is to identify the nature and quality of any stated relationship, and how this affects the issues. Where, for example, there is a family business dispute between siblings or parent and child, or between business or professional partners, the presenting dispute may well just be "the tip of the iceberg". In such cases, and indeed sometimes in cases that do not overtly appear to have any emotional content, there may well be a history of conflict and emotional entanglement that could significantly affect the dispute and its possible resolution.[29]
- Whether third parties' views or decisions may affect the outcome of the mediation: if, for example, insurers or a governing board needs to approve settlement terms or to provide funds, the mediator should be aware of this as it may affect who attends the mediation or how it is to be approached.
- Whether there are significant disputes of fact: where there is a direct conflict of fact such that one or other party must be lying, with no possibility of misunderstanding or other explanation, it can be more difficult to reach a settlement. The mediator may have to work with both parties to find creative ways of dealing with that situation.
- Each case is likely to involve the mediator obtaining particular information, which will be a matter for the mediator's judgment, in consultation with the parties as appropriate.

Acquiring specialist information

10–099 A mediator may or may not be an expert in the subject-matter of the dispute. Where the mediator does not have substance expertise and needs this for a particular case, this can be achieved in a few different ways:

- The mediator can liaise with the parties' experts. If the experts differ in their respective views, however, the mediator may not be in a position to know which view should prevail. This may or may not matter, depending on the extent to which expertise is critical to the outcome of the mediation and to what extent the process is evaluative.
- By arrangement with the parties and at their shared cost, the mediator can consult an independent expert, introducing such expertise for the benefit of the parties jointly.

---

[29] For further consideration of this aspect, see Stage 2 in Ch.9.

- In appropriate cases, the missing expertise can be furnished by using the co-mediation mode. For example, if the dispute involves complex legal, fiscal and accounting principles, it may be decided to have a lawyer and accountant as co-mediators, rather than either as a sole mediator consulting with the other.

STAGE 4: CONDUCTING SUBSTANTIVE NEGOTIATIONS

In this stage, the mediator assists the parties with their substantive discussions and negotiations towards settlement.   **10–100**

The mediator may ordinarily have started with a joint meeting with the parties, at which they will have made oral presentations and had some further discussions. The mediator must then decide whether and when to hold separate and private meetings (caucuses) with each party.   **10–101**

If the parties are communicating productively, explaining their positions and exchanging views, the joint session can continue: it may be a useful forum in which to explore options. Some mediators work extensively in this way, with excellent results.   **10–102**

However, at some point it may be better to end the joint meeting and move into separate meetings with each party, at which confidential exchanges may be more useful.   **10–103**

The first separate meetings

The mediator must decide whom to see first. This decision will be made on the basis of the mediator's judgment of the parties and the issues, and his or her sense as to who is more likely to get negotiations more productively under way. Some mediators decide to start by seeing the party who appears to be bursting to be heard. Others choose to see the claimant first, which is a sequence that can always be logically explained to the parties. Alternatively, where one party carries a key to the resolution, it may be sensible to meet that one first.   **10–104**

If there are tight time constraints, or if the mediator wishes to get directly into the negotiations, the first meeting will be used to start formulating settlement terms immediately. However, as indicated above, significant benefit can be obtained by using the initial meeting simply to acquaint the mediator with the parties and their thoughts generally. The mediator can tell the parties that the first separate meeting will be used to help get an understanding of respective positions, rather than to formulate specific terms. That will avoid the parties having unrealistic expectations of the initial session.   **10–105**

The mediator may have to ask questions thoughtfully and selectively, and be able to help each party to express his or her thoughts and feelings while being contained in time and content. It can be counter-productive to spend a long time with either party at this point.   **10–106**

Initiating discussions and negotiations

10–107   When the mediator has obtained a preliminary feeling for the parties' positions, it will be necessary to start the negotiating process with a view to constructing settlement terms.[30]

10–108   The most usual way of getting the negotiations going is for one of the parties to submit proposals to the other, through the mediator. The mediator will carry these to the other party. Negotiations then take place sequentially, with the mediator shuttling between the parties carrying proposals and counter-proposals, trying to narrow and eliminate any differences.

10–109   An alternative, but less common, way of approaching the negotiations is to have both parties furnish their proposals to the mediator who formulates terms to put to both parties for consideration, discussion and negotiation. This has the benefit of ensuring that neither party gets an advantage from seeing the other's proposals before formulating their own; and it gives the mediator greater scope to create a framework of composite terms. On the other hand, it can be difficult for the mediator to reflect the differences that inevitably exist, bearing in mind that the mediator's function is to help the parties with their negotiations rather than to become a personal principal in the negotiations. It also runs the risk of the mediator inadvertently favouring one party or the other in constructing the proposals.

Option development and reality testing

10–110   Where parties are not able to formulate settlement terms, or where a fresh approach is desirable, the mediator is likely to encourage the parties to explore possible options for settling the issues. The mediator should help the parties to develop as many options as they can, and to examine them to see which are realistic and which are not.

10–111   In a problem-solving mode, the mediator would help the parties seek creative solutions to what they accept is a problem that they need to address jointly and individually, and not antagonistically. This is the mode that mediators try to encourage, though in practice it may be difficult to shift parties to this mode to any substantial degree (though they can benefit from edging towards it).

10–112   The parties usually develop the options, but there is no reason why the mediator should not help them to do so and put forward some of his or her own, provided that any options that the mediator puts forward are not presented as "the mediator's solution". One way to assist with option development is through brainstorming, where all ideas are noted without initially rejecting or commenting on any, for later evaluation.

10–113   Options can be discussed, narrowed and converted into concrete proposals; or they can be put to the other party more generally to encourage a response in a similar mode. Eventually, of course, terms will have to be extracted from them.

---

[30] Edward de Bono refers in his book *Conflicts: A Better Way to Resolve Them* (Harmondsworth: Penguin, 1986) to a constructive "design idiom" through which the neutral can help the parties to design their own outcome to the problem. This may be seen as helping the parties to "craft" settlement terms out of the material that they provide but cannot themselves manage.

STAGE 4: CONDUCTING SUBSTANTIVE NEGOTIATIONS

The mediator serves a reality-testing function at various stages. One of these is to help parties to appreciate the factual situation, rather than the misconceptions that can often arise when conflict exists. Another is to help them to consider whether options that they are exploring, and proposals into which these may translate, are realistic. In this way, they can act as a sounding board for ideas and possible solutions which each side may be considering putting to the other, indicating ways in which this could most effectively be done and encouraging movement. 10–114

Shuttle mediation

As previously indicated, the mediator commonly uses a form of shuttle mediation to move between the parties, carrying messages and proposals from one side to the other, trying to assess how proposals could be varied or amplified to make them more mutually acceptable. 10–115

While the mediator is engaged in meeting one party, it can be helpful if there is a genuine task for the mediator to ask the other party to undertake. That uses time effectively, and lessens the opportunity for the party who is left alone to become too anxious about what is happening in the other room. Parties left alone often comment on how long the mediator has been away. Mediators should be aware of this, so that if they find that they are spending longer with one party than they expected, they can pop into the other and briefly indicate how long they expect to be. If a session is likely to take a long time, the mediator may wish to indicate this in advance to the other party, who can take an agreed break. 10–116

Shuttle mediation can continue as long as it is proving to be useful in narrowing differences.

Although it is usual to shuttle between parties during the course of the mediation day, this can take place over a more extended period. In one case, the day fixed for the mediation had ended without a settlement, but with terms still being discussed. Instead of adjourning to another fixed date (which would not have been practicable for some time), arrangements were made for the mediator to shuttle between the parties at their respective lawyers' offices from time to time over the following week. This resulted in a settlement. 10–117

Working with parties' lawyers and other professionals

Although parties may be unrepresented in the mediation process, it is usual for them to have their solicitors, and not uncommonly also barristers, with them at commercial mediation sessions, especially where litigation is pending or threatened. Parties may also bring other advisers such as accountants to mediation sessions. 10–118

It is a matter for the parties as to whether they wish to deal with the negotiations themselves or through their lawyers. Mediators should respect the parties' decision, but should also be aware that they do not need to be hidebound by the convention of communicating through representatives. To the contrary, the mediator is likely to address the party directly, or the party and representative jointly, rather than just the lawyer. 10–119

10–120 In some situations, the mediator may wish to meet both parties' lawyers together without the parties present. This can speed up the process, rather than shuttling, and can help to ensure that the same message is taken simultaneously to both parties, where necessary. Also, if lawyers are posturing for their clients, the mediator may want to separate them briefly to enable them to deal more candidly with issues that need to be straightforwardly addressed.

10–121 Sometimes it can help for the mediator to arrange for each party's professional advisers to meet separately, either during the mediation or during any adjourned period. For example, where the issues relate to accounting matters, the mediator may propose that the accountants meet together to consider and identify their differences, and to consider ways of resolving these (for example, asking them to try to agree conflicting records, accounts or valuations). They may not be able to resolve the differences themselves, but they may for example suggest machinery for doing so. Similarly, other experts or valuers may be able to find ways of narrowing their differences.

10–122 Professionals accompanying their clients in the mediation are there to support not to undermine a negotiated outcome. If they seem not to appreciate the adverse effects of negative interventions, the mediator may wish to discuss this with them (though respectful of the fact that the representative is there to protect the client's interests).

Arranging a series of meetings

10–123 As previously indicated, there are some situations in which the default procedure of expecting matters to be resolved in a single block of time would be inappropriate. In such cases, parties and lawyers would know at the outset that the initial substantive meeting was not intended to be final or definitive, and the expectation would be that it would serve a limited purpose and that one or more further meetings would follow.

10–124 Generally, the procedures outlined above, and the principles set out in relation to this stage would all nevertheless be applicable, including for example, having an opening joint meeting and oral presentations, using the initial session to establish the parties' views and any underlying issues and concerns, and commencing negotiations. However, these suggested procedures could be varied to meet the needs of the particular situation. The essence of the process should be an ability and readiness to adapt procedures flexibly to the needs of each individual situation.

10–125 An example of a situation in which a series of meetings was necessary was a complex inheritance dispute, in which the initial meeting was fixed to provide an introduction to the issues and a preliminary exploration of available options and their implications. The parties then met on a later occasion to explore and develop a particular option and to consider whether it was viable. Further time was needed to consider ancillary aspects and to prepare draft documents that would be needed as part of any final terms. Some of the negotiation was done by way of email communications. Everyone knew at the outset that matters would be dealt with over time, and had realistic expectations of each meeting and of the process.

STAGE 4: CONDUCTING SUBSTANTIVE NEGOTIATIONS

Another example was a fundamental disagreement and falling out between shareholders in a company that provided specialised property services in a particular region.

10–126
In that case, an initial meeting, again, allowed the parties to explain their respective positions, wishes and concerns and to explore and narrow a range of available options, which included (among others) either one buying out the other; splitting the company and each continuing to run the business in different parts of the territory; splitting the company's functions and each providing different, non-competitive elements of the business within the whole territory; and splitting the company's assets and each running a competitive business. The parties needed time to consider options and check with accountants and bankers which options were viable. Following some interim communications and exchanges of ideas, the second meeting explored and developed one particular (buy-out) option, which then received much of the focus of attention. A later, final meeting was necessary to deal with all the details and formalities of the deal, which was amicably concluded.

If arrangements have not been fixed in advance for a series of meetings, they can nevertheless be arranged at the initial meeting, once it becomes clear that this would be a beneficial way to proceed.

Dealing with emotions: the myth of rationality in civil and commercial disputes

There is a widespread notion that, unlike parties in family disputes, commercial disputants tend to deal with matters in a reasonable, business-like and rational way without what is seen as the diversion of emotions. While sometimes true, this is in many cases a myth.

10–127

Many civil and commercial disputes involve strong feelings. In some kinds of cases, this may be obvious. For example, family business or partnership disputes are highly likely to be emotional. This may be extended to most situations in which a working relationship existed but has broken down, such as disputes between former principals and their agents, franchisors and franchisees, manufacturers and their former distributors or employers and former employees.

10–128

Where the relationship breakdown arose because of an alleged breach of duty such as negligence, the sense of grievance and distress can be great. So, for example, a clinical negligence dispute commonly contains elements of patient anger, distress, anxiety and blaming. The medical practitioner in turn may experience other possible emotions including anger and disappointment at the patient's apparent disloyalty, indignation at being accused of error in often difficult circumstances, fear, regret and distress. Similar feelings may arise in negligence actions against other professionals, and perhaps in most fields of activity.

10–129

There may similarly be strong feelings where contractual relationships have ended in dispute. An apparently straightforward construction dispute may involve disagreement, anger, frustration and ill will between, for example, a contractor's manager and an employer's representative. What appears to be a straightforward disagreement about a technical matter may disguise an element of personal blaming and conflict between individuals.

10–130

10–131 Even if a disagreement itself might initially have been a straightforward issue capable of rational disposal, the way in which it developed can have created antagonism and distress. For example, excuses and attempts by parties to exculpate themselves and avoid liability may create hostility that did not initially exist. Factual disputes can cause anger (and denials in statements of case, though perhaps technically justified in a narrow sense, can exacerbate antagonism). The challenging tone adopted by some insurers and litigation lawyers can result in reasonable people becoming entrenched in their adversarial positions.

10–132 Parties who hold strong feelings may or may not demonstrate these in the mediation and may not necessarily even be aware of their existence. Whereas overt anger can be addressed, suppressed anger is far more difficult to deal with, especially if the party concerned does not acknowledge its existence. Yet suppressed anger can sabotage deals. The anger may manifest itself indirectly, surfacing unexpectedly and in disguise. It may come out in snide comments, unwillingness to co-operate with the mediation, criticism of the mediator or the process, or resistance to agreeing terms.

10–133 Sometimes the emotional responses that occur in a civil dispute can mirror those in family disputes. Some of the same factors that arise in the breakdown of a commercial relationship are similar to those in the breakdown of a couple's relationship. This is especially so where one party or both (or all) remain emotionally entangled in the continuation of the relationship.

10–134 Mediators need to be aware of how parties' emotions can be a block to resolution of their issues. Mediators should be sensitive to these as far as they can. Every individual copes differently with the expression of feelings, or with managing certain kinds of feelings, such as anger. A few guidelines may be helpful:

- It may not help to try to contain the expression of emotions. This may just bottle up the problem, which then surfaces in some other form and inhibits resolution. However, expressing the emotions can rekindle and reinforce them rather than releasing them, so this needs to be handled with care and sensitivity.
- If emotional issues arise in a joint meeting, it can sometimes be important for the other party to experience the strength of feeling that exists. However, the other party may not wish to experience this in the mediation forum. The mediator must use his or her discretion in deciding how far to allow these feelings to be expressed in the joint meeting. Up to a point, it may be important to allow: beyond that it may become unhelpful to everyone.
- The mediator can give sympathetic acknowledgment of the emotions (though not necessarily of the factors causing it), taking care not to compromise his or her neutrality. The mediator may need to mutualise by acknowledging the emotional effect on both the parties, if indeed this is the case.
- If, however, the expression of emotions is causing undue distress or looks likely to destabilise the process, the mediator should try, with the necessary sensitivity, to bring the more emotional party back to task.

STAGE 4: CONDUCTING SUBSTANTIVE NEGOTIATIONS

- In any event, when strong emotions have been expressed, it is commonly a relief if the mediator gently and non-judgmentally brings the parties back to the task of seeking a solution to their substantive issues.
- It is often easier to manage strong feelings when these are expressed in the separate meeting with a party. For this reason, it may be better to defer issues likely to arouse strong feelings until the separate sessions. Mediators must take care not to be drawn into the emotional maelstrom, or to overreact in empathising with either party.
- The mediator may perhaps meet the parties without their professional advisers, for example, where personal or emotional aspects need to be privately aired. This should, however, be undertaken with the greatest caution, if at all.
- Where emotional aspects have clearly affected the dispute and seem likely to affect the mediation, the mediator may consider touching on this in a joint meeting, perhaps at the outset. Where sensitively delivered, and where everyone realises that it is a factor, it can help to normalise this, for example:

    "It is clear from reading the papers that there are some strong feelings on both sides. That is not surprising, given that this dispute has been running for the last x years. Indeed, it would be surprising if that were not the case. I am just mentioning this, because in my experience strong feelings can sometimes block settlements and I would like to be able to come back to this if necessary."

- There are however risks in the mediator airing emotional aspects. Parties may wish to avoid their usual patterns of emotional response in the mediation, and an introduction referring to their feelings may be inappropriate. It may be safer to hold such observations until they become obviously appropriate in the separate meetings, when the mediator can decide whether and to what extent to touch on them.
- Sometimes inter-personal conflict may be resolved as a by-product of the mediation, either within the process or in the fullness of time after the dispute has ended. Mediators cannot resolve parties' underlying emotional issues, which may well be complex and seldom exclusively related to the dispute. If their contract with the parties is to help them resolve the dispute, that is what their role should be. If strong feelings get in the way of this, the mediator can acknowledge the feelings and can sometimes cautiously help parties to an awareness of the effect of their feelings on negotiations. With empathy and sensitivity, the mediator can help bring parties back into the process of business-like negotiation.

Other permutations of meetings and ways of working

Joint meetings and separate confidential meetings on a shuttle basis are by no means the only strategies that a mediator might employ during the negotiation phase. Other ways of working may include the following:

10–135

CIVIL AND COMMERCIAL MEDIATION

- As indicated above, the mediator may meet with the lawyers without their clients present. This is especially useful when the mediator wants the same message carried to both or all parties.
- Alternatively, the mediator may meet with the parties, jointly or individually, without the lawyers present, for example, when discussing personal matters.
- Sometimes parties may benefit from meeting with one another alone, without the mediator or lawyers present. Some mediators are anxious about doing this, others regard it as a useful strategy to use, where appropriate—but remaining nearby in case needed.
- Where experts are in attendance, the mediator may meet with them, jointly or individually, and may arrange for them to meet one another to see whether they can narrow technical issues or agree on any of the aspects under discussion. Experts can sometimes be less than helpful in relation to overall settlement, as they can have a narrow, specialist view and cannot necessarily see the bigger picture that the parties may need to have.
- Joint meetings can be reconvened between separate sessions as necessary.
- The mediator may liaise with third parties, for example, a party's accountant or other professional advisers, by arrangement with the relevant party.
- Between mediation meetings, the mediator may continue to liaise with the parties and/or their lawyers by telephone, email or in any other way, and may continue negotiations between meetings. Indeed, sometimes it may be difficult to set up meetings and once the parties have had an initial meeting or two, and are familiar with the process and with the mediator, negotiations and other communications can be conducted in this way.
- Any other permutation, meeting or communication that the mediator considers helpful can be flexibly used.
- Where agreement has been reached, the joint meeting can serve as an opportunity to summarise and check the terms and to discuss the formalities that will be followed to record and implement the agreement.

Using facilitation and communication skills

10–136   The mediator will facilitate communication and negotiation between the parties and the formulation of concrete proposals that reflect their interests, concerns and requirements, and will assist them in maintaining a practical, business-like approach.

10–137   Throughout the process the mediator will use communication and other mediation skills. This will include listening carefully to the parties, reframing their communications to enhance constructive dialogue, acknowledging movement, mutualising concerns and interests, questioning each to clarify, probe and test how realistic their ideas are, helping to develop options and generally facilitating negotiations.[31]

---

[31] See Ch.14 for the mediator's skills and attributes.

STAGE 5: DEALING WITH IMPASSE

As the mediator demonstrates an authentic involvement in the process and a patient commitment to helping the parties, they are likely to develop increasing trust in the mediator and the process. This in turn can have a positive effect on the movement towards resolution. 10–138

Adopting an evaluative mode[32]

Sometimes the facilitative procedures outlined above do not prove to be sufficient, especially where parties have different perceptions of the strengths of their case, and make different assessments as to the likely outcome. In such cases, some models of civil and commercial mediation provide for an element of evaluation to be used. 10–139

Many mediators do not introduce evaluation at all, while others might perhaps do so unwittingly. There are many misconceptions about what evaluation involves. It seldom involves a formal declaration by the mediator as to the likely outcome of the case if it were to be taken to trial. Rather, it may (and commonly does) involve a questioning of parties' certainties, or a reference to relevant case law or precedent, or an informed challenge to assumptions of outcome. 10–140

Mediators who are willing to introduce an element of evaluation into their mediation are well aware that this could potentially antagonise one of the parties and compromise the mediator's role, though if done thoughtfully, skilfully and with appropriate expertise, it should be regarded as a facilitative step, supporting both parties in reaching an appropriate outcome. Evaluation is accordingly not lightly undertaken. 10–141

STAGE 5: DEALING WITH IMPASSE

Where progress comes to a halt and the parties are deadlocked, the mediator may need to use impasse strategies to help regain movement. The following may be particularly relevant: 10–142

Addressing risk perception

An impasse can sometimes arise or be perpetuated by the nature of the advice or support being given to a party by his lawyer, accountant or other professional adviser. It is entirely proper and appropriate for the adviser to have a supportive role that is partisan.[33] However, in some cases, the adviser may have difficulty in confronting his or her client with options or views that the client is set against wanting to hear. The adviser may need support in dealing with this issue, and the mediator may need to accept the role of a scapegoat in helping to achieve a necessary shift.[34] 10–143

---

[32] For a more detailed consideration of evaluation, including specifically evaluative models of mediation, see Ch.19.

[33] See the value of the partisan role in Gwynn Davis, *Partisans and Mediators: Resolution of Divorce* (Oxford: Clarendon Press, 1988).

[34] One role of the mediator is sometimes to be a scapegoat for the decisions that the parties need to make. If a party can "blame" the mediator for having to reach a particular decision, the mediator will need to have sufficiently broad shoulders to accept that as part of his or her function.

10–144 There is also another aspect to this, which relates to the fact that people's risk intuition may commonly be skewed by innate biases and heuristics, or mental "shortcuts" that everyone takes in arriving at decisions. These biases can influence parties and lawyers in the way that they view the strength of their case.[35]

10–145 Research in the US has indicated that in cases where predictions were compared with actual outcomes, "lawyers frequently made substantial judgmental errors, showing a proclivity to over-optimism".[36] There is, it appears, an element of wishful thinking and a consistency with findings in previous studies in which judgments about probability and likelihood were significantly influenced by whatever side of the issue individuals thought about first. The authors of this research suggest that lawyers should consider obtaining third-party views on their litigation goals on behalf of their clients and how realistic these are to be achieved.

10–146 Although it is not clear how far this particular research would apply in other countries and legal traditions, there is some consistency with other studies, and with the broad principles of risk intuition. Viewed pragmatically, it is self-evident that where two lawyers assessing the same set of facts against the same legal principles can arrive at opposite conclusions, one or the other—or perhaps in some respects both—must be working on some mistaken element, whether of fact, law, judgment or intuition.

10–147 One question for mediators is how far to challenge these perceptions. Mediators who are purely facilitative may raise questions that challenge the party's perceptions (though this itself may be a form of evaluation); but this may not necessarily resolve the impasse. Indeed, merely drawing attention to the risks and costs of litigation is unlikely to have any real impact and may be perceived as patronising. In a report on court mediation, Professor Hazel Genn refers to one respondent as saying:

> "... the mediator kept banging on about the dangers of going on to appeal, asking 'has your solicitor advised you about the costs consequences?' Well frankly that's insulting. Of course we had considered the consequences...."[37]

10–148 It can be more helpful, and may sometimes be necessary, to challenge perceptions more directly, for example by asking how they reconcile their views with particular legal provisions or judicial precedents, or by considering aspects of the case that do not stand up well to scrutiny. The mediator can raise questions and challenge perceptions that may help the party and the adviser to reassess their views and to shift stuck positions. The mediator will not want to undermine the lawyer, but may facilitate the party and lawyer reviewing their views and certainties.

10–149 Sometimes when a mediator raises such a challenge in a private meeting, the lawyer is quite relieved and even supportive of the mediator. The lawyer may

---

[35] See, for example David G Myers, *Intuition: Its powers and perils* (Yale University Press, 2002).
[36] Jane Goodman-Delahunty, Pär Anders Granhag, Maria Hartwig and Elizabeth F. Loftus, "Insightful or wishful: Lawyers' Ability to Predict Case Outcomes" (2010) 16(2) *Psychology, Public Policy, and Law* 133.
[37] Professor Hazel Genn, *Court-based ADR Initiatives for Non-Family Civil Disputes: The Commercial Court and the Court of Appeal* (London: Lord Chancellor's Department, 2002), p.94.

STAGE 5: DEALING WITH IMPASSE

well have issued cautions to his or her client, but might not have wanted to press these too strongly. The lawyer may not want to have been perceived as being too negative or may have wanted to support the client in maximising the client's position, while looking for settlement opportunities.

Another useful device is to provide material that will help parties to focus more specifically on risk, cost and the implications of proceeding to trial in those cases where court proceedings have started or are in prospect. The mediator may prepare a risk analysis form for parties to consider with their lawyers and complete.[38] There are many possible forms and versions of this, and it can either be provided in a general form or adapted for the specific case by inserting for consideration a list of the key issues that would need to be decided in the event of a trial, for example, by following a sequential analysis of issues, broadly along the lines of a decision-tree analysis in part of it.[39] It can be useful to prepare this document in advance of the substantive meeting, and keep copies in reserve in case ever needed. They can then be produced and handed to the parties and their lawyers in the event of impasse.

10–150

It is not necessary for the parties and their lawyers to return the completed document to the mediator, though if they do, this can provide useful insights and provide a basis for further discussion. The point of the document is rather to help the parties focus on the implications of not resolving the dispute and of having to continue with court proceedings. Sometimes the mediator may find that the form has not been completed, but the parties, having reflected on the issues raised in it, are readier to engage further with the process.

10–151

BATNA and WATNA[40]

Flowing from the question of risk assessment, a useful strategy is to help the parties to examine their best and worst alternatives to reaching a negotiated agreement. This involves:

10–152

- Facilitating the examination by each party of the realistic best outcome they might achieve in any other forum such as litigation. In assessing this, positive and negative factors need to be taken into account, for example, the additional costs that would be incurred including those which would be irrecoverable. Delay and publicity factors, and any other relevant

---

[38] An example of such a form is set out in the Appendix at A1-047. Mediators can vary this however they see fit, or may obviously use their own version of this—simplified or amplified.

[39] A decision tree graphically examines alternative options with uncertain consequences, by developing and exploring its different branches and sub-branches, and assigning subjective probabilities to each of the items listed on the branches. Decision trees can be helpful in focusing on individual issues, but can be misleading: ultimately they involve subjective judgments that can give the illusion of being scientific, and the process does need great care to avoid flaws of logic creeping into it.

[40] BATNA is the best alternative to a negotiated agreement. The term arises from Roger Fisher and William Ury, *Getting to Yes: Negotiating Agreement Without Giving In* (Boston: Houghton Mifflin, 1981); Lax and Sebenius prefer the term "no-deal option" for the same concept: see their *3-D Negotiation: Powerful Tools to Change the Game in Your Most Important Deals* (2006). WATNA is the worst alternative to a negotiated agreement. For further discussion of the BATNA and WATNA concepts, see Ch.4, paras 4–006 to 4–008.

- considerations, would be taken into account. Each party will then have some idea of the best result that could be achieved if agreement is not reached.
- Similarly, facilitating the examination of the worst alternative to an agreement, assuming the realistic worst outcome in any other forum such as litigation. Here again, all relevant factors must be taken into account, including total costs payable by the losing party to his own solicitor, and any likely costs payable to the winner. Delay and publicity factors, and other relevant considerations, are again taken into account. Each party will then have some idea of the worst result that might follow if agreement is not reached.
- Facilitating the parties and their lawyers assessing the likelihood of winning or losing in the event of adjudication.
- Helping the parties to review the negotiations with the benefit of knowing their best and worst alternatives and having a better idea of their prospects of success.

10–153   The BATNA/WATNA exercise is potentially useful for each party (rather than the mediator) to undertake. It makes it clearer whether determination in another forum is a better option; if not, then a negotiated agreement should be pursued. Clearly this cannot ordinarily be undertaken by the parties jointly.

Examining underlying issues

10–154   If it is not apparent what is causing the deadlock, the mediator may wish to consider what underlying issues may be inhibiting resolution. For example, in a clinical negligence case, the claimant may not be satisfied merely with financial proposals. There may also be a need for some form of acknowledgment, explanation, apology or accountability.

10–155   The mediator may need to probe gently with each party to establish the underlying issues and requirements. Once these are identified, the mediator can try to consider with the parties what would need to be done or said that would satisfy those underlying issues and concerns. This can sometimes help to unblock stuck attitudes.

Exploring creative options

10–156   The mediator can help the parties explore creative ways of overcoming the impasse. These may be put forward by the parties themselves, encouraged by strategies such as brainstorming; or they may be suggested by the mediator—though this should be done with care so that the parties do not perceive this as the mediator's recommendation.

10–157   For example, in a case in which parties were considering terms for a settlement of a farming dispute, one particular farm was on offer but the person considering accepting it as part of a comprehensive deal (M) was uncertain whether the lie of the land would be really suitable for his farming plans. A stalemate arose on this, until the mediator suggested to both parties the possibility that M should take the land, farm it for a year and see if it suited him, and have

STAGE 5: DEALING WITH IMPASSE

the option at the end of the year to sell the farm, with an agreed adjustment of certain other payments in the event of such sale. This broke the deadlock and a formula was found along these lines. In the event, the farm did suit M, and he retained it after a year.

Symbolism

The mediator may need to consider whether a deadlock is caused by some symbolic issue, or whether perhaps some symbolic solution may be found to an impasse. 10–158

In a clinical negligence claim arising from the death of a baby in childbirth, an important element in moving towards resolution was addressed when the defendants offered to provide a headstone for the baby. In a commercial dispute, a deadlock about a residual payment was resolved when the parties agreed that it should be paid to a charity chosen by the parties. 10–159

Brackets

Increasingly in mediations held in the US parties and mediators find it useful to offer each other brackets. The party offering the bracket is effectively offering to move to a particular figure on condition that the other party responds by moving to the other end of the bracket. Thus a claimant might suggest a bracket of $15 million to $20 million. He is thereby offering to accept $20 million but his offer is conditional on the paying party lifting his offer to $15 million. The response may be by means of a different bracket or simple agreement. This technique and approach has not found particular favour in the UK as yet. 10–160

Where parties are deadlocked, it can help for the mediator to prepare written notes for the parties to consider: 10–161

- This may be a summarised analysis of the issues, reflecting those aspects on which there is some measure of agreement and those where there are differences, with the range of solutions put forward by each party.
- The mediator may add his or her own thoughts on the possible ways in which stuck issues can be approached consistently with the aspirations of each of the parties. This can be done non-judgmentally, merely by outlining available options; or if the circumstances necessitate, the mediator could add his or her views as to possible directions which the negotiations could take to become more effective.
- Depending on the specifics of the situation, the mediator may create a written note that creatively assesses the stuck aspects. The key requirements of such a strategy would be, first to bring a greater awareness of the issues to the parties, and secondly to offer some constructive ways to overcome the deadlock.

Adjournment for non-binding third-party evaluation of an issue

10–162 If the sticking point relates to a dispute about a legal or technical aspect, one possible strategy is to adjourn the mediation and arrange to obtain a non-binding evaluative opinion from some agreed authoritative third party. In such event, the parties or their lawyers may liaise with the mediator in preparing joint instructions to the third party, for example a specialist barrister; and if required, each party may be given the opportunity to attach an addendum outlining their respective views and contentions.

10–163 The third party's non-binding opinion can help to guide the parties in the mediation. It could be discussed at the next mediation session, and might help matters to move forward, even if it is not accepted by both or all the parties.

Making non-binding settlement proposals

10–164 A procedure that can be effective in helping to overcome deadlock is for the mediator to offer the parties the following option:

10–165 The mediator will meet the lawyers or the parties together, and will suggest terms that he or she thinks may be mutually acceptable as a way of resolving the dispute. Those terms will not be based on the merits or endeavour to anticipate the outcome if the matter were to go to court, nor are they an evaluation or non-binding determination. Rather they will just be proposed terms that the mediator thinks may pragmatically settle the issues.

10–166 The parties or their lawyers will be invited to consider these proposals and to revert to the mediator individually and confidentially. If both accept, the mediator will announce that the matter is settled. If both reject the proposals, the mediator will announce that there is no settlement. If one accepts and the other does not, the mediator will similarly announce that there is no settlement. This means that if one party accepts and the other does not, the refusing party will not know that the other was willing to agree, leaving the latter in no way compromised by agreeing.

10–167 If the parties agree to this procedure, the mediator will make his or her proposals. These will need to be thoughtfully crafted, based on an understanding of the parties' contentions, needs and views. It is certainly not just a matter of "splitting the difference" although there may sometimes be occasions when that might be appropriate. If the proposals are complex, it may be that composite terms will be set out in writing and provided to the parties.

10–168 There is experience of this procedure working in one of two ways. In some cases, the terms are accepted by both parties. In some other cases, one party may accept and the other may reject, but confidentially tell the mediator that while the mediator's proposals are not acceptable, he would agree to some alternative specified compromise. In that event, the mediator, as promised, announces that there is no settlement; but then suggests that negotiations might nevertheless continue, as he has another aspect he would like to explore. In this context, the mediator can discreetly test whether the alternative proposals might form the basis for a settlement, which may well be the case. The main point, however, is that the impasse strategy has been effective in ending the stalemate and getting discussions going again, on a basis that might potentially resolve the matter.

STAGE 5: DEALING WITH IMPASSE

Other strategies

Deadlock can arise for other reasons, such as differing perceptions of fairness. In such event it can help for each party to have an opportunity to address this issue. Although unlikely to persuade the other, this sometimes allows each to see that there are different perspectives, and that the matter needs to be dealt with pragmatically.   10–169

A basic impasse strategy is simply to pause and reflect. The mediator may need time to reflect on the cause of the deadlock. Self-examination is part of this process: the mediator may find that his or her own attitudes and assumptions are contributing to the problem, rather than helping to overcome it. This may, for example, concern the way the mediator relates to one of the parties. The mediator may have to change his or her approach or attitudes to create a new dynamic. Or the parties may need more time to reflect on matters themselves. Sometimes things take on a different hue after a few days of reflection.   10–170

As an adjunct to this, if the substantive mediation ends with the issues unresolved, the mediator may arrange for the parties to leave their respective proposals open for an agreed period, say 72 hours, with the opportunity for either to accept the other's proposals within this time. If this is done, it is important for the respective proposals and the terms of the extended time to be clearly noted, so that there is no room for misunderstanding. It should also be specified that this is part of the mediation process, and that the terms of the Agreement to Mediate continue to apply. The mediator may, before the end of the agreed period, contact each party to see if there is any interest in accepting the proposals. This provides an opportunity to check whether, with the benefit of reflection, either party may perhaps find some way to close the gap even if the other's proposals are not accepted.   10–171

Wade refers to a number of strategies for "crossing the last gap".[41] These include some of those mentioned above, and also simply splitting the difference; resolving matters by chance, such as spinning a coin, which saves face, or drawing a range of options from a hat; placating the fear of incremental increases by arranging that a proposal will only be considered if a party can be sure that it will be final and accepted; sub-dividing the last gap—as where for example one person makes a payment and the other pays the delivery and insurance costs; deferring the deadlocked item and implementing the rest of the settlement; and fixing a time for final discussions with limited and specific proposals.   10–172

Preparing for adjudication

If attempts to resolve the impasse are not successful, the parties will have reserved their right to proceed to adjudication. Sometimes coming face to face with that serves as an effective impasse strategy itself, and brings parties back into negotiation. However, a mediator should not use this as a strategy unless genuinely intending to end the mediation if there is no further movement: this should not be used by way of brinkmanship, but rather as a genuine last resort.   10–173

---

[41] John H. Wade, "Crossing the Last Gap" in Andrea Kupfer Schneider and Christopher Honeyman, *The Negotiator's Fieldbook: The Desk Reference for the Experienced Negotiator* (Washington DC: American Bar Association, 2006), Ch.54, pp.467–474.

10–174　In this event, the mediator can help the parties to prepare for adjudication in as constructive a way as possible. Issues and formal arguments can be addressed and simplified, and the parties can be encouraged to view the adjudication as a way of resolving the dispute by getting a third party to make a determination, rather than as an act of hostility.

Adjournment and "after-care"

10–175　When mediations do not result in settlement on the day there is increasingly an expectation that the mediator will remain involved. Mediations often continue through a mixture of written communication, telephone calls and face to face meetings for weeks, even months after the mediation day. The parties and the mediator always have the option of reconvening for a full further day of mediation.

STAGE 6: CONCLUDING MEDIATION AND RECORDING THE OUTCOME

10–176　As in all other fields of mediation, the process will end either when an agreement has been reached, or when the parties or the mediator conclude that, although resolution may not have been reached, nothing further can be achieved in the mediation process.

10–177　The mediator will have to consider and perhaps discuss with the parties whether a written record of the outcome is needed, and if so, in what form and by whom it should be prepared.

10–178　It is standard practice in civil and commercial mediation that if agreement is reached, a written memorandum of settlement terms should immediately be prepared and signed by the parties before they leave, if at all practicable. It will ordinarily be immediately binding, and this should be clear and explicit. If it is only to become binding after some further stage has been reached, such as after ratification by a board of directors or confirmation by an insurer, this must be clearly stated. It must also reflect any conditions in the case of a conditional agreement.

10–179　The memorandum should contain all the material terms of settlement, with no missing or vague essential elements, however complex this makes the memorandum and however long it takes.

10–180　Lawyers representing the parties may undertake or help with the necessary drafting. The mediator's role may be to undertake the drafting, to lead or support it, to review it or perhaps just to receive a copy of the agreement.

10–181　Where the parties are not legally represented in the mediation, or where for any other reason the mediator needs to be more closely involved in drafting, for example, where the mediator has kept notes that will facilitate drafting, the mediator may prepare an initial draft of the agreement. If only partial resolution has been achieved, the mediator might prepare a non-binding without prejudice summary of the position for the parties, which could usefully indicate the common ground and the differences between the parties, to facilitate further discussion in the future.

Where court orders or arbitration awards are required as part of the settlement, the mediator would not be expected to draft the relevant order or award. Indeed, it would generally be inappropriate to do so. This would be the responsibility of the parties' lawyers. 10–182

The memorandum might, however, need to record in clear terms what kind of order is needed and what time-scale, formalities and procedures are envisaged for obtaining and implementing the agreement. 10–183

ADDRESSING POST-MEDIATION ISSUES

The mediator can assist in various ways with any settlement the parties may enter into. For example, the mediator may supervise implementation of the settlement terms, although this would be very uncommon, act as stakeholder, mediate any issues that may arise, or perhaps even act in an adjudicatory capacity in relation to the implementation of the settlement.[42] Some of these functions may be undertaken by the ADR organisation that arranged the mediation. 10–184

The extent to which the mediator or the ADR organisation that arranged the mediation can have a post-settlement role in relation to civil and commercial mediation will depend on a number of considerations, including for example: 10–185

- the settlement terms, and whether and to what extent they involve a deferred implementation, or one that would benefit from neutral supervision or involvement;
- the relationship between the mediator and the parties including the level of trust established and the readiness of the parties to allow a third party a supervisory role in the implementation of their settlement;
- the additional cost factor of having further neutral involvement, balanced against the perceived benefits of such involvement.

A supervisory function could be useful, for example, in the implementation of a construction industry dispute where the work is continuing, or in the supervision of some physical activity which forms part of a settlement, such as the stocktaking of a business. The mediator might retain documents in escrow or care for physical items pending the payment of funds payable on completion of a transaction, to be released on specified terms.[43] 10–186

The mediator's post-settlement functions may either be contained in the written terms of settlement or can be arranged on an ad hoc basis if and when the need arises. 10–187

---

[42] This would though be unusual. It would not be med-arb, as the adjudicatory function would relate to the settlement terms and not the dispute. It changes the nature of the neutral's role, and care would be needed in agreeing these provisions, drafting the terms of adjudication and implementing them.

[43] For example, it was a term of settlement in one case that confidential documents held by a party had to be lodged with the mediation organisation that arranged the mediation, for destruction after the terms of settlement had been fully implemented (but not before).

DEAL MEDIATION

10–188 This chapter has dealt with the resolution of civil and commercial disputes, but mediation has the capacity to facilitate the creation of contractual arrangements, where there is no dispute at all, but rather where parties seek third-party support in negotiating contractual terms at the start of a relationship. This is particularly applicable where the proposed transaction is complex and global; but the principle is equally applicable in any domestic commercial contract where a flexible, creative and problem-solving approach by a third party would help them address a range of matters that might otherwise be difficult to resolve.

10–189 A number of mediators, in particular those with a commercial background, whether or not also legal, have been offering deal mediation. CEDR Solve offers third-party assistance in the negotiation of a deal, as well as other forms of assisted negotiation.[44] The International Mediation Institute, IMI, supports the concept and has published material relevant to the process.[45] It points out that mediation has far wider values in terms of enabling negotiators to do their job on a collaborative rather than confrontational or positional basis.

---

[44] See for example Graham Massie's 2016 article "Deal mediation—Neutral chairing for contract negotiation" at *https://www.cedr.com/blog/deal-mediation/* [accessed 16 May 2018].

[45] See *http://imimediation.org/deal-mediation* [accessed 16 May 2018].

CHAPTER 11

Divorce and Other Family Mediation

INTRODUCTION[1]

This chapter will focus on the breakdown of couples' relationships, which is what the term "family mediation" often refers to. It will also touch on other kinds of family disputes. 11–001

While family mediation is a form of ADR, it differs from other dispute resolution processes in that it does not focus on disputes as such, but rather deals with the consequences of relationship crisis or breakdown. Mediators will generally be as engaged in helping parties to make decisions that affect their futures and those of their children, and to formulate ways of adapting to changed circumstances in their lives, as in dealing with straightforward dispute resolution. There is accordingly a different culture in the field of family and divorce mediation than in other ADR fields. Nevertheless, there is also a substantial overlap of process. 11–002

Family mediation is not discreet and self-standing, but operates within a number of systems, including family systems, the legal and court systems and the mental healthcare system. It is accordingly necessary to view it in a holistic context, particularly in conjunction with lawyering, the courts and support resources such as counselling and therapy. 11–003

OVERVIEW OF FAMILY MEDIATION IN THE UK

Brief history

In essence, family mediation in the UK started in the 1970s with the courts and voluntary services providing mediation (then called conciliation) primarily for children's issues. District Judges (formerly Registrars) and court welfare officers mainly provided court services. Out-of-court services, working largely but not exclusively alongside the courts, were similarly mainly geared to child issues. 11–004

Most not-for-profit services were, and still are, affiliated to National Family Mediation (NFM).[2] Initially under their 1983 Code of Practice, property and financial issues could be discussed in outline in mediation only where these were inextricably linked with issues relating to children; otherwise they were to be 11–005

---

[1] The authors are grateful to Cressida Burnet for her contribution to this chapter.
[2] *http://www.nfm.org.uk* [accessed 16 May 2018]—previously called the National Family Conciliation Council and the National Association of Family Mediation and Conciliation Services.

referred to solicitors. Conciliation was not then used to address financial issues, except perhaps very incidentally to children's issues.

11-006 The concept of dealing in mediation with all issues, not just child-related, was developed in a co-mediation pilot scheme undertaken by a small group of practitioners. This led to the establishment in 1988 of the Family Mediators Association (FMA).[3] Its membership comprised family lawyers and counsellors, psychotherapists, social workers and other professionals working with couples or families going through relationship breakdown.

11-007 In addition to the FMA and NFM, which adopted all-issues mediation, other bodies entered the field, including family lawyers through the Solicitors Family Law Association (now called Resolution), CALM Scotland, and the Law Society, which developed recommended standards of training and a Code of Practice for solicitors who practise as family mediators.

11-008 The Family Law Act 1996 introduced the concept of counselling and mediation as processes standing alongside the legal process in dealing with marriage breakdown. Mediation was brought within scope for legal aid and in 1999[4] it became obligatory, subject to certain specified exemptions, for people who wished to obtain legal aid for various family issues to undergo a preliminary mediation assessment meeting to see whether mediation might be appropriate.

11-009 The Civil Partnership Act 2004 granted similar rights in a wide range of legal matters to same sex couples who registered their partnership under the Act, as married couples. This includes the Court's power on dissolution of a civil partnership to make financial provision for either party, which may include periodical payments by way of maintenance, lump sum payment(s), property adjustment and pension sharing.

11-010 Family mediation is also used to deal with issues arising from the breakdown of unmarried couples' relationships. There are some important differences from divorce mediation, for example with regard to financial disclosure and the applicable law. This is dealt with below.

11-011 There was a major development in 2011, when the principle of a mandatory preliminary meeting, the Mediation Information and Assessment Meeting (or MIAM as it has become known) until then only required for public funding, was extended to cover all disputes coming before the divorce courts in England and Wales.[5]

Mediation and conciliation through the courts

11-012 Court-based conciliation—which is a form of confidential mediation undertaken by a District Judge and/or a CAFCASS Children and Family Reporter[6]—deals with disputes about children in the county court. The judge does not make any

---

[3] *https://thefma.co.uk/* [accessed 16 May 2018].
[4] By the Access to Justice Act 1999.
[5] Practice Direction 3A (Pre-application protocol for mediation information and assessment)—supplementing the Family Procedure Rules 2010, came into force on 6 April 2011. This does not apply in Scotland.
[6] The Reporter, formerly called a court welfare officer, is attached to the Children and Family Court Advisory and Support Service, CAFCASS. This body was set up in 2001 under the provisions of the Criminal Justice and Court Services Act 2000 which brought together the family court services

substantive order except by agreement. If no agreement is reached, the District Judge will give directions dealing with evidence and reports and for a further hearing. Any further hearing will be before a different judge, and a different Children and Family Reporter would prepare a report to the court as required.

The conciliation scheme in the Principal Registry of the Family Division specifically provides for children over the age of 9 years to attend, but not in court: they will usually speak to the Children and Family Reporter. Some county courts do not have a conciliation scheme but may have a court welfare or CAFCASS officer who can discuss matters with a couple. 11–013

Currently, mediation by the court deals with children's issues only. Issues involving finance and property are referred to outside mediation bodies. 11–014

Financial Dispute Resolution (FDR)

FDR is a court-assisted process in which the parties meet with a District Judge who helps them to reach settlement terms. The parties inform the judge of their respective offers, even though these might be "without prejudice"; and if necessary the judge predicts what would be likely to happen if the case went to trial. 11–015

This is not mediation, but a facilitated and evaluative form of negotiation. The judge can only make an order by agreement. If the parties do not agree, the judge would not hear the case when it eventually came to trial: a different judge would need to do so. The FDR has had a good record of successful outcomes. 11–016

The Family Mediation Council (FMC)

The Family Mediation Council[7] is an umbrella organisation, established in 2007, which works for greater public awareness of and access to family mediation. Its members include the UK's national family mediation organisations, namely: 11–017

- IDR Europe Limited (ADR Group)
- College of Mediators
- National Family Mediation (NFM)
- Resolution
- The Family Mediators Association (FMA)
- The Law Society

The Council works closely with the Legal Services Commission and Ministry of Justice on family mediation related projects and negotiates with government and other interests on issues concerning family mediation. Through its members, it aims to achieve agreed minimum professional and training standards and compliance with a Code of Practice. 11–018

---

previously provided by the Family Court Welfare Service, the Guardian ad Litem Service and the Children's Division of the Official Solicitor's Office.

[7] See: *https://www.familymediationcouncil.org.uk/* [accessed 16 May 2018].

Family Mediation Standards Board (FMSB)

11-019   This body has delegated authority to advise upon and oversee the implementation of the FMC's professional standards. This includes maintaining and publishing a register of mediators and Professional Practice Consultants; ensuring standards of foundation training courses; maintaining and administering a robust system for accreditation; and considering and making decisions on complaints and disciplinary matters relating to the FMC's member organisations.

Mediation Information and Assessment Meetings (MIAMs)

11-020   As outlined above, the principle of a mandatory preliminary meeting to inform parties about mediation and check its suitability was extended in April 2011 from public funded cases to cover all cases involving children and finance going through the courts. From that time, a Mediation Information and Assessment Meeting (or MIAM) with an approved mediator became part of court procedure.

11-021   The object of a MIAM is to explain the mediation process and assess its suitability. However, in certain circumstances, parties will be exempted from it, including for example where there has been domestic abuse,[8] where one of the parties is bankrupt, where child protection issues exist, where there are urgent matters to be resolved by the court or where the mediator for any other reason considers that mediation would be inappropriate.

COUNSELLING/PSYCHOTHERAPY

11-022   The consequences of relationship breakdown may involve dealing with a mixture of personal and emotional issues, matters concerning the future of the children, practical questions of housing and finance, and coping at a personal and pragmatic level with substantial change, as well as trying to decide on respective "rights". This often occurs against a background of different perceptions of fairness and conflicting legal advice.

11-023   Counselling and psychotherapy have long been available to help families, couples and individuals to examine difficult personal issues and to cope with the personal consequences of ending the relationship. Counselling is still regarded by some as a process to help a couple to save their relationship. While that may well be its consequence, its objective is not generally so prescriptive. Rather, it helps people in a non-judgmental and non-directive way to explore their issues and to arrive at their own outcome.

11-024   The distinction between counselling and psychotherapy is not clear. Counselling generally tends to help with shorter term and more focused issues, whereas psychotherapy may deal over a longer term with more fundamental personal issues. However, therapy is available on a short-term basis, and may deal with specific issues; and longer-term counselling may deal with fundamental life issues. "Counselling" often embraces specific areas such as relationship endings, sexual problems, grief or addiction. Perhaps the distinction is less important than establishing what a particular counsellor or therapist offers and

---

[8] Though not all domestic abuse would make mediation inappropriate: see below.

whether the party or couple feel that he or she can establish an effective and empathetic relationship with them. Given that the terms "counselling" and "therapy" may still connote some sense of malfunction, the concept of seeking "professional support" in times of personal crisis may help to introduce people to available resources.

Some counsellors and therapists only work with individuals, others undertake individual, couples, family or group work. Each serves a different function. There is some concern that where only one of a couple undertakes individual counselling or therapy, this can feel threatening rather than supportive to the other, unless the other wholly supports the intervention.[9] Couple's counselling or therapy tries to maintain the balance, helping both to explore necessary changes.

11–025

A practitioner in the field of relationship breakdown will need to be aware of the availability of different counselling and therapeutic resources. Many lawyers and mediators will develop networks of counsellors and therapists, both individual and organisational, who may be able to assist in dealing with the stress of relationship breakdown.

11–026

Family mediation has incorporated some elements of counselling within its practice, including for example "working within a family system", "acknowledging", "mutualising" and "reframing", but of course the processes are fundamentally different in aims and objectives, and in all other material respects.

11–027

SOLE OR ANCHOR MEDIATION AND CO-MEDIATION

Family mediators can work as sole mediators or co-mediators. In the latter event, co-mediators might replicate the couple's gender: male and female mediators for a hetero-sexual couple, mediators of the same gender for a same-sex couple.

11–028

Within family co-mediation, further choices exist. A lawyer may for example work with a professional from a different discipline, experienced in couple and family dynamics; but neither needs to be a lawyer or a professional from a family dynamic background, as there are mediators from a range of backgrounds working in family mediation.

11–029

In "anchor mediation" one mediator starts the mediation and brings in a co-mediator later, if necessary. This may occur if for instance a specialist in a particular field is needed, including for example accredited financial mediators. However, this may raise questions for the couple about the initial mediator's ability to cope with the process. It may help for the mediator to indicate at the first enquiry that he or she generally mediates alone but that a co-mediator may be brought in later if that seems advisable.

11–030

---

[9] Robin Skynner and John Cleese, *Families and How to Survive Them* (London: Methuen, 1983) identify how individuals hide awkward emotions behind a "screen" (repression) and that many couples are secure in not looking behind their own or one another's screens. Healthy couples will help one another to bring feelings out into the open. However, if one is determined to change while the other resists change, that will inevitably lead to stresses in the relationship.

LAWYERS AND RIGHTS IN FAMILY MEDIATION

11-031 Periodically there are calls for marriage and relationship breakdown to be dealt with on the basis of parties' own values rather than on legal principles. For example, Marlow takes issue with the assumption that divorcing parties have a legal problem necessitating looking at legal rules for its resolution. If freed from the hegemony of the law, they can base their decisions on common sense and their own and not the law's sense of fairness.[10]

11-032 Marlow is correct in that divorce mediation is not necessarily dispute resolution—as this work has identified. It may well help people work constructively through a relationship breakdown and establish new ways of structuring their families and their finances. Also, it is open to them to import their own values and sense of fairness into the process, and the mediator should help them do this.

11-033 However, suggesting that parties in general should ignore legal principles in arriving at their decisions disregards the fundamental reality that parties "negotiate in the shadow of the law"[11] and that importing their own principles in ignorance of the legal position is to ask one or other of them to give up "blindfold" such benefits as they might have been entitled to receive had they worked through the legal system, as they would otherwise be able to do.

11-034 It is one thing to give up an entitlement on the basis of an informed decision to do so, if a party prefers to adopt his or her own sense of fairness. That is commonly done. It is arguably unrealistic and inappropriate to expect that everyone should do so without knowing what they are giving up, as a general practice.

11-035 It is a fundamental principle of family mediation that parties should be properly informed (by their lawyers) as to what adjudicated outcome might reasonably be expected. Mediators will not do so, though in some models, if parties are seeking a consent court order mediators will inform them if they are proposing an outcome which falls outside of the limits that a court would be likely to approve.

11-036 It is also a principle that parties who attend the mediation without their lawyers will have the opportunity to check any proposed settlement terms with their lawyers afterwards before any such proposals become binding. It is generally accepted that the ultimate professional responsibility for a party's acceptance of settlement terms lies with that party's individual lawyer; yet in many models parties' lawyers are excluded from the mediation process. There is however a model (sometimes called the "hybrid" model, because it combines elements of the civil and commercial model of practice with the family model) that does involve lawyers more closely in the process, which is further described below.

11-037 There is a consensus between mediators of all disciplines, including lawyers, that rights should not dominate the mediation process, though parties may inevitably have regard to them, among other considerations. It is generally

---

[10] Lenard Marlow, "Is Divorce Mediation a Form of Dispute Resolution?" (Spring 2011) *Family Mediation News*, published by the Family Section of the US Association for Conflict Resolution.
[11] R. H. Mnookin and L. Kornhauser, "Bargaining in the Shadow of the Law: The Case of Divorce" (1979) 88 Y.L.J. 950.

accepted that mediators should not advise parties on their rights or try to indicate what the outcome might be if litigated in the courts. Mediators should also not direct the parties towards any particular outcome, but may provide even-handed legal and other information to assist couples in making informed decisions.[12]

Lawyers as mediators

11–038 Many lawyers work as mediators, either as part of their legal practices, or separately, outside of legal practice. The Law Society of England and Wales allows them the option to work in either way, as long as they make it clear which way they are working. If conducting mediation outside their role as solicitor and outside their practice, they should comply with the Law Society's rules concerning "separate businesses" including not representing, directly or indirectly, that their mediation practice is regulated by the Solicitors Regulation Authority (SRA).[13] If mediating as a solicitor, it is clearly accepted that the function and conduct is different from the lawyer's traditional advisory role.

11–039 Family lawyers have knowledge of law and procedure, and experience of working with family issues and negotiation. They can provide information without influencing couples towards any particular outcome or advising. Those with a directive approach will have to "unlearn" this through mediation training. Their skills can then be re-assembled in a non-directive way that recognises and respects the couple's autonomy.

INCLUDING CHILDREN AND YOUNG PEOPLE IN MEDIATION AND DISPUTE RESOLUTION PROCESSES[14]

11–040 The United Nations Convention on the Rights of the Child 1989, adopted by the UK in 1991, states that in any matter or procedure affecting the child, the views of the child should be given due weight, in accordance with their age and maturity. Those capable of forming opinions should be assured of "the right to express their views freely" and should be given opportunities to express their views "either directly or through a representative or an appropriate body" (art.12).

11–041 In 2010 the UK government set up the Family Justice Review to examine the effectiveness of the family justice system and make recommendations for reform. The Review observed that

> "children's interests are central to the operation of the family justice system. Decisions should take the wishes of children into account.... Children and young people should be given age-appropriate information to explain what is happening

---

[12] This is accepted in Principle III(x) attached to the Council of Europe's Recommendation No.R (98) 1 on Family Mediation (1998).
[13] SRA Handbook—see *https://www.sra.org.uk/solicitors/handbook/code/part5/rule12/content.page* [accessed 16 May 2018].
[14] The authors are grateful to Lisa Parkinson for her substantial contribution to this section and for her permission to draw partly from Ch.8 in her book *Family Mediation*, 3rd edn (2014) Family Law.

and should be supported and enabled to make their views known. Older children should be offered 'a menu of options, to lay out the ways in which they could, if they wish, do this.'"[15]

11–042 The UK government endorsed the recommendations of the Family Justice Review and agreed initially that there should be "a non-legal presumption that all children and young people aged 10 and above should be offered the opportunity to have their voices heard in dispute resolution processes, including mediation, if they wish."[16] However, the proposed non-legal presumption has since been dropped and the Ministry of Justice seems unlikely to take it further. In contrast, the Family Mediation Council is taking a proactive approach in requiring nationally accredited family mediators to explain to those considering or taking part in mediation that their children aged 10 and above (and possibly younger) should be offered the opportunity to have their voices heard, if they wish, during the mediation process.[17] Paragraph 5.7.2 of the FMC Code of Practice provides as follows:

> "The Mediator must encourage the Participants to consider the children's wishes and feelings. All children and young people aged 10 and above should be offered the opportunity to have their voices heard directly during the Mediation, if they wish."[18]

If, as many experienced mediators understand, this is intended to require mediators to explain the options to parents and carers and encourage them to invite children and young people to participate in the process, rather than suggesting that such an invitation is obligatory for the mediator to extend in all cases, this paragraph would benefit from being revised accordingly.

11–043 There are a number of ways in which this may be arranged appropriately for and with the child or young person concerned, such as talking with a professionally qualified child counsellor or taking part in some way in the process of mediation. In practice, children and young people are rarely included in mediation directly, for a number of reasons. One of the main reasons is that the child is too young to be involved directly. A study of contested family law proceedings concerning children commissioned by the Ministry of Justice[19] found that 76 per cent of the children were under 10 years of age.

11–044 Older children, on the other hand, express great frustration and distress about their experiences of being drawn into their parents' battles and pressed to take sides, or ignored on the sidelines. A 12-year-old girl said: "I couldn't get my ideas heard; mum wouldn't let me go to court."[20] Another child said: "We needed to know what was going on, what was happening, how things would work out ... We needed help from outside, but there just didn't seem to be the right person to

---

[15] Family Justice Review, Final Report, 2011, Executive Summary, paras 8–9.
[16] Government Response to Final Report of the Voice of the Child Dispute Resolution Advisory Group, March 2015.
[17] See: *www.familymediationcouncil.org.uk/2017/06/09/child-inclusive-mediation/* [accessed 16 May 2018].
[18] FMC Code of Practice for Family Mediators, September 2016, s.5.7.2.
[19] Cassidy and Davey (2011) Ministry of Justice Research Summary 5/11, p.8.
[20] Office of the Children's Commissioner, *Don't Just Listen. Act* (Consultation Response to the Family Justice Review, July 2011), p.22.

turn to. No one seemed to be there to help us, especially us, the children. Mum and Dad had the lawyers, but we had no one".[21] During and following their parents' separation, older children and young people overwhelmingly report that they need information and want to be consulted on arrangements that affect their lives and well-being.[22] The opportunity to have their voice heard, if they wish, and to have their concerns and suggestions taken into account by their parents, offers considerable benefits for children and young people and also for their parents and carers in improving communication between children and parents.[23]

There are also potential disadvantages and pitfalls that require very careful attention and consideration. In June 2017 the FMC accepted the recommendations of an FMC working group on child-inclusive mediation.[24] These recommendations include essential principles (assessment of the suitability of mediation, safeguarding where needed of a child at risk or vulnerable adult, voluntary participation, informed consent, confidentiality, non-legally binding outcomes) and prerequisites for offering and undertaking child-inclusive mediation. Mediators must not only hold current FMC accreditation but must also have completed additional FMC approved training for child-inclusive mediation, must have a professional practice consultant with this additional specialist training and must comply with the FMC's standards and requirements. 11–045

Lisa Parkinson, who led the FMC working group on child-inclusive mediation, has written about the potential benefits and potential difficulties of this process, the competencies that mediators need to have and a checklist to work through in considering with parents the objectives and different ways in which a conversation with a child or young person can be arranged. Mediators help parents to consider the encouragement and reassurances their children may need about the invitation that is being offered to them.[25] 11–046

Research in Australia has compared child focused mediation with child-inclusive mediation.[26] In child focused mediation, the mediator helps parents to focus on their children's needs and provides relevant information. Children are not directly involved. In the Australian model of child-inclusive mediation, a child specialist meets with the child separately, possibly undertaking some form of play with a younger child, and then gives feedback to the parents in a subsequent mediation session on their interpretation of the child's experience, feelings and needs. The mediators then help parents to consider what they have heard and to incorporate the "children's agenda" into their negotiations about parenting plans. Experience in the UK suggests that parents appreciate being offered a range of options for child-inclusive mediation, rather than one fixed model. Older children and adolescents often ask to meet with the same mediator 11–047

---

[21] Lyon, Surrey and Timms, *Effective Support Services for children and young people when parental relationships break down—a child-centred approach* (University of Liverpool, 1998), p.5.
[22] J. Fortin, L. Scanlan and J. Hunt, "Taking a longer view of contact: the perspectives of young adults who experienced parental separation in their youth" [2013] Fam Law 104.
[23] Mediation Task Force Report, June 2014, Appendix A.
[24] See: www.familymediationcouncil.org.uk/2017/06/09/child-inclusive-mediation/ [accessed 16 May 2018].
[25] Lisa Parkinson, *Family Mediation,* 3rd edn (Family Law, 2014).
[26] Jennifer E. McIntosh, Caroline M. Long and Yvonne D. Wells, *Children beyond dispute: A four-year follow-up study of outcomes from Child Focused and Child Inclusive post-separation family dispute resolution* (Australian Attorney General's Department, with Family Transitions, Relationships Australia and La Trobe University, 2009).

who is meeting with their parents, because the mediator understands their family situation, whereas a counsellor does not have this knowledge and is not in contact with both parents. Alternatively, a different mediator may be involved.[27]

11–048 Research in Australia and the UK has shown that although there were inevitably variables, child inclusive mediation resulted in better outcomes than child-focused mediation in which the child did not take part.[28] Child-inclusive mediation led to more stable patterns of care and contact with which children were more content. There was a greater reduction in parental acrimony, children felt less caught in the middle, and parents were more able to resolve disputes that occurred post-mediation. Parents reported having learned more about their child and children confirmed the positive benefits they personally experienced.

11–049 The need to listen to the voice of the child and the benefits of child-inclusive mediation emerge clearly from research. All accredited mediators in England and Wales should have the knowledge and skills to be able to explain and discuss constructively with parents whether their children should be offered "the opportunity to have their voices heard directly during the Mediation, if they wish", as required by the FMC Code. The decision whether to involve their children directly, and if so, in what way, must be taken by the parents and agreed by them both, before any invitation is conveyed to the child. It must also be clear that the child is free to decline the invitation. In some cases it would be clearly inappropriate to involve a child directly and careful consideration is needed in all cases. Guidance on essential pre-conditions and contra-indications forms part of the additional training needed by mediators to obtain FMC recognition to undertake child-inclusive mediation.[29]

ISSUES AROUND MEDIATING WITH DOMESTIC VIOLENCE OR ABUSE

Abuse between the couple

11–050 A mediator is responsible for providing a secure environment, ensuring fairness of process and preventing manipulative, threatening or intimidating behaviour by either party. It is inherent in the mediation process and in many Codes of Practice that it cannot take place if one party conducts themselves in such a violent or abusive way towards the other that the process cannot be fairly or effectively carried out.

11–051 Concerns have been expressed whether mediation can protect the interests of those who are vulnerable to abuse and threat. There is a view that an abuser and victim can never negotiate on an equal footing. It is essential for mediators to be sensitive to such issues, which reflect a concern about power imbalances that most mediators would share.

11–052 There are different kinds of abuse. In 2013, the UK government provided a new definition of domestic violence and abuse as: "any incident or pattern of incidents of controlling, coercive, threatening behaviour, violence or abuse

---

[27] Parkinson, *Family Mediation*, Ch.8, para.8.6.
[28] See fn.26 above.
[29] See fn.24 and fn.25 above.

ISSUES AROUND MEDIATING WITH DOMESTIC VIOLENCE OR ABUSE

between those aged 16 or over who are, or have been, intimate partners or family members regardless of gender or sexuality. The abuse can encompass, but is not limited to:

"• psychological
• physical
• sexual
• financial
• emotional.[30]"

Abusive behaviour obviously includes direct violence, physical and sexual abuse and threatening or harassing behaviour. It also includes controlling or coercive conduct and emotional abuse such as ridicule and humiliation or any behaviour designed to undermine confidence or self-respect; economic abuse such as unilaterally closing a joint account, cutting off sources of cash or cancelling credit or bank cards; social abuse such as being insulting or offensive to friends, neighbours or family; and psychological abuse, where someone behaves subtly in a way that knowingly causes distress but which is not overtly objectionable, then dismisses the complaint as unreasonable or irrational. The last category includes for example "gaslighting" (named after the film "Gaslight"), where one person falsely denies his behaviour, and suggests that the other is becoming mentally disturbed.

11–053

Mediators need to have some form of screening mechanism for identifying cases where abusive behaviour exists that could affect the safety of a party or impact on the fairness and effectiveness of the mediation process. Screening may take place at different stages and in different ways:

11–054

- First indications may arise in the initial phone calls when the parties speak to the mediator to set up preliminary arrangements.
- There may then be an initial meeting (MIAM) when the mediator must undertake screening for domestic abuse in separate sessions. This allows a vulnerable party to discuss abuse more easily than in a joint meeting. It does, however, raise questions about confidentiality and practicalities: if a separate meeting indicates that mediation is not appropriate, the mediator would not ordinarily give the reason, though it might suggest itself.
- Indications may be given in the preliminary information or referral forms that the parties send to the mediator, which might have direct or indirect questions to help identify abuse.
- The issue may arise, directly or indirectly, during a mediation session. For example, a readiness by one party to make inappropriate concessions or admissions, especially if coupled with any other indications, might provide a clue to the possibility of abuse, threat or intimidation. Mediators should constantly be alert for signs of domestic abuse throughout the mediation process and screen as necessary.
- There may be physical signs of abuse.

---

[30] UK Home Office Guidance published 26 March 2013, updated 8 March 2016.

- Demeanour and non-verbal behaviour of either or both parties may provide an indication. Mediators should be on the lookout for tell-tale signs, such as one party being dominant and the other submissive (though of course, that does not necessarily indicate abuse).
- Patterns that exist in the relationship are likely to replicate themselves in the mediation, including for example high emotions, or abusive or sarcastic comments.
- If the mediation is being conducted in joint session, it may be appropriate to move into separate meetings to check the position if indications of possible abuse arise. Direct or indirect questions could be raised to check the position. Signals or halting revelations or admissions need to be gently eased out. People who are subject to abuse will not necessarily acknowledge this: they may be afraid or ashamed to do so. Indirect probing may take the form of asking each party whether he or she or the other has difficulty in coping with the stressful situation in the home. They may also be asked how they handle their own or the other's anger. It is ultimately necessary to establish whether one party is afraid of the other and how that affects the ability to arrive at decisions in the mediation fairly and effectively.

11–055 While the views and feelings of individuals who do not wish to enter mediation once there has been any violence should be respected, and any official rules or guidelines must be followed, the question of suitability for mediation may involve wider considerations including especially the following:

- *What is the severity of the abuse and in what circumstances did it occur?* There are qualitative differences between a minor one-off incident in a moment of anger and mutual provocation, and a pattern of serious and severe assaults. There is also a question as to the ability of the abuser to control his behaviour. Where, for example, an abuser is socially or emotionally dysfunctional, or suffers from alcoholism or substance abuse, mediation is unlikely to be appropriate (unless undertaken in conjunction with counselling, therapy or treatment for the problem condition, and then only with great care).
- *Does the perpetrator admit the abuse?* If the abuser acknowledges that abuse took place (even if details are not fully agreed) it allows the mediator and the parties to consider the possibility of mediation and any conditions. If however there is a dispute of fact about whether the occurrence took place or not, then mediation is very unlikely to be possible.
- *What is the genuine view of the victim in relation to the continuation of the mediation?* By ending the mediation, the mediator may force the couple into the courts, which may be the last thing that the victim wants. On the other hand, even a relatively "minor" incident may have a profound effect on someone sensitive to any such situation. The victim of abuse or threat may not be free to express a view, and therefore the mediator may not be able to establish whether a decision to continue is genuine.
- *How does the abuse relate to other power issues between the couple?* Abuse is a blatant, crude and immediate form of power imbalance. It is

likely in most cases to outweigh all other kinds of power disparities. Sometimes however other power issues may re-balance the abuse.
- *Is there a risk to the victim (or the mediator) if the mediation continues?* If the mediator believes that there is a real risk of harm to the victim or the mediator, that is the strongest indication that mediation is inappropriate.
- *Could the mediation continue if parallel steps were taken to protect the victim?* The parties may be able to agree on protection for either or both of them. For example, the perpetrator may agree to give undertakings to the other or through the court not to do certain things, or perhaps may consent to an injunction being taken out, even in agreed terms.[31] It may be helpful in appropriate cases to arrange for each party to have their lawyer present in the mediation to provide support and re-balance power. If any court order exists regulating the couple's relationship, for example, a non-molestation order, it is important for the mediator to see this to ensure that its terms are properly observed.

A person who has been subjected to abuse may well wish to have independent advice on whether or not mediation should take place. Other support services, including counselling (for either or both parties) may be available. A mediator who continues with the mediation where there has been violence or abuse must remain personally non-judgmental while making it clear to both parties that domestic violence and abuse are not acceptable. **11–056**

Mediators should have regard to continuing safety issues[32] such as ensuring that couples are not left together unsupervised and that a victim of abuse is allowed to leave the mediation first if appropriate. Machinery can also be established in the mediation to reduce the risk of conflict and to monitor arrangements for avoiding abusive behaviour. **11–057**

Child abuse

Mediators should also be alert to any possible indications that a child may have suffered or is at risk of suffering significant harm, and have a responsibility to deal with this issue. **11–058**

Most Codes of Practice cover this issue. For example, the FMC Code, adopted by its member organisations, provides that any specific allegation that a child has suffered significant harm is to be properly investigated, and that where the mediator suspects that a child is suffering or is likely to suffer significant harm, he or she must ensure that the appropriate agency or authority is notified. Wherever possible, the mediator should make such a notification after consultation with his or her Professional Practice Consultant—as mentioned below.[33] Any pending mediation would almost certainly need to be suspended pending the outcome of any such investigation. **11–059**

---

[31] This must be properly done, and must not become an abuse of court process.
[32] See Sherri L. Schornstein, *Domestic Violence and Health Care: What Every Professional Needs to Know* (California: Sage Publications, 1997), pp.117–135. Her concerns relate to hospitals and health care institutions, but the principles are adaptable to other circumstances. See also Helen L. Conway, *Domestic Violence: Picking up the Pieces* (Oxford: Lion Publishing Plc, 1997) which deals with issues concerning domestic violence and outlines options available for victims.
[33] Paragraph 5.5.3 of the FMC Code, September 2016.

11–060 The Agreement to Mediate should have a provision overriding confidentiality of the process in cases where children or others are at risk of significant harm. In any event, public policy provisions may override the duty of confidentiality.[34]

PROFESSIONAL CONSULTANCY OR SUPERVISION

11–061 Unlike civil and commercial mediation, which does not require mediators to have a supervisor or consultant for their practices, family mediation in the UK requires mediators to have someone working as a consultant to them, who can support their practices. The consultant supports their practices, having regard especially to the sensitivities of the subject-matter and the vulnerability of the parties and any children concerned.

11–062 Although initially viewed as supervision, it became clear that the "supervisor" had no real supervisory role and that this term could be misleading to the public. Hence the concept of consultancy was adopted, which led to the role of a Professional Practice Consultant (PPC).

11–063 The PPC supports a family mediator in entering practice, in dealing with challenging issues, in drafting summaries as required and generally in establishing a family mediation practice. There is a mandatory minimum number of hours meeting per annum, and optional communications and support throughout the year. The requirement of a PPC continues as long as a family mediator is practising in the UK, however senior the mediator becomes.

11–064 This consultancy requirement is not universal. In the US, for example, the Family Section of the Association for Conflict Resolution (ACR), formerly the Academy of Family Mediators, does not require this. Instead it provides in its Model Standards of Practice that "Mediators should participate in programs of peer consultation and should help train and mentor the work of less experienced mediators".[35]

MEDIATING UNMARRIED COHABITING COUPLES

11–065 The broad principles and models of family mediation will apply to unmarried couples, including same sex couples,[36] in a similar way to their application to married couples. However, in the UK, a number of differences apply to unmarried couples:

- The laws concerning finance and property relating to divorce and civil partnerships do not apply to unmarried couples.

---

[34] See Ch.15 for further consideration of confidentiality issues.
[35] Standard XIIIB.
[36] See, for example, S. Bryant, "Mediation for Lesbian and Gay Families" (1992) 9(4) *Mediation Quarterly* (M.Q.) 391. See also Douglas H. McIntyre, "Gay Parents and Child Custody: A Struggle Under the Legal System" (1994) 12(2) M.Q. 135; Isabelle R. Gunning, "Mediation as an Alternative to Court for Lesbian and Gay Families: Some Thoughts on Douglas McIntyre's Article" (1995) 13(1) M.Q. 47; Alan Campbell, "Mediation of Children Issues When One Parent is Gay" (1996) 14(1) M.Q. 79; Betsy J. Walter, "Lesbian Mediation: Resolving custody and visitation disputes when couples end their relationships" (2003) 41(1) *A.F.C.C. Family Court Review* 104–121.

- Unmarried cohabiting relationships may be governed by contractual arrangements or understandings, express or implied—which may sometimes be difficult to establish.
- However, s.8 of the Children Act 1989 does apply to unmarried couples, and orders under this section, for example relating to residence, contact and specific issues.
- The Trusts of Land and Appointment of Trustees Act 1996 (TOLATA) may be relevant in land disputes. This Act concerns co-owned real property and allows the court to make a declaration as to the respective beneficial interests, and where appropriate to order a sale of the property on the application of a joint owner.
- There could potentially be many other causes of action, based for example on contract, company law, partnership law or other principles; and more extensively, on trust law where constructive, resulting or implied trusts may be alleged; under the doctrine of proprietary estoppel; or under Sch.1 to the Children Act 1989.

As the legal principles differ between married and unmarried couples, some procedural differences will also arise, primarily that full financial disclosure is not required, as with divorce, though it may sometimes be voluntarily given. This is something that mediators might wish to clarify with parties to avoid any misapprehension. In other respects, as indicated above, the procedures outlined below for mediating on divorce and dissolution of civil partnerships will generally apply to unmarried couples. 11–066

FAMILY ISSUES OTHER THAN SEPARATION AND DIVORCE

There are also many other kinds of issues of a family nature which mediation can cover, especially using hybrid models that incorporate family and commercial ways of working. These include for example family business disputes; shareholder disputes involving family members; inheritance disputes (which may of course go beyond just family members); and a wide and varied range of family disputes, including for example siblings jointly administering inherited property, or parents in dispute with their children, or grandparents seeking contact with grandchildren. 11–067

Mediation can also address issues arising from parental abduction of children. In the US, Child Find of America, Inc has developed a programme using mediation to help prevent and resolve parental abductions.[37] In Europe, a number of initiatives have similarly been undertaken. The UK organisation *reunite*[38] offers a specialist mediation service dealing with international parental child 11–068

---

[37] See Helen D. Millar, "Resolving Parental Abduction: Child Find of America's Mediation Program" (1996) 13(3) *Mediation Quarterly* 207–216.
[38] See *http://www.reunite.org/* [accessed 16 May 2018].

abduction and wrongful retention; prevention of abduction where a family is separating and there are links with another country; contact across international borders; and relocation.[39]

THE STAGES OF FAMILY MEDIATION

11–069   The following outline will reflect various of the methods and approaches, rather than one distinct model.

PRE-MEDIATION: CONSIDERING MEDIATION, ASSESSING SUITABILITY AND OBTAINING COMMITMENT

11–070   This pre-mediation stage involves helping parties to decide whether mediation is likely to be appropriate and suitable for them.

11–071   Enquiries made at this initial stage may include a telephone discussion, email communication and providing the inquirer with written explanatory material.

11–072   Mediators should respond patiently, sensitively and in an informed way to specific inquiries about the process. It requires empathy and skills: people inquiring may be anxious, distressed and uncertain about the process or the best way to proceed.

11–073   As in other fields, increasing enquiries emanate from initial web research, so that people may have an idea of the process and the mediator's qualifications.

Intake sessions and MIAMs

11–074   Mediators provide an "intake" session to explain the process, obtain preliminary information and answer questions. This was, and remains, a requirement for the publicly funded process, also serving as screening for domestic violence and abuse. It has, however, now been more widely adopted in all cases and not just publicly funded, in the form of a Mediation Intake and Assessment Meeting (MIAM), as outlined above.

11–075   The procedure on MIAMs is generally to outline and explain the mediation process and to consider its suitability. The mediator conducting the meeting is also required to check that there has been no domestic abuse making mediation inappropriate. To this end, the mediator will ordinarily have a separate and private discussion with each party, as well as a joint discussion. If mediation is found to be inappropriate, the mediator is not obliged to give a reason, and would not ordinarily do so if abuse was the reason for refusal.

11–076   Even where a MIAM is not obligatory some mediators will nevertheless have an initial meeting along the lines of the MIAM. If the couple decide to go ahead with mediation, the Agreement to Mediate can be signed up and the process converted into an initial meeting. Other mediators do not have an initial

---

[39] A Revised draft Guide to Good Practice under the Hague Child Abduction Convention—Mediation—was published in 2012—see: *https://assets.hcch.net/upload/wop/abdguide5_mediation_en.pdf* [accessed 16 May 2018].

pre-mediation session, but use the initial mediation meeting as an opportunity to combine informal screening and discussion with making substantive progress.

Preliminary meeting with lawyers

Where both the couple have instructed lawyers, it is sometimes mutually helpful for the lawyers to have an initial meeting with the proposed mediator, without the parties attending. That meeting can serve a number of functions. The mediator can explain the process and can deal with any queries. The mediator can outline the lawyers' role, and where the mediator follows the "hybrid" model, with its separate confidential meetings with each party, this can be discussed as fully as necessary. The lawyers can decide whether they think that mediation would be suitable and whether they would propose to their clients to appoint that particular mediator. If everyone agrees that mediation will go ahead, they can take the opportunity to formulate an outline programme and timetable.

11–077

The meeting with lawyers does not replace the meetings that the mediator would have with the couple themselves, which would go ahead in the ordinary course. Nor does it disempower the couple: on the contrary, having given power over to the lawyers, it serves to re-empower the couple, while respecting their decision to be legally represented.

11–078

The Agreement to Mediate

It is standard practice, and generally required in Codes of Practice, for parties to enter into a written Agreement to Mediate before the formal process starts. This should apply even if the process is suggested by the Court or follows a MIAM. The terms may be agreed in advance, and the Agreement signed and exchanged at the first meeting.[40] Parties' lawyers and anyone else who may join the process should also sign the agreement to indicate acceptance of its terms, particularly with regard to confidentiality and privilege.

11–079

The Agreement will be likely to set out the ground-rules of the process, matters such as confidentiality and its exclusions, evidential privilege, and practical matters such as fees and complaints procedures. It may require each party to give commitment to the mediation and to provide full information relevant to their financial circumstances.

11–080

DURING THE MEDIATION: STAGE 1: PRELIMINARY COMMUNICATIONS AND PREPARATION

During this stage, the mediator obtains preliminary information from the parties, commonly in a form that is sent to the parties for completion and return before the initial session. This form may include personal information, details about children, initial data about finances, particulars of pending proceedings and legal representation, the matters that each wishes to deal with in the mediation, and any other relevant details.

11–081

---

[40] A specimen agreement is contained in the appendix.

11–082 Practical arrangements are usually made with the parties for the initial meeting, generally on the telephone and perhaps by email. Lawyers do not ordinarily attend the sessions, although they might do so by specific arrangement. There may be a number of different process options, for example:

- If there are limited issues, for example child contact only, one or two meetings may be sufficient.
- In all-issues mediation, three to six joint meetings of one and a half to two hours each are common. These may take place at agreed intervals, commonly fortnightly, or as needed. However, where the issues and financial circumstances are complex and/or the parties have difficulty in reaching agreement, more meetings or longer sessions may well be needed. Timing may be varied according to individual needs.
- The "hybrid" model mentioned below may be suitable for various kinds of issues, especially complex financial and property disputes, unmarried couples, those involving high conflict, and generally situations in which parties wish to have their lawyers more closely involved in the process, especially also if they have difficulty in negotiating directly with their partners themselves. In this model, lawyers play a greater role in supporting their clients. The mediator may, in addition to the usual procedures and meetings, arrange for an extended meeting which lawyers attend, and at which the mediator may in addition to any joint meeting, conduct a series of separate, confidential meetings with each party and their lawyer.[41]

11–083 Couples are not usually asked to make written submissions outlining their claims and the issues. It is also generally unhelpful to ask them to provide documents in advance, which if prematurely sought could meet with resistance or misunderstanding.

11–084 Where parties are legally represented, it is courteous (and in the hybrid model, standard) for the mediator to arrange with the parties to inform their lawyers of his or her involvement. Sometimes a meeting between the mediator and the lawyers might be a helpful initial step. This could usefully clarify the aspects that the mediation was going to cover, identify any reserved issues and the lawyers' role, and generally enable procedural matters to be addressed. If legal issues were likely to arise, these could also be identified. This can provide a good opportunity to establish a constructive framework for the mediation: lawyers commonly tend to cooperate with the process and to support it. An initial meeting with lawyers has not been common in family mediation in the UK, as it is in some other jurisdictions.[42]

---

[41] See below for further particulars of these separate meetings, and the special rules about confidentiality that will need to be agreed.

[42] For example, B. Landau, M. D. Bartoletti and R. Mesbur, *Family Mediation Handbook* (Toronto: Butterworths, 1987), p.48 say that in Canada "where both parties are represented at the outset of mediation, it is desirable to hold a meeting with both counsel present prior to beginning the mediation". In the US, lawyers do not usually meet with the mediator. However, in a survey of family lawyers in Florida, a relatively small responding sample indicated that over 55 per cent attended some mediation sessions with their clients, and that 14.8 per cent only did so for the first session to satisfy themselves about the mediator's training, skills and experience. (Susan W. Harrell, "Why Attorneys Attend Mediation Sessions" (1995) 12(4) *Mediation Quarterly* 369–377).

The mediator will arrange a suitable venue for the initial meeting with the couple, ideally a room with a sympathetic but business-like ambience.   **11–085**

The reception arrangements should ensure that the mediator is notified as soon as each party arrives, so that they are not left alone together for any length of time (and where tensions are high or there is any risk of confrontation or abuse, not at all). Some mediators have two separate reception areas so that where appropriate, couples can be kept apart at this sensitive and sometimes volatile stage. Alternatively, the first party to arrive might be shown straight into the mediation room while the other waits in the reception area.   **11–086**

STAGE 2: COMMENCING THE MEDIATION, ESTABLISHING THE ISSUES AND SETTING THE AGENDA

At the first substantive meeting, the mediator will welcome the couple and bring them into the joint meeting room. Offering refreshments at the beginning of the meeting can make the process somewhat less formal.   **11–087**

As to seating arrangements, where no table or only a small coffee table is used, the couple will usually face the mediator, with both chairs turned slightly inwards. It is however usually more practical and business-like for the parties to be seated around a table.   **11–088**

The mediator should have all necessary equipment and material in the room. This may include a flip chart, calculator, tissues, diary and reference material such as information and tax tables.   **11–089**

The mediator may start by acknowledging the forms that the couple have sent in and reiterating the ground-rules for the mediation, especially concerning privilege and confidentiality. The agreement to mediate, previously approved, will be signed. The use of first names all round may be agreed with the parties.   **11–090**

The mediation is undertaken on the basis that no agreement arrived at by the couple in the mediation is to be binding until they have both had an opportunity to take independent legal advice at the end of the process. That will be re-affirmed.[43]   **11–091**

In most family mediation, parties are not ordinarily asked to make presentations of their respective positions, as parties in civil or commercial mediation would be. Bearing in mind that the couple may sometimes find it difficult to meet together, and may need help in managing the conflict between them, any decision to focus on their differences, especially in a presentational form, could well be counter-productive.   **11–092**

The mediator does not usually seek the reasons for the breakdown of the relationship, though these may be established at some stage if this becomes relevant.[44] The dynamic between the couple and the factors leading to their differences often become apparent during the course of the mediation.   **11–093**

---

[43] The FMC Code para.6.15 provides: "The Mediator must inform the Participants of the advantages of seeking independent legal or other appropriate advice whenever this appears desirable during the course of the Mediation. The Mediator must advise the Participants that it is in their own interests to seek independent legal advice before reaching any final agreement, and warn them of the risks and disadvantages if they do not do so."

[44] Some mediators, while accepting the value of future-focus, place value on parties talking about past issues that have been important to them in forming present attitudes.

11–094 In some models the mediator meets each party at this stage to hear their views without the other one present and paraphrases their comments to the other in joint meeting.

11–095 The mediator establishes the parties' issues in a number of ways. They may briefly be mentioned or inferred during the initial phone enquiry. Then parties may be invited to say in the preliminary information form what they hope the mediation will achieve. The main occasion for establishing the issues will be during the initial joint meeting. The mediator will elicit the issues from the parties and establish an agenda, commonly writing this up on a flip chart in a non-contentious way. If the parties start engaging in substantive discussion about the issues, the mediator will try to maintain the focus on the agenda until it has been comprehensively prepared (unless there is a genuinely urgent issue needing immediate attention). The issues may then be prioritised according to the preference of the parties.

11–096 It is good practice to check the agenda with the parties at the start of each subsequent meeting as new issues may emerge or priorities may change.

STAGE 3: INFORMATION GATHERING

11–097 The culture of family mediation differs from other kinds of mediation in the information-gathering stage for a number of reasons:

- In relation to divorce and the dissolution of civil partnerships in the UK financial arrangements are not normally made without complete reciprocal disclosure of financial means and circumstances (though this does not ordinarily apply to unmarried couples).
- A court asked to make an order on financial aspects will ordinarily require an outline of the parties' respective financial positions. If the court reviewing a proposed order has any query it may decline to make the order until having clarified and resolved any such query.
- Any financial arrangements on divorce may be vulnerable to being set aside if a material non-disclosure or misstatement is subsequently discovered.
- Information gathering may be particularly important to enable the couple to make informed decisions about their futures and those of any children.
- It is not uncommon for there to be a discrepancy of knowledge about finances between the couple, redressed through the information exchange stage.

11–098 Mediation is not a soft option so far as disclosure is concerned. Divorcing couples are expected to make the same full disclosure as they would in adversarial proceedings. Mediators cannot undertake to verify such disclosure, though they will ordinarily provide the opportunities for such disclosures to be discussed and tested. They may mention ways in which verification can, if required, take place, for example by the production of documentary evidence or through the couple's own solicitors or on oath, as may be appropriate.

11–099 There are different kinds of information in family matters. Some will be factual, such as facts about the marriage, children and financial circumstances.

STAGE 4: CONDUCTING SUBSTANTIVE NEGOTIATIONS

Some will be technical, such as valuations of property, insurances or pensions, tax implications and legal considerations. Some may underlie the observable facts, such as the relationship between the parties and with their children, the underlying emotions of the parties and their respective aspirations, expectations, wants and needs. Inevitably parties will agree on some information, and not on others; and there will be views and perceptions that differ.

One area where a particularly structured approach is taken to information gathering is that of finance. There are different ways of gathering this information; but whichever method is used, it is essential that this should be carefully and effectively garnered and pooled. **11–100**

Parties are ordinarily each given a financial disclosure form, which embodies an extensive questionnaire covering all aspects of their financial affairs in considerable detail.[45] This is to be completed and returned to the mediator by an agreed date. It is generally sensible for parties to check this form with their lawyers especially where the finances are substantial or complex. The information which each party furnishes in completing this form is jointly considered, displayed on a flip chart (or an electronic screen) and used as the basis for any amplification or particularisation that may be required, and for the further discussions and negotiations that will then take place. **11–101**

There is no standard form or financial documentation for unmarried couples, though some may voluntarily complete the divorce financial forms. Others will only provide information relevant to their legal obligations, which a court would and could enforce. **11–102**

Information may continue to emerge throughout the mediation. Details or documents which are not initially available may come to hand; valuations may be obtained; assets may be sold or acquired; circumstances may change. **11–103**

Care must be taken that the parties do not make substantive decisions before sufficient information is available. This does not mean until total and complete particularisation is achieved. There is no reason why discussions cannot take place while the information is being collected together, and preliminary directions and options can be examined parallel to the information-gathering process. **11–104**

STAGE 4: CONDUCTING SUBSTANTIVE NEGOTIATIONS

This is the substantive stage of mediation. The mediator helps the parties to communicate with one another and to negotiate acceptable terms. This is usually done with the couple in joint sessions, but may be done in separate meetings at any time during the mediation. **11–105**

Option development

One of the mediator's primary functions is to help parties to identify and develop options for dealing with their issues, and then to prioritise and narrow these down to those that both would find acceptable. **11–106**

---

[45] A standard disclosure form (Form E) is used in UK divorce practice.

11–107 This could apply to any aspect of the relationship. Where housing arrangements are being considered, for example, options may include the family home being retained or sold (if it is owned); and if retained, either party remaining in it, and in that event, either indefinitely or for a limited period, with options as to the nature of the limitation. If it is sold, there will be options for dealing with the proceeds of sale to enable both parties to acquire new housing.

11–108 If the issues relate to children, different parenting possibilities can be explored. These do not have to be limited by the legal concepts of "residence" and "contact" but can rather be more generally embraced under "arrangements for the children". Other options for each having proper time and good communications with the children may be considered. Parents usually share common concerns about the well-being of their children, and it can help to focus on this and to acknowledge the mutuality of these concerns.

11–109 Whatever issues are being discussed, the generation of options is a freeing exercise. The parties would usually put options forward, through brainstorming or in the course of discussing possibilities generally. They need not, however, be limited to the parties' ideas: the mediator can add to the options, provided that these are not seen as his or her recommendations.

Providing information

11–110 The family mediator's role may include some element of providing an educative function for the parties. A line must, however, be drawn when that information becomes "advice", which is not an acceptable part of the mediation process.

11–111 Clear and general legal principles would be regarded as proper information that can be given to a couple by the mediator; but if the mediator tries to anticipate what a court would order in their particular circumstances, that would be advice not information, and would not be proper mediation practice. Some models provide for the parties to be informed if the mediator considers that their proposals fall outside the parameters that a court would be likely to approve.

11–112 As a general principle, decisions in family mediation should be made on an informed basis. Consequently, parties should ordinarily be encouraged to obtain advice or information from their lawyers or other professional advisers, and mediators may need to inform parties when they should do so—particularly before any proposed resolution is to be formalised.

Using communication skills

11–113 These skills are used throughout the mediation. To facilitate discussion and negotiation, the mediator has to be able to listen effectively and to help the couple to hear one another; to summarise and reframe effectively, sensitively and accurately; to acknowledge parties and help one another to do so where appropriate; to mutualise concerns and interests and normalise their feelings and anxieties. These and other skills are considered in greater detail in Ch.14.

STAGE 4: CONDUCTING SUBSTANTIVE NEGOTIATIONS

Dealing with the expression of emotions

11–114 Inevitably, when a marriage or relationship is going through the crisis of breakdown, parties will experience many emotional reactions. These will obviously vary between individuals, and will shift from time to time and sometimes rapidly within each individual.

11–115 Emotions commonly experienced may include anger, disbelief, grief, distress, sadness, loss, humiliation, hatred, hurt, fear, anxiety, guilt, blaming, self-doubt and relief. Some people may be in a state of denial about what is happening, as their way of coping. Some may suffer depression, which is manifested as an inability to feel other emotions. Others may feel a loss of self-confidence and self-worth.

11–116 People may experience many of these emotions within the mediation forum, especially during this phase of substantive discussions. The intensity of such feelings will depend on various factors including how much time has passed since the breakdown arose, how well each person has adjusted to it and whether they have had professional support such as counselling or therapy.

11–117 Where any of these emotions are manifested in the mediation, mediators have to be able to respond appropriately. Their personal attributes, including empathy and sensitivity, will help, as will their training and professional background. Expressions of emotion should be acknowledged and treated as normal and neither suppressed nor stimulated by the mediator. If the emotions are intense the mediator may have a short break and/or help the person concerned to regain his or her cognitive functions, which can be impaired by the intensity of feeling. There is a view that "venting" emotions may be helpful, but this is not necessarily correct: rekindling emotions may preclude effective cognitive functioning. Counselling in another forum may be useful, but that is not the role of the mediator. Parties often appreciate being gently and sensitively brought back to the task in hand in these circumstances. Where appropriate, however, the mediator's role does include "sign-posting" parties to other services, including counselling.

Managing the process

11–118 The mediator needs to be a proficient manager of the mediation process. This necessitates having an agenda for each session, albeit informal; controlling the procedure; constantly making decisions what to address; setting an appropriate pace for the process; controlling negative or abusive behaviour; and generally acting as a firm but fair chairperson.

11–119 If a mediator loses control of the management of the process, whether by allowing any party to dominate the proceedings or merely by a general inability to maintain authority, trust and confidence are likely to be eroded. The corollary of this is not domineering regulation by the mediator, but gentle, firm, impartial and effective management control.

Helping with reality testing

11–120 A party may have a misconceived impression about the other or about any factual situation. The mediator can help to redress distortions of fact, by thoughtful questioning, and by facilitating accurate information being brought into the process.

11–121 A party may have a misconceived idea about the implications and effect of proposals that he or she is making or considering, or of a course of action under consideration. The mediator can help the parties to consider such proposals and to try to ensure that they are realistic—and where appropriate that they will stand the test of time. This may be done in joint meetings. If done in separate meetings, the mediator can help to filter such proposals by acting as an informal sounding board for the party thinking of putting them forward.

Care must always be taken to ensure that the mediator is not imposing his or her version of reality on the couple.

Facilitating negotiations and decision-making

11–122 Certain common themes run through all kinds of issues. These are facilitating communications; encouraging a problem-solving approach; helping with the generation, development and exploration of options; and assisting in translating needs, interests and concerns into concrete proposals and terms.

11–123 The mediator can help in many practical ways. For example, if a divorce is being discussed, the mediator can help the parties to consider who will file the petition, when and on what grounds, and may also discuss the actual contents of the petition so that when received it will not be viewed as a hostile document.

11–124 If the issues relate to property and finance, there are a number of possible approaches. One is to invite the couple to examine their respective needs. Another is to review their capital, income and expenditure with them and to help them explore how their respective future living plans can be financed. It can be helpful for mediators to provide parties with budget/expenditure sheets as a practical tool to facilitate this examination and discussion. Where there is a shortfall of financial resources, the mediator can assist the couple to examine how that will be met; and where there is a surplus to both of their needs, a division needs to be discussed which is acceptable to both.

11–125 These approaches are by no means free from difficulty: individual perceptions of fairness may vary, and legal principles may not necessarily accord either with notions of fairness or with respective needs.[46]

---

[46] For example, the landmark House of Lords case of *White v White* [2001] 1 A.C. 596; [2000] 3 W.L.R. 1571 established a yardstick of equal financial division, within the court's discretion, rather than simply on the basis of needs. Parties in mediation may not wish to consider needs but might rather argue for broad equality; or one may argue for this where the other does not accept the principle. These issues may need to be addressed in the mediation forum, as part of the overall discussions.

STAGE 4: CONDUCTING SUBSTANTIVE NEGOTIATIONS

Children's issues and parenting plans

Family mediators are generally very mindful of the need to help parents consider the voices of any children of the family if they are not participating in the mediation. In working with issues concerning children, the parents' focus may be on their own rights, and the mediator may need to help them also consider the position from the children's perspective.   11–126

It is sometimes very useful to help the couple construct a parenting plan for the children.   11–127

This may cover a range of aspects including for example detailing the time the children will spend with each parent, who else will have a role in looking after children, educational arrangements and how school and extra-mural activities will be dealt with, holiday arrangements, agreed "house rules" to establish consistency of parenting, decision-making, and dealing with any health issues. Future contingencies might be covered such as how to introduce any new partner to the children and moving house or country. Provision may be made for periodical reviews, particularly in the early stages, either by the parties themselves or with third party support. Each parenting plan has to be individualised to the needs of each family. It can be a very helpful document for parents to work on, to give them a clear sense of shared responsibility, and to have as a guide for the future—with sufficient flexibility to allow for changes as they arise.

Separate meetings (caucuses): using the "hybrid" model

Although some models of family mediation in the UK involve having separate meetings with each party, this has not been widely used in family mediation. It may be used for intake and as an impasse strategy, but there is now an increasing adoption of this way of working in the family mediation process.   11–128

This "hybrid" model of practice is not separate from the standard model described above. It is rather an extension of the standard model that can be incorporated in a bespoke way, as required. It involves the following: 11–129

- Parties' lawyers tend to be more directly involved in the process, either from the outset, or brought in as the parties require. The mediator will liaise directly with them, and they may attend some or all meetings.
- The parties may involve their lawyers in the provision of financial information, including helping with the completion of the financial disclosure documentation (Form E). Lawyers will commonly also attend some sessions, especially those involving separate meetings.
- The mediator will meet the parties separately, and is likely to ask them to agree that separate confidences can be maintained, save as they may authorise, and save also that any financial information given to the mediator, which would be open in the standard model, will not be confidential but will be disclosed to the other, and will be treated as open and not privileged from disclosure to the court. This needs to be provided for in the Agreement to Mediate.

- As in the civil-commercial model, the mediator may shuttle between the two parties carrying messages and proposals. This caucusing process may also allow the mediators to examine the underlying issues and concerns more carefully.[47]
- Caucusing is more time-consuming than joint meetings. At least three or more hours should ordinarily be allowed for sessions involving separate meetings.

11–130　The "hybrid" process is a valuable and ethically proper way of working, and sits well alongside the standard model. It may be less useful for issues such as parenting, which need to focus on the improvement of communications and the strengthening of joint discussions. It may have greater use in resolving issues such as property and finance, especially where these are complex and each party wants more time on his or her own to consider matters and perhaps to reality test with the mediator. It places greater power in the hands of the mediator, and should be used with circumspection, care and sensitivity.

STAGE 5: DEALING WITH IMPASSE

11–131　An impasse strategy is one designed to help a couple to resolve deadlock. The general principles and strategies outlined in relation to mediation generally may be similarly applicable to family mediation. It will also be helpful to consider some impasse strategies specific to family mediation:

Pausing and reflecting

11–132　When an impasse surfaces, the mediator may want to pause and consider what it is about. What has caused it? Does it arise because of the parties' personal or emotional needs, or is it a matter of substance? Has the mediator contributed to the impasse by his or her comments or attitude? Might the mediator's approach or attitude towards either party fuel rather than resolve the dispute? Although the temptation may be great to try to find a quick solution to the impasse, it may help just to take time to pause and reflect on it.

Allow the parties to absorb the progress

11–133　Sometimes parties need time to absorb the progress that they have made. Each may feel that he or she has gone too far and given away too much. It may help just to review the position, to acknowledge the progress that has been made, and to mutualise by making it clear that both have shifted from their original positions (which is invariably the case). Instead of pressing them, the mediator may give them time to reflect on the position.

---

[47] See Christopher W. Moore, "The Caucus: Private Meetings That Promote Settlement" (1987) 16 *Mediation Quarterly* 87.

STAGE 5: DEALING WITH IMPASSE

Addressing underlying fears and concerns

An impasse may be caused by a party being blocked, often unwittingly, by his or her underlying fears and concerns. Once this is identified, these can be discussed and addressed. 11–134

An impasse may mask anxiety about the future. Will I be able to cope, will I feel very lonely, will it be possible to maintain a proper relationship with the children? These may not be articulated in these ways, but they may be the concerns that are blocking progress. The mediator may articulate these and examine them with the couple. By helping underlying issues to surface, the mediator can put them into perspective and help to see that they are addressed. 11–135

Addressing unresolved emotional blocks

In some cases, the impasse may arise because of unresolved emotional blocks that prevent the mediation from continuing effectively. The mediator should consider whether he or she can deal with this in the mediation or whether it is appropriate to discuss with the couple the possibility of their seeing a counsellor or therapist, either together or separately. 11–136

One of the most difficult kinds of couples to deal with are those where either or both of them have not emotionally separated from one another. They have been referred to as "undifferentiated" or "enmeshed" spouses. Undifferentiated couples can be among the most difficult to mediate because commonly their boundaries are blurred, their objectives are confused, their communications are intense but superficial, their ability to make and implement decisions is poor and their emotions are raw.[48] Conflict and polarised positions are likely to be high with such couples. 11–137

The mediator dealing with such couples needs to be pro-active and maintain firm control of the process, providing a clear structure and highly defined rules. Professional support in therapy or counselling may be necessary. Sometimes formal adjudication may be essential for such couples. 11–138

Dealing with cyclical patterns of behaviour

Patterns of behaviour that operated during the relationship are likely to be repeated in the mediation process, such as cycles of conflict and mutual recrimination. One of the mediator's functions is to identify such patterns and help the couple to break from them and use the mediation more effectively. In appropriate situations the mediator may draw the couple's attention to their patterns and ask them if they would create their own rules for overcoming those patterns which block their objective of arriving at an agreed resolution. 11–139

---

[48] See Richard D. Mathis, "Couples from Hell: Undifferentiated Spouses in Divorce Mediation" (1998) 16(1) *Mediation Quarterly* 37.

Considering perceptions of fairness

11–140   An impasse may exist because of different perceptions of fairness. The problem is that it is very difficult to help people to agree on fairness when they start from different viewpoints. It may help to discuss the issue in terms of fairness. What aspect is not fair? What would need to be done to make it fair? If these differences of perception cannot be reconciled, it may nevertheless make it clear to the couple how people can see things in different ways, and that this is not unnatural or wrong.

11–141   People do not necessarily change their perceptions of fairness by listening to others; but they may gain a better understanding of the other's perspective. Perhaps they may each have to maintain awareness that there are other perspectives.

Recognising the power of words and symbolism

11–142   Sometimes deadlocks arise because of terminology or the symbolic implications of some aspect of the proposed agreement. Seeking to retain a key to the door of the family home after moving out is an example: in addition to practical implications, it carries symbolic meanings including recognition of ownership and a right to enter at will. The corollary carries corresponding symbolism including not having personal autonomy and privacy in one's home and life. This may be addressed at a practical level, but the symbolism may need to be recognised, for example by recording the basis on which practical arrangements are made. The leaving partner may, for example, agree to leave the key with a neighbour rather than give it up, and it may be agreed that he or she will only use it in emergencies, and otherwise will call at the house by prior arrangement, while also recording his or her underlying rights as a co-owner of the property. The solution may lie in a mixture of practicality and symbolism. And in this context, it may be noted that the term "family home" itself is likely to have symbolic overtones, which can be avoided by referring instead to the property address.

11–143   "Residence" and "contact" in relation to children could be words with symbolic overtones that may be avoided by instead referring to "arrangements for the children". It may in some cases be necessary to acknowledge and record the concept of equality of parenting, and help parties to agree principles based on this concept, including in relation to joint decision-making, while not necessarily dividing time on an absolutely equal basis, which may not be practicable. The concept of "co-parenting" may be emphasised.

11–144   Similarly, certain items or events may have a symbolic meaning to one party, not necessarily identified in the mediation (perhaps not even appreciated by the party). A relatively minor point may be fought over just so that each can show the other who was actually right about the ending of the relationship.

Short term experiments and reviews

11–145   If there is disagreement about a proposed course of action, the parties could test it out over a short term before deciding whether to commit themselves to it. They could give reciprocal assurances as necessary; and a review date could be agreed

STAGE 5: DEALING WITH IMPASSE

when they could examine how matters worked during the test period. This may feel less threatening and more creative than immediately implementing untested proposals about which one party is uneasy. The parties could undertake the review themselves, and be able to call on the mediator again at that stage to help them with the review if necessary.

Managing differences of legal perception

An impasse may arise if the parties have received conflicting advice from their independent legal advisers. On the assumption that both views cannot be correct, the mediators could consider a number of possible strategies for helping the couple to resolve this impasse without undermining the individual advisers: **11–146**

- The mediator could help the parties to formulate questions to take to their lawyers, for example, as to prospects of success and likely costs of proceeding to trial. These particulars can help the parties to evaluate whether or not it is worth continuing in mediation.
- An option for both parties might be to seek a second opinion through their solicitors, for example from a barrister, on the points in issue. The mediator can help the parties to formulate the questions to be raised with counsel. In the UK, facilities exist for parties to have direct access to barristers without having to engage a solicitor to arrange this.
- Alternatively, the mediator could assist the parties in getting a joint opinion from a neutral barrister or a solicitor. This could be done through the parties' own legal advisers by their collaborating on jointly briefing counsel, perhaps (if required) coupled with an addendum from each party outlining their respective contentions. Such a non-binding evaluation could help the parties and their advisers to shift from entrenched positions and negotiate more realistically. The non-binding opinion could be brought into the next mediation meeting and could serve as a helpful basis for further discussion, and for movement from the stalemate. Further alternatively, a single issue obstructing progress could be dealt with through family arbitration, and the parties could then continue with mediation.[49]
- The mediator might suggest that respective legal advisers attend a mediation meeting with the couple to examine matters more fully. Both legal advisers could then expand on their respective views with everyone present. They would, however, be encouraged thereafter to move into a problem-solving mode, and the opportunity could be taken to explore ways of resolving the deadlock, including caucusing if necessary.

Using draft summaries

The mediator can provide a draft summary of the position to date for use at the following meeting. This would cover the issues already resolved and those remaining in contention and unresolved, in the latter case outlining alternatives based on ideas already put forward. By seeing what has already been achieved, **11–147**

---

[49] See para.11-154 below.

and having an outline of what remains outstanding, with parameters for discussion, parties have a clearer visual grasp of what needs to be done.

11–148 This ties in with the fact that at an early stage of the process, people may be inclined to be bullish, but as terms take shape and a momentum is established, they increasingly have more to lose by the deal falling through. At some point, the balance tilts towards resolution. Parties who are stuck at this later stage would particularly benefit from having a visual reminder of what has been achieved so far and what is at risk of being lost. They may not necessarily accept these terms, but may be loath to lose them, and this may serve as a spur to breaking the impasse.

Risk assessment (BATNA/WATNA)[50]

11–149 The mediator may suggest that the parties each examine their best and worst alternatives to reaching agreement in the mediation. BATNA calculates the position if everything went in the best way in an alternative forum. It explores outcome, cost, time factors, effects on family and relationships, and all other factors if that party chose to go down a different route from settling in mediation.

11–150 The WATNA exercise calculates the position if things went badly in an alternative forum for a party who decided not to settle in mediation. Assuming the worst result, it explores the outcome, cost, time factors, effects on family and relationships, and all other factors if that party chose to go down a different route from settling in mediation and was unsuccessful.

11–151 With the benefit of best and worst alternatives, calculated separately by each party, they will have a better idea of what faces them at best and at worst if they decided not to settle. This can help them to re-examine any stuck issues.

11–152 However it is done, effective risk assessment is an important element of helping people to reach a resolution of the issues. The mediator would not ordinarily be involved in this exercise, but can assist parties and their lawyers by discussing with them the aspects that they may wish to consider—not just the obvious ones such as risk, cost and delay, but also the other effects of litigating, including stress, effects on children and family, and indirect costs through lost time.

Separate meetings (caucuses)

11–153 If the couple have only been meeting in joint session, the use of separate confidential (caucusing) meetings may be a useful option to break a deadlock, allowing each to take the mediator into their confidence about how matters could move forward. With these insights, the mediator may be able to help them craft terms that meet their respective needs. Lawyers might well attend these meetings, and would be likely to do so in the "hybrid" model.[51] Where separate meetings might potentially be offered, this should be provided for in the Agreement to Mediate, and parties informed of the option at the outset.

---

[50] See Ch.4, paras 4-006 to 4-008.
[51] Note the special rules about confidentiality mentioned above.

STAGE 6: CONCLUDING MEDIATION AND RECORDING THE OUTCOME

Family arbitration

In this process, parties can appoint a specialist family arbitrator to make a final and binding determination of any financial and/or property disputes or in some cases, child-related issues, arising from family relationships. The parties may participate in arranging the procedures relevant to their circumstances. Organisations that provide this form of arbitration include the family lawyers' organisation Resolution and The Institute of Family Law Arbitrators, as well as individual arbitrators.[52] 11–154

Preparing for adjudication

Where an impasse cannot be resolved, the mediators can sometimes help the couple to prepare for adjudication in a constructive way. This may involve narrowing the issues, and helping them to take a non-hostile view of the fact that a third party adjudication is needed. That, after all, remains their right and is an entirely appropriate choice in some circumstances. In some cases, dealing with the deadlocked issues in this way can also serve as an impasse strategy in its own right. 11–155

STAGE 6: CONCLUDING MEDIATION AND RECORDING THE OUTCOME

Concluding the mediation

Family mediation may be ended by either party or by the mediator. It will ordinarily end when the parties have resolved their issues: but it may end without the parties reaching consensus on all issues. Outstanding issues would need to be dealt with by their respective legal advisers, and through the court if necessary. In this event, they may decide to endorse any partial agreements reached in the mediation, limiting their dispute only to the unresolved points; or they may disregard the partial resolution and deal in the adversarial process with all issues. Even if resolution is not reached, the mediation may have helped by dealing with information gathering, and narrowing the issues. Settlement possibilities discussed in the mediation, although initially rejected, often come back into focus at a later stage. 11–156

The mediation may end or be suspended because the parties decide to go to counselling or therapy. Mediators must keep the possibility of reconciliation in mind.[53] Counselling may address the possibility of reconciliation, or it may aim to help couples with other issues, such as coming to terms with the separation or considering children's needs. 11–157

Alternatively, mediation may be discontinued because the couple have gone as far as they can or want to at that time, perhaps deferring any further discussion 11–158

---

[52] See Ch.6, paras 6-061 to 6-066, for further reference to this process.
[53] This is required under many Codes of Practice.

pending the happening of a certain event such as a child completing a particular stage of education, or the couple first selling a property.

11–159   In some cases, the mediator may initiate the termination. This could happen if, for example, the mediator felt that it was inappropriate to continue with the mediation for any reason such as one party abusing the process or the couple reaching a stage where it became clear that no further progress was likely. Most Codes of Practice will specify circumstances in which mediation should be discontinued by the mediator.

Preparing summaries and memoranda

11–160   As any proposals reached in mediation are ordinarily subject to the parties having the opportunity to take professional advice on them before they become binding agreements, any document recording these proposals would not be an agreement.[54]

11–161   The mediator usually drafts a non-binding memorandum of understanding[55] on a without-prejudice basis, setting out the proposed terms, as well as an open summary of financial information, both of which the couple can take to their respective solicitors.

11–162   Where the mediation ends without complete resolution, it may still be appropriate and helpful to the parties for an off-the-record written memorandum or summary to be prepared. This can set out the issues that were resolved and those that remained unresolved, perhaps indicating the alternative options put forward by each and the parameters of any outstanding disagreement. This can serve both as an informal note to prevent misunderstanding as to the status of any partially resolved aspects, and as an agenda for any settlement discussions that the respective solicitors may wish to enter into.

11–163   Mediation memoranda and summaries are usually written in non-legal style, informal but clear, precise and sufficiently specific to avoid any ambiguity or misunderstanding. They should though cover all points in such a way that the independent lawyers acting for the parties can prepare any necessary documents based on the clarity and sufficiency of information. Lawyer mediators do not ordinarily draft the legal documents flowing from the mediation, though this policy has periodical reconsideration.[56]

11–164   Each solicitor can then advise their client on an individual basis, and may liaise with the other party's solicitor to arrange for the preparation of any formal documentation or court order and for any necessary formalities to be complied with.

---

[54] Care needs to be taken in relation to the concept of "agreement". Once there is "agreement" (perhaps even conditional), without prejudice communications may be looked into and may be treated as if open. It is therefore advisable to avoid the notion of "agreement" until parties are ready to bind themselves, having had independent legal advice, and merely refer to "proposals".
[55] Terminology varies. The term "memorandum of understanding" (or MoU) is widely used. "Summary of proposals" is preferred by some, but less frequently used.
[56] They might though help the couple to draft otherwise contentious aspects, such as behaviour clauses in divorce petitions. Where solicitors mediate as part of their solicitor's practice, the question is bound to arise as to their being able to prepare Deeds of Separation and draft court orders. The ethical and practical implications of this remain to be considered, but the current consensus is that they should not do so.

If both parties' lawyers attended the mediation or the concluding stage when mutually acceptable terms were arrived at, it might not be necessary for the mediator to prepare summaries: the respective lawyers would be in a position to undertake the drafting themselves. 11–165

Concluding formalities

Where the mediator has drafted and sent out summaries, any query or reservation about the proposed terms may be resolved between the parties themselves, or by their respective legal advisers. 11–166

In general, while respective solicitors will examine proposals and may raise questions, they are not generally obstructive of their client's wishes. If legal advisers raise matters which seem to merit any review of the proposed agreement, these can be brought to another mediation meeting for discussion; and if necessary, the respective legal advisers can be invited to attend the meeting. In such event, the mediators might ask them to assist in adopting a problem-solving approach to help find ways to allow the parties to achieve an agreed resolution while accommodating as far as possible any concerns raised. 11–167

Mediators may be willing to discuss the summaries with the individual lawyers, but should obtain the consent of both parties to do so if not previously given. With the approval of the parties, there is no reason why the mediators cannot clarify any drafting questions that may be raised by the parties' solicitors. In the "hybrid" model, the mediator is likely to have been liaising with the lawyers in any event, and communications between the mediator and the lawyers would be part of the process, whether substantive or drafting-related. 11–168

ADDRESSING POST-MEDIATION ISSUES

After the mediator has sent the final summaries and the parties have dealt with any necessary formalities, the role of the mediator will usually be at an end. 11–169

Family mediators may in some circumstances continue to be involved with a couple after the conclusion of the mediation. For example: 11–170

- certain issues concerning the children and their arrangements may be subject to later review;
- financial issues may also be subject to later review, including for example, maintenance provisions;
- making short-term rather than long-term arrangements can sometimes be helpful to a couple;
- couples sometimes agree that if there is any problem with the implementation of settlement terms they will revert to the mediator to assist them in overcoming the problem;
- a couple may resolve to return to mediation if at any time they find that any continuing aspect of their affairs is causing contention between them which they cannot resolve themselves.

CHAPTER 12

Neighbourhood and Community Mediation and Restorative Justice

INTRODUCTION TO NEIGHBOURHOOD AND COMMUNITY MEDIATION

Community mediation developed in the UK with the aim of bringing inter-personal or social disputes arising within local communities under community control rather than using the legal system. This is based on the notion of "grass-roots community self-help schemes" using local volunteers to bring disputing parties "face to face to discuss their allegations and grievances in a controlled way" and "to explore ways in which they could get on in future without conflict."[1]   12–001

The modern day concept originated in the US[2] and was latterly adopted by many other countries, including the UK and often adapted from traditional societies (such as the Indian panchayat) and older European village moots, which have survived in Norway, for instance, in the shape of "conflict councils". This community mediation concept has become established as an integral part of the conflict resolution process.   12–002

The adaptation of these traditional concepts has inevitably been accompanied by radical changes in the process. It has become more informal, individualised (or private), and imbued with values (such as gender equality, acceptance of change, inter-group tolerance) not necessarily characteristic of the traditional manifestations. In some places, for example Singapore, the process is a blend of traditional and contemporary approaches, taking into account the local cultural context and promoted as being consonant with Asian tradition and culture.[3] Wherever it is offered its essence is adaptation to and respect for local conditions and needs.   12–003

Community mediation is generally taken to include as part of its remit neighbour mediation, which in fact comprises by far the greatest part of its work. However, as the issues it addresses often go wider than immediate neighbours, extending to people living in the same area or community, the term "neighbourhood and community mediation" has been adopted. As outlined   12–004

---

[1] T. Marshall, *Reparation, Conciliation and Mediation* (Home Office Research and Planning Unit, 1984).
[2] The Carter Administration established Neighbourhood Justice Centers. See D.D. Cahn, *Conflict in Personal Relations* (New York: Routledge 2009).
[3] N-T Tan, "Community Mediation in Singapore: Principles for Community Conflict Resolution" (2002) 19(3) *Conflict Resolution Quarterly* 289–301.

241

12–005 In Scotland community mediation is organised through two umbrella bodies: Scottish Community Mediation Network (which is purely community based), and the Scottish Mediation Network (which covers all fields of activity including community).[4] The Scottish Community Mediation Network is closely connected to SACRO (Safeguarding Communities—Reducing Offending), which in addition to providing community mediation services, also provides services in restorative justice.

12–006 Various examples of neighbourhood and community disputes are outlined below.

NEIGHBOUR DISPUTES

12–007 Certain kinds of issues commonly arise between neighbours and people living in close proximity to one another, even if not immediately adjoining households. These are listed separately, but there may often be an overlap between them, as one problem becomes the basis for disagreement or conflict in another field:

Noise problems

12–008 In cities, this tends to be the most frequent cause of disputes between neighbours. A survey of community disputes in 2001 indicated that 45 per cent of all neighbour disputes originated with noise issues, almost as much as all other issues combined. According to a study by DEFRA,[5] 52 per cent of all SACRO mediation referrals in Scotland during 2005–6 related to noise issues.

Verbal abuse or harassment

12–009 In some cases, disputes arising from noise or other problems, or from mildly anti-social behaviour, can escalate into verbal abuse and forms of harassment and vandalism. It is usually aimed at a specific person, family or group (perhaps because of their race, culture or sexual orientation). Sometimes the harassment is by adults, who might become the principals in any mediation; but sometimes it may be by children, in which case whole families may be drawn into the dispute and the attempts to resolve it.

---

[4] See Scottish Community Mediation Network at:
http://www.scmc.sacro.org.uk/training/accreditation/mediator-accreditation [accessed 17 May 2018] and the Scottish Mediation Network at *https://www.scottishmediation.org.uk/* [accessed 17 May 2018].

[5] Department for Environment, Food and Rural Affairs Report: *Review of use of Mediation Services by Local Authorities and Housing Associations* (HMSO, 2006).

Children's behaviour

Children's behaviour may also give rise to complaints, even where it does not constitute harassment. Playing ball against a neighbour's wall, mischievous behaviour or excessive exuberance can create conditions in which antagonism can fester. This is most common where the "disturbed" party is elderly and may be afraid to approach young people about their behaviour. The lack of interaction between them may lead to the young people being projected as perhaps criminal or aggressive; and if this results in the police being called in, the conflict escalates. Also, people who do not have children in their household may sometimes have a different perception of "normal" levels of noise from family households where there are children. This can similarly lead to conflict.

12–010

Pets and other animals

Problems with animals can create enormous conflict between neighbours. These may, for example, include dogs that bark late at night or early in the morning or that are not kept under proper control, cocks that crow at dawn in urban or suburban areas, or birds that are fed excessively and create a nuisance to surrounding properties.

12–011

Boundary issues

The way in which neighbours maintain and position their property boundaries, can provoke anger and distress. One person may consider that a fence encroaches on his land, even by just a few inches, and he retaliates by moving or damaging it. Another objects to the height of the fence, which she perceives as a deliberately offensive act. Trees overhang a boundary wall and create problems, or are not trimmed and block a neighbour's light. Common walls are not properly maintained. Disputes such as these have involved people in costly litigation.

12–012

Eyesores and other environmental issues

People who do not maintain their properties acceptably, who erect unsightly signs or unusual structures on their property, or whose taste in colour or style cause upset in the neighbourhood, may find themselves involved in dispute. A man who truly enjoys allowing his garden to become overgrown with weeds may contend that "his home is his castle" but his neighbours may become aggrieved. Issues of hygiene may arise where there is serious lack of care.

12–013

Parking and other neighbour issues

Vehicular parking can become a cause for disagreement for example where a common driveway is blocked. Rights of way can also become contentious, both as to the way in which they are entitled to be used, and their abuse. Almost any issue that involves contact between people who live in close proximity to one another can give rise to problems and misunderstanding.

12–014

Mediation of social conflicts and inter-group disputes

12–015 Community mediation services may from time to time be asked to assist in inter-group conflict, such as conflicts between estate residents and groups of youths, or in relation to major social conflicts, including for example environmental disputes, planning negotiations, racial conflict, police-community antagonisms and public policy issues. Mediation is also used where anti-social behaviour orders have been made or are being contemplated, whether in relation to individuals or groups.

MEDIATION IN SCHOOLS AND PEER MEDIATION

12–016 Peer mediation involves pupils in schools taking responsibility for resolving disputes among themselves. It presupposes that they will be able to do so, with suitable training and support.

12–017 Mediation can provide life skills for peer mediators, particularly affirmation, communication and co-operation. Affirmation in current youth culture may be translated into the word "respect", which would be an important part of peer mediation.[6]

12–018 Training is an essential part of this process, in terms of providing the necessary skills, knowledge and awareness. Peer mediators need to appreciate what kinds of issues they can deal with, and what kinds of matters would be best dealt with by the school authorities. There are many practical matters that need to be considered, including engaging the school staff and pupils in the process, setting up structures and procedures appropriate for each individual school, setting aside time and suitable space for the process to take place, selecting the pupils to become peer mediators, and creating a school culture in which the process may be taken up by pupils in dispute.

12–019 US research has indicated that peer mediation programmes are successful in reducing disciplinary problems and violence and in improving the overall atmosphere. Reports show that the programmes among adolescent pupils also produced an improvement not only in behaviour and attitudes, but also academic results.[7] Baginsky's UK analysis of the benefits of peer mediation, with reference to various writings, indicate that peer mediation is said to:

> "'improve pupils' self-esteem and relationships, give children a greater sense of responsibility, reduce conflicts, promote academic achievement, develop life-skills, allow teachers to focus on teaching and create an environment in which pupils can learn and socialize safely and constructively".

---

[6] W. Baginsky, *Peer Mediation in the UK: A guide for schools* (NSPCC Publications and Information Unit, 2004). Daphne is a European Union project to combat violence against children, young people and women. Available at: *http://creducation.net/resources/peermediationintheuk.pdf* [accessed 17 May 2018].

[7] K.O. Wilburn and M.L. Bates, "Conflict Resolution in America's Schools" (1997) 52(1) *Dispute Resolution Journal*.

Tyrrell however sounds a word of warning, emphasising that any such programmes will not be effective unless a whole-school approach is adopted, an approach that addresses relationships at every level of the school.[8]

12–020

A number of mediation schemes in the UK have been introduced in schools, training both pupils and teachers in the skills of handling conflict. Teachers and other school staff such as meal supervisors may also be able to act as mediators within a school. Various organisations supporting the peer mediation and schools training process include Leap, Confronting Conflict[9]; SACRO[10]; Quakers (Peer mediation)[11]; Peaceworks Peer Mediation Network[12]; Peer Mediation at the National Association for Peer Mediation[13]; Common Ground Mediation[14]; and Peer Mediation Network.[15] This is not a comprehensive list, but merely a cross-section of some of the organisations in the field.

12–021

The general learning effects of school mediation are regarded by many as being as important as the facility for resolving specific inter-personal disputes: improving school management with regard to handling conflicts, including those between pupil and teacher or between parent and school, changing the attitudes of pupils and teachers, and giving children skills that enable them to avoid violence and fighting.

12–022

ELDER MEDIATION

Elder mediation is offered by community services and private mediators and organisations offering specialist elder mediation services dealing with conflicts affecting older people. These may be community conflicts, family conflicts, residential care conflicts or special conflicts (for example when old people become confused and are inconsistent in their ability to make decisions).

12–023

Elder mediation allows conflictual issues involving older people to be resolved with dignity and creativity.

GANG MEDIATION

Urban street gangs are a problem in many parts of the world and are becoming more widespread. Predominantly male—though there are female gangs and followers—and based on features such as age, locality and ethnicity, they function with a code and culture of their own that is commonly hierarchical, and can be secretive, violent and criminal. Membership loyalty can be fierce, and any disloyalty—including seeking to leave the gang—can result in violent reprisals. They are commonly territorial, and anyone from a rival gang treading on a gang's territory or "manor" is at risk of serious harm. Anti-social and commonly

12–024

---

[8] J. Tyrrell, *Peer Mediation: A Process for Primary Schools* (London: Souvenir Press, 2002).
[9] See *http://www.leapconfrontingconflict.org.uk/* [accessed 17 May 2018].
[10] See *http://www.sacro.org.uk/* [accessed 17 May 2018].
[11] See http://www.quaker.org.uk/news-and-events/news/peer-*mediation* [accessed 17 May 2018].
[12] See *http://peaceworks.org.uk/schools-peer-mediation/* [accessed 17 May 2018].
[13] See *http://www.peermediation.org/* [accessed 17 May 2018].
[14] See *http://www.commongroundmediation.co.uk/* [accessed 17 May 2018].
[15] See *http://www.peermediationnetwork.org.uk/* [accessed 17 May 2018].

carrying knives or guns, sometimes involved in drug trafficking and taking and other criminal activity they are likely to cause fear and anxiety among ordinary members of the public.

12–025   Various interventions are being made to try to counter and contain gang culture, including youth programmes and clubs, mentoring support, sports and recreational facilities and other community youth projects. One of the most challenging interventions is through gang mediation, in which mediators facilitate negotiations that aim to reduce or end gang violence, and in other ways ameliorate or end dangerous situations between individuals and groups.[16]

12–026   Gang mediation may be aimed not just at resolving immediate issues such as these, but moving to truces between gangs and more fundamentally, at shifting gang members away from violence and crime. Gang "summits" have been held to move gangs towards reconciliation, and some mediation is directed at preventing groups becoming gangs.

UK gang mediation developments

12–027   The following are some of the gang mediation developments in the UK:

The Centre for Conflict Transformation, formerly the West Midlands Mediation and Transformation Services, was based on the Good Friday initiative in Northern Ireland and a gang peace initiative in New Jersey. The project aims to help gang members and others who cannot be seen to be communicating with one another to enter into communication, to improve understandings, to explore accommodations, and—"the De Luxe version of mediated outcomes"—to facilitate parties reaching agreement.

12–028   *Capital Conflict Management*[17] is a London-based not-for-profit Community Interest Company (CIC). Wholly independent, it works closely with the Metropolitan Police Service, statutory agencies and local authorities to diffuse difficult and/or dangerous situations between groups and individuals.

12–029   *"Leap" Confronting Conflict*,[18] which works with youth and conflict and has developed gangs training programmes and its specialist gang workers, when appropriate, mediate between groups in conflict.

12–030   *The Aasha Gang Mediation Project*[19] in Tower Hamlets in East London has a programme to support young people in resisting gang culture, and with staff members and community volunteers, helps to "mediate, prevent and often resolve many gang conflicts".

12–031   Gang mediators work in a highly challenging environment and need to function in a way that is sensitive to the needs of the parties, affording them dignity and respect if this is to be reciprocated. Indeed, a lack of due respect—or the perception of this—is commonly one of the issues causing conflict.

---

[16] See as an example the Aasha Gang Mediation Programme in East London, which offers conflict mediation between rival neighbourhood gangs and conflict prevention to steer young people away from the gang culture and gangster lifestyle, *at http://www.osmanitrust.org/projects/aasha/* [accessed 17 May 2018].
[17] *http://capitalconflict.com/* [accessed 17 May 2018].
[18] *http://www.leapconfrontingconflict.org.uk/* [accessed 17 May 2018].
[19] See fn.16.

OTHER COMMUNITY MEDIATION

Victim-offender mediation, which was the forerunner of many of the community mediation developments, and which will be considered later in this chapter, addresses the wider issues of restorative justice. Other kinds of community conflict resolution services include services that provide homelessness mediation for young people; mediation services to address disputes between landlord and tenant; mediation services at a number of universities; mediation services to help young people who are estranged from their families, and to work with adults who are estranged from one another; and multifaith and multicultural mediation services specialising in dispute resolution in situations of religious, spiritual or racial conflict.

12–032

COMMUNITY MEDIATION SERVICES

Community mediation has played a major role in the development of alternative forms of dispute resolution alongside civil and commercial mediation, family mediation and other processes. However, whereas other forms tend to be at least partly, if not entirely, self-financing, community mediation is inherently non-commercial, generally being offered at low or no cost, and hence depends on others for its funding, rendering it vulnerable to forces over which it generally has little or no control.[20]

12–033

Community mediation funding depends at least in part on the model of service provision. The primary UK model tends to be an independent registered charity with trustees who may comprise local community members, agencies, funders, referring sources and mediators, with volunteers working at a grass-roots level. Another model is the provision of the service by a managing agency, usually a local authority, which may engage employed staff and/or volunteer mediators for its services.[21] Sources of funding include Community Trusts or other charitable trusts, local authority funding, or special Government schemes. In some instances, parties can contribute a voluntary donation after mediation if they wish.

12–034

In the UK the first community mediation centres were set up in the early 1980s, initially in Newham, London (the Conflict and Change Project, with wide aims for community development). Many inner London boroughs are now served, and they are prevalent in other metropolitan areas around England such as York, Leeds, Cambridge, Manchester, Plymouth, Liverpool and the Merseyside, Brighton and Hove, and Leicester. As indicated above, there are many community services in Scotland, as well as in Wales and Northern Ireland.

12–035

---

[20] It has been difficult for some community mediation services to survive financially and consequently some have closed down, notably in Southwark and Medway.
[21] See M. Liebmann, (ed.), *Community and Neighbour Mediation* (Oxford: Cavendish, 1998), pp.80–81, expressing concern at the danger perceived by some people that the agency-led model might lead to the process becoming too solution geared, rather than helping people to achieve greater mutual understanding. Over the years, this concern does not appear to have materialised, as both models have provided excellent service to communities.

12–036　Mediation services are common in all types of districts, rural as well as inner city areas, although rates of conflict in the latter can be relatively high because of the population density and the general stresses of life there.[22]

THE MEDIATION PROCESS IN COMMUNITY DISPUTES

12–037　Neighbourhood disputes tend to be highly marked by emotions and personal prejudices, which means that mediators may have to spend time on allowing parties to express their feelings and paying as much attention to psychological healing as material agreements. In some cases, the original material dispute may have entirely disappeared with the passage of time, but the conflict continues to escalate through acts of animosity and revenge.[23]

12–038　Two co-mediators commonly carry out community mediation. This provides support during the mediation, and allows newly trained mediators to obtain experience in conjunction with more seasoned colleagues. It also allows differences between disputants to be matched, for example if one is black and one is white, or one is male and the other female. This may be helpful to the parties' perceptions of empathetic understanding from the mediators if there are issues in the dispute related to the racial, gender or age differences between the parties.[24]

12–039　The process of mediation of community disputes will be described using the broad framework of stages outlined in Ch.9.[25]

PRE-MEDIATION: CONSIDERING MEDIATION, ASSESSING SUITABILITY AND OBTAINING COMMITMENT

12–040　Referrals to community mediation services tend to come from individuals themselves, or from a range of community agencies, such as Citizens Advice Bureaux, the police, environmental health or housing departments of the local authority, and solicitors.

12–041　The first step is to arrange a meeting to discuss the issues with the person who raised the issue and to get some understanding of the problem.[26] If mediation is considered appropriate, the mediators will explain the process and inquire whether they may approach the other party to suggest and explain mediation. If the initial party is unwilling for the mediators to make such an approach to the

---

[22] See M. Liebmann, "Community and Neighbourhood Mediation: A UK Perspective" in J. Macfarlane, *Rethinking Disputes: The Mediation Alternative* (London: Cavendish Publishing, 1997).
[23] T. Marshall, "Power of Mediation" (1990) 8(2) *Mediation Quarterly* 115.
[24] However, some mediators feel that such "matching" may be a token practice, especially if there are no issues in the dispute relevant to such racial, gender or age differences.
[25] These stages are used as a framework for all mediation reviewed in this book. J.C. Patrick, "*The Mediation Process*" in Liebmann, see fn.21, uses a 7-stage model: the first two relate to contacting each party, then the further stages are preparing, setting the scene (hearing the issues), exploring the issues, building agreement and closure, with follow-up.
[26] Services sometimes call the person who approached them "Party 1" and the other "Party 2". Many disputes involve counter allegations of one kind or another, so the term "complainant" is not necessarily useful or relevant.

DURING THE MEDIATION: STAGE 1: THE PRELIMINARIES

other party, the mediators can help the person analyse the situation dispassionately. This may present a new perspective that helps the person resolve the issue or at least to come to terms with it. Merely listening actively can help relieve tensions and anger that prevented that person from directly approaching the other party.

If the first party is willing, the mediators attempt to contact the other party and introduce the idea of mediation. In some cases, the second party may be quite unaware that a conflict exists, because the first party has been too afraid to raise the issue directly with him. Some disputes can be quickly resolved at this stage, once the mediators contact the second party to establish that person's concerns and views.[27] In other cases, the second party does not want mediation and the mediators must fall back on simply assisting the first party with reviewing and analysing the situation. Mediators would not in these (or any other) circumstances give advice to either party; but they may give information about where to go for support or for legal advice, such as a Citizens Advice Bureau. **12–042**

If both parties agree to mediation, it remains necessary to consider with each party whether they will have a joint meeting, or whether either of them prefers not to have a face-to-face meeting. In the latter event, the mediators may offer to shuttle between the parties (though many community mediators find that if parties are unwilling to discuss a dispute, shuttle mediation is unlikely to be any more successful). **12–043**

The parties may then be asked to sign a written agreement setting out the terms and ground-rules on which the mediation will take place. Alternatively, they may be given or sent a written note outlining the procedure and ground-rules for the process. **12–044**

DURING THE MEDIATION: STAGE 1: PRELIMINARY COMMUNICATIONS AND PREPARATION

If a joint meeting is agreed, an informal arrangement will be made as to the place and time for the mediation. If shuttle mediation is to take place, the mediators will liaise with the parties as to convenient times for doing this. **12–045**

As previously indicated, in some cases, because of the intensity of the emotions involved, it will not be possible to contemplate an immediate meeting of the parties. In such event, the mediators will talk separately to each party. This may result in an agreement without a face-to-face meeting occurring at all, especially if the parties do not need to have any significant contact with one another in the future. Alternatively, the shuttle mediation may lay the groundwork for an eventual meeting. **12–046**

The parties are not usually asked to prepare written summaries of their positions or to produce documents in advance. If they have relevant papers that **12–047**

---

[27] There are differences of practice as to whether the second party is informed of the first party's complaint. While some may do so, others feel that the second party visit has the same function as the first party visit, namely to hear of any concerns that person may have about their neighbour. On either approach, the mediator would need to guard against being seen as an advocate for the first party rather than an impartial intermediary.

12–048 they wish to mention in the mediation, they may be asked to bring them to the meeting if this is thought appropriate. This would not, however, be dealt with in a formal or legalistic way.

Much of the preparation will have been covered by the preliminary discussions with each party, and establishing their wish to mediate. The mediators may send them procedural information. By the time the parties reach the mediation forum, they should understand what is involved and be committed to trying to deal with the issues there.

STAGE 2: COMMENCEMENT ESTABLISHING THE ISSUES AND SETTING THE AGENDA

12–049 Joint mediation sessions in the community context are informal in style. They should take place in a comfortable, neutral venue. Usually the parties and the mediators sit round a table, alongside one another rather than facing one another. The placing of the parties has to be considered in advance in the light of the information gathered by the mediators on the state of the relationship between them.

12–050 In some cases, the mediators will be different from those who prepared the case: practice in this respect differs between services.[28]

12–051 The conduct of a mediation session itself is similar to mediation in other fields. The mediators will welcome the parties and make a brief introductory statement, outlining the process. They may re-affirm their neutrality, and the parties may be asked to confirm that they wish to proceed if any reservations are expressed. Ground rules are established and agreed.

12–052 Following the introductions, each party in turn will be given a chance to give their own account of the dispute. The mediators will not allow these presentations to be interrupted. The mediators during this phase will try to ensure that parties express their feelings as well as the material facts of the case as they see them, but they will deter abusive, harassing or threatening remarks. They may summarise each presentation by way of feedback, to ensure that the parties are satisfied that they have each been heard correctly.

12–053 At some convenient point, clarification may be sought on points of detail. This is unlikely to be done before both parties have completed their presentations, in order to avoid an imbalance in the time given to either party, especially for example one who is less articulate or who has brought more issues. Mediators will be aware of the build-up of frustration while parties wait to make their own presentations, and will avoid exacerbating this by inappropriately timed questions.

12–054 Consideration will be given as to who should make the first presentation. It has been suggested that the timid participant or less articulate or powerful person might feel more comfortable if given the opportunity to speak first, or that an agitated party may need to be asked to start. The mediator may otherwise decide

---

[28] These matters and community mediation practice generally are covered in J.E. Beer and C.C. Packard, *The Mediator's Handbook*, 4th edn (Canada: New Society Publishers, 2012); J.C. Patrick, "*The Mediation Process*" in Liebmann, see fn.21.

to ask the original complainant to commence, or may ask who wishes to start. Speakers can be limited in time, or asked to summarise if they become repetitive.

An agenda is likely to be implicit from the issues raised by the parties, rather than necessarily explicitly decided upon. The mediators may however discuss fixing an informal agenda, especially where the issues identified by the parties are complex; or at least they should identify the parties' priorities. 12–055

STAGE 3: INFORMATION GATHERING

This is not done as a distinct stage but rather information is gathered as the process unfolds. The mediators will obtain some relevant information during their initial communications with the parties, some in separate meetings with them, and some during the course of the process itself. 12–056

One of the most useful ways of gathering information in informal mediation of this nature is through effective questioning. This may help to elicit the necessary information and clarify any areas of misunderstanding. It is not, however, in the nature of cross-examination. The mediators will need to listen with care to what is being said, and should pay attention to body language and other non-verbal communications. 12–057

STAGE 4: CONDUCTING SUBSTANTIVE NEGOTIATIONS

After the presentations, there will be a phase of free discussion and exchange, exploring differences and clarifying the nature of the principal issues. During this phase the mediators will try both to establish a common view of the nature of the problem and to ensure that the parties are able to communicate freely and constructively. They will also attempt to identify the main differences, the nature of each party's real needs (as distinct from their negotiating positions), their priorities, any underlying problems that need to be encouraged into the open and emotions that may have to be addressed.[29] 12–058

It should now be possible to enter the phase of generating and examining options for settlement and working towards arrangements that would best meet all needs.

All the mediators' skills outlined in Ch.14 are relevant to this stage. Mediators need to effectively manage the mediation process in order to help the parties to adopt a problem-solving mode. They will also need to maintain control of the process, keep discussions focused, provide a model for the conduct of the parties, balance negotiating power if necessary, maintain a constructive climate for discussions,[30] and where necessary deal with unproductive behaviour.[31] The generation by the parties of suggestions and options for solving the problems is a key part of the process. 12–059

---

[29] See J.E. Beer and C.C. Packard, *The Mediator's Handbook*, fn.28, pp.36–54.
[30] See J.E. Beer and C.C. Packard, *The Mediator's Handbook*, fn.28, pp.117–147.
[31] See J.E Beer and C.C. Packard, pp.133–135: Beer and Packard recommend that mediator intervention be considered if the parties' behaviour is considered unproductive. However, they emphasise that a discussion can still be productive even when the parties are being loud, rude or upset as long as they are learning from each other and the level of hostility is trending down not up.

12–060 As in other mediation, this process, while acknowledging that the issues relate to past events, is future-focused and problem-solving, aiming to move the parties from past grievances towards new ways for the future. There is, however, some tension between this approach and the transformative one described by Folger and Bush.[32] The latter approach questions the emphasis on future-focus and problem-solving, concentrating instead on helping parties to a better understanding, with acknowledgment and empowerment.

12–061 Once parties have an understanding of one another's positions, practical solutions may need to be considered and perhaps brainstormed. Can noisy activities be curtailed, or limited to certain hours, or advance warning be given of them? Can carpeting or wall insulation be organised to dull sounds? If people inadvertently or forgetfully breach understandings, can a formula be agreed for communicating about this without giving offence?

12–062 Options will at this stage be narrowed and prioritised, and the feasibility of each considered. The parties will need to have felt heard and acknowledged, on any model, and engaged in the practical search for a solution that meets their needs, which by now should be mutually understood.

STAGE 5: DEALING WITH IMPASSE

12–063 When parties reach impasse in community mediation, the deadlock is generally likely to relate to issues of practical workability, perceptions about the other person or people and their attitudes, continuing differences about fairness and values, a sense of grievances not being taken fully on board and emotional reactions rather than differences of technical or legal opinion or differences of perception of the outcome in the event of adjudication.

12–064 Some of the strategies identified in Ch.9 and in relation to other fields of activity may be equally relevant here, but the following may be particularly appropriate:

- If separate meetings with the parties, as outlined in Chs 9 and 10 have not been used, the mediators may try these. The rules as to confidentiality need to be clear.[33] The parties feeling able to speak more freely in separate meetings may help provide the mediators with the insights about the issues and perhaps any underlying concerns that may help the parties towards better understandings, and hence to craft a mutually acceptable agreement.
- If parties are still feeling unheard or not understood, it may be necessary to give them each a fuller opportunity to express themselves, and to help reframe their concerns in ways that the other(s) can appreciate and relate to.
- If there is uncertainty about the feasibility of certain options, or if there is any lack of confidence that they will be properly implemented, it can be helpful to have a trial period, perhaps over a couple of months or as

---

[32] R. A Baruch Bush and J. P. Folger, *The Promise of Mediation: Responding to Conflict through Power and Recognition* (San Francisco: Jossey-Bass, 1994). Some community mediators may find this useful.

[33] Mediators should clarify whether separate confidences will be maintained unless authorised to the contrary (in accordance with the usual civil-commercial model), or whether the mediators will share information exchanged in the separate meetings.

- appropriate, to see how they might work, with arrangements to reconvene and to discuss them and any possible adaptations.
- In some cases, symbolism can be powerful. An expression of understanding and perhaps regret can shift attitudes. Offering to do some act, however small, like joining together to remove graffiti or walking together to inspect a disputed boundary and suggesting some concessionary act, like cutting back shrub growth, can provide a basis for future cooperation. Forms of words and acknowledgments should not be underestimated.
- If there are a number of issues, and not all are stuck, it can sometimes help to move to other issues and to try to generate progress there, and come back to the deadlocked points as the issues are narrowed.
- Sometimes it can also help for the mediators to acknowledge that they are stuck and to invite the parties' ideas. This can be done through the introduction of brainstorming.[34] Some mediators may offer their own ideas, but if this is done it should be "impersonally, not as advice".[35]

Care should always be taken by the mediators to avoid exercising authority which may inhibit the parties from reaching their own conclusion or choosing to move to other alternatives. Indeed, exploring those alternatives with them can sometimes be a helpful role, if thoughtfully and sensitively done, in the nature of BATNA and WATNA[36] and not by way of implicit threat.

12–065

STAGE 6: CONCLUDING MEDIATION AND RECORDING THE OUTCOME

Where the mediation results in an agreement, the mediators will ordinarily acknowledge the parties' achievement. They may then need to formalise the agreement. Where no agreement is reached, they may want to consider with the parties what further options they have, and may offer further help in the future if required.

12–066

In most neighbourhood disputes the issues are not necessarily clearly separable. Facts and feelings may be interrelated, and care needs to be taken to prepare an agreement that similarly balances the issues and parties' obligations, not identifying clear winners and losers. The agreement should also include provisions for future disputes, for example:

12–067

> "If A is disturbed in future by B's dog, than A agrees to tell B about this in a calm manner, and not go straight to the police."

Although in some cases the parties may not require any written record of the understandings reached by them, agreements are normally recorded in writing and signed by the parties, because this acts symbolically as an assurance of the

12–068

---

[34] See J.E. Beer and C.C. Packard, fn.30 at p.158.
[35] See J.E. Beer and C.C. Packard, *The Mediator's Handbook*, fn.28, p.161. They recommend that mediators avoid suggesting or critiquing options on the basis that the parties may develop a stronger agreement and working relationship if mediators let them take the lead in developing and evaluating solutions. Ultimately it could come down to a matter of "mediator style" approach.
[36] See Ch.4, paras 4-006 to 4-008, for a definition and explanation of these acronyms.

parties' sincere intentions. Such an agreement is not normally intended to carry any special legal status but of course it might have legal consequences and should therefore be drafted with care. The position would be different if a solicitor or a court referred the case with the express purpose of formulating a legal agreement. In such a case, the settlement would need to be binding if so required by the parties. In this event the parties may in some cases want their legal advisers to review it before they sign it, though obviously much depends on what issues and obligations are involved. Where legal rights are actually or potentially involved, the mediators may in any event advise parties to seek legal advice before entering into any agreement.

ADDRESSING POST-MEDIATION ISSUES

12–069 It is accepted as good practice for the mediators to offer a follow-up service by getting in touch with the parties after a specified time to see whether the agreement is working successfully, and if not to offer further mediation. This follow-up may also be helpful to the mediation service in getting feedback on the process. Such follow-up contacts would normally only take place, however, if the parties gave prior agreement to them.

GENERAL OBSERVATIONS

12–070 Many difficulties may occur in this kind of mediation because of the various extrinsic factors that may can impinge upon a resolution of the problem. These may include the nature and history of the relationship between the parties, the influence of common acquaintances, the nature and culture of the area where they live, personal and social problems unrelated to the immediate issues, power struggles, attitudes and styles of living. A dispute may sometimes occur because of the isolation of one of the parties and their use of complaints to stimulate some kind of personal relationship, even if it is a negative one. Parties may blame one another for a problem caused by a third party, such as local authority housing with party walls that provide inadequate sound insulation.

12–071 Power imbalances may need to be addressed by the mediators by ensuring parity of opportunity in discussion, or helping less articulate parties to express their needs or opinions. In extreme cases, mediators may decide to discontinue mediation because there is no way in which a fair outcome can result.[37]

12–072 Sometimes it will be necessary to involve other parties in the mediation because the ramifications of the dispute make it insoluble for the original parties alone. Racial and other cultural animosities may be present, which can be particularly difficult for mediators to deal with; but much experience has been accumulated in relation to such problems, and special training programmes are available on handling prejudice.

12–073 The complexity and diffuse character of community disputes necessitate a high degree of flexibility and informality in the structure of such mediation. Periods of face-to-face discussion may be interspersed with separate meetings.

---

[37] See Ch.16, Ethics and values, fairness and power.

For community mediation, mediators need to be trained in the principles and skills of conflict resolution, and not a rigid set of procedures, so that they are able to adjust action to the exigencies of each dispute.

INTRODUCTORY OVERVIEW OF RESTORATIVE JUSTICE[38]

The restorative concept has at its root the principle that where a person has been harmed by the wrongful actions of another, opportunities should be provided for (i) some form of healing and possible restitution for the harmed person and any others affected by those actions; and (ii) some way to engage the wrongdoer more directly with his actions and their consequences, and prevent any repetition. 12–074

There are three forms of restorative processes: 12–075

- *Restorative justice:* This is perhaps the best known, referring to the restorative process in relation to the criminal justice system. An important kind of restorative justice is victim-offender mediation, which combines concerns for the victims of crime, the rehabilitation of offenders and the notion of appropriate reparation.
- *Restorative practices:* This refers to restorative processes other than in relation to the criminal justice system and includes situations in which one person harms another non-criminally, for example in workplace or school bullying, or anti-social behaviour. It refers to the interventions that a facilitator may make in these circumstances.
- *Restorative approach:* This refers to the underlying ethos of a group, institution or organisation, in adopting the principles and ideas of restorative practice in the way that it functions and relates to its personnel and constituents.

The International Institute for Restorative Practices[39] reflects the fundamental hypothesis of restorative practices as being the proposition that: 12–076

> "human beings are happier, more cooperative and productive, and more likely to make positive changes in their behaviour when those in positions of authority do things *with* them, rather than *to* them or *for* them".

On this hypothesis, people respond better to participating and being involved in the process of addressing issues arising from the wrongful actions of others than when these are imposed in a punitive and authoritarian or paternalistic mode. 12–077

Like divorce mediation, restorative justice and practices may not necessarily be dispute resolution. Indeed, there may be no dispute as such between the person harmed and the wrongdoer. However, the objective of facilitating an accommodation between parties and the processes of third-party intervention run parallel in many respects to the mediation process, albeit with the distinction that in mediation, "parties are assumed to be on a level moral playing field…." whereas 12–078

---

[38] The authors are grateful to Lawrence Kershen QC, erstwhile Chairman of the UK's Restorative Justice Council, for his contributions to early editions of this chapter and its concepts.
[39] See para.12-081 for more information about restorative justice and practice organisations.

in restorative justice and practice, it is fundamental that one person has done something wrong and the other has been harmed.[40]

12–079   In England and Wales restorative justice and restorative practices are delivered by a range of different service providers including: community mediation services,[41] police forces,[42] police crime commissioners,[43] private initiatives,[44] youth offender services and various charitable organisations.[45]

RESTORATIVE JUSTICE

12–080   Restorative justice has developed in the field of criminal justice, combining concern for those harmed and the rehabilitation of wrongdoers with the notion of reparation.

12–081   Examples of victim and offender schemes have been established in North America and Europe, including the UK, under which victims meet their offenders in the presence of a third party to afford them an opportunity for discussion and to arrive at agreed terms for restitution, whether financial or by way of services to be performed for the victim or the community. These were known in the UK as "reparation schemes" and in the US as "victim offender reconciliation programs" (VORPS). However, the view held by some that victims should not be pressed to forgive and become reconciled with their offender until ready to do so, and consequently the term "victim and offender mediation" schemes became more common.

12–082   According to Zehr, whilst the terms "victim" and "offender" are widely used, there is also a view that it is better not to label people in either of these ways.[46] Terms such as "person harmed" and "wrongdoer" may therefore be preferable. In this work, these alternative terms are used interchangeably.

Restorative justice: the rationale

12–083   The criminal justice system is largely based on the proposition of crime being an offence against the State. Consequently, the State prosecutes offenders and exacts retribution by way of punishment. This, however, overlooks the relationship that

---

[40] H. Zehr, *The Little Book of Restorative Justice* (Good Books, 2012), pp.15–16.
[41] For example CALM *http://calmmediation.org/* [accessed 17 May 2018] based in London, Maidstone Mediation Scheme *http://www.maidstonemediation.co.uk/* [accessed 17 May 2018] based in Kent.
[42] Notably Thames Valley Police who were pioneers of Police Service restorative justice delivery, which is now the responsibility of the local Police & Crime Commissioner in that area of England. See *https://www.thamesvalley-pcc.gov.uk/victims-first/victims-services/restorative-justice/* [accessed 17 May 2018].
[43] The Essex Restorative and Mediation Service was set up by the Police & Crime Commissioner for Essex to work in partnership with agencies across Essex to support victims of crime, reduce offending and support communities, see *http://www.essex.pfcc.police.uk/* [accessed 17 May 2018].
[44] Project Salus http://salusgroup.org.uk/service/restorative-justice/ [accessed 17 May 2018] and Restorative Solutions http://www.restorativesolutions.org.uk/ [accessed 17 May 2018] are examples of privately run initiatives, the latter delivers restorative justice across a number of counties in England and Wales.
[45] Such as Victims First Northumbria *https://victimsfirstnorthumbria.org.uk/*.
[46] H. Zehr, *The Little Book of Restorative Justice*, fn.40, p.12.

the victim has with the crime and the offender and sometimes neglects the victim in the process. For this reason, the system has re-balanced itself by introducing the concept of victims' rights and support.[47]

Restorative justice involves a different way of viewing crime, by focusing on the injury to the victim and the community, rather than to the State, and by aiming for restitution rather than punishment as a primary goal. 12–084

The movement towards a system of restorative justice has grown internationally, but remains diverse in the ways in which it might achieve its broad aim of transforming the way society responds to crime and other forms of troublesome behaviour, and there are competing ideas about its nature. Even the term "restorative justice" has no universally accepted meaning, but is used in a range of different ways.[48] 12–085

The aim of restorative justice has been described as "repairing (as far as possible) or making up for the damage and hurt caused by the crime".[49] The following are its main principles: 12–086

- the offence is primarily against the victim and secondarily against the state;
- society's values should be recognised such as respect for others;
- the needs of the victim resulting from the wrongdoing are important; and restitution may be required to restore the relationship between victim and offender—achievable by way of reparation, usually in the form of compensation, apology or community service;
- reconciliation between victim and offender is also seen as an objective of restorative justice, but not universally so;
- communication and negotiation between the victim and others affected by the crime, and offender, is possible and often desirable to consider how to redress the wrong;
- offenders are required to take responsibility for their actions and have the opportunity to make amends;
- there is an element of empowerment of those affected by the crime.

These broad principles of restorative justice are promoted as an alternative to the present criminal justice system based on punishment and deterrence ("retributive") or the "rehabilitative" approach, both of which have the potential shortcoming that they may not afford offenders the experience of observing the consequences of their wrongdoing. McCold and Wachtel consider that the restorative approach "confronts and disapproves of wrongdoing while affirming the intrinsic worth of the offender". It involves collaborative problem-solving and 12–087

---

[47] Concern for the victim developed in the 1970s and early 1980s, and manifested in the Victim Support movement and the National Association of Victim Support Schemes. See H. Reeves, "The Victim Support perspective" in M. Wright and B. Galaway, *Mediation and Criminal Justice: Victims, Offenders and Community* (London: Sage Publications, 1989). See also D. Quill and J. Wynne, *Victim & Offender Mediation Handbook* (London: Save the Children, 1993).

[48] G. Johnstone & Daniel W Van Ness, *Handbook of Restorative Justice* (Devon: Willan Publishing, 2007), pp.6–9.

[49] M. Wright, *Justice for Victims and Offenders: A Restorative Response to Crime* (Bristol: Open University Press, 1991), p.41 (as mentioned in G. Robinson, *Victim-Offender Mediation: Limitations and Potential* (Oxford: Centre of Criminological Research, University of Oxford, 1996).

allows the people affected by an offence to "share their feelings, describe how they were affected and develop a plan to repair the harm done or prevent a reoccurrence".[50]

Victim-offender programmes

12–088   These programmes allow victims and offenders an opportunity, either directly or indirectly, to work with a facilitator to discuss the crime, its consequences and effects, and to consider how the offender can best make amends for the offence. This may be by way of apology, reparation, community service or any other agreed form.

12–089   The history of these programmes has been traced in a number of works and articles.[51] The forerunner is said to have been an experiment conducted by a court in Kitchener, Ontario, in 1974, in which a probation officer invited the court to see whether the victims of a vandalism spree would be willing to meet the offenders to discuss the crime. The offenders made restitution to the victims: the experiment "was successful beyond everyone's expectations".[52]

12–090   In the UK, interest in victim-offender schemes developed in the 1970s. Compensation orders were introduced by the Criminal Justice Act 1972; and community service schemes started around the same time. By the 1980s there was an increasing awareness of victims' rights and needs, and the National Association of Victims Support Schemes had been launched. The Home Office established four experimental reparation schemes. These were in Coventry, Wolverhampton, Carlisle and Leeds.[53]

Restorative cautioning

12–091   Traditionally, cautions consist of a formal warning to an offender by a police officer. Thames Valley Police developed a restorative cautioning initiative in which everyone affected by an offence, including family members, were invited to participate in the conference, which was facilitated by trained officers following a script. Research in 2002 for the Joseph Rowntree Foundation found

---

[50] P. McCold, and T. Wachtel, *In Pursuit of Paradigm: A Theory of Restorative Justice*, Paper presented at the XIII World Congress of Criminology, 10-15August 2003, Rio de Janeiro, Brazil.
[51] See for example T. Marshall, *Reparation, Conciliation and Mediation* (London: Home Office Research & Planning Unit, Paper 27, 1984); T. Marshall, and S. Merry, *Crime and Accountability* (London: HMSO, 1990); M. Wright and B. Galaway, *Mediation and Criminal Justice: Victims, Offenders and Community* (Sage: London, 1989); M. Wright, above, fn.49; G. Robinson, *Victim-Offender Mediation: Limitations and Potential* (University of Oxford Centre for Criminological Research, 1996) and its bibliography.
[52] See D. E. Peachey, *"The Kitchener Experiment"* in Wright and Galaway, *Mediation and Criminal Justice: Victims, Offenders and Community*, fn.49.
[53] For a more detailed history of these schemes, see John Harding, "Reconciling Mediation with Criminal Justice" in Wright and Galaway, Mediation and Criminal Justice: Victims, Offenders and Community, fn.49.

that "offenders, victims and their respective supporters were generally satisfied with the fairness of the process and the outcomes achieved".[54]

A Revised Code of Practice for Conditional Cautions (Adults) was issued in 2010 by the Secretary of State for Justice.[55] It allows a prosecutor to offer a caution with conditions attached for certain offences and suspends any criminal proceedings while the offender is given an opportunity to comply with the agreed conditions. Where the conditions are complied with, the prosecution is not normally commenced.[56]

12–092

Restorative justice for young offenders

Some projects are geared specifically for juveniles, including for example Youth Restorative Disposal projects, which hold 10- to 17-year-olds to account for minor crime and disorder by using restorative justice. The victim takes an active role in the way an offender is dealt with. This concept was jointly created by the Youth Justice Board, the Ministry of Justice and the Association of Chief Police Officers. Typically, a trained police officer acts "on the spot" where circumstances allow and oversees a meeting between the two parties to resolve the offence. The victim may talk about the effect it had on them and there is an apology—sometimes with a plan to make good any damage.[57]

12–093

In Northern Ireland restorative justice has entered the mainstream of the criminal justice system through legislation providing for it in youth justice disposals. Youth Conferencing was brought in by the Justice (Northern Ireland) Act 2002, and since then almost all youth crime in Northern Ireland is dealt with through a restorative justice process, the Youth Conference. It is available both as a diversionary option and as the default option for almost all youth offending in the courts.

12–094

Kinds of offences dealt with by restorative justice programmes

Offenders may be subject to an official caution, currently in the course of being prosecuted, or already sentenced. Many police forces are now using restorative justice as part of their neighbourhood policing approach, training officers to resolve conflict and low level crime informally on the street—"street restorative justice". The police are also key in referring cases on to community-based restorative justice providers—Community Justice Panels and Community Mediation Services. Some forces are also training officers to deal with more serious offences, including with prolific and priority offenders post-sentence.

12–095

---

[54] H. Hoyle, R. Young and H. Hill, *"Proceed with Caution: An evaluation of the Thames Valley Police initiative in restorative cautioning"* (York: Joseph Rowntree Foundation, 2002) available at *https://www.jrf.org.uk/report/evaluation-implementation-and-effectiveness-initiative-restorative-cautioning* [accessed 17 May 2018].

[55] Office for Criminal Justice Reform, *A Revised Code of Practice for Conditional Cautions (Adults)* (The Stationery Office: London, 2010), and available at: *https://www.gov.uk/government/uploads/system/uploads/attachment_data/file/228971/9789999098144.pdf* [accessed 17 May 2018].

[56] See para.7.7 of the Revised Code.

[57] The Youth Out-of-court Disposals: Guide for Police and YOTs published by Ministry of Justice, Youth Justice Board for England and Wales, and Crown Prosecution Service is available at: *https://www.gov.uk/government/publications/youth-out-of-court-disposals-guide-for-police-and-yots* [accessed 17 May 2018].

12–096 The wrongdoers will all have admitted guilt or accepted responsibility: mediation is not appropriate where this is in dispute. They may be feeling remorse to variable extents prior to the meeting. Those with obviously cynical attitudes will not be accepted. It is a given that the victims have expressed a willingness to participate.

12–097 The various victim-offender mediation and restorative justice schemes each have their own policy about the nature of the offence that can be brought to them. Many exclude serious violent and sexual offences, though some have no restrictions and may even gear themselves to cases that are more serious.[58] Facilitators will be careful to screen out parties who are too emotional or disturbed to handle direct meetings.

12–098 Some believe that it is in more serious cases, such as aggravated burglary or sexual assault, that victims may have most to gain from being able to express their feelings and come to some sort of resolution of the aftermath of the crime. The view that restorative justice is more effective in more serious crime is supported by the independent evaluation of restorative justice by Shapland.[59]

12–099 Some Probation Victim Liaison Units offer restorative processes as part of their statutory service to victims of offenders sentenced to more than 12 months in custody; and in some areas Probation Services will refer cases to local Mediation Services. Organisations like Prison Fellowship, SORI, and the Forgiveness Project provide courses in prisons based on restorative principles, which often lead to offenders wanting to make amends to the victims of their crimes.

12–100 Mediation and restorative justice processes have even been used in manslaughter and murder cases between the offender and relatives of the victim (usually some considerable time after the event). Mark Umbreit, writing about the transformative and healing power of mediation, observes that these powerful, if controversial to some, qualities of mediation have been observed in the use of mediation and dialogue in the US between parents of murdered children and the offender.[60]

12–101 A significant proportion of crimes involving personal victims are committed by someone who is acquainted with the victim. A Home Office study[61] showed that in half of the cases it considered, the victim and offender already knew one another, at least by sight and often lived in the same neighbourhood. Such situations offer opportunities for better understanding through mediation. Other offences that are brought into restorative justice schemes include vandalism, assault, antisocial behaviour orders (ASBOs) and road traffic offences.

---

[58] See G. Robinson, fn.49, p.23.
[59] J. Shapland, A. Atkinson, H. Atkinson, et al, *Does restorative justice affect reconviction? The fourth report from the evaluation of three schemes* (London: Ministry of Justice Research Series 10/08, June 2008). The earlier three reports examined how the schemes were implemented (Shapland et al, 2004; 2006), participants' expectations and take-up rates (Shapland et al, 2006) and victims' and offenders' views on the process and outcomes (Shapland et al, 2007).
[60] M. Ubreit, "Humanistic Mediation: A Transformative Journey of Peacemaking" (1997) 3 *Mediation Quarterly*.
[61] T. Marshall and S. Merry, fn.51.

RESTORATIVE PRACTICES

There is a blurring between some aspects of restorative justice and restorative practices. For example, family group conferences, which are dealt with below, are used both for child welfare in general and youth justice in particular and are equally applicable to restorative justice and restorative practice. Indeed there is no real need to make any distinction.

12–102

Family Group Conferencing and youth restorative justice

A family group conference is a group meeting in which family members meet together in order to address and resolve conflictual or behavioural issues and problems, including criminal conduct. The model was developed in New Zealand and is based on Maori traditions and methods of conflict resolution.[62]

12–103

These conferences have mainly been used in two ways:

12–104

- For both juvenile and adult offenders, they allow victims the chance to confront the offender and express their feelings, and allow the offenders the chance to apologise and make amends. A trained facilitator will assist the process.
- For family crises in a welfare context, they allow a young person to attend with his extended family, and any relevant agencies, to consider the issues, problems and available resources, followed by an opportunity for the young person and his family to discuss and formulate an appropriate action plan.

Thames Valley Police were one of the first police forces to use the restorative conference as a key feature of their work. Typically, those present at the conference might include victims and their families and friends, offenders and their families and friends, and, if appropriate, representatives of the community affected by the crime. A trained person facilitates discussion. In this way, offenders hear from those affected details of the harm that they have caused. The conference usually provides the opportunity for an agreement to be reached about reparation.

12–105

Restorative justice is not a soft option as many offenders find it difficult to face up to the impact of their crimes, and that victim participation is always voluntary.

12–106

Another restorative justice project for youth offenders was the Young Offenders Mediation Project, established in Fife, Scotland in 1996 by SACRO (Safeguarding Communities—Reducing Offending). This is now the Youth Justice Mediation Service, an independent service which works with young people aged between 11 and 16 years, who have been charged by the police and referred to the children's reporter.

12–107

---

[62] R. Mutter, D. Shemmings, P. Dugmore and M. Hyare, "Family group conferences in youth justice" (2008) 16(3) *Health and Social Care in the Community* 262.

Circles

12–108 The concept of a circle is effectively a group of people sitting round a room and speaking and listening to one another with an acceptance of certain values such as mutual respect, empathy, active listening and acceptance of differences in a problem-solving environment. It is used in a variety of circumstances, including schools, communities, workplace discussions and youth conferences. The formalisation of the process, and sometimes a ritualisation of it, invests the process with a greater opportunity for genuine and respectful exchanges of views and the resolution of differences.

Restorative practice in schools

12–109 Restorative practices in schools may relate to bullying and other forms of harm that children may experience, or to the whole range of conflicts that can arise in a school environment, from classroom discipline and exclusions to parent/teacher and other disputes, known as a "whole-school" approach. It is also being used proactively to build relationships, develop discipline and prevent harm occurring.

12–110 A report commissioned by the Department for Education found that restorative processes had a positive effect in tackling bullying, and recommended that schools consider developing restorative ethos and culture, which supported the development of social and emotional skills.[63] The range of processes under consideration covered problem-solving circles; restorative discussions; restorative meetings between staff and students; restorative thinking plans; mini-conferences; and restorative conferences.

12–111 Another project specifically addressed the use of restorative practice in schools, outlining the values underpinning it (including empowerment, honesty, respect, engagement, voluntarism, healing, restoration, personal accountability, inclusiveness, collaboration and problem-solving) and setting out the applicable principles and the issues to consider in practice.[64]

---

[63] F. Thompson, and P. Smith, *The use and effectiveness of anti-bullying strategies in schools* (Goldsmiths report for the University of London, April 2011), pp.21–22, s.2.2.9, p.34, s.2.5 and pp.93–112, s.4.3.

[64] Restorative Justice Consortium, *Statement of Restorative Justice Principles—As applied in a school setting*, 2nd edn (London: Restorative Justice Consortium, 2005).

CHAPTER 13

Workplace and Employment Dispute Resolution

BRIEF UK HISTORICAL BACKGROUND

Industrial conciliation in Britain dates back to the time of Pitt the Younger, with the so-called "pretentious legislation" of 1867 and 1872. A. J. Mundella, a 19th century industrial entrepreneur, established joint boards for the hosiery industry in Nottingham, with the proposition that "masters and men should get around the table and 'talk it out' on a footing of equality".[1] The experience in Nottingham was one of reduced strikes, lock-outs and industrial violence, which encouraged the spread of these boards into other areas and other industries. Even when the boards were overtaken by the rise of the national trades unions, the agreements the boards had achieved remained. The boards were almost always replaced by a different form of autonomous dispute resolution machinery, which enjoyed early TUC support. These experiences set the agenda and established the basis for future industrial dispute resolution. **13–001**

The policy in the 20th century was to encourage autonomous institutions with the option of recourse to an independent arbitration and conciliation service funded by the state. Notwithstanding the institutional expansion of government regulatory agencies, including employment (formerly industrial) tribunals, the Central Arbitration Committee, and Acas,[2] most dispute resolution activity was conducted outside state-supplied machinery. **13–002**

The 21st century saw the reassessment of dispute resolution in the employment field. In 2006 the Department of Trade and Industry commissioned a review of the options for simplifying and improving all aspects of employment dispute resolution. This was produced in 2007 by Michael Gibbons,[3] who recommended that "the measures to be used in future should be much simpler and more flexible" and who expressed a "vision of a greatly increased role for mediation". **13–003**

The outcome of the review was the passing of the Employment Act 2008, which came into force in 2009, and which represented a change in disciplinary and grievance procedures, focusing on fairness and transparency, with a new **13–004**

---

[1] I. G. Sharp, *Industrial Conciliation and Arbitration in Great Britain* (London: Allen and Unwin, 1949), p.466.
[2] The Advisory, Conciliation and Arbitration Service.
[3] Michael Gibbons, *Better Dispute Resolution: A review of employment dispute resolution in Great Britain* (Department of Trade and Industry, 2007)—available at: *http://webarchive.nationalarchives. gov.uk/20090609022048/http://www.berr.gov.uk/files/file38516.pdf* [accessed 17 May 2018].

non-prescriptive, principles-based statutory Acas Code. One of the features of the new system is pre-claims conciliation designed to encourage the speedier and earlier resolution of disputes.

ACAS

13–005 The Conciliation and Arbitration Service was established in 1974 as a separate service "at arm's length from government".[4] It became a statutory body in 1976[5] and renamed the Advisory, Conciliation and Arbitration Service (Acas).

13–006 Acas is publicly funded, but impartial and independent from government. According to its website, in addition to specialised training and other resources and services it:

> "provides expert and impartial advice on good practice, and support in finding solutions when relationships go wrong."

PROCESSES AND TERMINOLOGY

13–007 Employment Tribunals constitute the main forum for making decisions about employment disputes, including issues such as unfair dismissal, redundancy and discrimination. The three primary elements of ADR envisaged by the Employment Rights (Dispute Resolution) Act 1998 as alternatives to employment tribunals are conciliation, mediation and arbitration.

Conciliation

13–008 There is no consistency of usage of the term "conciliation": in many fields it tends to be used interchangeably with "mediation", though some organisations and practitioners use "conciliation" to refer to a more proactive and evaluative form of process, whereas, the reverse usage is sometimes employed. In employment, the term "conciliation" refers to a facilitative and non-evaluative mediatory process.

13–009 Individual conciliation is the term used for the conciliation of individual disputes, such as claims for unfair dismissal or other complaints by individuals that their employment rights have been infringed.

13–010 Collective conciliation relates to collective disputes, for example concerning pay or working conditions where employers and trade unions are in dispute. These are usually referred by trade unions or employers, separately or jointly, though occasionally Acas may at its own initiative offer conciliation to disputing parties.

---

[4] See the ACAS article in K. J. Mackie, *Handbook of Dispute Resolution: ADR in Action* (Routledge, London, 1991), p.100.
[5] By the Employment Protection Act 1975.

Early conciliation is a free, impartial service offered by Acas to people who have a workplace disagreement likely to lead to a tribunal claim. The offer of the service prior to claims being submitted to the tribunal represents proactive early dispute resolution. **13–011**

Mediation

Mediation is available from Acas, which also runs training programmes in workplace mediation, including a programme leading to a Certificate in Internal Workplace Mediation. There are also many private, independent, specialist workplace mediators and organisations in the marketplace. **13–012**

The concept of an evaluative mediator, as distinct from a facilitative conciliator, is no longer adopted in relation to individual workplace mediation. Indeed, the Acas website says that "mediators do not make judgments or determine outcomes." However, as indicated below, this concept of a mediator making recommendations continues to exist in relation to "collective mediation". **13–013**

Arbitration

Although Acas has always had the power to offer arbitration for industrial disputes, this power was extended by the 1998 Act to cover individual employment disputes concerning unfair dismissal. The Acas Arbitration Scheme is an alternative to employment tribunal hearings. Only cases of alleged unfair dismissal or claims under flexible working legislation may be decided. Arbitrators, who are chosen from the Acas panel of independent arbitrators and who are not employed by Acas, make awards binding on all parties. By entering into an arbitration agreement, parties contract out of the jurisdiction of the employment tribunals.[6] A similar scheme is run by the Labour Relations Agency in Northern Ireland. **13–014**

Employment and workplace issues distinguished[7]

Although the terminology is not always clearly distinguished, employment issues are generally about employment rights, often in the context of the potential or actual ending of a relationship and the terms of a settlement agreement (previously but no longer called a compromise agreement). Lawyers tend commonly, but not necessarily, to be involved in these claims and in any consequent negotiations. **13–015**

Workplace issues, on the other hand, tend to occur in the context of ongoing relationships, perhaps between colleagues or teams, or between management and staff, and may for example involve interpersonal issues or working practices. They may also involve re-establishing working relationships following grievance or disciplinary proceedings. Lawyers are not usually involved in these kinds of disagreements. **13–016**

---

[6] Employment Rights (Dispute Resolution) Act 1998 s.8.
[7] The authors are grateful to Liz Rivers for her contribution to this section and chapter.

RATIONALE FOR ADR IN EMPLOYMENT AND WORKPLACE DISPUTES

13–017 Employers and employees are in a special relationship, which will often have to continue after the dispute has been resolved. Their disputes are not necessarily amenable to judicial pronouncement, especially where complex and many-sided agreements are concerned and where it may not be appropriate for the solution to involve having one party as a winner and the other a loser, as occurs in most traditional court litigation.

13–018 It is generally accepted that the best solutions to both employment and workplace disputes are those arrived at through negotiated agreement tailored to the needs of the parties, rather than imposed upon them. This creates the optimum conditions for a satisfactory continuing working relationship.

13–019 Arbitration, despite its advantages over litigation of relative informality and specialised knowledge of the context of the dispute, still involves the same limitation as other forms of adjudication including litigation. This is that it must provide a winner and a loser, without scope to create a resolution that takes into account the varying needs, interests and concerns of the different parties and the nuances so often inherent in a complex consensual settlement. The confrontational context of arbitration and its win-lose outcome can often have negative consequences in terms of parties' satisfaction, perceptions of fairness and compliance with decisions.[8]

13–020 Workplace disputes and disagreements often arise from miscommunication and misunderstandings which if not effectively addressed may result in formal grievance procedures. However, these formal processes may lead to an escalation of the conflict and may not resolve fundamental issues, while leaving the aggrieved party still having to work with those with whom he or she has been in disagreement. Workplace mediation can help to address problems in communication and resolve inter-personal conflict more effectively than formal processes and can help restore working relationships.

13–021 In their CIPD (Chartered Institute of Personnel and Development) conference paper "Workplace Mediation—Transforming the Culture of Conflict Management?" Saundry and Wibberley explore whether and to what extent there may have been a shift in the culture of employment relations through the use of workplace mediation. They find some evidence that the use of mediation has increased, though it has not become embedded in the culture of conflict handling. After analysing its key advantages and challenges and having regard to some case studies, they conclude that in-house mediation schemes can have an effect on conflict management, particularly where there is organisational recognition of its importance and early intervention, and where key staff are actively involved.[9]

---

[8] Deborah M. Kolb, "How Existing Procedures Shape Alternatives: The Case of Grievance Mediation" (1989) *Journal of Dispute Resolution* 6(1): 59–87.

[9] Professor Richard Saundry and Dr Gemma Wibberley, "Workplace Mediation—Transforming the Culture of Conflict Management?" CIPD Applied Research Conference 2015. See: *https://www.cipd.co.uk/Images/workplace-mediation-transforming-the-culture-of-conflict-management_2015_tcm18-15587.pdf* [accessed 17 May 2018].

CONCILIATION PRACTICE AND PROCEDURE

As indicated, there are two kinds of conciliation: individual conciliation and collective conciliation. 13–022

Individual conciliation

In individual Early Conciliation, the conciliator will talk through the issues with both sides to help them each understand how the other side views the case, may help them establish the facts, and will explore how the issues may be resolved without a hearing. Any settlement proposals will be carried from one to the other and discussed. The conciliator will not offer advice or any opinion as to the likely outcome of the case at a tribunal hearing, but may explain the relevant law and may outline what a tribunal would take into account when deciding a case.[10] 13–023

Where a party has an authorised representative and wishes the conciliator to deal with them, the conciliator will do so, and will not necessarily deal with the party directly. 13–024

Individual conciliation generally takes place over the telephone. However, in some cases telephone contact does not satisfactorily meet parties' needs, especially where legal information is complex or parties are conducting the discussion in difficult circumstances. Email is sometimes also used. 13–025

If face to face meetings are held, these may be conducted by way of separate confidential meetings with each party, the conciliator adopting a peripatetic role, moving between the parties, trying to establish common ground and to narrow the issues. There may be joint meetings, though in situations of high tension, these might be avoided. 13–026

If the parties agree on settlement terms, the conciliator will, insofar as may be required, help them to record the terms in a binding written agreement known as a COT3. If they do not reach agreement, their negotiations and discussions in conciliation cannot be used in evidence at a tribunal hearing, and are confidential. Conciliation will continue to be available until all matters of liability and remedy have been determined by the employment tribunal. 13–027

Collective conciliation

Collective conciliation refers to negotiations between representative groups (typically trade unions) and employers, facilitated by a neutral and independent conciliator. Matters most commonly referred to collective conciliation are disputes about pay, working hours and other terms of employment, job losses and redundancy, and Trade Union recognition.[11] 13–028

If parties agree to use the process, a conciliator will liaise with both sides to see how best to help and what procedure would work best in the situation. Each side would need to have an opportunity to hear and understand the other's point of view, directly or indirectly, and to reflect on this quietly and privately. 13–029

---

[10] See: *http://www.acas.org.uk/media/pdf/h/o/Early-Conciliation-explained.pdf* [accessed 17 May 2018].

[11] See: Research Paper "Acas Collective Conciliation Evaluation 2016" (Ref: 06/16) August 2016 by Caroline Booth, Michael Clemence and Sara Gariban (Ipsos MORI).

13–030　The process that then follows is likely to involve some permutation of joint and separate meetings, in the latter case with the conciliator shuttling between the parties carrying thoughts and proposals, and aiming to find terms that everyone may find acceptable. Parallel with this, the conciliator is likely to try to resolve misunderstandings and misperceptions, and to help the parties restore trust in one another.

13–031　Even if the conciliation does not achieve an agreed resolution during the process, it may sometimes help resolve any deadlocks that might have arisen, allowing the parties to move forward, and able to continue their negotiations themselves without the need for the conciliator to remain involved. Alternatively, the parties may decide to move to some other form of dispute resolution such as binding arbitration.

Settlement (Compromise) agreements

13–032　A settlement agreement (formerly and sometimes still called a compromise agreement) is a document in which an employee agrees not to pursue a claim against his or her employer.

13–033　For a settlement agreement to be binding, it must be in writing, must relate to a specific claim or claims, actual or potential, and the employee must have had proper legal advice from an independent adviser. The agreement, which may be subject to confidentiality provisions and mutual undertakings, will ordinarily identify the payments to be made to the employee, and if any part is payable free of tax, this will be reflected. It may confirm any existing post-termination restrictive covenants and any new ones that might have been negotiated and agreed. It will contain any other agreed provisions, and will be in full settlement of all claims, including the right to bring tribunal proceedings.[12]

MEDIATION PRACTICE

13–034　Acas distinguishes between "mediation" and "collective mediation", with a concept for the latter that has a special meaning in the employment field that it does not necessarily have in other spheres of activity.[13] Collective mediation is dealt with briefly below.

13–035　Acas has indicated that mediation can be used "to address a range of issues including relationship breakdown, personality clashes, communication problems, bullying and harassment."[14] This is, however, not a limitation, and mediation is in fact used to address a wide range of workplace and employment issues, including by an increasing number of private, independent mediators and commercial

---

[12] For further details about settlement agreements, see Acas Code of Practice 4: "Settlement Agreements (under section 111A of the Employment Rights Act 1996)", July 2013, published by TSO (The Stationery Office).

[13] "When I use a word" Humpty Dumpty said, in a rather scornful tone, "it means just what I choose it to mean—neither more nor less." Lewis Carroll, *Through the Looking-Glass* (London: Macmillan, 1871).

[14] See: "Mediation: An Approach to Resolving Workplace Issues—A guide February 2013" produced for Acas and the Chartered Institute of Personnel and Development (CIPD) by Sarah Podro and Rachel Suff of Acas.

services, many of whom are registered with the Civil Mediation Council or the Scottish Mediation Register. Indeed, it can also be used to address disputes that might otherwise be dealt with through individual conciliation, such as unfair dismissal, or those which might be dealt with through collective conciliation, such as pay disputes.

The pre-mediation phase in employment and workplace mediation involves all concerned assessing its suitability, especially where there may be a wish or need to have a third-party decision, when clearly mediation would not be appropriate. Other preliminary questions that a mediator may want to address include establishing whether other informal attempts have been made, or can still be made, to resolve the issues at management level, or whether there is any other more suitable process available. The mediator will want to ensure that all concerned genuinely wish to participate and understand that the process is entirely voluntary. They may be asked to sign an agreement to mediate. 13–036

The stages adopted in this work then continue as follows: 13–037

STAGE 1: PRELIMINARY COMMUNICATIONS AND PREPARATION

This involves explaining to the parties the ground-rules and how the process will work and the rules about confidentiality and privilege. The mediator will ordinarily liaise with both parties separately to set up the arrangements and the preliminary documentation, will organise a suitable venue and an agreed timetable for exchanging information and for the substantive mediation. 13–038

The timetable needs to be realistic, recognising that it needs to take place as speedily as possible while ensuring that nobody will be prevented from presenting their positions adequately. Fixing the substantive meeting(s) for one or two days is common, though some are dealt with in less than a day, and some may take more than two days. 13–039

Parties may be represented in workplace mediation, though this is not generally encouraged, on the basis that the process is designed to facilitate direct communication, and that representatives may tend to move towards positional bargaining rather than problem-solving. Attitudes and policies on representation vary: trade union representatives and other advisers may, for example, play a supporting role behind the scenes. However, legal representatives are more likely to be involved in employment mediation, especially where there are formal claims arising from the ending of a relationship. 13–040

Some mediators will arrange for the parties to provide and exchange case summaries, comprising a brief history of the events and issues giving rise to the mediation. 13–041

STAGE 2: COMMENCEMENT, ESTABLISHING THE ISSUES AND SETTING THE AGENDA

13–042　Before having a joint meeting, the usual procedure is for the mediator first to meet each party separately, more than once if necessary, to allow each party to explain their position and perceptions to the mediator privately, enabling the mediator to get a grasp of the presenting issues, and also of any underlying issues. This will also provide an opportunity for the mediator to check that mediation is suitable and to re-affirm the ground-rules.

13–043　The parties will then commonly meet the mediator for a joint meeting, at which each will ordinarily be given an opportunity to explain their position and concerns. The mediator will create an environment in which this can be done respectfully and without interruption. After each party has done so, the mediator may ask some questions to help clarify the issues and to establish an agenda of matters to be addressed in the mediation.

STAGE 3: INFORMATION GATHERING

13–044　The mediator will establish the necessary information in a number of ways, initially by preliminary discussion with each party, and then through the exchange of written statements (and relevant copy documents, if any) in those models where this is done. Some mediators prefer not to have this written exchange, or to avoid doing so in situations where this would be likely to be unhelpful and might perhaps be unnecessarily inflammatory. Some mediators ask parties to submit an initial referral form containing relevant information.

13–045　The mediator gains most information in the separate meetings with the parties before the joint meeting, and then through the respective explanations that each will give in the joint meeting. Thereafter, information may continue to emerge as the process develops: further facts may come to light, and also feelings and attitudes affecting the position may surface, which the mediator may need to address.

13–046　As in all other fields, the mediator needs to remain alert throughout the process for hidden signs and indicators, which may be discovered by picking up on the odd remark or by a careful observation of non-verbal communication, and taking up and sensitively probing any aspect that the mediator may—perhaps intuitively—feel could inform the process and help to move matters forward.

STAGE 4: CONDUCTING SUBSTANTIVE NEGOTIATIONS

13–047　During this substantive phase, the mediator will explore the issues with both parties and will encourage open communication. The approach will often be to encourage "future focus" rather than dwelling on the past; but obviously the past will inform the future, so it may also be necessary to consider how past events have affected each of the parties so as to identify ways of overcoming similar problems in the future.

As the parties begin to gain some better understanding of one another's viewpoints and concerns, they would be encouraged to start exploring options for addressing the issues in the future. The mediator will try to gather together a range of options and to develop these for consideration. This may be done by encouraging the parties to suggest options, perhaps through a brainstorming session if appropriate; and there is no reason why the mediator should not also suggest options provided that this is done in a sensitive and tentative way. It can then be productive to work on exploring and narrowing the options in a problem-solving mode. 13–048

Where relationships will continue in the future, one of the main objectives of the process will generally be to develop better ways of functioning more effectively rather than necessarily just reaching settlement terms. This indicates a need to help the parties towards a greater awareness of various elements of the issues under discussion, for example, how their way of functioning may affect the other and how this may be dealt with in the future. Changes may need to be organisational and structural, or they may also need to be personal. 13–049

Where the mediation relates to the potential or actual ending of an employment relationship and agreeing the terms of a settlement agreement, the substantive negotiations may follow some of the approaches and procedures applicable to civil and commercial mediation, as outlined in Ch.10, appropriately adapted to the context of an employment relationship. 13–050

Ideally, the discussion and negotiations during the mediation will not only help the parties to overcome problems that they have experienced in the past, but (particularly in the context of workplace issues, where parties may continue in their ongoing relationships) will provide them with the necessary skills and insights that will enable them to address any difficulties that might emerge in the future. 13–051

STAGE 5: DEALING WITH IMPASSE

If discussions become deadlocked, all the strategies outlined in Ch.9 may be considered, but there are some that may be particularly relevant to employment and workplace mediation. 13–052

One impasse strategy is to have one or more separate, confidential meetings with each party, to try to establish privately what the underlying issues are that are blocking resolution, with a view to developing some possible ideas that might accommodate both sides' concerns. Using this strategy, the mediator may either reassemble in joint meeting after having had a separate meeting with each, or may continue for a while shuttling between the parties in their separate rooms, carrying thoughts, ideas and proposals back and forth. 13–053

Although this is reflected here as an impasse strategy, there may well be situations where this procedure may be used at an early stage, and indeed in some cases perhaps instead of a joint meeting, where the parties feel, initially in any event, unable to meet together in the same room. If using this procedure, the mediator will need to agree the confidentiality rules applicable: they are likely to be similar to the commercial model in which the mediator undertakes not to 13–054

13–055 disclose anything to the other party discussed in the separate confidential meeting, save with specific authority, which may be sought where appropriate.

13–055 Mediators might also consider whether either or both parties feel unheard, particularly with regard to fairness. It can sometimes help to devote a little time specifically to discuss issues of fairness, and to allow each to address this topic. People may not necessarily persuade one another that their perceptions of fairness are correct, but they can feel heard and can also appreciate that there may be more than one perspective on this, allowing them to move forward with pragmatic solutions.

13–056 This ties in with the need that people may have to address symbolic aspects. There are situations in which people may want some form of acknowledgment or recognition, or to have some symbolic act to reinforce agreed aspects, apart from financial compensation. This partly explains the power of apology and public statements, or reinstating a holiday period or other benefit—that may go well beyond cash value.

13–057 Helping parties with risk assessment can also be a useful function where discussions have reached deadlock. Exploring BATNAs and WATNAs (Best and Worst Alternatives to a Negotiated Agreement) can be useful—though the mediator would not generally undertake this exercise for the parties, but would rather help them to do so themselves where appropriate and arrive at their own conclusions. Outcome perceptions may be unrealistic, both as to the position if taken to a tribunal or any other form of adjudication, and also as to the likelihood of achieving vindication in some other forum.

STAGE 6: CONCLUDING MEDIATION AND RECORDING THE OUTCOME

13–058 If the parties reach agreement in mediation, the agreed terms will be recorded in a document signed by them both, which will be binding in law. The wording should clearly reflect their terms and avoid legalese. There may be a focus on future conduct and communications, and how these will be handled.

13–059 Mediators will check that the agreements are unambiguous and workable, and will also check who else might be allowed to have sight of the document, notwithstanding its confidential nature, for example, senior management or as the case may be.

If the parties are unable to reach agreement in the mediation, they will have reserved all their rights to have the matter dealt with in another forum, as appropriate to the issues.

POST-MEDIATION

13–060 At the end of the mediation and after the parties have signed an agreement embodying the settlement terms if this occurs, the mediator may need to report to management, but strictly only if so agreed between the parties. In the case of an Acas appointment, reporting will accord with Acas policy and the terms of the arrangement with the parties.

Some mediators or providers will maintain contact with the parties after the end of the process in order to ensure that matters are proceeding smoothly and to offer any further support that may be required. 13–061

COLLECTIVE MEDIATION

This is a concept used by Acas as a step beyond collective conciliation, where the latter has been tried and not succeeded and the parties do not wish to move to arbitration but remain committed to trying to resolve the issues in some agreed way. 13–062

Acas mediators, drawn from their independent panel, may "offer the parties recommendations designed to settle the dispute. Although these recommendations are not binding, parties are expected to seriously consider them as a basis for resolving the dispute".[15] 13–063

EMPLOYMENT ARBITRATION

Acas maintains an arbitration scheme as an alternative to a tribunal hearing in order to deal with unfair dismissal cases and claims under flexible working legislation. It aims to do so expeditiously, and to produce outcomes equivalent to those given by tribunals. 13–064

An agreement to enter into arbitration ousts the jurisdiction of the tribunal, so there are limitations on being able to do so, namely that parties must either do so with the assistance of an Acas conciliator, or through an effective Settlement Agreement signed after the employee has taken advice from a relevant independent adviser.[16] 13–065

Acas also offers a free collective arbitration service, which is an option in which parties voluntarily enter into the arbitration, which is not legally binding but in which they submit agreed terms of reference, and undertake in advance to accept the decision of the arbitrator. The parties exchange statements of case containing their respective submissions which also forward to the Arbitrator. The hearing is private and informal, and the arbitrator makes an award within three weeks thereafter. 13–066

---

[15] See: "Collective mediation" at *http://www.acas.org.uk/index.aspx?articleid=2013* [accessed 17 May 2018].
[16] See fn.12.

CHAPTER 14

Mediator Attributes, Skills and Roles

INTRODUCTION

This chapter addresses one of the most important aspects of ADR practice: the skills and attributes of the facilitator handling the process. These will be considered in the context of mediation, but the principles outlined here will be equally applicable to all consensual and agreement-based ADR processes facilitated by an impartial third party. Whilst party autonomy underpins such a procedure, the role of the facilitator may be influential on its shape, aims, content, and successful outcome, and hence the significance of the role should not be downplayed.[1]   **14–001**

While mediators draw on experiences and skills developed elsewhere, mediation demands a different approach than is needed for many occupations of origin. Existing attributes and qualities may need to be re-examined and fresh understandings may be required. Practical skills may be used in a different way. Mediators need to develop a new ethical awareness and discard some old habits. This can be a challenging process.   **14–002**

As already observed, there is a range of models of, and approaches to, mediation. Mediators from different fields of activity and disciplines are likely to work in different ways. This chapter seeks to extract common principles that are important for the mediator.   **14–003**

The chapter introduces a mediation construct designed to identify some of the main features that, ideally, facilitators bring to the mediation process. Hence it sets out what may be described as foundational knowledge, suggests desirable attributes, and discusses possible leadership traits that may assist in facilitation of the mediation process. It cannot, and does not pretend to be, a comprehensive and exhaustive chronicle of all relevant attributes and qualities of a mediator.   **14–004**

Skills, in this context, refer to the ways in which people relate to and communicate with others. Attributes refer to inherent characteristics and qualities that may be a product of personality and psychological make-up but may be developed and honed over time. While there may be a relationship and overlap between the two, they are also distinguishable; and for the purpose of considering and analysing the attributes and skills of a mediator, they will be dealt with separately.   **14–005**

---

[1] "Some disputes are more intractable than others. Some mediators are more skilled than others": Lord Justice Dyson in *Halsey v Milton Keynes General NHS Trust* [2004] EWCA Civ 576 [27] in support of his statement that it should not be "overlooked that the potential success of a mediation may not depend only on the willingness of the parties to compromise".

14-006 The chapter will also consider the different roles that the mediator performs and the different functions that the mediator has in carrying out these roles.

THE CONCEPT OF THE CONSTRUCT

14-007 The construct is built on three fundamental or foundational blocks of knowledge. These are theoretical understanding, skills, and ethical awareness. Without a proper understanding of these aspects, mediators will be ill-equipped to deal appropriately with the range of circumstances and situations which they may encounter in mediation processes. The second layer of the construct focuses on desirable attributes of the mediator: sound judgment, and sensitivity, empathy or understanding. These characteristics together ensure that parties are properly heard and that due attention is paid to relevant issues. This leads to the top of the construct: this has to do with the conduct of the process which may require creativity, flexibility and balance or even-handedness.

Foundational knowledge

Theoretical understanding

14-008 There is no single theory of mediation. Each field, model and approach may have different theoretical orientations. However, mediators should have an understanding of these theoretical perspectives in order to understand and communicate the possibilities of the process and to enable participants to adopt the most appropriate process for their situation. The following are highlighted here, and discussed in more detail elsewhere in this book, as examples of matters of which a mediator should have theoretical knowledge:

- *A theoretical perspective:* for example, mediation as a set of stages,[2] or a communications perspective,[3] or a transformative theory of mediation.[4]
- *The mediator's role and function:* the way in which the mediator's even-handed facilitative role is put into practice is outlined below.
- *Conflict and dispute:* understanding the distinction between these and how they can be addressed and resolved.[5]
- *Adversarial and consensual dispute resolution processes:* how mediation fits in.[6]

---

[2] Mediation writers variably suggest 5 to 13 stages of the mediation process. These may be divided into two broad categories: preparation (prior to the mediation) and process (stages within the procedure): see, e.g. C.W. Moore, *The Mediation Process: Practical Strategies for Resolving Conflict*, 4th edn (Jossey Bass, 2014), Ch.6.

[3] See, e.g. A Zariski, "A Theory Matrix for Mediators" (2010) (26) *Negotiation Journal* 203, 215–218.

[4] Ch.1, paras 1-042 to 1-046; Ch.3, paras 3-052 to 5-053; Ch.9, paras 9-016 to 9-019; and Ch.16, paras 16-105 to 16-106; see R.A. Baruch Bush and J.P. Folger, *The Promise of Mediation: The Transformative Approach to Conflict*, rev edn (Jossey-Bass, 2005).

[5] For discussion on this, see Ch.1, paras 1-022 to 1-027.

[6] Discussed briefly in Ch.1, paras 1-002 to 1-003.

The Mediation Construct

Leadership Traits or Style		
Creativity	Balance	Flexibility

Desirable Attributes		
Sound Judgement	Sensitivity and Empathy	Other e.g.: Patience, Authority, Trustworthiness

Foundational Knowledge		
Theoretical Understanding	Practical Skills	Ethical Awareness

- *The principles of mediation:* common principles run through all kinds of mediation.[7]
- *Confidentiality and legal privilege:* the principles that regulate mediation practice.[8]
- *Power:* its manifestations, imbalances and empowerment.[9]
- *Negotiation:* theories and approaches.[10]
- *Evaluation:* its advantages, limitations and problems.[11]
- *The dynamics of mediation*[12]*:* the relationship between the parties and the mediator, the mediator's creative and facilitative functions,[13] and issues such as triangulation and alliances,[14] culture and gender.[15]
- *Cautions, limits and reservations:* when mediation may be inappropriate, or when to proceed with caution.[16]

Practical skills

14-009   A mediator must not only have a theoretical grounding, but also the practical skills necessary to work effectively. Most mediation training programmes recognise this and provide opportunities for mediators to observe and practise these skills through a combination of DVDs, demonstrations and role play exercises with feedback from trainers and participants.

14-010   Practical mediation skills comprise a combination of management and facilitation abilities. The mediator must be able to manage the process firmly but not autocratically, and with due sensitivity; to facilitate communication and negotiation; to combine pragmatism and vision; to help move the parties to resolution of the dispute; and to ensure that the outcome is properly recorded as the parties and process require. Important skills are discussed in more detail below.[17]

---

[7] For a fuller discussion, see Ch.8.
[8] For a fuller discussion, see Ch.15.
[9] For a fuller discussion, see Ch.16.
[10] For a fuller discussion, see Ch.4.
[11] For a fuller discussion, see Chs 8 and 19.
[12] See D. De Girolamo, *The Fugitive Identity of Mediation: Negotiations, Shift Changes, and Allusionary Action* (Routledge, 2013).
[13] For example, see M. Deutsch, P.T. Coleman and E.C. Marcus, *The Handbook of Conflict Resolution: Theory and Practice* (Jossey Bass, 2006) Pt 4: Creativity and Change.
[14] Discussed further at paras 14-085 to 14-091. Also see, e.g. W.F. Regina, *Applying Family Systems Theory to Mediation* (University Press of America, 2011), Ch.6.
[15] For example: C. Rack, *Latino Anglo Bargaining: Culture, Structure and Choice in Court Mediation* (New York & London: Routledge, 2006); T Grillo, "The Mediation Alternative: Process Dangers for Women" (1991) 100 *Yale Law Journal* 1545–1610, 1550.
[16] Two different approaches by experienced mediators to a hypothetical case study is set out in C Menkel-Meadow & H. Abramson, "Mediating Muliculturally: Culture and the Ethical Mediator" in E. Waldman (ed.) *Mediation Ethics: Cases and Commentaries* (San Francisco: Jossey Bass, 2011), pp.305–338.
[17] See Mediation Skills at paras 14-042 to 14-101.

THE CONCEPT OF THE CONSTRUCT

Ethical awareness[18]

The role of mediator carries the responsibility, not only to provide effective assistance to the parties, but to do so in an ethically proper manner. A mediator intervenes in a private dispute with significant power and opportunity to affect the outcome. Mediators must undertake their practice with awareness of that ethical responsibility. Mediators should have regard to the following ethical considerations in carrying out their functions: 14–011

- The Code of Practice under which they mediate. This will usually provide clear ethical and practical guidelines for their practice.
- The ethical rules of any professional body to which they belong.
- The principles of fairness of process.[19]
- When not to mediate: there are circumstances in which it would be inappropriate for the mediator to mediate, or having started, to continue.[20]
- When they should be conscious of cautions and reservations about mediation.
- When people external to the mediation may be identified in the mediation as being vulnerable to harm.
- When fairness to the parties requires that the mediator needs an understanding of cultural issues that are relevant to the mediation process.
- When there are power imbalances and/or vulnerable parties involved in the mediation.

This aspect of the foundational knowledge required for mediators may lead, on occasion, to the need for at least a basic understanding or awareness of more *specific* or *substantive knowledge*. For example, where parties are from minority and majority cultures, it may be advisable to have an awareness of any cultural issues that may impact on the mediation or that may lead one party to more readily accede to suggestions from the other party.[21] At times specific knowledge of the subject-matter, also, may be useful.   14–012

In general, if there is a choice between process expertise and substance expertise, one would choose as a mediator someone who is skilled in the mediation process rather than an expert in the subject-matter of the dispute. However it is now possible in many fields of activity to have a mediator who has both substantive knowledge and process expertise.   14–013

Substantive knowledge can mean expertise in a specialist field. So, for example, a mediator required for a dispute about the construction of a bridge may be an engineer with detailed and specialist knowledge of bridge construction or a lawyer who specialises in construction law and practice. However, substantive knowledge does not necessarily mean specialist expertise, but may, for example, mean a mediator with knowledge of the general field of the dispute. So, for example, a generalist commercial mediator with a background in business would have substantive knowledge of commerce and be well able to deal with a wide   14–014

---

[18] For a fuller consideration of ethics, as set out in this section, see Ch.16.
[19] A. Gerami, "Bridging the Theory and Practice Gap: Mediator Power in Practice" (2009) (26) *Conflict Resolution Quarterly* 433: discussing the influence of mediators in ensuring fair process.
[20] See Ch.16 for ethical issues, when not to mediate, and cautions and reservations.
[21] C. Rack, *Latino Anglo Bargaining: Culture, Structure and Choice in Court Mediation,* see fn.15.

14–015 range of specialist issues in a commercial dispute. Parties would be unlikely to choose a mediator who worked in a neighbourhood, community or family context who had neither specialised knowledge of their industry nor even substantive general commercial experience.

14–015 Similarly in the family field, mediators may bring substantive knowledge into the process. They may have expertise in working with children or may be therapists or counsellors with a specialist knowledge about relationship breakdown or they may have a background as a family lawyer with experience in dealing with separating and divorcing couples and their children. Some may not have a background in working with families, but may have been specifically trained to do so, with a knowledge base about couple's dynamics, children's needs and legal issues. The required substantive knowledge base might in some cases be very specific, for example, where appropriate to the issues, a mediator might need to have knowledge of or access to relevant social security legislation.

14–016 General mediators with no substantive knowledge of couples or families and their issues, and no specialised substantive training, could not realistically and effectively be expected to undertake divorce mediation involving children, finance and the other issues that couples bring into the process.

14–017 In the community and neighbourhood field, mediators are often drawn from members of the local community and are commonly not professionals. In a sense, they could be said also to have substantive knowledge: they are likely to know about the local community, to have experience of the kinds of problems that local people face, and to understand the needs of the disputants better than, for example, a specialist construction industry mediator.

14–018 In most fields of activity, a well-rounded mediator will bring some substantive knowledge to the table, and will be expected by the parties to do so.

Desirable attributes

14–019 The second layer of the construct highlights the important personal attributes of the mediator. Attention is paid here to two aspects in particular but it should be noted that mediation websites, blogs and institutions suggest a wide variety of desirable attributes.[22]

Sound judgment

14–020 This is a subjective attribute that might be honed with practice, but cannot easily be taught or learned. It is nevertheless an extremely important one for mediators to have and to use. Mediators who are used to exercising their judgment are likely to have developed this facility and to be able to bring it into play for the benefit of disputants.

14–021 There is a link between the exercise of sound judgment and an ability to trust intuitive responses. Many professionals, especially lawyers, place a high premium on the value of logic and are loath to acknowledge the significance of

---

[22] One such site lists "212 qualities of a good mediator": Kluwer Mediation Blog at: *http://mediationblog.kluwerarbitration.com/2012/02/19/212-qualities-of-a-good-mediator/* [accessed May 2018].

intuition. In truth, both of these have their places in the exercise of judgment. Intuition is more immediate, logic and reason underpin decisions based on intuition.[23]

14–022 Every step in the mediation process demands the exercise of judgment. How much time should be allowed to each party for different aspects of the process, such as presenting or explaining their positions? How should the mediator handle interruptions or provocative statements? When is it appropriate for the mediator to offer personal observations? How should the mediator conduct the process? There are a myriad of decisions that the mediator needs to make, consciously or intuitively, that affect the process and perhaps the outcome.

Sensitivity and empathy

14–023 These aspects may be considered as the mediator's ability to function relationally with the parties to the proceedings and to deal with the strong feelings that may inevitably arise in any dispute, even between commercial parties.[24]

14–024 Emotional sensitivity does not mean that the mediator must have the skills and expertise of a counsellor or that the mediation should be confused with counselling or any process that deals with the resolution of personal emotional issues. Neither does this run counter to the assertion that mediators should remain objective,[25] rather it requires emotional maturity and means that the mediator can offer the parties the following:

- an ability to cope with the emotions expressed by the parties in the mediation in a way that accepts them normally and non-judgmentally;
- an ability to work sensitively with parties in exploring issues and concerns underlying those that they present in the mediation;
- recognition of the possible impact of the emotional aspect on the process, and an ability to acknowledge parties' feelings in a non-patronising way;
- assistance in getting back to the task of finding a resolution to the issues when the parties or any of them are caught up with the strength of their feelings;
- an understanding of the network of resources available to help parties where the strength of their emotions is so great that it impairs their ability to resolve matters in the mediation;
- some understanding of high conflict and the strategies to help parties in this category.

---

[23] See H. Brown, N. Dawson and B. McHugh, *Psychology, Emotion and Intuition in Work Relationships: The Head, Heart and Gut Professional* (Routledge, 2018).
[24] For perspectives on the need to engage with emotion in negotiation and other dispute resolution processes see: D.L. Shapiro "Negotiation Emotions" (2002) (20) *Conflict Resolution Quarterly* 67; A.N. Isen "Positive Affect and Decision Making" in J.K. Haviland-Jones and A.G. Johnson (eds), *Handbook of Emotions* (New York: Guildford Press, 2000); and Fisher and Shapiro, *Building Agreement: Using Emotions as You Negotiate* (London: Random House Business Books, 2007).
[25] See, e.g. J.B. Stolberg "Must a Mediator be Neutral? You'd Better Believe It" (2012) (95) *Marquette Law Review* 829; M. Coyle "Defending the Weak and Fighting Unfairness: Can Mediators Respond to the Challenge?" (1998) (36) *Osgoode Hall Law Journal* 625.

14-025   Closely related to sensitivity is empathy. This is an attribute that cannot readily be taught, though it is possible to develop an attitude that makes it easier to be genuinely empathetic to parties even when one does not readily find them likeable.

14-026   Empathy is defined in the Shorter Oxford dictionary as "the power of identifying oneself mentally with (and so fully comprehending) a person or object of contemplation". A mediator tries to identify with both or all parties and to "fully comprehend" their positions, concerns and aspirations. Yet such identification has to be properly boundaried, to maintain the necessary professional balance.

14-027   Parties can generally sense whether a mediator is genuinely empathetic. If they appreciate that the mediator is trying to help them to achieve an outcome that attempts to meet their requirements, they will feel able to work with that mediator. The fact that the mediator is also seeking the same outcome for the other side does not diminish that willingness to co-operate. If, however, they sense that the mediator does not understand or comprehend their situation and cannot relate to them, their willingness to work constructively with that mediator is likely to be adversely affected.

14-028   Inevitably mediators will come across parties who conduct themselves in a way that the mediator may find unattractive. It can sometimes be difficult to be empathetic towards parties whose behaviour and approach feel offensive to the mediator's sense of justice and propriety.[26] However, it is important that the mediator develops an understanding of the positions of all parties and approaches the mediation with balance.

14-029   Sometimes it may be necessary for a mediator consciously to review his or her attitude towards a party. One impasse strategy requires the mediator to consider whether he or she is perpetuating the problem by perhaps being stuck in one approach or by unwittingly supporting one position. In that situation, it is possible that the mediator has lost empathy with one of the parties, and the result may be that the mediation has gone off track. Balance and empathy are probably related in this way.

14-030   In addition to the qualities already discussed, a mediator will ideally also have other attributes. There can be no definitive list of these nor can they be easily distinguished because of their overlap, and the amalgam of inherent attributes and qualities, of learned and intuitive skills and techniques, of cultural and professional influences. They might, however, include the following:

- *Understanding:* the ability to understand with sensitivity the issues, often complex, and the concerns and aspirations of the parties, explicit and implicit.
- *Intuition:* an ability to sense information without any rationalisation, obtained through perceptiveness to verbal and other signals received.
- *Trustworthiness:* integrity coupled with a sense that trust can be reposed in the mediator.

---

[26] A study by Wing suggests that where a minority party's narrative within a mediation runs counter to the dominant cultural discourse, this may be less understood by mediators and may lead to disengagement with that party's story and, hence, to disadvantage in the mediation process. L. Wing, "Mediation and Inequality Reconsidered: Bringing the Discussion to the Table" (2009) 26(4) *Conflict Resolution Quarterly* 383–404.

- *Patience:* regarded by many parties as one of the most important qualities, to help them through what can often be testing times for everyone.
- *Vision:* being able to see that a resolution exists even to complex and fraught situations.
- *Authority:* firmness of touch in managing the process effectively and constructively.
- *Constructiveness:* a practical turn of mind that sees positive possibilities and can motivate the parties to deal constructively with settlement options.
- *Independence:* this includes an ability to work autonomously, without support or feedback, and to maintain a neutral and independent stance.

Leadership traits or style

The mediator needs to be a proficient manager of the mediation process itself. This necessitates organising the meetings and preparation for it including documentation, conducting preliminary and interim communications, maintaining control of all procedural aspects and deciding how to conduct each element of the process, making and implementing the agenda and deciding how best to deal with the issues. It involves acting as a firm but fair chairperson of the process and ensuring that time is used effectively. It also includes managing power imbalances as appropriate, ensuring procedural fairness and compliance with any Code of Practice and ethical rules.   14–031

If a mediator loses control of the management of the process, whether by allowing any party to dominate the proceedings or by an inability to maintain authority or effectiveness, the trust and confidence of the parties is likely to be eroded, with potentially adverse consequences on the outcome of the process. The corollary of this is not domineering regulation by the mediator, but gentle, firm, impartial and effective management control. Thus, the final layer of the construct identifies aspects of leadership that can aid facilitation of the mediation process.   14–032

Creativity

De Bono considers creativity to be an essential part of the process of designing dispute resolution outcomes.[27] In his view, people in dispute and involved in dialectic argument are least likely to be able to adopt a creative approach to the resolution of their issues. This is likely to be the experience of many practitioners.   14–033

An impartial practitioner will ordinarily be in a good position to help people to see beyond the confines of their argument. That role is expected of the mediator or other ADR facilitator. One of the benefits of ADR is its ability to help parties to examine matters beyond their immediate dispute, and to consider their wider interests. Certainly, disputes may be resolved by finding a point somewhere between their respective positions, and that is a perfectly good and honourable   14–034

---

[27] Edward de Bono, *Conflicts: A Better Way to Resolve Them* (Harmondsworth: Penguin, 1986). He prefers the term "lateral thinking" because of the vagueness of the term "creativity" and its artistic connotations: creative people can be rigid in their thinking, whereas "lateral thinking" opens up new ways of looking at things and doing things. Nevertheless, he does use the term "creativity".

14–035 Creativity may manifest itself in many ways. Brainstorming may help parties to explore a range of options and to come up with a range of ideas. However, it may often be up to the mediator to develop creative ideas, taking care to test them tentatively with the parties and not to promote them. Levine considers that facilitators will have a vision of the outcome, and that they must be careful not to drive the result to that vision. However, as he points out, the neutrality of the facilitator does not mean a lack of involvement and there may be times, when parties are at an impasse, that mediators might suggest their vision, albeit gently.[28]

Flexibility

14–036 One of the great advantages of ADR is its flexibility, albeit within certain structured frameworks. Instead of facing the rigid structures of litigation, disputing parties have the benefit of processes that are adaptable to their specific needs. An ADR practitioner can create a process that responds to the requirements of the parties and their issues. This is the origin of the various hybrid processes of ADR.

14–037 This flexibility also extends to the way in which each process is conducted and to the range of options that may be explored, which can go out of the usual range of settlement discussions in conventional negotiation. This flexibility of approach is inherent in ADR.

14–038 Of course, there cannot be flexibility of process or of the topics under discussion without flexibility on the part of the mediator. One of the hallmarks of a good mediator is the ability to be flexible where the situation requires it.

Balance

14–039 Balance involves impartiality and even-handedness between the parties and is critical to the facilitation of a mediation process. It demands an ability to see both sides of the conflict, and to maintain that even-handedness at all times.

14–040 A mediator maintains a centred position in relation to the parties, showing favour to neither. This even-handedness does not mean that the mediator might not lean one way or another during the process: on the contrary, this is almost inevitable as the mediator probes here, questions there, prevents abusive behaviour perhaps from one and then from the other.[29] However, balance involves the mediator maintaining and returning to a centred position.

14–041 Another concept of balance refers to the mediator being in a balanced frame of mind. A mediator who is personally off-balance is likely to be less effective. This

---

[28] S. Levine, *Getting to Resolution: Turning Conflict into Collaboration* (San Francisco: Berrett-Koehler, 2009), pp.134–135.

[29] Indeed, even-handedness may require mediators to ensure substantive equality between parties to a mediation where a particular party may require longer time to articulate their story due to disadvantage, such as a member of a minority group where cultural norms are not familiar or where a party has a disability that affects participation. L. Mulcahy, "The Possibilities and Desirability of Mediator Neutrality: Towards an Ethic of Partiality" (2001) 10(4) *Social and Legal Studies* 505–527.

reference to personal balance in mediation has led to some comparisons with the practice of the form of aikido, a Japanese martial art, which requires a practitioner to be balanced, centred, perceptive and decisive, moving responsively with the flow of the challenger.[30]

MEDIATION SKILLS

In addition to those outlined above, the mediator also needs to use various skills in conducting the mediation. These skills may be learned or intuitive, enhancing communication, negotiation, flexibility and creativity within a secure, well-managed environment, and include the following: 14–042

Listening

This is a fundamental but often neglected communication skill. It involves allowing the parties to speak without interrupting, anticipating or contradicting them, and then absorbing those words and ideas before responding. 14–043

Some people, while listening, are thinking of a response, perhaps even responding before the speaker has finished the sentence. To some this may be viewed as a strength. As a mediator, however, except where the circumstances require the mediator to interrupt a party or to stop a line of discussion for a specific reason, it is important to exercise patience and restraint, to listen carefully and to hear what is being said before responding. 14–044

Active listening involves a number of elements: 14–045

- giving proper, uninterrupted and focused attention to the speaker;
- acknowledging that one is doing so, whether verbally or non-verbally;
- keeping an open mind rather than offering one's own thoughts and comments;
- understanding and evaluating what is being said;
- responding appropriately.

Observing non-verbal communications

A skilled mediator will have highly-tuned antennae which can pick up things that have not only been said, but are merely hinted at. A grimace or flicker of the eye may lend a clue as to how a party feels about some issue, and an observant mediator will notice this and either respond to it in some way, or perhaps store it as data received. 14–046

---

[30] US martial arts practitioner Thomas Crum draws on the principles of aikido in conflict resolution. See *The Magic of Conflict: Turning a Life of Work into a Work of Art* (New York: Touchstone, 1987); and *Journey to Center: Lessons in Unifying Body, Mind and Spirit* (New York: Touchstone, 1997). He believes that a centred neutral is more likely to be stable, sensitive and effective. Another mediator, Donald Saposnek, describes in "Aikido: A Systems Model for Maneuvering in Mediation" (1987) 14/15 *Mediation Quarterly* 119 the parallels between the processes, including the stages of defence: perception, evaluation, decision and reaction.

14-047 Much has been written on how non-verbal communications such as body language can inform one about a person's underlying feelings.[31] This includes eye signals, facial expressions, gestures, body postures, tone of voice and maintenance of personal space.[32] The mediator needs to draw on all kinds of skills, and to supplement the information formally provided by the parties with additional data that may not be volunteered but which may be relevant to the resolution of the issues. An ability to pick up non-verbal as well as verbal communications can be most helpful.

14-048 If the mediator is so engaged with taking notes, asking questions and managing the process that he or she becomes insensitive to the nuances of the parties' communications and cannot listen carefully to the parties and note their unspoken responses, something of value in assisting the resolution of the issues may be missed.

Helping parties to hear

14-049 People do not always hear what is being said, especially when they are in a stressful situation. They may hear the words but are so caught up with what they are planning to say, or with their own perceptions of the position, or are so emotionally troubled in relation to issues, or to the person speaking, that they cannot take in what has been said.

14-050 It is not surprising that people who are caught up in the heat of the process might not hear something that is important and perhaps beneficial to them, such as an acknowledgment or concession. The mediator can ensure that it registers, for example, by reiterating the statement, by acknowledging it, or perhaps by asking it to be repeated.

14-051 Similarly, the mediator needs to ensure that parties do not misunderstand one another. The mediator has a role to help people to hear and to understand one another. (In one example, in a family business dispute between a father in his 70s and his 50-year-old son, the mediator in private session with the son drew attention to some favourable comments that the father's lawyer had made in his opening address about the son's achievements in the company. Reminded of these, the son said he had been pleased that his father had given this acknowledgment and added that he had learned a lot about the business from his father. With permission, the mediator carried that sentiment to the father, who was delighted with the acknowledgment and responded very positively. This paved the way for useful joint and separate discussions, resulting in a settlement.)

---

[31] See for example A. and B. Pease, *The Definitive Book of Body Language: How to Read Others' Attitudes by Their Gestures* (London: Orion, 2005); M. L. Knapp and J. A. Hall, *Nonverbal Communication in Human Interaction*, 6th edn (California: Wadsworth Publishing, 2005); and Desmond Morris, *Peoplewatching: The Desmond Morris Guide to Body Language* (United Kingdom: Vintage Books, 2002).

[32] Allan Pease refers to personal space, comprising zones determined by cultural factors, status and personal factors. These are the intimate zone (into which only those emotionally close to the person are allowed); the personal zone (acceptable for social occasions); the social zone (for communicating with people not well known to the person); and the public zone (relevant to addressing a group of people). He identifies social rules and rituals relating to such zones.

Questioning

Skilled questioning is a fundamental tool of the mediator. Haynes has suggested that the mediator accomplishes most of his or her work through questions and has drawn attention to the value of questions in allowing the mediator the opportunity to frame statements as questions, minimising the scope for mediator error, and giving parties the opportunity to correct invalid assumptions. This also allows the parties to shift their positions themselves as they review the problem after answering questions.[33] Hence questions can be used for a number of purposes, for example:

14–052

- In their ordinary usage to help the mediator to gather information and get a better understanding of the issues, to clarify facts and to probe unclear aspects.
- To test reality: to help a party to examine whether his position or assessment or his understanding of the issues is realistic, or whether a proposed option or course of action is workable in practice. Confronting a party's perceptions, positions or preconceived notions with questions that present alternative ways of viewing the situation may be essential in getting necessary and proper understanding and movement.
- To promote reflection by a party on any aspect of his or her circumstances or proposals and thus to become more fully aware of the issues involved in any situation.
- To encourage a party to review a position or to focus on specific issues.
- To redirect the way in which discussions are moving and as a form of intervention in conflict management to divert parties away from heated discussion to a more productive field.
- A question may be strategic, where the mediator knows the answer but wishes the party to arrive at the answer himself.
- Instead of a mediator expressing a personal view on a situation, questions can be asked which allow parties to consider issues needing to be examined without compromising the mediator's neutrality.[34]

Questions may take different forms and may be:

14–053

- *Open*, allowing for any kind of answer, for example "What do you think will happen?"
- *Closed*, and more specific, usually calling for a yes or no response, for example "Did you pay the filing fee?"
- *General*, which allows for a general response, for example, "What happens when you try to discuss these matters with Fred?"

---

[33] See J. M. Haynes and G.L. Haynes, *Mediating Divorce: Casebook of Strategies for Successful Family Negotiations* (San Francisco: Jossey-Bass, 1989), pp.32–34. Haynes acknowledges the pioneering work of Karl Tomm, "Interventive Interviewing: Intending to Ask Lineal, Circular, Strategic, or Reflexive Questions" (1988) 27(1) *Family Process* 1.

[34] But see Ch.19, paras 19-014 to 19-017 for the possibility of questions and reality-testing being used as a vehicle for evaluation. This is not necessarily inappropriate, but needs to be undertaken with care, awareness and responsibility.

- *Focused*, which calls for a relevant and precise reply, for example "Can you describe what he was wearing at the time?"
- *Directed*, to a specific party.
- *Undirected*, asked to both or all the parties, allowing any party to respond.
- *Circular*, to draw connections between people or groups, as where one asks a party "How do you think that Fred would answer that?"
- *Minimal prompts*, which help parties to develop more fully what they are saying, such as repeating as a question a word or phrase used by a party, or even just nodding.
- *Leading*, which makes assumptions or suggests the answer such as "How much do you think the overspend will be?" where there has been no acceptance of an overspend, or "You saw him arguing with her, did you not?"
- *Reflective*, which encourage people to contemplate on what has been said or on some issue, for example, "Do you think that this proposal will promote cohesion within the group?"
- *Hypothetical*, used to stimulate possibilities or test reality, for example, "What would happen if you stopped paying?"
- *Rhetorical*, to which no answer is expected, generally used for effect, for example, "Why do some people have to go through such hardships?"

14–054 Questions have many purposes and can be framed in a variety of ways. While they may be neutral, it will be apparent from the above that they may also be formulated and presented with specific objectives in mind. What is asked, of whom, when, in what tone of voice, and for what underlying purpose—these all challenge the proposition, often heard from mediators, that they do not express opinions, they merely ask questions. Mediators need to be aware of and acknowledge the range and power of questions.

Summarising

14–055 Summarising can be important and helpful. First, it helps the mediator to ensure that he or she has a correct understanding of what has been said. Secondly, the mediator can be seen to have understood what has been said, which may help to establish confidence. Thirdly, it crystallises and focuses the issues to facilitate decision-making. Summarising is not, however, mere parroting what has been said, but involves careful, accurate and succinct paraphrasing.

14–056 It is not necessary or appropriate to summarise everything a party says to the mediator. That would be excessively laborious and annoying. There are times, however, when a mediator may find it useful to summarise. For example, the mediator may do so at the end of a party's presentation of his case particularly if complex issues have been covered that need to be checked, or when concluding a separate meeting with a party, especially where some aspects are to be kept confidential and others may be carried to the other party.

Acknowledging

One of the mediator's functions is to hear a party's views, feelings and grievances about the issues, even though the mediator's role is not to adjudicate on them. Sometimes what is needed is an acknowledgment that they have been heard and recognised. This does not mean that the mediator needs to agree with them: on the contrary, that may not be at all appropriate and could damage impartiality. It also does not mean patronising the party. A simple acknowledgment that the mediator has heard and understands the views or feelings will usually suffice.

14–057

Acknowledgment may also be appropriate in other respects. If one party makes a creative suggestion or is willing to make even a small concession, it may be appropriate to acknowledge the helpfulness of that, again without being patronising. The corollary is that if people feel that their concessions are unacknowledged, or worse still are being treated dismissively, they may be less emotionally ready to make further concessions in the future.

14–058

Acknowledgment may be verbal, but it may be no more than a nod of response to a party, an indication that he or she has been heard, though care needs to be taken that it is not construed as agreement, which it might not be. There is a difference between "I understand what you're saying" and "I agree with what you're saying" which may need to be made clear.

14–059

A mediator may also help parties to acknowledge one another where appropriate. This does not always come naturally where they are locked in dispute.

14–060

Mutualising

It is no surprise that parties to a dispute tend to see the issues from their own point of view, and that each is likely to have quite different perceptions of the same facts. One way that a mediator can help to bridge this discrepancy of perception is to make observations that tend to show that there are similar concerns, interests or doubts on both sides.

14–061

So, for example, where a lack of trust in the other is expressed, the mediator may observe that where relationships break down it is not uncommon for both sides to feel concerned about putting trust in the other. Mutualising each side's concerns can help to remove the focus from the party's own position and serve as a gentle reminder that similar concerns exist on both or all sides.[35]

14–062

The term "mutualising" is not a familiar one and may be dismissed as jargon, however it is a useful concept. It means clarifying that the other party shares a similar feeling, and that concerns are mutually felt.

14–063

Using language effectively and reframing

Mediators have to take special care with the words they use. Language needs generally to be neutral, and the mediator should be careful about adopting the words or images of one party. The mediator has to avoid language directing

14–064

---

[35] John Haynes refers to mutualising statements as "powerful creators of doubt" about individual positions, bringing the focus back on overlapping self-interests. See J.M. Haynes and G.L. Haynes, *Mediating Divorce: Casebook of Strategies for Successful Family Negotiations,* see fn.33.

parties ("I think you should..."). The mediator may need to acknowledge a party, but must take care that this is not patronising. Some words and ideas are best avoided: for example, asking for a "bottom line" in negotiation is unhelpful, because the words carry a connotation of ending the negotiations if the proposed terms are not agreed.

14–065 It is difficult enough to conduct the mediation process without also having to watch every word with care. Nevertheless, it is essential to be aware of the importance of how words are used: it becomes second nature to do so.

14–066 Words also have to be used with particular care when carrying messages, ideas and proposals between parties in the course of shuttle mediation. Sometimes it is necessary to do so in the exact words of the party. Sometimes, however, paraphrasing is necessary without distorting the meaning of what has been said. A party may for example tell the mediator privately that he considers a claim to be grossly inflated and typical of the claimant's greed, and that he will not pay it, but that he may explore settlement at a more realistic level. The mediator need not parrot those words back to the other party. It may be more productive if the mediator were to paraphrase this into something like:

> "It may not surprise you to hear that X does not agree with the level of your claim. He thinks that it is much too high; but he tells me that he would be willing to explore settlement possibilities at a rather lower level, which he thinks would be more realistic..."

Such re-wording is sometimes called reframing, but this is not the strictly correct technical usage of the term "reframing".

14–067 The term "reframing" has been adopted from the language of family therapy. It refers to a technique that assists people to change the frame of reference against which a person views an event, so that the judgment placed on that event takes a different meaning or perspective. So, for example, in a partnership disagreement, professional partners may see one partner's actions as constantly and deliberately provocative. If, however, the "provocative" partner is anxiously trying to force the partners to confront certain issues which are damaging to the firm as a whole, and this can be made clearer to all concerned, the actions in question may be seen in a somewhat different light. This is the essence of a reframe.

14–068 The use of reframing in mediation should not distort the meaning of a party's actions, but rather allows those actions to be seen in a positive rather than negative way. It is essential that a reframe should resonate with all parties if it is to be effective. If the mediator reframes in a way that does not sound right to the parties, they will reject the reframe.

Use of metaphor

14–069 One of the other ways of framing thoughts and ideas is by the use of metaphor, which can be helpful in mediation. Haynes has advocated the use of metaphors and explains their use as:

"importing the descriptive language of physical things and applying it to ideas we wish to convey. The listener, hopefully, hears our description and translates it into a conceptual understanding."[36]

Metaphors may be used to emphasise conflict, such as: or "having a number of good points in our armoury" or "shooting down their arguments" or "dropping a bombshell". Metaphors that suggest reconciliation, constructiveness and creativity are likely to create a more positive environment: such as "crafting a resolution", "laying the foundation", "building an agreement block by block", "weaving the different requirements together". **14–070**

There are two ways that metaphors may be used in mediation. The first is for the mediator to introduce it to help build the imagery of what is planned. This might for example be a crafting or construction image as outlined above, or travel imagery, as in "we've come a long way" or "this has been a difficult path, but we're getting towards the end of it". The other way is for the mediator to be conscious of any imagery introduced by a party and if practicable to respond appropriately by maintaining the party's own imagery—though Parkinson's caution is salutary: an inappropriate metaphor can be patronising, insensitive or just ridiculous.[37] **14–071**

The example of a metaphor quoted in Ch.19 was effective in an actual mediation: **14–072**

> "You know that in order to win the lottery you need six numbers. With five numbers you win something, but nowhere near the big prize. It seems to me that you may have five rather than six numbers here. If you think you have the sixth number, perhaps we should adjourn so that you can come back demonstrating that you have the sixth number."

Normalising

People may feel that their situation is an unusual and extraordinary one that no-one else could have encountered and that may be beyond their (or the mediator's) capacity to resolve. In a divorce, for example, a couple may feel very troubled and distressed about particular aspects and may not realise that such feelings are not unusual. The mediator may want to reassure them of the normalcy of such feelings, while taking care not to minimise or be dismissive of those feelings. That can help to put their minds at rest, and allow them more easily to address the issues facing them. **14–073**

A mediator should not try to normalise inappropriately, and should be careful not to patronise parties. The effective use of normalising, however, can be a relief to parties. **14–074**

Managing conflict and the expression of emotions

As some element of conflict is invariably likely to be inherent in mediation, a mediator will need to have some proficiency in the skill of conflict management. This involves the ability to intercede between two opposing sides and to channel **14–075**

---

[36] At *http://www.mediate.com/articles/metaphor.cfm* [accessed 6 June 2018].
[37] L. Parkinson, *Family Mediation,* 2nd edn (Bristol: Jordan Publishing, 2011), p.159.

14–076 their energies, which may have been devoted to sustaining the conflict, into a more productive and creative mode. This role is not required by an adjudicator, such as a judge or arbitrator, in the traditional adversarial process: he may suggest to the parties that they should try to settle, but must protect his judicial role and cannot enter into the maelstrom of the dispute itself.

14–076 Sometimes the parties need to be diverted from their conflict on an immediate basis, when they are engaged in a high level of conflict with one another during the meeting. A mediator may need to be able to distract the parties from their immediate altercation and to direct them towards a more productive line of discussion.

14–077 This raises a number of questions about the mediator's task in managing conflict and parties' emotional states. Situations of conflict and dispute can involve a high level of emotional content. This is not limited to family and inter-personal disagreements: whenever relationships break down or are under strain feelings can run high, as anyone involved in a business or professional partnership dispute or a professional negligence claim will confirm. Indeed, strong feelings are likely to exist in most commercial and civil disputes.[38]

14–078 In such situations, a mediator needs the skill of handling parties in conflict. If a party is upset or angry, or is experiencing any other strong feelings, the mediator needs to consider how best to manage that situation.

14–079 It may be necessary to allow those feelings to be expressed rather than trying to keep them bottled up. If this happens in a private meeting, the other party is unlikely to be affected, at least directly. If, however, it happens in a joint meeting, there is a risk that the other party may also become upset, angry or emotional. That may also be necessary. At some point, however, the expression of emotions may move from being necessary and sometimes cathartic and restorative, to being unhelpful to the process and even destructive.

14–080 There is a further consideration to be put onto the scale here. When people are engaged in anger-inducing thought, this could trigger more cascades of anger, and have an escalating rather than ameliorating effect. On the one hand, suppressed anger sabotages deals. On the other hand, anger-inducing thought may produce more anger. This is a dilemma that a mediator faces in handling such situations.

14–081 There is a balance to be struck in these situations. The mediator will generally need to allow parties to express their emotions, but must remember that the object of the exercise is dispute resolution not counselling. The mediator will have to judge how far emotions can be expressed before the party is gently, or if necessary briskly, brought back to the business at hand. Until a party has been able to express the feelings experienced, discussions and negotiations may often be unproductive; but afterwards matters may settle down more easily into a constructive mode.[39] It is equally important in a joint meeting that the other party should understand that such expression of feelings will not continue unchecked but will be eased towards an end.

---

[38] See the section "Dealing with emotions: the myth of rationality in civil and commercial disputes" in Ch.10.

[39] Most mediators recognise the need to address emotional aspects, if only to be able to move on from them. Christopher Moore, for example, has devised a "Circle of Conflict": value problems, relationship problems (including emotional issues) and data problems need to be dealt with before substantive issues can be addressed. Parties tend to move back and forth between the two areas: C.

Conflictual situations may be defused in a number of ways.[40] This may call on the mediator's empathetic skills, or may involve acknowledgment, mutualising or other skills as outlined in this section. The expression of feelings may be necessary, or distraction may be required to divert a crisis. A short break may be needed to let feelings cool, or a light or humorous touch to help break the tension, where appropriate.[41]

14–082

Lateral thinking

Lateral thinking involves thinking differently by changing perceptions and concepts and seeking new perspectives, ideas and alternatives.[42] The Penguin Dictionary of Psychology refers to it as a heuristic for solving problems in which the individual attempts to look at a problem from many angles rather than searching for a direct, head-on solution. This is what mediation is often about, so the development of skills that enhance this process must be valuable.

14–083

De Bono identifies methods of developing lateral thinking skills, which include finding ways of generating alternatives; testing and challenging assumptions, especially where people are hidebound by existing dogmatic structures, ideas or positions; suspending judgment; "fractionation" (his terms for breaking situations down to their basic components in order to restructure); using a "reversal" method of standing ideas on their heads; brainstorming; and designing problem-solving solutions.

14–084

Understanding triangulation and avoiding alliances

Relationship triangles arise in many ways. In families, this may happen when a third party intrudes on a couple's relationship; but it may arise in other ways, for example with the birth of a baby or when a child plays one parent off against another, or when siblings form alliances with one another.

14–085

A mediator entering the arena of a dispute creates a new dynamic by his or her very presence. In a dispute between two parties, the mediator is the third party in a triangular relationship, which creates a dynamic containing both benefits and potential risks.

14–086

In this context, De Bono coined the term "triangular thinking" to describe the input of a third party who helps disputing parties to create a design for the resolution of their issues. He distinguished his method of conflict resolution from both the confrontational approach and from the negotiating or bargaining approach. In De Bono's view, the third party has an essential role in conflict resolution since disputing parties cannot usually undertake problem-solving themselves, due to the nature of conflict situations and/or they may not be trained

14–087

Moore, *The Mediation Process: Practical Strategies for Resolving Conflict,* 2nd edn (Jossey Bass, 1996), pp.60–61. (See also the 4th edn, Jossey Bass, 2014).
[40] For further consideration of these issues, see Ch.10, paras 10-127 to 10-134; and Ch.11, paras 11-114 to 11-117.
[41] Humour when appropriately used can be valuable in mediation. This does not mean facetiousness; but a warm, apt, humorous remark can sometimes help to defuse tension and give parties an opportunity to step back from tense and hostile confrontation.
[42] See Edward De Bono, *Lateral Thinking: A Textbook of Creativity* (London: Ward Lock Educational, 1970); also his many other works.

in lateral thinking and the problem-solving mode. In De Bono's model the third party has a more significant role than a go-between but is an active participant in the creative process of designing appropriate solutions.[43] The cornerstone of mediation is party autonomy and mediators must be careful not to assume that parties are unable to think laterally. Indeed, the ideal behind transformative mediation is to provide parties with the tools to resolve their own disputes and conflicts going forward. However, this is clearly an important function of a mediator.

While this third-party intercession can be beneficial there is also a risk of triangulation and the formation of alliances between two parties against a third.

14–088 The most common form of triangulated alliance is one between the mediator and one of the parties. This may happen consciously, but more usually develops unwittingly. It may arise from different causes, for example:

- The mediator may be protective of one party, perhaps perceived to be the weaker one facing a more dominant opponent. This could for example arise when a mediator believes that a power imbalance is occurring in the mediation, and takes steps to redress that imbalance, and this develops into an unwitting alliance.[44]
- The mediator may have greater sympathy for one party's position and unconsciously slips into supporting that party.
- There may be greater rapport with one party than with the other because of common backgrounds, professions, ideas or interests.
- The mediator may develop some antagonism or competitiveness towards one of the parties, leading to an unconscious alliance with the other.
- There may be a same gender bias, especially when dealing with family matters.
- Or there may be some element of personal attraction with one of the parties.
- A party may deliberately or unconsciously try to engage the mediator on his or her side.

14–089 Triangulation as outlined above can be blatant, or more usually may be subtle and barely perceivable: sometimes no more than a collusive glance between the party and the mediator while the other is talking, or a difference in tone in discussions with the parties. Any such triangulation must inevitably have adverse implications for mediator impartiality, and is likely to be damaging to the process and its effectiveness, as well as the perceptions of both parties. Mediators must be alive to the risk of being triangulated into an alliance, and the need to avoid this conscientiously, for example by not holding the knowing and collusive glance and by constant awareness of the risk of this happening.

14–090 Parties may form an alliance against the mediator ("We'll show the mediator how stuck we are!") leaving the mediator feeling excluded or ineffective. This is

---

[43] E. De Bono, *Conflicts: A Better Way to Resolve Them* (1986), which develops the concept of "triangular thinking" and argues for the "design idiom". He puts forward interesting and challenging notions as well as practical ways of working.

[44] See Ch.16 for discussion on how to address power imbalances in mediation.

rarely done as a deliberate act, but can be defence mechanisms of couples, business partners or others with a personal or working relationship.

One of the advantages of co-mediation is that there is less risk of triangulation occurring or alliances forming, though this does not entirely follow: one of the co-mediators can still triangulate or form an alliance with the parties, though this may be less likely to happen. **14–091**

Encouraging a problem-solving mode

While some parties may enter mediation receptive to a problem-solving mode of negotiation, many others, perhaps most, tend to be in a competitive mode, because of their strong views or feelings about the dispute or because they believe that to be the most effective way to negotiate. One of the mediator's skills is to help the parties to move towards a more creative and problem-solving negotiating approach, if working on a mediation model that considers this approach to be beneficial. Some models, such as the transformative approach with its primary focus on empowerment and recognition rather than problem-solving, would not regard this as a necessary or appropriate skill. **14–092**

Even when encouraging problem-solving, parties would not be expected to abandon their self-interest. Rather, the mediator would help the parties to realise, or where appropriate to reinforce their awareness, that each party's aspirations may be more readily achieved in the context of an approach which seeks imaginative and resourceful solutions that can benefit both or all parties. As indicated by Lax and Sebenius,[45] negotiation even in a problem-solving mode will still involve tensions between the needs, wants and aspirations of the parties. Seeking the best individual outcome is not necessarily incompatible with also seeking a mutually advantageous resolution. **14–093**

One of the skills of the mediator lies in encouraging a problem-solving mode while recognising that parties also aim to achieve positive individual outcomes—creating a balance between these different negotiating tensions. **14–094**

Being silent

There are times when a mediator may want to say something when it would be better to maintain silence. Professionals whose traditional roles involve giving advice or assistance may find this a difficult skill to develop, but an essential one on some occasions.[46] **14–095**

There may for example be a significant moment in a joint meeting when one person tells the other something critically important and perhaps personal. That may need time and silence to absorb, especially if it is painful. Some professionals may want to leap in at such a time with words of comfort or **14–096**

---

[45] D. Lax and J. Sebenius, *3-D Negotiation: Powerful Tools to Change the Game in Your Most Important Deals* (Boston: Harvard Business School Press, 2006); and see Ch.4 under "The essential tension between interest-based and competitive approaches" at paras 4-026 and 4-027.

[46] See J. E. Beer, *Peace-making in Your Neighbourhood: Mediator's Handbook* (Canada: Friends Conflict Resolution Program, 1990), p.34 (also the Handbook's 4th revised edition, 2012).

digression, to rescue the party from the pain. Yet mediators must be able to allow people the space they need, including time to hear and to take in what is said. Quiet empathy may follow.

14–097 At other times, there may be a need for silence while a party is considering some aspect, perhaps something that has been said or proposed or perhaps just a few moments for reflection. Mediators must be able to respect silence when it is appropriate.

Constructive facilitation

14–098 This summarises the essence of the mediator's role: in a myriad of ways to devise and implement strategies to help the parties communicate and negotiate effectively with one another, to encourage them to develop and consider options, and to help direct the process towards a consensual resolution.

14–099 The skills and attributes outlined in this chapter will enhance the mediator's facilitation repertoire. Alongside these specific skills and attributes, other matters covered in this book will also come into play, for example, preparing and planning effectively, maximising relevant information exchanges, and helping parties to develop a shared vision of resolution.

14–100 The mediator may take an active facilitation role or may prefer a lower key role, allowing the parties themselves to reflect and initiate thoughts and ideas, and managing the process with an occasional and light touch. Sometimes a mediator may move between these different ways of working, as appropriate. The degree of facilitation and involvement will reflect the style of the mediator, the preferences of the parties, express or perceived, the needs of the situation, the strategy decided on by the mediator and the model of mediation being followed.

14–101 Underlying all these attributes, skills and other factors is the mediator's commitment to the parties, the process and its outcome. This does not mean that the mediator should be invested in the outcome in any way, which would be inappropriate, but rather that the mediator should have an authentic wish to help the parties achieve their best outcome. Coupled with the skills, attributes and awareness outlined above, this will provide a sound base for effectively carrying out the mediator's facilitative role.

THE MEDIATOR'S ROLES AND FUNCTIONS

14–102 Mediators perform a number of different roles and functions at different times during the mediation process, sometimes consecutively, sometimes simultaneously. Some may be more relevant to one model of mediation than another; nor are they as clearly defined in practice, where they overlap and blur, as they may be in theory.

The mediator as manager of the process

14–103 There are various ways in which the mediator manages the mediation process:

- by making the practical and administrative arrangements for the mediation meeting(s) which may cover matters such as obtaining any intake forms, arranging the venue, and agreeing how the process should be conducted and what documents are required;
- by acting as an informal chair of the meetings and ensuring that there is an orderly and secure environment in which discussion can take place effectively and constructively;
- by assuming responsibility for the conduct of the mediation process in accordance with ground rules accepted by the parties;
- by formulating, implementing and varying as necessary an agenda for the mediation, where appropriate in consultation with the parties;
- by managing the meetings, regulating the time spent on different aspects, deciding whether and when to meet parties separately, deterring abusive conduct, allowing or preventing interruptions, and generally assisting the parties in using the time productively.

Newly practising mediators, conscious of their impartial, facilitative role, are sometimes uncertain about the extent of management authority they should exercise. This may to some extent depend on the model of mediation being used, the culture within which it is taking place and the style and strategy of the mediator. It is, however, generally accepted that the management of the mediation process is the mediator's responsibility; and this needs to be authoritatively, even if gently, asserted in order for the process to be most effective. **14–104**

The mediator as information gatherer

The mediator needs to establish the issues and obtain relevant information from the parties: **14–105**

- Sometimes parties will complete intake forms or provide preliminary information about themselves and the issues.
- Parties will generally be required to furnish copies of documents relevant to the issues. Where the model allows confidentiality between the parties, there must be a clear distinction as to which documents are shared between the parties and which are confidential to the party supplying them.
- In some models, particularly civil and commercial, parties send written submissions to the mediator and to one another, setting out the facts and issues that each party considers relevant and material, and their contentions on the issues.
- In joint meetings with the parties, the mediator can seek clarification and amplification of any unclear aspects, being careful to maintain neutrality in doing so.
- Where each party makes an oral presentation in the joint meeting, appropriate questions can be asked which may help to inform the mediator and to clarify or highlight matters for the other party.
- In private meetings with each party, the mediator may receive information on a confidential basis. Any information received on this basis must of

- course be maintained confidentially, but the mediator may seek permission to make some disclosure to the other party if this may assist with the negotiations.
- The mediator also receives information in a more indirect way, through hints given by the parties, body language and other non-verbal communications, and through data obtained from third parties such as experts and advisers.

To enable the mediator to facilitate effectively, careful impartial information-gathering is necessary.

The mediator as facilitator

14–106 This is the mediator's primary role. The range of facilitative actions for a mediator is significant. Merely by way of example, the following are some of the facilitative functions that a mediator might perform:

- helping each party to listen to, hear and understand the other party's position;
- defining and prioritising the issues and working to some kind of agenda;
- helping the parties to generate, explore and narrow options for resolving the issues, encouraging brainstorming, and consistently seeking ways to create additional resources that may assist in achieving a resolution;
- acting as a sounding board for a party to test whether possible proposals may be useful and viable before they are communicated to the other party;
- examining common interests and aspirations, and possibilities for future relationships where appropriate, and endeavouring to seek common ground between the parties which will facilitate resolution;
- examining mutual concerns, including underlying issues and anxieties, and exploring how these can most effectively be dealt with;
- allowing the parties to express their feelings such as anger, distress or frustration about various aspects of the dispute or towards the other party, without letting this become counter-productive to the process;
- reframing statements when communicating them from one party to another, to put them into a more understandable context or to minimise the risk of polarisation where a negative statement has to be communicated;
- acknowledging the strength of views and feelings held without necessarily agreeing with these;
- using a range of other communication skills and strategies;
- suggesting outside resources that may assist the parties, such as their seeking valuations or specialist third-party advice or expertise relevant to the issues;
- using impasse strategies if the parties are deadlocked;
- exploring the alternatives to negotiated resolution and their implications.

The mediator as reality tester and evaluator

Testing the realism of a party's views, position or proposals is a different function from evaluation, though there can be a continuum between them.

14–107

A mediator may wish to check whether a party is realistic about the viability of proposals for resolution, the strength of his position, or any other aspect. Helping the parties to test realism is widely regarded as being an integral part of the mediation process, even following an exclusively facilitative model. This may involve no more than asking the parties questions ("What if?") to help ensure that they have correctly understood the matter or proposal under discussion and its implications and consequences.

14–108

Additionally, an evaluative mediator may go further and express a non-binding view on the merits of one or more of the issues between the parties, or of any matter under discussion. It may be based on the mediator's own expertise and knowledge, or on third-party expertise imported into the mediation.[47]

14–109

The mediator's evaluative view may influence parties to adjust their outcome expectations, negotiating positions and settlement aspirations. For this reason, where evaluation is undertaken at all, it needs to be done with the utmost care, sensitivity and responsibility:

14–110

- Under a model that uses evaluation, the mediator may test one party's views or perceptions by reference to the other party's position and views, to objective criteria where these are known, or to the mediator's own perceptions of the position.
- Even if an evaluation of the issues is not specifically requested by the parties, the mediator may in some situations make some evaluative comment, perhaps informally and in a separate confidential meeting to challenge an entrenched view and to help a party to reassess a view or position that may not be sustainable.
- The mediator may be specifically asked by the parties in some cases to undertake an evaluation. This may range from a formal non-binding opinion given to both or all parties as to the likely outcome, to merely expressing an informal and confidential view to one party as to the strength of a particular point or argument.

Even where evaluation is an accepted part of the model being used, there is always a risk that an evaluation will damage the perceived neutrality of the mediator. A mediator will need to consider in the circumstances of each individual case whether or not it would be appropriate and helpful to provide any such evaluation, and if so, in what form and at what stage of the process.

14–111

The mediator as host

One of the perhaps unacknowledged but important functions of the mediator is that of host: the person who welcomes the parties to the venue, puts them at ease and ensures that they have adequate rooms and facilities when they will be

14–112

---

[47] See Ch.19 for discussion about neutral, non-binding evaluative processes.

meeting the mediator separately during the day. The mediator arranges adequate and appropriate seating for the joint meeting.

14–113 The mediator should also ensure that the parties, lawyers and others accompanying them have suitable refreshments on arrival and during the day: tea or coffee—even biscuits perhaps—and a supply of water. If the meeting continues through lunchtime, the mediator needs to arrange for meals for the parties. These may be held in separate rooms or if appropriate, perhaps by everyone together (though that is a strategic decision for the mediator, and may depend on an assessment as to the relationship between the parties, whether or not it is likely to be comfortable and whether time constraints militate against it.)

14–114 Similar principles apply if the mediation continues after hours. Can the venue provide an evening meal or can it be ordered externally for delivery to the venue? They also apply to other aspects of the venue: is the heating adequate in winter, are the parties comfortable?

14–115 The costs of these facilities—venue, refreshments and meals—may well ultimately be met by the parties, but the notion for the mediator to bear in mind is the hosting responsibility and function and the need to create a comfortable and secure environment in which the parties can conduct their discussions and negotiations.

14–116 There are indeed reports of mediators who have taken the parties to a restaurant for lunch, which helped facilitate informal discussions; of a mediator who took parties to the opera at the end of a long working day (when reportedly, matters got resolved during an interval); and of mediators who as a matter of practice offer the parties a drink together at the end of the mediation, after they have signed a settlement agreement.

The mediator as scribe

14–117 While the process is under way, the mediator should maintain essential notes, for example, of matters that need to be further investigated, undertakings given by the parties or the terms of settlement proposals under discussion:

- The mediator may provide the parties with a note of outline settlement proposals under consideration to focus them on these and to maintain an impetus towards resolution.
- Where the issues are resolved, one of the mediator's tasks may well be to help them prepare a note of the terms of settlement for signature, though the responsibility for this may belong to the parties themselves or their lawyers. In some models, particularly where the parties do not wish to be bound right away, this may comprise a summary of the proposed terms which the parties may wish to consider further, either by themselves or with the benefit of professional advice.
- It may be left to the parties' lawyers to draft the settlement agreement, particularly if they attended the mediation proceedings. The mediator may assist with the drafting of the settlement agreement or may wish to check its drafting to ensure that it correctly reflects the position. Alternatively, the mediator may prepare a first draft, or heads of agreement, for the parties' own lawyers to finalise.

The mediator as settlement supervisor

The mediator can assist in various ways with regard to the supervision or implementation of any settlement the parties may enter into: 14–118

- the mediator (or the appointing ADR organisation) may act as a stakeholder, with explicit directions as to the circumstances under which the stakeholding may be released (or, as occurred in one specific case, certain documents were to be destroyed);
- the mediator may be appointed to supervise a settlement and to ensure in a specified way that the terms of settlement are being properly implemented;
- if any dispute arises in the course of implementing a settlement, the mediator can be given authority to liaise with the parties in order to help resolve that issue.

Under some circumstances, the mediator can be given limited or general adjudicatory powers to deal with matters arising during the implementation period.

MEDIATOR TRAINING

The facilitator is central to ensuring that agreement-based ADR processes are conducted appropriately and fairly and that the parties have adequate opportunity to present their narratives, interests, and to contribute to the design of any resolution. In order to ensure that mediators are adequately equipped with the relevant knowledge, skills, and have the opportunity to hone and develop the desired attributes, it is important that mediators are well-trained. The requirements of training for mediators varies considerably across jurisdictions. Relevant European legislation requires Member States to implement mediation training but does not suggest any particular content or duration.[48] Currently, in the UK, the Civil Mediation Council (CMC) holds a list of registered training course providers.[49] Registered course providers must provide a minimum of 40 hours' training, to include a performance assessment,[50] whereas various other European Member States are required to undertake longer training.[51] The content of such 14–119

---

[48] E.g. Directive 2008/52/EC art.4(2) on certain aspects of mediation in civil and commercial matters (Mediation Directive); Directive 2013/11/EU art.6(6) on alternative dispute resolution for consumer disputes.

[49] http://www.civilmediation.org/join-cmc/49/registered-training-courses [accessed May 2018]. Individual mediators can be registered with the CMC if they have completed an assessed training course, have mediator experience, and adhere to a mediator code of conduct: http://www.civilmediation.org/join-cmc/36/individuals.

[50] Legal and Parliamentary Affairs European Parliament Study "'Rebooting' the Mediation Directive: Assessing the Limited Impact of its Implementation and Proposing Measures to Increase the Number of Mediations in the EU" (Directorate General for Internal Policies, Policy Department C Citizens' Rights and Constitutional Affairs 2014) by G. de Palo, L. D'Urso, M. Trevo, B. Branon, R. Canessa, B. Cawyer, L. Reagan Florence 69–70.

[51] E.g. Austrian mediators must study 150 hours of theory, undertake practical seminars and a case study: Legal and Parliamentary Affairs European Parliament Study "'Rebooting' the Mediation Directive: Assessing the Limited Impact of its Implementation and Proposing Measures to Increase

training is not necessarily stipulated by the national legislation. As mediation takes a more prominent place in the dispute resolution landscape, and as mediators are required to maintain an even-handed approach with all the requisite knowledge, skills, and attributes to help disputing parties towards satisfactory resolution, it is important to ensure that the training is sufficient and is kept under review.

---

the Number of Mediations in the EU" (Directorate General for Internal Policies, Policy Department C Citizens' Rights and Constitutional Affairs 2014) by G. de Palo, L. D'Urso, M. Trevo, B. Branon, R. Canessa, B. Cawyer, L. Reagan Florence 19; Bulgaria requires mediators to study for a minimum of 60 hours at an accredited institution (30 hours of which must be practical training): "Rebooting the Mediation Directive" 24–25.

CHAPTER 15

Confidentiality and Privilege

INTRODUCTION

The issues of confidentiality and privilege are of fundamental importance to mediation and other ADR processes. Parties using these processes will usually do so on the basis that they can discuss matters freely in the expectation that they will be disclosed neither publicly, nor to a court in the event of the process not resulting in an agreed outcome.

15–001

Confidentiality and privilege are different concepts and either one can exist in relation to material without the other being present. However, because they are likely to overlap in respect of the same material, they are sometimes blurred.

15–002

Whereas English law relating to confidentiality is relatively straightforward, the position concerning privilege in relation to mediation and other ADR processes is less clear. This situation is not peculiar to England and Wales, as the subject has been and continues to be grappled with in many jurisdictions throughout the world where ADR is used.

15–003

Earlier editions of this work expressed the view that any doubt about these matters needed to be resolved and replaced with certainty, and that there did not seem to be any logical reason why the English Law Commission's 1990 proposal for the provision of a statutory privilege in family proceedings[1] should not be extended to all mediation. Since then, there have been a number of developments affecting these issues, indicating a need for clarity and providing a strong case for some form of legislation to supplement ethical and contractual provisions. However, a mediation privilege remains tantalisingly in prospect but somehow never implemented.

15–004

In other jurisdictions and fields, the need to deal effectively with these questions has been or is being addressed.

15–005

In Scotland, a 1992 Scottish Law Commission paper "Evidence in Family Mediation"[2] led to legislation in 1995 and 2006 that provided for the inadmissibility in civil proceedings of information as to what occurred during family mediation in relation to certain specified matters arising out of the breakdown or termination of their relationship or concerning mediation about children.[3] This has not, however, been extended to other kinds of mediation.

15–006

---

[1] English Law Commission, *Family Law: The Ground for Divorce* (London: HMSO, 1990), Law Com. No.192.
[2] Scottish Law Commission, *Report on Evidence: Protection of Family Mediation* (Edinburgh: HMSO, 1992) Scot. Law Com. No.136.
[3] The Civil Evidence (Family Mediation) (Scotland) Act 1995, as amended by the Civil Partnership Act 2004 and the Family Law (Scotland) Act 2006.

CONFIDENTIALITY AND PRIVILEGE

15–007 In the US, the 2001 Uniform Mediation Act (UMA) provided rules on the issue of confidentiality and established an evidential privilege for mediators, parties and non-parties participating in mediation. Available for adoption by individual states, it has been taken up by most but not all US states. The United Nations Commission on International Trade Law (UNCITRAL) has adopted a Model Law on International Commercial Conciliation (2002) which provides at art.10 that:

> "a party to the conciliation proceedings, the conciliator and any third person, including those involved in the administration of the conciliation proceedings, shall not in arbitral, judicial or similar proceedings rely on, introduce as evidence or give testimony or evidence"

regarding various aspects of the conciliation proceedings. This includes the fact of participation, views expressed or statements or suggestions made in those proceedings, proposals made by the conciliator or any indication of willingness to accept these, and any document prepared solely for such proceedings.

15–008 In the Republic of Ireland, the Mediation Act 2017 includes a section on confidentiality and privilege.[4]

15–009 It is widely accepted—and certainly by the UMA in the US, by UNCITRAL and by the Irish Mediation Act[5]—that any confidentiality or privilege attaching to mediation cannot be absolute, but is subject to exceptions. As will be apparent from this chapter, the provisions concerning confidentiality and evidential privilege are complex and cannot be regulated by a simple overriding provision.

15–010 The EU Directive on Cross-Border Mediation[6] has brought the issue of confidentiality and privilege closer to more general application throughout Europe by requiring that, where the Directive applies, mediation is to take place in a manner which respects confidentiality. Member States are required by the Directive to ensure that, unless the parties agree otherwise, mediators and others involved in the administration of the mediation process are not to be compelled to give evidence in subsequent proceedings regarding information arising out of or in connection with the mediation process, except where this was necessary for overriding considerations of public policy, or for the implementation or enforcement of settlements. The Directive has been implemented in the UK, although its application is limited to cross-border disputes and its principles have not been extended to the country's domestic jurisdiction, as some other countries have done.[7]

15–011 This chapter will consider principles of confidentiality, privilege and "without prejudice" communications separately, and also the overlap between them particularly with regard to those aspects where a court would wish to override confidentiality or claims of privilege. It will then turn to consider the more specific topics of the Proceeds of Crime Act 2002; issues in drafting ADR

---

[4] See s.10. The Act implements many of the recommendations made by the Law Reform Commission in its Report on Alternative Dispute Resolution: Mediation and Conciliation 2010. The Act is available at *http://www.irishstatutebook.ie/eli/2017/act/27/enacted/en/html* [accessed 18 May 2018].
[5] See Mediation Act 2017 s.17.
[6] Directive 2008/52/EC of the European Parliament and of the Council of 21 May 2008 on certain aspects of mediation in civil and commercial matters.
[7] See below at paras 15-118 to 15-122: Privilege and confidentiality under the EU Directive. The Directive invited Member States to extend the principles to their domestic jurisdictions.

agreements; developments at a European level; and, finally, the recurring debate about the adoption of a mediation privilege.

CONFIDENTIALITY

General principles

15–012 As a result of developments in the law of privacy, there are now two separate frameworks for determining if a breach of confidence is actionable. The first covers the disclosure of confidential information of a non-personal nature, the second relates specifically to the disclosure of personal information.

15–013 Turning to the first, if someone communicates information not generally available to the public to another person in confidence on the basis, either explicit or implicit, that it will not be disclosed to anyone else or used for an unauthorised purpose, any unauthorised use or disclosure can lead to an action under English law for breach of confidence.

15–014 The claimant can establish a cause of action by showing:

- that he communicated information of a confidential nature to the defendant;
- that the circumstances under which it was communicated imposed an obligation on the defendant to maintain confidentiality;
- and that the defendant used or disclosed the confidential information in a way which was not intended and without authority.[8]

For a private individual to bring such an action, it is also necessary to show that he has suffered some actual or potential detriment.[9]

15–015 The duty to keep information confidential may arise explicitly or by implication. To make it explicit, the person communicating the information specifies in terms before giving it that it will be furnished on a confidential basis. This may be oral or contained in a written communication, such as a letter or agreement. Alternatively, it may be implied by the circumstances surrounding the communication. For example, an employee who receives secret information in the course of his employment will ordinarily be expected to maintain it confidentially and a duty of trust and confidence would be implied, as well as "an obligation binding his conscience" quite apart from contract.[10]

15–016 Where information is widely known then it will not ordinarily acquire confidential status sufficient to found a cause of action merely by the person disclosing it adding a stipulation for confidentiality. Similarly, information which was confidential but which has been made public cannot be protected by an injunction.[11]

---

[8] See *Halsbury's Law of England*, 4th edn (London: Lexis Nexis), para.1455; *Coco v A N Clark (Engineers)* [1969] R.P.C. 41; *Fraser v Evans* [1969] 1 Q.B. 349; [1968] 3 W.L.R. 1172 CA (Civ Div); *Vestergaard Frandsen A/S v Bestnet Europe Ltd* [2013] UKSC 31.
[9] *Attorney General v Observer Ltd* [1990] 1 A.C. 109; [1988] 3 W.L.R. 776 HL.
[10] See *Halsbury's Law of England*, fn.9, para.1455; and *Saltman Engineering Co v Campbell Engineering Co Ltd* [1963] 3 All E.R. 413 (Note) CA.
[11] *O Mustad & Son v S Allcock & Co; sub nom. Mustad v Dosen* [1964] 1 W.L.R. 109; [1963] 3 All E.R. 416 HL.

15-017 More protection is offered to personal information, as a result of developments in the English law of privacy following the implementation of the Human Rights Act in 2000. English law now recognises the right to privacy in accordance with art.8 of the European Convention on Human Rights (ECHR), which provides that "[e]veryone has the right to respect for his private and family life, his home and his correspondence." This right must be balanced, however, against art.10, which provides that:

> "Everyone has the right to freedom of expression (which) shall include freedom to hold opinions and to receive and impart information and ideas without interference by public authority...."

The freedom contained in art.10 is in turn subject to various qualifications, including specifically a reference to "preventing the disclosure of information received in confidence."

15-018 That the tort of breach of confidence has to some extent changed its nature as a result of the ECHR is clear from the House of Lords' decision in *Campbell v MGN Ltd*,[12] where Lord Nicholls plainly stated that:

> "The time has come to recognise that the values enshrined in articles 8 and 10 are now part of the cause of action for breach of confidence."

In the same case, Lord Hoffmann referred to

> "a shift in the centre of gravity of the action for breach of confidence when it is used as a remedy for the unjustified publication of personal information..."

As Sedley LJ observed in a perceptive passage in his judgment in *Douglas v Hello! Ltd*,[13] the new approach takes a different view of the underlying value which the law protects. Instead of the cause of action being based upon the duty of good faith applicable to confidential personal information and trade secrets alike, it focuses upon the protection of human autonomy and dignity—the right to control the dissemination of information about one's private life and the right to the esteem and respect of other people".[14]

15-019 As indicated above, the courts have had to strike a balance between arts 8 and 10 of ECHR. In *McKennitt v Ash*,[15] for example, the claimant sought to restrain publication of a friend's book on the basis of breach of privacy and/or breach of confidence. Eady J held that a significant shift had taken place in the law's view of the appropriate balance between freedom of expression and the legitimate interest of the citizen to have their private life protected. A number of passages in the book infringed the claimant's reasonable expectation of privacy and she was

---

[12] [2004] UKHL 22.
[13] [2001] Q.B. 967; [2001] 2 W.L.R. 992 CA (Civ Div).
[14] *Campbell v MGN Ltd* at [51].
[15] [2006] EWCA Civ 1714; [2008] Q.B. 73.

entitled to an injunction and damages. On appeal it was held that there had been no error of principle in carrying out the balancing exercise between the rights under arts 8 and 10.[16]

Still more recently, the law of privacy has been to some extent thrown into disarray by social networking and the developments in technology allowing millions of people to exchange information with one another virtually instantly. Confidential information can thus be disseminated without necessarily attributing it to any one source. This came into particular focus in the case of *CTB v News Group Newspapers Ltd*[17] in which a married footballer with a family sought to enjoin *The Sun* newspaper from naming him or publishing a report of an alleged extra-marital relationship. He based his case on art.8, respect for his family life. There was no explicit counter-argument that there was a public interest in publishing, and the court granted the injunction, observing that:

15–020

> "It has recently been re-emphasised by the European Court of Human Rights that the reporting of 'tawdry allegations about an individual's private life' does not attract the robust protection under Article 10 afforded to more serious journalism."

Some tens of thousands of people used social networking to identify the name of the footballer, which was then confirmed by a Member of Parliament identifying him under the cloak of parliamentary privilege (which provides an immunity from civil or criminal liability).[18] There were conflicting views as to whether or not this was a proper use of parliamentary privilege. In any event, the courts continued to uphold the injunction, although it had been widely frustrated.

15–021

It is against this ever-changing backdrop that the specific subject of confidentiality in ADR falls to be considered.

Confidentiality in ADR

Confidentiality may arise in at least two different ways in ADR. The first relates to the confidentiality of the process and the matters dealt with in it, so that all those involved will maintain confidences on these matters. The other aspect relates to the confidentiality that a neutral may maintain as between the parties, that is, that the neutral receives information in confidence from one party that may not be disclosed to the other. These different kinds of confidentiality will be considered in turn.

15–022

---

[16] An analysis of the balancing exercise and case law is to be found in an article by Michael G. Doherty, "The Right to Tell One's Own Story? Balancing Privacy and Expression Claims" [2007] 5 *Web Journal of Current Legal Issues* (at *http://webjcli.ncl.ac.uk/2007/issue5/doherty5.html#_Toc184032933* [accessed 18 May 2018]).

[17] [2011] EWHC 1232 (QB).

[18] The limitations on confidentiality in the context of social networking have been particularly highlighted by revelations about alleged misuse of personal data by Facebook and Cambridge Analytica, the implications of which remain to be established as at the time of publication of this book.

CONFIDENTIALITY AND PRIVILEGE

Confidentiality of matters dealt with in the process

(a) Mediation

15–023   One of the features of mediation is that, unlike most litigation, it is usually confidential. A mediator is likely to have a duty of confidentiality towards the parties, which may arise by explicit agreement, perhaps in the Agreement to Mediate or the relevant Code of Practice, or implicitly. Some forms of ADR are not confidential in nature, for example, the mediation of public policy issues which may positively require public exposure; or there may be some private processes in which the parties agree disclosure is required because of the nature of the issues or for other particular reasons. In most cases, however, the parties will expect, and the mediator will offer, privacy and confidentiality.

15–024   In some jurisdictions, this has been rendered explicit—in the US, for example, most statutes and court rules establishing court-annexed mediation programmes include confidentiality provisions, for example, in Arizona, Florida and Texas. Some states, for example, California and Massachusetts,[19] have mediator confidentiality provisions as part of their rules of evidence, or otherwise independent of a court-annexed programme (though in some cases written agreement between parties is also required).

(b) Arbitration

15–025   There may not be a presumption that confidentiality is implicit in arbitration, however, albeit that one of the reasons for preferring the process over litigation is the proposition that it is private whereas litigation is generally public. Estreicher and Bennett raise this question[20] noting that most arbitration bodies include a reference to confidentiality in their arbitration rules, but point out that these rules generally only offer limited protection and that it may be necessary to balance confidentiality against the public interest. In this respect, the position is not dissimilar to the principles applicable to other forms of ADR, and indeed to the general law on confidentiality in the UK and many other jurisdictions.

15–026   The position in the UK has been developing over the years. In 1995 the High Court of Australia rejected the view that a general duty of confidence existed in arbitration, a decision later described as "nuclear" by Lord Neill QC (commenting in the 1995 Bernstein lecture),[21] in *Esso Australia Resources Ltd v Plowman (Minister for Energy and Minerals)*.[22] The shock waves of the *Esso Australia* decision were felt outside Australia.

15–027   In England, the Court of Appeal considered the issue in *Ali Shipping Corp v Shipyard Trogir*.[23] Citing the *Esso Australia* case, the Court of Appeal held that

---

[19] See by way of example s.23C of the General Laws of the Commonwealth of Massachusetts, relating to work product of mediator confidential; confidential communications; exception; mediator defined, available here: *https://malegislature.gov/Laws/GeneralLaws/PartIII/TitleII/Chapter233/Section23c* [accessed 18 May 2018].
[20] US lawyers, Samuel Estreicher and Steven C. Bennett, "The Confidentiality of Arbitration Proceedings" (2008) 240(31) *Arbitration*.
[21] Lord Neill QC, "Confidentiality in Arbitration" (1996) 12 *Arbitration International* 287.
[22] (1995) 128 A.L.R. 391.
[23] [1999] 1 W.L.R. 314; [1998] 1 Lloyd's Rep. 643 CA (Civ Div).

the English position was that the arbitration agreements in that case included terms implied as a matter of law which obliged the parties to maintain confidentiality in the proceedings, but could in the "interests of justice" be circumvented, but on evidential grounds alone.[24]

The *Esso Australia* decision came as the Departmental Advisory Committee advising the Secretary of State on the development of new arbitration legislation was in the final stages of its work. The Committee was emphatically of the view that confidentiality was fundamental to the conduct of arbitration as traditionally presented in England. However, it was felt that to attempt a comprehensive statutory definition of confidentiality in English arbitration was fraught with difficulty and that it was best left to the courts to develop a pragmatic theory in the light of actual cases. Consequently, there is no provision for confidentiality in the UK's arbitration legislation.

15–028

In *Emmott v Michael Wilson & Partners Ltd*,[25] the English Court of Appeal reaffirmed the *Ali Shipping* approach of "categories of exceptions" with some revision. The categories now cover disclosure following an order or leave of the court; where it is in the public interest; where reasonably necessary to protect a party's legal rights; and where there is express or implied consent. The English Commercial Court decision of *Teekay Tankers Ltd v STX*,[26] certainly seems to suggest that confidentiality in arbitration proceedings within the jurisdiction of England and Wales is far from absolute, and reaffirms *Ali Shipping Corp v Shipyard Trogir*, suggesting that the disclosure of otherwise confidential documents could be ordered using the "interests of justice" argument.

15–029

The extent of arbitration confidentiality is likely to depend on a number of considerations, including primarily the law applicable in the governing jurisdiction, the rules of the arbitral organisation under whose auspices it takes place and any ad hoc rules adopted by the parties, the terms of any written agreement between the parties regulating the arbitration, and the question as to whether there may be any overriding consideration of either public policy or matters which may be in the interests of justice.

15–030

(c) Conclusion

The result is that in all ADR, whether mediation, arbitration or otherwise, there cannot be an absolute guarantee of confidentiality, and most Codes, guidelines, model procedures and standard forms of Agreement to Mediate should reflect the qualified nature of this obligation. The circumstances when a court might wish to override a confidentiality agreement and examine confidential data will be further considered below. It should though be emphasised that these are by and large exceptional circumstances and that in the overwhelming majority of matters confidentiality provisions will be respected.

15–031

---

[24] Footnote 22, per Potter LJ who stated that the "interests of justice" exception is primarily concerned with ensuring that the judicial decision in a particular case is based on accurate evidence rather than a focus on a broader, global public interest.
[25] [2008] EWCA Civ 184; [2008] Bus. L.R. 1361.
[26] [2017] EWHC 253. See fn.22, and Potter LJ's obiter in *Ali Shipping Corp v Shipyard Trogir*, in which he considered obiter that the interests of justice argument should be favoured over that of the "wider public interest".

Confidentiality of separate meetings or caucuses

15–032   In a number of ADR processes, the neutral will not maintain separate confidences as between the parties. In arbitration and adjudicatory forms that require due process and natural justice, it would be improper to do so. In various models of mediation, most of the process is conducted jointly or in any event without maintaining separate confidences.[27]

15–033   In those models of mediation where the mediator meets the parties separately by way of caucusing or shuttle negotiations, there is commonly a further duty to each party to maintain confidentiality in relation to the separate matters confided to the mediator by the separate parties. A common practice is for the mediator to undertake to each party that anything that is said to him or her in the separate confidential meeting will be maintained confidentially unless authority to disclose it is given. The mediator uses the information gained in this way to help craft mutually acceptable terms and to facilitate a resolution.

15–034   The risk, however, of inadvertently breaching the duty of confidentiality owed to each party could be considerable, and practitioners must act with the greatest of care to avoid any such lapse. In practice, they should check the limits of their authority to disclose information at the end of each separate meeting. Some mediators are understood to reverse the onus of disclosure, by arranging with the parties that, unless specifically asked not to do so, they will assume that they are authorised to disclose what has been discussed. This, however, creates a different dynamic in the process and is not commonly used.

15–035   As to disclosing confidential information in other circumstances, for example, if required by a court, similar principles to those applicable to confidentiality in mediation generally are likely to apply to confidentiality maintained in the separate meetings, particularly if the agreement to mediate deals with confidentiality in both situations in the same way. Or a mediator may be faced with having to decide whether he or she is able or perhaps even has a responsibility to disclose confidential information, for example, concerning a child or other person being at risk of significant harm.

Some general principles where confidentiality is not applicable

15–036   Confidentiality may not apply even if initially agreed or expected in some circumstances. These will be further considered below together with exceptions to rules concerning privilege. In general, the considerations relating to confidentiality qualifications and exclusions are as follows:

- The exceptions to confidentiality may be specifically identified in the agreement to mediate or arbitrate or in the rules, Code or model procedure governing the relevant mediation or arbitration. To be contractually effective, such provisions should be incorporated into the agreement. It is little use a mediator being bound by the terms of a Code regulating confidentiality if those terms are not known and accepted by the parties.

---

[27] However, where separate meetings are held with couples to check for possible abusive situations, the mediator will not necessarily inform the abusing party that the person harmed or at risk has told the mediator about the abuse, for fear of recrimination and further abuse.

- One common exception relates to the fact or risk of violence, abuse or any other harm to children or anyone else revealed in the process. Agreements to mediate often specify this exception in terms.
- Criminal acts or intent may be excluded, though this may depend on the seriousness of these. Would a statement in a mediation by a party that he sometimes accepted cash payments for work done (and hence evaded payment of tax) be a disclosable criminal activity? Almost certainly not, unless there were some overriding statutory obligation to disclose, for example in money laundering laws.[28]
- Balances may need to be struck between competing rights, for example the right to privacy under art.8 of ECHR and the right to freedom of expression under art.10.
- Generally, there is an overriding test as to whether public interest justifies disclosure notwithstanding what would otherwise be a duty of confidence.[29] It has been said that the confidential information will not be restrained from being disclosed where there is a just cause for such disclosure.[30]
- "The true doctrine is that there is no equity in the disclosure of iniquity".[31] It may be more difficult to decide what constitutes iniquity, and whether its nature is such that it overrides the duty of confidence—particularly where personal information is involved.
- ADR does not of itself constitute an exception to the general law of confidentiality, nor does it provide a cloak to protect a party from an iniquity disclosed during its course.

PRIVILEGE

15–037 A distinction needs to be made between confidentiality, which concerns the withholding of information from all sources including the public and the courts, and privilege, which relates specifically to the admissibility of information in the courts. While the same information may be subject both to duties of confidentiality and privilege, different though often overlapping principles apply to each.

15–038 The general rule of evidence is that all persons are both competent (legally qualified) to give evidence and compellable (obliged by law) to answer all questions put to them which are competent (do not contravene any rule of law) and relevant.

15–039 There is a small category of witnesses who are deemed not to be competent such as those who through youth or mental or physical incapacity are unable to understand or answer questions; and judges are not competent witnesses in proceedings before them, nor are jurors as to their deliberations and arbitrators as to their awards.

---

[28] This may raise some ethical dilemmas for a mediator. See below under Proceeds of Crime Act.
[29] See *W v Egdell* [1990] Ch. 359; [1990] 2 W.L.R. 471 CA (Civ Div).
[30] *Fraser v Evans* [1969] 1 Q.B. 349.
[31] *Gartside v Outram* (1857) 26 L.J. Ch. 113.

CONFIDENTIALITY AND PRIVILEGE

15–040 In criminal proceedings s.80 of the Police and Criminal Evidence Act 1984 (PACE) governs the competence and compellability of the spouse or civil partner of an accused. Broadly, a spouse or civil partner is competent to give evidence for the prosecution against the accused if not also charged, but only compellable in respect of certain offences of violence and sexual abuse. For the defence, a spouse or civil partner is competent and compellable unless jointly charged.

15–041 Two categories of witnesses are deemed competent but are able to choose whether to testify. First, there are those who are not compellable such as the sovereign, foreign heads of state and holders of diplomatic immunity, who may not be compelled to give *any* evidence. Secondly, there are those who are in possession of privileged information, who may not be compelled to give evidence relating to privileged matters unless authorised to do so by the privilege holder.[32]

15–042 The ground for allowing the information to be withheld is that to answer the question or to supply the documents would infringe some interest, the protection of which is more important in the eyes of the law than the ascertainment of the truth and administration of justice in the particular case.[33]

15–043 The law of England and Wales traditionally recognises three classes of privilege:

- first, the exclusion of evidence on the grounds of public policy, known as public interest immunity[34];
- secondly, a party will not be compelled to disclose documents or answer questions that tend to incriminate or expose the party to proceedings for a penalty;
- thirdly, the exclusion of certain information, principally litigation related communications, on the grounds of confidentiality.

15–044 The House of Lords has emphasised that this area of the law has developed over the years and the categories are not closed and are at times interlinked.[35]

15–045 To establish public interest immunity the claimant needs to be able to show that the public interest requires that the information shall not be disclosed and that the public interest is so strong as to override the ordinary right and interest of the litigant that he should be able to lay before the court all relevant evidence.[36] Such claims are not restricted to departments or organs of central government.[37]

15–046 The second head of privilege, the "privilege against self-incrimination", protects an accused from the need to give evidence which may incriminate and

---

[32] Law Reform Committee, *Sixteenth Report on Privilege in Civil Proceedings* (London: HMSO, 1967), para.1, Cmnd.3472, defines privilege as "the right of a person to insist on there being withheld from a judicial tribunal information which might assist it to ascertain certain facts relevant to an issue upon which it is adjudicating".

[33] C. Tapper, *Cross and Tapper on Evidence*, 12th edn (Oxford: OUP, 2010).

[34] This is not, strictly speaking a "privilege", as it is not capable of waiver, but instead a rule of evidence which will exclude evidence of certain facts where it is not in the public interest for these to be admitted—see *Rogers v Home Secretary* [1973] A.C. 388, per Lord Reid at 400.

[35] *D v National Society for the Prevention of Cruelty to Children (NSPCC)* [1978] A.C. 171; [1977] 2 W.L.R. 201 HL.

[36] *R. v Lewes Justices Ex p. Secretary of State for the Home Department* [1973] A.C. 388; [1972] 3 W.L.R. 279.

[37] *D v National Society for the Prevention of Cruelty to Children (NSPCC)* [1978] A.C. 171.

was authoritatively formulated by Goddard LJ in *Blunt v Park Lane Hotel Ltd*.[38] It is, however, not an absolute rule. It is subject to numerous statutory exceptions, for example those in the Criminal Evidence Act 1898 (no privilege in respect of the offence for which the accused is being tried) and s.14 of the Civil Evidence Act 1968 (no privilege in respect of liability for penal proceedings abroad).

As to the third head, the mere fact that information may be regarded as confidential by reason of a contractual, professional or moral obligation does not of itself create a right or privilege to withhold it in legal proceedings.[39] The primary heads of privilege that arise from the concept of confidentiality are:

15–047

Professional privilege

Communications between a professional legal adviser and his client, made for the purpose of obtaining advice as to the client's legal rights and obligations, are privileged although they may not relate to any suit pending or one which is contemplated or apprehended.[40] The reason for this privilege is that it is believed that it promotes the public interest because it assists and enhances the administration of justice by facilitating the representation of clients by legal advisers.[41]

15–048

The privilege lies with the client and if waived the lawyer must testify and produce any documents sought. Communications made to or by a litigant or his legal adviser to a third party about a matter relevant to litigation at hand are privileged only if made for the sole or dominant purpose of furthering commenced or contemplated litigation.[42]

15–049

Once the privilege has been validly claimed, it ordinarily continues to have permanent effect, irrespective of, for example, a change of legal representative. It has been upheld in relation to a new claim by a different claimant, even if the subject-matter differs. So, in *The Aegis Blaze* a survey report prepared on behalf of the defendant for one claim remained privileged when a different claimant sued the defendant.[43]

15–050

The privilege may be waived expressly or by implication or it may be lost. If part of a document is disclosed, privilege will be waived for the whole unless the remaining part deals with a different subject-matter.[44]

15–051

Privilege may be lost by inadvertent disclosure of documents which would otherwise have been privileged. The applicable rules were summarised by Slade LJ in *Guinness Peat Properties Ltd v Fitzroy Robinson Partnership*.[45]

15–052

---

[38] [1942] 2 K.B. 253 CA at 257.
[39] *Santa Fe International Corp v Napier Shipping SA (No.1)*, 1985 S. L.T. 430. This distinction between confidentiality and privilege is a significant one.
[40] *Three Rivers DC v Bank of England (No.4)* [2004] EWCA Civ 218; [2004] Q.B. 916.
[41] *Grant v Downs* [1976] H.C.A. 63; (1976) 135 C.L.R. 674.
[42] *Alfred Crompton Amusement Machines Ltd v Customs & Excise Commissioners (No.2)* [1972] 2 Q.B. 102; [1972] 2 W.L.R. 835 CA (Civ Div).
[43] *The Aegis Blaze* [1986] 1 Lloyd's Rep. 203 CA (Civ Div).
[44] *Great Atlantic Insurance Co v Home Insurance Co* [1981] 1 W.L.R. 529; and *Pozzi v Eli Lilley & Co, The Times,* 3 December 1986.
[45] [1987] 1 W.L.R. 1027; [1987] 2 All E.R. 716 CA (Civ Div) at 729.

Without prejudice

15-053 Admissions made by a party in a course of abortive negotiations for settlement of a dispute will generally not be admitted as evidence in future proceedings. This is normally referred to as the "without prejudice" rule.

15-054 In *Cutts v Head* Oliver LJ noted that the without prejudice rule rests on:

> "...[the public policy]...that parties should be encouraged so far as is possible to settle their disputes without resort to litigation and should not be discouraged by the knowledge that anything that is said in a course of such negotiations (and that includes, of course, as much the failure to reply to an offer as an actual reply) may be used to their prejudice in the course of the proceedings. They should...be encouraged freely and frankly to put their cards on the table."[46]

15-055 The term "without prejudice" is sometimes misunderstood and used inappropriately. For example, where parties are communicating about a matter which does not involve settlement negotiations, they wrongly use the term, perhaps intending to import confidentiality. However, communications will not be privileged simply because they are marked "without prejudice". The test is not the description used by the parties, but whether or not the communications are actually directed towards reaching a settlement. Only such communications will be protected, whether or not they are stated as being "without prejudice". Such communications may, however, be admissible where the issue is whether or not there was a settlement.

15-056 In the case of *Rush & Tompkins Ltd v Greater London Council*,[47] the Court of Appeal cited with approval the principle expressed in *Tomlin v Standard Telephones & Cables Ltd*[48] which was originally propounded in *Walker v Wilsher*[49] that:

> "... I think they mean without prejudice to the position of the writer of the letter if the terms he proposes are not accepted. If the terms proposed are accepted a complete contract is established, and the letter, although written without prejudice, operates to alter the old states of things and to establish a new one."[50]

15-057 This quotation was approved as an accurate statement of the meaning of "without prejudice" with the qualification "if that phrase be used without more."[51] Parties could give the phrase a somewhat different meaning, for example where they reserved the right to bring a without prejudice offer to the attention of the court on the question of costs if the offer should not be accepted. Subject to any such modification, the court held that:

---

[46] *Cutts v Head* [1984] Ch. 290 CA (Civ Div) at 306; also [1984] 2 W.L.R. 349 and [1984] All E.R. 597 CA (Civ Div).
[47] [1989] A.C. 1280; [1988] 3 W.L.R. 939 HL.
[48] [1969] 1 W.L.R 1378; [1969] 1 Lloyd's Rep. 309 CA (Civ Div).
[49] (1889) L.R. 23 Q.B.D. 335 CA.
[50] *Walker v Wilsher* (1889) L.R. 23 Q.B.D. 335, per Lindley LJ at 1287.
[51] *Walker v Wilsher* (1889) L.R. 23 Q.B.D. 335, per Balcolmbe L at 1297.

> "the parties must be taken to have intended and agreed that the privilege will cease if and when the negotiations 'without prejudice' come to fruition in a concluded agreement."

15–058 The Court of Appeal in *Rush & Tomkins* established a number of principles as to the nature of the without prejudice privilege. These are outlined as follows:

- its purpose is to enable parties to negotiate freely without the risk that their proposals could be used against them if the negotiations failed; but that once a settlement is concluded, the privilege goes, having served its purpose[52];
- parties could use a form of words enabling without prejudice correspondence to be referred to, even if a settlement was not concluded, for example, on the question of costs[53];
- on the other hand, parties could use a form of words to preclude reference to any such correspondence even after a settlement had been reached;
- the privilege does not depend on the existence of proceedings;
- even before any settlement, and while the privilege continued to subsist, there are a number of real or apparent exceptions to it;
- the privilege extends to the solicitors of the parties to such negotiations.

15–059 The *Rush & Tomkins* case was taken on further appeal to the House of Lords,[54] on the question as to whether the without prejudice privilege did indeed end once a settlement was achieved. Lord Griffiths, expressing the unanimous view of the House of Lords, disagreed with the proposition that if the negotiations succeed and a settlement is concluded, the privilege ends. The cases considering the without prejudice rule show that "the rule is not absolute":

> "Resort may be had to the 'without prejudice' material for a variety of reasons when the justice of the case requires it."[55]

15–060 Lord Griffiths held that as a general rule the without prejudice rule:

> "renders inadmissible in any subsequent litigation connected with the same subject matter proof of any admissions made in a genuine attempt to reach a settlement."

He concluded that (subject to having recourse to the without prejudice material when the justice of the case required it) without prejudice communications between parties to litigation needed to be protected from production to other parties in the same litigation.

---

[52] But this principle was varied on appeal, as amplified in the text below.
[53] The principle was established in *Calderbank v Calderbank* [1976] Fam. 93; [1975] 3 W.L.R. 586 CA (Civ Div) that an offer (a *Calderbank* offer) could be made on a without prejudice basis, while expressly reserving the right to produce the letter to the court on the issue of costs. Without fettering the court's discretion, if the offer is rejected and the court order is for no more than the *Calderbank* offer, the court would be invited to order costs from the time of the offer against the party rejecting the offer. *Calderbank* offers ceased to be relevant in family ancillary relief proceedings in 2006.
[54] *Rush & Tomkins* [1989] A.C. 1280 HL at 1292.
[55] *Rush & Tomkins* [1989] A.C. 1280 HL at 1300.

CONFIDENTIALITY AND PRIVILEGE

15-061 In *Unilever Plc v Procter & Gamble Co*,[56] Laddie J considered the scope of information arising in the course of without prejudice discussions which were protected from subsequent disclosure by the without prejudice rule. In line with what may be seen as a tentative but developing support for party-based resolution of disputes, the court held the without prejudice rule to be of wide application. "[Parties] should be encouraged fully and frankly to put their cards on the table". Laddie J noted that the Civil Procedure Rules, though not in force at the date of his judgment, represented:

> "the current policy aimed at making litigation a last resort the policy in favour of encouraging prelitigation settlement is now much stronger than it has been".

15-062 In *Ofulue v Bossert*[57] the House of Lords reaffirmed importance of the public policy principle underlying the without prejudice rule and the protection provided by it to parties engaging in genuine settlement negotiations. However, in subsequent decisions, the position in relation to the extent of without prejudice protection (WPP) can apply, suggests that there are limitations. In *Avonwick Holdings Ltd v Webinvest Ltd*,[58] in which the Court of Appeal examined the substance of the negotiations between the parties in order to decide that WPP did not apply in the circumstances of that case. In *Property Alliance Group Ltd v Royal Bank of Scotland Plc*,[59] a first instance decision, Birss J held that the content of the without prejudice settlement discussions had become admissible because WPP-type protection of negotiations does not prevent a regulator (in this case the FCA) from acting on information received in those negotiations. Furthermore, the WPP-type protection of negotiations cannot be maintained in civil proceedings if the basis on which certain evidence (in this case a Final Notice) was decided is itself put in issue in the proceedings. This appears to be an exception to the general rule that WPP is usually treated as being a joint privilege which cannot be waived unilaterally.

15-063 On appeal, the Court of Appeal in *Unilever* set out eight exceptional situations in which without prejudice correspondence negotiations might be revealed.[60] These are:

1) when the issue is whether without prejudice communications have resulted in a concluded compromise agreement;
2) to show that an agreement should be set aside on the ground of misrepresentation, fraud or undue influence;
3) where a clear statement made by one party, and on which the other party is intended to act and does in fact act, may be admissible as giving rise to an estoppel[61];

---

[56] [1999] 2 All E.R. 691 Ch. D.
[57] [2009] UKHL 16; [2009] 1 A.C. 990.
[58] [2014] EWCA Civ 1436.
[59] [2015] EWHC 1557 (Ch).
[60] *Unilever Plc v Procter & Gamble* [2000] 1 W.L.R. 2436; [2001] 1 All E.R. 783 CA (Civ Div).
[61] Estoppel is a rule that in certain circumstances a person cannot deny the truth of something that he or she has previously asserted. This would, for example, apply where the other person has acted on that assertion and would be prejudiced by the denial, or where the assertion was made in a deed.

4) if the exclusion of the evidence would act as a cloak for perjury, blackmail or other "unambiguous impropriety";
5) if necessary to explain delay or apparent acquiescence;
6) whether a party has acted reasonably to mitigate his loss in his conduct and conclusion of negotiations for the compromise of proceedings;
7) where an offer is expressly made "without prejudice except as to costs";
8) in matrimonial cases, where a privilege is applicable extending to communications received in confidence with a view to matrimonial conciliation.[62]

An additional exception was established in *Oceanbulk Shipping & Trading SA v TMT Asia Ltd*.[63] In that case, the Supreme Court decided that without prejudice communications—facts that led to a settlement agreement—should be admitted to resolve the issue of construction of a settlement agreement and to clarify the meaning of the terms. To this list should perhaps be added the reasoning behind the first instance decision earlier mentioned in *Property Alliance Group Ltd v Royal Bank of Scotland Plc*, although at the time of this work going to press, this decision is the subject of appeal. **15–064**

The without prejudice rule is very important in the ADR context, because it is one of the main bases on which privilege is commonly claimed for communications made in ADR processes. Parties will usually be required to agree to this in the agreement to mediate. The without prejudice basis is as effective in ADR as it would be in analogous bilateral negotiations.[64] In addition to and apart from the without prejudice rule, however, as outlined below, a public policy "privilege" could also be sought for mediation. **15–065**

The without prejudice rule is intended to provide a privilege to the parties rather than to any third party through whom they may conduct their negotiations or communications, and the parties may agree to waive it and treat any such communications as open, without requiring any consent from a mediator or any other third-party intermediary. **15–066**

However, there may be alternative provisions which could affect the mediator's personal position, including for example a contractual provision regulating the mediation whereby the parties agree not to call the mediator to testify,[65] or perhaps a mediator's privilege in those jurisdictions where this exists. **15–067**

Reconciliation

Another limb of privilege has arisen out of the concept of confidentiality, which as Lord Hailsham observed: **15–068**

---

[62] See "Mediation about children" below. Whereas the first seven items are clear exceptions, this eighth exception is more of a hybrid and not clearly an exception in the same way as the other seven.
[63] [2010] UKSC 44; [2011] 1 A.C. 662.
[64] Indeed, mediation has been described as an "assisted without prejudice negotiation"—see *Brown v Rice* [2007] EWHC 625 (Ch) at 12; and *Aird v Prime Meridian Ltd* [2006] EWCA Civ 1866.
[65] But would this be enforceable? In the interests of the integrity of the mediation process, it is to be hoped that the courts would respect such a provision.

"has now developed into a new category of a public interest exception based on the public interest in the stability of marriage".[66]

15-069 This privilege relates to the intervention of a third party who acts as an intermediary with the object of bringing about a marriage reconciliation and reflects the fact that "in matrimonial disputes the state is an interested party. It is more interested in reconciliation than divorce".[67] It seeks to overcome the established principle that communications between parties in dispute are not privileged unless they are without prejudice.[68]

15-070 There has been a series of decisions in which the courts have supported the notion of privilege for communications between spouses made with a view to establishing a reconciliation, including those made through a third party acting in a mediatory capacity. In one of the earliest of these,[69] Denning LJ took the view, in relation to spouses' discussions with a probation officer, that even if nothing specific was said in this regard, the parties must be taken to have held their discussions on the basis that what they said would not be disclosed. He extended this in *Mole v Mole*[70] to cover not only probation officers, but also other persons such as clergy, doctors or marriage guidance counsellors to whom either or both parties may go with a view to effecting a reconciliation.

15-071 This principle has been applied to communications made through a vicar[71]; a priest acting as marriage guidance counsellor,[72] and even to a private individual who tried to assist spouses to move towards reconciliation.[73] It applies also to third-party witnesses of such efforts.[74]

Mediation about children

15-072 In a significant decision for mediation, *Re D (minors)*,[75] the Court of Appeal acknowledged the growth and evolution of conciliation concerning children, in court and out of court. Bingham MR stated:

> "In our judgment the law is that evidence may not be given in proceedings under the Children Act 1989 of statements made by one or other of the parties in the course of meetings held or communications made for the purpose of conciliation save in the very unusual case where a statement is made clearly indicating that the maker has in the past caused or is likely in the future to cause serious harm to the well-being of a child."

15-073 The case of *Re D (minors)* relates only to children and not to financial and other issues arising on divorce. Until a more general mediation privilege is

---

[66] *D v NSPCC* [1978] A.C. 171.
[67] *Mole v Mole* [1950] 2 All E.R. 328 CA, per Bucknall LJ.
[68] *Grant v South Western and County Properties Ltd* [1975] Ch. 185; [1974] 3 W.L.R. 221 Ch D.
[69] *McTaggart v McTaggart* [1948] 2 All E.R. 754.
[70] [1950] 2 All E.R. 328 CA, per Bucknall LJ.
[71] *Henley v Henley* [1955] 2 W.L.R 851; [1955] 1 All E.R. 590 (Note) PDAD.
[72] *Pais v Pais* [1970] 3 W.L.R. 830; [1970] 3 All E.R. 491 PDAD.
[73] *Theodoropoulas v Theodoropoulas* [1963] 3 W.L.R. 354; [1963] 2 All E.R. 772 Assizes (Winchester).
[74] *Slade-Powell v Slade-Powell* (1964) 108 S.J. 1033.
[75] *Re D (Minors) (Conciliation: Disclosure of Information)* [1993] Fam. 231; [1993] 2 W.L.R. 721 CA (Civ Div).

established, parties in mediation will have to rely on the without prejudice principles to provide evidential privilege for their communications concerning matters other than children and reconciliation.

A further development in confidentiality in proceedings concerning children was made in *Re C (A Minor) (Care Proceedings: Disclosure)*.[76] A parent was persuaded to admit to causing the death of a child in care proceedings concerning her sister, with the assurance of protection from admissibility of that evidence in criminal proceedings. It was a matter for the court's discretion whether material covered by the protection (under s.98(2) of the Children Act 1989) should be released to the police. In the case, the public interest in promoting frankness, which was in the interests of the child, predominated and material covered by s.98(2) would not be released to the police.

15–074

Part 36 of the Civil Procedure Rules: Without prejudice save as to costs

Part 36 of the CPR introduced a concept of an offer to settle, which is treated as being "without prejudice save as to costs" (r.36.13). If an offer to settle or payment into court is made in accordance with the provisions of Pt 36, the court will take any such offer into account when making any order as to costs. Nothing in Pt 36 prevents the parties from pursuing settlement strategies outside of the Civil Procedure Rules, in the normal way.

15–075

Employment conciliation provision, family court practice

Statute has ascribed privilege to the conciliation of employment disputes: s.18(7) of the Employment Tribunals Act 1996 provides that anything communicated to a conciliation officer shall not be admissible in evidence before an Employment Tribunal.

15–076

Under Practice Directions in the Family Division, communications made in the mediation of children disputes are to be privileged and are not to be disclosed in any subsequent application. A Child Arrangements Programme Practice Direction contains provision for parenting plans, MIAMs (Mediation Information and Assessment Meetings) and dispute resolution services, including mediation and stipulates that, subject only to safeguarding issues, neither the parties nor the mediator may inform the court as to the content of any discussions held in mediation and/or the reasons why agreement was not reached.[77]

15–077

Also, under the Financial Dispute Resolution (FDR) scheme in divorce proceedings,[78] anything discussed with a District Judge dealing with the FDR cannot be used in evidence in any subsequent hearing before another judge. The President of the Family Division, in setting up this procedure, stipulated that:

15–078

"In order for the FDR appointment to be effective, parties must approach the occasion openly and without reserve. Non-disclosure of the content of such

---

[76] [1996] 2 F.L.R. 123; [1996] Fam. Law 603.
[77] Family Procedure Rules 2010. Practice Direction 12B—at para.5.11. See *http://www.justice.gov.uk/courts/procedure-rules/family/practice_directions/pd_part_12b* [accessed 18 May 2018].
[78] Chapters 5 and 11 both address aspects of the FDR.

meetings is accordingly vital and is an essential prerequisite for fruitful discussion directed to the settlement of the dispute between the parties."[79]

The courts have upheld this aim: in the Court of Appeal, Lord Justice Thorpe has said that:

"litigants distrustful of each other and made anxious by the complex tactics of contested litigation must be confident that conciliation within the court proceedings guarantees them the same confidentiality that they would enjoy had the dispute been referred by the judge to mediation by a mediation professional."[80]

COURT EXCLUDING CONFIDENTIALITY AND PRIVILEGE

15-079 Exceptions to confidentiality and privilege have been outlined above. The following situations amplify some of the circumstances in which courts may decline to uphold confidentiality or privilege, and may require to be told what happened in mediation or other ADR process:

The court stipulates for mediation and wishes to know what happened

15-080 Courts that order mediation or adjourn proceedings to enable mediation to be undertaken may wish to know what happened in the mediation if there is no settlement. This may be to enable the court to consider whether or not a costs sanction might be appropriate against a party for failure to enter into the mediation, properly or at all.

15-081 While in some circumstances a costs sanction for failure to agree to mediate would be appropriate,[81] the position is more complex if a party does in fact enter mediation, but does so in such a negative and uncooperative way that it negates any attempt to resolve the matter. Does that amount to bona fide mediation?

15-082 In accordance with the principles of confidentiality, a mediator would not inform the court as to what happened or whether a party cooperated, provided that the mediation took place at all. The mediator's duty would be to report that the mediation took place and that the matter was not resolved.

15-083 In one reported case, one of the parties behaved outrageously at the mediation that a Florida court had ordered. Joe Francis (founder of the adult video series *Girls Gone Wild*) is said to have arrived at the mediation four hours late, barefoot and wearing sweat shorts and a backwards baseball cap, all the while playing with an electronic device, and then constantly erupting with expletives and threats. The other party sought court sanctions contending that in effect, Francis did not attend the mediation, and if he did attend, he failed to negotiate in good faith, and accordingly had violated the Court's order. Appropriately, the mediator

---

[79] By Direction dated 25 May 2000: *Practice Direction (Ancillary Relief Procedure)* [2000] 1 F.L.R. 997.
[80] *Myerson v Myerson* [2008] EWCA Civ 1376 at [26]; [2009] 1 F.L.R. 826.
[81] According to the *Halsey* principles: see Ch.17.

merely reported that the mediation had taken place and had resulted in an impasse.[82] In the event, Francis was jailed for contempt.

In a rather less dramatic case, an English court reviewed what happened in a mediation—albeit with the consent of both parties—and concluded that:

15–084

> "the claimant's position at the mediation was plainly unrealistic and unreasonable. Had they made an offer which better reflected their true position, the mediation might have succeeded For a party to agree to mediation but who then causes it to fail by reason of his unreasonable position in the mediation is in reality in the same position as a party who unreasonably refuses to mediate. In my view it is something which the court can and should take into account of on the costs order in accordance with the principles considered in *Halsey*."[83]

These cases raise the question as to how far parties have to go in order to comply with an order or requirement to mediate and how reasonable a party needs to be in order to be regarded as having complied with a direction to mediate, whether in the form of an order or recommendation, or simply under the *Halsey* principles. Is it arguable that if a party attends mediation but does not mediate in good faith, this is equivalent to a failure to mediate?

15–085

This question is addressed by Zimmerman, analysing the Joe Francis case.[84] She suggests a two-tiered approach. The first tier clarifies what is expected of participants in court-mandated mediation, with guidelines and standards, for example as to documentation, time limits, dress code and other provisions. The second tier, if an allegation of bad faith still remains, would be to have an in camera hearing before a judicial officer other than the one who would make a substantive decision on the merits of the case in due course.

15–086

Until the question of mediation privilege is resolved these issues will continue to arise, and courts will continue to wish to know if there has been an abuse of process where mediation has been ordered, or whether a party has cooperated sufficiently to warrant avoiding a costs sanction. Even with a privilege, there may be circumstances where the court will want and be entitled to a report. The challenge will be how to balance the fundamental principles of confidentiality with the right of the court to be informed of matters arising in the process, in the very limited circumstances when this might be appropriate.

15–087

Allegations are made of fraud, misrepresentation, economic duress or undue influence

Although the underlying facts and grounds may differ, this raises similar issues to those outlined in the previous section.

15–088

---

[82] Victoria Pynchon, "Mediating? Bring Your Toothbrush". Joe Francis and "Girls Gone Wild" at Negotiation Law Blog at *http://www.negotiationlawblog.com/conflict-resolution/mediating-bring-your-toothbrush-joe-francis-and-girls-gone-wild/* [accessed 18 May 2018].
[83] Per Mr Justice Jack in *Carleton (Earl of Malmesbury) v Strutt & Parker* [2008] EWHC 424 (QB) at 72.
[84] Samara Zimmerman, "Judges Gone Wild: Why Breaking the Mediation Confidentiality Privilege for Acting in 'Bad Faith' should be Re-evaluated in Court-Ordered Mandatory Mediation" [2009] 11 *Cardozo Journal of Conflict Resolution* 353.

15-089 An example arose in the case of *Farm Assist Ltd (In Liquidation) v Secretary of State for the Environment Food and Rural Affairs*[85] in which Farm Assist Ltd sought to set aside a settlement agreement with the Secretary of State for the Department for Environment Food and Rural Affairs (DEFRA) on the grounds of economic duress. To enable the court to decide whether there was any duress, Farm Assist sought to examine what took place in a mediation that had been conducted some five years earlier.

15-090 Despite the mediator observing that she did not have any notes or sufficient recollection of the matter, and a provision in the agreement to mediate that the mediator would not be called as a witness, DEFRA sought to compel her attendance at court and issued a witness summons. She sought to have it set aside on the grounds, inter alia, that her evidence would be confidential, legally privileged and/or irrelevant. The judge, Mr Justice Ramsay, considered the provisions in the agreement to mediate, which included a confidentiality clause and a statement that the process would be without prejudice and privileged, as well as the relevant authorities, and concluded that that the court could order disclosure of the otherwise confidential material if it was in the interests of justice to do so.

15-091 The judge also expressed the view that although the parties could agree to waive confidentiality, the mediator was also a party to the confidentiality provision and they would need her consent to do so. There was clearly a without prejudice privilege, but it was less clear whether there was any specific "mediation privilege". In any event, despite the mediator's general right to rely on the confidentiality provision, the court had the power to override it if it was in the interests of justice to do so—as the judge found it was in this case.

15-092 In the event, the parties did not find it necessary to pursue the witness summons so it remains unknown as to what the mediator might have been pressed to address in evidence. In analysing the case, Cornes[86] considers it to be a:

> "worrying aspect of this decision that no protection was afforded even to private conversations between the mediator and one party alone in private…"

15-093 Would the court have allowed "mediation secrets" in the separate private meetings to be disclosed? Cornes rightly regards this:

> "an important aspect of mediation (that) needs further consideration either by a court or by the provision of some rules about mediator evidence in the Civil Procedure Rules or by statute".

The court wishes to determine whether an agreement was concluded

15-094 In *Brown v Rice*,[87] there was an issue as to whether or not the parties had reached an agreement to settle. In that case, the judge, Isaacs QC (sitting as a deputy High Court Judge) overrode a confidentiality provision in the agreement to mediate in

---

[85] [2009] EWHC 1102 (TCC); [2009] B.L.R. 399.
[86] David Cornes, "Mediator Fails to Have Witness Summons Set Aside: *Farm Assist Ltd v Secretary of State for the Environment Food and Rural Affairs (No.2)*" (2009) 75 *Arbitration* 4.
[87] [2007] EWHC 625 (Ch).

order to determine the issue of whether a concluded settlement had been reached by the parties at mediation. The judge stated that "as a matter of practicality" the confidentiality provisions would not prevent the court from looking into the mediation to determine the issue of whether or not there had been a concluded settlement.

The judge accepted the: 15–095

> "clear public policy now reflected in the CPR (Civil Procedure Rules) to encourage mediation as a preferred means of dispute resolution to litigation";

but this did not mean that mediation should have any greater status in the context of without prejudice privilege than bilateral negotiations. He was entitled to look at what happened at a mediation to decide whether settlement terms had been agreed, as would have been possible in any without prejudice negotiation. In this, he drew support from Jacob LJ in *Reed Executive Plc v Reed Business Information Ltd (Costs: Alternative Dispute Resolution)*[88] that no distinction was to be made between party to party negotiations and negotiations conducted within a mediation: both were to be treated as subject to the without prejudice rule.

The judge also considered the possibility of the existence of a distinct mediation privilege, something which he felt might need to be further considered by the legislature or the courts; but as the case could be dealt with on without prejudice principles, he did not find it necessary to make any decision in that regard. 15–096

Where there is an allegation of negligence

If there is an allegation of negligence against the mediator in relation to any aspect of his or her conduct of the process, it would be odd if the mediator would not be allowed to defend him or herself by way of reference to what happened. Similar principles would presumably apply in relation to any other allegation of negligence relating to the mediation proceedings, for example a claim by a party against a professional adviser, though much would depend on the individual circumstances and the balancing of rights. 15–097

The position in *Cumbria Waste Management Ltd v Baines Wilson (A Firm)*[89] was somewhat more complex. The claimants alleged that their solicitors had been negligent in connection with the drafting and negotiation of agreements with DEFRA relating to the amounts payable to them for services. They had settled with DEFRA following a series of without prejudice communications between solicitors and two mediations and now sought compensatory damages from the solicitors. 15–098

The claimants alleged that the dispute with DEFRA occurred entirely as a result of their solicitors' negligence and that DEFRA's case in the dispute with them was based on ambiguities and inconsistencies in the drafting of the contract for which the solicitors were responsible. They contended that, if the solicitors 15–099

---

[88] [2004] EWCA Civ 887; [2004] 1 W.L.R. 3026.
[89] [2008] EWHC 786 (QB); [2008] B.L.R. 330.

15–100   had performed their obligations and ensured that the contract was clear and unambiguous, the position taken by DEFRA on the construction of the contract would not have been possible.

The solicitors, who had not been parties to the mediation, contended that the claimants should not have settled in the mediation on the terms that they had, and that if the claimants had chosen to do so, the claimants could not now seek the shortfall in their expectations from them. Relying on an earlier Court of Appeal decision in *Muller v Linsley & Mortimer*[90] (in which disclosure of without prejudice documents was permitted in a negligence action in order to establish the reasonableness or otherwise of a party's actions), they wished to see certain mediation documents which they contended were vital to understand the conduct of the claimants in the mediations. DEFRA, although not a party to the litigation with the solicitors, opposed this on a number of grounds, including confidentiality, with practical implications concerning other cases that it faced.

15–101   Kirkham J (sitting as a High Court judge) distinguished the facts from *Muller* and declined to order disclosure of the documents, citing public policy reasons why DEFRA should be allowed to assert the privilege to protect themselves from disclosing material that might embarrass and compromise them in other disputes. The judge found that there were:

> "clear public policy reasons to encourage mediation in place of litigation. The court should be slow to find exceptions to the without prejudice rule….the court should support the mediation process by refusing, in normal circumstances, to order disclosure of documents and communications within a mediation."

15–102   There is, here again, a balance to be struck whenever someone wishes to go behind a mediation in order to support or defend an allegation of negligence relating directly or indirectly to the process. It is the balance between achieving fairness and justice where disclosure calls for this, and maintaining the integrity of the mediation process and the proper expectation of parties that their affairs and communications will be maintained privately.

Where the court wishes to interpret an agreement

15–103   As outlined above, *Oceanbulk Shipping & Trading SA v TMT Asia Ltd*[91] added another exception to the maintenance of the without prejudice rule, namely that access to privileged material should be allowed to resolve the issue of construction of a settlement agreement and to clarify the meaning of the terms.

15–104   The judgment demonstrates the difficulty in finding the right balance between competing rights and arguments. The judge at first instance in the Commercial Court held that certain representations made during without prejudice discussions could be admitted in evidence. On appeal two of three Lord Justices of Appeal (Longmore and Burnton LJJ) decided that the judge had erred, and allowed the appeal, upholding the without prejudice rule. Ward LJ dissented in strong and unequivocal terms.[92] The further appeal was heard by seven judges of the

---

[90] [1996] P.N.L.R. 74 CA (Civ Div).
[91] [2010] UKSC 44.
[92] *Oceanbulk Shipping & Trading SA v TMT Asia Ltd* [2010] EWCA Civ 79; [2010] 1 W.L.R. 1803. In dissenting, Ward LJ said: "If you can use the antecedent negotiations to prove the agreement, to

Supreme Court, who unanimously supported the views of the first instance judge and Ward LJ in allowing the without prejudice material to be used in evidence. Had this matter been left at the first appeal, the law would have been very different.

Lord Clarke, delivering the Supreme Court's judgment, addressed the question of whether extending the exceptions would undermine the without prejudice rule. He accepted the contention that: **15–105**

> "if a party to negotiations knows that, in the event of a dispute about what a settlement contract means, objective facts which emerge during negotiations will be admitted in order to assist the court to interpret the agreement in accordance with the parties' true intentions, settlement is likely to be encouraged not discouraged."

He added that "this approach is the only way in which the modern principles of construction of contracts can properly be respected."

PROCEEDS OF CRIME ACT 2002

A serious issue about confidentiality arose when the Proceeds of Crime Act 2002 came into force and provided, among other things that a person committed an offence if he: **15–106**

> "enters into or becomes concerned in an arrangement which he knows or suspects facilitates (by whatever means) the acquisition, retention, use or control of criminal property by or on behalf of another person" (s.328).

Responsibility could however be avoided by making "an authorised disclosure" to the authorities, which was to be done without telling the party concerned, which would itself constitute an offence of "tipping off". There was a flurry of activity with mediators drafting clauses in agreements to mediate that would inform parties of this position and of the risk that confidentiality would not apply in these circumstances. **15–107**

The Civil Mediation Council (CMC) gave an example on its website of one such clause, used by a mediation provider, that read: **15–108**

> "...the mediator has an absolute obligation under the Proceeds of Crime Act ('POCA') 2002 to report to the NCIS any knowledge or suspicion relating to the involvement of the proceeds of crime (including tax evasion) and is precluded by law from informing the Parties of his intention to do so."

Clauses along those lines were not uncommon. Mediators were alarmed that these anti-money-laundering provisions would have an adverse effect on parties' willingness to discuss matters openly in mediation. **15–109**

---

rescind it, or to rectify it, why on earth can you not use the negotiations to establish the truth of what the concluded contract means? Not to do so would strike my mother as 'barmy'. It goes to prove what every good old-fashioned county court judge knows: the higher you go, the less the essential oxygen of common sense is available to you."

15–110   It seems that this concern has largely but not entirely receded as a result of the judgment in *Bowman v Fels*,[93] which has provided some reassurance that s.328 was "not intended to cover or affect the ordinary conduct of litigation by legal professionals...." This has been widely construed as extending to the conduct of mediation by mediators, though that has neither been confirmed nor refuted over the years that have passed since the judgment. It does though seem that there needs to be a link to existing or contemplated proceedings.

15–111   The CMC provides guidance on its website,[94] which suggests that mediators should act with caution where there are no existing or contemplated legal or arbitration proceedings or where the link between the mediation and such proceedings is tenuous and where (even if there are existing or contemplated proceedings) the settlement:

> "[did] not reflect the legal and practical merits of the parties' respective positions in the proceedings and was known or suspected to be no more than a pretext for agreeing on the acquisition, retention, use or control of criminal property".

15–112   With regard to reporting to the Serious Organised Crime Agency, the CMC points out[95] that while disclosures authorised by the Act will not provide grounds for an action for breach of confidence, a disclosure that is not required by the Act might do so. Mediators who "act on the safe side" by reporting concerns may well face an action for breach of confidence.

15–113   The CMC guidance refers to the Chartered Institute of Arbitrators, which also provides very helpful POCA guidelines on its website, which analyse the provisions relevant to mediators and arbitrators.[96] It also points out that the offence of "tipping off", which it considers was never likely to be committed by an arbitrator, mediator or adjudicator, ceased to have any relevance when it was limited in 2007 to cases where the "information on which the disclosure is based came to the person in the course of a business in the regulated sector".

CONTRACTING FOR CONFIDENTIALITY AND PRIVILEGE

15–114   Parties negotiating on a without prejudice basis in mediation or any other ADR process do so on the assumption that what they discuss is both confidential and unavailable for use in any later court proceedings. That is the basis on which the process is generally offered. Given the uncertainties inherent in the upholding of this assumption, albeit that exceptions arise only rarely, mediators and mediation organisations may need to revisit the basis on which they offer the process, and the terms of their agreements to mediate.

---

[93] [2005] EWCA Civ 226; [2005] 1 W.L.R. 3083.
[94] See the guidance note dated 15 October 2010 "Guidance on the obligations of mediators under the Proceeds of Crime Act (POCA) 2002: *http://www.civilmediation.org/downloads.php?f=46* [accessed 18 May 2018].
[95] Acknowledging that this point is made by the Chartered Institute of Arbitrators.
[96] *http://www.ciarb.org/docs/default-source/ciarbdocuments/other-practice-guidelines/ proceedsofcrimeact2012.pdf* [accessed 18 May 2018].

The CMC has issued guidance on this,[97] namely that agreements to mediate should continue to stipulate that the proceedings will be conducted on a without prejudice basis and that what is said during such proceedings will be confidential; also that agreements should not restrict the circumstances in which a mediator cannot be compelled to give evidence in court. 15–115

In the *Farm Assist* case, the agreement to mediate provided that the parties would not call the mediator or require any records or notes relating to "the dispute" that is, the original dispute being mediated. The CMC draw attention to the fact that CEDR, the Centre for Effective Dispute Resolution, now use the following wording to meet this situation, namely: 15–116

> "The Parties will not make an application to call the Mediator or any employee or consultant of CEDR as a witness, nor require them to produce in evidence any records or notes relating to the Mediation, in any litigation, arbitration or other formal process arising out of or in connection with their dispute and the Mediation; nor will the Mediator nor any CEDR employee or consultant or agree to act as a witness, expert, arbitrator or consultant in any such process"[98]

which widens the provision. The relevant clause goes on to require the party applying to call the mediator or other CEDR employee or consultant to indemnify him or her in respect of any costs incurred in resisting and/or responding to such application.

The question arises as to how explicit agreements to mediate should be in outlining the circumstances in which the proceedings and communications may not be confidential or privileged; and similarly how explicit explanatory material should be. This requires a balance between on the one hand being explicit about the relevant circumstances when confidentiality may not apply, and on the other hand not overwhelming the parties with details particularising every possible contingency.[99] 15–117

PRIVILEGE AND CONFIDENTIALITY UNDER THE EU DIRECTIVE[100]

Commentary seems to suggest that it is unlikely that the UK Parliament will repeal EU Regulations concerning cross-border mediation in light of Brexit (see below at para.15-124).[101] The EU Directive dealing with the mediation of cross-border disputes deals with confidentiality at art.7 as follows: 15–118

> "1. Given that mediation is intended to take place in a manner which respects confidentiality, Member States shall ensure that, unless the parties agree otherwise, neither mediators nor those involved in the administration of the

---

[97] Civil Mediation Council Guidance Note No.1, *Mediation Confidentiality* (CMC, 8 July 2009).
[98] *https://www.cedr.com/about_us/modeldocs/* [accessed 18 May 2018]
[99] An example may be found in the Agreement to Mediate (family) in Appendix I at para.A1-044, which may be too explicit for some, but not explicit enough for others.
[100] Directive 2008/52/EC of the European Parliament and of the Council of 21 May 2008 on certain aspects of mediation in civil and commercial matters [2008] O.J. L136/3.
[101] See the views of Nadja Alexander at: *http://mediationblog.kluwerarbitration.com/2016/07/18/brexit-and-london-as-a-mediation-venue/* [accessed 18 May 2018].

mediation process shall be compelled to give evidence in civil and commercial judicial proceedings or arbitration regarding information arising out of or in connection with a mediation process, except:
(a) where this is necessary for overriding considerations of public policy of the Member State concerned, in particular when required to ensure the protection of the best interests of children or to prevent harm to the physical or psychological integrity of a person; or
(b) where disclosure of the content of the agreement resulting from mediation is necessary in order to implement or enforce that agreement.
2. Nothing in paragraph 1 shall preclude Member States from enacting stricter measures to protect the confidentiality of mediation."

15–119 The UK Government has implemented the Directive for cross-border disputes with reference to confidentiality and privilege as follows[102]:

15–120 *The Cross-Border Mediation (EU Directive) Regulations 2011*[103]: in relation to what is described as "mediation evidence" (defined as "evidence arising out of or in connection with a mediation process"), these provide at reg.9 that, subject to reg.10, "a mediator or mediation administrator has the right to withhold mediation evidence in civil and commercial judicial proceedings and arbitration." Regulation 10 allows a court to order the disclosure of mediation evidence where all parties agree, or where this is necessary for overriding considerations of public policy, or where the mediation evidence relates to the mediation settlement and disclosure is necessary to implement or enforce the settlement.

15–121 *The Civil Procedure (Amendment) Rules 2011*[104]: these provide in Sch.2 s.III r.78.26, that where a person seeks disclosure or inspection of mediation evidence in the control of a mediator or mediation administrator, that person must apply in accordance with a prescribed procedure. There must be evidence in support that all parties agree to such disclosure or inspection, or that this is necessary for overriding considerations of public policy, or that disclosure is necessary to implement or enforce the settlement. The Rules outline the procedures for applying for a witness summons and the representations that may be made. These provisions do not apply to proceedings allocated to the small claims track.

15–122 It would seem that further harmonisation of the provisions for confidentiality and privilege across European jurisdictions is both possible and desirable. In an informative analytical chapter about the history and implications of the EU Directive,[105] Kallipetis points out that there is a conflict between common law and civil law jurisdictions because the concept of privilege is not common to both and is not a feature of civil law systems. On the other hand, the concept of confidence—protecting commercial confidence, confidential information and trade secrets and confidential communications with their lawyers—is common to

---

[102] In relation to family mediation, see rr.35.3 and 35.4 in the Family Procedure Rules.
[103] The Cross-Border Mediation (EU Directive) Regulations 2011 (SI 2011/1133).
[104] The Civil Procedure (Amendment) Rules 2011 (SI 2011/88 (L.1)).
[105] Michel Kallipetis QC, "Mediation Privilege and Confidentiality and the EU Directive" in Arnold Ingen-Housz, *ADR In Business* (New York: Wolters Kluwer, 2011), Vol.2.

all jurisdictions. Prior to the UK's decision to leave the EU he, perceived a need for EU countries to develop a common and uniform approach to confidentiality and privilege.[106]

A MEDIATION PRIVILEGE?

It remains to be resolved definitively by the UK courts or by the legislature whether there is a privilege attaching to the whole mediation process, including all communications passing within that process, whether the mediation relates to family matters, civil or commercial disputes or any other kind of issue. 15–123

As indicated above, the courts from *McTaggart* onwards have supported the existence of a privilege where parties are negotiating towards achieving a reconciliation, on the broad principle that as a matter of public policy this is a desirable end and that the state is more interested in reconciliation than divorce. 15–124

Re D (minors) was a major step forward towards the development of a general mediation privilege. There is a clear public policy consideration that settlement is a desirable end to disputes and that settlements are preferred to litigation, as appears from *Cutts v Head*.[107] Given this, it would not be a very substantial step for the courts to extend the privilege established in *Re D (minors)* to cover also financial, property and other aspects discussed in family mediation and settlement negotiations in civil or commercial mediation. 15–125

The *Re D (minors)* principles suggest that the courts might well decide in the future that a privilege should attach to other aspects of the mediation process that should be similarly protected on the grounds of public policy. In that case, the Court of Appeal said that: 15–126

> "in this field as in others it is undesirable that the law should drift very far away from the best professional practice"

and that a practice existed which followed the law "in recognising the general inviolability of the privilege protecting statements made in the course of conciliation".

The extension of the *Re D (minors)* principles into a more general mediation privilege was in fact considered by Ramsay J in the *Farm Assist*[108] case, when he observed that Sir Thomas Bingham's outline of the law in *Re D (minors)* and the decision of the House of Lords in *D v National Society for the Prevention of Cruelty to Children (NSPCC)*[109] lent some support for the existence of such a privilege. He also said that: 15–127

---

[106] The European Parliament passed a resolution on 25 October 2011 supporting a wide range of ADR proposals and stated that it was considering, where applicable, more far-reaching measures, such as creating a professional privilege in parallel with that provided for in art.7 of Directive 2008/52/EC. Any developments in this regard are still awaited.
[107] [1984] Ch. 290 CA (Civ Div) at 306; also [1984] 2 W.L.R. 349 and [1984] All E.R. 597 CA (Civ Div) and the comments of Oliver LJ.
[108] [2009] EWHC 1102 (TCC); [2009] B.L.R. 399.
[109] [1978] A.C. 171.

> "in mediation where existing concepts of legal advice privilege, litigation privilege and without prejudice privilege can be applied, I consider that those principles provide sufficient guidance but there is also the need for a further 'privilege' which arises other than the Mediator's right to confidentiality in relation to the mediation proceedings".

However he did not go so far as to decide that such a privilege existed.

15–128 The 1990 Law Commission inquiry into grounds for divorce[110] referred to the principle that it was in the public interest for disputes to be settled and litigation avoided.[111] It expressed the view that there should not be doubt about this question of privilege, and recommended that a statutory privilege should be conferred on statements made during the course of conciliation or mediation processes. Its reference was to processes connected with separation or divorce, but it saw no reason in principle why the privilege should not be extended to all disputes that are or may become the subject of family proceedings.[112]

15–129 The Law Commission's view that doubt needs to be resolved and replaced with certainty is beyond question. Equally, there is no logical reason why their proposal for the provision of a statutory privilege should not be extended to all mediation, not just family. If the principle is accepted that it is in the public interest for disputes to be settled and litigation avoided, then support is needed for processes that promote the non-adversarial resolution of disputes.

15–130 Support for a mediation privilege appears to be widening. Cornes expresses the view that:

> "we need to create a statutory special privilege for mediation that not only brings fairness and consistency but admits of the reality that mediation is more than assisted negotiation and which advances the position of the United Kingdom as a respected centre for international and domestic mediation".[113]

15–131 Kallipetis argues that within the EU, Member States cannot have conflicting and different approaches to the fundamental principle of confidentiality:

> "This emphasizes that there is a need for a privilege that is recognized by all Member States and will protect the integrity of the mediation process, thereby producing an effective resolution mechanism for its citizens."[114]

He further argues:

---

[110] English Law Commission, *Family Law: The Ground for Divorce* (London: HMSO, 1990), Law Com. No.192: October 1990.
[111] English Law Commission, *Family Law: The Ground for Divorce*, fn.110, para.5.40.
[112] English Law Commission, *Family Law: The Ground for Divorce*, fn.110, para.5.44.
[113] David Cornes, "Mediation Privilege and the EU Mediation Directive: An Opportunity?" (2008) 74 *Arbitration* 395.
[114] See Kallipetis, "Mediation Privilege and Confidentiality and the EU Directive" fn.105 in which he says that this does not necessarily require legislation: all that is required in the common law countries is a definitive judicial decision. This may be affected by the UK's Brexit decision, but the principle of mutuality of recognition remains valid.

"it is clear that the time has come to press for a distinct mediation privilege to preserve the integrity of the process".[115]

Allen and Mackie address the issue of confidentiality, which they describe as being "in the heart of the mediation process."[116] Pointing out that there is no statutory protection for mediators in the UK, as had been envisaged in an earlier draft of the EU Mediation Directive, or even to provide the qualified protection of the Directive, they say that "we need legislation to achieve even this limited requirement we need to establish a higher standard and greater clarity." Allen, following implementation in May 2011 of the EU Directive, identifies the uncertainties in the law on confidentiality, and the need to have each issue settled by the court through "happenstance", unless the government pre-empts the process by legislation. Implementing the law in piecemeal fashion could have far-reaching negative impacts.[117]

Briggs states that:

15–132

15–133

"there is an ongoing debate as to whether, even if a mediator is ordered to give evidence, he/she may rely on a so-called mediation privilege and decline to give evidence about 'confessional exchanges' he/she had with either party. Such an approach has recently received authoritative support."[118]

In the US, the Uniform Mediation Act (UMA) Committee, in presenting the draft Act in 2001,[119] referred to a mediation privilege contained in the Act. The official Reporter noted that:

15–134

"virtually all state legislatures have recognized the necessity of protecting mediation confidentiality to encourage the effective use of mediation to resolve disputes state legislatures have enacted more than 250 mediation privilege statutes."

The Reporter further observed:

"As with other privileges, the mediation privilege must have limits, and nearly all existing state mediation statutes provide them. Definitions and exceptions primarily are necessary to give appropriate weight to other valid justice system values."

Strong US support for a mediation privilege is also displayed by McCrory, who regards immunity from disclosure as essential to the proper functioning of matrimonial mediation.[120]

15–135

It should be said that while there is extensive support for the legislature to introduce a statutory privilege, this is not universal. There are those in the US

15–136

---

[115] Michel Kallipetis QC, "Should there be a distinct 'Mediation Privilege'?" *Standing Committee of Mediation Advocates* 26 October 2007.
[116] Tony Allen and Professor Karl Mackie, "Moves in mediation: confidentiality, the EU Directive and regulation" *The Barrister* 43.
[117] Tony Allen, *The EU Directive Now Implemented*, available at: *https://www.cedr.com/articles/?item=The-EU-Directive-now-implemented* [accessed 18 May 2018].
[118] Sir Michael Briggs, "Mediation Privilege?" *New Law Journal*, 3rd and 10th April 2009.
[119] Uniform Mediation Act (UMA) Committee, "June 2001 Draft of the Uniform Mediation Act" at: *http://www.mediate.com/articles/umaJune01draft.cfm* [accessed 18 May 2018].
[120] John P. McCrory, "Confidentiality in Mediation of Matrimonial Disputes" (1988) 51 MLR 442, 454, quoted in Scottish Law Commission Discussion Paper No.92 of March 1991 at para.5.50.

15–137   whose views are widely respected who question whether it is advisable to seek legislation on confidentiality.[121] They query whether blanket legislation could properly cover all forms of ADR and believe that there is adequate protection under existing law. They also express concern about the rights of third parties unless the terms of the privilege were most carefully expressed and delimited. Similar reservations about the introduction of a mediation privilege have been strongly expressed in the UK by a number of senior and respected practitioners.

15–137   Certainly, if any privilege were to be formulated, it would need to have regard to these concerns. Cornes says:

> "I believe that, on balance, it is better to have privilege in mediation regulated by legislation, with all the difficulties of drafting that entails, rather than leaving it to the common law to develop it case by case using tools rooted in rules relating to without prejudice negotiations *simpliciter* and not always appropriate to the task of creating a clear and consistent approach to mediation."[122]

The mediator's position

15–138   As the law stands, any privilege that might exist attaches to the parties and not to the mediator. Consequently, the parties can agree to waive that privilege and allow the mediator to provide the court with any information that arose in the mediation process. However, if the mediator and the disputing parties all enter into an agreement to mediate, with confidentiality provisions, then the mediator needs to agree to any waiver of those confidentiality provisions. A mediation privilege would need also to protect the process and should not be variable by the parties without the agreement of the mediator.

15–139   Another question may arise with regard to the appropriateness or otherwise of a possible immunity for mediators in relation to the risks to which they may be exposed as a consequence of an actual or alleged breach of confidence, or other matters such as defamation or negligence.

15–140   Some contracts for mediation specifically seek to exempt mediators from liability for breaches of contract, negligence or other tortious conduct. Where this is not the case, or even where it is, should there be a statutory immunity for mediators, or should the nature and limit of any immunity be a matter for the common law? A similar debate took place in the preparatory work for the Arbitration Act 1996. Initially, the Departmental Advisory Committee advising the Secretary of State for Trade and Industry, in its second report of May 1991 considered that no statutory immunity should be given to arbitrators. However, such a provision was enacted together with the complementary provision for arbitrators' instructions.

15–141   There is a strongly arguable case for mediators to be immune from liability for mediation undertaken by them other than for fraud or gross abuse of their position and trust. There is in principle no difference between the protection of a mediator and an arbitrator in this respect and the policy reasons that led to

---

[121] For example, Professor Eric Green, "A Heretical View of the Mediation Privilege" (1986) 2 *Ohio State Law Journal* 1.
[122] David Cornes, "Mediation Privilege and the EU Mediation Directive: An Opportunity?" (2008) 74 *Arbitration* 395.

statutory immunity being given to arbitrators apply with equal force to mediators. Some statutory protection is desirable, especially if mediation develops as part of, or as an adjunct to, court procedures.

Clarification and reform

It is clear that there is still scope and need for clarification and reform of the law relating to privilege in mediation. A statutory privilege for mediation in all fields of activity would achieve this, and would enhance the process. Undoubtedly much care would have to go into both the questions of principle and the pragmatic formulation of the terms and effect of the privilege, as well as any mediator immunity that may, as a separate issue, be considered. **15–142**

The Scottish Law Commission has addressed the question of confidentiality and privilege in relation to mediation.[123] Although limited to family matters, their discussion document and the subsequent papers cover many issues relevant to matters other than family. They pose the general question as to whether, in principle, some kind of privilege should attach to information acquired in the course of family mediation; and their provisional conclusion is in the affirmative.[124] They examine whether the scope of the privilege should be left to be developed by judicial decision or defined by statute; and in the latter event, to what extent and with what implications. They suggest for consideration that "the scope of the privilege should be defined by legislation in conventional terms."[125] Their further consideration of the various issues relevant to the subject is comprehensive and thorough, and well worth attention by anyone concerned with the reform of the privilege applicable to any form of mediation. **15–143**

These issues were raised in the first three editions of this work and remain relevant in this fourth edition. The use, understanding and importance of mediation have developed and increased over the years. To some extent, practice continues to be likely to lead the law; but the issues do need to be addressed thoughtfully and carefully and initiatives to enhance the mediation process by clarifying and unifying the law and practice on confidentiality and privilege would be very welcome and not before time. **15–144**

---

[123] Scottish Law Commission, *Confidentiality in Family Mediation*, fn.120.
[124] Scottish Law Commission, *Confidentiality in Family Mediation*, fn.120, para.5.1.
[125] Scottish Law Commission, *Confidentiality in Family Mediation*, fn.120, para.5.16.

CHAPTER 16

Ethics, Values, Fairness and Power

INTRODUCTION

The matters introduced and discussed in this chapter relate primarily to mediation. Providing impartial third-party assistance in the field of dispute resolution or management raises a number of ethical and practical questions for practitioners, which will be addressed under the following heads: 16–001

Rules of underlying professional bodies: professional issues concerning dispute resolution practice may arise from the rules of a practitioner's traditional practice. 16–002

ADR ethics and Codes of Practice: professional questions may arise in relation to the practitioner's ADR practice, whether arising from a code of practice or from ethical standards that should be inherent in any neutral dispute resolution practice. 16–003

The practitioner's values, attitudes and beliefs: these could affect issues of fairness, practice and ethical responsibility. What does "neutrality" or "impartiality" mean in this context? 16–004

Fairness: the question arises to what extent a practitioner has responsibility for the fairness of any agreement reached and for fairness of the process. 16–005

Conflicts of interest: the impartiality and the parties' perceptions of the impartiality of mediators and other practitioners are critical to the mediation process. Conflicts of interest, imputed bias and situations that suggest a lack of impartiality need to be avoided. 16–006

Ethics of confidentiality: this relates to the issues and dilemmas facing practitioners in dealing with sensitive information received on a confidential basis. 16–007

Power imbalances: this relates to the question whether, to what extent and how a practitioner can and should deal with the question of power imbalances between the parties. 16–008

Mediator cautions: this considers the circumstances in which a mediator should not act, or should do so with caution. 16–009

RULES OF UNDERLYING PROFESSIONAL BODIES

Professional organisations have rules regulating the conduct of their members in their professional capacities. Insofar as any dispute resolution practice may overlap the traditional practice of the practitioner, consideration may have to be given to ensuring that there is no conflict between the two sets of practices. 16–010

16–011 The legal profession is the main profession whose members engage in dispute resolution, and the rules applicable to solicitors and barristers will be considered. Other professional bodies may also regulate their members who engage in dispute resolution, and this may need to be individually checked.

The Law Society of England and Wales and the Solicitors Regulation Authority

General provisions

16–012 The professional body for solicitors in England and Wales is the Law Society, which maintains specialist accreditation schemes, including the Family Mediation Accreditation Scheme and the Civil and Commercial Mediation Accreditation Scheme, with approved panels of mediators in each scheme.

16–013 The Law Society delegated its regulatory powers in 2007 to the Solicitors Regulation Authority (SRA), which is part of the Law Society, but operates separately from it.

16–014 Before considering specific rules that relate to mediation, reference should be made to SRA Principle 1, which effectively replaces r.1 of the Solicitors' Practice Rules 1990. This mandatory principle provides, among other things, that a solicitor must:

> "1. uphold the rule of law and the proper administration of justice;
> 2. act with integrity;
> 3. not allow your independence to be compromised;
> 4. act in the best interests of each client;
> 5. provide a proper standard of service to your clients…"

16–015 Like the rules that these principles replace, these provisions may apply in a number of ways. A solicitor has a duty to ensure that any dispute resolution activities undertaken comply with the requirements as to integrity, independence and standards. When representing a client in traditional practice, he or she must also act in the best interests of that client, by being aware of all appropriate processes available and properly advising the client about them so that an informed choice can be made.

16–016 Given especially the sanctions against failing to explore and possibly use alternative processes before embarking on litigation, as summarised in the *Halsey* case,[1] it would be remiss, and possibly negligent, for a solicitor not to advise a client about all relevant dispute resolution processes. An analogy might be the failure of a solicitor to advise a client about the availability of public funding in circumstances where it is available and could be appropriate.

Specific mediation provisions

16–017 Solicitors who mediate need to decide and make clear whether they are mediating in their legal professional role—"as solicitors"—or outside that role, hence "not as solicitors". In the latter event, they should not refer to themselves in this

---

[1] See Ch.17 for the *Halsey* criteria.

context as "solicitors" and are not covered by their solicitors' professional indemnity insurance. The SRA does not regulate them in their mediation practices, though it retains control over solicitors who fundamentally breach professional rules, for example, by committing a crime.

The Law Society/SRA have specific requirements for solicitors who mediate as such. They will be expected to undertake specific training in mediation in accordance with prescribed training standards, and they will be expected to observe the Society's Mediation Codes of Practice.

The Law Society's Mediation Panels

The Law Society has established specialist panels of family mediators and civil-commercial mediators, each with a Chief Assessor, with the power to appoint supporting assessors. The panels have two-tier membership. The first tier is intended to provide for those who work and have experience in the relevant practice and who have completed the designated training (General Members). The second tier covers those who have completed an accreditation process involving prescribed practice, consultancy, peer group, and further education requirements (Practitioner Members).

The Bar

The General Council of the Bar has not published any ethical standards specifically for barristers acting as mediators. Its view was that the standards applicable to barristers contained in the Bar's Code of Conduct would apply whatever their function, be it as barristers in practice or barristers acting in any part-time judicial function. If they breach the fundamental principles set out in para.301 of the Code, which relates to discreditable conduct or conduct likely to bring the profession into disrepute a complaint can be made.

The Bar Council website includes a list of barrister mediators who have all completed training with a mediation provider which adheres to prescribed standards.

ADR ETHICS AND CODES OF PRACTICE

Acting as an impartial practitioner in a dispute resolution process carries with it a substantial ethical obligation to act in a responsible, competent and effective way with principle and integrity. It is possible for practitioners to influence the course of proceedings by the way in which they conduct the process, the questions they ask and the options they help the parties to examine.[2] However, they must not,

---

[2] Cobb and Rifkin have pointed out that the way in which the facilitator frames questions may significantly impact the dominant discourse of the process: S. Cobb & J. Rifkin, "Practice and Paradox: Deconstructing Neutrality in Mediation" (1991) 16 *Law & Social Inquiry* 35–62: This is discussed in some depth in S. Shipman, L. McGregor and R. Murray "Human Rights Claims, Process Standards and Agreement-Based ADR", *Human Rights Quarterly* (forthcoming).

directly or indirectly, try to impose their own views or settlement terms on the parties. Abusing this ethical rule could be harmful to the practitioner's reputation and that of the process.

16–022 The high ethical standards that a practitioner should observe have a number of sources:

- As observed above, the practitioner's traditional occupation may stipulate standards and requirements.
- Mediation and other dispute resolution organisations generally stipulate the standards of conduct required of their members, which may be informally regulated, or may be in the form of a Code of Practice or Model Procedure.
- Individual practitioners may subscribe to their own practice and ethical rules, either informally or as part of an agreement with the parties.
- Properly trained practitioners should be aware of the ethical considerations and the need to work with integrity and should do so as part of a personal ethos irrespective of any formal document regulating these activities. They should be imbued with a sense of the need to conduct the process in a fair, effective and even-handed way.

16–023 A Code of Practice is likely to reflect an organisation's ethical values and practical ground rules. It may outline the organisation's policy or guidelines on various matters such as mediator qualification, mediation practice, values and principles underlying practice, confidentiality and privilege. It is likely to address other ethical issues such as conflicts of interest and circumstances in which the mediation should be ended as well as practical matters including payment of fees and mediator indemnity insurance.

16–024 Ethics constitute a cornerstone of ADR practice. A third party is given substantial power to influence the resolution of disputes, in many cases affecting the lives of the people concerned. That practice is carried out largely privately, out of the public gaze, and without the same kind of protections provided by the court system, such as the possibility of getting reasoned judgments or appealing. Practitioners owe it to the public and to their profession to observe a strong sense of ethical awareness.

16–025 Given the range of fields within which ADR is practised and the variety of skills, styles, cultures and approaches that it encompasses, some controls are desirable in the public interest. In the interests of diversity, however, those controls should not be rigid. That would replicate the rigidities and problems of the legal system that ADR intends to avoid. Rather, the controls should be maintained by a keen and clear sense of ethical propriety. If an ethical framework is in place, practitioners have a sound theoretical understanding, and are practised in facilitative skills, there should be scope for creativity and flexibility.

THE PRACTITIONER'S VALUES, ATTITUDES AND BELIEFS

The concept of neutrality

The term "neutral" runs through the literature on ADR. It is extensively used both as a noun, to refer to the impartial practitioner ("the neutral") who works in ADR, and as an adjective, to refer to the "neutral" quality of the practitioner or as a part of the process, as in "early neutral evaluation". However, there is a view that nobody can be strictly "neutral" because they cannot function in any way as human beings without bringing their own personal values, attitudes and beliefs into what they do, whether consciously or not. Hence they cannot truly operate strictly "neutrally".[3]

16–026

For this reason, instead of referring to "neutrality" in relation to the ADR practitioner's role, many people prefer to use the terms "impartiality" and "even-handedness", which refer to an absence of bias or partiality and do not imply any reference to the presence or absence of the practitioner's values.[4]

16–027

Personal values, attitudes and beliefs

Mediators and other dispute resolution practitioners working in a neutral role will inevitably have values,[5] attitudes and beliefs that affect how they approach their work. Rather than imagining that they can abandon all of these, it is probably more useful for practitioners to be fully aware and conscious of them. With that awareness, they can try to ensure that these do not impinge on the process and unconsciously affect what they do and how they work.

16–028

Various aspects can usefully be brought into awareness:

16–029

Attitude to conflict

Dispute resolution practitioners bring into the dispute their underlying views and responses to conflictual situations. These will generally have been formed in their families of origin, based on early experiences. If family conflict was well managed, the practitioner may be able to address conflict in later life more easily. If conflict was avoided, commonly by one member of the family (perhaps even the practitioner) being the peace-maker, the practitioner may in later life tend towards adopting a conflict-avoidance approach to conflict management and resolution.

16–030

These and other related attitudes, developed over years, will invariably affect the practitioner's approach to particular disputes.

---

[3] For further discussion of neutrality see Christopher W. Moore, *The Mediation Process, Practical Strategies For Resolving Conflict*, (New Jersey: John Wiley & Sons, 2014), p.9 and pp.21–22.
[4] See for example: L. Mulcahy, "The Possibilities and Desirability of Mediator Neutrality: Towards an Ethic of Partiality" (2001) 10(4) *Social and Legal Studies* 505–527. See also S. Shipman, L. McGregor and R. Murray, "Human Rights Claims, Process Standards and Agreement-Based ADR", fn.2.
[5] See for example: R. Goldberg, "How our Worldviews Shape our Practices" (2009) 26(4) *Conflict Resolution Quarterly* 405–431, 427. See also S. Shipman, L. McGregor and R. Murray, "Human Rights Claims, Process Standards and Agreement-Based ADR", fn.2.

16-031 A practitioner does not need to formalise this self-enquiry, but may consider his or her attitude to conflict on a reflective basis. Formal tests do exist. For example, the Myers-Briggs Type Indicator (MBTI) classifies sixteen psychological types, which it identifies through a specific questionnaire. Some people find that this typology helps towards self-understanding and to identify sources of conflict. Less formal self-analysis generally suffices, though guidance in undertaking it can always be helpful.[6] With the benefit of these insights, a practitioner's ability to address conflictual situations can be improved. Also, practitioners may remind themselves that their attitudes and responses are not universal, and that each party may be better able, or less able, to cope with the conflict than the practitioner.

Rationality-emotionality

16-032 Dispute resolution practitioners may also find it helpful to have an understanding of their broad positioning between rational and emotional responses, on a notional continuum, though there are inherent risks in referring to rationality-emotionality on this basis. First, people are more complex than this, and may at times be rational and at other times emotional (and sometimes both). Secondly, people may make inappropriate and generalised gender assumptions and identify general principles of emotionality with women and rationality with men.[7] Social conditioning and other factors may result in patterns that have observable gender similarities; but it is risky and unsustainable to create theories or generalisations based on any such patterns. Thirdly, there is no real continuum between rationality and emotionality.

16-033 Parties, especially in inter-personal disputes including marital issues, but also in a range of other conflicts, may well have their own different positions on this notional divide. One party may seek a calm, logical and ordered approach to resolving the issues, whereas the other party may be more emotional and unready to resolve matters purely on the basis of a business-like approach, preferring to deal with personal issues. A mediator in such a situation who adopts a rational, business-like approach is in some respect failing to acknowledge the party who is more emotional. Correspondingly, if the mediator resonates with the more emotional approach, the "rational" party may be troubled. Practitioners (not just in the family field) need to be aware of this division and of their own natural

---

[6] A useful self-analysis exercise in assessing one's attitudes to conflict is the Conflict Mode Exercise developed by Thomas and Kilmann, see: R.H. Kilmann and K.W. Thomas, "Developing a Forced-Choice Measure of Conflict-Handling Behavior: The Mode Instrument" (1977) 37(2) *Educational and Psychological Measurement* 309–325. For sources of conflict, see Bernie Mayer, *The Dynamics of Conflict: A Guide to Engagement and Intervention*, 2nd edn (Jossey-Bass, 2012) Ch.1, pp.1–33 and the wheel/circle of conflict hypothesis which he developed in conjunction with Christopher Moore.

[7] Writers such as John Gray have commented on gender differences along similar lines to these, for example in his book, *Men are from Mars, Women are from Venus* (London: Element, 1993). Works such as his offer insights into gender differences, but run the risk of all generalisations, namely that they do not apply universally.

inclinations in response.[8] They may need to find an approach that recognises and acknowledges the validity of both ways of functioning.

Practitioners also need to be aware of their own individual capacities to cope with the emotions of the parties. Some people can tolerate parties' anger, distress or frustration more easily than others. They should have this awareness when entering the field of conflict. They should also remember that the parties themselves may well have different tolerances from one another and from the practitioner. These limitations need to be borne in mind when following the skills process of "allowing parties to express their emotions".[9] 16–034

Much that practitioners do in conflict and dispute resolution is intuitive. Many lawyers and other professionals tend to place a premium on logic and rationality, but in fact have well-developed intuitive responses that are not readily acknowledged. They may have a sense that something is not quite right or a feeling about what they are being told. Skilled questioning relies on this sense about what to pursue and what to leave unasked. Similarly, skilled mediation involves intuitive as well as reasoned responses. There is a balance to be struck, which the mediator hopes to achieve. 16–035

Values, beliefs and assumptions

All people have their own individual values and belief systems, on which their assumptions about behaviour are based. It is impossible to divorce ethical awareness from individual beliefs, if ethics are to be observed at a fundamental level. 16–036

People start forming their values and beliefs from the earliest age and develop them as they grow older. Many factors will shape these. They include, of course, individual experience, the culture of one's nuclear and extended family, community and religion, the influence of schools and teachers, and the media. Practitioners enter the conflict arena with an array of beliefs, assumptions, biases and in some cases prejudices. It will not be easy to identify these with particularity, but at least the practitioner should understand that they exist, to be ready to guard against the effect that they may have if they intrude on the dispute resolution process. 16–037

Crawley says: 16–038

> "belief systems are sensitive, personal and absolutely necessary. They provide us with a basic framework from which to relate to the people and situations we encounter. An effective conflict manager possesses a strong set of positive values

---

[8] The authors wish to acknowledge Neil Dawson and Brenda McHugh, family therapists and mediators, for their contributions to these insights. See also Benjamin on the "Myth of Rationality" at Ch.19 fn.36.

[9] The term "venting" emotions is commonly used in dispute resolution literature. Although not intended to be disrespectful to the parties, it could have that connotation. The "expression" of emotions does not just happen in family and inter-personal issues. Underlying emotions can be strong in many civil and even commercial disputes. Practitioners should also be aware of the risk that when people express their emotions, this may rekindle underlying feelings, which will need to be handled with care and sensitivity.

about other people, but also needs to examine and be in control of his or her own beliefs, assumptions, stereotypes and prejudices".[10]

FAIRNESS

Fairness of process or fairness of outcome

16–039 An issue that sometimes arises is whether and to what extent the mediator is responsible for fairness in mediation. The principles that apply to mediation will generally also apply to other forms of consensual dispute resolution.

16–040 It is a fundamental principle of mediation that the parties are the negotiators and that the mediator serves as a facilitator. The parties are responsible for all their decisions including their settlement terms. In arriving at their decisions, the parties may have regard to any considerations they may consider relevant. The mediator may provide information and may in some models help with evaluation; but none of this allows a mediator to impose his or her decisions or preferences on the parties or to influence them unduly in their decision-making.

16–041 In these circumstances, given that parties make their own decisions however much the mediator may have a different view, it is clear that mediators cannot be responsible for the fairness of the outcome agreed between the parties. This is not always understood. Ensuring that parties enter into a fair agreement is not within the power or function of the mediator.

16–042 What mediators can do and need to do, however, is to establish fairness of process. This means that they should manage the mediation process in such a way that the procedure is as fair as possible to both or all parties. When people refer to mediation being a "fair" process, it is this quality of procedural fairness to which they refer and not necessarily fairness of substantive outcome.

16–043 Fairness of process implies certain requirements:

- Even if they are required to attempt mediation, as some mandatory schemes may require, there should be no coercion on parties to settle, but merely a requirement to try using the process. Parties should not be penalised for example by the withholding of public funding if they try to use mediation and do not find it helpful.
- Mediators must be even-handed and impartial in their dealings with parties. This does not mean that the mediator may never say anything that one or other party may not like to hear. At times a mediator may need to challenge one party or the other. This does not imply partiality, which should be viewed in the round.
- Mediators should create conditions in which both or all parties can be properly heard. If one party dominates the process, that would ordinarily create a sense of unfairness. In some situations, more attention may need to

---

[10] John Crawley, *Constructive Conflict: Managing to Make a Difference* (London: Nichols Brealey, 1992), p.31.

- be given to one of the parties than to another, but that may be necessary, and should be carefully explained as appropriate.[11]
- Power imbalances exist in most situations, and are likely to continue in all forms of dispute resolution. Mediation cannot and does not pretend to eliminate power imbalances, but mediators may have strategies to help prevent these from distorting the process. Mediators may address power imbalances where appropriate, but should decline to mediate where the power imbalances are so severe that the mediation process cannot be fairly or effectively conducted.[12]
- The mediator needs to ensure that as far as practicable parties negotiate and decide freely. If there is any harassment, abuse or violence, the mediator must take steps to deal with that to ensure that negotiations are not induced by fear or made under duress, otherwise the mediation will have to be ended. In a contentious situation, many people may be influenced by fears and concerns. They may be afraid of the risks and costs of litigation, or of the animosity that proceedings may cause. They may fear that their losses will be even greater if they do not concede during negotiations. These and other concerns may be inherent in the situation and would arise in any forum. The mediator's task is to try to ensure that a party is not forced into a decision by improper pressure or duress.
- Mediators should not unduly influence the parties in their decision-making. Mediators sometimes say that they do not influence the parties because they do not make statements, but primarily work through questions. However, the way in which questions are used and their choice can be very influential. Mediators should not seek to escape responsibility by suggesting that questions are neutral.
- Parties must be capable of decision-making and of understanding the issues. If any party, through illness, mental incapacity or for any other reason cannot properly participate in the process, it should not take place.
- A sense of fairness and respect should permeate the whole process. The mediator should be aware of this in his or her interventions, questions and comments; in any information provided; in the procedures used; in the arrangements made for meetings; and in the conduct of the process generally.

In whatever model may be used, the mediator needs to be able to control the process sufficiently to ensure that fairness of process prevails.

---

[11] See L. Wing, "Mediation and Inequality Reconsidered: Bringing the Discussion to the Table" (2009) 26(4) *Conflict Resolution Quarterly* 383–404 for a discussion that symmetry in terms of aspects such as equal time for caucuses for each party may impact negatively on parties. This may occur, for example, where there is dissonance between one party's story and a dominant cultural narrative. See also S. Shipman, L. McGregor and R. Murray, "Human Rights Claims, Process Standards and Agreement-Based ADR", fn.2.

[12] A fascinating portrayal of two different approaches by experienced mediators to a hypothetical case study relating to this question is set out in C. Menkel-Meadow and H. Abramson, "Mediating Multiculturally: Culture and the Ethical Mediator" in E. Waldman (ed), *Mediation Ethics: Cases and Commentaries* (San Francisco: Jossey Bass, 2011), pp.305–338.

ETHICS, VALUES, FAIRNESS AND POWER

What constitutes fairness?

The parties' views guiding fairness

16–044 The fairness that applies in mediation is the parties' sense of fairness and not the mediator's. This means that if the parties regard a resolution as fair, the mediator should not be troubled by the fact that it does not accord with his or her sense of fairness. The mediator may wish to check that the terms and their implications are fully understood by the parties; but subject to doing this, the mediator's views as to their fairness would not be relevant.

16–045 This is not a difficult proposition for mediators to accept. The problem, however, is that parties in dispute often find it difficult to agree on a mutual definition of fairness in their circumstances. They may have different perceptions of fairness. How, then, does a mediator address fairness? What are the criteria or factors that apply?

Legal principles guiding fairness

16–046 The legal system is concerned with justice and fairness. Unfortunately, two problems exist in this connection. First, while these principles constitute an ideal, the system is not always able to deliver on its promise of these principles. Secondly, the principles of fairness adopted by the law are not necessarily the principles adopted by people generally. Lawyers tend to use legal principles of fairness as their starting point for testing fairness; yet many agree that this is an inadequate measure.

16–047 As mediation is conducted "in the shadow of the law"[13] and parties can generally turn to the court system for redress if they are not satisfied with the mediated outcome, legal principles and rights tend to guide parties in deciding what they think is fair. Yet this may not meet people's needs. So, for example, in a financial dispute on divorce, it is quite common for each party to have a different perception of the guiding principles and factors as to how the finances should be divided. Each may seek to draw on different legal principles to support their position. Or in dealing with residential arrangements for children, one may draw on the law to support equality of residential time as being fair, while the other may contend that the children need a solid base and that it is unfair to require them to move about to meet the needs of a parent wanting equality. These examples are drawn from family situations, but the need for fairness permeates all fields of activity and dispute.

Workability guiding fairness

16–048 Mediators sometimes take the view that fairness is an elusive concept, and that if the parties cannot agree on it, all that they can do is to test the workability of proposals. If proposals are viable and workable in practice, that is as close to

---

[13] See Ch.19, para.19-006 and fn.1 of that chapter.

fairness as mediators may feel that they can take matters. Mediators would test workability by asking the parties questions about implementation, in the form of "reality-testing".

Legal representation guiding fairness

Where parties are both or all represented by lawyers in the mediation process, a mediator may perhaps consider it less necessary to be concerned about the fairness or otherwise of the terms of the settlement. There is a view that lawyers create an equality of bargaining power, and can help their client to assess all relevant factors in deciding whether or not to accept settlement terms. It is true that legal representation for all parties tends to help reduce certain kinds of power imbalances, but it cannot achieve full equality of power nor can it guarantee fairness. **16–049**

Other fairness considerations

Other attempts are sometimes made to devise fair principles to guide dispute resolution negotiations. An example is the mathematical formula devised by Brams and Taylor.[14] The authors have adapted the cake-cutting procedure of "I cut, you choose" with mathematical formulae to try to create what they call "envy-free" allocations. **16–050**

Sometimes practitioners can do no more than allow parties to express their views of fairness, try to help them to hear and understand one another, and then, if necessary, to agree to differ.

Manifest unfairness

Many mediators take the view that however unfair the settlement of the issues might seem, that is a matter for the parties. Others would not wish to participate in a resolution that they felt to be manifestly and fundamentally unfair and unconscionable, even if both parties agreed to it.[15] In the absence of any specific provision in a Code of Practice, this must ultimately be a matter for the mediator's individual conscience. **16–051**

CONFLICTS OF INTEREST

Impartiality, even-handedness and the mediator's neutrality to the outcome of the mediation are essential components of mediation. It is vital to the integrity of the process that mediators should neither have any conflict of interest, nor should they be perceived as having any interest or potential bias, even if no actual conflict of interest exists. **16–052**

---

[14] Steven J. Brams and Alan D. Taylor, *Fair Division: From cake-cutting to dispute resolution* (Cambridge: Cambridge University Press, 1996). For a brief outline, see Ch.4, under "Other theories and models".

[15] For an account of two very different approaches to this type of situation refer to fn.12.

16–053 Three aspects need to concern mediators. Similar principles will apply to practitioners in other kinds of consensual processes:

- *actual conflicts of interest*, where the mediator has or has previously had another role, relationship or interest that is inconsistent with his or her impartial, even-handed and neutral function as mediator;
- *potential conflicts of interest*, where a conflict does not yet exist but the possibility of it arising is inherent in the situation;
- *perceived conflicts of interest*, where there is no actual or potential conflict of interest as such, but where the situation or circumstances nevertheless may cast doubt on the mediator's ability to act impartially and may give rise to imputed bias.

Regulating conflicts of interest and perceived conflicts

16–054 Mediators need to have rules regulating whether or not they can mediate where a conflict of interest exists. Generally, subject to the possibility of obtaining informed consent, they should not do so; and they should carefully observe the restrictions and qualifications on mediating in situations where perceived conflict exists.

16–055 Mediation Codes of Conduct usually make provision for mediators to disclose any conflict of interest, which will preclude a practitioner from being appointed or continuing with an existing appointment, save for some where parties may agree to the appointment continuing notwithstanding the conflict—depending on its nature.

16–056 In addition, professional bodies such as the Solicitors Regulation Authority, the Bar Council and the British Association of Counselling and Psychotherapy may have their own stipulations regulating conflicts of interest in their professions. The Legal Services Commission also has conflict rules that need to be observed where appropriate.

The wider net covering conflicts and perceived conflicts

16–057 Rules that regulate actual and potential conflicts and perceived conflicts may also affect other people who are, or are perceived to be, in certain kinds of close relationships with the mediator, including those that involve a sharing of information. In certain situations, information known by one person is deemed to be known by others who have an actual or potential information-sharing relationship with that person. For example, all members of a law firm or other partnership are deemed to have knowledge that one member of that firm or partnership acquires, notwithstanding that the person with actual knowledge may be at pains to keep it confidential from others within the firm or partnership. The principle that applies is that "Chinese walls" to keep information confidential cannot ordinarily be erected within a relationship where there are possibilities or duties of information-sharing.[16]

---

[16] See the landmark House of Lords case of *Bolkiah v KPMG* [1999] 2 A.C. 222; [1999] 2 W.L.R. 215 HL relating to the unqualified duty that attaches to confidential information imparted during a professional relationship that has to be retained confidentially after the ending of that relationship.

Similarly, there will be other working relationships, such as mediation services and certain kinds of consortia, where knowledge of facts by one person may create the presumption that all other members of that service or consortium similarly have that knowledge. The effect of this is that if one member of the firm, service or consortium is precluded from acting as a mediator because he or she has relevant information about the parties, then all other members of the firm, service or consortium will be similarly precluded. 16–058

The term "firm, service or consortium" includes the following: 16–059

- all partnerships, associations or consortia in which people hold themselves out as partners (but not generally including a consortium of practitioners who are clearly independent of one another but who merely join together in a loose association for mutual marketing or support);
- any other association or relationship which involves people working or co-operating with one another in a way that includes actual or potential sharing of profits and/or access to one another's confidential information.

Absolute and relative bars to mediating by reason of conflicts and perceived conflicts

In some situations, mediators will be absolutely barred from mediating even if the parties wish to release the mediator from that bar. In other situations, it may be possible for the parties to decide that they do want the mediator to mediate for them notwithstanding the existence of a perceived conflict. In the latter case, however, consent to mediate can only be effectively given by parties who are fully aware of the circumstances of the perceived conflict. Consent can only be effective if it is informed consent. 16–060

Each organisation or regulatory body needs to formulate applicable rules. The following are examples of how such rules might be adopted, but are not intended to be definitive: 16–061

Absolute bar to mediating

It is suggested that a mediator ought not to mediate for parties in the following circumstances even if the parties specifically request him or her to do so and are willing to give consent: 16–062

- where the mediator or member of his or her firm, service or consortium has a personal or financial interest in the outcome of the mediation;
- where the mediator or a member of his or her firm, service or consortium has at any time provided legal, counselling or any other professional advice, support or representation for any party in relation to issues that may arise in the mediation;
- where the mediator has or at any time has had a therapist/client or counsellor/client relationship with any of the parties;

Lord Millett referred to the "Chinese walls" and expressed the view that "an effective Chinese wall needs to be an established part of the organisational structure of the firm, not created *ad hoc*" ([1999] 1 All E.R. 517 HL at 530).

- where the mediator or a member of his or her firm, service or consortium advises or acts for or has previously advised or acted for either party on a matter unrelated to the likely issues in the mediation, as long as the other party is unaware of this;
- where the mediator or a member of his or her firm, service or consortium advises, acts for or counsels or has previously advised or acted for any third party whose interests may conflict with those of either party to the mediation (such as the trustees of a family trust of which either party is a beneficiary, discretionary or otherwise);
- where the mediator is aware that for personal or other reasons he or she will not be able to mediate in an impartial way, or notwithstanding informed consent is likely to be perceived as being unable to do so.

16–063 This last category covers situations in which the mediator is in a position where his or her duties and responsibilities to the parties are or may potentially be compromised. Or a mediator may have such strong feelings or views about a situation that he or she feels unable to be impartial and neutral. Mediators may feel able to overcome personal blocks of this nature; but there may well be times when this is not the case, and in such event the mediator will be acting properly in declining to mediate.

16–064 In such a case, even if the mediator felt that he or she would be impartial and even if the parties agreed, the mediator might well decline to act. The test for the mediator would be whether the perception is likely to continue that he or she will not be able to be impartial.

Qualified bar to mediating

16–065 It is suggested that in the following circumstances, a mediator ought not to mediate for parties unless they specifically request him or her to do so and give informed consent:

- Where the mediator or a member of his or her firm, service or consortium advises or acts for or has previously advised or acted for either party on a matter unrelated to the likely issues in the mediation and the other party is aware of this.
- Where the mediator or a member of his or her firm, service or consortium has acquired information, not in the public domain, relevant to any issue likely to arise in the mediation, then the mediator should not act unless the nature and source of such information is known to all parties and they consent to the mediator acting.
- Where the mediator or a member of his or her firm, service or consortium advises, acts for or counsels or has previously advised, acted for or counselled any third party on a matter related to the likely issues in the mediation and the parties are aware of this. (However, where the third party's interests may conflict with those of either party to the mediation, it is suggested that there should be an absolute bar on mediating.)

- Where the mediator has a social or other personal relationship with either party or with any third party materially affected by the mediation, the mediator should not act unless full disclosure is made to the parties and they consent to the mediator acting.
- Where circumstances exist and are known to the mediator in which a party aware of such circumstances might reasonably be concerned about the mediator's ability to act impartially as a mediator, but which do not constitute an actual or potential conflict of interest. In such event, if full disclosure of the circumstances is made to both parties and they give informed consent, the mediator should be able to act as such.

The distinction between the absolute bar and the qualified bar to mediate is clear. In the case of an absolute bar, the conflict of interest or perceived conflict is so fundamental that it cannot be overcome, even with the consent of the parties. In the case of a qualified bar, however, the conflict, potential conflict or perceived conflict, while serious enough to raise concerns, is capable of being accepted where all parties agree to do so, with full knowledge of all relevant facts and concerns. This allows parties proper freedom of choice, where a mediator might be entirely suitable and is not conflicted out, but where circumstances exist that the parties can properly overlook if they choose to do so. 16–066

Conflicts or perceived conflicts arising or identified after mediation has started

If a mediator starts to mediate in the good faith belief that no conflict or perceived conflict exists, and either of these subsequently arises or is identified, the mediator must be guided by his or her organisation's rules as to whether he or she can continue to act. 16–067

Where there is an absolute bar, the mediator must withdraw from the mediation. Where there is a qualified bar, the mediator must either withdraw or inform the parties of all relevant facts and circumstances and should establish whether the parties wish him or her to continue. In some circumstances, the mediator may consider that even where a qualified bar exists, he or she should not continue to act as mediator. In such event, the mediator should withdraw from the mediation. Mediators should not lightly withdraw where there is only a qualified bar and the parties wish him or her to continue, especially if they have already spent significant time or made significant progress in the mediation. 16–068

Changing roles after the conclusion of mediation

Organisations and regulatory bodies need to make it clear whether mediators can change role after the end of the mediation. Some bodies provide that the mediator may not represent, advise or counsel either party in relation to any issues dealt with in the mediation. This would mean that a solicitor mediator could not act as solicitor for either party or for the parties jointly, in relation to any matter that arose in the mediation. In such event, he or she could not bring court proceedings in any consequent divorce or deal with the conveyancing of any property that was required to be transferred from one to the other. 16–069

16–070   There seems to be a broad consensus, though not necessarily unanimity, that a mediator should not be precluded from subsequently acting in another role (such as solicitor) for a party to the mediation in relation to any issue or matter that is unrelated to the issues in the mediation. However, he or she should not do so or even discuss or agree to do so until the settlement terms have all been implemented. This would ensure that the parties are able to revert to mediation if any problems or issues arise during the course of implementation. It would be invidious and improper for a mediator during the mediation to agree or even to discuss the possibility that he or she will after conclusion of the mediation act for one party albeit in an unrelated matter.

ETHICS OF CONFIDENTIALITY

16–071   The legal implications of ADR confidentiality are dealt with in Ch.15. However, certain ethical issues arise in relation to the subject of confidentiality which, although they overlap with the legal aspects, will be considered separately from them in this chapter. These arise, first, in relation to the broad issue of confidentiality within the ADR process, and secondly, in relation to the subject of maintaining confidences in private meetings with the parties.

Ethics of confidentiality in ADR generally

16–072   An ethical issue may arise where a practitioner is bound by an agreement to maintain confidentiality in ADR proceedings and comes across a situation in which he or she feels morally or ethically obliged to breach that duty of confidentiality. This may, for example, arise where parties in a mediation inform the mediator in confidence that a public structure or a product being marketed is unsafe or a couple tell the mediator confidentially that a child is being subjected to physical or sexual abuse.

16–073   Whether or not there is a legal obligation to maintain confidentiality will depend upon the conditions under which the process takes place, and on the applicable law. So, for example, in some states in the US there is an obligation on the part of the mediator to report to the authorities any serious allegations of abuse or neglect in family mediation.[17] In the UK, the terms of many agreements to mediate and relevant Codes of Practice may exempt the mediator from maintaining confidentiality in relation to certain kinds of information, for example where there is significant risk of serious harm to anyone.

16–074   If there is no legal duty of confidentiality, or if the circumstances of the matter and a legal duty of disclosure override the obligation to maintain confidentiality, the mediator can consider the ethical position without legal constraints. The mediator's dilemma will, however, arise where there is a legal duty to maintain confidentiality with no clear exemption from that duty, and yet the facts are such that the mediator feels obliged to make a disclosure. There is no standard answer to that dilemma. The mediator must be guided by the applicable law; the terms of the agreement to mediate; the terms of any relevant Code of Practice; his or her

---

[17] See "Confidentiality and Privilege in Divorce Mediation" in J. Folberg and A. Milne, *Divorce Mediation—Theory and Practice* (New York: Guilford Press, 1988), p.323.

duties to the parties; the nature, seriousness and implications of the information; any applicable public policy considerations; and ultimately the mediator's own conscience.

This moral issue has been addressed in an article by Gibson.[18] He challenges a perception that exists among some writers that everything in mediation is necessarily strictly confidential and incapable of being examined. He believes that few mediators are "absolutists" with regard to the question of confidentiality, but rather that "there is a broad spectrum of opinion about what should be revealed" and with what justification.

16–075

The Code of Practice under which a mediator works may guide this question, particularly if it is incorporated explicitly or by indirect reference into the contract for mediation between the mediator and the parties. It follows that organisations establishing such codes or individuals creating their own contracts could make their own choices as to what degree of freedom from confidentiality they wish to provide.[19]

16–076

Gibson considers the moral aspect of confidentiality, including the distinctions between the law and morality, where "legal acts are sometimes immoral, and moral acts are sometimes illegal".[20] Consequently:

16–077

> "mediators who face difficult or novel questions about whether or not to disclose client confidences are unlikely to find plain guidelines in the law"

though an examination of the law may be helpful.[21] Gibson analyses the various bases for mediator confidentiality and decides that these "do not support a clear-cut rule for mediators to always keep their client's confidences."[22] He analyses the cases where there may be a duty to break confidences, for example, warning victims of intended violence, child abuse and public interest and concludes that:

> "mediation confidentiality is only as strong as the justifications that can be made on its behalf...There are two (crucial) elements...one is the policy element which supports the institution of mediation and the related role obligation; the second is the mediator's own ethical judgment."

He argues for public accountability, substantial and adequate rather than absolute confidentiality, an external review mechanism and a review of codes of practice to allow mediators more scope to make their own considered judgments about disclosure.

16–078

---

[18] Kevin Gibson, "Confidentiality in Mediation: A Moral Reassessment" (1992) *Journal of Dispute Resolution* 25.
[19] The Codes referred to in the appendix of precedents provide examples of confidentiality clauses.
[20] Gibson, fn.18.
[21] The legal, as distinct from the ethical and moral, issues concerning confidentiality are dealt with in Ch.15. In practice, the law on public policy disclosure and the contractual provisions increasingly inserted into agreements to mediate may well cover many situations.
[22] Gibson, fn.18, p.4.

Ethics of confidentiality in private meetings

16–079 Caucusing is the process of meeting the parties separately and privately in the mediation process, often combined with "shuttle mediation" in which the mediator moves between the parties, carrying messages and helping to facilitate their negotiations with one another.

16–080 The holding of separate meetings with the parties is by no means used in all models of mediation. Some mediators only have joint meetings with the parties and do not consider it right to maintain separate confidences. However, where separate meetings are held, there are three principal ways of dealing with the confidentiality aspect:

1) parties may agree that there will be no separate confidences, and that anything said in the separate meeting will be brought back to the joint meeting;
2) they may agree that matters discussed in the separate meetings will be maintained confidentially, save as the mediator may be authorised to disclose;
3) there may be special rules or individual circumstances applicable to separate meetings.

Each of these will be considered.

Disclosure of information from separate meeting into joint meeting

16–081 Where mediators work on the principle of not maintaining separate confidences, there may nevertheless be occasions when they need to meet each party separately, for example, where a party feels uneasy about discussing something in the joint meeting. Separate meetings then enable each party to speak more freely to the mediator, who will bring the separate information into the joint meeting, having perhaps discussed with each party separately how this will be done. This maintains the principle that all matters discussed will be made available to all parties.

16–082 Ethical problems can arise if notwithstanding the agreement for open disclosure of matters discussed separately, a party may say something in the separate meeting which he or she does not after all want disclosed to the other. This may place the mediator in a difficult position, especially where the information could be embarrassing or inflammatory. In that situation the mediator would have to reinforce the need to disclose the information according to the agreed procedure, and perhaps help to deal with any concerns relating to such disclosure. If the party is adamant that there cannot be disclosure, the mediator may feel unable to continue acting in that mediation. The mediator can avoid such a situation by emphasising at the outset the need to bring back all information to the joint session and that no separate confidences can be maintained.

16–083 Mediators will not necessarily report back verbatim to the joint meeting, but will commonly summarise and paraphrase. Many consider that they do not need to repeat non-material statements. This is understandable and generally unobjectionable; but it leaves the discretion as to materiality with the mediator and risks potentially material information being withheld.

There may also be some risk that the mediator, in carrying the information back from the separate meeting to the joint meeting, may summarise or paraphrase it inaccurately and consequently not fully comply with the agreement for disclosure. The mediator needs to ensure that communications are carefully and accurately conveyed when this model is used.

16–084

Agreement to maintain confidentiality of separate meetings

The practice of maintaining confidentiality—subject to obtaining permission to disclose aspects as appropriate—is a common way of working in civil and commercial disputes, as also in some models of family mediation.

16–085

An ethical dilemma can arise where the mediator receives confidential information in the separate meetings and is subsequently required to arbitrate formally, in med-arb mode. Can the mediator do so using confidential information not known to the other side?[23] The ethical aspect can probably best be addressed by ensuring that either the parties have an opportunity to opt out of the process if there has been any confidential information given to the mediator.

16–086

Another ethical dilemma could arise if the mediator receives confidential information that indicates that another party is under some material misapprehension. Clearly, the mediator would not wish to allow any misunderstanding to remain if it arose as a result of anything said by the mediator or the other party. The situation may be more complicated if the error arose without any fault or misleading element on the part of the mediator or any other party, and if the mediator is required to maintain strict confidentiality about the correct position. In that event, the mediator may need to seek permission to correct the misunderstanding (being sure not to breach any confidence the other way round). The mediator may perhaps point out where relevant that the erroneous understanding could result in an unsatisfactory and unworkable agreement being reached. If confidentiality is still insisted upon, and the misunderstanding is significant and material, the mediator would have to consider whether or not to continue with the mediation. This would depend on the circumstances, the nature of the misapprehension and its effects, whether the other party is being professionally advised, and other relevant factors.

16–087

Another ethical dilemma might arise if a mediator learns confidentially that a party would pay more than the other party has privately said he would accept. How does the mediator deal with the surplus? Concluding on either the higher or the lower amount would result in the mediator aligning with one party. Is the mediator justified in taking a mid-figure? Or should the mediator ignore the information and leave the parties to reach their agreement? Views have been expressed that it would be appropriate to discuss the dilemma with the parties and to see whether they would "split" the surplus. There is no right answer to this dilemma: the mediator may need to make a judgment based on each individual case.

16–088

Ethical dilemmas of this kind occur infrequently. The mediator can invariably deal with them by following sound principles and acting with integrity. It is

16–089

---

[23] The practicalities of med-arb are addressed in Ch.19.

Separate meetings with special rules

16-090   In the UK, some family mediators extend the joint meeting model by also having separate confidential meetings with each party.[24] However, in view of the standard rule in family practice that financial information is evidentially open and available to be used in court, whereas attempts to resolve the issues are without prejudice, this principle is also applied to the separate private meetings. Consequently, a party cannot maintain confidentiality from the other about financial information in a private meeting. The mediator would need to insist on the disclosure as the fundamental basis on which the whole process is undertaken, and indeed this is addressed in the Agreement to Mediate where this model is used.

16-091   Another special situation may arise in relation to the Mediation Information and Assessment Meetings in family matters.[25] These may be held jointly and also separately in order to check privately whether there has been violence or abuse that may make mediation inappropriate. If the mediator is told in a separate meeting that there has been violence or abuse that would make the matter unsuitable for mediation, the mediator may retain this information confidentially for the protection of the party disclosing it, and may simply decline to mediate without giving reasons. This may raise some ethical questions as well as practical difficulties if the party alleged to be abusive enquires why the mediator is unwilling to proceed. However, it seems that pragmatic issues of safety and well-being may predominate in these circumstances: the risk of any further violence or abuse needs to be minimised.

16-092   Separate meetings may arise spontaneously even where joint meetings without separate confidences are the norm, as for example where something distressing or provocative arises and parties need to be temporarily separated. Clearly the broad understanding of no separate confidences needs to be maintained, and the joint meeting re-established as soon as practicable.

POWER IMBALANCES

Forms of power

16-093   The issue of power understandably gives rise to many concerns. It is perhaps summed up by the question:

> "How does ADR, which depends upon consensual resolution, deal with the situation where one party to a dispute is more powerful than another and can accordingly use that power to influence the outcome?"

---

[24] As outlined in Ch.11.
[25] As referred to in Ch.11.

POWER IMBALANCES

To address this question, the notion of power in dispute resolution should be considered.[26]

16–094 Because power exists in different forms and is often subtly exercised, it is sometimes difficult to describe and identify. It is affected by the perceptions that parties have of their own power and the power of others, which may or may not be accurate. Power is not necessarily static, but may shift as circumstances change. Power relationships may be complex, and different elements of power may reside in different ways in the parties to provide a more complicated balance than may be obvious.

16–095 Analysis of any dispute will reveal this. For example, in a commercial dispute between a multi-national corporation and a small franchisee, there is apparently a clear power imbalance. The multi-national company is likely to have very substantial resources to fight a case, will engage top lawyers, and may be unaffected by the outcome whereas the small franchisee may be crippled by an adverse outcome. That could well be the true power position. Other factors might, however, balance the power between them. For example, the legal merits of the dispute might favour the franchisee, so that the franchisee might well succeed in a trial. There may be other franchisees interested in the way the multi-national company deals with its franchisees, which could make its handling of the situation politically sensitive. The multi-national company might also be sensitive to adverse publicity if it crushed a small company in what could be portrayed as a "David and Goliath" encounter. The financial collapse of the franchisee in the event of the multi-national company winning at a trial may be a less satisfactory outcome for the multi-national company than working out a solution that allows the franchisee to continue in business. The circumstances and factors comprising the total power relationship between the parties may not be as one-sided as first impressions may have suggested.

16–096 In this example, mediation of the dispute between the parties could well provide them each with what they need, namely a mutually acceptable, agreed resolution of their differences. The suggestion sometimes made that litigation would be more effective in redressing power disparities would not necessarily be valid in this situation. The power imbalance would be manifest in litigation, which might operate to favour the multi-national company with its ability to extend and prolong the dispute. The smaller company would perhaps be hard pressed to sustain and fund lengthy and expensive litigation, which in the final analysis it could not be assured of winning, given the uncertainties and risks inherent in the litigation system.

16–097 Similarly, a husband who is a businessman with a domineering manner may appear to have a power imbalance over a wife who does not work and who has a quiet manner. This may well be a true reflection of the power balance; but there may be other factors making the situation more complicated. For example, the wife's quiet manner may conceal strength and determination which may have supported the family in stressful times, and the wife may have a more powerful position, actual or perceived, with regard to the children of the family. ("Do not use the children as pawns in your disagreement" is a very proper admonition to

---

[26] For a brief discussion of this concept, see Ch.4 "Negotiation" under the sub-heading "Power".

couples; but this may not recognise the complex and subtle nature of power relationships and family dynamics.) Power imbalances are not always what they seem.

16–098　Practitioners need to be aware of the different forms of power and the way in which these are manifested. Power can be overt or covert. Maintaining silence and declining to co-operate effectively with the process can be very powerful. Practitioners cannot make premature assumptions about power because it can be more complex than may initially be appreciated.

Power imbalances: the mediator's role

16–099　In circumstances where there is an apparent power imbalance between the parties, the mediator's role is to effectively manage the mediation process to ensure that the power imbalance does not adversely affect the dynamic of the mediation.

16–100　Where parties have equal power, they may be expected to behave more co-operatively, function more effectively and behave in a less exploitative or manipulative manner than when the relationship is unequal.[27] In most cases, there is likely to be some power disparity between parties. This raises some questions for mediators.

Should a mediator try to redress a power imbalance?

16–101　Employment mediators and conciliators who facilitate issues between employers and employees commonly take the view that it is not their function to redress power imbalances. The power balances, for example between large employers and trade unions representing employees, can be delicately poised. At times one side may have greater power, at times the other. Mostly, their joint interests are served by finding solutions that do not test their power balance. In this context, employment mediators and conciliators consider that the parties have to continue working with one another and that it would be inappropriate to contemplate trying to redress the power balance between them.

16–102　Analogous points may arise in other kinds of mediation. If parties engage the mediator to help them resolve specific issues, does that entitle the mediator to assume the role of redressing their power balance (even if he or she could do so, which is seldom the case)? On the other hand, if power imbalances exist, can mediation, which depends on parties being able to negotiate with one another, work effectively and fairly?

16–103　This issue has been debated among mediators. Moore outlines the difficult position mediators face when confronted with a discrepancy in parties' power relationship and the means of influence which a mediator can impose as follows:

---

[27] Christopher W. Moore, *The Mediation Process: Practical Strategies for Resolving Conflict*, fn.3, pp.518–521.

POWER IMBALANCES

"The independent mediator, because of his or her commitment to neutrality and impartiality, is generally ethically barred from direct advocacy for the weaker party, yet is also ethically obligated to assist the parties in reaching a relatively fair, acceptable and durable agreement".[28]

The following thoughts may be useful in this regard: 16–104

- Mediators cannot assume that they can or should automatically try to address issues of power balancing that arise in the mediation. They should consider whether this is part of the brief required by the parties, and whether it would be proper and possible for them to do so.
- The mediator's responsibility is not to seek to change the power relationship between the parties, but rather to ensure that any power disparity that exists does not impact on the process in such a way as to make it unworkable or unfair.
- The mediator should appreciate that power imbalances are complex and that superficial appearances of imbalance may not give the whole picture. However, mediators can initially take power imbalances at their face value and need not delay in dealing with those that present themselves. If other facets of the imbalance manifest themselves, the mediator can then consider whether and how to address those.
- Where imbalances are observed, the mediator should always be vigilant in guarding against any abuse of the process. He or she will be likely to observe as the process unfolds whether the parties can use the process effectively and can suggest procedures or use strategies which help to exclude these imbalances from the communications and negotiations between the parties.
- If power imbalances are severe, affect the process and cannot be redressed, they will almost certainly prevent one of the parties from being able to negotiate with the other effectively in the mediation forum. This may for example occur where one party consistently dominates, harasses, threatens or abuses the other. In such event, the mediation is unlikely to be able to continue and the mediator would have a responsibility to end it. However, power imbalances that do not affect the process, such as financial power, would not ordinarily be a reason to end the process.

The transformative model of mediation[29] does not directly address the issue of power imbalances. Instead, it does so indirectly through its twin approach of empowerment and recognition. Instead of viewing disputes as problems, it sees a conflict as: 16–105

> "first and foremost a potential occasion for growth in two critical and interrelated dimensions of human morality. The first dimension involves strengthening the self. This occurs through realizing and strengthening one's inherent human capacity for dealing with difficulties of all kinds by engaging in conscious and deliberate reflection, choice and action. The second dimension involves reaching beyond the self to relate to others. This occurs through realizing and strengthening one's

---

[28] Above, p.519.
[29] See Ch.3.

inherent human capacity for experiencing and expressing concern and consideration for others, especially others whose situation is 'different' from one's own."[30]

16–106 Transformative mediators would therefore not approach the issue of power from the perspective of seeking ways to balance power. Their approach would be to see the conflict as an opportunity for parties to discover and strengthen their resources for dealing both with the substantive issues and the relationship questions, to develop their inherent capacities for strength of self and relating to others. Power would arise in a very different way from the concept of a mediator helping to redress imbalances. Rather, it would arise through the concept of empowerment, which, in general terms, is said to be:

> "achieved when disputing parties experience a strengthened awareness of their own self-worth and their own ability to deal with whatever difficulties they face, regardless of external constraints".[31]

16–107 All people engaged in conflict (even "powerful" executives) are said to feel unsettled, fearful and vulnerable, and can be empowered as to goals, options, skills, resources and decision-making, irrespective of outcome. By empowerment and by giving recognition (by voluntarily becoming more open, attentive, sympathetic and responsive) based on this empowerment, parties will experience the:

> "strengthening of self and greater actualization of their capacity for relating to others, and they will advance in both critical dimensions of moral development".[32]

16–108 Bush and Folger say:

> "As we are using the term, empowerment does not mean 'power balancing' or redistribution of power within the mediation process itself in order to protect weaker parties. Indeed, empowerment is always practiced with both parties. Of course, empowering *both* parties, in our sense, may indeed change the balance of power, if one party starts off with greater self-confidence and self-determinative ability. That, however, is a side effect of empowerment and not a conscious objective."[33]

What steps could a mediator take to redress power imbalances?

16–109 A mediator may consider it necessary to try to redress power imbalances insofar as these are adversely affecting the fairness and efficacy of the process. If the weaker party is unable to function effectively in the mediation forum, the mediator may wish to intervene to make it more possible for him or her to be more effective. The problem about this is that it could become or be perceived as partial and lacking the even-handedness that should characterise proper mediation practice.

---

[30] R. A. Baruch Bush and J. P Folger, *The Promise of Mediation* (San Francisco: Jossey-Bass, 1994), p.81.
[31] See fn.30, p.84.
[32] See fn.30, p.95.
[33] See fn.30, pp.95–96.

POWER IMBALANCES

Moore distinguishes between: 16–110

> "the situation in which a mediator assists in recognizing, organizing, and marshalling the existing power of a disputant and that in which a mediator becomes an advocate and assists in generating new power and influence. The latter strategy clearly shifts the mediator out of his or her impartial position, whereas the former keeps the mediator within the power boundaries established by the parties".[34]

Moore acknowledges that "there is no easy answer to this strategic and ethical problem".

The mediator might use any of the following strategies for addressing unequal power positions between parties that affect the process: 16–111

- trying to ensure that proper and relevant information is brought into the process to redress any imbalance in the possession of data (because having and controlling information is a form of power);
- assisting parties in considering any such information;
- where appropriate, providing legal or other information on an even-handed basis, while being careful not to advise the parties as to their respective rights or generally;
- allowing both or all parties a proper opportunity to express their views and to be heard;
- preventing abusive, threatening or harassing behaviour including sarcasm or other forms of belittling or ridicule;
- helping a party to articulate their views and proposals, always ensuring that they remain the party's views and proposals, and not becoming the party's spokesperson;
- agreeing rules with the parties to make communications and negotiations more effective;
- helping the parties to deal with their concerns and interests in a way that is constructive and not unduly threatening to them;
- discussing and agreeing rules that prevent a party from exercising undue power or influence that could improperly affect the outcome of the mediation, either inside the process or, as far as practicable, outside it;
- if the parties are not legally represented, suggesting that they take independent legal advice, or suggesting that legal advisers join them in the process, where appropriate.

A practitioner who remains concerned about the issue of power imbalance, either initially or perhaps after having worked with the parties for a while, could discuss this issue with the parties in some appropriate manner, to establish their views about it. While eventually having to make his or her own decision, the practitioner may be guided by the parties' views and preferences, in particular the genuine preference of the party perceived as having less power, so far as these can be effectively established. 16–112

If a practitioner believes that a party is participating unwillingly in the process or is in any respect not acting in a voluntary way, or if despite all reasonable 16–113

---

[34] Christopher W. Moore, *The Mediation Process: Practical Strategies for Resolving Conflict* (1996), p.69.

16–114 As mediation and other ADR processes are voluntary and consensual, a party who feels that a power imbalance or any other consideration is leading to an unacceptable or unfair result can refuse to continue with the process or to enter into an agreement.

16–115 If the existence of power imbalances between parties meant that they could not negotiate settlements of their disputes with one another, but would have to get those resolved by the courts, no cases would ever be settled unless parties had equal power. That, of course, is not the reality of the position. In fact, parties are constantly settling their cases, many of them finding that the litigation system does not in practice offer them power equalisation any more than any other process could do so.

16–116 Nevertheless, litigation does offer those who can afford it or who are publicly funded the opportunity to come to court with their more powerful opponents on relatively even terms. Where the disparities in power are so great that no agreement could realistically be negotiated, either between parties and their lawyers bilaterally or in an ADR process, litigation may well be the way to proceed. Most cases are, however, amenable to ADR processes despite the fact that power disparities may exist, as long as these do not preclude effective negotiation and agreement.

Opening paragraph (continuation): steps, the issue of power imbalance remains an obstacle to proper and effective negotiation, that would need to be dealt with, and if necessary, the process should be terminated. In this regard, a Code of Practice would help to inform the mediator's actions.

MEDIATOR CAUTIONS

16–117 There are some situations in which mediation would be entirely inappropriate, others in which it might be appropriate, but with some caution.

When mediation is inappropriate

16–118 There cannot be a comprehensive list of all the situations where mediation is inappropriate. The following are some of the circumstances in which mediation should not be undertaken:

- Where because of mental or other incapacity or for any other reason a party is unable to participate in the negotiation and decision-making process. This does not refer to negotiation inexperience or reticence about participating, but an inability to cope with the process notwithstanding the mediator's intercession and assistance. However, this should not preclude properly appointed representatives such as Mental Capacity Advocates choosing to mediate in appropriate cases.
- Where a party is unable to participate properly because of fear directly or indirectly engendered by the other, for example through violence, abuse, threat or intimidation.

- Where power imbalances are so great and irremediable that the mediator does not believe that the process can be fairly conducted and an equitable result achieved.
- Where the parties require the mediator to act illegally, improperly or in a way that would infringe public policy or breach material provisions of the relevant Code of Practice.
- Where fundamental and non-negotiable rights are in issue, for example relating to constitutional rights or personal freedom.
- Where it is necessary for a party to take urgent action to protect their position, for example to obtain immediate injunctive relief (though there may be circumstances in which this can be negotiated, but the mediator cannot take responsibility for this).
- Where it is essential to obtain a binding precedent (though there may be circumstances where this can be agreed and a consent order obtained).
- Clearly some matters require a court order that affects the status of either party, such as a divorce decree, though this can of course be agreed in principle.

When mediation needs to proceed with caution or reservation

There are situations in which mediation may not be precluded, but the mediator needs to check whether it might be inappropriate to proceed, or where he or she needs to proceed with care and circumspection. Here again, this is a matter for individual judgment and there cannot be a comprehensive list, but the following are some of the considerations that may signal an amber light:

16–119

- Where there is any past record of abuse, intimidation or threat, but where both parties indicate that they wish to proceed with mediation nonetheless. Mediation may well be possible and appropriate, but the mediator does need to assess the position with care.[35]
- Where it appears that any of the circumstances set out in the preceding section may perhaps exist, but this is uncertain. In this case, the mediator may wish to have a preliminary meeting to help him or her and the parties assess whether or not mediation would be suitable and appropriate.[36]
- Where it appears that a party may have no genuine intention of negotiating in good faith with a view to reaching a resolution, but seems to have some other motive in wishing to mediate, such as seeking to establish details of the opponent's case or causing delay.[37]

---

[35] Considerations about mediating in these circumstances are set out in Ch.11, in the section "Issues around mediating with domestic violence or abuse".

[36] For example, where there are issues of principle that appear to be irreconcilable, and may indeed be so, mediation may still be useful to help parties to manage the dispute rather than necessarily resolve it. See Mayer, *Staying with Conflict: A Strategic Approach to Ongoing Disputes* (San Francisco: Jossey-Bass, 2009)—in Ch.8, paras 8-051 to 8-053 and fn.37 in that chapter.

[37] But even when a party is perceived as untrustworthy and not genuinely committed to resolution there may be times when negotiation might still be productive. See Mnookin, *Bargaining with the Devil: When to Negotiate, When to Fight* in Ch.4, paras 4-034 to 4-036 and fn.27 in that chapter.

- In civil or commercial disputes, if it appears from the *Halsey* principles, as outlined in Ch.17, that mediation might not be appropriate, the mediator may wish to check this, though these are factors that parties, rather than the mediator, would ordinarily consider.
- If working with a model that involves a joint meeting of the parties for part or all of the process, the mediator would ordinarily check with all concerned that the parties feel able to meet with one another in this way. If not, whether because of strong antagonism or for any other reason, a process should be followed that does not involve a joint meeting, at least until everyone feels ready for it.

16–120 As will appear from the above, where there are uncertainties about the suitability of the mediation process, or indeed any other, a preliminary meeting with parties and/or lawyers as appropriate might often help the mediator and the parties to decide whether or not to go ahead. If the mediation continues thereafter, it is in any event a useful step in the process.

CONCLUSION

16–121 The issues addressed in this chapter are important in private and public sector mediation of all kinds. They are particularly important in court-related mediation especially if there is an element of compulsion, whether through a mandatory process or one ordered or proposed by the court.

16–122 Practitioners should be imbued with the ethical principles outlined in this chapter; but for the public to have the confidence in them, there also needs to be some element of accountability to an organisation or body with the power to ensure that these ethical rules are observed.

CHAPTER 17

Lawyers' Role Representing Parties in Mediation

INTRODUCTION

This chapter considers how lawyers can best represent their clients in mediation, with particular reference to civil-commercial and family practice. Similar principles may apply to representing parties in other fields and non-adjudicatory ADR processes.   **17–001**

Representing a client in mediation does not change the lawyer's basic duty to act in the best interests of the client. There are, however, differences in the way in which that duty can most effectively be carried out. The lawyer must have regard to the fact that the client has chosen to try to resolve the dispute in a consensual and not an adjudicatory manner or forum, which requires a suspension of the adversarial mode of practice. Results can be achieved for the client in a way that does not necessarily involve having to defeat the other side but rather by seeking solutions that are mutually beneficial, as far as this is possible. These all involve a difference of approach on the part of the lawyer.   **17–002**

On the other hand, each party will invariably still wish to achieve the best possible result in mediation, and strong positions and tough negotiations may well take place. The lawyer's task is to balance these competing requirements and tensions in a way that produces the best outcome for the client.   **17–003**

DIFFERENCES BETWEEN CIVIL-COMMERCIAL AND FAMILY MEDIATION

There are differences of both process and culture between civil-commercial mediation and family mediation, which will be reflected in the way that lawyers represent their clients in each field of activity. However, processes are starting to overlap and the distinctions are not as rigid as they used to be.   **17–004**

So, for example, the role of the party's lawyer in family mediation on separation and divorce has tended to be one of advising outside the mediation meetings rather than participating directly in them, though with developing and overlapping models, this is changing. In civil and commercial mediation the lawyer's role usually involves direct participation in the mediation proceedings.   **17–005**

In this chapter, general principles and practice applicable to both fields will be stated. Differences will be indicated where applicable.   **17–006**

SPECIALIST MEDIATION ADVOCACY

17-007 Mediation advocacy has become a specialist skill attracting a body of specialist practitioners and, in the UK, there are organisations which promote best practice in mediation representation and advocacy and provide mediation advocacy training and seminars.[1] The subject has also been addressed in a number of conferences, and has been written about.[2]

17-008 Mediation advocacy is not a soft option but relates to a sophisticated process with its own internal dynamic that advocates need to be aware of in order to achieve the goals desired by their clients.[3] With mediators coming from specialist sectors and risk analysis assuming a role in the resolution of disputes, particularly in the civil and commercial fields, so the role of the skilled mediation advocate is likely to increase.

DECIDING ON THE MEDIATION FORUM

17-009 Lawyers representing clients who are engaged in a dispute need to consider with their clients in what forum the dispute can most effectively and appropriately be addressed. It is no longer acceptable to assume that litigation will automatically be required.[4]

Is the dispute suitable for mediation?

17-010 To assess whether a dispute is suitable for mediation, the following questions may need to be considered:

17-011 *Is it essential to have a court order?* Clearly, mediation would be inappropriate in cases where a binding precedent has to be established[5] or where an urgent injunction regulating behaviour is needed. Some issues, relating to constitutional rights or personal freedom, are not amenable to mediation at all. However, sometimes mediation may be possible after or in conjunction with the obtaining of an interim injunction or a court order.

---

[1] See the Standing Conference of Mediation Advocates (SCMA) at *http://scmastandards.com/*, an organisation which has also taken European and other international initiatives, the ADR committee of the Bar Council, the Centre for Effective Dispute Resolution (CEDR), and the ADR Group.

[2] A. Goodman, *Effective Mediation Advocacy (Student Edition)* (St Albans: Mediation Publishing, 2017). A. Goodman, *Effective Mediation Advocacy—A Guide for Practitioners*, 3rd edn (St Albans: Mediation Publishing, 2016); S. Walker, *Mediation Advocacy; Representing Clients in Mediation* (London: Bloomsbury Professional, 2015).

[3] See Goodman, fn.2 (2016 and 2017).

[4] See generally; F.E.A. Sander and S.B. Goldberg, "Fitting the Forum to the Fuss: A User-Friendly Guide to Selecting an ADR Procedure" (1994) 10 Neg. J. 49, 66; or (2005–2006) 7 Cardozo J. Conflict Resol. 83.

[5] There is a view that ADR deprives the civil system of precedents by settling disputes. Individual litigants do not need to sacrifice their best interests for the public good; but sometimes issues of principle need to be established to guide future disputes of a similar nature. See arguments against settlement in O. Fiss, *"Against Settlement"* (1984) *Yale Law Journal* 93; N. Andrews, "A New Civil Procedural Code for England" (2000) C.J.Q. 19–38 and; J. Wade, "Don't Waste My Time on Negotiation and Mediation: This Dispute Needs a Judge", (2001) 18(3) *Conflict Resolution Quarterly* 259–280.

*How do the Halsey principles apply?*⁶ The guidelines set out by the Court of Appeal in *Halsey* can help lawyers decide on the appropriateness of mediation in civil and commercial cases. These are: 17–012

- The nature of the dispute: although the court in *Halsey* observed that "most cases are not by their very nature unsuitable for ADR", there may be some which are unsuitable, such as those mentioned above where a court order, injunction or binding precedent is needed, or where a point of law needs to be resolved.
- The merits of the case: if one party has a patently weak case and is using mediation as a tactical ploy, mediation may not necessarily be appropriate. This is, however, an objective and not a subjective judgment: belief in one's case must be reasonable. In any event, mediation may provide a relatively low cost alternative to trial that allows the issues to be aired and a resolution broadly appropriate to the merits to be reached.
- The extent to which other settlement methods have been attempted: if previous attempts to settle have been made and one party is unresponsive, that is a factor militating against the use of mediation.
- Whether the costs of the ADR would be disproportionately high: it is not indicated if the amount in issue is relatively small and the costs of mediation would be disproportionate.
- Whether any delay in setting up and attending the ADR would be prejudicial: this might be particularly applicable if an offer to mediate comes very close to a trial date.
- Whether ADR has a reasonable prospect of success: this is a test on the basis of objective reasonableness.

Is there a time limit within which litigation must be started? If there is a statutory limitation period within which a claim must be brought, a lawyer may need to bring court proceedings to prevent the claim being statute-barred (time-barred). However, once limitation is interrupted, for example by the institution of proceedings, a choice of fora for dealing with the issues may again be available. 17–013

This question is addressed by the European Directive on certain aspects of mediation in civil and commercial matters⁷ which regulates the mediation of cross-border disputes, and which has been adopted by some countries for their domestic mediation as well. The UK has adopted the Directive for cross-border disputes only.⁸ 17–014

---

⁶ In the case of *Halsey v Milton Keynes General NHS Trust* [2004] EWCA (Civ) 576; [2004] 1 W.L.R. 3002, the Court of Appeal set out guidelines for deciding whether costs sanctions should apply in the event of a refusal to mediate. See Ch.10.

⁷ Directive 2008/52/EC of the European Parliament and of the Council of 21 May 2008 on certain aspects of mediation in civil and commercial matters. Article 8.1 provides that Member States are to ensure that parties who choose mediation in an attempt to settle a dispute are not subsequently prevented from initiating judicial proceedings or arbitration in relation to that dispute by the expiry of limitation or prescription periods during the mediation process.

⁸ The Cross-Border Mediation (EU Directive) Regulations 2011 (SI 2011/1133). Part 3 amends primary legislation in relation to various limitation and prescription periods (which should be individually checked where this may be relevant), so that neither party is prevented from initiating proceedings simply because a limitation or prescription period expired during the course of mediation.

17–015 *Is the case being brought or defended for strategic reasons?* Are there objectives that cannot be met through settling, such as attracting public interest or delaying the fulfilment of obligations? These are contra-indicators to mediation, though sometimes objectives such as these can be met through a mediated outcome.

17–016 *Does the dispute involve a past or present relationship that has broken down?* Mediation is strongly indicated where a personal, professional or working relationship has broken down or is in crisis. However, it is not limited to those kinds of issues and is also suitable for most other kinds of disputes.

17–017 *Does a lack of trust preclude mediation?* This fundamental question is addressed by Mnookin,[9] who considers that while there are situations where one should properly decline to negotiate—and therefore to mediate—more often than not negotiation may well be appropriate and productive despite concerns about the other party's trustworthiness.

What kind of mediation is required?

17–018 Some thought needs to be given as to what kind of mediation and mediator is required. Some mediators are purely facilitative and will not express any view as to the merits of the dispute, directly or indirectly. Others may introduce an evaluative element on a spectrum that ranges from minimal and indirect questioning or observation through to expressing a view to the parties as to the likely outcome of the dispute if taken to litigation. Between these two parameters, there is a range of practice that may include "reality testing" (checking if perceptions match up to objective reality by selective questioning), or playing "devil's advocate".

17–019 There are many misperceptions as to what facilitation and evaluation comprise, so when considering appointment, rather than simply using these terms, it may be prudent to establish how the mediator would react if he or she thought that the mediation was deadlocked through one party misperceiving the strength of his position.[10]

Does the mediator need to be an expert?

17–020 The most important requirement of a mediator is to be an expert in the mediation process. If a choice has to be made between process expertise or expertise in the subject matter of the dispute, then process expertise will always prevail.

17–021 It may, however, be possible to engage a mediator who has expertise in the subject-matter of the dispute, as well as process expertise. Although a competent general mediator of civil-commercial disputes could effectively mediate on a range of issues (as a competent general litigator could do in litigation), some parties may feel more comfortable with a competent mediator with a specialist knowledge and experience in the field of activity of their dispute.

---

[9] See Mnookin, *Bargaining with the Devil: When to Negotiate, When to Fight* (Simon & Schuster, 2010). See Ch.4, paras 4-034 to 4-036 providing guidance on these issues.
[10] For a more detailed consideration of the concept of evaluation, see Ch.19.

DECIDING ON THE MEDIATION FORUM

Commercial and civil disputes

So, for example, people involved in construction disputes are more likely to choose a mediator with specialist knowledge of the construction industry. Similarly, there are specialist mediators in most civil and commercial fields of activity.

17–022

There are a number of reasons for this, relating to understanding the industry in which the dispute arises, personal authority in the field, more effective "reality testing" and risk analysis, and perhaps a greater ability to challenge stuck and mistaken perceptions. On the other hand, someone unconnected with their industry may bring a fresh and creative view; and in many cases, the issues do not necessarily turn on the specialist topic.

17–023

Where the substance or complexity of the dispute warrants it, co-mediators might be considered. For example, a medico-legal issue might benefit from having a team comprising a doctor and a lawyer. Or an accountant and a lawyer might be appropriate as a joint appointment for a complex corporate dispute involving share valuations.

17–024

Family issues

There are two different views about the relevance of the mediator's background expertise in relation to the mediation of family issues, particularly those arising on separation and divorce.

17–025

One view is that mediators who have an aptitude for mediation and who are properly trained, will be able to acquire sufficient generic skills to enable them to work effectively with couples. On this view, the mediator's background expertise (if any) is irrelevant. While therefore mediators may be drawn from legal, social work, counselling or other professions concerned with families, they may also be drawn from any other background irrespective of its relevance to family issues.

17–026

The other view is that the mediator's professional background has some relevance. On this view, family lawyers and counsellors, psychotherapists and others with experience and expertise in working with families who are trained to mediate bring their experience, knowledge and awareness to bear in the mediation process.

17–027

Here again, co-mediation is a viable option, which may involve combining mediators of different background professions and/or a male and female mediator to provide a gender balance. This may be a preferred option where, for example, there are complex financial, children and emotional issues.

17–028

Even where the mediator has relevant background professional expertise, he or she would not seek to influence the couple as an "expert". This would be inappropriate on any view. Rather, the mediator could draw on his or her professional background experience to provide even-handed legal or other information to the couple, to help develop options, and to help couples check whether their ideas and proposals are effective, workable and (where appropriate) within the parameters that a court would approve.

17–029

ENGAGING THE OTHER PARTY IN MEDIATION

17–030   In those jurisdictions, such as England and Wales, where mediation and other ADR forms are reasonably well established, the task of engaging the other party in mediation involves little more than approaching them with this suggestion. Indeed, as outlined in Ch.9, there is commonly an expectation that mediation will be considered in all civil and commercial disputes, with potential court sanctions for failing to do so. Similarly in the family field there is provision for a preliminary meeting—a Mediation Information and Assessment Meeting or MIAM—in relation to all disputes in the courts.

17–031   In those jurisdictions where mediation is less well established, there may be a concern that mediation would not be properly understood or that suggesting it might be viewed as a form of weakness or lack of confidence in one's case. Inasmuch as mediation does imply some willingness to find a mutually acceptable solution, there would be little point in suggesting it if there were no willingness at all to compromise. However, even if one is confident of success at trial, the process can allow the other party a graceful and low-cost opportunity to withdraw from the litigation. In suggesting mediation, parties can indicate that they are sufficiently confident in their prospects of success to agree to a mediation. A proposal to mediate can be accompanied by expressions of confidence in one's case, in the same way that this may be done when entering into bilateral negotiations.

UNDERSTANDING THE MEDIATION PROCESS

17–032   Lawyers representing parties need to understand the principles and procedures of mediation. This will enable them to use it to best effect, knowing when and how to adapt negotiations to the needs of each situation, to enter the problem-solving mode without necessarily having to concede individual advantage and to gain the maximum benefit from using the dynamic of mediator intervention.

17–033   To assist in considering the process, this book views the process in three phases. It considers an initial pre-mediation phase, before the substantive mediation starts. Then there is a second phase involving the substantive mediation process. Finally, there may sometimes be a post-mediation phase.[11]

THE PRE-MEDIATION PHASE

17–034   This phase includes considering mediation and assessing suitability, engaging the other party and selecting the mediation forum (addressed above), selecting a mediator and entering into an Agreement to Mediate.

---

[11] Chapter 9 covers the stages of mediation, and the individual chapters dealing with specific fields of activity do so in greater detail relevant to each field.

Preliminary meetings

In some cases, the mediator may hold a preliminary meeting other than a MIAM with the parties and/or their lawyers. This may take place in civil-commercial cases if the mediator thinks it would be useful, or in family cases though this is not widely done in privately-funded matters in England.[12]

17–035

The preliminary meeting may serve a number of functions:

17–036

- It allows the lawyers an opportunity to form a view about appointing the mediator.
- The mediator can explain the process and deal with any procedural queries or concerns.
- If a decision is taken during the meeting to appoint the mediator and go ahead with the process, the meeting can be converted into a preliminary meeting within the mediation. The mediator and the lawyers can discuss and agree procedural aspects such as preparing and submitting the parties' statements and documents, the mediation timetable and other procedural matters. In family mediation, they may be able to agree on the way in which financial disclosure particularisation (if required) and other matters can be dealt with.

Selecting a mediator

In the civil and commercial field, ADR organisations commonly have case managers who will provide preliminary information about the process including timing, procedures and costs, as well as panels of mediators, who might be generalists or specialists. The case manager may help parties select a short-list of suitable potential mediators. The organisation will also arrange the venue and facilities, provide the framework for the mediation including its rules and Agreement to Mediate, and will deal with all necessary formalities and practicalities.

17–037

Alternatively, parties may choose a mediator independently of any specific organisation, who will similarly deal with the necessary practicalities.

17–038

Family mediation organisations vary in their practice. There are groups or services who can help set up the process, whereas some will provide a list of mediators regulated by them, leaving it to the parties to contact the individual mediator direct.[13]

17–039

The agreement to mediate

Parties should enter into an Agreement to Mediate before the process begins. Lawyers for the parties should ensure that they have an opportunity to consider the agreement and to discuss it with their clients before the mediation meeting. If

17–040

---

[12] In some jurisdictions preliminary meetings involving lawyers in family cases are more common. B. Landau, M.D. Bartoletti and R. Mesbur, *Family Mediation Handbook* (Toronto: Butterworths, 1987).

[13] In the UK, the Family Mediation Council approves mediator bodies with individual mediator members. See its website *http://www.familymediationcouncil.org.uk/* [accessed 21 May 2018] for member organisations with their own mediator panels.

they have any queries, these should be discussed and clarified with the mediation organisation or the mediator who sent the document to the parties. The parties will be expected to sign the agreement by or at the commencement of the mediation meeting. The agreement will usually deal with matters such as evidential privilege, confidentiality, mediation costs and other practicalities.[14]

THE SUBSTANTIVE MEDIATION PHASE

Preliminary meetings and communications

17–041 A preliminary meeting once the mediation has started deals with the practicalities for the substantive mediation meeting(s). The mediator would meet with the parties, or in civil-commercial mediation more usually their lawyers, and arrange matters such as venue, documents, timetable, procedures, authority, representation and anything else that might help the substantive process to take place more efficiently and smoothly.

17–042 However, the more usual practice is for these matters to be dealt with by telephone or email given especially the cost and logistics of arranging a meeting. With the improvement of electronic and other communications including virtual meetings, it should become increasingly practicable for these useful meetings to take place.

Dealing with the documentation

Civil-commercial disputes

17–043 The lawyer in consultation with his or her client will usually prepare a without prejudice case summary for the mediator and the other party, setting out, in simple and non-legal terms, the relevant facts, issues and submissions.

17–044 The case summary may include an outline of the legal propositions and facts supporting parties' respective contentions, in an informative rather than combative way. It is usual for one copy to be sent to the mediator and one copy simultaneously to the other party.

17–045 A bundle of relevant documents is usually also provided. Where possible, a common bundle of documents may be agreed. This bundle does not have to follow the selection or disclosure process that would be used in traditional litigation. Selection is based rather on including relevant documents that may clarify the position for the purpose of the mediation. If parties cannot agree on a common bundle, each party may prepare their own separate bundle for the other party and the mediator.

17–046 Where a case is pending in the court or in an arbitral or other adjudicatory forum, the mediator may wish to have a set of documents from the other forum, or at least those that outline the respective cases such as statements of case.

17–047 All necessary documentation is ordinarily exchanged before the mediation starts, and should be available at the mediation meeting. Occasionally a party

---

[14] Specimen Agreements to Mediate can be found online. See Appendix I paras A1-009 to A1-011 for a brief outline and paras A1-043 and A1-044 for reference to sample agreements.

may show a mediator a document on a confidential basis. (Some mediators and organisations also provide for a supplementary case summary to be delivered to the mediator on a confidential basis, "for the mediator's eyes only", which may outline confidential information that the party does not wish to share with the other side. More usually, though, this is covered in the separate confidential meeting that the mediator will have with each party.)

Family issues

Family mediators may obtain preliminary information from the couple before starting the mediation, commonly through a standard referral form, which provides basic information about the parties and any children, a brief outline of their financial position and their legal representation. It can also serve as an initial step in the process of screening for domestic abuse. This preliminary information may be disclosed to the other party, though addresses and telephone numbers may be confidentially maintained.[15]

17–048

Unlike civil-commercial mediation, a bundle of documents would not be prepared at this stage. Where financial issues are to be dealt with in the mediation, a detailed financial disclosure is required. This is usually discussed and arranged during the mediation, rather than beforehand.

17–049

Preparation

Civil-commercial cases

The lawyer will be expected to prepare and present his or her client's case effectively, signalling a need to prepare carefully and thoroughly for the mediation, with an ability to demonstrate on facts, law and any technical aspects reasonably good prospects of success at a trial.

17–050

Wulff, an American litigation lawyer, mediator and mediation advocate considers that "skimping on preparation for a mediation is myopic".[16] He questions "what better quality time" could be spent than in preparing for what will probably be "the most important event of the case". Another US mediator, Jansenson, points out that:

17–051

> "mediations are less formal than arbitrations or hearings, but they require no less preparation. Not only should the client be thoroughly prepared for the mediation, but every statute, case deposition transcript and document supporting the party's position should be brought to the mediation".[17]

Hanger, an Australian barrister and mediator, points out that:

---

[15] The mediator does not ordinarily maintain separate confidences as between the couple, save that special confidentiality rules may in some cases, and in some models, be agreed if the mediator has separate private meetings and/or communications with each party.
[16] See R.W. Wulff, "A Mediation Primer" in J.H. Wilkinson, *Donovan Leisure Newton and Irvine ADR Practice Book* (New York: Wiley Law Publications, 1990), p.124.
[17] D.R. Jansenson, "Representing Your Clients Successfully in Mediation: Guidelines for Litigators" (1995) 1(2) *The NYLitigator*.

> "Although not necessarily as extensive, preparation for a mediation is just as important as preparation for a trial. If the mediation is unsuccessful, experience indicates that most of the preparation is not wasted and is useful by way of trial preparation."[18]

17-052 This preparation is not inconsistent with adopting a problem-solving approach to the issues. There is an "essential tension" between a problem-solving approach that seeks joint gains and a competitive approach that seeks the best outcome for each individual party.

Family cases

17-053 Where the mediator meets the couple without their lawyers, there would not ordinarily need to be any preparation by the lawyer. It is, however, good practice for a party to have preliminary legal advice before attending the initial mediation meeting. Even where mediators offer legal information on an even-handed basis, this is not a substitute for each party being advised individually and specifically as to their legal position and rights.

17-054 Where the lawyer participates in the process at any stage, it will clearly be beneficial to support the process and the parties' aims. The lawyer should be prepared to explain any legal contentions in a clear and understandable way.

The substantive meeting

17-055 During this phase, the mediator will welcome the parties and the substantive mediation process will commence. In most models, the mediation will start with a joint meeting. In family mediation, joint meetings commonly continue throughout the process, though in some models separate meetings may well take place. In civil and commercial mediation, it is usual for the parties to break into separate meetings and for the mediator to undertake shuttle mediation between them and other permutations of meetings, after the conclusion of the preliminary joint meeting.

17-056 In civil and commercial mediation, the parties will ordinarily be asked to make an oral presentation of their respective cases, but that is not usually done in family mediation.

Presentation of the case in civil commercial mediation

17-057 Ordinarily, the task of presentation will fall to the lawyer where there is one, although it can be powerful for a party to do so, or to add a personal statement following a lawyer's presentation.

17-058 Whereas in adjudicatory processes, the primary object of the presentation is to persuade the adjudicator to make a determination in one's favour, that focus shifts in non-adjudicatory forms of dispute resolution because the decision-making power does not lie with the neutral, but with the other party or parties. The parties

---

[18] I. Hanger QC, "The Role of Lawyers in Mediation": address to the 1st Asian Mediation Association Conference, Singapore, June 2009.

may feel that the mediator has a moral authority and perhaps some evaluative role. However, it is ultimately the other party who has to be persuaded by the presentation.

This shift in approach means that the presenter, while addressing the mediator, must present the argument in such a way that it is persuasive but not aggressively combative or provocative. The aim is not only to persuade the mediator of the rightness of the case, but also to explain one's views to the other party so as to create a climate for negotiations in which the other party will consider making reasonable concessions. 17–059

The following practical observations may be helpful in formulating a presentation strategy: 17–060

- An aggressive approach could be counter-productive in mediation, where the parties are going to have to arrive at their own resolution. This does not mean that the strength of a party's views and feelings should not be made clear. Rather, that there must be an awareness of the effect that the presentation can have on the other parties. The object of the exercise is persuasion rather than belligerence, and exacerbating antagonism by the content, manner or style of presentation is unlikely to have a beneficial effect on the process that will follow.
- A presentation is more likely to influence the other party if based on a version of the case which that party can recognise, confronting the issues in an understandable context, rather than one perceived to be misrepresented. Differences may arise because of good faith disagreements, recollections or perceptions; different technical opinions; values or ideas of fairness which do not accord with one another; miscommunications and misunderstandings. Presentations can be made in a context that allows and helps the parties to appreciate the possible validity of conflicting viewpoints.
- Consideration may be given to ways of supporting or enhancing the presentation, where appropriate, for example, by reference to documents. Although in most mediations presentations will just be by way of summary of the case, technical devices may be used, such as flip charts, audio-visual devices or slides.
- Time-limits agreed between the parties or stipulated by the neutral should be observed as closely as possible, and time used efficiently and effectively.
- It is unusual to have responses following the initial presentation. Lawyers should not expect the right of response unless there is some special reason to do so. Usually there will be an opportunity to deal in the separate meetings with any matters raised.

Presentations in family mediation

There is not usually a presentation in family mediation. It is often said to be "future focused" so that the history of issues and grievances is not primarily addressed. However, it is sometimes necessary to look at past issues, because they may contain the reasons for present positions and attitudes. Indeed, there is a view that it is essential to allow the past its space in working out the future. Relevant past issues are likely to emerge during the course of the mediation. 17–061

17–062　In some situations and models, the parties' lawyers may attend a mediation meeting after the parties have had some sessions. In such event, the lawyers may sometimes be asked to give a brief outline of the position, as they see it. This would require the lawyer to balance two competing priorities. The one is to present the client's case clearly. The other is to avoid being unnecessarily contentious, which may not help the negotiating process.

Providing information

17–063　In civil and commercial mediation, relevant information is provided at the outset, through the written statement and the bundle of documents. The mediator may obtain supplementary information as the process develops. In family mediation, information is provided at different stages. Some is obtained in the preliminary telephone conversations, some through the preliminary information form, some through more detailed financial forms, and some through documents provided, questions asked and developments that take place during the substantive mediation.

Negotiating and communicating during the mediation

17–064　One of the strengths of mediation is that it lends itself to problem-solving approaches rather than the purely competitive approaches which so often typify adversarial proceedings.[19] The intercession of an impartial third party makes this more possible.[20]

17–065　However, even in mediation, there may not always be scope for a problem-solving approach, and in any event, for many negotiators the tendency will be to negotiate in the most familiar way: the competitive approach. Problem-solving and competitive approaches are likely to co-exist within any ADR process, requiring a lawyer to be able to shift between them as necessary.

17–066　The following may be helpful in conducting negotiations and communications in mediation:

- Even if using a competitive negotiating method, lawyers should be aware of the problem-solving approach and should be willing to consider constructively with their clients any approaches that enable all parties to gain an advantage from a suggested outcome.
- Proposed settlement proposals should be examined from the vantage point of all parties. What is the incentive to the other party to accept the proposals? Can anything be added or varied to make the offer more acceptable without eroding any material aspect? Is there any outcome that could bring gains to all parties? Are there any beneficial side-effects to resolving the dispute which could be incorporated into the proposals, such

---

[19] See Ch.4 "Negotiation".
[20] E. de Bono, *Conflicts: A Better Way to Resolve Them* (Harmondsworth: Penguin, 1986) considers that certain functions, relating to "the design of an outcome" must be carried out by a third party. This is because he considers that the parties themselves, for practical reasons and flowing from the logic of their maintenance of opposing positions, generally cannot do so themselves.

- as the continuation or extension of an existing business relationship? A constructive and creative approach does not need to be at the expense of the client's best interests.
- "Bottom lines" or "final offers" are usually unhelpful unless these are genuinely meant. The problem about taking positions is that it is often very difficult to move from them, and parties will not wish to lose face or to feel discredited by having to extricate themselves from a position that was previously reflected as immovable. Positional bargaining does not necessarily produce the best results, and parties may prefer in many cases to engage in principled negotiation aiming for a fair outcome using objective criteria.[21]
- Confidential separate meetings provide a good opportunity to test settlement ideas and options in discussion with the mediator, without being committed to developing them. The mediator may be able to indicate whether a particular line of thought is helpful or not, or whether intended proposals might more effectively be structured in an alternative way. Negotiators should use this resource to maximum effect.
- Courtesy, respect for opposing views even while disagreeing firmly with them, a willingness where appropriate to acknowledge the correctness of an opposing position and perhaps to shift one's own position, and the establishment of common ground can be of positive assistance in creating the climate for progress in mediation.
- An important element in successful negotiation is for the lawyer to have an understanding of and respect for his or her client's position, concerns and interests and for the client to trust the lawyer sufficiently to appreciate that the lawyer may sometimes need to give advice which the client will find unwelcome. That relationship can be as important for lawyers as their negotiating skills. The lawyer will need to prepare for the mediation by analysing the case, understanding its strengths and weaknesses and expressing a frank and honest opinion to the client. Supporting the client does not involve taking an inappropriately optimistic view of the position, but rather identifying with the client's aims and concerns and trying to achieve the best result realistically consistent with these.

17–067 The mediator's availability can assist the lawyer in the task of helping the client to assess the position realistically. Where the client has reservations about the lawyer's advice, or perhaps where the lawyer is tentative about views that the client may not be happy to hear, the lawyer may raise such issues with the mediator in caucus in order to get the mediator's reactions to these. This may allow both the lawyer and the client an opportunity to consider and discuss the issue, with the benefit of the mediator's comments where the mediator is willing to give these.

17–068 While bearing these matters in mind, negotiators will be guided by their own experience, instincts and instructions to conduct effective negotiations. They will probe, make judgements about the way in which their clients' proposals are made

---

[21] See R. Fisher, and W. Ury, *Getting to Yes: Negotiating Agreement Without Giving In* (Boston: Houghton Mifflin, 1981) and the discussion about this work and the various theories of negotiations in Ch.4.

and the timing of them, draw conclusions from what is said to them and will react as they then consider proper. They will, in short, draw on all the skills which they have, but will be aware that there are additional benefits that can be achieved by working flexibly and creatively.

Strategies

17–069 Negotiators in the traditional process are likely to have a negotiating strategy of some kind, even if informal. They will know what their clients' aspirations are, what the other side's expectations are likely to be, how they envisage movement might proceed, at what point they will call off discussions and generally at what pace and in what direction they wish to move. The situation is similar in mediation negotiations, though the mediator's role and function may change the dynamic of negotiations.

17–070 The following points arise for consideration:

- Is it possible that either side is strategically using the mediation to achieve some gain that would not have been available in the traditional process? If, for example, the mediation may be used to delay litigation, terms may have to be agreed, such as fixing a time-limit or arranging that court proceedings will run parallel to the mediation. Or if the concern is that a party may only be using mediation to establish how the case will be argued at the trial and not to engage in good faith negotiations, then this may affect the way in which the case is presented; and mediation may be discontinued if there are no signs of bona fide movement.
- The mediator may invite the parties to indicate confidentially their proposals and parameters for negotiation. Should the party tell the mediator his outer limits right away, even if restricting the mediator's authority to use that data? Or should the party rather hold back, aiming for the best outcome and only easing into improved offers when pressed by the mediator? There are no absolute answers to these questions. In practice, it is unlikely that parties will make their best offers initially. A natural inclination must exist to test the process and the possibilities. If, however, in the judgment of the party and the lawyer, that party's best interest will be served by confidentially telling the mediator the best offer right at the outset, even if controlling the pace at which that is released to the other side, that would be a matter of individual judgment. Negotiations can develop their own dynamic, with new ideas emerging as time passes; so it would be understandable if parties moved slowly forward, waiting to see how far they needed to go, where time and other factors permitted.
- Each party and lawyer may need to consider to what extent the client should play a leading role in the mediation and to what extent it is to be lawyer led. This decision will depend at least in part on the client's skill as a negotiator, the nature of the issues, and the relationship between lawyer and client. On any version, close teamwork and collaboration are needed.
- The decision whether to settle on terms arrived at in mediation is the same as it would be in bilateral negotiations and will, as in all such situations, involve assessing the client's best and worst alternatives to a negotiated

outcome and analysing the client's realistic prospects of success in litigation and the costs and outcome risks.

The lawyer's role during substantive family mediation

Family mediation very largely takes place with the couple themselves, without direct lawyer participation. That can feel uncomfortable for some lawyers. They may feel anxious on their client's behalf, especially if the client is perceived as vulnerable and the other party as strong or manipulative. 17–071

The following principles are relevant to the representation of clients in family mediation: 17–072

- Family mediation involves an element of personal empowerment of the parties by working directly with them. Lawyers should respect this and allow their clients to formulate their own thoughts how to resolve their issues, as far as they may wish and be able to do so.
- On the other hand, clients may not have chosen mediation to empower themselves, but rather to achieve the resolution of their issues in a fair, effective and expeditious way. They may wish to be supported by their lawyers through the process.
- Lawyers should therefore be available to advise and support their clients as required through the mediation process. Some clients may wish to discuss matters between every meeting, and get guidance as it progresses. Others may prefer to consult their solicitors only as specific issues arise.
- There are some points at which the lawyer should be consulted. The first might be for general advice before embarking on mediation. The next important stage is usually the formulation of the financial disclosure form, especially if their financial circumstances are at all complex.[22] Other stages may arise as specific issues are addressed, and certainly when settlement terms are being formulated.
- If lawyers believe that the process is prejudicing their client in any way, then they should be explicit in advising their client accordingly. Some way may need to be found to rectify the problem so that the process can be more effective and fair. In the final analysis, they may need to suggest to the client that the process is inappropriate and should be ended.

Lawyers may be uncertain whether it is proper for them to communicate with the mediator while a family mediation is pending. This is not surprising, since some family mediators do not encourage communications from lawyers. If there is any aspect that a lawyer feels should be mentioned, it may be preferable for the client personally to do so. If, however, the issue feels too sensitive or the client feels unable to raise it, then it may well be necessary for the lawyer to communicate with the mediator direct. It must though be borne in mind that this will be on a non-confidential basis, and that any such communications will be 17–073

---

[22] In England, a complex form, Form E Financial Statement, is used. Lawyers should probably assist their clients in completing this form especially where finances are complex or substantial.

17-074 It should be noted that the concept of separate confidences between the mediator and the parties is gradually increasing in use and availability, with two of the FMC's six organisational members supporting it and a third member having specifically authorised it in the past.[23] In this context, more direct lawyer involvement is envisaged in the process generally, including for example in assisting with preparation of financial disclosure and in attending some sessions, particularly where separate confidential meetings take place, though this is certainly not essential.

shared with the other party. An exception would be if this was done pursuant to an agreement that the mediator could have separate and confidential communications with each party.

Drafting and formalising

17-075 If total or partial resolution is achieved, some record of the terms will have to be prepared. In civil and commercial mediation, it is generally regarded as a primary aspiration for a binding settlement agreement to be signed before the parties leave the meeting. In family mediation, it is usual for the mediator to prepare a without prejudice memorandum of the terms after the meeting, and to send it on to the parties for consideration. They would not ordinarily be bound until having had the opportunity of taking independent legal advice on the proposed terms.

17-076 The drafting of the settlement agreement in civil and commercial mediation will usually be the responsibility of the parties or their lawyers. The mediator may have a supporting role, perhaps providing notes and comments, and checking drafts as they are prepared.

17-077 The settlement agreement must be drafted with care and precision, even if informal: the parties will not want any later arguments or misunderstandings about the settlement terms.

17-078 The following checklist may be helpful to a lawyer drafting civil-commercial settlement terms:

- Are the terms to be binding immediately? If not, when and under what circumstances do they become binding?
- Are the terms unconditional? If not, what specific and unambiguous conditions are to apply?
- Are all dates, periods, amounts, methods of calculation and other directions and formulae clear, specific and unambiguous?
- Does the agreement need to specify the consequences of non-compliance?
- What format is appropriate for the settlement agreement? A formal document, heads of agreement, a letter of agreement, a deed or some other?

---

[23] The ADR Group and Resolution have both provided training in this model, and the Law Society's Code of Practice for Family Mediation, 2nd edn (1999) provided specifically at para.5.7.2 for mediators to have an option to "maintain separate confidences: provided that if separate confidences are to be maintained, they must not include any material fact which would be open if discussed in a joint meeting." This was dropped when the Law Society adopted the FMC Code, but the principle was not reversed and as this 4th edition goes to press, the Family Mediators Association will be discussing and reviewing standards and models at its forthcoming conference.

THE SUBSTANTIVE MEDIATION PHASE

- Do the parties envisage that a further and more comprehensive document will be entered into later? In such event, what is the status of the document meanwhile being entered into? What will the effect be if no such further document is executed?
- Is an order of the court required? If so, are its terms to be drafted and agreed immediately or will this be done later, and with what consequences if there is a later problem in relation to the drafting and finalising? Who will deal with the formalities of getting the order made?
- If court proceedings are pending, is the agreement clear as to what is to happen with such proceedings? Are they to be discontinued? Is there any agreement as to costs?
- Are there any special requirements as to confidentiality of the settlement terms?
- Are there any aspects that involve a neutral third-party role after execution of the agreement, such as acting as a stakeholder? Are documents to be held in escrow or items to be retained pending completion? Is there to be any supervision by the mediator?
- Does the agreement need to specify which country's laws are to apply to the construction of the settlement agreement? Do the parties wish to submit to the jurisdiction of any court or provide for arbitration or any other form of adjudication if any further disagreement arises? Or for further mediation?
- Will the parties be executing the agreement in personal or representative capacities? In the latter event, do the signatories have the necessary authority?

17–079   The role of the lawyer in finalising and formalising any settlement arrived at in mediation is similar to the role where the parties have arrived at an agreement following without prejudice bilateral negotiations. However, the mediator can add a significant resource in helping with the drafting and in overcoming any obstacles to finalisation.

Vetting family mediation proposals

17–080   Parties will ordinarily be given the opportunity before finalising any agreement to take independent advice from their solicitors about the proposed terms. For this reason, agreements as such are not reached in family mediation (in England and Wales in any event), but rather mutually acceptable proposals are formulated, which are subject to independent advice.

17–081   To enable parties to obtain such advice, the mediator will usually prepare two summaries: an open statement of financial particulars (where appropriate) with relevant supporting documents, and a privileged summary of settlement proposals, commonly known as a Memorandum of Understanding.

17–082   Where a lawyer has had little or no role during the mediation process, it may be challenging and difficult to endorse the settlement terms without the benefit of working through the process and understanding the reasons for the terms having been arrived at, albeit that the mediation summary may help to explain these reasons. The lawyer has responsibility and might be liable in negligence if

17–083 allowing the client to enter into disadvantageous terms; yet the lawyer could be regarded as obstructive advising against agreeing such terms.

The lawyer's duty is to advise fairly and effectively on the proposed terms and to draw attention to any deficiencies. The client will often be able to explain why certain terms were accepted, and the lawyer will no doubt wish to respect decisions that are well considered. There are, after all, many reasons for agreeing terms that may be perceived as less than ideal, and many parties have found themselves doing so "at the doors of the court". A client may choose to accept terms in the face of advice that better terms might be achieved in court. Lawyers may wish to protect against negligence claims by recording their advice in writing, as they would do in similar circumstances in traditional negotiations.

17–084 Mediators may invite parties to return to mediation for further discussion if either lawyer considers the proposals inappropriate. Some will also invite the lawyers to attend, if that is thought to be helpful. Having lawyers vet proposed terms is the safeguard built into the family mediation process, and lawyers should not shy away from challenging terms where they consider them to be inappropriate. Equally, they should where appropriate support clients who have gone through an arduous process and who have arrived at terms that they wish to accept.

THE POST-MEDIATION PHASE

17–085 Even if the matter is resolved in the mediation, there is scope for the mediator to have a continuing role in two respects. The first relates to the mediator's role in implementing any settlement terms, the other relates to a possible role thereafter in appropriate circumstances.

17–086 The settlement agreement can, if required, provide for the mediator to facilitate any aspect of implementation should any problems arise during that phase. In addition, there may be other ways in which the mediator, or any mediation organisation concerned, may have a role. For example, the mediator or organisation may act as a stakeholder in relation to funds to be released on agreed terms, or may hold documents in escrow pending the implementation of the settlement. An example of the latter role was a term of the settlement agreement that confidential documents held by a party were lodged with the mediation organisation, on terms that they were to be destroyed only when the terms of settlement had been fully implemented.

17–087 It is possible for the mediator to be given a future role under the terms of settlement. For example, the terms of an agreement on divorce might include future financial reviews or review of arrangements for children, which could provide for these matters to be dealt with by negotiated agreement, failing which, by mediation. Commercial arrangements may similarly envisage a future review with a backstop appointment of the mediator to help facilitate any problems that may arise if bilateral negotiations are not successful.

17–088 If the mediator has worked successfully with the parties and has established trust and a good understanding and working relationship with them, and if the

THE POST-MEDIATION PHASE

settlement terms provide for any possibility of their needing any further facilitation of issues in the future, it does seem sensible to build an option for this into the agreement where appropriate.

CHAPTER 18

Ombudsman

THE OMBUDSMAN[1] CONCEPT

As various forms of dispute resolution alternative to traditional adversarial processes continue to gain traction in the UK and elsewhere, one such procedure that has attracted huge support, though not without some criticism as well, is the ombudsman institution—or enterprise.[2] Referrals to ombudsmen now outstrip all other forms of ADR. 18–001

For example during the third quarter of the financial year 2017/2018 the UK's Financial Ombudsman Service (FOS) handled 147,775 enquiries, taking on 80,958 new cases.[3] The Parliamentary and Health Service Ombudsman received 10,558 enquiries between April and June 2017, completing 1,184 investigations[4]; and during 2016–2017 the Local Government and Social Care Ombudsman received 16,863 complaints and upheld 54 per cent of them. 18–002

The ombudsman institution combines a number of features. It addresses public grievances, promotes good administration and provides "a 'third way' between the courts and various forms of alternative dispute resolution".[5] 18–003

---

[1] There are questions as to whether the term "ombudsman" is discriminatory and should be "ombudsperson". This issue was addressed in a Research and Information Service Briefing Paper written in June 2015 by Tim Moore for the Northern Ireland Assembly entitled "Ombudsman—Gender Neutral?" It considered the etymology and usage of the word and noted that the word "Ombudsman" is Scandinavian and gender-neutral in origin. (See: *http://www.niassembly.gov.uk/globalassets/documents/raise/publications/2015/ofmdfm/8115.pdf* [accessed 10 June 2018]). There are however other views. For example, in an online Ombuds Research article in June 2015 entitled "'Manning' the ombuds barricades", Margaret Doyle undertook an analysis and questioned the conclusions reached about the etymology. She considered other alternatives such as "ombud/s" and "ombudsperson" and invited a wider conversation about this subject. (See: *https://ombudsresearch.org.uk/2015/06/09/manning-the-ombuds-barricades/* [accessed 10 June 2018]).

[2] The concept of the ombudsman as an "enterprise" was suggested by Trevor Buck, Richard Kirkham and Brian Thompson in the title and content of their book, *The Ombudsman Enterprise and Administrative Justice* (Routledge, 2010), in which they explain that an enterprise is defined as "a project or undertaking, especially a bold one" *(OED)*—and that this reflects the proactive approach adopted by the ombudsman community in the UK in providing a significant role in the delivery of public services and in the country's constitutional arrangements.

[3] See *http://www.financial-ombudsman.org.uk/publications/ombudsman-news/143/143-ombudsman-focus-complaints-statistic.html* [accessed 10 June 2018].

[4] See *https://www.ombudsman.org.uk/about-us/corporate-information/how-we-are-performing/performance-statistics/july-2017-performance-statistics* [accessed 10 June 2018].

[5] As described by Nick O'Brien and Mary Seneviratne in *Ombudsmen at the Crossroads: The Legal Services Ombudsman, Dispute Resolution and Democratic Accountability* (Palgrave Macmillan, 2017).

The ombudsman's role and function

18-004 An ombudsman is an independent person whose primary role in the public sector is to deal with public complaints against administrative injustice and maladministration, with the power to investigate, criticise and make issues public. Although having no power to alter a decision when a complaint is found to be justified, he or she may persuade the relevant department or authority to alter its decision or to pay compensation to the complainant. The ombudsman has become an important part of the administrative justice system in the UK and elsewhere. The ombudsman's role is also an accepted and significant form of ADR, which includes investigative and in some cases determinative and mediatory functions, as well as using various forms of ADR as part of its operations.[6]

18-005 Although the ombudsman institution is predominantly in the public sector, it is also found in the private sector, including for example the Legal Ombudsman and the Financial Ombudsman Service, and a national private sector ombudsman scheme, Ombudsman Services.[7] However, the distinction between these sectors is not considered to be helpful as there is a cross-fertilisation of practice and ideas.

18-006 The office of ombudsman was originally established in Sweden early in the nineteenth century and from there moved to various other countries in Scandinavia, New Zealand, Australia, Germany, parts of the US and elsewhere. In the UK the first ombudsman was appointed under the Parliamentary Commissioner Act 1967, with the title of Parliamentary Commissioner for Administration, with lesser powers than the ombudsman under the Swedish system. This has become the Parliamentary and Health Service Ombudsman (PHSO), which describes its service to the public as follows:

> "We make final decisions on complaints that have not been resolved by the NHS in England and UK government departments and other UK public organisations .... We look into complaints where someone believes there has been injustice or hardship because an organisation has not acted properly or has given a poor service and not put things right."[8]

The range of ombudsman institutions[9]

18-007 The ombudsman concept has been adopted in over 70 countries. In the UK there is a range of ombudsman services, which include the following (in addition to the PHSO mentioned above):

- Agencies dealing with complaints relating to departments of the UK's devolved administrations, such as the Scottish Public Services Ombudsman, the Northern Ireland Ombudsman and the Public Services Ombudsman for Wales.
- The Legal Ombudsman (LeO), established in 2010 pursuant to the Legal Services Act 2007, replaced the Legal Services Ombudsman—a role that had been established under the Courts and Legal Services Act 1990. The

---

[6] See Buck, Kirkham and Thompson, *The Ombudsman Enterprise and Administrative Justice*, fn.2.
[7] See *https://www.ombudsman-services.org/* [accessed 10 June 2018] and see below at para.18-008.
[8] See *https://www.ombudsman.org.uk/about-us/what-we-do* [accessed May 2018].
[9] This list is not comprehensive, but merely reflects a cross-section of some of the available services.

THE OMBUDSMAN CONCEPT

LeO deals with public complaints about legal services covering all legal service providers. It describes its job as "look[ing] at complaints about service providers in a fair and independent way."[10]

- The Financial Ombudsman Service "set up by Parliament to resolve individual complaints between financial businesses and their customers...looks into problems involving most types of money matters."[11]
- The Housing Ombudsman ensures the fair and impartial resolution of housing disputes, helping landlords and tenants to resolve disagreements.[12]
- The Property Ombudsman "has been providing consumers and property agents with an alternative dispute resolution service since 1990."[13]
- The Waterways Ombudsman scheme provides impartial and independent dispute resolution for unresolved complaints of injustice suffered as a result of maladministration or unfair treatment by the Canal & River Trust or its subsidiaries.[14]
- The Prisons and Probation Ombudsman investigates complaints made by prisoners, young people in detention, offenders under probation or supervision and immigration detainees, and investigates deaths in prison or detention and of immigration detainees.[15]

The second edition of this book observed that there might be scope for extending the ombudsman's role in the private business sector, suggesting that businesses could appoint ombudsmen to investigate consumer complaints, or particular industries could appoint them to investigate a range of matters from complaints about quality to procedural grievances. Since then private companies including The Ombudsman Service Limited (Ombudsman Services), a not-for-profit company limited by guarantee, have been established providing ombudsman services.[16] The sectors they cover include a wide range of communication, energy and property companies, as well as others such as copyright licensing and home improvement. Ombudsman Services also has an independent reviewer who considers complaints about the standard of service provided by the Solicitors Regulation Authority and about companies that are members of UK Finance, covering various finance, banking, markets and other services. **18–008**

The Retail Ombudsman was a service provided by another not-for-profit company, Consumer Dispute Resolution Limited (CDRL), which has been converted to a non-ombudsman service RetailADR providing complaints-handling ADR services apparently modelled on the ombudsman process. They similarly deal on a non-ombudsman basis with complaints relating to the aviation industry (AviationADR), utility providers (UtilitiesADR) and the communications industry (CommsADR).[17] **18–009**

The Ombudsman Association, formerly called the British and Irish Ombudsman Association, is a professional association for ombudsmen and complaint **18–010**

---

[10] See *http://www.legalombudsman.org.uk/helping-the-public/* [accessed 10 June 2018].
[11] See *http://www.financial-ombudsman.org.uk/* [accessed 10 June 2018].
[12] See *http://www.housing-ombudsman.org.uk/* [accessed 10 June 2018].
[13] See *https://www.tpos.co.uk/about-us* [accessed 10 June 2018].
[14] See *http://www.waterways-ombudsman.org/* [accessed 10 June 2018].
[15] See *https://www.ppo.gov.uk/* [accessed 10 June 2018].
[16] See *https://www.ombudsman-services.org/* [accessed 10 June 2018].
[17] See *https://www.cdrl.org.uk/about-us/* [accessed 10 June 2018].

handlers, their staff and others interested in the work of independent complaint resolution. It has as its central objectives the supporting and promotion of an effective system of complaint handling and redress and encouraging, developing and protecting the role of an ombudsman in both the public and private sectors as the "best practice" model for resolving complaints.[18]

18–011 There is also an Office of the European Ombudsman, established in 1995, which considers complaints about maladministration in EU institutions, bodies and agencies. It also conducts enquiries on its own initiative. Vogiatzis considers that this ombudsman role has contributed to the EU's democratisation, transparency and accountability.[19]

HOW THE OMBUDSMAN OPERATES

Ombudsman procedures

18–012 Procedures and policies vary between the different ombudsmen. However, all tend to commence with the receipt of a formal complaint lodged with them, alleging some administrative fault or shortcoming and/or some failure to provide a proper service. The ombudsman service will generally need to be satisfied that the complaint falls within their remit and jurisdiction and that an individual (or in some cases a group of individuals) has suffered injustice, hardship or financial loss because of the action or lack of action complained of.

18–013 A complaint to the ombudsman should only be made after the organisation complained of has been afforded an opportunity to address the issue through its own complaints process. Submitting a complaint before that will ordinarily be considered premature.

18–014 Even where these preliminary matters are complied with, certain kinds of complaints would not ordinarily be dealt with by the ombudsman. These might for example include complaints which are pending in the courts, or which could be taken to a court or tribunal; complaints which relate to matters earlier than a prescribed period; or disputes relating to the supply of goods or services.

18–015 Once an ombudsman is satisfied that a complaint falls properly within his or her remit, it may be dealt with immediately if the facts are not in issue and the evidence is clear that the complaint should be upheld, otherwise it will need to be investigated. Procedures for investigation vary. The public service ombudsmen have powers similar to those of a High Court judge with regard to the attendance and examination of witnesses and the production of documents.

18–016 The Legal Ombudsman arranges to investigate complaints against solicitors, barristers, registered European lawyers, trade mark attorneys and others carrying out legal services and the investigator will form an independent view about what happened. Attempts will then be made to find an agreed resolution. If agreement is not possible, the investigator will write a report that may propose a remedy or action the service provider should take. This may take the form of a Preliminary Decision, which the parties may accept to resolve the issues. If the Preliminary

---

[18] See *http://www.ombudsmanassociation.org/index.php* [accessed 10 June 2018].
[19] Nikos Vogiatzis, *The European Ombudsman and Good Administration in the European Union* (Palgrave Macmillan, 2018).

Decision is not accepted by the parties, the ombudsman may be required to make a formal decision, which is final and binding.

18–017 The UK's Financial Ombudsman Service (FOS) will initially check that a complaint has been referred to the relevant business in case direct resolution may be possible. If direct resolution is not possible, a case handler will be appointed to consider it. If the complaint falls outside the scope of the ombudsman's function, it will be dismissed. Otherwise the complaint will be further investigated. The case handler will give a view of the case and proposals for resolution that are considered fair and reasonable in the circumstances. Informal attempts may be made to reach a resolution, including the use of mediation. If these do not result in agreement, the ombudsman may become directly involved, carrying out an independent review before making a final decision. If the consumer accepts the ombudsman's decision, it is binding on the business; if not, the consumer is free to take court proceedings against the business.

18–018 The FOS's 2014–2015 annual review reflected that "405,202 cases [were] resolved by our adjudicators through mediation, recommended settlements and adjudications".[20] In Ireland, it was reported that "the vast majority of complaints to the Financial Services Ombudsman [in 2017] were resolved through mediation."[21] Of 3,867 complaints closed in 2017, a total of 2,370—more than 60 per cent—were resolved using mediation.

18–019 These are examples of procedures adopted by ombudsmen. Specific procedures should be checked with each individual ombudsman.

18–020 Buck, Kirkham and Thompson refer to the benefits of ADR and the informal processes embodied in the ombudsman concept, including the fact that it provides a fitting forum in accordance with the principles of proportionate and appropriate dispute resolution, providing informality, accessibility, flexibility and cost-effectiveness.[22] In contrast, court procedures and rigorous formality are often deemed disproportionate to the kind of complaints commonly brought and the potential remedies available.

Remedies

18–021 Ombudsmen will ordinarily furnish reports outlining their decisions and the actions that they propose should be taken.

18–022 Remedies vary according to the provisions applicable to each individual scheme. They may include requiring a respondent organisation or authority to do any of the following:

- to apologise;
- to provide better facilities or procedures, as appropriate;
- to remedy a problem or repay any money received;
- to pay compensation of a specified or maximum amount for loss suffered;
- to pay interest on that compensation;

---

[20] See *http://www.financial-ombudsman.org/publications/ar15/index.html#a2*.
[21] Irish Legal News. See: *http://www.irishlegal.com/11981/vast-majority-complaints-financial-ombudsman-resolved-mediation/* [accessed 10 June 2018].
[22] Buck, Kirkham and Thompson, *The Ombudsman Enterprise and Administrative Justice* (2011), fn.2, pp.8, 40, 223 and 226.

- to ensure (and pay for) putting right any specified error, omission or other deficiency;
- to take (and pay for) any specified action in the interests of the complainant;
- to pay a specified amount for costs the complainant incurred in pursuing the complaint.

ONLINE AND COMMUNICATION OMBUDSMEN AND ADJUDICATORS

18–023   Inevitably, there will be an increasing need for dispute resolution services in relation to issues arising online, and for services to be provided online and/or electronically.[23] Ombudsmen and complaints mechanisms have been developing and some examples are outlined below.

18–024   An early development, the Online Ombuds Office was established in the US in 1996, and established as the Center for Information Technology and Dispute Resolution at the University of Massachusetts in 1997. The Online Ombuds Office no longer functions as such, though the Center continues to operate.

18–025   Although the idea of a specific UK Internet Ombudsman has occasionally been floated,[24] this has not yet been adopted (at the time of publication of this 4th edition of this work) and online complaints processes have been linked together with communications complaints generally, and dealt with through Ofcom.

18–026   Ofcom is the UK's communications regulator, covering aspects including radio, television, fixed-line phones, mobiles and postal services. It has stipulated that communications providers offering services to individuals and small businesses (up to 10 employees) must be members of an ADR Scheme; and has authorised two ADR schemes that provide complaints resolution services in relation to the sector that it covers.

18–027   The two schemes authorised by Ofcom, and which operate independently of Ofcom and of the communications providers, are CISAS (the Communications and Internet Services Adjudication Scheme), operated by CEDR (the Centre for Effective Dispute Resolution); and a scheme operated by Ombudsman Services in its communications sector. Individual service providers will generally belong to one or the other of these two schemes, and customers with complaints will need to direct these to whichever scheme their communications provider belongs to.

18–028   These schemes can order the service provider to fix the problem, make a payment or take other practical steps. Their decision is final and binding on the provider, but not on the consumer who is free to decide whether to accept the decision or to seek a remedy elsewhere.

18–029   The Internet Services Providers' Association (ISPA UK) is the UK's Trade Association for providers of internet services. Membership is voluntary but the companies who choose to become members of ISPA agree to abide by the ISPA

---

[23] See Ch.20.
[24] For example in an article in *The Guardian* in August 2017 entitled "UK considers internet ombudsman to deal with abuse complaints". See: *https://www.theguardian.com/technology/2017/aug/22/uk-considers-internet-ombudsman-to-deal-with-abuse-complaints* [accessed May 2018].

UK Code. Under the Code, all ISPA members are required to belong to an ADR scheme approved by ISPA Council: at the time of publication, both CISAS and Ombudsman Services are the approved schemes.[25]

EU DIRECTIVE ON CONSUMER ADR: IMPLICATIONS FOR OMBUDSMEN

In 2013 the European Union published a directive requiring member states to make provision by June 2015 for consumer disputes to be dealt with through ADR processes.[26] The objective was to ensure that consumers would have recourse to an ADR scheme in the event of any complaint about goods or services not being resolved to their satisfaction. In particular, the aim was to provide access to "simple, efficient, fast and low-cost ways of resolving domestic and cross-border disputes which arise from sales or service contracts".[27] 18–030

The directive also referred to the variable quality levels of available ADR procedures, and observed that disparities in ADR coverage, quality and awareness in Member States constituted a barrier to the internal market.[28] These concerns and the wish to improve the handling of cross-border disputes to increase confidence in the internal market were motivating factors for the directive. 18–031

The UK gave effect to the directive by way of the Alternative Dispute Resolution for Consumer Disputes (Competent Authorities and Information) Regulations 2015, as amended by The Alternative Dispute Resolution for Consumer Disputes (Amendment) Regulations 2015, which came into full effect in January 2016.[29] Among its other provisions, these Regulations required all traders to provide information about ADR whenever there was an unresolved complaint relating to a sales or service contract. ADR providers (called "ADR entities" in the regulations) in turn are obliged to seek accreditation from a competent authority, such as the Chartered Trading Standards Institute, which will monitor their performance. 18–032

ADR entities must meet specified requirements which include maintaining an up-to-date website and providing relevant information about its ADR procedures; providing expertise, independence and impartiality; ensuring that it does not have 18–033

---

[25] ISPA Code of Practice para.8.2. See *https://www.ispa.org.uk/about-us/ispa-code-of-practice/* [accessed 10 June 2018].

[26] Directive 2013/11/EU of the European Parliament and of the Council of 21 May 2013 on alternative dispute resolution for consumer disputes and amending Regulation (EC) No.2006/2004 and Directive 2009/22/EC (Directive on consumer ADR). For a full transcript, see: *https://eur-lex.europa.eu/legal-content/EN/TXT/?uri=celex%3A32013L0011* [accessed 10 June 2018]. See Ch.20, paras 20–027 to 20–031 for further discussion of the European Directive on Consumer Alternative Dispute Resolution, the Alternative Dispute Resolution for Consumer Disputes (Amendment) Regulations 2015, the Statutory Instruments incorporating the EU Directive into UK law, and in particular the aspects relating to the resolution of online disputes.

[27] Directive, see fn.26—preamble para.(4).

[28] Directive, see fn.26—preamble paras (5) and (6).

[29] Respectively Statutory Instrument 2015 No.542 and 2015 No.1392 Consumer Protection.

any conflicts of interest; being transparent, effective and fair; and ensuring the legality of any proposed solution and that it does not deprive the consumer of his or her rights.[30]

18-034 The EU directive does not specifically refer to ombudsmen, but covers their activities by implication. The UK regulations refer to ADR entities, which include ombudsmen, in some cases quite specifically.[31] However, the principles and requirements of the regulations cover the activities carried out by ombudsmen, irrespective of their being named as such or not. The effect has been to bring the ombudsman process directly within the ambit of the EU directive and the corresponding regulations. Services provided by ombudsmen are covered by and subject to those regulations.

OMBUDSMAN DEVELOPMENTS, CHALLENGES AND CRITICISMS

18-035 Walter Merricks, erstwhile Chair of the British and Irish Ombudsman Association (now the Ombudsman Association) and founding chief ombudsman of the Financial Ombudsman Service, has observed that whereas ombudsmen were originally seen as quite distinct from the civil justice system with very little cross over between the two, public sector ombudsmen were now dealing with many cases that could equally be dealt with through the civil justice system.[32] This observation continues to be valid.

18-036 There are other processes that can similarly address consumer complaints effectively, whether or not described as ombudsmen, such as consumer conciliation. So, for example, issues arising under the Renewable Energy Consumer Code (RECC) are dealt with by the Independent Conciliation Service (RECC) through CEDR subsidiary IDRS, who describe the conciliation process as "a private and structured form of negotiation between the parties, facilitated by an independent conciliator, who may propose a solution for the parties' consideration in order to reach agreement".[33]

18-037 Ombudsmen do not have unfettered discretion and their decisions are subject to judicial review like any other public body. If their decisions are irrational or unreasonable, they may be set aside. So, for example, in *R (Crawford) v Legal Ombudsman*,[34] the High Court held that the Ombudsman's decision was irrational[35] and that no reasonable person could have made it. Consequently the court quashed the decision.

---

[30] Statutory Instrument 2015 No.542, see fn.29: Sch.3, with reference to reg.9(4): Requirements that a competent authority must be satisfied that the body meets.

[31] Regulation 8 mentions the Pension Ombudsman; and Pt I of Sch.1 mentions the Financial Ombudsman Service and the Office for Legal Complaints, which established the Legal Services Ombudsman.

[32] Presentation to the ADR Committee of the Civil Justice Committee, April 2003.

[33] IDRS: Independent Conciliation Service (RECC) June 2015. See: https://www.cedr.com/idrs/documents/150721142401-independent-conciliation-service-june-2015.pdf [accessed 18 June 2018].

[34] [2014] EWHC 182 (Admin).

[35] The test used was the one set out in *Associated Provincial Picture Houses Ltd v Wednesbury Corp* [1948] 1 KB 223—the test of *Wednesbury* reasonableness.

18-038 Similarly, the High Court quashed a decision of the Legal Ombudsman in *Hariz & Haque Solicitors v Legal Ombudsman & Tahira Quereshi*[36] which it found to be irrational and unlawful. In *R. (on the application of Rosemarine) v Office for Legal Complaints*[37] the Court again applied the Wednesbury test,[38] but in this case did not find the ombudsman's decision to be unreasonable.

18-039 Although there has been substantial support for the ombudsman function, there have also been critics, including activist consumer groups ("ombudsman watchers"). This was considered by Creutzfeldt and Gill in their policy briefing paper for the Economic and Social Research Council (Impact Acceleration Account), *Critics of the Ombudsman System: Understanding and Engaging Online Citizen Activists*.[39] Workshops related to this project identified four broad themes in terms of the groups' critiques of ombudsman schemes, notably lack of accountability, procedural and practice issues, staffing and qualifications and the impact of the system on complainants. The preliminary conclusions of the paper were that there appeared to be interesting and wide ranging critiques, useful for those interested in the ombudsman institution by identifying consumer perspectives and indicating how the ombudsman institution might be misunderstood by the public. Ombudsman schemes were responsive to these critiques in various ways, while there was also perceived to be a risk of privileging unrepresentative opinions by devoting too much resource to engagement.

18-040 In March 2018 the Financial Times newspaper reported growing dissatisfaction with the UK's ombudsman system.[40] It referred to accusations of services serving consumers badly, lacking enforcement powers, confusion in some sectors and a perception that some—funded by their members—might favour those members. The report also referred to an undercover television programme critically investigating the Financial Ombudsman Service[41] and indicated a "general groundswell for reform".

COMPLAINTS ADJUDICATION

18-041 Alongside the ombudsman system, and closely related to it, is the complaints adjudication system. So, for example, the Registrar of Companies has Complaints Adjudicators to investigate complaints about delay, discourtesy and mistakes and the way in which these complaints have been handled at Companies House. There is also an Adjudicator who acts as an unbiased referee looking into complaints about HM Revenue & Customs and the Valuation Office Agency. Certain complaints about the police can be referred to The Independent Office for

---

[36] [2014] EWHC 1539.
[37] [2014] EWHC 601 (Admin).
[38] See para.18-037 and fn.35.
[39] Naomi Creutzfeldt & Chris Gill, December 2015—See: *https://www.law.ox.ac.uk/sites/files/oxlaw/critics-of-the-ombudsmen-system-understanding-and-engaging-online-citizen-activists-dec15.pdf*.
[40] "Complaints put consumer watchdogs on watch"—report by Lindsay Cook, 16 March 2018. See: *https://www.ft.com/content/510b5344-279b-11e8-b27e-cc62a39d57a0* [accessed May 2018].
[41] A Channel 4 Dispatches investigation at the Financial Ombudsman Service found that staff with inadequate training or understanding of financial products and without properly reading case files were judging cases. See: *http://www.channel4.com/info/press/news/investigation-at-fos-finds-staff-with-severe-lack-of-training* [accessed 10 June 2018].

Police Conduct (formerly the Independent Police Complaints Commission), and complaints in relation to television and radio can be referred to the Broadcasting Standards Commission.

18–042 The relationship between the complaints adjudication system and ADR is underscored by the fact that the Independent Complaints Adjudication Service for Ofsted (ICASO), the Office for Standards in Education, Children's Services and Skills, is administered by CEDR, the Centre for Effective Dispute Resolution, described in its website[42] as a leading ADR service provider specialising in the resolution of conflict deadlock, and that CEDR's Director of Consultancy, Graham Massie, is ICASO's Senior Independent Complaints Adjudicator.

---

[42] *https://www.cedr.com/* [accessed 10 June 2018].

CHAPTER 19

Non-Binding Evaluative ADR and Hybrid Processes

INTRODUCTION TO NON-BINDING EVALUATION

In ADR, there is a clear and fundamental distinction between adjudicatory processes, in which thwhich stressed their merely facilitativee neutral makes a binding determination of the issues, and non-binding, consensual processes, in which the neutral has no adjudicatory function but helps the parties arrive at their own resolution. However, in some consensual ADR processes, the neutral may also have an evaluative role, albeit non-binding, and questions arise as to the nature and limits of that role. **19–001**

There are differing views in this regard. Some practitioners contend that a mediator or other neutral in a consensual process should do no more than pure facilitation of the parties' communications and negotiations. However, there are differences as to what constitutes "facilitation", with many practitioners extending the definition of this to include challenging parties' perceptions indirectly through selective questioning, probing, challenging and "reality testing". Some, almost certainly a small minority, at the other end of the spectrum, might express a non-binding view as to the likely outcome in the event of a trial, if the parties require them to do so. In between, there are practitioners who will facilitate communications and negotiations, probe, challenge and test reality as necessary, and in the event of the parties being deadlocked because of competing perceptions of the merits of the dispute, may go further down the road of evaluation, for example by being devil's advocate, or in the privacy of a separate meeting, challenging perceptions by reference to specific case law, factual issues, technical shortcomings or other relevant factors. **19–002**

There are those who consider that any non-binding evaluation in mediation converts the process into a form of adjudication. Patently that is not the case; but there are legitimate issues about the effectiveness and propriety of mediators or other neutrals evaluating the circumstances in which, and the extent to which, they may properly do so, which this chapter will address. **19–003**

This chapter will also review the following forms of non-binding evaluative ADR processes: **19–004**

- evaluation in mediation;
- the mini-trial (Executive Tribunal);
- the summary jury trial;

- Early Neutral Evaluation including case evaluation and Financial Dispute Resolution.

Before examining these processes, it is necessary to consider the motivation for evaluation and what it entails.

REASONS FOR EVALUATING

19–005 Purely facilitative processes may help parties in dispute to communicate and negotiate, to adopt problem-solving rather than competitive approaches, and to explore options for resolution based on interests, needs, concerns and considerations other than just legal rights. For some parties, this will suffice, coupled especially with their own assessments of cost and risk.

19–006 For others, however, that may not be enough. They may find themselves stuck because of differing perceptions as to the strength of their positions. Parties negotiate "in the shadow of the law"[1] and problem-solving and interest-based solutions may not get them round that fundamental impasse.

19–007 It is generally in this kind of situation that the question of possible evaluation may arise. Understandably, third-party neutrals will be wary of doing or saying anything that may compromise their objectivity and impartiality, and will generally resist being drawn on the question as to which party would be likely to succeed in the event of the matter going to trial.

19–008 However, where an evaluative intercession could help break a deadlock, where parties accept that this would be appropriate and beneficial, where this can be done privately and sensitively and without compromising impartiality or ethical boundaries, and where the neutral is suitably qualified to do so, the question must arise as to why it should not be done. Indeed, some processes are set up specifically to provide this kind of guidance to the parties to help them with their decision-making, as in neutral evaluation and some forms of mini-trial—and nobody would question their entitlement to have such third-party guidance in those circumstances.

19–009 ADR has a number of processes that can help parties towards realistic settlement terms by providing non-binding evaluation in some or other form, including combining this with a facilitative process. This includes an evaluative form of mediation.

19–010 Evaluation as part of a consensual and non-binding ADR process has potential advantages and disadvantages, and must be carried out with great care and sensitivity. Subject to these cautions, ADR processes can help parties to evaluate their positions in appropriate cases and situations.

---

[1] As observed by Robert Mnookin and Lewis Kornhauser, "Bargaining in the Shadow of the Law, The Case of Divorce" (1979) 88 Y.L.J. 950, parties know that if they cannot agree in negotiation, they have the ability to obtain redress through the legal process.

WHAT CONSTITUTES NEUTRAL EVALUATION?

Neutral non-binding evaluation may be defined as an "off-the-record" expression of opinion or view by a mediator or other third-party neutral about any aspect of the merits of the issues between parties, whether formulated as a statement, question, non-verbal sign or other indication however conveyed.

19–011

A non-binding evaluation provided neutrally to any party to a dispute is obviously not intended to be partisan, but is invariably likely to support one party more than the other, and this may create some ambiguity about the evaluator's neutrality and impartiality. Can an ADR practitioner express a view on the merits and remain neutral and impartial?

19–012

There seems little doubt that the expression of a view on merits does not of itself erode a practitioner's impartiality. A judge or arbitrator may rule on an interim or final aspect of a case while retaining impartiality. The question is one of subjective perception. If a party forms a view that the ADR practitioner is no longer neutral and impartial, that will inevitably damage the process, possibly fatally.

19–013

Evaluation can take different forms. Its object is not that a practitioner should sit in judgment but rather that the evaluation should help any or all parties to view the case with a better awareness of the merits of certain aspects. In this sense, it may be regarded as itself being facilitative: facilitating a better understanding of the situation. A neutral, non-binding view may be expressed in a number of different ways:

19–014

- It may involve giving all or any of the parties a comprehensive opinion on the respective prospects of success of the parties in the event of the matter going to trial. This is at the far end of the non-binding evaluative spectrum, and is rarely done in the UK,[2] though may sometimes be more readily done in the US.[3]
- It may involve a more qualified, indirect, informal and generalised view as to outcome, given privately, and perhaps hedged with reservations, for example:

    "I can see why you feel strongly on the first three legs of your claim, but I do have some difficulty seeing how you can feel so bullish on the fourth and fifth legs."

    Or:

    "You know that in order to win the lottery you need six numbers. With five numbers you win something, but nowhere near the big prize. It seems to me that

---

[2] Models of UK training tend to emphasise a facilitative approach.
[3] US mediator Jonathan Marks (who was a mediator in the Microsoft anti-trust case) says in "Evaluative Mediation—Oxymoron or Essential Tool" (AMN. LAWYER, May 1996, at 48A) that although he mostly does not have to express a view, in a substantial minority of cases, where skilful questioning and focused devil's advocacy are not sufficient to shift parties from their outcome predictions, "I think the mediator's responsibility is firmly to step over the threshold from facilitator to evaluator. If, but only if, the parties agree (and have so stated in a pre-mediation agreement), I'll tell them (with reasons) what I think a fair settlement is and what I think will happen in court if they don't settle."

you may have five rather than six numbers here. If you think you have the sixth number, perhaps we should adjourn so that you can come back demonstrating that you have the sixth number. If you want to go on with the mediation today, I think that it would be on the basis of five numbers."[4]

- An evaluation may be formal or informal, given to all parties or only to one privately, and may relate only to some part of the case, and not necessarily the outcome if adjudicated. For example, it may relate to a preliminary aspect or to an application for interim relief; or it may cover just one of a number of points in issue that would not decide the whole case.
- Without overtly expressing a view, a neutral may postulate counter-arguments as "devil's advocate" with arguments put forward or expected to be submitted by the other party. This may or may not constitute evaluation: insofar as it indicates an underlying point of view that is intended to influence a party to change his opinion on the merits, it would fall within a broad definition of evaluation.
- Similarly, a neutral may challenge a party's assessment of the merits of his or her case in other ways, for example, by asking probing questions. Some practitioners believe that questioning is a non-directive way of working with parties; but it may be just as directive and just as evaluative. "Have you read the latest case on this point, X v Y?" may be just as evaluative as outlining the principles of that case. There are shades of grey, but practitioners who challenge parties' views on merits by selective questioning may find that they are evaluating.

19–015 There is still a widespread tendency to refer to mediation as being either "facilitative" or "evaluative",[5] but that is not a valid distinction. All mediation is facilitative, whether or not a mediator introduces an element of evaluation into it, unless that evaluation becomes adjudicatory and removes the decision-making power from the parties. Indeed, it is arguable that evaluation enhances the parties' decision-making and is a facilitative function.

19–016 Some ADR practitioners who think that they are purely facilitative may find that they are actually introducing an element of evaluation into their work, albeit subtly and often unwittingly.[6]

19–017 Mediators who believe that they do not influence the parties with their own views because they only ask questions, probe and challenge indirectly and do not offer comments, may be avoiding the responsibility that in fact they have. It would be better to recognise and acknowledge that responsibility and to ensure that it is exercised with due care and propriety.

---

[4] See Ch.14 for the use of metaphor in mediation.
[5] The first edition of this book in 1993 made that distinction, in common with the general thinking at that time. That was changed in the second edition.
[6] In Professor Hazel Genn, *The Central London County Court—Pilot Mediation Scheme Evaluation Report* (Lord Chancellor's Department Research, 1998 Series No.5/98), she found that "many mediators were explicitly evaluative during the course of mediations, despite their introductions which stressed their merely facilitative role." (Para.7.6.4).

SOME CONSIDERATIONS RELEVANT TO NEUTRAL NON-BINDING EVALUATION

The following matters are relevant to neutral non-binding evaluation: 19–018

- Some ADR processes are specifically designed with the aim of providing a neutral evaluation independently of any facilitation. Examples of these are the mini-trial (Executive Tribunal), the summary jury trial, and neutral evaluation.
- Most ADR processes such as mediation place their primary focus on facilitation, and in some cases may introduce an element of evaluation mainly to assist the facilitative process. If the parties can resolve the matter on the basis of their interests, concerns and their own evaluations of the issues and risks, then neutral evaluation is unnecessary.
- The main aim of neutral evaluation is to help parties to gain a more objective and realistic view of the position, and where appropriate to shift from unrealistic positions.
- If required and agreed, a neutral other than the mediator or ADR practitioner may be asked to undertake the evaluation (for example a barrister or other lawyer jointly instructed by the parties for this purpose).
- A neutral evaluation as to the likely outcome of the case given to both or all parties may contain inherent potential problems in that it may well entrench or harden the position of the party considered to be likely to succeed. This may make it more difficult rather than easier to arrive at a negotiated resolution.
- The value of the evaluation also depends on the level of expertise and experience of the evaluator. As a matter of ethical propriety, no mediator should undertake any form of evaluation in mediation unless competent to do so, and practised in facilitation.
- There is a substantial responsibility in altering the parties' perceptions by an evaluation that is necessarily personal. It is not to be lightly undertaken and requires a high standard of professional care.
- Any evaluation should be consistent, even if the manner of presentation varies.[7] It is not, however, necessary for a practitioner to discuss the same issues with each party. Indeed, it may well be appropriate for evaluative challenges or observations to be made confidentially to one party without informing the other that this has been done.
- If an evaluation is undertaken, it should be done competently and sensitively, at an appropriate time and in a way that is neither determinative nor coercive, and which leaves decision-making control squarely with the parties.

---

[7] A mediator should not give inconsistent views, for example suggesting to each party in turn that they are likely to fail in litigation, in order to try to persuade each to settle.

EVALUATION IN MEDIATION

19–019 It is not feasible or appropriate to expect people to negotiate with one another in mediation unless they have some realistic idea of the value of the subject matter of their negotiations. "Value" does not necessarily only mean financial value, but might refer to the weight to be placed on the claim or obligation.

19–020 Nor is it sufficient to contend that parties place their own value on the subject-matter. People commonly accept less than they may be entitled to, but this needs to be done on an informed basis. If one party discovers that there is an objective or measurable value, and that he or she has negotiated in ignorance of it, there could well be an understandable disappointment coupled with a feeling of having been let down by the mediator or the process.

19–021 In some cases, value may be irrelevant, for example, in neighbourhood or community disputes, such as noise or environmental issues. The same would probably apply to inter-personal issues, where parties are trying to resolve disputes that would not be likely to be adjudicated. In many other cases, however, assessing the value of parties' rights may be necessary to enable effective negotiations to take place.

No idea of the parameters

19–022 Parties may have no real idea of the parameters within which to negotiate. This might be the case, for example, in divorce mediation where a party may not know what level of capital, income or other financial adjustment is appropriate.

19–023 In English law, legislation and precedent prescribe various factors to be taken into account in dealing with financial issues on divorce. Parties commonly wish to be guided by what these are likely to be before they agree on terms to settle their own issues. This necessitates an evaluation, which is made by the parties' own advisers outside the mediation.

19–024 However, in many cases parties do not engage lawyers, at the outset in any event, especially with public funding not necessarily being available. In that event, they may expect some kind of guidance from the mediator. Some models that are purely facilitative would not regard it as appropriate for mediators to give such guidance, others, despite also being virtually entirely facilitative, might offer some help, for example:

- The mediator could provide information about the applicable legal principles, without trying to predict what the court would be likely to order in their particular case. This does not constitute evaluation. An awareness of the applicable legal principles might help the couple to arrive at their own preliminary assessment of the position.[8]
- Where appropriate, the mediator could inform the couple if the proposals they are considering seem likely to fall outside the parameters that a court

---

[8] It is widely accepted that the mediator may provide neutral information (which does not constitute evaluation), but should not give specific advice to the parties or try to apply that information to specific circumstances for example so as to predict how a court might apply it. So, for example, the couple may be given a copy of the relevant section of the law containing a list of factors to be taken into account in making financial arrangements or decisions.

might order or approve. The mediator, having informed the couple of the position, would not ordinarily elaborate by indicating his or her view as to the likely court order. It would be up to the parties to seek their own advice or to decide to settle outside court parameters. At least they would do so consciously and not unwittingly.[9]

Deadlocked by differing outcome perceptions

During the course of mediation, parties may become deadlocked because of their different views as to the likely outcome if the case were to be adjudicated. All attempts to achieve an agreed resolution may be frustrated by the strength of these respective perceptions. In these circumstances, it may be necessary for the mediator, particularly in civil or commercial mediation, to help break the deadlock.   19–025

Parties sometimes maintain unrealistic outcome predictions notwithstanding having been given realistic advice by their lawyers. Whatever the reason for this, mediators will know that when they challenge a party's outcome perceptions in a separate meeting, the party's lawyer will sometimes support the mediator and indicate a sense of vindication of advice given previously. It is as though the party needed to hear the reservations from a neutral person, despite having already heard it from his or her own lawyer. In such circumstances, shifts can occur in the negotiations.   19–026

Family mediators are far less likely to want to introduce their own views, and may be precluded from doing so by their Codes of Practice. Some will introduce evaluation by suggesting or facilitating the joint appointment by the parties of an outside neutral to provide the evaluative element, such as a neutral barrister's or solicitor's opinion. Others may do so indirectly by the way they ask questions and deal with "reality-testing". More debate is probably needed as to whether, when, in what circumstances and how family mediators might properly introduce evaluative elements into family issues.   19–027

US mediator John Bickerman, writes that: 19–028

> "Without sacrificing neutrality, a mediator's neutral assessment can provide participants with a much-needed reality check. Counsel will often look to a mediator to reduce a client's expectations by providing frank assessments of the risk. Parties do not lose trust in mediators or consider them biased because mediators talk frankly with them about their cases While pure facilitative mediation may work in certain contexts, parties often want—and expect—a mediator to explore strengths and weaknesses of the case."[10]

---

[9] For example, the Law Society of England and Wales provided in its previous Code of Practice for family mediators, at para.5.10 that "The mediator should, if practicable, inform the parties if he or she considers that the resolutions which they are considering are likely to fall outside the parameters which a court might approve or order. If they nevertheless wish to proceed with such resolutions, they may do so." This provision, however, has not been repeated in the Code of the Family Mediation Council, which the Law Society has adopted.

[10] See John Bickerman, "Evaluative mediator responds" in "Alternatives" (1996) 14(6) *CPR Institute for Dispute Resolution*. Bickerman is an attorney and adjunct professor at Georgetown University Law Center.

Opposition to evaluation in mediation

19–029　"Mediation training programmes in the UK tend to teach a substantially facilitative, non-evaluative approach, the rationale here perhaps being that this is the 'pure' model, that mediation should not be evaluative (at all, or in some views at least until practitioners gain more experience and can exercise discretion about how and when to introduce a measure of evaluation) and that in any event mediation is about party decision-making and that the mediator should not influence the outcome by expressing a view on the merits These policies of training and practice have substantial merit, but there (is not) usually enough consideration about the different ways in which evaluation takes place, with the result that instead of having this as a structured development in their training, they are left to their own devices in adapting the process and in deciding whether, when and how to evaluate. For some, this may follow naturally and effectively; but this is a hit-and-miss process; and mediators do not necessarily have norms against which to judge their individual approaches to evaluation."[11]

19–030　There is significant opposition to evaluation, albeit that for many the resistance may be based on a perception of evaluation that might not be shared by all. For example, Freddie Strasser and Paul Randolph say that a specialist mediator will have a propensity to offer advice and an opinion "creating a problematic mix of roles: mediator/professional adviser" and can easily descend into "trashing" a case.[12] And an opponent of evaluation in mediation, writing to resist an extension of the mediation rules in Florida, said that if mediators could give advice and opinions during a mediation, that would damage the structure of mediation. Mediation, in his view:

> "could, and probably would, quickly devolve into an undelineated combination of mediation, arbitration, early neutral (or perhaps not so neutral) evaluation, early expert (or perhaps not so expert) evaluation and private judging".[13]

19–031　To some extent, a mediator's attitude to the introduction of evaluation into mediation will be influenced by a combination of his or her personal predilection, experience, view of the culture of mediation and ADR, professional and organisational background, and mediation training. Practitioners who see ADR as a flexible process, offering parties a range of options that might mix elements of non-binding evaluation with mediation and negotiation are likely to accept an evaluative element in mediation with relative equanimity. Others properly prefer to keep the processes separate. There does not seem necessarily to be a "right" answer to this issue, but rather a number of possibilities, each with its own validity and reservations. Perhaps the different views can be reconciled by having a range of ADR processes, purely facilitative, evaluative and hybrid, ensuring that they are clearly distinguished, so that consumers can make an informed choice.

---

[11] From Henry Brown's paper "Creating confidence in mediators and the process: an exploration of the issues" (2010) Chartered Institute of Arbitrators, 3rd Mediation Symposium.

[12] F. Strasser and P. Randolph, *Mediation: A Psychological Insight into Conflict Resolution* (London/New York: Continuum International Publishing Group, 2004), pp.67–68.

[13] Charles N. Castagna, "Mediation: Leave Well Enough Alone" (November 1997) *Newsletter of the Clearwater, Florida, Bar Association*.

THE MINI-TRIAL (EXECUTIVE TRIBUNAL)

The mini-trial concept

The term "mini-trial" was coined by the New York Times in a report on the first known case using that procedure: a major US patent infringement action in 1977 between Telecredit Inc and TRW Inc. Despite its name it is not a trial but a non-binding ADR process which assists the parties to a dispute to gain a better understanding of the issues, thereby enabling them to enter into settlement negotiations on a more informed basis.   19–032

The concept of traditional negotiation is that each party, with his lawyer next to him, faces the other party and his lawyer across the table. Notionally, the mini-trial changes this arrangement by putting both parties, or in the case of corporations, their chief executive decision-makers, on the same side of the table, and the lawyers on the other side of the table. By virtue of this change, the parties effectively become a "tribunal", assisted in most cases by a neutral expert who sits between them; and the lawyers take turns to present an abbreviated version of the case to them, in accordance with procedural rules devised and agreed in advance.   19–033

No determination is made, though the neutral may express a non-binding opinion to the parties about the case. In this way, the parties have an opportunity of "hearing" the case and forming their own views about it, with the benefit of the neutral's assistance, enabling them to convert the problem to a business one rather than a legal one. They can then bring their business judgment into the settlement discussions that usually follow the presentations and which may be facilitated by the neutral.[14]   19–034

This notion of the parties constituting the tribunal to listen to the presentations and to formulate their views on the case has led CEDR (the Centre for Effective Dispute Resolution) to name this process "Executive Tribunal".   19–035

The mini-trial is really an elaborate and stylised form of evaluative mediation, providing a structured settlement process.[15] Although there is no evidence of it being used in the UK to any significant degree, it is a valuable process for gaining an understanding of the issues, arguments and sentiments on both sides more accurately; a resource for reviewing outcome predictions; a way to obtain an independent and informed third-party view; and an opportunity, with the benefit of these insights, to resolve the dispute with third-party support. With individual adaptations for each case as appropriate, it has a valued place in the dispute resolution repertoire.   19–036

---

[14] This brief outline is based on an informal explanation given by Jonathan Marks who was a lawyer in the original mini-trial case (*TRW and Telecredit*, 1977) and helped to design the process together with Professor Eric Green, whose article "Growth of the Mini-trial" (Fall 1982) 9 *Litigation* 1 helpfully describes the process. Eric Green wrote the *Mini-trial Handbook* (New York: Center for Public Resources, 1982). Another counsel involved in the original case has written a description of the procedure used in it: R. L. Olson "An Alternative for Large Case Dispute Resolution" (Winter 1980) 6 *Litigation* 22.

[15] Eric Green, one of the originators of the mini-trial, has informally described it as "a kind of evaluative mediation".

The mini-trial procedure

Appointment of neutral adviser

19–037   The neutral adviser, who may be a neutral lawyer, a retired judge or any other person with authority in the field of the dispute, is an important figure in this process, some might say a key figure.

19–038   A view does exist, however, that the neutral is not essential to the process. Indeed, in the US mini-trials are sometimes conducted without one. This approach may be favoured by some parties or lawyers, both because of cost-effectiveness and because they may prefer to have all the opportunities offered by the process without a neutral expert expressing a view on the merits or otherwise interceding.

19–039   The concept of the mini-trial is that it allows the parties to hear the presentations and to obtain an informed neutral view about the merits of the case. The role of the neutral adviser in chairing the process, asking appropriate questions, helping the parties to a better understanding of the issues and if necessary forming and expressing a view on the merits, is thus widely regarded as being a central one.

Preparation

19–040   The parties will need to enter into an agreement to initiate a mini-trial. The Agreement to Mediate can be adapted as necessary, or some organisations provide a bespoke form of mini-trial agreement.[16]

19–041   The mini-trial needs to be carefully planned and the following matters need to be considered:

- The venue, date(s) and length of time allowed for the process, allocating a time frame to each component part including the oral presentations by each party and any responding statements after initial presentations have been made.
- The form and time-scale for exchanging written submissions and any bundle of relevant documents.
- Whether witnesses and/or technical experts will be called, and if so, how many on each side and what time each may have; and whether and how questions may be put to the experts. The usual rules of evidence do not apply to mini-trials.
- Whether any further information should be furnished, and if so, what and how.
- Who should attend the mini-trial to represent corporate parties. They should be senior personnel used to making decisions, and authorised to make binding decisions about settlement within their own discretion, albeit within any fixed limit of authority. It is also preferable that they should be detached from the dispute, though this may not always be practicable.

---

[16] See for example CEDR's Executive Tribunal model procedure and agreement with the relevant link at Appendix I, Document 12, para.A1-046.

- The role of the neutral adviser in the mini-trial, in explaining the issues and his or her views to the parties and in relation to any subsequent settlement negotiations.
- The non-binding, confidential and privileged nature of the proceedings.
- Practical matters such as responsibility for costs, which are usually shared between the parties equally. Other matters might include temporary suspension of pending litigation if applicable; an agreement not to call the neutral adviser in any subsequent proceedings; and whether the mini-trial process can be terminated before it has run its full course, and if so, by whom and under what circumstances.
- Any other matters specifically relevant to the individual case.

The conduct of the mini-trial

The procedure and timetable will have been agreed by the parties with the neutral adviser to meet the individual needs of the case. The following is a typical example of how a mini-trial might proceed:

- The neutral adviser welcomes the parties, addresses them about the process and its confidential, privileged and non-binding nature and chairs the proceedings which follow.
- The claimant's lawyer presents the claimant's case, summarising the evidence, and making submissions. Use may be made of photographs, films, charts and other devices in making this presentation. This may take an agreed period of, say, two or three hours.[17]
- An expert then summarises the technical position on behalf of the claimant, similarly using projectors, diagrams and any other devices that may be useful to explain and clarify the technical aspects. This may take an agreed period of, say 90 minutes.
- Key witnesses may outline relevant aspects of the claimant's case. (Alternatively, the lawyer may instead summarise the proposed evidence in his or her presentation.)
- The neutral adviser may ask the claimant's lawyer and witnesses any questions to clarify the case. This is not generally done by way of cross-examination or to help make good shortcomings, but rather by way of genuine enquiry to assist understanding. Of course, such questions may have a probing effect. The parties may also put questions; and the defendant's lawyer may ask some questions of the claimant's lawyer and in some cases to the witnesses, if this has been agreed.
- The defendant's lawyer then presents the defendant's case for the same agreed period, similarly using any useful devices; and the procedures and timetable for experts, witnesses and questions will be reciprocated.
- If so agreed, time may be allowed for the experts to have a brief dialogue in front of the tribunal, perhaps responding to questions asked by one another.

---

[17] See Lewis D. Barr, "Whose Dispute is this Anyway?: The Propriety of the Mini-trial in Promoting Corporate Dispute Resolution" (1987) *Journal of Dispute Resolution* (Missouri) 133. Barr suggests that the presentations, concisely made, should take no more than six hours for the case and two hours for the rebuttal. It is likely that presentations would generally be significantly shorter than this.

NON-BINDING EVALUATIVE ADR AND HYBRID PROCESSES

- Winding-up statements may be made, taking an agreed period of, say, one hour each.
- The neutral adjourns with the parties to discuss the matter.

The neutral adviser's role

19–043 The neutral acts as a chairperson, manages the process, keeps the lawyers to their time-limits, asks pertinent questions and generally obtains sufficient information to be able to form a view about the issues and to assist the parties in doing the same.

19–044 At the end of the presentations, the neutral may adjourn with the parties to discuss the presentations with them and help them to gain a better understanding of the issues and the merits, and if required, giving an indication of his or her view of the respective strengths and weaknesses on each side, on a privileged and non-binding basis.

19–045 The settlement discussions following the mini-trial may be held between parties and lawyers, without necessarily requiring the intervention of the neutral; or if required, the neutral may facilitate the negotiations, in mediator mode.

19–046 As an alternative, a different person may be engaged to act as mediator. That person would, in such event, also attend the mini-trial. If the issues are substantial and there is a preference to separate the expert function from the mediatory role, this may be considered to be a worthwhile cost.

The settlement negotiations

19–047 These take place on a without prejudice basis after the conclusion of the mini-trial. Having a senior executive decision-maker of corporate parties attend the process and the negotiations brings commercial judgment into it so that, working with their lawyers, they can help to find a realistic business-like solution to the dispute.

19–048 If the matter is settled, the terms will be recorded in a formal agreement; and if there is a case pending in the court or in an arbitration tribunal, a formal consent order or award may be obtained. If the matter is not settled, all rights will have been reserved, and the parties can revert to the adjudicatory system for the resolution of their dispute. They will not ordinarily be allowed to refer in such formal process to any of the matters that arose in the mini-trial.

19–049 Experience in the US has shown that if the mini-trial and subsequent negotiations do not result in a settlement, a "cooling-off" period can be useful before litigation is commenced; and that during this period, settlement is often achieved.[18]

---

[18] See "A Primer on Mini-trials" in J. H. Wilkinson, *Donovan Leisure Newton and Irvine ADR Practice Book* (New York: Wiley Law Publications, 1990), p.173.

THE MINI-TRIAL (EXECUTIVE TRIBUNAL)

Kinds of cases suitable for mini-trial

Mini-trials are used most often in the US for substantial business disputes covering mixed issues of fact and law, and also those involving technical disputes and in cases involving contract, tort, infringement of patents, insurance claims and construction disputes. **19–050**

Where the parties are in deadlock because of a good faith disagreement, particularly as to the respective perceptions of their rights, the mini-trial is particularly apt.[19] Indeed, it is suitable for most kinds of issues that could be settled by negotiation; but because of the cost of preparing for and running the mini-trial, it would normally only be used where the costs are justified relative to the amount in issue, in accordance with the concept of proportionality. **19–051**

The mini-trial is less suitable for cases which turn exclusively on credibility and which necessarily have to be tested by way of cross-examination; or for cases in which a binding precedent is required; or where fundamental non-negotiable rights are concerned. It is, like most other consensual ADR processes, unsuitable if either party does not genuinely wish to settle but has an interest in delay or in abusing the process. It is also unsuitable if a party cannot produce "an effective decision-maker who can negotiate a settlement".[20] **19–052**

Timing of mini-trial usage

A mini-trial can take place at any stage of a dispute, though some parties prefer to wait until after pleadings have closed and all documents disclosed under the discovery procedure. They consider that this provides the best balance between on the one hand identifying the issues and documents under the strict rules of the adversarial system, and on the other hand obtaining the benefits of the mini-trial relatively early, before steps are taken and costs incurred in preparing for trial.[21] In this event, the formal pleadings and an abbreviated bundle of relevant documents are then used in the mini-trial. **19–053**

A mini-trial can however be effectively run at an early stage of the dispute.[22] This not only maximises cost savings, but allows the parties to consider the position with greater flexibility, before attitudes have hardened and become entrenched. It might ordinarily, however, be premature to do so before the issues have clearly crystallised.[23] **19–054**

---

[19] S. Goldberg, E. Green and F. Sander, *Dispute Resolution* (1985), p.272. The mini-trial focuses on the legal merits while "reconverting into a business problem" what has become a legal fight.

[20] Per Philip Naughton QC in an address given in December 1988 for the Chartered Institute of Arbitrators, the Inns of Court and the Bar Council.

[21] Barr, "Whose Dispute is this Anyway? The Propriety of the Mini-trial in Promoting Corporate Dispute Resolution" (1987) *Journal of Dispute Resolution* (Missouri) 139. He considers that the issues need to be sufficiently developed for the mini-trial hearing to be useful, and that the more complex the subject-matter of the dispute, the more documentary disclosure will be necessary before using the abbreviated discovery of the mini-trial.

[22] Philip Naughton QC expressed the view (see fn.20 above) that it was not essential to wait for discovery to conduct a mini-trial. He suggested that there could be a limited discovery of documents identified to be relevant. He cited the Industrial Tribunal as a precedent for this.

[23] Barr, fn.21 above, quotes Green, "Corporate Alternative Dispute Resolution" (1986) 1 Ohio St J.D.R. 238 as suggesting that parties should base their decision as to timing on a cost/benefit analysis on the value of obtaining additional information.

General observations about mini-trials

19–055   Mini-trials are said to be substantially successful in the cases in which they are used. A survey of lawyers who had participated in mini-trials reflected that 24 out of 28 cases using this process had ended in settlement, with 16 of the 19 lawyers satisfied with the process and enthusiastic about using mini-trials again.[24] It is also said that most parties who have been engaged in mini-trials feel that even if the case does not immediately settle, they do not regard the money spent on it as wasted, because the focused work done on it is so useful as a preparation for the trial.[25]

19–056   On the other hand, the cost factor is relatively high, though the costs of a full-scale trial and its preparation may be averted. There is also a high time investment required by the parties and their senior personnel. A risk exists that parties may inform their opponents of their trial strategies and of the weaknesses in their opponent's case, enabling them to anticipate the trial more accurately and to make good at the trial any shortcomings disclosed.[26] This is generally felt to be outweighed by the potential advantages of an early and effective settlement, and by the ability of most experienced lawyers to conduct a mini-trial effectively without giving away any strategic information, but rather using it with considered judgment.

19–057   The absence of probing the case by cross-examination and the need to present it in an abbreviated form, may also result in some important elements being missed; but here again, these are matters which can be guarded against by lawyers alive to risk.

19–058   Like all ADR, the mini-trial is not a panacea and is not suitable or helpful for all cases. It is, however, a substantially useful and effective process: it:

> "returns the dispute to the businessmen, educates them, and then allows them to use their developed skills—assessing risk and negotiating—to resolve the dispute."[27]

THE SUMMARY JURY TRIAL

19–059   The mini-trial procedure can be adapted as required. One American variation is the "summary jury trial", which is in effect a mini-trial conducted before a mock jury who give a verdict which is not binding, but which helps to inform the parties of the likely reaction of a real jury. This is used in relation, for example, to personal injury cases and reflects the American preference for jury trials.

19–060   Two articles in the Donovan, Leisure, Newton and Irvine: *ADR Practice Book*[28] express different views about the summary jury trial. Federal District Judge Hon. Thomas D. Lambros, in whose court the process was first used,

---

[24] Barr, fn.21 above, at p.134, referring to *The Effectiveness of the Mini-Trial in Resolving Complex Commercial Disputes: A Survey* (American Bar Association's Litigation Section, ADR Sub-committee, 1986).
[25] Goldberg, Green and Sander, *Dispute Resolution* (1985), p.277.
[26] Annie Billings mentions this in her article "The mini-trial: misunderstanding and miscommunication may short-circuit its effective use in settlements" (1990) 2 *Journal of Dispute Resolution* 417.
[27] Olson, "An Alternative for Large Case Dispute Resolution" (Winter 1980) 6 *Litigation* 22.
[28] Wilkinson, *Donovan Leisure Newton and Irvine ADR Practice Book* (1990).

describes its benefits. However, in the chapter "Personal Experiences with Corporate ADR", Howard J. Aibel and Edwin A. Kilburn, both counsel to ITT, describe having found the summary jury trial unsatisfactory and prefer the mediation process. That divergence of view has been replicated elsewhere, reflecting a concern that while the process has benefits, these may be outweighed by its drawbacks.

The summary jury trial is unlikely to be relevant in the UK because of the limited use of civil jury trials. It does, however, demonstrate how ADR processes can be adapted to meet particular needs, whether of procedure generally or of individual disputes.

19–061

EARLY NEUTRAL EVALUATION, CASE EVALUATION, FINANCIAL DISPUTE RESOLUTION AND THE COURT SETTLEMENT PROCESS

Outline of neutral evaluation

Although Early Neutral Evaluation (ENE) has been available in the UK for many years, interest in it has increased more recently with its adoption and incorporation into Court procedures in the Chancery Division, the Commercial Court and the Technology and Construction Court (TCC).[29]

19–062

ENE originated in 1985 in the United States District Court for the Northern District of California, with cases referred at an early stage to a third-party lawyer for non-binding evaluation, with a mandate to look at the strengths and weaknesses of the case and to consider how best to conduct the litigation rapidly and economically.

19–063

The scheme was initially designed to force parties to confront the merits of the case more carefully and to develop an efficient approach to the issues and to discovery. Subsequently settlement facilitation was added to the scheme, and the evaluator may now have the authority at the evaluation session to help the parties, in joint or separate meetings, to explore the possibility of settlement.

19–064

Clearly in any form of evaluation the person agreed as evaluator will need to be someone whose opinion and authority are respected by the disputing parties, such as a lawyer or other dispute resolver with appropriate experience and expertise. This principle has been firmly adopted in some courts by offering an option of judicial ENE.

19–065

ENE through the courts

As mentioned above, ENE has been directly adopted within the court system in England and Wales in the Chancery Division, the Commercial Court and the TCC, and it is also indirectly followed in the Family Division through the established Financial Dispute Resolution procedure (FDR).[30]

19–066

---

[29] For links to the relevant court guides, see Appendix II at paras A2-001, A2-002 and A2-004.
[30] See Ch.11, paras 11-015 and 11-016.

NON-BINDING EVALUATIVE ADR AND HYBRID PROCESSES

19–067 Part 3 of the Civil Procedure Rules (CPR) relates to the court's case management powers. Paragraph 3.1(2)(m) specifies that "Except where these Rules provide otherwise, the court may ... take any other step or make any other order for the purpose of managing the case and furthering the overriding objective, including hearing an Early Neutral Evaluation with the aim of helping the parties settle the case."

19–068 The Chancery Guide describes ENE as follows:

> "ENE is a simple concept which involves an independent party, with relevant expertise, expressing an opinion about a dispute or an element of it. It is unlike mediation because a mediator acts primarily as a facilitator. Although the mediator may undertake some 'reality testing', there is no requirement to do so. The person undertaking ENE provides an opinion based on the information provided by the parties and may do so without receiving oral submissions if that is what they wish.... An essential feature of ENE, apart from being consensual, is that unless the parties agree otherwise, the opinion is non-binding and the process is without prejudice (it being treated as part of a negotiation between the parties)."[31]

19–069 As the Guide indicates, the Chancery Division does not have set procedures for ENE. Directions for its preparation and conduct will be given by the judge who is to act as the neutral evaluator. The judge's opinion may be based solely on written position papers provided by the parties and a bundle of core documents or there may also be a short hearing of up to half a day. The judge will deliver his or her evaluation informally.

19–070 The Commercial Court similarly addresses the use of ENE in its Guide.[32] However, here the neutral may, but will not necessarily be a judge. Provision is made for the neutral evaluator to be an appropriate third party. As in the Chancery Division, if a judge is appointed, he or she will give appropriate directions for its preparation and conduct and will take no further part in the case unless the parties agree otherwise.

Neutral evaluation procedure

19–071 There is no standard ENE procedure, but the following would be a typical way of obtaining an evaluation in a private context:

- The parties enter into an agreement to obtain an evaluation.[33]
- The parties furnish the evaluator with summaries of their case and submissions, together with a bundle of relevant documents, which may include pleadings (statements of case) in any pending litigation or arbitration.
- The evaluator considers these summaries and documents and may convene an evaluation session, unless the parties have agreed that the evaluation should be made on a documents-only basis.

---

[31] See paras 18.7 and 18.8 of the Chancery Guide, February 2016.
[32] See para.G2, 10th edn, 2017.
[33] For reference to a specimen agreement, see Appendix I, document 11, para.A1-045.

EARLY NEUTRAL EVALUATION AND OTHER PROCESSES

- If there is an evaluation session, the parties themselves, or their legal representatives, make oral presentations. Experts or witnesses do not ordinarily participate unless exceptionally this is agreed.
- The evaluator assesses the relative strengths and weaknesses of the case, explaining his or her reasoning for the views expressed. This may be done at the session, or in writing, as may be agreed.
- In some models, and if so agreed with the parties, the evaluator may obtain expert input from a specialist on any particular aspect of the dispute, which will be disclosed.
- If the evaluator thinks that it might be helpful and appropriate to have any follow-up activities after the initial session, these can be arranged. This might be in the form of written or telephone communications, and perhaps, with the consent of the parties, a second evaluation meeting.

General observations about evaluation

Evaluation provides an independent and objective assessment of risk and prospects, which is off the record and not binding, hence affording everyone the opportunity to explore ways of resolving the issues realistically before parties become entrenched in their positions and extensive commitment and costs are invested into defending those positions. 19–072

The ENE procedure has been extensively researched in the US and the findings show that the process works satisfactorily, and that it is widely viewed as being fair and valuable, with some qualifications.[34] The positive benefits include making parties and their lawyers examine the case more carefully and systematically; giving them a better understanding of the issues; improving information exchange; improving communications; and creating opportunities for early settlement discussions to be conducted. On the other hand, evaluations remain the subjective opinions of the evaluators and are not necessarily reinforced by the eventual outcomes. 19–073

Case evaluation was successfully used in the major reconstruction and renewal plan for Lloyd's insurance syndicates. Part of the process necessitated valuing reinsurance cover, which would have been almost impossible with many disputes pending. An expeditious process was needed, which was provided by a case evaluation procedure, involving a group of some 15 senior lawyers and market experts co-chaired by Lord Ackner and Lord Templeman. From this group, panels dealt with individual disputes, evaluating them on a range between "very strong" and "hopeless". Evaluations were based on documents submitted, and in some cases, a one-day hearing. They did not affect the parties' legal rights.[35] 19–074

Evaluations of merits will not resolve all the issues facing parties in dispute. They may not shake opinions obtained from other experts and indeed may not be correct. They may be trumped by factors other than purely legal ones including commercial, emotional, personal and risk considerations. They may imbalance 19–075

---

[34] See Professor David I. Levine, "Early neutral evaluation: a follow-up report" (1987) 70(4) *Judicature*; and Professor David I. Levine, "Early Neutral Evaluation: The Second Phase" (1989) *Journal of Dispute Resolution* 1.

[35] See the article by Sarah Scarlett, "Use of ADR in Lloyd's R&R plan" *Insurance Day*, 25 February 1997. The Lloyd's process was dealt with by the City Disputes Panel, using its case evaluation procedures.

NON-BINDING EVALUATIVE ADR AND HYBRID PROCESSES

negotiations by favouring one party over another. And as Robert Benjamin observes, people do not necessarily resolve their disputes on a logical basis.[36] But ultimately, realistic assessments of outcome predictions provide one of the best ways of helping people arrive at sensible and realistic solutions where they may believe that their remedies will be better in other fora if they have them adjudicated.

Financial dispute resolution

19–076   In the courts of England and Wales, this concept originally related to a hearing of this name in the family court, in which a District Judge meets the parties and their lawyers and tries to help them to arrive at a resolution of any differences by predicting what would be likely to happen if the matter were to be decided at a final hearing. The broad consensus is that this proved to be a successful and helpful initiative.[37]

19–077   The concept of "financial dispute resolution" has been adopted by the Chancery Division (Ch FDR), acknowledging that its origins lie in the family courts. It is described as "a form of ADR in which the judge facilitates negotiations and may provide the parties with an opinion about the claim or elements of it."[38] The process is consensual and will not be imposed by the court. It is non-binding and without prejudice.

19–078   The procedure for Ch FDR is set out in the Chancery Guide[39] and involves the court giving directions that will help the process to be successful, such as directing the parties to exchange and file without prejudice position papers and to lodge a bundle of relevant documents. Parties may hold initial discussions before the substantive meeting before the meeting with the judge begins. The meeting with the judge is "a dynamic process" which may resemble an initial mediation meeting. At the request of the parties the judge may express an opinion about the issue or the claim as a whole. As with the ENE, if the dispute is not resolved, the judge who conducts the Ch FDR meeting has no further involvement with the case.

Court Settlement Process

19–079   This is a procedure in the TCC carried out by judges in appropriate cases and where all parties consent. It is a facilitative process, along the broad lines of mediation, but providing an evaluative element in that if the parties do not reach a settlement during the process, they may request a non-binding assessment from the Settlement Judge, who of course has no further role in the case if the parties do not reach a settlement and continue to trial.[40]

---

[36] See his articles at *http://www.rbenjamin.com/pg226.cfm* [accessed 21 May 2018] including for example "On Becoming a Rationally Irrational Negotiator/Mediator: The 'Messy' Human Brain and the 'Myth of Rationality'".
[37] See fn.30 above.
[38] See the Chancery Guide, February 2016, paras 18.16 to 18.18—link in Appendix II below, para.A2-001.
[39] See para.18.17.
[40] For further details, see Ch.5 at paras 5-015 to 5-018.

HYBRID PROCESSES

Non-binding evaluative processes, as outlined above, straddle the territory between adjudicatory and consensual processes. So too do a range of other processes, but these are somewhat different in that rather than combining both aspects in a particular permutation, they adopt the elements of each approach and follow them consecutively. Generically, these are often referred to as "hybrid" processes, though this term suffers from a lack of precision and could cover many other processes that "mix and match" elements of different approaches. 19–080

The following hybrid processes will be considered in this chapter: 19–081

- med-arb (mediation-arbitration);
- arb-med (arbitration-mediation);
- neutral fact-finding expert.

The ombudsman role may also be regarded as hybrid, but a separate chapter will be devoted to that.[41]

MED-ARB (MEDIATION-ARBITRATION)

Outline and issues for consideration

Med-arb is an extension of the mediation process in which the mediator changes role if the matter does not settle in mediation, and becomes an arbitrator with the task of making a binding determination. 19–082

The decision to move to an arbitration mode if mediation is unsuccessful, is one to which the parties commit themselves before the process commences. This offers the advantage that the process will produce a resolution, one way or another. It may also be considered advantageous that if adjudication is needed, there will be no loss of time or cost in re-acquainting a new neutral with the facts of the case and the issues. 19–083

There is however perceived to be a corresponding disadvantage, namely that mediator's ability to function in either mode, as a mediator or as an arbitrator, may be compromised by having both roles. Whether and to what extent this can be overcome is addressed below. 19–084

Parties in mediation must not only trust the impartiality of the mediator. They must also be able to make disclosures to the mediator either in the separate caucus meetings or in the joint meetings, which they know will be maintained confidentially and could not be used in evidence if the dispute went to adjudication. They also know that they can make concessions in an evidentially privileged situation. If however the parties know that the mediator is to become the adjudicator if the case does not settle, this may well inhibit effective negotiation and change the whole dynamic of the mediation process. 19–085

Corresponding questions arise in the arbitration mode. Does the neutral ignore information received during the mediation phase that may be prejudicial to a 19–086

---

[41] See Ch.18.

19–087 party? Even if the neutral is able to do this, what would the perceptions of the parties be, once they are faced with the reality of it and with the neutral making a finding against one of them?

Where the same person serves as mediator and then as arbitrator, serious reservations have been expressed as to whether, in addition to damaging his efficacy as a mediator, he will not have "fatally compromised the integrity of his adjudicative role."[42]

Meeting the concerns

19–088 Although these are widely accepted as valid concerns, some practitioners feel that they tend to be theoretical and not supported by what actually happens in practice. For example, Megan Elizabeth Telford reports in an article for the Industrial Relations Center at Queens University in Ontario, that she conducted interviews with experienced med-arbiters at the Grievance Settlement Board (for Crown employers and trade unions) and concluded that doubts about the abilities of med-arbiters to perform their role were unfounded and that experienced med-arbiters were able to move from one role to the other and ensure that arbitration was not affected adversely by information learned during mediation.[43]

19–089 Those who see value in the med-arb process have formulated various alternative forms of med-arb to meet the concerns outlined above.

19–090 In one of these, if the mediation does not result in an agreed outcome and needs to proceed to adjudication, the mediator checks at that stage with all the parties whether they are agreeable to his or her continuing to act, henceforth in the different role of arbitrator. If any party does not wish him or her to do so, they have the right to opt out of the process, and the mediator ceases to act in any capacity. If however the parties trust the mediator and want him or her to adjudicate the issues, there is a view that they should be allowed to agree to this. This process has been called "med-arb-opt-out".[44]

19–091 This principle is enshrined in the Commercial Arbitration Act 2010 of New South Wales, which affords disputing parties the opportunity to "opt out" after the mediation phase, in which case a different person will arbitrate.[45] The Act also provides that, before proceeding to arbitrate after the mediation has terminated without resolving the dispute, the arbitrator must disclose to all parties any confidential information learned in the mediation that is material to the arbitration. If the parties decide to give their consent in these circumstances,

---

[42] See the comments of S. Goldberg, E. Green and F. Sander, *Dispute Resolution* (1985) quoting in turn from an article by Professor Fuller "Collective Bargaining and the Arbitrator" (1962) Proceedings, Fifteenth Annual Meeting, National Academy of Arbitrators 8.
[43] Megan Elizabeth Telford, *Med-Arb: A Viable Dispute Resolution Alternative* (Canada: IRC Press, 2000).
[44] S. Goldberg, E. Green and F. Sander, *Dispute Resolution Supplement 1987*, p.69.
[45] Section 27D(4) of the NSW Commercial Arbitration Act 2010 No.61, which provides that "an arbitrator who has acted as mediator in mediation proceedings that are terminated may not conduct subsequent arbitration proceedings in relation to the dispute without the written consent of all the parties to the arbitration given on or after the termination of the mediation proceedings".

parties will not readily be able or justified in challenging the arbitrator's decision on the basis that the arbitrator was influenced by representations to which they had no opportunity to respond.[46]

19–092 Brett and Goldberg devised another alternative, under which the neutral would be a "mediator-adviser" and would conduct the mediation in the ordinary course, trying to shift the parties from a rights emphasis to an examination of their respective interests, and would endeavour to facilitate a settlement. If agreement could not be achieved, the mediator would become an advisory arbitrator, furnishing a non-binding opinion for the guidance of the parties, but not a formal arbitrator making a binding decision: the parties would need to engage someone else to arbitrate formally if they wished to do so. This process seemed to produce highly satisfactory outcomes, with costs and time savings, and a high level of party satisfaction.[47]

19–093 Med-arb should not be confused with the concept of parties attempting to mediate their differences and agreeing in advance to proceed to arbitration if settlement is not achieved in mediation. In that event, different people have the roles of mediator and arbitrator. That is a common and non-contentious procedure.

ARB-MED (ARBITRATION-MEDIATION)

19–094 This is the reverse image of med-arb, in which arbitration takes place, as it would if there were no mediation element attached to it, but the award is not published. It is instead sealed and maintained by the arbitrator confidentially, and the parties then move into mediation in an attempt to reach an agreed resolution without knowing what the award is.

19–095 The arbitrator then becomes a mediator, and neither the arb-mediator nor the parties are constrained by any of the concerns outlined above regarding med-arb, since the award has been made and sealed and nothing said in the mediation would affect it. In this event, there may be less point in having a different person mediate the issues, and indeed some of the possible benefits—knowledge of the issues and costs savings—would be lost.

19–096 However, some parties may be more comfortable having a different person as mediator, which does overcome the problem that any reality-testing comments of the arb-mediator, however carefully and neutrally formulated, may be interpreted by the parties as providing an indication of what the award contains.

19–097 The dynamic in arb-med is likely to change once the arbitration has been concluded, as the parties may then feel better able to anticipate the outcome than they were before it. One party may feel more confident, another less so, and this

---

[46] Section 27D(7). The authors are grateful to Sydney mediator Alan Limbury for drawing their attention to the information contained in this paragraph and for other contributions to this chapter.

[47] Deborah M. Kolb, "How existing procedures shape alternatives: the case of grievance mediation" (1989) *Journal of Dispute Resolution* 73, referring to two articles by J. M. Brett and S. Goldberg, namely "Grievance Mediation in the Coal Industry: A Field Experiment" (1983) 37(1) Indus. & Lab. Rel. Rev. 49 and "Mediator-Advisers: A New Third Party Role" in M. Bazerman & R. Lewicki, *Negotiating in Organisations* (California: Sage Publications, 1983).

19-098 A 2002 study found that disputants using arb-med settled in the mediation phase more frequently and achieved settlements of higher joint benefit than disputants in using med-arb.[48]

19-099 Some arbitrators are reported to contain the length of the arbitration element, for example, limiting it to a half-day for each party. This is intended to deflect some of the criticism of arb-med that it is an unnecessarily expensive process, losing the cost-saving benefit of mediation that takes place before a full-scale hearing and may accordingly avoid it. This abbreviated arbitration—a sort of mini-arbitration rather than a mini-trial—may well suffice in many cases, but will not be appropriate for those cases which require detailed evidence and probing.

19-100 Another possible advantage of arb-med, or some abbreviated form of it, is that any settlement that may be arrived at can, if required, be made into a consent award, with the enforcement advantages that this has over a contractual agreement. The corollary would not necessarily apply, since if the parties were able to settle in mediation, they would not then be able to initiate arbitration or court proceedings to record the outcome as an award or order, since that could constitute an abuse of the court or of the arbitration process.[49]

SOME FURTHER OBSERVATIONS ABOUT MED-ARB AND ARB-MED

19-101 There is a dearth of recorded experience of the use of med-arb and arb-med, in the UK in any event. This may not be surprising because of the confidentiality of the processes, and also because of the concerns that have been widely expressed about the way in which the combination of mediation and arbitration might perhaps compromise both elements.

19-102 There is however, some informal experience of both these processes having been effectively undertaken in a number of cases and based on these, some observations may be made:

- Parties generally approved of the concept of having a mechanism that would allow them to try to resolve the issues themselves by agreement, but having a fall-back procedure that would provide a binding outcome if they failed to do so.
- Most parties selected the arb-med mode, and the best outcomes were achieved using this process. The arbitrator-mediator heard the arguments and sealed the award in an envelope, then conducted the mediation. Where cases settled, the envelopes did not need to be opened.

---

[48] D.E. Conlon, H. Moon and K.Y. Ng, "Putting the cart before the horse: The benefits of arbitrating before mediating" (2002) 87(5) *Journal of Applied Psychology* 978.

[49] The Cross-Border Mediation (EU Directive) Regulations 2011 and the corresponding Civil Procedure (Amendment) Rules 2011 (SI 2011/88 (L.1)) which gave effect to the Directive, allow for applicable mediated settlements to be subject to a mediation settlement enforcement order (r.78.24). This has limited application.

- The disputes for which the parties selected arb-med, and also med-arb, tended to be very substantial commercial issues involving international parties. The subject-matter was varied, including commercial contract disputes, product liability, banking, insurance and intellectual property. A common theme was that most were perceived as being intractable and not readily amenable to resolution by mediation alone.
- In almost all the cases, the parties entered the process at a late stage of the dispute, when litigation or arbitration was already well advanced. None undertook med-arb or arb-med pre-action.
- Despite successful outcomes, the trend has been a significant reduction in the referrals to med-arb and arb-med. One explanation is that there was an initial accumulation of suitable cases, and that as these were disposed of, others of a less intractable nature chose conventional mediation. Another possible explanation is that the novelty of the process wore off. It is also possible that fewer international contracts are selecting English law and jurisdiction to resolves disputes arising under them.
- A major difficulty in sustaining continuing interest in the processes is that there is no organisation that embraces and promotes these hybrid forms, and hence there is no organisational drive to market them.
- A further difficulty is that although professional indemnity insurance is readily available for the mediation process, it is very expensive for the adjudicatory element, making it uneconomic for the mediator to provide the linked option as a matter of course, particularly in large commercial disputes.

NEUTRAL FACT-FINDING EXPERT[50]

Where a case involves technical, scientific, accounting or other specialised issues, the parties and the court will generally depend on expert evidence in arriving at a proper conclusion. In traditional practice, there are two main ways of engaging expert support:

19–103

- The individual parties each engage different experts, who are expected to maintain professional objectivity in the way they function.[51] This helps to get matters resolved, where the respective experts are able to cooperate with one another in discussing the issues arriving at a consensus. In practice, however, this does not happen as commonly as might perhaps be hoped. Courts have had to choose between the views of experts expressing opposing opinions.
- A single joint expert may be appointed, whose duty is to the court, to which any expert report must be addressed.[52]

---

[50] The authors are grateful to Michael Cohen of the Academy of Experts for providing background information about sole joint experts.
[51] The Civil Justice Council has published Guidance for the instruction of experts in civil claims, August 2014.
[52] See Pt 35.8 of the Civil Procedure Rules.

19–104 A further option used in the US is the Neutral Fact-finding Expert. This is a sole expert jointly appointed by the parties, whose function is not only to provide a non-binding opinion, but who may also be required to investigate the relevant facts and to report on these, and have regard to his or her fact-finding in arriving at an opinion. Not being partisan, the expert can make an independent enquiry and a neutral evaluation of the facts, which can assist a court in adversarial proceedings, and can help the parties by narrowing the issues and promoting settlement—and indeed the expert, after reporting, may play a facilitative mediatory role if required.[53] In the UK, the expert's role is determined by contract: in some cases it may include fact-finding and testing, in others it does not. A key issue is whether the expert's opinion is determinative and binding on the parties, or a non-binding evaluation.

19–105 Where the parties participate in the selection of the expert and in the formulation of his instructions, this itself can help to narrow and define the issues.

19–106 The parties commonly agree that the expert's non-binding opinion will be admissible in any court proceedings between the parties, but that it is not conclusive. If this is agreed, it allows each party to adduce any other expert evidence to try to controvert the neutral expert's views. This gives the neutral expert's opinion a persuasive quality without making it decisive. It is this factor which keeps it a non-adjudicatory form of ADR, and distinct from expert determination or private judging. The information provided by the neutral expert will quite commonly cause either or both parties to re-assess and perhaps modify their prediction of their probability of success, with consequent impact on settlement attitudes.

---

[53] In the US, the Federal Rules of Evidence may lend themselves to the appointment of such an expert. For a detailed consideration of the subject of court-appointed neutral experts, see Professor Eric Green, "The Complete Courthouse" in A. Leo Levin and Roscoe Pound-American Trial Lawyers, *Dispute Resolution Devices in a Democratic Society* (Washington D.C.: Roscoe Pound ATLA Foundation, 1985), pp.44–51.

CHAPTER 20

Online Dispute Resolution

INTRODUCTION

It seems extraordinary to think that in 1990 there were no Internet Service Providers, online services and inter-communication availability were limited and networks could not exchange information with one another. The developments over the following three decades have been astonishing and happened—and continue happening—at an exponential rate.

20–001

Information technology has developed into Information Communication Technology (ICT) to include the increasingly wide range of available communications such as email, data sharing, VoIPs (Voice over Internet Protocols), video conferencing, virtual meetings, communications-enabled applications and other information sourcing and usage technologies.

20–002

As these developments occurred, and as online activities increased, and especially with the introduction and extension of e-commerce, the need emerged for appropriate dispute resolution mechanisms to deal with the issues that would arise in this new world. It was logical that these would be located within the same technological environment as the disputes themselves, namely online and incorporating ICT. As observed by the earliest of the writers about online dispute resolution, Professor Ethan Katsh, the resources of the internet provided opportunities for creative approaches and responses to problem-solving.[1] Consequently, with there being much more of an emphasis on dispute avoidance and resolution generally, ICT platforms are being developed and used with increasing frequency to assist the problem-solving process.

20–003

However, ICT and Online Dispute Resolution (ODR) resources are not limited to dealing with disputes arising online, but are increasingly used and available for disputes arising in the real world. They are also used alongside traditional ADR processes to complement and enhance those processes.

20–004

DISPUTES ARISING ONLINE

Katsh and Wing observe that until the 1990s, many college students had access to university mainframes and to the internet, which was not yet widely available to the general public. As a result, some early dispute resolution services were university-based including the University of Massachusetts which established a

20–005

---

[1] E. Katsh and L. Wing, "Ten Years of Online Dispute Resolution: Looking at the Past and Constructing the Future" (2006) 38 *University of Toledo Law Review* 19.

Center for Information Technology and Dispute Resolution in 1997 and ran the "Online Ombuds Office", which sought to adapt the ombudsman's role to cyberspace issues.[2] It became The National Center for Technology and Dispute Resolution, described as being "at the intersection of technology and dispute resolution".[3] It provides information, supports ODR initiatives and has a list of ODR providers.

20–006 A number of other first generation online services that aimed to facilitate the resolution of online disputes no longer exist. A new paradigm is apparently being sought for the next generation.

20–007 E-bay for example used to employ a specialist company, Square Trade, to handle some hundreds of thousands of disputes between its buyers and sellers, but in 2008 e-Bay took this service over itself through its Resolution Centre to deal online with matters that could not be resolved between the parties directly. The seller may for example be required to issue a refund, or the buyer may be required to pay for an item, or the sale may be reversed.

20–008 Other internet retailers are using different mechanisms to address disputes arising with their customers. One favoured procedure is to invite customers to register a complaint or claim, and to facilitate communications, with the sanction of refunding any amount in issue. Credit card companies also have a role, in making a chargeback of any disputed sum to the account-holder where services or products have not been satisfactory. These procedures facilitate pragmatic arrangements for the avoidance and quick settlement of any disputes.

20–009 As observed in Ch.18, complaints machinery and the ombudsman have been other ways in which online disputes are addressed. An Internet Ombudsman has been piloted in which consumers can register their complaints about products or services that they have purchased on the internet and have them resolved by neutral conciliators and adjudicators. Its two-stage process starts with mediation, and if this does not resolve the issues, then adjudication which is not binding on the consumer, but may be binding on the supplier. The Internet Services Providers' Association has a Code and complaints scheme involving resolution of disputes by CISAS (the Communications and Internet Services Adjudication Scheme), in which an independent adjudicator makes a decision which is binding on the member company but not on the complainant.

20–010 Where disputes arise in relation to domain names, these can be dealt with under the Uniform Domain Name Dispute Resolution Policy (UDRP) created by the Internet Corporation for Assigned Names and Numbers (ICANN). Evaluative panels can transfer or cancel domain names and are said to have dealt effectively with tens of thousands of domain name disputes.

20–011 In the UK, Nominet, the internet registry for .uk domain names, offers a Dispute Resolution Service to resolve .uk domain name disputes. It initially offers mediation, and where this does not resolve the matter, then an independent expert decision by a different person, who can order suspension or (more unusually) cancellation of the domain name and can also declare that the

---

[2] See the UMass Center for Information Technology and Dispute Resolution Online Ombuds Office at *http://www.ombuds.org/center/ombuds.html* [accessed 22 May 2018]. See also information about the Online Ombuds Office under "Ombudsman" in Ch.18.

[3] See the National Center for Technology and Dispute Resolution at *http://www.odr.info/index.php* [accessed 22 May 2018].

complainant was "reverse domain name hijacking"—using the service in bad faith in an attempt to get a good domain name without justification.

"REAL WORLD" DISPUTES DEALT WITH BY ODR

Online resources are also being made available in different ways to facilitate "real world" disputes rather than those arising online. Galves suggests that ODR has all of the same cost-saving and efficiency advantages of traditional ADR because "it is simply ADR on the Internet"[4] and can be faster, more convenient and more cost efficient. 20–012

ODR processes for resolving real world disputes range between fully automated programmes through to providing incidental support for mediators and arbitrators ("flesh and blood" practitioners, as one online commentator has called them). 20–013

ODR began its existence as "Online ADR" and was intended to be a network-based equivalent of offline face-to-face dispute resolution processes, such as negotiation, mediation and arbitration, according to Rabinovich-Einy and Katsh.[5] Proponents of ADR have met with much success in encouraging disputing parties to work together through various forms of mediation and negotiation using interests rather than rights or power to frame their disputes. While the "real world" dispute resolution system remains essentially a rights- and power-based system, proponents of ADR seek to introduce mediation and negotiation using models that tend to be more mutually satisfying, value-creating, and "win-win" than polarised, zero-sum rights-based approaches. As internet users have gained understanding of encryption and how that can protect important ADR principles such as trust and confidentiality, use of such systems by governments, courts and court users has increased since the start of the millennium. 20–014

Double-blind bidding

At the automated end, one of the main ODR mechanisms is double-blind bidding, which is generally used where the quantum payable is in dispute. Parties are invited to submit their respective figures online, and these are maintained confidentially by the system. If the bids come between a pre-agreed range for example 20 per cent, the system confirms a deal at the midpoint figure. If they are outside that range, parties may be given further opportunities to bid again, until an agreement is reached. 20–015

---

[4] F. Galves, "Virtual Justice as Reality: Making the Resolution of E-commerce Disputes More Convenient, Legitimate, Efficient, and Secure" (2009) (1) *Journal of Law, Technology & Policy*.

[5] O. Rabinovich and E. Katsh, "Digital Justice: Reshaping Boundaries in an Online Dispute Resolution Environment" (2014) 1 *International Journal of Online Dispute Resolution* 1.

Visual blind bidding

20–016 An alternative automated process is visual blind bidding, in which the parties reveal their proposals to one another at the outset, but maintain confidentiality about the levels at which they would settle. The system then calculates and generates suggestions, which may anonymously include suggestions made by the parties, or parties may openly contribute suggestions. The dispute is resolved when the parties agree on a set of proposals. This process is said to be suitable both for simple and complex issues.

Online arbitration

20–017 Online arbitration services can involve a range of ICT processes including for example the downloading of forms, the use of email for communications and the submission and exchange of documents, and the use of telephony, video-conferencing and virtual meetings. These services may offer paperless case submission processes, with evidence submitted electronically by secure email. In some services, arbitrators make their award electronically.

20–018 One example of an online arbitration service is the US-based net-ARB, which claims to be the world's first and only Small Claims Court for the internet, breaking jurisdictional boundaries by providing for non-appearance dispute resolution by email: the "hearing" is conducted by email over time, usually between a couple of days to a week or more. The arbitrator, or panel if so agreed, will then issue an award.

Supporting traditional ADR

20–019 Other forms of ODR technology assist mediators and arbitrators in their traditional process, for example an online mediation service such as Juripax, operated by a company based in the Netherlands, offers support for individual mediators, or for businesses with large volumes of cases, in relation to divorce, employment, e-commerce and small claims. This includes online intake forms, online discussion room and conference facilities, digital document and case management systems, and the use of networked software (ASP).

20–020 In the UK, the Mediation Room has developed technology to enable all forms of dispute resolution to be undertaken online, whether wholly or partially, using an interest-based mediation approach. They provide licences for the use of their software and other appropriate tools, enabling the creation of case files with multiple collaborative forums, anonymous brainstorming, audio-visual teleconferencing and desktop sharing, blind bidding facilities and psychometric profiling. They also provide mediators from their panel, and distance training courses in ODR.

20–021 The WIPO (World Intellectual Property Organisation) Arbitration and Mediation Center provides ODR facilities for use in connection with dispute resolution procedures such as the arbitration of intellectual property disputes. Digital communication tools allow parties to file requests by completing electronic forms and to submit documents and exchange correspondence online through secure channels, with automatic notifications and databases to support the logging and archiving of documents and secure fee payment facilities. WIPO has also developed an internet-based online dispute resolution facility to deal with disputes arising out of the registration and use of an internet domain name.

OTHER USAGES OF ICT IN DISPUTE RESOLUTION

Given the rapid development of ICT, any list of usages is likely to look dated within a few years. The ways in which ICT is used in ADR generally, in addition or complementary to the ODR usages outlined above, include the following: 20–022

- Email and document scanning have become an indispensable means of communication and of transmitting documents in ADR processes.
- Methods of communication with multiple parties include phone and video conferencing and virtual meetings, making it easier for parties in different countries to "meet" one another. Access to the web provides a source of instant information as well as alternative forms of communication such as internet telephony.
- Data storage and retrieval is also instant; documents can be drafted and amended by multiple parties; standard and bespoke forms can be completed and exchanged online; and many other resources are available and constantly being added.
- Websites provide not only marketing opportunities for practitioners and organisations, but offer the extensive delivery of relevant information and links.
- Professional and social networks have extended to include information exchange and advice seeking. The uses of these resources, combined with mobile phone technology, have had a profound impact on the nature of communicating news and events around the world, changing the whole paradigm of information dissemination and marketing.

As support for human practitioners, ICT resources are likely to have increasing value, though it is unlikely that practitioners, who attach importance to personal connections with disputing parties, would wish to see the automated aspect of their roles predominating over the personal element. As Humpty Dumpty observed in *Alice Through the looking-Glass* "The question is, which is to be master—that's all".   20–023

REGULATION OR HARMONISATION OF ODR

Consumer protection for citizens in European Member States was a topic of focus during the early part of the 21st century. Concerns over the inconvenience and disproportionate expense that consumers experienced in dealing with disputes arising from e-commerce, particularly as these were commonly likely to involve cross-border jurisdictional problems, informed the debate about the need for a   20–024

20-025 regulatory framework for cross-border consumer-related disputes and the use of ICT to develop ODR systems to assist with this.[6]

20-025 On 25 October 2011 the European Parliament passed a wide-ranging ADR resolution, strongly supporting ADR processes, inter alia seeing "great potential for online ODR, in particular for small claims [and emphasising that] where traditional ADR is carried out online, procedural standards should not be lowered, and that issues such as the enforceability of awards should also be resolved".

20-026 UNCITRAL, the United Nations Commission on International Trade Law, had been considering ODR since 2000. It undertook research into the subject, and received periodical reports from an ODR Working Group that it established. In 2010, the Commission agreed that a Working Group should be established to undertake work in the field of online dispute resolution relating to cross-border electronic commerce transactions, including business-to-business and business-to-consumer transactions. Reviewing legal standards, the Working Group developed draft procedural rules in 2011, with a focus on low-value, high-volume cross-border electronic commerce transactions. There was a recognition that procedural rules should be forward-looking and able to accommodate any changes in technology and practice that might arise in the long-term future. The work of the ODR Working Group helped inform the European Parliament's decision to introduce of legislation in this area.

20-027 The European Directive on Consumer Alternative Dispute Resolution and the Regulation on Online Dispute Resolution of 21 May 2013[7] was fully adopted into UK law on 9 January 2016.[8] As well as promoting consumer protection within Member States, the directive is also designed to encourage efficient, fast and low-cost ways of resolving domestic and cross-border disputes which arise from sales or service contracts. Foremost is the promotion of ADR for the resolution of online as well as offline transactions for disputes which arise from cross-border consumer transactions. An ODR platform launched in February 2016 offers consumers and traders a single point of entry for the out-of-court resolution of online disputes arising from purchases made over the internet, through ADR entities which are linked to the platform and offer ADR through quality ADR procedures.

20-028 The EU Alternative/ODR platform has been developed and is operated by the European Commission for consumers and traders in Member States and involves the consumer filling in an online complaint form and submitting it via the internet. Once the consumer and trader agree on an ADR entity to handle their dispute, the EU ODR platform transfers the complaint automatically to that entity. The ADR entity then handles the case entirely online and reaches an outcome in 90 days without the parties present.[9] Currently this system is only available to those consumers living in and traders based in the EU.

---

[6] P. Cortés, *Online Dispute Resolution for Consumers in the European Union* (Routledge, 2011).
[7] http://eur-lex.europa.eu/LexUriServ/LexUriServ.do?uri=OJ:L:2013:165:0063:0079:EN:PDF [accessed 22 May 2018].
[8] See SI 2015/1392 Consumer Protection: The Alternative Dispute Resolution for Consumer Disputes (Amendment) Regulations 2015, which is the Statutory Instrument incorporating the EU Directive into UK law. Available at: *http://www.legislation.gov.uk/uksi/2015/542/pdfs/uksi_20150542_en.pdf* [accessed 22 May 2018].
[9] The EU Online Dispute Resolution Platform at: *https://webgate.ec.europa.eu/odr/main/index.cfm?event=main.home.show&lng=EN* [accessed 22 May 2018].

Whilst Cortés suggests that consumer ADR entities are an important development for many Member States who do not necessarily see their court system as being the primary route to resolving consumer disputes, he does make the point that although traders are required to provide information about certified consumer ADR entities, they cannot be compelled to participate and mandating trader participation by Member States may be the answer.[10]

Since implementation of the EU Directive, the requirement to make the the link to the ODR platform easily accessible has been tested in the courts. The decision of a German district court has now extended the requirement to websites. The district court of Bochum decided that an online trader of watches (applicant) who requested a preliminary injunction against another online trader of watches (defendant), who did not include a link to the ODR Platform, should be granted a preliminary injunction, for the defendant's breach of German Unfair Competition Law. The defendant watch trader was prohibited from further trading online until such a link was made accessible.[11]

The question of enforcement of cross-border consumer disputes is however vague, as the EU Alternative/ODR platform does not make the procedure clear. It seems that this will be left to Member States to determine themselves and may give rise to distortions in the Internal Market, due to the lack of incentives it creates for traders.[12]

SOME PRACTICAL ODR ISSUES

Confidentiality

Rules regulating confidentiality in mediation or other ODR processes should be agreed before the process is started. This should cover both a contractual commitment to confidentiality by the parties and technological assurances about confidentiality and privacy in the ICT system.

Technological developments, such as digital signatures using encryption technology, are likely to improve levels of security and confidentiality, both in relation to e-commerce and more specifically to ODR processes, video-conferencing and virtual meetings.

---

[10] P. Cortés (ed.), *The New Regulatory Framework for Consumer Dispute Resolution* (Oxford University Press, 2016), pp.37–38.
[11] In District Court Bochum (Germany), Decision 31 March 2016—No: 14 O 12/16, the court held that the defendant was obliged to include an easily accessible link as of 9 January 2016—when the Regulation went into force—even though the ODR Platform was not online at the time. Since the defendant did not provide such link, they violated s.3a of the German Unfair Competition Act in connection with art.14 para.1 sentence 1 of the Regulation (No) 524/2013.
[12] See P. Moreno in Cortés, *The New Regulatory Framework for Consumer Dispute Resolution*, fn.10, p.403.

Enforcement

20–034 The enforceability of online arbitration awards and ADR outcomes has understandably been considered since the early days of ODR. Much depends on the process itself and the nature of the outcome, whether arbitrated or agreed, and how recorded.

20–035 Arbitrated outcomes in the shape of awards are expected to be enforceable under the 1958 New York Convention on the Recognition and Enforcement of Foreign Awards, notwithstanding that they are conducted partly or totally online. If there were a serious irregularity in the conduct of the arbitration, there might well be enforcement challenges under the Convention; but the mere fact that ICT was by agreement used in the process should not of itself constitute irregularity.

20–036 The enforcement of other forms of consensual outcome in ODR would be no different from the position if they were resolved in the ordinary course, without ICT, subject again to the proviso that there was no serious irregularity—which would in any event also be applicable in those ordinary ADR processes.

20–037 As in ordinary practice, enforcement would depend on having a contract or award that would be recognised by a real court, this issue should be considered and agreed in any agreement to participate in ODR.

Law and jurisdiction

20–038 Until ODR establishes its own enforceable rules and jurisdiction, all indications are that parties contracting online would be well advised to agree on a legal system that will be applicable to their transaction. It would also be sensible to agree on any territorial jurisdiction that would apply, though some of the benefit of using ODR processes might be to avoid jurisdictional problems.

20–039 Practitioners may find that the disputants have already agreed these matters in their contract that forms the subject matter of the dispute. Online providers of goods or services might well have stipulated standard terms regulating the transaction.

ODR AND THE COURTS

Money Claims Online

20–040 The Money Claim Online (MCOL) service is the HM Courts & Tribunals Service internet-based service for claimants and defendants.[13] It became operational in 2012 and enables claimants to commence certain types of county court claims electronically.[14] The issue of a MCOL or by the SDT system for bulk claims leads to the claim being handled, initially, in Northampton but then (only if disputed) being transferred to an appropriate County Court hearing centre in accordance with protocols which pay attention to, but which are not bound by, the claimant's choice or party preference.[15]

---

[13] See *https://www.moneyclaim.gov.uk/web/mcol/welcome* [accessed 22 May 2018].
[14] See Practice Direction 7E.
[15] See Lord Justice Briggs, *Civil Courts Structure Review: Final Report*, July 2016 available at:

The MCOL service is for a fixed sum under £100,000 against no more than two people or organisations. The claimant must be over 18 to use the service and it can be used from anywhere in the UK, but only against someone with an address in England or Wales. A court fee must be paid using a debit or credit card. The service cannot be used for personal injury claims or claims for return of deposit from a landlord. 20–041

The Civil Justice Council has developed plans to introduce an internet-based dispute resolution service for low value claims of less than £25,000.[16] The proposed Online Court (HMOC) would have three tiers: 20–042
Tier 1: Online evaluation to assist a user to categorise and understand options regarding a claim;
Tier 2: A facility for reviewing case papers to support either negotiation or mediation; including automated negotiation tools;
Tier 3: A judicial decision making tool for judges to hand down judgments based on submissions received online.

While the proposed model does have some similarities with ombudsman procedures, Hodges argues that it fails to emulate the individualised response to people who seek advice, and the objective triage of facts presented, that ombudsmen offer.[17] The model follows existing online systems in operation in Canada, Germany and The Netherlands and is designed to provide a new model for flexible and cost-effective access to justice rather than simply supporting existing court services electronically.[18]

---

https://www.judiciary.gov.uk/wp-content/uploads/2016/07/civil-courts-structure-review-final-report-jul-16-final-1.pdf [accessed 22 May 2018] p.74.

[16] See the Civil Justice Online Dispute Resolution Advisory Group's Report of February 2015: *Online Dispute Resolution For Low Value Civil Claims*, available at: *https://www.judiciary.gov.uk/reviews/online-dispute-resolution/* [accessed 22 May 2018]. This follows the vision also set out by Lord Justice Briggs in his Report *Civil Courts Structure Review: Final Report*, July 2016 available at: *https://www.judiciary.gov.uk/wp-content/uploads/2016/07/civil-courts-structure-review-final-report-jul-16-final-1.pdf* [accessed 22 May 2018]. The Ministry of Justice introduced the online court for claims of up to £10,000 on 6 April 2018. It will allow an action to be commenced in the county court, settle disputes online and recommend mediation services.

[17] C. Hodges in Cortés, *The New Regulatory Framework for Consumer Dispute Resolution*, fn.10, p.361.

[18] S. Blake, J. Browne and S. Sime, *A Practical Approach to Alternative Dispute Resolution* (Oxford University Press, 2016), p.77.

CHAPTER 21

Jurisdiction, Forum and Law

ADR JURISDICTION

In traditional litigation, the courts obtain their jurisdiction from legislation, from rules made pursuant to such statutory provisions and from the concept of inherent jurisdiction.[1] Non-adjudicatory ADR processes, however, depend largely on the agreement of the parties for their authority, though this may be derived from mandatory procedural requirements.

21–001

AUTHORITY ARISING FROM STATUTE

As outlined in Ch.6, the statutory provision for arbitration in England arises under the Arbitration Act 1996. There is also statutory provision for adjudication, which was introduced through the Housing Grants, Construction and Regeneration Act 1996. There is, however, no statutory regime for consensual processes like mediation. There is a case for the passing of a mediation statute, but that seems likely to be some way off and would need a consultation process to identify what it should cover.[2]

21–002

It would seem that principles and procedures for adjudicatory forms are easier to prescribe than those for consensual processes. The latter vary as to model and methodology, and generally rely as much on the skill, style and approach of the neutral as on the rules of the process. Also, the outcome of adjudicatory forms will necessarily be a determination, whereas consensual processes will only have a binding outcome if the parties reach agreement. Consequently, adjudicatory processes and their outcomes can probably be more easily regulated by statute than consensual processes.

21–003

The following are some examples of ADR based directly or indirectly on statutory provisions:

21–004

- Statutory arbitration, arising under various laws such as the Telecommunications Act 1984 and the Water Industry Act 1991.

---

[1] In England and Wales the Civil Procedure Act 1997 introduced the Civil Procedure Rules.
[2] See the US Uniform Mediation Act 2003 (UMA) which seems to be one of the primary pieces of consolidating legislation present in westernised jurisdictions concerning mediation regulation.

- Court-annexed (or court-ordered) arbitration.[3] This kind of arbitration is not available in UK jurisdictions. Whether the arbitrator's decision is binding on the parties, (either initially non-binding but becoming binding under certain circumstances), and what rules or limits to jurisdiction apply will depend upon the model of court-annexed arbitration provided for by the statute.
- Arbitration in the UK under the Arbitration Act 1996. Although the procedures are governed by statute, amplified by common law and judicial precedent, arbitration requires the agreement of the parties in order for this procedure to be used. Once parties have agreed to arbitrate, either by way of general consent before or after any dispute has arisen, the arbitrator will have authority to consider the dispute and to make a binding decision. This is subject only to the discretion of the court to intervene in the very limited ways permitted by the Arbitration Act 1996, for example, under ss.67, 68 and 69.
- Private judging.[4] This procedure for the appointment of an impartial third-party referee with various prescribed judicial powers requires specific legislation. While unavailable in the UK, it is used in certain jurisdictions such as California and Texas.
- Mandatory (court-imposed) ADR and mediation schemes. While these do not exist in the UK, they are stipulated by statute in some jurisdictions around the world.[5]
- Mediation may be voluntarily entered into, but then regulated by statute, rules and regulations. A number of jurisdictions, but not England and Wales, have enacted ADR legislation which does not compel parties to enter into those processes (and certainly cannot compel them to use them effectively by concluding agreements) but which governs the way in which such processes are employed within that jurisdiction.[6]

AUTHORITY ARISING FROM AGREEMENT

21–005 Save where there is statutory or court-imposed provision for arbitration or mediation, ADR processes generally require the consent of all parties for the process to be used. In the absence of such agreement, litigation is the usual way for a dispute to be determined.

21–006 Agreement to engage in mediation or another ADR process can be given before any dispute is envisaged, for example stipulated in a contract as a dispute resolution procedure to be used in the event of any dispute arising on that contract. Alternatively, it can be agreed in relation to a specific disagreement after it has arisen, that is, on an ad hoc basis.

---

[3] See Ch.5 for a description of this process. In the US, it usually refers to arbitration by an arbitrator appointed by the court, who hears the parties and makes a determination. If neither party appeals, the decision becomes binding. If either party appeals, the decision is non-binding and a fresh hearing takes place before a judge.
[4] See Ch.19 for a description of this process.
[5] See Ch.5 for some examples of international court-related schemes, including those with a statutory foundation.
[6] See fn.2 and the US.

CONTRACT CLAUSE STIPULATING FOR ADR

Once a dispute arises in relation to a contract, parties commonly assert their respective positions, often with little inclination by either to explore creative and constructive ways of trying to resolve their differences. Neither side wishes to give an impression of weakness. On the contrary, in order to assert their rights each may wish to demonstrate the strength of their case, the justness of their cause and their determination to pursue the matter until a satisfactory outcome is achieved. Consequently, both sides often feel they must pursue their respective positions through the adversarial process, even if privately they may hope for an opportunity to be able to resolve the issues without a decision being imposed upon them.

21–007

Having observed this, it should be said that in jurisdictions with established ADR regimes, the concern about showing weakness through proposing ADR is no longer a major issue. On the contrary, it is an increasingly common requirement for parties in dispute to consider mediation or other forms of ADR, with potential costs sanctions for failing to do so.[7] Agreeing to mediate is no longer a sign of weakness. In any event, there are many lawyers and disputants who are well able to initiate a settlement discussion without seemingly losing face.

21–008

Nevertheless, in anticipation of possible disputes, it is prudent for contracts to incorporate a dispute resolution clause, which either side can invoke without any suggestion of weakness. These clauses can offer process options for dealing with disagreements at an early stage before the parties become too entrenched in their respective positions.

21–009

Such a clause may provide for arbitration instead of litigation. Or it can go further and stipulate that parties are not to pursue arbitration until having endeavoured to resolve the issues through a stipulated non-adjudicatory ADR process.[8]

21–010

While non-adjudicatory ADR procedures are being used, all rights are ordinarily reserved to revert to litigation or arbitration, as the case may be. If court proceedings need to be started or pursued in the meantime, this may well be done parallel to ADR. For example, it may be essential to issue a summons to avoid statute barring by limitation, or injunctive remedies may need to be pursued without delay. In any such event, parties might wish to protect their positions through court proceedings without necessarily precluding the possibility of trying to resolve matters through ADR.

21–011

---

[7] See Ch.5.
[8] Examples of such clauses are contained in the appendix, which may need to be appropriately adapted.

Arbitration clause

21-012 If a contractual arbitration clause exists, parties will generally be held to the arbitration procedure, and the courts will ordinarily decline to deal with the issues until the parties have exhausted the agreed arbitration procedure.[9] In some circumstances the court may, however, override such agreement and nevertheless accept jurisdiction.[10]

21-013 An arbitration clause can take various forms. The principal requirements are that the parties must commit themselves clearly and unconditionally to arbitration of the issues as stipulated in the clause and that the issues are arbitrable. Any limitations on the kinds of issues that may be so referred should be explicit. An arbitrator may be specifically identified, by name or by reference (such as a person nominated by the President for the time being of a stated professional body). If any system of law or institutional or ad hoc arbitration is to apply, that should also be stated (such as the rules and regulations of the International Chamber of Commerce or the UNCITRAL rules). If this is not done, the provisions of the Arbitration Act may apply where the parties are subject to English law and procedure. In international contracts, it is vital to provide for a venue.

Clause for non-adjudicatory ADR

21-014 Parties may wish to go beyond an arbitration clause and stipulate also for a non-adjudicatory form of ADR, often but not necessarily mediation. Clauses may reflect the sequence of process that the parties intend to follow to try to resolve any dispute. First they will usually select negotiation, then mediation and if that does not succeed, then arbitration, or litigation if that is preferred.

21-015 Dispute resolution clauses in contracts may be in a short form, just setting out the fundamental requirements. In this event, the commitment to the process is given and sufficient information to give the clause meaning, but procedural and other details are left for the parties to address in the event of a dispute. Alternatively, they may be in a longer form, setting out procedural details in advance.

21-016 The advantage of the short form is that it makes simple provision for ADR, leaving it to the parties to agree details appropriate to the actual issues. The disadvantage is that the detailed machinery is not settled, and it may be difficult to agree this later.

21-017 The advantage of a long form is that it will minimise later scope for procedural disagreement and may enhance the possibility of a court treating it as enforceable. The disadvantages, however, are that the details may not necessarily be appropriate to the actual dispute when it arises; and trying to agree detailed

---

[9] Such a clause may but need not necessarily be in the form of a *Scott v Avery* clause, based on the case of that name, (1856) 5 H.L. Cas. 811, which makes the award of the arbitrator a condition precedent to the right to litigate in the courts to enforce the rights under the contract.

[10] The court will do so where all parties agree that despite the arbitration clause, the court should deal with the matter. Where one party wishes to abide by the arbitration clause, but another wants to be released from it and prefers the court to adjudicate, the court will examine all relevant considerations and will decide whether or not to override the arbitration clause and to accept jurisdiction.

CONTRACT CLAUSE STIPULATING FOR ADR

dispute resolution provisions in advance, which may never arise in practice, may not be considered commercially desirable by parties when entering into a contract.

21–018
A further question arises as to whether or not it is necessary to provide specifically that a party is free to take formal steps, such as issuing a summons if this is for example necessary to prevent limitation, or seeking injunctive relief, notwithstanding the existence of an ADR clause. Arguably, this is inherently possible, notwithstanding the existence of a reference to ADR. In view, however, of a possible trend to try to enforce ADR clauses and to prevent litigation until they have been followed, it may be desirable, where appropriate, to insert such a provision for the avoidance of doubt.

21–019
Clauses in contracts need to be devised with due regard to the specific requirements of the parties. The following matters may be considered for such a clause:

- A description of the kinds of disputes and different circumstances which may be covered by the clause.
- Provision for the parties first to try to negotiate in good faith, using their best endeavours, perhaps with a time limit.
- Provision for the dispute then to be referred to mediation or to some other ADR form, perhaps listing the other possibilities and allowing the parties to choose.
- If the name of the mediator or the organisation providing the mediation or other ADR services is agreed, this may be specified; alternatively, the machinery for appointing a neutral practitioner should be stated.
- The rules, procedures and/or code of practice that will apply to the mediation or other ADR form could be specified, either in specific terms or indirectly, by reference, for example to an ADR organisation.
- A requirement for confidentiality and any other relevant terms may be indicated. If the process is to be treated as without prejudice or otherwise privileged that might usefully be stated.
- The clause can specify whether the mediator is required to provide a report, opinion, recommendation or evaluation, which would be off the record and non-binding.
- The timetable for the mediation or ADR process can be specified, providing also for it to be extended or amended by agreement.
- Provision can be made, if required, for an obligation on the parties to negotiate in the process in good faith.[11]
- The rights of the parties can be reserved in the event that no agreement is reached. It can specify that parties are free to pursue formal steps if required to protect their positions and that this will not prejudice the continuation of the mediation.
- If the process does not result in an agreement within a specified period, to be extended or amended by agreement, the clause can specify the adjudicatory process that is to follow, for example, arbitration (or litigation).

---

[11] See Ch.4 regarding the implications and efficacy of a commitment to negotiate in good faith.

- If the clause provides for arbitration, it may specify the name of the arbitrator or how or by whom such arbitrator is to be appointed and in international contracts the venue should be specified. It may also specify the rules of arbitration that are to apply and confirm that such arbitration is to be final and binding.
- The contract will usually stipulate which system of substantive law applies to the contract, but in case not, this may need to be specified in this clause.

ADR AGREEMENT AFTER DISPUTE HAS ARISEN

21–020 If parties in dispute have not agreed in advance what procedure is to apply to the resolution of their differences, and in the event that the dispute cannot be settled through negotiation, the court will be required to determine the outcome through the litigation process.

21–021 However, parties are free at any time to agree to some alternative procedure for the determination or resolution of their dispute, for example by way of arbitration or some other form of adjudication such as expert determination. If they first want to try to resolve it by negotiated agreement with the help of an impartial third-party facilitator, they can agree to attempt mediation or any other non-adjudicatory form of ADR, while reserving their right to revert to litigation or arbitration if the consensual process is unsuccessful.

21–022 The form of an agreement to submit to arbitration after a dispute has already arisen may follow the form of an arbitration clause in a contract, adapted to the actual requirements of the case.

21–023 The form of an agreement to submit to mediation or any other ADR process will also broadly follow the contractual form discussed above. It will usually need to be more detailed, to include for example the agreed terms relating to confidentiality, privilege, timetable, whether or not agreements reached in the process are immediately binding, non-liability of mediator (if applicable), terms of payment of mediator's fees and various other such matters.[12]

21–024 A wide range of possibilities exists as to what matters may be covered by the agreement, whether to have a simple form and perhaps just append a code of practice, as to drafting style and as to the terms of engagement.[13]

ENFORCEABILITY OF ADR CLAUSES IN CONTRACTS

21–025 The court has an inherent power to stay an action where it considers it appropriate to do so. This power is explicitly confirmed in r.3.1(2)(f) of the Civil Procedure Rules (CPR), which states that except where the Rules provide otherwise, the court may "(f) stay the whole or part of any proceedings or judgment either generally or until a specified date or event". Also, CPR r.26.4 provides:

---

[12] Contracts providing for mediation or other non-adjudicatory forms of ADR are more likely to be effective if these detailed terms are agreed in advance, either specifically or by reference to the standard terms of agreement or practice of a specified ADR organisation.

[13] Specimen agreements and relevant web links are contained in the appendix of precedents.

"(1) A party may, when filing the completed directions questionnaire, make a written request for the proceedings to be stayed while the parties try to settle the case by alternative dispute resolution or other means."[14]

21–026 Where parties have agreed in a binding contract clause that disputes are to be resolved by way of arbitration, it is well established that the courts will, in the absence of any compelling reason to the contrary, respect that decision by declining to allow one party to use the court instead of arbitration. This is generally done by staying any court proceedings so that the parties can use the agreed arbitration procedure. This power is expressly confirmed in the Arbitration Act 1996 s.9(1) of which reads as follows:

"A party to an arbitration agreement against whom legal proceedings are brought (whether by way of claim or counterclaim) in respect of a matter which under the agreement is to be referred to arbitration may (upon notice to the other parties to the proceedings) apply to the court in which the proceedings have been brought to stay the proceedings so far as they concern that matter."

21–027 This power has been considered in many cases, and courts have ordinarily upheld the arbitration provisions by ordering a stay, save where for specific reasons this was not considered appropriate. For example, in *Birse Construction Ltd v St David Ltd*[15] the question arose as to whether or not there was a valid arbitration agreement in existence and whether the court could rule on this. In the absence of a valid agreement to arbitrate, a stay would be refused. In *Sun Life Assurance Co of Canada v CX Reinsurance Co Ltd*[16] the Court of Appeal held that although the parties had orally agreed to arbitrate, no binding written agreement had been concluded and the decision to refuse a stay was upheld.

21–028 In *Nokia Corp v Interdigital Technology Corp*[17] there was an application to stay patent proceedings to give effect to an arbitration clause. The stay was refused, and upheld by the Court of Appeal, on the basis that the validity of the patent, which was the subject of the court proceedings, was a critical factor in the issues that would need to be arbitrated, hence the arbitration could follow after the court's determination on the patent.

21–029 There have been numerous decisions in which the courts have stayed proceedings to enable arbitration to take place. In *Bilta (UK) Ltd (In Liquidation) v Nazir*[18] the High Court ruled that, provided a party had expressly reserved its rights, an application for an extension of time to serve a defence would not constitute a waiver of the right to seek a stay of proceedings pending arbitration. It also ruled that the time period set out in CPR Pt 11 for challenging the court's jurisdiction did not apply to applications to stay for arbitration.

21–030 On the other hand, it is clear that under English law an agreement to enter into negotiations is not enforceable. In *Courtney and Fairbairn Ltd v Tolaini Brothers (Hotels) Ltd*, Lord Denning MR said that it was "too uncertain to have any

---

[14] See S. Sime, *A Practical Approach to Civil Procedure*, 20th edn (Oxford: OUP, 2017), Ch.15, for discussion of the court's powers in relation to granting stays for ADR to allow for settlement and the practicalities thereof.
[15] [1999] EWHC Technology 253.
[16] [2003] EWCA Civ 283; [2004] Lloyd's Rep. I.R. 58.
[17] [2004] EWHC 2920 (Pat).
[18] [2010] EWHC 1086 (Ch); [2010] Bus. L.R. 1634.

binding force".[19] After being followed in a number of subsequent cases, this decision was considered in *Walford v Miles* in the House of Lords, which confirmed that "a bare agreement to negotiate has no legal content" and is unenforceable.[20] In that case, Lord Ackner also said that the concept of a duty "to carry on negotiations 'in good faith' is inherently repugnant to the adversarial position of the parties when involved in negotiations." This could be distinguished from an agreement "to use best endeavours" which could be enforced.[21]

21-031 For courts to enforce an ADR clause, the ADR provision must be clear, certain and detailed in its terms. In *Tubeworkers v Tilbury Construction*,[22] Lord Justice Kerr approved and applied the principles enunciated in *Northern RHA v Derek Crouch Construction Co Ltd*[23] in order to uphold and enforce the dispute resolution mechanisms upon which the parties had agreed.

21-032 In 1998, in *Beaufort Developments (NI) Ltd v Gilbert-Ash NI Ltd*, the House of Lords overruled the Court of Appeal's decision in *Northern Regional Health Authority v Derek Crouch Construction Co.*[24] However, this did not undermine the principle that parties could agree on the dispute resolution machinery regulating their contractual relationship. Lord Hope of Craighead observed that:

> "the Court of Appeal in the *Crouch* case, having started from the correct principle, fell into error in its application to the facts".

21-033 The issue of enforceability of an ADR provision again came under scrutiny in *Cable and Wireless Plc v IBM United Kingdom Ltd,*[25] In that case Mr Justice Colman upheld the enforceability of an ADR clause in a contract and granted a stay of proceedings until after mediation had taken place. In his analysis, the judge said:

> "The reference to ADR is analogous to an agreement to arbitrate. As such, it represents a free-standing agreement ancillary to the main contract and capable of being enforced by a stay of the proceedings or by injunction absent any pending proceedings. The jurisdiction to stay, although introduced by statute in the field of arbitration agreements, is in origin an equitable remedy. It is further a procedural tool provided for under CPR 26.4 to encourage and enable the parties to use ADR."

Of interest with this case is the fact that the contract was not specific about the mode of ADR to follow, merely stating that the parties should, through "good faith negotiations", attempt to resolve their dispute using an ADR method recommended by the Centre for Dispute Resolution.

---

[19] *Courtney and Fairbairn Ltd v Tolaini Brothers (Hotels) Ltd* [1975] 1 W.L.R. 297 CA (Civ Div) at 301–302.
[20] *Walford v Miles* [1992] 2 A.C. 128; [1992] 2 W.L.R. 174 HL, per Lord Ackner at 181–182.
[21] *Walford v Miles* [1992] 2 W.L.R. 174 HL, per Lord Ackner at 181. See Ch.4 for more detailed discussion of this case and of "good faith" negotiation in general.
[22] (1985) 30 B.L.R. 67 CA (Civ Div).
[23] [1984] Q.B. 644; [1984] 2 W.L.R. 676 CA (Civ Div).
[24] *Beaufort Developments (NI) Ltd v Gilbert-Ash NI Ltd* [1999] 1 A.C. 266; [1998] 2 W.L.R. 860 HL (NI).
[25] [2002] EWHC 2059 (Comm).

ENFORCEABILITY OF ADR CLAUSES IN CONTRACTS

Clarity has been provided in *Holloway v Chancery Mead*,[26] in which Ramsey J suggested that to be enforceable such ADR clauses must meet at least the following three requirements: first, that the process must be sufficiently certain in that there should not be the need for an agreement at any stage before matters can proceed; secondly, the administrative processes for selecting a party to resolve the dispute and to pay that person should also be defined; and thirdly, the process or at least a model of the process should be set out so that the detail of the process is sufficiently certain.

21–034

In 2008 Mr Justice Coulson reaffirmed the use of the case management stay provision under r.3.1(2)(f) CPR in *Balfour Beatty Construction Northern Ltd v Modus Corovest (Blackpool) Ltd*[27] in which, citing *Cable and Wireless*, he said:

21–035

> "I take it as settled law that if the parties have agreed a particular method by which their disputes are to be resolved, then the Court has an inherent jurisdiction to stay proceedings brought in breach of that agreement even where the term of the contract on which the claiming party is said to be in breach was a general agreement to refer disputes to ADR".

It is clear from these cases that there is a line to be drawn between on the one hand merely agreeing to negotiate or loosely agreeing to try to resolve issues through ADR, both of which would be unenforceable, and on the other hand specifying a dispute resolution mechanism with sufficient particularity to render it enforceable. Another point that emerged from the *Balfour Beatty* case was that the court would also consider whether or not there was an arguable case. If there was, and if summary judgment was not appropriate, and if the court felt that mediation would be an appropriate way to proceed, then it might in any event have adjourned the case to enable mediation to take place.

21–036

On the issue of ADR clause enforceability where mediation is the contractual process choice, clarity has been further provided by the Court of Appeal's decision in *Sulamerica CIA Nacional de Seguros SA v Enesa*,[28] in which the court refused to uphold an ADR clause because it imposed no legal obligation on the parties. However, in that case, Moore-Bick LJ gave clear guidance on the drafting of mediation clauses to ensure enforceability. First that a clear explanation of the procedure to be followed should be provided when seeking to have the dispute resolved by mediation. Secondly, there should be clear provisions to appoint a particular mediator. Thirdly, a clearly defined mediation process must be provided.

21–037

The question must inevitably be asked why a party would seek to insist upon any other party being compelled to enter into negotiations, even in an ADR context, where the latter can effectively frustrate all attempts to resolve the matter by simply declining to agree to anything substantively. The answer is that a clause for mediation or ADR does seem to have an effect. It contains a moral and ethical requirement to comply with the terms of the contract in good faith and provides agreed machinery to facilitate resolution. The anecdotal experience of a number of mediators is that people who are compelled by the court to mediate

21–038

---

[26] [2007] EWHC 24.
[27] [2008] EWHC 3029 (TCC).
[28] [2013] 1 W.L.R. 102.

ADR FORUM

21-039 The notion of a forum in which a dispute is resolved is fundamental to the traditional processes of litigation, in that without first deciding upon the forum there cannot be an adjudicator or rules governing the process.[29] The parties may have agreed in their contract which forum would apply to the resolution of disputes. They might, for example, stipulate that:

> "The Courts of England shall have exclusive jurisdiction to resolve any dispute or disagreement arising from or by virtue of this Agreement".

Or they might provide that:

> "All disputes arising in connection with the present contract shall be finally settled under the Rules of Conciliation and Arbitration of the International Chamber of Commerce by one or more arbitrators appointed in accordance with the said Rules. The venue of the arbitration shall be Geneva, Switzerland."

21-040 In the absence of agreement, whether private or by the application of a convention such as the EU Regulation for the jurisdiction, recognition and enforcement of judgments in civil and commercial matters, No.44/2001 ("Brussels I"), various factors may apply to the choice of forum for traditional litigation. Where there are competing claims, as for example where the courts of more than one country might arguably or in fact have jurisdiction, the forum will be the one which according to the relevant principles of law,[30] is judged to be the most appropriate: the "forum conveniens".

21-041 In arbitration of international disputes, agreement on the venue is vital, for upon that choice may depend the enforceability of the arbitration agreement itself, the efficacy of the arbitral process and the ease of enforcement of any award. If parties to international contracts do not stipulate a venue, then the venue will depend either upon the decision of any arbitral institution upon which the parties may have agreed or upon the decision of the arbitrator or arbitrators themselves who have been appointed. A court may become seized of the matter if, for example, one or other of the party seeks to enforce the arbitral agreement in a given jurisdiction and the Court in question exercises supportive powers to give effect to the intention of the parties to arbitrate.

---

[29] See generally Frank E. A. Sander and Stephen B. Goldberg. "Fitting the Forum to the Fuss: A User-Friendly Guide to Selecting an ADR Procedure" (1994) 10(1) *Negotiation Journal* 49–68.

[30] For a statement of the applicable principles of English law in such cases see *Spiliada Maritime Corp v Cansulex Ltd ("The Spiliada")* [1987] A.C. 460; [1986] 3 W.L.R. 972. There is a two-stage test: what is the natural forum, with which the case is most closely connected; and are there any considerations of justice which should prevent the court from declining jurisdiction in favour of the natural forum?

In consensual ADR, the forum for the process is necessarily a matter of agreement between the parties. For this purpose, "forum" may mean the kind of process, the arena in which the ADR process is conducted, and the venue where this happens.   21–042

APPLICABLE LAW

The use of ADR does not necessarily remove the need for the parties to know the substantive legal system within which they are operating, as it may be vital to their rights and obligations, which may differ under different systems of law, apart from the procedural implications of such system.   21–043

As to procedure, where the parties are using an adjudicatory form, the legal system of the venue may regulate such procedure, as for example applying the Arbitration Act 1996, rather than the arbitration laws of some other country. Where they are using a consensual, non-adjudicatory form, the legal system may be less relevant, as the process will often have its own procedures, which may not be dependent on the applicable legal system. The organisation or practitioner responsible for implementing the process is likely to have a set of rules and procedures, perhaps in the form of a code of practice or a contract. Nevertheless, the legal system may as a matter of public policy prescribe what kinds of procedures are permissible and enforceable, and there may be an element of judicial oversight, so the system does have a relevance even to procedure. Some countries have an ADR statute that affects the system in which the process is undertaken.   21–044

Parties may agree which country's laws will apply to their transaction. It is commonplace for a contract involving international aspects to contain a provision stipulating which system of law is to apply to their agreement. So, for example, the contract may provide for disputes to be resolved by arbitration under the rules of arbitration of the International Chamber of Commerce, the arbitration to take place in Geneva, and for the system of law applicable to the contract to be English.   21–045

If the parties to an ADR contract have not stipulated for an agreed system of law, then if there is no international aspect and the parties are both or all in England and Wales, English law will generally apply; or if both or all in Scotland, Scots law. If, however, there is an international element, then the question as to which law applies to the provision for ADR will be resolved by the principles applicable to the conflict of laws. The factors that will primarily be taken into account will be the relevant international conventions and agreements, including those which affect Member States of the European Community in so far as these may be applicable, the countries in which the parties reside or carry on business, and the places where the terms of the agreement are to be performed.   21–046

CHAPTER 22

Future Directions

ADR 25 YEARS ON

It is now 25 years since the first edition of this work was published and it may be of some interest to reflect on changes and developments since then. 22–001

The first edition referred in the preface to "an increasing awareness that there is a denial of justice to the vast majority of the population as far as the civil justice system is concerned whose procedures and delays cause unacceptable levels of cost, beyond the reach of all save the wealthiest individuals and companies." *Plus ça change, plus c'est la même chose*: the more things change, the more they stay the same. Twenty-five years on and all the considerations indicating a need for alternatives to the court system remain at least as valid as they were at that time. 22–002

On the other hand, however, there has been significant progress in the development of ADR processes in the UK and public and professional awareness and acceptance of it. For example: 22–003

- While a small number of ADR organisations that were active at that early stage[1] continue to be among the leaders in the field, civil-commercial ADR has expanded. For example, the Civil Mediation Council (CMC),[2] created in 2003, at the time of publication of this 4th edition has 58 organisations registered as mediation providers in the civil-commercial field, including regional groupings, commercial bodies and charities.
- Family mediation has become an integral part of the process of addressing family issues. The Family Mediation Council (FMC) serves as an umbrella body for family mediation in England and Wales with six major organisational members[3] and with The Family Mediation Standards Board (FMSB) having delegated authority to advise on and oversee the implementation of, and adherence to, the FMC's professional standards.

---

[1] Such as CEDR (The Centre for Effective Dispute Resolution), CIArb (the Chartered Institute of Arbitrators), the ADR Group and the Academy of Experts.
[2] See the CMC's website at: *http://www.civilmediation.org/index.php* [accessed 10 June 2018].
[3] The six organisational members of the FMC are ADR Group, the College of Mediators, the Family Mediators Association, the Law Society, National Family Mediation and the family lawyers' body Resolution. See the FMC's website at: *https://www.familymediationcouncil.org.uk/* [accessed 10 June 2018].

FUTURE DIRECTIONS

- Mediation and other forms of ADR have become integrated into the court system though, perhaps to a greater extent, in areas like family and employment than in civil and commercial cases.[4]
- The use of ombudsman[5] and similar processes to address complaints against administrative injustice and maladministration, extended also into the private sector, has increased considerably over the period, incorporating the use of mediation and other forms of alternative dispute resolution.
- The whole concept of dispute resolution has changed from being primarily adversarial to embracing a range of alternative options. Consequently many solicitors now describe themselves as "dispute resolution lawyers" rather than "litigation lawyers" and many law firms have changed their "Litigation Departments" to "Dispute Resolution Departments"; various barristers' chambers offer mediation services. Additionally, as observed below, ADR is being integrated into legal education and training in the UK[6]; and, while litigation through the courts underpins parties' rights and will remain the option chosen by many, there has been some cultural shift towards adopting other approaches alongside or instead of litigation, with a greater expectation that ADR may be relevant.

22-004 Arbitration continues to be widely used, and contractual adjudication is increasingly employed and, as observed in Ch.7, may be the primary dispute resolution machinery in this field in the UK. Also, the use of international arbitration has increased significantly and is used for increasingly complex issues, including for example issues arising from bilateral investment treaties (BITs), Energy Charter Treaties as well as a range of financial and information technology disputes.[7] The trend over the last 25 years towards the use of processes, both adjudicatory and non-adjudicatory, other than through national courts is clearly continuing.

---

[4] See Ch.5 for the numerous ways in which ADR has increasingly permeated and intersected the court-based litigation system, including through rules, practice directions and protocols; Mediation Information and Assessment Meetings (MIAMs); some courts themselves adopting ADR processes such as Early Neutral Evaluation and Financial Dispute Resolution; Courts directing or recommending ADR processes; and judicial authority for Courts imposing sanctions where ADR should be and is not attempted.

[5] See Ch.18. As observed in that chapter, some prefer the term "ombudsperson". The word "Ombudsman" is Scandinavian and considered to be gender-neutral though questions remain about its etymology and usage.

[6] See paras 22-016 to 22-020.

[7] See for example the Report of the International Bar Association's Arb40 Sub-committee: "The Current State and Future of International Arbitration: Regional Perspectives" at *https://www.ibanet.org/Document/Default.aspx?DocumentUid=2102ca46-3d4a-48e5-aa20-3f784be214ca* [accessed 10 June 2018] published in August 2015, which analyses six primary regions of the world and indicates in its Executive summary "international arbitration is on the rise in all six regions". See also the reflections on international arbitration by leading arbitration practitioners and academics in anticipation of the conference "The Evolution and Future of International Arbitration: The Next 30 Years" at *http://www.law.qmul.ac.uk/media/qmul-images/Where-next-for-International-Arbitration.pdf* [accessed 10 June 2018].

BREXIT

The fourth edition of this work is published in anticipation of the UK's departure from the EU on 29 March 2019, following which there will be a transition period. What implications then does the EU withdrawal have for ADR? 22–005

With regard to mediation, the Cross-Border Mediation (EU Directive) Regulations 2011 (SI 2011/1133), which incorporates Directive 2008/52/EC of the European Parliament and of the Council of 21 May 2008,[8] came into force domestically on 20th May 2011. These Regulations cover issues of mediation evidence and extension of time limits with regard to mediation in certain cross-border disputes and makes amendments to particular primary legislation. 22–006

After Brexit, choice of applicable law will be important regarding matters such as mediation confidentiality and privilege, because the courts in civil law jurisdictions can interpret such issues very differently from those within our common law jurisdiction. For instance the "without prejudice" principle, which is a common law concept, is not recognised in EU countries where the civil jurisdiction predominantly operates.[9] 22–007

Where choice of jurisdiction in the event of a dispute is not made clear, the EU currently has two main Regulations that aim to achieve a harmonised set of rules for EU Member States in this regard, namely the Rome I and Brussels I Regulations.[10] Neither of these Regulations will apply when the UK leaves the EU and consequently there are implications. 22–008

As a result, there will be uncertainty as to how the applicable law, currently governed by the Rome I Regulations, will be determined. The UK will have to make clear how certain matters, including legal issues in relation to the mediation of cross border disputes, should operate after Brexit. 22–009

Choice of court is currently governed by the Brussels I Regulations and jurisdiction for this will have to be clarified after Brexit also, which otherwise leaves the possibility of parallel litigation. The withdrawal may also have an effect on the recognition of mediation clauses, mediation settlement agreements and their enforceability, as at present some EU Member States can treat mediated settlement agreements in the same way as a court order, court consent award or judgment. 22–010

Pursuant to Article 24 and/or 25 of Regulation No 805/2004 of the European Parliament and of the Council of 21 April 2004[11] creating a European Enforcement Order for uncontested claims, cross-border mediated settlement agreements of certain money claims can currently be enforced in the state of origin. This is done by application of Art.65 of the EC Treaty,[12] the aim of which 22–011

---

[8] See: *https://eur-lex.europa.eu/legal-content/EN/TXT/PDF/?uri=CELEX:32008L0052&from=EN* [accessed 10 June 2018].
[9] And principles of good faith generally carry greater weight in civil law systems: see Ch.4, paras 4-076 to 4-085.
[10] See: *https://eur-lex.europa.eu/legal-content/EN/TXT/PDF/?uri=CELEX:32008R0593&from=EN* [accessed 10 June 2018] and *http://eur-lex.europa.eu/LexUriServ/LexUriServ.do?uri=OJ:L:2012:351:0001:0032:EN:PDF* [accessed 10 June 2018].
[11] See: *https://eur-lex.europa.eu/legal-content/EN/TXT/PDF/?uri=CELEX:32004R0805&from=EN* [accessed 10 June 2018].
[12] See: *https://eur-lex.europa.eu/legal-content/EN/TXT/PDF/?uri=CELEX:12002E/TXT&from=EN* [accessed 10 June 2018].

is to improve and simplify the recognition and enforcement of decisions in civil and commercial cases, including decisions in extrajudicial cases (which includes mediation settlement agreements). The Article promotes the compatibility of the rules applicable in the Member States concerning the conflict of laws and of jurisdiction and eliminates obstacles to the good functioning of civil proceedings, if necessary by promoting the compatibility of the rules on civil procedure applicable in the Member States.[13] This may all change after the UK's withdrawal from the EU on 29 March 2019.

22–012 UNCITRAL's Working Group II (Dispute Settlement) and their Working Group II (Arbitration and Conciliation), are looking into enforceability of cross-border settlement agreements arising out of international commercial arbitration, conciliation and mediation, including the future possible development of a multi-lateral convention similar to New York Convention in relation to foreign arbitral awards.

REGULATION

22–013 A further issue concerns the regulation of mediation. The arguments for regulation are strong: these include the interests of the parties (including effective complaints mechanisms and the adequacy of available legal remedies); national interest (including the facilitation of cross-border disputes, attracting dispute resolution to the UK); and public interest (in the good administration of justice, the need to ensure accountability in relation to particular types of mediated claims—such as human rights).[14] This may be considered particularly important if mediation becomes, de facto, compulsory. However, there are convincing arguments against regulation: in particular, the need to ensure that the growth of the mediation sector is not adversely impacted by excessive regulation and rigidification, and the potential for costs increase which would pass to parties (due to indemnity insurance, for example). The consensus appears to be leaning towards light-touch regulation.

22–014 Another consideration is what form, if any, regulation should take. The argument for legislation can be based on the need to ensure consistency across mediation bodies and practitioners so that mediators require accreditation and a minimum base level of training, together with entrenchment of the core principles of mediation. This ensures a base level of protection for parties. The alternative is for professional bodies or affiliated groups of mediators to set base level standards and to have an accountability mechanism in place, such as a complaints procedure. The Civil Mediation Council takes this function within the UK for civil and commercial mediation, through its registration of mediator groups who are approved by the CMC to offer training and through individual mediator registration. However, without legislation in place to ensure that training is only offered by approved providers and that individuals are registered with a mediation group and/or with the professional body, this may not be sufficient on its own to protect individuals from unregistered mediators who lack either

---

[13] Treaty Establishing the European Community Art.65 (a), (b) and (c).
[14] See M. Whitehouse "Regulating Civil Mediation in England and Wales: Towards a Win-Win Outcome" (2017) (2) *Mediation Theory and Practice*, pp.69–83.

experience or training. Hopt and Steffek, in their excellent comparative work, have outlined two models of regulation: "extensive regulation" and "restrained regulation".[15] The light-touch or restrained regulation model ensures that the key principles of mediation are entrenched—this offers protection for the parties in that such regulation aids enforcement of those principles. However, heavier regulation (particularly if this takes the form of legislation) may thwart the effectiveness of mediation as a flexible and informal process.[16]

The EU Mediation Directive arguably adopted a light-touch approach. The Directive requires Member States to encourage the training of mediators and the introduction of effective quality control mechanisms in relation to the provision of mediation services.[17] Further the training is to ensure that "mediation is conducted in an effective, impartial and competent way".[18] However, the means by which to ensure effective quality control of mediation services provision was left to the Member States to use "whatever means they consider appropriate", including voluntary codes of conduct and other mechanisms.[19] Brexit will provide a further opportunity to consider this issue.

22–015

EDUCATION AND ACADEMIC DEVELOPMENTS

ADR, or dispute resolution, as an identifiable academic subject, has not been traditionally viewed as a key element or component of the general principles of legal education for undergraduate or postgraduate law students in the UK. The focus has generally been on the adversarial nature of dispute resolution and consequently, the syllabus has traditionally focused on advocacy during the practical stage of training on both the Legal Practice Course for those students intending to qualify as solicitors, and the Bar Professional Training Course for aspiring barristers.[20]

22–016

This is in contrast to the approach generally taken by law schools outside the UK. In other common law jurisdictions, there is evidence of enlightened liberal education approaches; of the top 10 ranked US Law Schools in 2018, all of them taught stand-alone courses on negotiation, mediation and arbitration, and some have live clinics linked with these areas of the taught curriculum.[21] Similarly, in Canada the top ranked law schools all offer conflict/dispute resolution, mediation

22–017

---

[15] Klaus J. Hopt and Felix Steffek, *Mediation: Principles and Regulation in Comparative Perspective* (Oxford: Oxford University Press 2013) 17–19.
[16] See Chan's review of Hopt and Steffek's work: P.H. Chan "Book Review: Klaus J. Hopt and Felix Steffek, *Mediation: Principles and Regulation in Comparative Perspective* (Oxford, Oxford University Press 2013)" (2013) (14) *European Business Organization Law Review* 613.
[17] Preamble [16] Directive 2008/52/EC on certain aspects of Mediation in civil and commercial matters.
[18] Directive 2008/52/EC art.4(2) on certain aspects of Mediation in civil and commercial matters.
[19] Directive 2008/52/EC art.4(1) on certain aspects of Mediation in civil and commercial matters.
[20] B.D. Waters, "The Importance of Teaching Dispute Resolution in a Twenty First Century Law School", (2017) 51(2) *The Law Teacher*.
[21] The top 10 law schools as listed in the US News and World Report Rankings 2019 were: Yale, Harvard, Stanford, Columbia, The University of Chicago, New York University, The University of Pennsylvania, The University of Michigan, The University of California Berkeley and The University of Virginia, available at: *https://www.usnews.com/best-graduate-schools/top-law-schools/law-rankings?int=9c0f08* [accessed 10 June 2018].

FUTURE DIRECTIONS

22–018 and negotiation courses as part of their curriculum. In the UK there are negotiation and mediation competitions for law students, however relatively few UK teams enter the law student ICC Mediation Competition held annually in Paris.

In recent years, however, ADR has become more integrated into legal education and training in the UK and this is reflective of many legal practitioners' attitudes to the subject.[22] Law students wanting to become legal practitioners need to have an awareness of the ethical implications of the Civil Procedure Rules (CPR)[23] as well as their professional codes of conduct.[24] This is particularly the case for future solicitors who are required to provide legal advice in the general area of dispute resolution. As observed above, in the world of legal practice, many law firms have adopted the words "dispute resolution" to replace their "litigation" departments.

22–019 The Legal Education Training Review (LETR)[25] Committee, whose remit was to consider the future of legal education and to make recommendations to ensure that England and Wales has a system of legal education fit for the future, reported its findings and recommendations in July 2013. The Committee's Report mentioned little about ADR and only in relation to advocacy within the practical training stage for barristers.[26] However, in July 2017 the Solicitors Regulation Authority (SRA) released its syllabus requirements as part of wholesale changes to training regulations for students seeking admission as solicitors. The study of dispute resolution now appears as a requirement within the syllabus for both parts

---

[22] Whilst the Legal Practice Course, the practical stage of a solicitor's training, does not include any compulsory elements associated with ADR, the Bar Professional Training Course requires future barristers to learn about the various alternative methods of dispute resolution which fall outside the usual judicial process, including mediation, negotiation, arbitration, early neutral evaluation, expert determination, and other alternative dispute resolution processes. See the *Resolution of Disputes Out of Court* module included within the BPTC Syllabus and Curriculum 2017/18, p.72, available at: *https://www.barstandardsboard.org.uk/media/1914855/2017-18_bptc_syllabus_-_full_syllabus_nov_2017.pdf* [accessed 10 June 2018].

[23] The following Rules and associated Practice Directions: Practice Direction (Pre-action Conduct) promote pre-issue settlement and requires parties to consider ADR. The Pre-action protocols require parties to consider whether some form of ADR is appropriate (there can be later costs sanctions); CPR 1.4 dealing with judicial case management extends to encouraging use of ADR; CPR 26.4 gives the court power to stay cases to enable ADR to take place; the Practice Direction to CPR 29 provides that the court can give directions regarding ADR on its own initiative without a case management conference (CMC); CPR 44.3 provides that the court can consider parties conduct on issues of costs (relating to the Pre-action Protocol period) and CPR 44.5 the court can consider parties' conduct on issues of costs during the proceedings.

[24] Pursuant to para.2.02(1)(b) of Solicitors Regulation Authority's (SRA) Code of Conduct 2011, when considering the options available to the client if the matter relates to a dispute between a client and a third party, a solicitor should discuss whether mediation or some other ADR procedure may be more appropriate than litigation, arbitration or other formal processes.

[25] LETR was undertaken on behalf of the Bar Standards Board (BSB), ILEX Professional Standards (IPS) and the Solicitors Regulation Authority (SRA). It was the first sector-wide review of legal services since the *Ormrod Report* of 1971 (*Report of the Committee on Legal Education*, Cmnd 4595). J Webb, J. Ching, P. Maharg and A. Sherr, *Setting Standards: The Future of Legal Services Education and Training Regulation in England and Wales* (London: Legal Education and Training Review, 2013) (LETR Report). Available at: *http://letr.org.uk/the-report/index.html* [accessed 10 June 2018].

[26] LETR Recommendation 13 stated that on the Bar Professional Training Course (for intending barristers), Resolution of Disputes out of Court should be reviewed to place greater practical emphasis on the skills required by ADR, particularly with regard to mediation advocacy.

1 and 2 of the Solicitors Qualification Examination (SQE). The SRA proposes to introduce these new training regulations for solicitors in September 2020 (at the earliest).

Hence, in the future, the foundational areas of legal knowledge which are incorporated into the current Qualifying Law Degree (QLD), will be replaced with what the SRA now calls "functioning legal knowledge" areas. The six areas of functioning legal knowledge proposed for SQE 1 will include Dispute Resolution in Contract and/or Tort. At SQE2, candidates must choose two practice contexts and one of the options from which to choose is Dispute Resolution. 22–020

These developments are likely to support the continuing establishment of a culture in the legal profession that regards the use of mediation and other forms of facilitated dispute resolution as standard rather than exceptional, and which increases the understandings and skills of practitioners in this regard. 22–021

REVIEW OF CIVIL JUSTICE AND ADR

As outlined in Ch.5, Lord Justice Briggs' Civil Courts Structure Review (CCSR), published in July 2016, provided a vision for the future, particularly online dispute resolution (ODR) and the Online Court. A pilot scheme, operating in England and Wales for claims of up to £10,000, has been established to test this online process. The two reports (Interim and Final) contain significant findings and recommendations in relation to ADR provision for the future.[27] In his final report, Briggs LJ stated the purpose of his review to be "to identify how best by structural change to preserve the strengths, address the weaknesses, maximise the opportunities and manage the threats of, and facing, the civil courts". Briggs LJ's recommendations for dispute resolution included: 22–022

- the creation of an Online Court, intended to be used by litigants mainly without the need for legal representation;
- there will be various nudges towards ADR in the tier 1 exchanges with the party during which he/she clarifies their case;
- at tier 2 a key task of the "case officer" will be not only to assist judges in dealing with routine box work but to assist the parties in making an informed choice between the available ADR options and possibly even to conduct a telephone mediation themselves;
- the use of a single County Court for the enforcement of all civil judgments and orders;
- the value threshold below which a claim cannot be issued in the High Court to be increased to £250,000 initially, then £500,000, with no distinction for personal injury claims.

The Online Court has been established and future developments will undoubtedly include the further recommendations outlined above.

---

[27] Lord Justice Briggs, *Civil Courts Structure Review: Final Report*, July 2016 available at: *https://www.judiciary.gov.uk/wp-content/uploads/2016/07/civil-courts-structure-review-final-report-jul-16-final-1.pdf* [accessed 10 June 2018].

FUTURE DIRECTIONS

22–023 In late 2017 the Civil Justice Council (CJC), the advisory non-departmental public body responsible for overseeing and co-ordinating the modernisation of the civil justice system, tasked its ADR Working Group with reviewing the ways in which ADR is currently encouraged and positioned within the civil justice system in England and Wales. This included reviewing current forms of ADR encouragement for mediation (and other suitable forms of ADR) in civil disputes, including practices in other jurisdictions, assessing proposals for reforms to rules or initiatives, monitoring, and contributing to the review of the EU Mediation Directive.

22–024 A major concern of the ADR Working Group was to complement and build upon the proposals introduced by Lord Briggs in his CCSR. The Group thought it striking that even 15 years ago a report on the structure of the civil courts might well not have contained any discussion of the role of ADR.

COMPULSION: WHERE ARE WE?

22–025 With the Children and Families Act 2014, we have seen the introduction and extension of the MIAM for private family related disputes as outlined in Ch.11. Not only is a MIAM effectively a pre-condition for beginning family proceedings but in applicable cases FDR hearings are also compulsory. The Employment Tribunals (Constitution and Rules of Procedure) Regulations 2013 introducing updated Tribunal Rules set out duties for the Employment Tribunal to encourage the use of ADR, including ACAS conciliation, mediation and judicial mediation. These developments since the last edition are the closest we have reached to anything approaching mandatory mediation in the UK.

22–026 Given the above developments there is a strong view that compulsion or automatic referral can no longer be said to cross an unacceptable constitutional line, though there are equally strong views questioning whether compulsory mediation is necessary or appropriate. Whether a move in that direction will ever be made in the wider civil and commercial field remains open to doubt. The Interim Report of the Civil Justice Council working group did not (by a majority) back compulsion but spoke of introducing an effective presumption that parties would have to put forward proposals for some form of ADR at the directions stage. Imposing MIAMs as a preliminary condition where the majority of claims are not disputed seems impractical. There could also be practical issues as to who in a civil dispute should attend a MIAM. All proponents of compulsion accept that there would have to be some opt-outs and that the Court would necessarily retain some discretion. There can also be legitimate disagreement as to when in the course of proceedings ADR is appropriate. Should the parties wait until the evidence is complete? Judicial sentiment still seems firmly set against compulsion.

BLACK SWANS AND THE GDPR

Some things that were not anticipated may appear to have been clearly predictable—after the event. This is one of the attributes of Black Swans, a concept developed by Taleb.[28] 22–027

Perhaps we might all have anticipated that the need to provide greater protection for people's private data might impact on dispute resolution procedures, both in terms of maintaining privacy and of a possible obligation to share information received confidentially about someone. How for example would this affect a mediator's ability to maintain the confidentiality of information provided in separate confidential meetings with parties if the other party requires to be told—at the time or perhaps later—what had been said or what information had been provided about him or her? What are the obligations of a dispute resolution facilitator in relation to data received during an ADR process? 22–028

These are largely unanticipated but perhaps predictable issues that have arisen because of the coming into force of the General Data Protection Regulation 2018 (GDPR).[29] 22–029

This 4th edition goes to print just as the GDPR comes into effect, so its implications for ADR are not yet fully appreciated, but the following preliminary observations may be made[30]: 22–030

- Mediators and all dispute resolution practitioners need to ensure that they are conversant and up-to-date with all data protection principles and requirements, which are likely to be amended from time to time, and that they are fully compliant with these.
- Personal data is protected by the GDPR and is identified on the ICO's website[31] as including information relating to natural persons who can be identified or who are identifiable, directly from the information in question or who can be indirectly identified from that information in combination with other information. Some data may be particularly sensitive.

---

[28] Nassim Nicholas Taleb, *The Black Swan: The Impact of the Highly Improbable* (London: Penguin, 2007). The title of the book arises from the fact that at one time people believed that all swans were white, and it was a shock to discover that black swans existed. In Taleb's view, we need to acknowledge that often we just "don't know" and cannot easily compute probabilities, though we may believe that we can do so mathematically or scientifically.

[29] The GDPR, which came largely into force on 25 May 2018, forms part of the UK's data protection regime, together with the Data Protection Act 2018. It supplements the EU's General Data Protection Regulation 2016/679 and is enforced by the Information Commissioner's Office (ICO)—see the ICO website generally at *https://ico.org.uk/* [accessed 10 June 2018] and its Guide to the GDPR at *https://ico.org.uk/for-organisations/guide-to-the-general-data-protection-regulation-gdpr/* [accessed 10 June 2018]. The UK Government has confirmed that the UK's decision to leave the European Union will not alter this: in this regard and generally see: *https://www.local.gov.uk/our-support/general-data-protection-regulation-gdpr* [accessed 10 June 2018].

[30] The authors are grateful to Angela Lake-Carroll and to the family lawyers' organisation Resolution for providing their Good Practice Guide (GPG) for mediators written by her. This, and the extensive guidance provided by the ICO on its website—see fn.29—largely provide the basis for this brief summary of some relevant aspects of the GDPR. It must be emphasised that readers need to be fully conversant with all relevant data protection provisions and cannot place any reliance on this brief and partial summary.

[31] See fn.29.

FUTURE DIRECTIONS

- Personal data about parties may not be shared without their expressed permission and must be stored securely. If held electronically, systems for both storing and deleting the data must be secure. The same applies to any paper information or data.
- Individuals have various rights under the GDPR, which cover the right to be informed; the right of access to data; the right to rectification and erasure; the right to restrict processing and data portability; the right to object; and rights in relation to automated decision making and profiling.
- The GDPR outlines the key principles underlying the processing of personal data. These include primarily principles of lawfulness, fairness and transparency, among others. Furthermore, practitioners must have a lawful basis for processing personal data and should document what it is. A privacy notice or policy, in clear, understandable and unambiguous language, should identify the basis and the purposes of the processing and how personal data is handled and managed. This might be included or referred to in any Agreement to Mediate.[32]
- Personal data must not be kept for longer than is necessary for the purpose for which it is processed. The Resolution guide[33] points out that that mediation is not a "legal activity".[34] Consequently, the requirements for retention of legal documents—commonly held for at least six years—will not apply in the same way to the retention of mediation documents, which should be considered on a case-by-case basis, and not retained for any longer than is necessary for the purposes of providing a mediation service.
- Parties or prospective clients may request information held about them, known as a "subject access request". A fee used to be chargeable for providing this, but that is no longer permissible. If that person's data contains information about another person, it cannot ordinarily be provided without that other person's consent. Responses to subject access requests need to be made with care on a case-by-case basis so as to ensure compliance with carefully balanced regulations and principles.
- The question may arise as to how a mediator may respond to a request for information obtained from the other party in a separate confidential meeting. Lake-Carroll points out that the Data Protection Act sets out several specific exemptions including an exemption in relation to negotiation where disclosure would be likely to prejudice the negotiations.[35] This may apply in relation to any subject access request made by a mediation party. In deciding on the appropriate response, the mediator must consider whether it would be proper to release information without the other person's express consent and whether the negotiation exemption is justified.

---

[32] Document 10 in Appendix I at para.A1-044, a specimen Agreement to Mediate in the family field, will require amplification to reflect the requirements of the GDPR, such as a reference to the mediator's privacy notice or policy with information about data protection, including privacy policy, the retention and destruction of notes and personal information and the circumstances under which data may be shared and/or released. The mediator's organisation might provide guidance or a precedent in this regard.

[33] GPG, see fn30.

[34] Defined in the Legal Services Act 2007s.12 (4).

[35] In Pt IV of and Sch.7 to the 1998 Act. See fn.30.

It is difficult to predict whether and to what extent the GDPR will affect mediation and other ADR processes. Meanwhile it would be advisable for practitioners to comply carefully and conscientiously with it.

THE WAY FORWARD

In the first edition of this work, there was doubt about ADR and its adoption into and participation within the mainstream of the dispute resolution continuum. With the government's response to Lord Woolf's Report in the form of the Access to Justice Act 1999, the attendant CPR and Practice Directions, we have witnessed by way of judicial activism a growth in extra-judicial dispute resolution. This has taken place through the imposition of costs penalties on litigants for unreasonably refusal of offers to explore alternative ways (other than litigation) to resolve civil disputes, as well as through directions provided to litigants to explore ADR processes whilst proceedings are stayed. There has also been a growth in ADR because of carefully drafted ADR clauses embedded within commercial contracts.

Since 2014 claims can be issued online through the HMCTS Money Claims Online Service (MCOL) and we have already witnessed the introduction of ODR via the ODR platform for consumer disputes, adopted into UK law in January 2016. As mentioned above, a new online claims system is being piloted in England and Wales for claims of up to £10,000, to be potentially further developed to include a three-stage process for disputes to be resolved "virtually", as envisioned by Lord Justice Briggs. Online legal services will undoubtedly form an important part of the future: these include free web-based services, subscription-based services for law firms, chargeable services for alternative business structures and publishers.[36]

In the critical area of public and professional awareness of ADR and mediation, the position is one of incremental progress. Mediation techniques, though not always described as such, are now being encountered by the citizen in a variety of contexts. These can include consumer conciliation, divorce, employment, workplace issues around stress and bullying, restorative justice in crime and neighbour disputes, as well as civil and commercial disputes. Anecdotally mediators report a slow but steady increase in the number of lay clients who attend mediation with, if not always direct experience, some concept of what the process might involve. Just as recently-appointed judges will have attended mediations in their professional lives, so lawyers now qualifying are more likely to have encountered mediation thinking during their training. The success of peer mediation when it is introduced in schools may even mean that students are leaving school and university, and entering adult life, having actually conducted a mediation. ADR is a dynamic and fascinating landscape though significant challenges still lie ahead.

---

[36] R. Susskind, *Tomorrow's Lawyers: An Introduction to Your Future* (Oxford: Oxford University Press, 2013), pp.84–91.

APPENDIX I

Drafting, Documents and Precedents

All precedents and documents provided or referred to in this Appendix are for general guidance and information only and no warranty or assurance is given as to their suitability for any particular usage or generally. It is up to readers to check and adapt them appropriately for their use and the publishers, authors, consulting editor and others providing the precedents and documents cannot accept responsibility for their use. Furthermore, it should be noted that they are provided as at the time of publication of this book, and may vary in the future.

Most if not all of the documents used in the processes covered in this book are "living" documents that may be updated or varied from time to time. Having regard to this and to the fact that many of them are available in updated form online, this appendix will provide web links to relevant documents rather than publishing the documents themselves. Note that copyright in the documents vests in any organisations mentioned. It should be emphasised that this list is by no means comprehensive or definitive. **A1–001**

Documents set out fully in this appendix may not be generally available online and are included for guidance. They will need to be adapted with judgment for individual use. **A1–002**

DRAFTING MEDIATION AND OTHER ADR DOCUMENTS

Effective documentation may be integral to mediation and other ADR processes. The mediator's appointment and agreement to mediate should be recorded. Some documents may need to be prepared during the mediation. After its conclusion, the outcome has to be effectively and appropriately recorded; and although this is the responsibility of the parties themselves in most situations, the mediator may need to assist and sometimes to take a role in the drafting. This may comprise a binding agreement (as, for example, in most civil and commercial settlements) or a non-binding memorandum or summary that can be used as a basis for the subsequent drafting of binding terms (as commonly required in family mediation). **A1–003**

Mediation organisations will usually have a Code of Practice and perhaps a procedural guide, and may provide precedent documents, such as standard terms of Agreement to Mediate, practice forms, draft summaries of outcome and settlement agreements. **A1–004**

Codes of Practice and Model Procedures and Standards

A1–005 Codes differ according to the field of activity of the mediation. In the civil and commercial field in the UK there is no standard Code, but each organisation may have its own Code.

A1–006 In addition to a Code of Practice for third party neutrals, CEDR Solve, the dispute resolution service of the Centre for Effective Dispute Resolution (CEDR) has published a Model Mediation Procedure applicable to civil and commercial disputes. A link to this is provided.

A1–007 In the family field, while different organisations may have their own Codes, the umbrella organisation in England and Wales, the Family Mediation Council (FMC), publishes a Code which applies to all mediation conducted or offered by mediators who are members of the organisations belonging to the FMC.

A1–008 The Rules for Expert Determination of the Academy of Experts can be found in a link to that body provided below.

The Agreement to Mediate

A1–009 Before the mediation process is started, the mediator should enter into an agreement with the parties setting out the terms and basis on which the mediation is undertaken.

A1–010 The agreement ought to cover various matters including the mediator's role, confidentiality, privilege and other relevant process matters. It should also deal with practical matters such as fees, time frame, venue and complaints procedure.

A1–011 The agreement to mediate can be formal, which is more common for civil and commercial work, or it can be relatively informal in style, which family and community mediators tend to prefer.

Contract clauses

A1–012 Commercial contracts commonly indicate which country's law is to apply to their terms and how disputes are to be dealt with. Dispute resolution clauses may state which courts are to have jurisdiction, but frequently set out machinery for addressing disputes without using the courts. So, for example, provision may be made for mediation and/or arbitration. The clause may outline a sequential procedure, which may start with negotiation, moving on to mediation or other consensual processes if necessary, and then to arbitration if still unresolved.

A1–013 Dispute resolution clauses in contracts allow parties to choose in advance how they want any disputes to be dealt with. That avoids the tendency for parties to become polarised if they try to agree this machinery only after a dispute has arisen.

DRAFTING, DOCUMENTS AND PRECEDENTS

Settlement Agreements

Who drafts and when?

This is likely to depend on the practice within the field of activity being mediated. In civil and commercial mediation, where agreements are commonly signed before the parties leave the process, the settlement agreement is ordinarily drafted "on the spot". However, this is not always practicable and appropriate and drafting may be undertaken afterwards. As to whether any understandings might be recorded in the meanwhile, see below under "Binding or non-binding". A1–014

Where lawyers represent the parties in the mediation, they may agree between themselves as to the procedure and responsibility for the drafting. In either event, the mediator may liaise with them as they do so and may view the document before signature in case of any misunderstanding or oversight. The mediator's role will usually be minimal, with the responsibility for drafting resting with the parties' lawyers. A1–015

Where parties are not represented in civil-commercial mediation, or where the mediator has kept notes that will facilitate drafting, the mediator may need to be more closely involved in the drafting and may well produce a first draft agreement. However, it should be made clear to the parties that it is their responsibility to check and ensure that the terms correctly reflect the agreed resolution and that all relevant details and conditions are incorporated. The mediator too would check this. The settlement agreement must be binding and enforceable if this is what is required, or non-binding or conditional if this is the requirement. A1–016

It is helpful for civil-commercial mediators to have a template or precedent settlement agreement to facilitate drafting if the matter is settled. This may be general or it may be specific to the case being mediated. A1–017

In family mediation, there is a different culture and expectation concerning the recording of settlement terms. Parties commonly attend mediation meetings without their lawyers present and would not ordinarily sign a settlement agreement in the meeting, but would expect a non-binding note of the proposed terms to be sent to them afterwards. Any such note would be non-binding to allow each party to take the document to their respective lawyers for individual advice and to have the terms converted into appropriate formal documentation. A1–018

It is usual for family mediators to draft a non-binding note or memorandum of the proposed terms, usually in the form of a "without prejudice" Memorandum of Understanding (MoU). If the respective lawyers approve the terms, they will arrange between themselves for those terms to be incorporated into a binding document, whether a formal agreement, deed or a court order. The mediator would not ordinarily be further involved in the drafting. Of course, if the lawyers attend the mediation, the settlement documentation may well be dealt with at that time. A1–019

In other fields of activity, drafting practice varies. Workplace mediation tends to follow the civil-commercial approach, whereas practice in neighbourhood and community mediation depends on the issues involved and the requirements of the parties. In some cases, a binding written agreement will be needed; but in some kinds of inter-personal or community mediation, oral agreements binding in A1–020 honour only may sometimes suffice or be preferred. Even if a mediation is informal, and the parties do not want their proposed agreement to be binding, it may be helpful to have a written record of their understandings for the avoidance of possible future good faith misunderstandings.

Format

A1–021 Formats for the recording of settlement terms vary according to the field of ADR in which one is working. Even within the same field, differences of approach and style exist.

A1–022 In the civil and commercial field, agreements tend to record matters in a businesslike way, as in an ordinary commercial agreement. It can be helpful for the mediator to prepare in advance an outline settlement agreement, providing the framework for the agreed terms to be attached as a schedule to it.

A1–023 In the family field, a different format tends to be used. The usual practice is for the mediator to prepare a non-binding, without prejudice MoU or Summary of Proposals, which contains a brief outline of the issues and the proposals. It is generally accompanied by an open (not privileged) Financial Disclosure Summary, setting out the financial circumstances of the parties.

A1–024 In community and neighbourhood mediation, settlement terms may remain oral. If recorded, the memorandum recording them would usually be brief and informal.

SOME PRINCIPLES OF MEDIATION DRAFTING

Binding or non-binding, principle or detail

A1–025 It must be clear whether the recorded terms are to be immediately binding. If not, will they become binding when some further stage has been reached or condition met?

A1–026 The agreement under which the parties entered into the mediation may make provision whether or not and in what circumstances the agreement reached in the mediation will be binding on the parties. It may for example stipulate that no agreement is binding unless and until reduced to writing and signed by the parties.

A1–027 A potential pitfall may arise where Heads of Agreement are signed which outline the main points and provide for it to be amplified in a later, more formal and detailed contract, to be drafted by the parties' lawyers. However, the Heads may well constitute a binding and effective agreement even though a later document does not get signed. The lack of detail may sometimes suit one party more than the other. The status and effect of any intended Heads of Agreement should be discussed with the parties and the intention as to whether and when it becomes binding should be clearly and explicitly recorded.

A1–028 As a rule, the document should be as detailed and precise as possible, for the avoidance of subsequent misunderstanding and disagreement. Unless all material terms are agreed, there is a risk that the court could subsequently find that no agreement exists.

Conditional or unconditional

This is not the same issue as whether an agreement is binding or non-binding. A conditional agreement is one that will come into effect contingently upon specified condition(s) being met; or particular terms of a binding agreement may come into effect in the event of certain conditions being fulfilled. For example, it is possible for parties to agree on a binding basis that X will pay Y a specified sum of money if some specified event occurs, say, if the profits of a company exceed a defined level within a prescribed period. In that event, the test is an objective one which may be outside the control or will of the parties. If the condition is met, the relevant term of the agreement will come into effect.

That is of course different from parties provisionally agreeing on terms that will not come into effect at all until the parties bring them into binding effect, for example, they are, and are expressed to be, subject to contract and non-binding until a formal contract has been prepared and executed by the parties.

Formality and style

The degree of formality of a settlement agreement or summary will depend on the style and preference of those drafting it, the requirements of the parties and the conventions of the field within which they are operating. However, whether formal or informal, the terms must be clear and precise, and all necessary provisions must be included and unambiguous, to enable it to be implemented without misunderstanding or further dispute. Informality of style should not be confused with imprecision or sloppiness.

In some cases the parties may want or need the agreement to be recorded as a deed, or it may need to be made into an order of the court, in which event the drafting of the documentation may be in the form of a Tomlin Order or other form of consent order.[1] Alternatively, in some circumstances an agreement may be filed and made a rule of court. Settlement terms that have to be made into court orders are likely to require legal input from the parties' lawyers.[2]

Inasmuch as ADR processes tend to be less formal than court processes, there is greater scope to avoid a legalistic approach to drafting and to make documents more understandable. It is worth mentioning the worldwide organisation "Clarity", which is committed to simplifying legal language, and which provides helpful guidelines.[3]

Authority to sign

Those who sign the agreement must have the necessary authority to do so if attending in a representative capacity. This ought to have been established by the mediator at an early stage of the process.

---

[1] A Tomlin Order provides for a stay of proceedings on agreed terms, save to carry such terms into effect, with liberty being reserved to revert to the court in relation to such terms.
[2] With regard to the drafting of consent orders, see *Foskett on Compromise* by David Foskett QC (8th edn, 2015).
[3] http://www.clarity-international.net/.

DOCUMENTS AND PRECEDENTS

Document 1: CEDR Solve Code of Conduct for Third Party Neutrals

A1–035 CEDR Solve, the Dispute Resolution Service of CEDR—the Centre for Effective Dispute Resolution (see www.cedr.com)—publishes model documents at *http://www.cedr.com/about_us/modeldocs/*.

Its Code of Conduct for third party neutrals (2018 edition) and any updates can be found at *https://www.cedr.com/about_us/modeldocs/?id=4*.

Document 2: CEDR Mediation Model Procedure (2018 Edition)

A1–036 This document may be found at *https://www.cedr.com/about_us/modeldocs/?id=21*.

Document 3: Code of Practice of the Family Mediation Council (FMC)

A1–037 This document may be found at *https://www.familymediationcouncil.org.uk/wp-content/uploads/2016/09/FMC-Code-of-Practice-September-2016-2.pdf*.

For further information about the FMC, see their website at *http://www.familymediationcouncil.org.uk*.

Document 4: Code of Practice of the Restorative Justice Council

A1–038 This document, which is renewed every three years, may be found at: *https://restorativejustice.org.uk/sites/default/files/resources/files/RJC%20Practitioner%20Code%20of%20Practice.pdf*.

For further information about the RJC, see their website at *https://restorativejustice.org.uk/*.

Document 5: Academy of Experts—Rules for Expert Determination

A1–039 This document may be found at: *https://www.academyofexperts.org/system/files/documents/ed_rules_booklet.pdf*.

These Rules provide a framework and timetable for the expert determination process, designed for use in virtually any dispute in any jurisdiction. For further information, see the Academy's website at *http://www.academy-experts.org/*.

Document 6: Mediation clause (short form)

A1–040 *This is a simple form of clause for civil or commercial mediation. See Ch.21 for considerations about the enforceability of contract clauses, which may need to have significant detail to be upheld by the courts in some jurisdictions. If* however, sufficient detail is inserted to give the clause effect, for example, an identified or identifiable neutral, organisation and procedure, it may well be upheld.

If any dispute arises out of this agreement, the parties shall in the first instance attempt to resolve it by mediation. In such event, the mediator shall be [name] [nominated by (mediation organisation)] and shall mediate in accordance with the [rules][mediation Code of Practice or model procedure] of [name of organisation].

Document 7: Arbitration clause (short form)

The following is a specimen short form for domestic arbitration[4]:   A1–041

If any dispute arises out of this agreement, including any dispute about its performance, construction or interpretation, it shall be referred to arbitration in accordance with the provisions of the Arbitration Act 1996. A single arbitrator [nominated by ... and arbitrating under the Rules of Arbitration of ....] shall conduct the arbitration, whose decision in relation to any such dispute shall be final and binding.

Document 8: Combined negotiation, mediation and arbitration clause

Parties may wish to stipulate in a contract that they will try to resolve differences   A1–042
by negotiation in the first instance. If that fails, it is to be followed by mediation if necessary. That would be followed by arbitration if the mediation were not to produce an agreed outcome. The following is a specimen of this[5]:

If any dispute arises out of this agreement, including any dispute about its performance, construction or interpretation, the parties shall in the first instance endeavour to resolve it by agreement through negotiations [conducted in good faith].[6] If they are unable to agree, the dispute shall be referred to mediation by [name] [nominated by (mediation organisation)] who shall mediate in accordance with the [rules][mediation Code of Practice or model procedure] of [name of organisation].

The parties reserve all their rights in the event that no agreed resolution is reached in the mediation. Neither party shall be precluded from [taking interim formal steps as may be considered necessary to protect such party's position] [commencing or continuing litigation, arbitration or other adjudication] while the mediation is pending.

If the dispute is not resolved by mediation within [28][42][60] days of its initiation, or such extended period as the parties may agree, the dispute shall be referred to arbitration in accordance with the provisions of the Arbitration Act 1996. A single arbitrator [name] [nominated by (relevant arbitral or other body)]

---

[4] This needs to be adapted to specific needs and circumstances. For examples of clauses suggested by specific arbitral organisations see e.g. the ICC clause at *https://iccwbo.org/publication/standard-icc-arbitration-clauses-english-version/* or the LCIA clause at *http://www.lcia.org/dispute_resolution_services/lcia_recommended_clauses.aspx*.

[5] See Ch.21 regarding the enforceability of contract clauses.

[6] As to the questionable effect of contracting to negotiate "in good faith", see Ch.4 under the heading "Good faith in negotiation".

shall conduct the arbitration, whose decision in relation to any such dispute shall be final and binding. In such event, the rules of the [relevant arbitral body] shall apply in relation to such arbitration.

The law of [England] shall apply to this agreement, which shall be interpreted and construed in accordance with such law.

Document 9: CEDR—model mediation agreement

A1–043　This document may be found at: *https://www.cedr.com/about_us/modeldocs/?id=31.*

It should be read together with the relevant notes at: *https://www.cedr.com/docslib/11th_edition_CEDR_Solve_notes.pdf.*

Document 10: Agreement to Mediate (family)

A1–044　Family mediation organisations tend to have or recommend their own form of Agreement to Mediate, which may commonly be adapted to individual circumstances. Members may have online access to these templates, which are currently not available to non-members. Examples may be found, for members of the family lawyers' organisation Resolution at *http://www.resolution.org.uk/* or for members of the Family Mediators Association at *https://thefma.co.uk/.*

The following sample has not been specifically approved by any mediation organisation, but provides an outline example of the kind of agreement that might be used in relation to a divorcing couple in England and Wales (where there is an obligation to provide complete financial disclosure when addressing financial issues)—subject to appropriate individual adaptation as necessary and subject also to any requirements under the General Data Protection Regulation (GDPR) 2018 in which regard, see Ch.22, paras 22-027 to 22-031. It would be signed by the mediator(s) and counter-signed by each party. If any lawyers and/or other participants are to be involved in the mediation, they too would counter-sign it by way of acceptance of the confidentiality and other relevant terms.

To [parties]

You have asked me to mediate certain issues concerning your relationship. I now record the terms on which I do so:

1. You appoint me and I agree to act as mediator in relation to these issues. I confirm that I do not have any conflict of interest in doing so or any interest in the outcome. I will try to help you both reach terms that you find acceptable, which does not mean trying to anticipate what the outcome would be if the issues were decided by the court.
2. I do not mediate as a solicitor but function as an independent and impartial mediator, and I do not advise or represent parties or give legal advice to you, jointly or individually.
3. We undertake to one another that, except as may be otherwise agreed in writing, we will each maintain confidentiality in respect of all statements, communications and matters arising in the mediation, subject to the following exceptions in which confidentiality will not apply:

- 3.1 insofar as there is a need for disclosure in order to comply with any statutory obligation and/or data protection provision, obtain professional advice or enforce any settlement agreement;
- 3.2 if any public policy requirement (including anyone suffering or appearing likely to suffer significant harm) exceptionally overrides the duty of confidentiality; or
- 3.3 if any obligation or requirement of law, whether under the Proceeds of Crime Act 2002 and/or under any related regulations and/or otherwise, requires a disclosure to be made to any relevant authority.
4. You both undertake to provide such financial and other information as may be relevant to your issues and to furnish any supporting documents reasonably required. All financial information (which may include personal information that would be relevant to a court in making a financial determination) is provided on an open basis, which means that it can be used in court whether in support of a consent application or in contested proceedings.
5. Subject to Paragraph 4 and to all relevant data protection laws (including in particular the General Data Protection Regulation (GDPR) 2018) to which this entire Agreement is subject, the mediation and our discussions and communications, for example about possible terms of a financial settlement, are conducted without prejudice and with a claim of evidential privilege. You may not have access to any of my notes or call me as witness in any proceedings relating to any aspect of the mediation.
6. As part of the mediation process, in addition to any joint or other meetings, you agree that I may have separate meetings or discussions with each of you and with your lawyers. Anything discussed separately will be maintained confidentially and not disclosed to the other, save as I may be authorised to disclose, subject to the following exceptions:
    - 6.1 The exceptions set out in Paragraphs 3 and 5 above;
    - 6.2 As set out in Paragraph 4: any financial information even if disclosed to me separately will be open and will not kept confidential from the other;
    - 6.3 Anything that may cause or risk causing any harm to a child or any unilateral action actually taken or intended to be taken that may fundamentally affect existing child arrangements without due consultation with the other party; and
    - 6.4 Any communication or information of which I may become aware indicating that any agreement or record being drafted or prepared by either/both of you and/or your legal representatives contains any error, ambiguity or misunderstanding
7. Any decisions arrived at in the mediation which may be significant to either or both of your positions (including any proposed settlement terms) will not be made into a binding agreement until you have each had the opportunity to seek advice on them from your lawyers (who may in some circumstances be in attendance). Any such terms will not be legally binding unless and until reduced to writing in an open, binding agreement or draft order signed by you or on your behalf. Your lawyers will prepare any such agreement and/or order and I may if required assist them in doing so.

8. You both reserve your respective rights (including the right to proceed to court) should the mediation not result in a settlement of the issues under discussion.
9. I will act in good faith throughout the process and will not be liable to you, individually or collectively, for any act or omission in respect of my services under this Agreement.
10. Either of you may terminate the mediation at any stage. If I think that the continuation of the mediation or my appointment is inappropriate, I may end the mediation without necessarily assigning any reason. However, as long as it is pending, you both agree to work in good faith towards seeking an acceptable outcome.
11. My fees, shared between you equally unless otherwise agreed, are charged at the rate of £x per hour for meetings, phone, e-mail and other communications, any agreed drafting and any other work necessarily undertaken in the mediation.
12. Apart from these fees you will be responsible for providing the mediation venue (which I can arrange on your behalf) and paying any other expenses necessarily incurred.
13. These fees and expenses are payable on presentation of my invoice or any interim invoice(s) that I may render.
14. You will each be responsible for your own costs and expenses of taking part in the mediation and your individual representation.
15. This Agreement shall be governed by and construed in accordance with English law.

Document 11: CEDR Model Early Neutral Evaluation Agreement—and guidance notes

A1–045   This document, including notes, may be found at *https://www.cedr.com/about_us/modeldocs/?id=9*.

Document 12: CEDR Model Executive Tribunal Procedure and Agreement

A1–046   This may be found at *https://www.cedr.com/about_us/modeldocs/?id=10*.

Document 13: Dispute risk analysis

A1–047   *The following fictitious example was inspired by risk analysis work done by Professor John Wade and developed from a model originated by a group comprising Heather Allen, Tony Allen, Henry Brown, Philip Naughton QC and Roger Tabakin, whom the authors wish to acknowledge. The form may be individually adapted: para.5 is based on the issues appearing from the parties' summaries and documents and may follow a decision tree sequence. Ultimately judgments tend to be subjective and this analysis is merely an aid to reaching those judgments.*

DRAFTING, DOCUMENTS AND PRECEDENTS

The form may be provided at the outset or reserved as an impasse strategy. Parties may return it to the mediator, but more usually it is provided for parties' own private analysis, not shared with the mediator.

DISPUTE RISK ANALYSIS

Dispute between	*ABC Agency Limited ("ABC")*
And	*DEF Traders Limited ("Traders")*
Risk analysis by	*[ ]*
On (date)	*[ ] January 2018*

Principal action and counterclaim (if any)	
1. How much is the claim (quantifiable)?	£
2. What are the unquantifiable elements of the claim (if any) e.g. injunction, accounting, rectification, declaration etc.?	
3. How much is the counterclaim, if any (quantifiable)?	£
4. What are the unquantifiable elements of the counterclaim (if any) e.g. injunction, accounting, rectification, declaration etc.?	
5. Regarding the important issues listed on 12 December 2017, how do you rate your chances of succeeding on each issue at trial? These are crystallised to include the following:	Prospects of success %
5.1 Were Mr Smith and/or Mr Jones "ABC personnel" such as to render ABC responsible for their actions?	
5.2 Were their actions such as to entitle Traders to terminate the 2015 Agreement summarily?	
5.3 Do the Commercial Agents Regulations apply?	
5.4 Is ABC entitled to an indemnity?	
5.5 Did Traders cause the destruction of ABC's business?	
5.6 If 5.2 answer is negative, quantification of ABC's claim.	
5.7 If 5.2 answer is positive, quantification of Traders' counterclaim.	
5.8 What is the appropriate contractual adjustment between ABC and Traders?	

Principal action and counterclaim (if any)		
6. Having regard to Question 5, and taking all other relevant factors into account, what are the % prospects of the main claim succeeding:	%	Sum receivable or payable
In full as claimed		£
A significant part of the claim		£
7. Having regard to Question 5, and taking all other relevant factors into account, what are the % prospects of any counterclaim succeeding:	%	Sum receivable or payable
In full as claimed		£
A significant part of the counterclaim		£

How much is it going to cost?		
8. Are you fully indemnified for your own costs to trial (for example by insurance or other arrangement?)	Yes	No
9. Are you fully indemnified for your opponent's costs to trial (for example by insurance or other arrangement?)	Yes	No
10. If you settle before trial, will your opponent's costs be fully covered by insurance or any other indemnification?	Yes	No
11. If the answer to Question 10 is "no", estimate your opponent's costs to date of settlement.	£	
12. Is your opponent indemnified for its/their costs?	Yes	No
13. What are your total costs and expenses to date?	£	
14. What are your estimated legal costs to the end of a trial? Consider witness expenses, expert costs, counsel's costs and all other cost items.	£	
15. If you succeed, estimate how much of your costs you are likely to recover.	£	
16. Even if you succeed, how much of your costs will not be recoverable? (How much of this will relate to future costs still to be incurred in getting to trial?)	£ (Future element £)	
17. If you do not succeed, estimate how much of your opponent's costs you are likely to have to pay.	£	

DRAFTING, DOCUMENTS AND PRECEDENTS

How much is it going to cost?		
18. If the matter goes to trial, estimate the time taken by your management, staff and others in preparing, seeing lawyers and attending court. Put a value on this.	Time:	Value: £
19. Estimate the value of resulting lost business/income.	£	
20. If you succeed at trial, what interest (if any) are you likely to receive?	£	
21. If you do not succeed at trial, what interest (if any) are you likely to pay?	£	
22. If either party appeals a trial judgment, estimate what extra costs you might incur.	£	
23. Estimate what costs and expenses you will need to lay out pending the trial?	£	

How long will it take?	
24. If a date of trial has been fixed, when is it?	
25. If not yet fixed, estimate when it is likely to take place.	
26. Estimate the length of trial (number of days in court).	
27. If either party appeals, estimate the further time involved in going through the appeal process.	
28. Is there any prospect that your opponent will not have the resources to meet a judgment, immediately or at all? If so, estimate the time, prospects and costs of enforcing a judgment.	£

Other factors	
29. Has the other party made an offer to settle (under Part 36 of the Rules or otherwise)? If so, what are your chances of "beating" that offer?	%
30. Have you made an offer to settle (under Part 36 of the Rules or otherwise)? If so, what are the other side's chances of "beating" that offer?	%
31. Is this dispute limited to the existing litigation, or is there any other dispute pending or potentially likely anywhere else (for example in courts abroad, tribunals, trade mark registries, or other dispute resolution fora)? If so, place an estimated value on resolving all such other disputes.	£

Other factors	
32. Put a (notional) value (positive or negative) on the benefit of settlement rather than trial, taking into account the possibility of publicity (positive or negative), impact on your and/or your opponent's reputation and goodwill, effect on working relationships and any other factors.	£
33. Is there any risk that even if you succeed at the trial, there will be other consequent negative repercussions? Place a value on such risk.	£
34. Put a (notional) value on the benefit for you and/or your employees and witnesses in avoiding the stress of preparing for and attending a trial (apart from the estimated cost in Question 18 above). Might issues arising in a trial risk damaging the credibility, reputation or authority of any party or witness?	£
35. Does this dispute have any non-pecuniary personal element? If so, might settlement terms address that element, for example, through some form of private or public acknowledgment and/or appropriately worded terms? (Particulars are not required here.)	
36. How damaging would an adverse trial decision be to you and/or your business? Put a (notional) value on the effect of losing the case.	£
37. How damaging would an adverse trial decision be to your opponent? Put a (notional) value to your opponent on the effect of losing the case.	£
38. Might there be any indirect benefits from a settlement (e.g. restoring or preventing further damage to goodwill; trading opportunities etc.)?	

© 2003 Heather Allen, Tony Allen, Henry Brown, Philip Naughton QC & Roger Tabakin

Document 14: Civil/commercial terms of settlement (framework)

A1–048   *Because of the range of possible agreements and the diversity of styles and requirements, this precedent will merely outline a possible template, which must be adapted according to the needs of each individual case. The substantive terms would be attached as a schedule.*

   The format and content of the agreement will vary, depending on whether a draft consent order is required, a deed, a complete formal agreement, heads of agreement, an exchange of letters or an even more informal record. Style will vary from one drafter to another.

   AGREEMENT made this   day of   between:
   (1) ABC   ("Mr. C")

DRAFTING, DOCUMENTS AND PRECEDENTS

(1) XYZ Investments Limited   ("XYZ")

PREAMBLE:

A. The Parties have been in dispute in relation to the 2017 Proceedings and the Section 994 Petition, as hereafter defined, and as outlined in the Parties' respective mediation summaries and in the agreed bundle of documents ("the Dispute").

B. The parties agreed to deal with their disputes in mediation with DEF as mediator. The mediation took place on [date]. Mr C was represented by [solicitor/counsel]. XYZ was represented by [solicitor/counsel].

C. In the mediation the parties settled their differences in relation to all pending disputes, and they wish to record the terms of such settlement on a binding basis in this Agreement.

IT IS AGREED:

1. Upon signature by the Parties, this Agreement shall immediately be fully and effectively binding on them by way of a complete and final settlement of all proceedings, and of the Dispute and all claims that either of them may have against one another in relation to the Dispute. Tomlin Orders and/or any other court orders shall be obtained by consent to give effect to these terms.

2. The following definitions shall apply in this Agreement:

"the Company"	XYZ Superior Holdings Limited
"the 2017 Proceedings"	The action, as amended, brought by Mr C against XYZ in the Chancery Division of the High Court, No.
"the Section 994 Petition"	The Petition under Section 994 of the Companies Act 2006 filed in the Chancery Division of the High Court, No.
"all Proceedings"	Collectively, the 2017 Proceedings and the Section 994 Petition

3. The terms of settlement agreed between the Parties are set out in [the schedule] [draft Consent Order with schedule] attached to this Agreement and signed by them.

4. This Agreement shall be immediately binding upon signature by the parties. The signatories to this Agreement on behalf of XYZ jointly and severally warrant that they are duly authorised to enter into this Agreement on its behalf.

5. In the event of any dispute or difference arising in relation to any aspect of this settlement, or the implementation or performance of its terms, the parties agree that before taking any formal contentious steps, they will first

attempt to resolve such dispute or difference by negotiation. If that fails, they agree to refer it to further mediation by DEF (subject to his availability, otherwise by a mediator appointed by [mediation organisation]). If it remains unresolved within 4 weeks of such referral to mediation, either party shall be free to take such action as he or they may see fit. These provisions shall not, however, preclude either party from taking any injunctive or other interim legal proceedings considered necessary for the urgent protection of such party's rights.

6. Each party will pay their own legal costs in relation to the mediation, and will share equally the costs of the mediation including the mediator's fees.

Document 15: Family—Memorandum of Understanding

A1–049 *The authors acknowledge Resolution for permitting the reproduction of this draft summary. The names, details and circumstances used are fictitious and are merely illustrative. Each summary will have to be adapted to its individual needs. An "open" financial summary setting out the couple's financial position fully would accompany this memorandum.*

Without prejudice

Miles Flurry and Katherine (Kate) Flurry, who have been married for 14 years, have been in mediation with [ ] regarding various matrimonial issues. They have had six mediation meetings, during which they have examined their respective financial and personal circumstances, and have looked at proposals for their financial settlement. They have also had regard to the position as it affects their children, Oliver (aged 10) and Tamsin (aged 8).

This memorandum is furnished on an evidentially privileged and "without prejudice" basis. It is intended to help Miles and Kate to consider and obtain advice on the current proposals and does not record or create a binding agreement. An agreement will only come into being should they both decide to commit themselves to it, and they execute an appropriate formal document, after having each had an opportunity to take independent legal advice.

Background circumstances

Miles is a director and shareholder in the company Manifest Occult Publications Limited which publishes fantasy and occult books. He has expressed concern about the future of this specialist field of publishing, but accepts that for the foreseeable future, the company is likely to continue to be profitable. Kate is a full-time primary school teacher. She is currently being considered as deputy-head of her school.

Miles and Kate are both living at 33 Aspinall Road, London N3, but are conducting their lives separately. They wished to separate and used the mediation to discuss how they could do so in an orderly way and on terms that they could both accept.

Kate and Miles had a number of factors in mind in formulating their proposals. They were concerned to ensure that any arrangements they might reach in the mediation would be best for Oliver and Tamsin and would provide them with the necessary security. They wanted to achieve a "clean break" settlement but recognised the difficulties in doing this. They wanted the settlement terms to feel fair to themselves and to one another.

Settlement discussions and proposals

The following are the matters discussed in the mediation, including the proposals which Kate and Miles find mutually acceptable:

Future of the relationship

1. Miles and Kate have resolved to separate. This will be achieved in practice when they sell their property at 33 Aspinall Road, London N3, and can buy separate homes.
2. They have accepted that their marriage has broken down and that a divorce is now inevitable. They do not regard this as urgent, though both wish to have this properly formalised in the ordinary course.

Recording the proposed terms

3. They propose to record their settlement terms in a Deed of Separation, or in whatever way their solicitors may advise; and they will implement such terms. They realise that until a court order is obtained, there is a possibility that either of them might seek to vary any such terms and that the court retains the power (if it considers it appropriate) to re-open matters. However, neither of them has any present intention to seek to vary the terms, and barring anything wholly unforeseen that might materially change the position, neither would expect or wish to do so in the future.

Arrangements for Oliver and Tamsin

4. Both Kate and Miles have expressed their concerns for the needs and interests of Oliver and Tamsin. They wish to maintain a good relationship with one another in the children's interests, and propose to arrange their separation, housing and future contact and communications generally in such a way that this is achieved.
5. Detailed practical arrangements concerning Oliver and Tamsin, including decision making, communications and other matters still need to be discussed and agreed. Kate and Miles have, however, arrived at a broad understanding as to how they will approach these aspects:
    5.1 Oliver and Tamsin will continue to reside with Kate when she moves into her new home.
    5.2 Kate and Miles will establish a framework for Oliver and Tamsin to spend time with Miles.
    5.3 The kind of pattern that Miles and Kate have in mind will be something like Miles spending time with Oliver and Tamsin for a weekend every fortnight. Provisionally, the idea is that he will fetch

them on Friday evening and bring them back on Sunday evening; but the details remain to be discussed. Miles will also speak to them freely on the phone between weekend visits, and may visit them if he is in the area. However, he will always check in advance whether interim visits will be convenient for them and for Kate. He will also arrange to have them with him for part of the holiday periods.

Kate and Miles both recognise that Oliver and Tamsin need a good relationship with them both. They want to support one another in achieving this.

5.4 Once the pattern is in place, both Kate and Miles accept that there will need to be flexibility. They will try to establish a mechanism for making changes without unduly inconveniencing the children or one another.

5.5 They have in mind to liaise with one another about Oliver and Tamsin as necessary, and where practicable to deal jointly with matters such as schooling, health needs and the like. They will try to devise a way to ensure that these communications take place, and how each will deal with emergencies in case they cannot contact the other.

5.6 The detailed arrangements concerning these matters have been deferred, partly because of time constraints and partly because both Miles and Kate will find it easier to discuss these matters more usefully when they have actually separated and have established themselves in their separate homes. Meanwhile they are satisfied that these broad principles will be able to guide them in their discussions. If necessary, they will arrange further mediation to deal with any difficulties, should they arise.

Sale of 33 Aspinall Road and division of proceeds

6. The house at 33 Aspinall Road is to be marketed immediately at an asking price of £980,000. Any genuine offer of £950,000 or more will be acceptable. (A tentative offer of that sum has already been received.) If that level cannot be achieved within three months, Kate and Miles will consider accepting less, as advised by their agents, Creative Sales (who are being given an initial three months sole agency).

Contracts will not, however, be exchanged on any sale or separate purchases until agreement between Kate and Miles has been reached and formalised.

7. The mortgage redemption, costs of sale and provision for both parties to move to their new homes are set out in the schedule provided by Miles and Kate. Provisionally, this is expected to total approximately £160,000. It is proposed that the net proceeds of sale will be paid to Kate absolutely, in settlement of all her capital claims against Miles. Assuming a price of £950,000, such net proceeds will be about £790,000. If there is any surplus over £790,000 this will be shared as to 67 per cent (Kate): 33 per cent (Miles).

8. Kate intends to use the proceeds of sale of 33 Aspinall Road to buy a house for herself and the children for about £700,000. She will pay all costs of

purchase and any other expenses out of her capital. It is not her intention to have a mortgage. She has seen a house in the nearby area, which will enable her to remain in the same catchment area for the school. The asking price is £725,000, which she believes will be negotiable: it requires about £25,000 of work to be done to it. She believes that it (or something similar) will be suitable.

9. Miles has made an offer of £420,000 on a flat for himself, which has been accepted, subject to contract. He will be using his capital towards this, and intends to borrow about £175,000 by way of mortgage.

10. If Kate and Miles wish to proceed with the sale of 33 Aspinall Road and the purchase of new homes for themselves, then they are aware that certain steps will be necessary before any binding legal commitments are made on the sale and purchases.

   10.1 Both Miles and Kate intend to obtain specific advice from their respective solicitors on the agreement they are proposing to enter into between themselves, to satisfy themselves about doing so.

   10.2 They propose to sign a written agreement on an open basis, in terms approved by their respective solicitors.

   10.3 If a comprehensive settlement is not yet reached, they know that an interim agreement should be entered into on an open basis. It will be expressed to be without prejudice to any further adjustment that might need to be made in the context of any overall resolution of the financial issues and to both of their rights generally. It will also be without prejudice to any argument that either of them may wish to pursue in any subsequent proceedings if matters are not settled by agreement. Its intention would be expressed as being to facilitate their separation, to be taken into account in any final resolution of the matter. The terms of the interim agreement would need to be agreed between the solicitors.

11. If final terms of settlement are now reached and approved by Miles and Kate after having been advised by their respective solicitors, then an interim agreement would not be necessary. In that event, all terms can be incorporated into a final agreement as advised by the respective solicitors (for example, in a Deed of Separation or in minutes of order if proceedings are envisaged).

Maintenance for Oliver and Tamsin

12. Miles proposes to pay Kate the sum of £675 per month as maintenance for each of Oliver and Tamsin, with effect from the first day of the month following completion of the sale of 33 Aspinall Road. That would be acceptable to Kate. This will continue until each child attains the age of 18 years or completes full-time schooling, whichever is the later, or further agreement or order. This offer is being considered within the context of Kate's income needs generally. It is not being considered within the provisions of the Child Support Act. Kate and Miles have declined to have CSA calculations informally made, but may revert to this if they wish.

Maintenance considerations for Kate

13. In consideration of the imbalance of payment of the proceeds of sale of 33 Aspinall Road in favour of Kate, Miles wished to be relieved of any further maintenance obligation towards Kate personally. He accordingly proposed that the settlement terms should constitute a "clean break", with Kate having no claims at all against him. The implications and effect of a "clean break" were considered and discussed.

   Having regard to her other financial resources, Kate was willing to consider these proposals, and to accept the capital imbalance and the maintenance figure of £1,350 per month for the children, with no personal maintenance for herself. However, she did not feel able to agree to waive her right to maintenance permanently, in case anything should arise while the children were still young, which might preclude her from working. She therefore proposed that Miles's offer would be acceptable if instead of an immediate clean break, he was willing to pay her a nominal sum of £1 per year in order to reserve her rights.

   Considerable time was spent in trying to find a solution to this issue. Ultimately, both agreed to consider the following formula:

   13.1 The above terms would be acceptable, with a nominal maintenance payment of £1 per annum to Kate, on the basis of the further matters set out below.

   13.2 It would be recorded that a capital payment had been made in consideration of Kate's personal maintenance being waived, and that although she was reserving her rights, that would only be against an unforeseen and serious problem arising, which could not be met in any other way. Maintenance would not be sought to meet any day-to-day difficulties that Kate might experience in managing on her income. (Both parties acknowledged that it would be difficult to know which way the court would exercise its discretion if the issue ever had to be dealt with by the court.)

   13.3 If and to the extent that Kate sought any future maintenance, either directly for herself or attributable to her within a Child Support Agency context, she would agree to credit Miles with a corresponding capital sum by way of an interest in her property, subject to a maximum of £25,000. She would hold that by way of a Declaration of Trust. (It was understood that this provision might not necessarily be legally enforceable.)

   13.4 Attempts would be made to cover Kate by way of sickness and if possible redundancy insurance for a period of 10 years. By that time, both children will have attained their majority. Miles would contribute 50 per cent of the premiums for the duration of this period (subject to these not being "loaded" in any way, otherwise 50 per cent of the unloaded level).

   13.5 Kate's claims for personal maintenance would be dismissed 10 years from the date of an Agreement being formalised on this settlement. She would not be entitled to apply for this term to be extended.

Division of assets

14. Miles and Kate will each retain their own motor car and other personal possessions. They will share the contents of 33 Aspinall Road, according to their respective needs, which they expect to be able to resolve without assistance. Broadly, they envisage that Kate will have all bedroom furniture for herself, Oliver and Tamsin, and that the remaining furniture will be divided approximately 3:1 in Kate's favour. If they have any difficulty in resolving this, they will arrange a further mediation meeting.
15. Miles will pay Kate's Visa and personal debts in full as listed in her financial statement.
16. Subject to the above, Kate and Miles will each retain as their sole property all assets respectively in their own name or under their individual control.

Full settlement of all capital claims

17. Subject to the above terms, Kate makes no further claim on Miles' assets, nor Miles on Kate's. This is a full and final settlement of all capital claims that either of them may have against the other, however arising. All capital claims are to be reciprocally dismissed in any court proceedings to be brought in due course. All claims under the Inheritance (Provision for Family and Dependants) Act 1975 are similarly to be dismissed as and when Kate's maintenance claims are extinguished: meanwhile will be reserved. The implications of that Act were briefly discussed, but Kate and Miles will discuss and consider these further with their solicitors.

Dealing with future issues

18. Miles and Kate have resolved to try to deal in a reasonable way with any issues that may arise in the future, whether to do with Oliver and Tamsin, or of a financial nature, so far as the latter aspect has been reserved. If they have any problems about doing so personally, they intend to revert to mediation.

   Miles and Kate will now wish to consult their respective solicitors for advice on these proposals. If, having received advice, they wish to enter into an agreement to settle all issues, the solicitors will prepare the necessary documents. Alternatively, the solicitors may assist with the preparation of interim documents (in discussion with me if so agreed) to enable the house sale and purchases to proceed in the meanwhile.

   If after seeing solicitors Miles and Kate wish to discuss matters further, then further mediation meeting(s) can be arranged for that purpose (attended by the solicitors as well, if that is considered helpful and necessary).

Document 16: Civil/commercial mediation checklist

A1–050 *Mediators may find it helpful to have a checklist, by way of an informal guide. The following checklist could serve in relation to the standard model of commercial and civil mediation, adapted as necessary to suit individual requirements:*

Mediation checklist

A. *Preliminary matters*

1. Have both/all parties agreed to the mediation? If not, is any assistance required in examining the process? Any documents to be sent? Discuss mediation with each party?
2. Has a formal agreement to mediate been submitted to the parties and agreed by everyone regulating the terms on which the mediation is to be undertaken, including mediation confidentiality, privilege, fees etc.?
3. The following matters may need to be discussed and agreed, either at a preliminary meeting of lawyers and/or parties, or by way of phone and/or e-mail communications:
    3.1 Arrange for case summaries and bundles of relevant documents. Outline requirements and timetable.
    3.2 Consider appropriate process and meeting arrangements. Is one block of time required, or might parties want an initial meeting with the possibility of further meetings? Fix initial or substantive meeting: date, venue and arrangements.
    3.3 Discuss parties' presentations.
    3.4 Check authority of representatives of parties. Will they be able to conclude an agreement or will they need to seek further authority? Will all necessary parties be present or contactable, e.g. insurers, sub-contractors? If not, do parties all agree to proceed in any event, and will this be viable?
    3.5 Consider whether any aspects can be addressed pending the substantive meeting. Anticipate and reduce issues for the main meeting.
    3.6 Discuss and check legal representation.
    3.7 Check whether there are any deadlines, e.g. limitation period shortly to expire, court hearing date or the like. If so, ensure that they are noted and built into timetable or that there is a binding agreement for limitation period to be suspended or otherwise covered.
    3.8 Discuss practicalities e.g. after hours availability? Are experts or specialist advisers contactable after hours if needed?
    3.9 Check process and ground rules understood, address any queries.
4. Arrange or check venue details including for example:
    4.1 Ensure that adequate accommodation is available. Is a room needed for each party? Are special reception arrangements needed? Set up practical arrangements for working lunches, refreshments, etc.

	4.2	Is the venue available after hours if required? Will printing, copying and any other necessary facilities be available?
	4.3	Any special circumstances requiring special preparation? Flip-chart, photocopying and printing facilities or any other facilities needed and available?
5.		Check summary and documents when received. Any supplementary documents or information needed before meeting?

B. *At the substantive meeting*

1. Mediators commonly welcome each party as they arrive, show them to their rooms, put them at ease.
2. Mediator's welcome and introduction, acknowledge summaries and documents, outline procedure (including in particular confidentiality aspect and without prejudice basis for discussions) and deal with any queries.
3. Where mediator considers appropriate, each party, personally and/or through their lawyer, to make a brief case presentation.
4. If any additional factual information is needed, consider whether this should be sought from the parties together, or whether considerations of confidentiality indicate that these should be obtained privately in caucus.
5. Consider (i) how long to continue with all parties together; (ii) when to caucus, for how long, and whether and when to meet together again; (iii) whether and how best to work with legal representatives; (iv) whether to seek expert input or other third party involvement and how to do so.
6. When any party is not with the mediator, is there any useful task that can be done while waiting, e.g. getting supplementary information or considering options?
7. Maintain notes sufficient to ensure that all aspects covered, confidentiality between parties preserved, tasks of parties noted, and terms recorded.
8. Consider whether and how to obtain any missing expertise, technical, legal or other. Engage an independent expert and at whose cost? Status of advice received?
9. If caucusing with one party takes longer than expected, check out periodically with other parties if necessary.
10. If issues unresolved at end of initial meeting:
    10.1 Consider procedure for future: Fix new appointment? Meet parties separately by appointment? Any other procedure or specific matter for agenda?
    10.2 Any practical tasks which the parties and/or the mediators need to undertake before next stage? Additional information or documents? Third-party inquiries? Legal or other professional advice? Specify, with timetable if appropriate.
    10.3 Any settlement-geared steps parties can take in the meanwhile, e.g. formulating proposals, considering existing options, looking at new settlement permutations?
    10.4 Check whether any interim matters need to be urgently resolved before next step in mediation, e.g. decisions which need to be taken in the meanwhile and which parties cannot resolve themselves?

10.5 Consider and check whether an interim summary would be helpful, covering the matters partially resolved and indicating outstanding issues. This could be prepared and sent after the meeting.

10.6 Any other matters that need to be discussed with the parties or arrangements made?

C. *In the event of impasse*

1. Can the issue in deadlock be deferred or dealt with on a temporary basis? Alternatively, is there a short-term basis for dealing with it for a trial period?
2. Have the parties undertaken a risk analysis? Have they examined their best and worst alternatives to a negotiated resolution?
3. If the deadlock issue arises in relation to a symbol or form of words, have the underlying needs and concerns been examined?
4. Do the parties have different perceptions of fairness in relation to the outcome? Has this been examined and might it be further discussed?
5. Will a non-binding evaluation of the sticking issue help the parties to budge? Or might this just entrench positions further? Who should provide this? The mediator or a third party such as counsel? Or perhaps a binding adjudication, limited to the sticking issue?
6. If strong emotional responses are creating a block, can it help for these to be expressed or for some other person to be asked to take over representing a corporate party or to join an adjourned meeting?
7. Will it help the parties if the mediator provides a written summary of the position setting out the aspects resolved and those awaiting resolution, with the alternative proposals and settlement parameters? Can and should the mediator suggest some possible permutations of existing proposals which may take matters forward?
8. Will it help and would it be appropriate for the mediator to make proposals for the settlement of the issues?
9. Are there any other impasse strategies that may be used? Consider the specific sticking issue, and examine the possibilities. Go back to basics: examine why the parties came to mediation, what they hope to achieve, what other advantages there are in continuing, can the proposals be reconstructed more acceptably? Can the parties themselves suggest any basis for breaking the deadlock or re-establishing the negotiations?
10. If dealing with a high conflict party or parties, have the special considerations relevant to these been considered and applied? Review approach in the light of these factors.
11. If the deadlock cannot be resolved and the mediation must come to an end, do the parties realise this and have they considered what the implications would be? Might it help them to have an opportunity to consider these?

D. *When issues resolved*

1. Arrange for the parties' lawyers to draft a careful note of matters resolved, for parties' immediate signature or draft terms of consent order if court

proceedings are pending. Be clear as to what is required: do parties want to be immediately and unconditionally bound on signature? Or is the agreement conditional upon the fulfilment of any stated contingency, and if so, exactly what? Or is there to be no binding agreement, but merely a note of acceptable proposals which the parties will finalise through their legal advisers? Or some other reservation or nuance? Parties and/or their lawyers may need support during the drafting process.

2. Are there any provisions in the agreement to mediate or in the ground rules which may affect the terms of settlement? Check this. If, for example, there is a provision that if a party does not give effect to a settlement, the other may be released from the settlement terms on written notice, check if this is required; if so, strict time scales should be specified; if not required, alternative provisions should be specified.

3. If legal representatives have not attended the mediation, do the parties want the mediator to communicate with those advisers? Clarify requirements.

4. Check with parties if anything else is required from the mediator or the ADR organisation. For example (i) mediator or ADR organisation to act as stakeholder, with specific directions; (ii) mediator to be supervisor of settlement terms, with specific instructions and authority; (iii) mediator being available if any issue arises during implementation of settlement; (iv) mediator to act as expert or adjudicator in relation to implementation.

E. *If mediation ends with issues unresolved*

1. Do not close the door on any particular options. Leave scope for parties to continue their own discussions. Consider whether parties wish and agree to leave any proposals and counter-proposals open for acceptance for an agreed period. If so, these will need very careful formulation and recording to be effective.

2. Check if the parties want a without prejudice summary of the position to facilitate any continuing discussions, or anything else from the mediator.

3. Do the parties want an evaluation and is it appropriate to furnish one? Or perhaps the mediator's proposals for settlement? Have appropriate explanations been given about these options and their implications?

4. Offer the parties the opportunity to return to mediation if required.

5. Check whether the parties would find it helpful to use the mediation to narrow and define the issues for adjudication.

Checklist caution

This checklist is for guidance only, and cannot be comprehensive or definitive. It must obviously be used with discretion and personal judgment. It remains the responsibility of individual mediators to ensure that all relevant matters are covered and properly dealt with, whether or not included in this checklist.

Document 17: Family mediation checklist

A1–051 *This checklist is broadly based on a model of mediation structured into stages as envisaged in this book. It is, however, obviously adaptable to any other way of working. It assumes that the couple are not publicly funded and that they have a range of issues and that they have not expressed any preference for prioritising, and that finance will be addressed first. It follows the model of meeting the couple together, at least for some meetings. It includes provision for the model in which the mediator may also meet parties separately and privately.*

As in all mediation, checklists are for guidance only and do not prevail over parties' wishes and preferences. It cannot be comprehensive or definitive and mediators must use their discretion and judgment in amplifying and adapting it appropriately.

Dealing with initial phone enquiry

- Deal with any procedural enquiries, and explain how mediation works and the need for a Mediation Information and Assessment Meeting in certain circumstances (where court proceedings are envisaged, subject to exceptions). Where appropriate, indicate costs and possible number of sessions.
- Do not accept information about the merits of the matter. Avoid this by saying that you prefer to find out more about the merits when both are together.
- Check that the other party will be contacting you. Explain that this will be needed before mediation can commence.
- Establish the name and contact details of the enquirer, and check whether explanatory written material is required.
- Check urgency and timetable if a meeting is requested in the telephone call.

The Mediation Information and Assessment Meeting (MIAM)

- Only mediators accredited by the Family Mediation Council (FMCA mediators) can conduct MIAMS.
- The MIAM can be conducted with the couple jointly, or more commonly if both attend, there may be separate meetings—or a combination of joint and separate meetings. However, in order to monitor for possible abuse or risk of harm, some time will have to be spent with each party alone. Sometimes only one party will attend the MIAM.
- Some mediators will conduct a MIAM by use of Skype or a similar electronic communication.
- Use this meeting to explain the mediation process to the couple, to deal with their questions about it and to explore their options. Consider their alternatives as well as cost and other implications, including perhaps the respective advantages and disadvantages.
- Inform the couple if you consider their issues suitable to be dealt with through mediation.

- If the couple decide not to continue into mediation or it is not suitable for them, sign the relevant court form to enable them to take court proceedings if that is what they wish to do.
- If the couple decide to enter into mediation, arrangements will need to be made to set up an initial mediation meeting and for them to be provided with the Agreement to Mediate and any preliminary information form (to be returned before the in initial meeting), if not already provided.

Arrangements for initial meeting

- Check that both parties have approved the agreement to mediate and have returned the preliminary information form. If not, consider contacting the party whose form is missing to check that it is being sent. Familiarise yourself with the information furnished.
- In co-mediation, ensure that the co-mediator is fully briefed.
- Have the following documents available for the meeting: a spare copy of the Agreement to Mediate, for signature, three sets of financial disclosure documentation (to hand to the parties and for yourself) and the completed preliminary information forms.
- Have the following available namely, flip chart and marking pens, tissues, diary, calculator and any relevant tax, financial, welfare benefits or other tables.
- Set up the room for the meeting. Clear files and papers, establish a professional but informal ambience. Ensure privacy, non-disturbance and diversion of calls.
- Establish reception arrangements. Ensure that you are immediately notified as each party arrives so that they are not left together for any length of time (and not at all if there is any actual or potential hostility). If the parties are thought to be hostile, arrange separate reception areas or place the first arriving in the mediation room.
- Arrange for the availability of tea/coffee/water.
- Ensure that any arrangements for payment of your fee and expenses, insofar as applicable, are made with the parties and clearly understood. If privately funded, some mediators arrange for the fee to be payable in advance, some collect this at the end of each session and some invoice the parties for payment afterwards.

Initial Meeting with the couple (See below for initial meeting with lawyers)

- Put the couple at ease, offer tea/coffee.
- Check permission to use first names all round (unless inappropriate).
- Reiterate key elements of the Agreement to Mediate, which should have been agreed in advance. If it has not already been signed, for example electronically, do so now.
- Consider whether the preliminary information form raises anything needing to be addressed at the outset.

- Insofar as not already done, for example at a MIAM, employ a screening mechanism for possible problems of abuse, violence or threat. These must be addressed. Ensure that mediation can properly and effectively take place. Consider seeing each party separately if this may allow freer discussion about abuse.
- Check and record parties' agenda and priorities. Avoid contention in doing so.
- Check if there are any urgent issues requiring attention in the first session. If so, address them, checking if there are competing priorities. If so, discuss how to allocate the time.
- Check the framework within which decisions are to be taken: exploratory, separation, divorce? Discuss and clarify options if required.
- Sole mediators who may co-mediate in some circumstances should consider whether the dynamics or issues indicate that co-mediation might be appropriate. If so, discuss it with the couple and make any necessary arrangements for the future.
- Acquaint yourself with the relevant facts especially regarding children, housing and general circumstances. Consider and discuss how best to establish the needs, wishes and feelings of any children involved.
- Hand the parties financial disclosure documentation for completion and explain how these are to be dealt with. Arrange how and when these should be returned to you.
- If either party is legally represented, and assuming lawyers are not present, seek permission to write to their solicitor(s), and clarify what may be said to them.
- Deal with concluding practicalities such as summarising matters to be dealt with by each, fixing date of next meeting, obtaining or arranging payment and any other matters.

Maintaining separate confidences

The family mediation model primarily used in England and Wales developed on the basis that mediators do not maintain separate confidences, save in some circumstances for private addresses and issues regarding violence and abuse.

However, there is an increasing use and acceptance of a development of process in which mediators have separate meetings with parties and/or their lawyers on the basis that separate discussions will not be disclosed to the other without authority. This is used as an additional resource alongside the standard model of conducting mediation through joint meetings, and not generally as an alternative. However, there are some exceptions to this, in particular that separate confidences will not be maintained in respect of financial information, which is evidentially open, will be openly disclosed and may be used in court; also other exceptions include the protection of children's rights, and especially protection for children or others who might be at risk of harm.

The checklist relating to separate private meetings is continued below, after an outline of the standard model. Any references to separate meetings obviously only apply to those models of practice where separate confidences are maintained.

DRAFTING, DOCUMENTS AND PRECEDENTS

After initial meeting

- If financial disclosure documents have not arrived by the agreed date, contact the defaulting party and check the position.
- When the financial disclosure documents are received, make copies to hand to the parties at the next meeting.
- If appropriate, prepare a flip chart by writing up any outline, but not any data, which should be done together with the couple.
- Consider information given by the parties and reflect on any further information likely to be needed.

Second meeting (if finances are to be addressed)

- Acknowledge the financial disclosure documents. Check if anything material has arisen since the last meeting and review agenda.
- Unless other issues are to be dealt with, continue with information disclosure. Take couple through documents. Start with capital position, writing up on the flip chart. Check for completeness. Indicate what further information is needed.
- After recording the financial disclosure, establish needs and wants against available resources. You may perhaps start with respective housing needs. This may inter-relate with children's accommodation needs and whom they will be primarily living with. Have preliminary discussion about the children (if any) and their needs.
- Are there any legal contentions about respective rights? Consider how these will be addressed. Perhaps invite lawyers to a meeting?
- Start helping the couple to generate options, including housing and finance.
- Consider what action parties can each take pending the next session, for example, checking property value(s), exploring prices and availability of alternative housing, taking legal advice etc.
- Is any urgent action needed before the next meeting? If so, discuss this with the couple.
- Deal with concluding practicalities, summarise matters to be dealt with by each, fix date of next meeting.

Further meetings

- Each meeting will have to be conducted according to the needs of the situation as it develops. No standard format can be given.
- Financial issues will be dealt with by generating, developing and exploring options and by assisting the parties with their negotiations.
- On children issues, establish a picture of the children and their circumstances, wishes, interests and needs. Consider how to bring those factors into the process. These issues can be dealt with through exploring alternative options. Mediators who have specifically trained to work with children in mediation will consider whether it would be appropriate and helpful to see the children and will arrange to do so in accordance with the principles and requirements of child-inclusive practice.

- Consider with the couple whether they want a parenting plan for the children (if any) and work through a precedent discussing and completing this as appropriate.
- Consider whether any third party assistance is needed, e.g. counselling, legal, financial or any other input, valuations or tax assistance, and how best this can be arranged.
- Consider possibilities of reconciliation throughout.
- Consider impasse strategies if necessary.
- Consider providing a written summary of partly resolved issues.

Separate private meetings

If working under a model that incorporates separate private and confidential meetings, and if appropriate, one or more separate meetings may be arranged, with or without lawyers, which may be in addition to joint meetings. Bear the following in mind:

- There is a common misperception that such meetings are only useful where there has been abuse and parties cannot meet together jointly. While this and any sense of intimidation are indeed indicators of such meetings, there are many other circumstances in which these might be useful, for example, where the couple's finances require complex planning and negotiation; where either party has difficulty with face-to-face negotiation and needs time to reflect on and respond to proposals; or where a party genuinely cannot understand the other's thinking or intent and needs time and support—perhaps from his or her own lawyer—to reflect on matters. Also, separate meetings can be a useful impasse strategy when negotiations in joint session are deadlocked.
- More time is generally needed than the usual one and a half hours—perhaps a half-day or longer (but check parties' ability to cope and avoid lengthy over-runs).
- Rules about confidentiality and the open nature of financial information and the other relevant exceptions to confidentiality must be agreed and clearly recorded.
- If parties are attending alone, prepare them for periods of waiting alone, including perhaps suggesting relevant aspects that they might consider.
- If lawyers are attending, liaise with them in advance to prepare them for a supportive rather than combative role.
- Separate meetings are sometimes more helpful after parties have had some joint meetings, shared financial data, identified, discussed and narrowed options.
- Separate meetings tend to be more useful for property and financial matters and less useful for dealing with children's issues, which generally require joint discussion and decision-making.

Parties' lawyers

In the model that has become standard in the UK, parties' lawyers tend to function outside the mediation, providing advice, commenting on the outcome and drafting any formal documentation. In many cases, parties do not have lawyers. However, where lawyers are appointed early on, there is an increasing opportunity for them to play a greater role in the process itself.

- In the model in which parties' lawyers advise outside the meetings, check with the parties that you can contact the lawyers as a courtesy to advise them of the mediation.
- Where lawyers are already instructed by the parties, a preliminary meeting with them, without the parties, can be useful to enable you to outline your process and your expectations, including how the lawyers can contribute, and to establish some rapport and some commonality about the issues.
- As the mediation proceeds, encourage parties to take advice as appropriate, especially on issues such as financial disclosure and different views about respective rights. The lawyers may have a significant role in helping to establish financial disclosure.
- Keep in mind the possibility of lawyers attending a joint session, even if you are not maintaining separate confidences.
- If necessary and if the parties request or agree, liaise with the lawyers about matters requiring attention.

If following a model that allows for separate confidences:

- The above points remain equally valid, but lawyers may have a greater role within the process including perhaps attending a preliminary meeting as outlined above as well as any others, dealing with financial disclosure and liaising with the mediator to try to narrow issues.
- The same rules about confidentiality, privilege and the open nature of financial disclosure that apply to the parties will extend to the lawyers.

When issues are resolved

- Check with the parties that the terms are understood and that they are acceptable.
- Ensure so far as possible that you have all necessary information on hand to enable the summaries to be prepared in sufficient detail to make it unnecessary for any further inter-party or inter-solicitor negotiations to take place.
- Arrange that summaries will be prepared by you. Estimate time-scale and cost, and practical arrangements for furnishing and checking the summaries, correcting any errors on the draft.
- If lawyers have not been directly involved, recommend the couple to see their respective solicitors with the summaries when finalised. Check if you are required to communicate the outcome to the solicitors.

- Remind the couple that the resolution is provisional and not binding until both parties confirm acceptance after having had legal advice (or declining to obtain such advice having had the opportunity to do so).
- Suggest that a further mediation meeting be held if there are any issues raised by solicitors that cannot be readily resolved between the parties or their solicitors. The solicitors can also be invited to attend that meeting.

APPENDIX II

Court-Related Documents and Directives

This appendix lists some relevant court-related guides, directives and documents, with web references, and includes a draft order (the "Ungley Order") not readily available online. This list is not intended to be comprehensive. Insofar as EU directives are concerned, these are provided as at the time of publication, but in view of the UK's imminent departure from the EU at the time of publication, these might well change over time.

CHANCERY GUIDE (CHANCERY DIVISION OF THE HIGH COURT OF JUSTICE)

See *https://www.judiciary.gov.uk/wp-content/uploads/2016/02/chancery-guide-feb-2016.pdf* with particular reference to Ch.18—Case management for settlement, which includes provision for "Stays for mediation", "Early Neutral Evaluation" and "Financial Dispute Resolution".   **A2–001**

THE TECHNOLOGY AND CONSTRUCTION COURT GUIDE

See *https://www.gov.uk/government/uploads/system/uploads/attachment_data/file/448256/technology-and-construction-court-guide.pdf* with particular reference to Ch.7—ADR.   **A2–002**

See also Appendix E of the Guide for a draft ADR order and Appendix G for a draft Court Settlement Order.

QUEEN'S BENCH DIVISION GUIDE

See *https://assets.publishing.service.gov.uk/government/uploads/system/uploads/attachment_data/file/587836/qb-guide-2017-final5.pdf* with particular reference to para.3.1, which refers to Settlement and Pre-action Protocols, and para.8.4, which deals with Alternative Dispute Resolution ("ADR"). And although not directly related to ADR, para.8.5 (Offers to settle and payments into and out of court) may be of relevance to those working as intermediaries in civil proceedings.   **A2–003**

COMMERCIAL COURT GUIDE INCORPORATING THE ADMIRALTY COURT GUIDE

A2–004   See   *https://www.gov.uk/government/uploads/system/uploads/attachment_data/ file/672422/The_Commercial_Court_Guide_new_10th_Edition_07.09.17.pdf* with particular reference to s.G, which covers ADR generally and Early Neutral Evaluation in particular. Section O covers arbitration. Appendix 3 provides a draft ADR order.

UNGLEY ORDER

A2–005   Order for ADR as approved in Halsey (See Ch.5).

"The parties shall by [date] consider whether the case is capable of resolution by ADR. If any party considers that the case is unsuitable for resolution by ADR, that party shall be prepared to justify that decision at the conclusion of the trial, should the judge consider that such means of resolution were appropriate, when he is considering the appropriate costs order to make.

The party considering the case unsuitable for ADR shall, not less than 28 days before the commencement of the trial, file with the court a witness statement without prejudice save as to costs, giving reasons upon which they rely for saying that the case was unsuitable."

PRACTICE DIRECTION: PRE-ACTION CONDUCT AND PROTOCOLS

A2–006   See *https://www.justice.gov.uk/courts/procedure-rules/civil/rules/pd_pre-action_ conduct#8.1* with particular reference to paras 8–11 (Settlement and ADR).

PRACTICE DIRECTION 3A: PRE-APPLICATION PROTOCOL FOR MEDIATION INFORMATION AND ASSESSMENT (FAMILY)

A2–007   See   *https://www.justice.gov.uk/courts/procedure-rules/family/pdf/practice_ directions/Web_pd_part_03a.pdf* for this Practice Direction, which supplements the Family Procedural Rules (FPR) Pt 3.

HM COURTS & TRIBUNALS SERVICE—MONEY CLAIM ONLINE (MCOL) SERVICE

A2–008   See *https://www.moneyclaim.gov.uk/web/mcol/welcome.*

COURT-RELATED DOCUMENTS AND DIRECTIVES

EU DIRECTIVES AND ONLINE PLATFORM

See *http://eur-lex.europa.eu/LexUriServ/LexUriServ.do?uri= OJ:L:2008:136:0003:0008:En:PDF* for the transcript of Directive 2008/52/EC on certain aspects of mediation in civil and commercial matters.

A2–009

See also *https://publications.europa.eu/en/publication-detail/-/publication/ 2f3efba7-fb97-41b2-953a-69c6080dfbcc/language-en* for the transcript of Directive 2013/11/EU on alternative dispute resolution for consumer disputes and amending Regulation (EC) No 2006/2004 and Directive 2009/22/EC (Directive on consumer ADR).

The EU Online Dispute Resolution Platform at: *https://webgate.ec.europa.eu/ odr/main/index.cfm?event=main.home.show&lng=EN.*

In the UK the relevant Statutory Instruments are:

Statutory Instrument 2015 No.542: The Alternative Dispute Resolution for Consumer Disputes (Competent Authorities and Information) Regulations 2015. See *http://www.legislation.gov.uk/uksi/2015/542/pdfs/uksi_20150542_en.pdf* for a transcript of the full document.

Statutory Instrument 2015 No.1392: The Alternative Dispute Resolution for Consumer Disputes (Amendment) Regulations 2015. See *http://www.legislation. gov.uk/uksi/2015/1392/pdfs/uksi_20151392_en.pdf.*

Following the UK's decision to withdraw from the EU ("Brexit") there may well be future changes to some aspects of the UK's relationship with any relevant EU Directives.

Glossary

TERMS AND ABBREVIATIONS

AAA: American Arbitration Association.

Acas: A statutory body, the Advisory, Conciliation and Arbitration Service, designed to provide an independent industrial relations service to industry.

ACR: The US organisation, Association for Conflict Resolution, with professional interest sections including commercial, community, environment, family, restorative justice, training and workplace.

Adjudication: Generically, a dispute resolution process in which a neutral third party hears each party's case and makes a binding decision as for example in litigation and arbitration—also in some jurisdictions private judging. There is also a more specific meaning in some industries, particularly the construction industry, of a procedure by which a neutral adjudicator is empowered and required by contract to make summary binding decisions about disputes arising under that contract without following litigation or arbitration procedures. This specialised meaning, also called "fast track adjudication" and "interim adjudication", generally provides for the determination to be binding only until the parties have reached some further agreement on the issue or have taken it to litigation or arbitration.

ADR: Alternative Dispute Resolution; but other ideas are promoted for this acronym, most commonly Appropriate Dispute Resolution.

Adversarial process: A process in which each party to a dispute presents his case to the other(s) and to a neutral adjudicator, seeking to demonstrate the correctness of his own case and the wrongness of the other(s). It may be distinguished from consensual ADR processes, which aim for an agreed outcome and may be more problem-solving, or from an inquisitorial approach, in which a neutral investigator seeks to establish the truth by making inquiries of the parties and others.

Alternative Dispute Resolution (ADR): This term covers an agglomeration of dispute resolution procedures that stand as alternatives to litigation. They usually entail helping the parties to arrive at a negotiated agreement, commonly using a third-party neutral. Arbitration and other forms of adjudication apart from

GLOSSARY

litigation are sometimes included in the term ADR and sometimes not. The developing consensus is that they are part of ADR. See also "Dispute resolution".

***Amiable composition*:** The power which may be given to arbitrators in certain civil law jurisdictions to render an award according to what they believe to be just and fair, so as to be able to introduce principles of equity to the applicable substantive law.

Arbitration: A dispute resolution process in which the issues are adjudicated upon by a neutral third party who is either selected privately by them or under some agreement for his or her private selection and/or who acts under the rules of arbitration, and whose decision is binding on them.

Arb-med: A process in which an arbitrator conducts arbitration proceedings, makes an award and seals it without informing the parties, then conducts a mediation. If the parties settle in mediation, the sealed award is not opened. If they do not, then the award is opened and takes effect.

Baseball arbitration: See "Final offer arbitration".

BATNA: "The Best Alternative to a Negotiated Agreement" or the best outcome which a party can achieve if the matter is not settled by negotiation. A concept introduced by Fisher & Ury in *Getting to Yes* as the standard against which a proposed settlement can be measured. See also WATNA.

Brainstorming: Putting forward as many ideas and options as possible as they come to mind without at that stage inhibiting their flow by examining them individually.

Case evaluation: See "evaluation".

Caucusing: One of the procedures used in mediation in which the mediator meets the parties to a dispute separately, as part of a strategy to assist in the resolution of the dispute. This is often part of a process in which the mediator shuttles backwards and forwards between the parties, caucusing each in turn, in order to try to narrow the issues between them with a view to eventual resolution. In the field of industrial relations, the term "caucus" has a different meaning, being used to relate to a private meeting that a conciliator has with negotiators from both sides.

CEDR: Centre for Effective Dispute Resolution.

CJC: The Civil Justice Council.

CMC: The Civil Mediation Council.

Collaborative law (or collaborative practice): A practice in which disputing parties each engage a collaboratively trained and committed lawyer, who contract

GLOSSARY

with their respective clients to deal with the matter by negotiation and not to embark on unilateral court action. There is a broad framework for negotiations in which the parties have an active role together with their lawyers. If parties cannot settle in the process and either wishes to proceed to litigation, the contract provides that the collaborative lawyers will stand down and will not act in the contentious proceedings.

Co-mediation: Mediation by two or more mediators who may be from the same or different disciplines and who may work in tandem and/or share different tasks.

Complementary Dispute Resolution: Court-related ADR processes, though also commonly used as an alternative term for Alternative Dispute Resolution.

Consensus building: This is a form of collaborative problem solving largely used to deal with complex, multiparty disagreements particularly in the environmental field, or to address public policy issues and social policies and programmes. It aims for a concord, and not necessarily unanimity, between interested parties through dialogue.

Conciliation: This term is often used interchangeably with mediation though conciliation is often viewed as being more facilitative and non-interventionist, whereas mediation is seen as allowing for more mediator proactivity. Sometimes however the reverse usage is employed: there is no consistency. It is sometimes used as a generic term to cover third-party facilitation generally.

Conflict: A state of incompatibility of interests, objectives or positions between people or groups. It may include a dispute, which is a form of conflict that is justiciable.

Consensual processes: Processes of dispute resolution based on the parties having to reach agreement in order for the issues to be resolved, such as negotiation and mediation. They are distinct from adjudicatory processes, in which a third party can impose a binding decision upon them, such as litigation and arbitration.

Court-annexed (or court-ordered) arbitration: A form of arbitration by a court-approved neutral. In various models of this, the neutral's finding is initially non-binding, but it will become binding if neither party seeks a rehearing by a judge. Sanctions, such as a costs award, may be applied to an applicant for a rehearing who does not materially improve his position at a trial.

Court-annexed (or court-ordered or court-related) mediation: Mediation ordered by or arranged through a court, and undertaken by a judicial or court officer, or by an outside third party approved by the court.

CPR: This may refer to the English court's Civil Procedure Rules. It is also an acronym for the US body CPR—originally called the Center for Public Resources and latterly the International Institute for Conflict Prevention and Resolution.

GLOSSARY

***Culpa in contrahendo*:** A doctrine developed by courts and commentators in some civil law systems under which the mere initiation of negotiation creates a pre-contractual relationship as a matter of law which, inter alia, imposes on the negotiating parties a reciprocal duty of care.

Dispute: A dispute is a disagreement about an issue or issues that are capable of being decided upon by a third party, that is to say, they are justiciable.

Dispute board (or dispute review board): A board set up at the commencement of a contract, particularly but no longer exclusively in the construction industry, to consider and try to deal with disputes as they arise, through informal meetings and discussions, and perhaps also by interim adjudication.

Dispute resolution: The determination of a dispute, which is generally achieved by adjudication or by an agreed settlement between the parties. A distinction is sometimes drawn between a "settlement" which merely indicates that terms have been agreed to end the dispute though the underlying issues may not have been disposed of, and "resolution" which infers that all issues have been satisfactorily resolved and determined. However, settlement is commonly equated with resolution. The term "dispute resolution" is also sometimes used instead of "alternative dispute resolution", indicating that ADR processes should not be regarded as "alternative".

Early neutral evaluation (ENE): A process developed in the Northern District of California for a neutral evaluator to meet parties at an early stage of a case in order to make a confidential assessment of the dispute. Partly this procedure helps them to narrow and define the issues, and partly it promotes efforts to arrive at a settlement. This term has been increasingly commonly used to refer simply to "evaluation". Provision for ENE is now incorporated into the Commercial Court Guide, the Chancery Guide and the Technology and Construction Court Guide.

Evaluation: This term has two usages. Generically, it is a non-binding expression of opinion about the merits of issues between parties. It is sometimes also used to refer to assessing the merits of proposed settlement terms. Specifically, as a process in its own right, evaluation (or "case evaluation") is used as a non-binding ADR process. Under it, a case may be submitted to an evaluator or an expert panel, who can consider submissions and if necessary hear witnesses. The evaluator or panel then makes a reasoned, non-binding evaluation of the case that can be used in attempts to facilitate settlement. See also "Early neutral evaluation".

***Ex aequo et bono*:** Principle of dealing fairly and in good faith.

Executive Tribunal: Term used by CEDR to describe the mini-trial.

GLOSSARY

Expert determination: A procedure whereby a dispute, perhaps of a technical nature, is to be resolved by an expert, nominated or identifiable, whose decision is to be final and binding on the parties, and who need not follow the rules of arbitration or litigation.

Facilitation: The assistance provided to the parties to a dispute by a third party, usually neutral, to help them to deal constructively with the issues between them.

Fact-finding expert: See "Neutral fact-finding expert".

Fast track adjudication: See "Adjudication".

Final offer arbitration: Also known as "pendulum arbitration", "flip flop arbitration" and as "baseball arbitration" because of its usage in relation to the resolution of disagreements concerning the salaries of baseball players in the US. Each party makes a final settlement offer and the arbitrator chooses the one considered more reasonable. This puts both sides under pressure to submit a reasonable offer.

Financial Dispute Resolution (FDR): A court hearing in matrimonial financial proceedings in which a judge helps the parties to explore their issues without any judicial determination and to arrive at an agreed resolution on a privileged and "without prejudice" basis. If agreement is reached, a consent order may be made. If not, the judge may give directions for trial but would not have any further judicial function in that case. The Chancery Division of the High Court also has a Financial Dispute Resolution process (Chancery FDR), a form of ADR in which the judge facilitates negotiations and may provide the parties with an opinion about the claim or elements of it.

FMA: Family Mediators Association.

FMC: The Family Mediation Council.

GEMME: European Association of Judges for Mediation.

High-low contract: A procedure used in the US in which parties agree to adjudication, but limit the parameters of the financial award. For example, a claim may be referred to court on the issue of liability only on the terms that if the finding is for the plaintiff, an agreed sum will be payable which will be less than the plaintiff was hoping for. If the finding is in favour of the defendant, there will nevertheless be a payment of an agreed smaller sum to the plaintiff. This allows each party to hedge against an adverse award.

Hybrid processes: Dispute resolution processes created by drawing on the primary processes and using them in different ways or permutations; such as mini-trial, med-arb or moderated settlement conference. A hybrid model of mediation is one that adopts and integrates elements from different fields of activity.

GLOSSARY

ICC: International Chamber of Commerce.

ICSID: The International Centre for Settlement of Investment Disputes.

IDRC: The International Dispute Resolution Centre.

IMI: The International Mediation Institute.

Impasse strategies: Strategies and tactics employed by a neutral to try to overcome a deadlock in negotiations.

Interest-based (or integrative) negotiation: Commonly involving joint problem solving, this focuses on parties' interests including needs, wishes, concerns and fears. It aims to find a resolution that meets such interests and needs. It is generally contrasted with "rights-based" negotiation, though these are not mutually exclusive.

Interim adjudication: See "Adjudication".

Intermediate dispute resolution: A procedure, especially in the construction industry, by which contracting parties provide in their contract for the appointment of a neutral third party or board to deal with or advise on the resolution of disputes progressively as they arise. This may be through mediation or informal adjudication.

Judicial settlement conference: A procedure used in US state and federal courts and elsewhere in which the judge convenes a meeting in his or her chambers to see whether the parties can find a basis for settlement by agreement without a trial. See also "Financial Dispute Resolution".

Kompetenz-Kompetenz: The extent of the arbitrator's power to decide upon his own jurisdiction, when the validity of an arbitration agreement is in question and the clause providing for arbitration is contained in that agreement.

LCIA: London Court of International Arbitration.

Litigation: A dispute resolution process in which the issues are argued before and adjudicated upon by a judge or other state-appointed official, whose decision is binding on them.

Med-arb: Med-arb refers to "mediation-arbitration" and is a composite of these two procedures. A neutral is required to mediate, and if this does not achieve a settlement, to go on to make a binding decision by way of arbitration. In some versions the parties are given the option to decide whether or not to proceed to arbitration before its commencement or there may be rules requiring the mediator to make certain disclosures before moving to the arbitration phase; in others the arbitration is non-binding, for guidance of the parties only.

GLOSSARY

Mediation: A facilitative process in which disputing parties engage the assistance of an impartial mediator, who has no authority to make any decisions for them, but who uses certain procedures, techniques and skills to help them to resolve their dispute by negotiated agreement without adjudication. Mediation is commonly interest-based (q.v.). In some models where rights are relevant, the mediator may, with the parties' agreement, evaluate the merits in some way, commonly informally and privately but many mediators do not regard evaluation as a function of mediation.

The term "mediation" is sometimes used interchangeably with "conciliation". Sometimes mediation is understood to be more pro-active and evaluative than conciliation, which is more facilitative; and sometimes the reverse usage is used. There is no national or international consistency of usage.

MIAM (Mediation Information and Assessment Meeting): This is a preliminary meeting required under court rules that parties may be required to have with a mediator in order to assess whether mediation might be suitable for their issues, and to obtain information about the process.

Michigan evaluation (Michigan mediation): A form of case evaluation developed in Michigan in which a panel meets the parties' lawyers separately to seek an agreed settlement. Failing agreement, the panel makes settlement proposals, which become binding if not objected to within a specified period. The use of the term "mediation" is said by its proponents to be misleading and is being dropped in favour of "evaluation".

Mini-trial: A procedure in which the parties (or in the case of corporations, their senior executives), with the help of a neutral, observe an abbreviated form of non-binding trial, presented by their respective lawyers so that they may assess relative strengths and weaknesses, and then enter into settlement negotiations. The neutral helps clarify the issues, assess the presentations, and evaluate the case; and may assist the parties with their negotiations and/or provide a non-binding opinion. Thus the mini-trial may be a form of evaluative mediation.

Moderated settlement conference: This is a modification of court-annexed arbitration but instead of an arbitrator, there is a panel of impartial third parties.

Multi-door courthouse: The concept of a court official making a preliminary case analysis and then providing or referring disputants to a wide range of dispute resolution facilities and processes and not merely litigation. A number of American cities or counties and some other territories offer multi-door programmes.

NFM: National Family Mediation.

Negotiation: Discussions or dealings about a matter, with a view to reconciling differences and establishing areas of agreement, settlement or compromise.

GLOSSARY

Neutral: A third party who is independent of the parties in dispute and neutral in relation to their issues, and who assists them in the resolution of their dispute by acting as a mediator or conciliator or other ADR practitioner. Neutrality may be thought to imply that personal values will not be brought into the process. Some only use the adjective "neutral" in relation to outcome rather than process.

Neutral fact-finding expert: A neutral expert appointed by parties to investigate facts and to form a legal or technical view either about certain specified issues, or on all issues generally, and to make a non-binding report to the parties. The neutral may facilitate subsequent settlement discussions. The neutral's report may by agreement be open to the court in any subsequent proceedings, without precluding any party from submitting further evidence and expert reports.

ODR: Online dispute resolution—the use of web-based and related technology to help with the process of dispute resolution. This may relate to disputes arising online, or simply to using online resources to work with "real world" issues.

Ombudsman: An independent person who deals with complaints by the public against administrative and organisational injustice and maladministration in certain specified areas, with the power to investigate, criticise, make issues public and sometimes with limited powers to award compensation.

Partnering: A voluntary, non-binding collaborative process used mainly in the construction industry that focuses on solving common problems between different groups, such as owners, designers and builders, working on the same project. It is primarily a means of dispute prevention.

Pendulum arbitration: See "Final offer arbitration".

Primary processes: The primary procedures used for dispute resolution, namely negotiation, mediation and adjudication—in its generic usage. (Adjudication is sometimes divided further into sub-categories including litigation, arbitration and statutory and administrative determination). When elements are drawn from the primary processes and rearranged into new permutations these are known as hybrid processes.

Private judging: A process introduced by law into certain jurisdictions in which the court refers the case to a referee chosen by the parties to decide some or all of the issues, or to establish any specific facts. The referee is given most of the powers of a judge, and the referee's report to the court stands as an enforceable, binding and appealable judgment.

Privilege: The right in the law of evidence of a person to insist on there being withheld from a judicial tribunal information which might assist it to ascertain certain facts relevant to an issue upon which it is adjudicating.

GLOSSARY

Reconciliation: Literally the restoration of friendly relations after an estrangement. In divorce or civil partnership terms, it is the decision by a couple to try to re-establish their relationship after a separation or other differences. It is sometimes confused with the similar sounding word "conciliation" which has a different meaning.

Reframing: This refers to a communication technique which changes the frame of reference against which an event is viewed by a person, so that the judgment placed on that event takes a different meaning or perspective and it can be seen in a different light. More loosely, it is a redefining of issues or of views in a more constructive way.

Reparation: A process in the criminal justice system in which an offender makes voluntary restitution to the victim by paying compensation, performing a service or apologising, which may be accomplished through restorative justice.

Restorative justice: A process used in the criminal justice system where a person has been harmed by the wrongful acts of another, for engaging the wrongdoer with his actions and considering possibilities for restitution and sometimes for healing. Victim-offender mediation is a form of restorative justice.

Restorative practices: These are interventions by a neutral facilitator in restorative processes outside the criminal justice system, for example in workplace or school bullying or antisocial behaviour. See "restorative justice".

Rights-based negotiation: This focuses on the parties' respective rights, as they are perceived, and aims for a resolution broadly in line with those rights. This is generally contrasted with interest-based negotiation, though as previously observed, these are not mutually exclusive.

Settlement: Conclusion of a dispute by agreement, generally but not necessarily implying some compromise between the parties.

Shuttle mediation: A term used where a mediator caucuses with each party in turn as part of a strategy to narrow and help resolve the issues between them. The term is based on the activities of diplomats who go back and forth between the representatives of countries or groups in dispute, to try to resolve their differences by agreement.

Summary jury trial: A US adaptation of the mini-trial in which cases are presented to mock juries, who make findings which indicate to the parties the likely reaction of a real jury to the issues, and which help them to engage realistically in settlement negotiations.

UNCITRAL: The United Nations Commission on International Trade Laws, which has developed a set of uniform arbitral rules, the UNCITRAL rules, for world-wide use. Although these rules have been adopted in Scotland, they have not been adopted in England.

GLOSSARY

WATNA: "The Worst Alternative to a Negotiated Agreement". A development introduced by John Haynes of Fisher & Ury's BATNA being the worst anticipated outcome if a dispute is not settled by negotiation. See also "BATNA".

Win-win: The concept that parties can arrive at settlements (often arrived at through using problem-solving techniques) in which each gains some advantage, rather than an adjudicated resolution in which generally one party will win and the other will lose. The opposite of a zero-sum game.

WIPO: The World Intellectual Property Organization.

Zero-sum game: A situation in which there is no room for a win-win resolution, because every penny gained by one party must necessarily involve a loss of that amount by the other without room for any advantage to accrue to the latter.

Zone of agreement: The parameters of the range of possible terms of settlement within which a particular dispute may be resolved.

Bibliography

The following authorities have been cited in this book or are considered to be of possible interest to readers:

Abraham, Ann, "The Ombudsman as Part of the UK Constitution: A Contested Role?" (2008) 61(1) *Parliamentary Affairs*.

ACAS-CIPD, Mediation: An approach to resolving workplace issues at *http://m.acas.org.uk/media/pdf/n/n/Mediation-an-approach-to-resolving-workplace-issues.pdf*) (Feb 2013).

Acland, Andrew Floyer, *A Sudden Outbreak of Common Sense: Managing Conflict through Mediation* (London: Random House Business Books, 1990).

—, *Resolving Disputes Without Going to Court* (London: Century Books, 1995).

—, *Dialogue by Design: A Handbook of Public and Stakeholder Engagement* (London: Dialogue by Design, 2010).

Adair, Wendi L. and Jeanne M. Brett, "The Negotiation Dance: Time, Culture, and Behavioral Sequences in Negotiation" (2005) 16(1) *Organization Science*.

Adler J., D. Hensler, and C. Nelson, "Simple Justice: How Litigants Fare in the Pittsburgh Court Arbitration Program" in J.S. Murray, A.S. Rau and E.F. Sherman, *Processes of Dispute Resolution: The Role of Lawyers* (New York: Foundation Press, 1989).

Alexander, Najda Marie, *Global Trends in Mediation*, 2nd edn (London: Kluwer Law International, 2006).

Allen, Tony and Karl Mackie, "Moves in mediation: confidentiality, the EU Directive and regulation" (2008) 43 *The Barrister*.

Andrews N., "A New Civil Procedural Code for England" (2000) *Civil Justice Quarterly*, 19–38.

Antes, James R., Donna Turner Hudson, Erling O. Jorgensen and Janet Kelly Moen, "Is a Stage Model of Mediation Necessary?" (1999) 16(3) *Mediation Quarterly*.

Axelrod R., *The Evolution of Co-operation* (New York: Basic Books, 2006).

Babcock, Linda and Sara Laschever, *Women Don't Ask: Negotiation and the Gender Divide* (New Jersey: Princeton University Press, 2003).

Baginsky, William, *Peer Mediation in the UK: A guide for schools* (written for the Daphne Project, NSPCC, 2004).

Barr, Lewis. D., "Whose Dispute Is This Anyway?: The Propriety of the Mini-trial in Promoting Corporate Dispute Resolution" (1987) *Journal of Dispute Resolution (Missouri)*.

Beer, Jennifer E., *Peacemaking in Your Neighbourhood: Mediator's Handbook* (Canada: Friends Conflict Resolution Programs, 1990; 4th revised edition, 2012).

BIBLIOGRAPHY

—, and Caroline C. Packard, with Eileen Stief, *The Mediator's Handbook,* 4th edn (Canada: New Society Press, 2011).

Benjamin, Robert, "The Mediator as Trickster: The Folkloric Figure as Professional Role Model" (1995) 13(2) *Mediation Quarterly* 131.

—, "The Use of Mediative Strategies in Traditional Legal Practice" (1997) 14(2) *Journal of the American Academy of Matrimonial Lawyers* 203.

—, "The Risks Of Neutrality—Reconsidering The Term And Concept" at *http://www.mediate.com//articles/benjamin1.cfm* originally published as "Peripheral Visions" (1998) 18(1) *Mediation News* 8.

—, "Swindlers, Dealmakers and Mediators: A Brief History of Ethics in Negotiation" (Spring 2004) *ACResolution Magazine.*

—, "On Becoming a Rationally Irrational Negotiator/Mediator: The 'Messy' Human Brain and the 'Myth of Rationality'" (2009) *http://www.mediate.com// articles/on_becoming_rationally_irrational_1.cfm.*

Berkovitch, J., V. Kremenyuk, and I.W. Zartman, *Sage Handbook of Conflict Resolution* (Sage Publications Ltd, 2008).

Bernstein, Ronald QC, John A. Tackaberry QC, and Arthur L. Marriott QC, *Bernstein's Handbook of Arbitration Practice*, 4th edn (London: Sweet & Maxwell, 2003).

Bevan, Alexander H., *Alternative Dispute Resolution* (London: Sweet & Maxwell, 1992).

Bickerman, John, "Evaluative Mediator Responds" (1996) 14(6) *Alternatives.*

Billings, Annie, "The Mini-Trial: Misunderstanding and Miscommunication May Short-Circuit its Effective Use in Settlements" (1990) 2 *Journal of Dispute Resolution.*

Blackaby, Nigel, Constantine Partasides, Alan Redfern & Martin Hunter, *Redfern and Hunter on International Arbitration*, 5th edn (Oxford: Oxford University Press, 2009).

Blake S., J. Browne and S. Sime, *A Practical Approach to Alternative Dispute Resolution* (Oxford University Press 2016).

Booth, Caroline, Michael Clemence, and Sara Gariban, "Acas Collective Conciliation Evaluation 2016", Research Paper, (Ipsos MORI Ref: 06/16).

Boulle, Laurence and Miryana Nesic, *Mediator Skills and Techniques: Triangle of Influence* (Haywards Heath: Bloomsbury Professional, 2010).

Brams, Steven J. and Alan D. Taylor, *Fair Division: From Cake-Cutting to Dispute Resolution* (Cambridge: Cambridge University Press, 1996).

Brett J. M. and S. Goldberg, "Grievance Mediation in the Coal Industry: A Field Experiment" (1983) 37(1) Indus. & Lab. Rel. Rev. 49.

—, "Mediator-Advisers: A New Third Party Role" in M. Bazerman & R. Lewicki, *Negotiating in Organisations* (California: Sage Publications, 1983).

Briggs LJ, Civil Courts Structure Review: Final Report, July 2016, available at: *https://www.judiciary.gov.uk/wp-content/uploads/2016/07/civil-courts-structure-review-final-report-jul-16-final-1.pdf.*

Briggs M., "Mediation Privilege?" *New Law Journal*, 3 and 10 April 2009.

British Academy of Experts, *Report of the Committee on the Language of ADR* (1992).

BIBLIOGRAPHY

Brown, Henry, Neil Dawson and Brenda McHugh, *Managing Difficult Divorce Relationships: A multimedia training programme for family lawyers* (Resolution, 2006).

—, "Creating confidence in mediators and the process: an exploration of the issues" *Chartered Institute of Arbitrators* (3rd Mediation Symposium 2010).

—, "Mediating high conflict couples" in Pia Deleuran (ed), *Conflict Management in the Family Field and in Other Close Relationships: Mediation as a Way Forward* (Copenhagen: DJÒF Publishing, 2011).

—, Neil Dawson and Brenda McHugh, *Psychology, Emotion and Intuition in Work Relationships: The Head, Heart and Gut Professional* (London and New York: Routledge, 2018).

Bryant, S., "Mediation for Lesbian and Gay Families" (1992) 9(4) *Mediation Quarterly* (M.Q.) 391.

Buck, Trevor, Richard Kirkham and Brian Thompson, *The Ombudsman Enterprise and Administrative Justice (Election Law, Politics, and Theory)* (Surrey: Ashgate Publishing, 2011).

Buckingham, Paul, "The effective use of experts and expert witnesses" (2009) at: (*http://www.mondaq.com/uk/x/71864/Arbitration+Dispute+Resolution/The+Effective+Use+Of+Experts+And+Expert+Witnesses*).

Bush, R A. Baruch and J.P. Folger, *The Promise of Mediation* (San Francisco: Jossey-Bass, 1994; Revised edn, 2004).

—, and J.P. Folger, "Transformative Mediation and Third-Party Intervention: Ten Hallmarks of a Transformative Approach to Practice" (Summer 1996) 13(4) *Mediation Quarterly*.

—, J.P. Folger and D.J. Della Noce, *Transformative Mediation: A Sourcebook—Resources for Conflict Intervention Practitioners and Programs* (New York: Association for Conflict Resolution and the Institute for the Study of Conflict Transformation, 2010).

Cahn Dudley, D., *Conflict in Personal Relations* (New York: Routledge, 2009).

Campbell, Alan, "Mediation of Children Issues When One Parent is Gay" (1996) 14(1) *Mediation Quarterly*.

Carnwath, Sir Robert, "Tribunals: A New Start" [2009] 1 *Public Law* 48.

Carr, L., M. Lacobini, M-C. Dubeau, J. C. Maziotta, and G. L. Lenzi, "Neural mechanisms of empathy in humans: A relay from neural systems for imitation to limbic areas" (2003) 100(9) *Proceedings of the National Academy of Sciences* 5497.

Carroll, Eileen and Karl Mackie, *International Mediation: The Art of Business Diplomacy* (Haywards Heath: Bloomsbury Professional (previously Tottel Publishing), 2006).

Castagna, Charles N., "Mediation: Leave Well Enough Alone" (November 1997) *Newsletter of the Clearwater, Florida, Bar Association*.

Chan, P.H., Book Review: Klaus J. Hopt and Felix Steffek, *Mediation: Principles and Regulation in Comparative Perspective* (Oxford, Oxford University Press 2013) (2013) (14) *European Business Organization Law Review* 613.

BIBLIOGRAPHY

Chapman, Peter, "Dispute Boards on major infrastructure projects" (June 2011) Proceedings of the Institution of Civil Engineers (ICE) *Management, Procurement and Law* 162, February 2009 Issue MP1.

Chern C., *Chern on Dispute Boards* (Abingdon: Routledge, 2015).

Chornenki, Genevieve, "Mediating Commercial Disputes: Exchanging 'Power over' for 'Power with'" in J. Macfarlane, *Rethinking Disputes; the Mediation Alternative* (London: Cavendish Publishing, 1997).

Cialdini, Robert B., *Influence: Science and Practice*, 5th edn (Pearson Education Inc/Allyn & Bacon, 2009).

Civil Justice Online Dispute Resolution Advisory Group's Report of February 2015: "Online Dispute Resolution for Low Value Civil Claims" available at: *https://www.judiciary.gov.uk/reviews/online-dispute-resolution/*.

Civil Mediation Council's Online Directory of Mediators, available at: *http://civilmediation.justice.gov.uk/*.

Civil Mediation Council Guidance Note No.1, Mediation Confidentiality, (CMC, July 8, 2009).

Cloke, Kenneth, *Mediating Dangerously: The Frontiers of Conflict Resolution* (San Francisco: Jossey-Bass, 2001).

Clout, Imogen, *"The Which?" Guide to Divorce: The Essential Practical Guide to the Legal and Financial Arrangements for Divorce* (London: Which? Books, 2005).

Coates, C.A. et al, "Parenting Coordination for High Conflict Families" (2003) 41 *Family Court Review* 1.

Cobb S. and J. Rifkin, "Practice and Paradox: Deconstructing Neutrality in Mediation" (1991) 16 *Law & Social Inquiry*.

Cohen I., "Apology Accepted" The Lawyer, 7 April 2003.

Coleman, P.T., M. Deutsch, and E.C. Marcus, *The Handbook of Conflict Resolution: Theory and Practice*, 3rd edn (San Francisco: Jossey Bass, 2014).

Communities and Local Government Department, *Mediation in the planning system* (London: HMSO, 2000).

—, *Planning applications: A faster and more responsive system, Final Report* (The Killian Pretty Review) (London: Communities and Local Government, 2008).

Conlon D. E., H. Moon and K.Y. Ng, "Putting the cart before the horse: The benefits of arbitrating before mediating" (2002) 87(5) *Journal of Applied Psychology* 978.

Construction Umbrella Bodies Adjudication Task Group, *Users' Guide to Adjudication: A guide for participants in adjudications conducted under Part II of the Housing Grants, Construction and Regeneration Act 1996* (London: Construction Umbrella Bodies Adjudication Task Group, April 2003).

Conway, Helen L., *Domestic Violence: Picking up the Pieces* (Oxford: Lion Publishing Plc, 1997).

Cook, Lindsay, "Complaints put consumer watchdogs on watch" (March 2018). At: *https://www.ft.com/content/510b5344-279b-11e8-b27e-cc62a39d57a0*.

Cooper, Christopher, *Mediation & Arbitration by Patrol Police Officers* (New York: Oxford University Press, 1999).

Core Solutions Group, *A Guide to the Use of Mediation in the Planning System in Scotland* (Edinburgh: The Scottish Government/Core Solutions, 2009).

BIBLIOGRAPHY

Cornes, David, "Mediation Privilege and the EU Mediation Directive: An Opportunity?" (2008) 74 *Arbitration* 395.

—, "Mediator Fails to Have Witness Summons Set Aside: Farm Assist Ltd v Secretary of State for the Environment Food and Rural Affairs (No.2)" (2009) 75 *Arbitration* 4.

Cortés, Pablo, *Online Dispute Resolution for Consumers in the European Union* (Abingdon: Routledge, 2011).

—, (ed.) *The New Regulatory Framework for Consumer Dispute Resolution* (Oxford University Press, 2016).

Council of Europe, *Convention for the Protection of Human Rights and Fundamental Freedoms*, as amended by Protocols No.11 and 14 (2010).

Coyle, M., "Defending the Weak and Fighting Unfairness: Can Mediators Respond to the Challenge?" (1998) (36) *Osgoode Hall Law Journal* 625.

Craver, Charles B. & David W. Barnes, "Gender, Risk Taking and Negotiation Performance" (1999) 5 *Michigan Journal of Gender & Law* 299.

Crawley, John, *Constructive Conflict Management: Managing to Make a Difference* (London: Nicholas Brearley Publishing, 1992, 1995).

Creutzfeldt, Naomi, & Chris Gill, "Critics of the Ombudsman System: Understanding and Engaging Online Citizen Activists" (December 2015 briefing paper for the Economic and Social Research Council); available at *https://www.law.ox.ac.uk/sites/files/oxlaw/critics-of-the-ombudsmen-system-understanding-and-engaging-online-citizen-activists-dec15.pdf*.

Crook, Jason A., and Julio César Betancourt (eds), *What is Alternative Dispute Resolution (ADR)?* (London: Chartered Institute of Arbitrators, 2010).

Crum, Thomas F., and John Denver, *The Magic of Conflict: Turning a life of Work into a Work of Art* (Touchstone, New York, 1987).

—, *Journey to Center: Lessons in Unifying Body, Mind and Spirit* (New York: Touchstone, 1997).

Davey, Barbara & Gill Dix, *The Dispute Resolution Regulations two years on: the Acas experience* (London: Acas Research and Evaluation Section, 2011).

Davies, Harry, "Alternative Dispute Resolution: Panacea or Anathema" 99 *Harvard Law Review* (1985–1986).

Davis, Gwynn, *Partisans and Mediators: The Resolution of Divorce Disputes* (Oxford: Clarendon Press, 1988).

—, & Marian Roberts, *Access to Agreement* (Milton Keynes/Philadelphia: Open University Press, 1988).

—, with Heinz Messmer, Mark Umbreit and Robert Coates, *Making Amends: Mediation and Reparation in Criminal Justice* (London: Routledge, 1992).

de Boisséson, Matthieau, *Le droit franpaise de l'arbitrage interne et international* (Paris: GLN-éditions, 1990).

De Bono, Edward, *The Use of Lateral Thinking* (London: Jonathan Cape, 1967).

—, *Conflicts: A Better Way to Resolve Them* (Harmondsworth: Penguin Books, 1986).

—, *New Thinking for the New Millennium* (London: Viking, 1999).

—, *Lateral Thinking: An Introduction* (London: Vermilion, 2014).

DEFRA, *Review of use of Mediation Services by Local Authorities and Housing Associations* (London: HMSO, 2006).

BIBLIOGRAPHY

De Girolamo, D., *The Fugitive Identity of Mediation: Negotiations, Shift Changes, and Allusionary Action* (Routledge 2013).

Deleuran, Pia (ed.), *Conflict Management in the Family Field and in Other Close Relationships: Mediation as a way forward* (Copenhagen: DJØF Publishing, 2011).

Della Noce, D.J., J.P. Folger, J.R. Antes, "Assimilative, Autonomous or Synergistic Visions: How Mediation Programs in Florida Address the Dilemma of Court Connection" (2002) 3 *Pepperdine Dispute Resolution Law Journal* 11.

Dendorfer, Renate, "One Continent: Many Methods: Mediation in Germany: Structure, Status Quo and Special Issues" (Paper to the 2011 Conference of the Chartered Institute of Arbitrators, European Branch, Paris). Available at: *http://docplayer.net/48518922-One-continent-many-methods-mediation-in-germany-structure-status-quo-and-special-issues-ciarb-chartered-institute-for-arbitrators-european-branch.html*.

De Palo G. et al, Legal and Parliamentary Affairs European Parliament Study *"'Rebooting' the Mediation Directive: Assessing the Limited Impact of its Implementation and Proposing Measures to Increase the Number of Mediations in the EU"* (Directorate General for Internal Policies, Policy Department C Citizens' Rights and Constitutional Affairs 2014).

Deutsch, M., P.T. Coleman, and E.C. Marcus, *The Handbook of Conflict Resolution: Theory and Practice* (Jossey Bass 2006).

Dingwall, Robert & John Eekelaar, *Divorce Mediation and the Legal Process* (Oxford: Clarendon Press, 1988).

—, Greatbatch, D. and L. Ruggerone, "Gender and Interaction in Divorce Mediation" (1998) 15(4) *Mediation Quarterly* 277.

Doyle, Margaret, *The Use of ADR in Ombudsman Processes* (2003): *https://www.researchgate.net/publication/322623046_The_Use_of_ADR_in_ Ombudsman_Processes_Results_of_a_survey_of_members_of_the_British_and_ Irish_Ombudsman_Association_2003*.

—,"'Manning' the ombuds barricades", at *https://ombudsresearch.org.uk/ 2015/06/09/manning-the-ombuds-barricades/*.

Ehrmann, John R. & Michael T. Lesnick, "The Policy Dialogue: Applying Mediation to the Policy-Making Process" (1988) *Mediation Quarterly* 20.

English Law Commission, *Family Law: The Ground for Divorce* (London: HMSO, 1990), Law Com. No.192.

Estreicher, Samuel and Steven C. Bennett, "The confidentiality of arbitration proceedings" (2008) 240(31) *Arbitration*.

Farnsworth, E.A., "Precontractual Liability and Preliminary Agreements: Fair Dealing and Failed Negotiations" (1987) 87 *Columbia Law Review* 217.

Faulks E.P.L., keynote speech at the Civil Mediation Conference 22 May 2014, available at: *https://www.gov.uk/government/speeches/mediation-and-government*.

Faure, G.O., *How People Negotiate: Resolving Disputes in Different Cultures* (Advances in Group Decision and Negotiation) (The Netherlands: Springer, 2003).

File, D. Jason, "United States: multi-step dispute resolution clauses" (July 2007) *Mediation Committee Newsletter* (IBA Legal Practice Division).

BIBLIOGRAPHY

Fisher, Roger, *International Mediation: A Working Guide* (Harvard Negotiation Project, 1978).

—, and William Ury, *Getting to Yes: Negotiating Agreement Without Giving In* (Boston: Houghton Mifflin; Penguin, 1981).

—, "Negotiating Power" in (1983) 27 *American Behavioural Science*.

—, and Scott Brown, *Getting Together: Building a Relationship that Gets to Yes* (London: Business Books, 1989).

—, Elizabeth Kopelman and Andrea Kupfer Schneider, *Beyond Machiavelli: Tools for Coping with Conflict* (Cambridge Massachusetts and London, England: Harvard University Press, 1994).

—, and Daniel Shapiro, *Building Agreement: Using Emotions as You Negotiate* (London: Random House Business Books, 2007).

Fiss, Owen, "Against Settlement" (1984) 93 *Yale Law Journal* 1073, 1075, 1085.

Folberg, Jay and Alison Taylor, *Mediation: A Comprehensive Guide to Resolving Conflicts Without Litigation* (San Francisco: Jossey-Bass, 1984).

—, and Ann Milne, *Divorce Mediation: Theory and Practice* (New York/London: The Guildford Press, 1988).

Folger, Joseph. P, & Tricia S. Jones, *New Directions in Mediation: Communication Research and Perspectives* (California: Sage Publications, 1994).

—, Robert A. Baruch Bush and Dorothy J. Della Noce, *Transformative Mediation: A Sourcebook—Resources for Conflict Intervention Practitioners and Programs* (New York: Institute for the Study of Conflict Transformation; and Association for Conflict Resolution, 2010).

Fortin J., L. Scanlan and J. Hunt, "Taking a longer view of contact: the perspectives of young adults who experienced parental separation in their youth" [2013] Fam Law 104.

Foskett, David QC, *Foskett on Compromise*, 8th edn (London: Sweet & Maxwell, 2015).

Freedman C., and J. Farrell, *Kendall on Expert Determination*, 5th edn (London: Sweet & Maxwell, 2014).

Fuller, Lon, "Collective Bargaining and the Arbitrator" (1962) *Proceedings, Fifteenth Annual Meeting, National Academy of Arbitrators* 8, 29–33, 36–48.

—, "Mediation—Its Forms and Functions" (1971) 44 S. Cal Law Review.

—, "The Forms and Limits of Adjudication" (1978) 92 *Harvard Law Review* 353.

Galanter, Marc, "The Day After the Litigation Explosion" (1986) 46 *Maryland Law Review* 3 in Murray, Rau and Sherman's *Processes of Dispute Resolution* (New York: Foundation Press, 1989).

—, "The Quality of Settlements" (1988) *Journal of Dispute Resolution*.

—, "Justice in Many Rooms: Courts, Private Ordering, and Indigenous Law" (1981) 19 *Journal of Legal Pluralism* 1.

—, "Against Settlement: Twenty-Five Years Later" (2009) 78 *Fordham Law Review* 1117.

Galves, Fred, "Virtual Justice as Reality: Making the Resolution of E-Commerce Disputes More Convenient, Legitimate, Efficient, and Secure" 2009 1 *Journal of Law, Technology & Policy*.

BIBLIOGRAPHY

Gavrila C.A., "212 qualities of a good mediator": Kluwer Mediation Blog at: *http://mediationblog.kluwerarbitration.com/2012/02/19/212-qualities-of-a-good-mediator/*.

Gelfand, Michele J. and Jeanne M. Brett, *The Handbook of Negotiation and Culture* (California: Stanford University Press, 2004).

Genn, Hazel, *Evaluation Report of the Central London County Court Pilot Mediation Scheme No.5/98* (London: Lord Chancellor's Department, July 1998).

—, *Court-based ADR initiatives for non-family civil disputes: the Commercial Court and the Court of Appeal* (London: Lord Chancellor's Department, 2002).

—, Fenn P., M. Mason, A. Lane, N. Bechai, L. Gray and D. Vencappa, *Twisting arms: court referred and court linked mediation under judicial pressure* (London: Ministry of Justice Research Series 1/07, 2007).

—, "What is Civil Justice For? Reform, ADR, and Access to Justice" (2013) 24(1) *Yale Journal of Law and the Humanities* 397.

Gerami A., "Bridging the Theory and Practice Gap: Mediator Power in Practice" (2009) (26) *Conflict Resolution Quarterly* 43.

Gibbons, Michael, *Better Dispute Resolution: A review of employment dispute resolution in Great Britain* (Department of Trade and Industry, 2007).

Gibson, K., "Confidentiality in Mediation: A Moral Reassessment" (1992) *Journal of Dispute Resolution* 25.

Gilkey, Roderick W. and Leonard Greenhalgh, "The Role of Personality in Successful Negotiating" (1986) 2(3) *Negotiation Journal*.

Glasl, Friedrich, *Konfliktmanagement. Ein Handbuch für Führungskräfte, Beraterinnen und Berater* (Bern: Paul Haupt Verlag, 1997).

—, *Confronting Conflict: A First-aid Kit for Handling Conflict* (Stroud: Hawthorn Press, 1999).

Goldberg R., "How our Worldviews Shape our Practices" (2009) 26(4) *Conflict Resolution Quarterly* 405–431, 427.

Goldberg, Stephen, Eric Green and Frank Sander, *Dispute Resolution* (Boston/Toronto: Little Brown & Company, 1985, Supplement 1992).

—, "ADR Problems and Prospects: Looking to the Future" (1986) 69 *Judicature* 291, 293.

—, Frank Sander, Nancy Rogers and Sarah Rudolph Cole, *Dispute Resolution: Negotiation, Mediation and Other Processes*, 5th edn (New York: Aspen Publishers, 2007).

—, Sander, F. E., N.H. Rogers, and S.R. Cole, *Dispute Resolution: Negotiation, Mediation and Other Processes* (Aspen: Wolters Kluwer Law & Business, 2014).

Goldman, B., "The Complementary Roles of Judges and Arbitrators in Ensuring that International Commercial Arbitration is Effective" in ICC, *60 Years of ICC Arbitration—A Look at the Future* (Paris: ICC Publishing, 1984).

Goldsmiths, University of London, *The Use and Effectiveness of Anti-Bullying Strategies in Schools* (Goldsmiths, University of London, April 2011).

Goodman A., *Effective Mediation Advocacy—A Guide for Practitioners*, 3rd edn (St Albans: Mediation Publishing, 2016).

—, *Effective Mediation Advocacy (Student Edition)* (St Albans: Mediation Publishing, 2017).

Goodman-Delahunty, Jane, Pär Anders Granhag, Maria Hartwig and Elizabeth F. Loftus, "Insightful or wishful: Lawyers' Ability to Predict Case Outcomes" (2010) 16(2) *Psychology, Public Policy, and Law* 133.

Gould, Nicholas, Claire King and Philip Britton, *Mediating Construction Disputes: An Evaluation of Existing Practice* (London: King's College, Centre of Construction Law and Dispute Resolution, 2010).

Grant, K, "The ICSID Under Siege: UNASUR and the Rise of a Hybrid Regime for International Investment Arbitration" (2015) Osgoode Legal Studies Research Paper Series Paper 108: *http://digitalcommons.osgoode.yorku.ca/olsrps/108*.

Gray, Ericka B., "What is 'Real Mediation?'" (1996) 15(2) *AFM Mediation News*.

Gray, John, with Moira Halliday and Andrew Woodgate, *Responding to community conflict: A review of neighbourhood mediation* (York: Joseph Rowntree Foundation/York Publishing Services, 2001).

Gray J., *Men are from Mars, Women are from Venus* (London: Element, 1993).

Green, Eric, "The CPR Mini-trial Handbook" in *Corporate Dispute Management* (New York: Matthew Bender & Co, 1982).

—, "Growth of the Mini-trial" (Fall 1982) 9 *Litigation* 1.

—, "The Complete Courthouse (Dispute Resolution Devices in a Democratic Society)" (Washington D.C.: Roscoe Pound Foundation—ATLA, 1985).

—, "A Heretical View of the Mediation Privilege" (1986) 2 *Ohio State Law Journal* 1.

Grillo, T., "The Mediation Alternative: Process Dangers for Women" (1991) 100(6) *Yale Law Journal* 1545.

Gulliver, P.H., *Disputes and Negotiations: a Cross-Cultural Perspective* (New York: Academic Press, 1979).

—, "Arbitration and mediation" in Adam Kuper and Jessica Kuper, *The Social Science Encyclopaedia* (London/ Boston: Routledge, 1985).

Gunning, Isabelle R., "Mediation as an Alternative to Court for Lesbian and Gay Families: Some Thoughts on Douglas McIntyre's Article" (1995) 13(1) *Mediation Quarterly*.

Hager, L., Michael and Robert Pritchard, "Deal Mediation: How ADR Techniques Can Help Achieve Durable Agreements in the Global Markets" (1999) *ICSID Foreign Investment Law Journal* 1.

Halsbury's Law of England, 4th edn (London: Lexis Nexis).

Hanger I., QC, "*The Role of Lawyers in Mediation*": address to the 1st Asian Mediation Association Conference, Singapore, June 2009.

Harding, John, "Reconciling Mediation with Criminal Justice" in Wright and Galaway, *Mediation and Criminal Justice: Victims, Offenders and Community* (London: Sage Publications Limited, 1989).

Harrell, Susan W., "Why Attorneys Attend Mediation Sessions" (1995) 12(4) *Mediation Quarterly*.

Harris, B, "The Arbitration Act 1996 – 10 Years On: Preliminary Observations of a Major Survey of Users' Views" (2006) at *https://www.biicl.org/files/2126_the_arbitration_act_1996_10_years_on.pdf*.

Haviland-Jones, J.K. and A.G. Johnson (eds), *Handbook of Emotions* (New York: Guildford Press, 2000).

BIBLIOGRAPHY

Hay, Carolyn, Katharine McKenna and Trevor Buck, *Evaluation of Early Neutral Evaluation Alternative Dispute Resolution in the Social Security and Child Support Tribunal* (London: Ministry of Justice, 2010).

Haygood, Leah V., "Negotiated Rule Making: Challenges for Mediators and Participants" (1988) *Mediation Quarterly* 20.

Haynes, John M., *Divorce Mediation* (New York: Springer Publishing Co, 1981).

—, & Gretchen L. Haynes, *Mediating Divorce* (San Francisco: Jossey-Bass, 1989).

—, with Thelma Fisher and Dick Greenslade, *Alternative Dispute Resolution: The Fundamentals of Family Mediation* (London: Old Bailey Press Limited, 1993).

Hellmuth, Theodore H., "Using ENE as a Gatekeeper Dispute Resolution Process" (1995) 13(8) *Alternatives*.

Hopt, Klaus J., and Felix Steffek, *Mediation: Principles and Regulation in Comparative Perspective* (Oxford, Oxford University Press, 2013).

Hoyle, Carolyn, Richard Young and Roderick Hill, *Proceed with Caution: An evaluation of the implementation and effectiveness of an initiative in restorative cautioning* (York: Joseph Rowntree Foundation, 2002).

Hwang, Michael S.C., Loong Seng Onn and Yeo Chuan Tat, "ADR in East Asia", chapter in J-C. Goldsmith et al, *ADR in Business: Practice and Issues Across Countries and Cultures* (Netherlands: Kluwer Law International, 2006).

Ingen-Housz, Arnold (ed.), *ADR in Business: Practice and Issues Across Countries and Cultures: Volume II* (Netherlands: Kluwer Law International, 2010).

Insurance Institute of London, *Alternative Dispute Resolution in Practice* (London: IIL, 2011), Research Study RS263.

International Bar Association (Arb40 Sub-committee), "The Current State and Future of International Arbitration: Regional Perspectives" at *https://www.ibanet.org/Document/Default.aspx?DocumentUid=2102ca46-3d4a-48e5-aa20-3f784be214ca* (August 2015).

Irving, Howard H. and Michael Benjamin, *Therapeutic Family Mediation: Helping Families Resolve Conflict* (California: Sage Publications, 2002).

Isen, A.N., "Positive Affect and Decision Making" in J.K. Haviland-Jones and A.G. Johnson (eds), *Handbook of Emotions* (New York: Guildford Press, 2000).

Jackson, Lord Justice (ed.) et al, *Civil Procedure: The White Book Service 2017* (London: Sweet & Maxwell, 2017).

—, "Review of civil litigation costs: final report." Office of the Judiciary of England and Wales (2009).

Jansenson D.R., "Representing Your Clients Successfully in Mediation: Guidelines for Litigators" (1995) 1(2) *The NYLitigator*.

Johnstone, Gerry and Daniel W. Van Ness, *Handbook of Restorative Justice* (Devon: Willan Publishing, 2007).

Jordan, Thomas, "Glasl's Nine-Stage Model Of Conflict Escalation", at *http://www.mediate.com/articles/jordan.cfm*.

BIBLIOGRAPHY

Kallipetis, Michel, QC, "Mediation Privilege and Confidentiality and the EU Directive", in Arnold Ingen-Housz (ed.), *ADR in Business: Practice and Issues Across Countries and Cultures: Volume II* (Netherlands: Kluwer Law International, 2010).

—, "Should there be a distinct mediation privilege?" (2008) Standing Conference of Mediation Advocates.

Katsh, Ethan and Janet Rifkin, *Online Dispute Resolution: Resolving Conflicts in Cyberspace* (San Francisco: Jossey-Bass, 2001).

—, and Leah Wing, "Ten years of online dispute resolution: Looking at the past and constructing the future" (Fall 2006) 38 *University of Toledo Law Review*.

Kennedy, Gavin, *Everything is Negotiable: How to Negotiate and Win*, 3rd edn (London: Arrow Books, 1997).

—, *Everything is Negotiable: How to Negotiate and Win*, 4th edn (London: Random House, 2008).

Kilmann, R.H. and K.W. Thomas, "Developing a Forced-Choice Measure of Conflict-Handling Behavior: The Mode Instrument" (1977) 37(2) *Educational and Psychological Measurement*.

Knapp, Mark. L. and Judith Hall, *Non-verbal Communication in Human Interaction*, 6th edn (California: Wadsworth Publishing Co Inc, 2005).

Koch, Richard, *The 80–20 Principle: The Secret of Achieving More with Less* (London: Nicholas Brealey Publishing Limited, 1997; and 10th anniversary edn, 2007).

Kolb, Deborah M., "How existing procedures shape alternatives: the case of grievance mediation" (1989) *Journal of Dispute Resolution*.

—, and Jean M. Bartunek, Hidden Conflicts in Organisations: Uncovering Behind-the-Scenes Disputes (California: Sage Publications, 1992).

—, et al, *When Talk Works* (San Francisco: Jossey-Bass, 1994, 1997).

Korobkin, Russell, "A Positive Theory of Legal Negotiation" (1999-2000) 88 Geo. L.J. 1789.

Krivis, Jeffrey, "Mediating in Cyberspace" [1998] *ADR Law Journal* 19 (and (1996) 14(10) *Alternatives*).

Lalive, Pierre, "The New Swiss Law on International Arbitration" (1998) 4 *Arbitration International* 2.

Landau, Barbara, Mario Bartoletti and Ruth Mesbur, *Family Mediation Handbook* (Toronto: Butterworths, 1987).

Lax, David A. and James K. Sebenius, *The Manager as Negotiator: Bargaining for Co-operation and Competitive Gain* (New York: Free Press, 1986).

—, *3-D Negotiation: Powerful Tools to Change the Game in Your Most Important Deals* (Boston: Harvard Business School Press, 2006).

Law Reform Committee, *Sixteenth Report on Privilege in Civil Proceedings* (London: HMSO, 1967).

Law Society of England and Wales, *Code of Practice for Civil and Commercial Mediation* (July 2009).

—, Henry Brown, *Report on Alternative Dispute Resolution for the Courts and Legal Services Committee* (London, 1991).

—, "Alternative Dispute Resolution" (2nd Report, June 1992).

BIBLIOGRAPHY

Leathes, Michael, "Mediator Competency is like Truth, Beauty and Contact Lenses Why the fifth mechanism to assure users about mediator quality really works" (2009) 24 *Ohio State Journal on Dispute Resolution* 191 at *http://www.mediate.com/articles/mediatorcompetency isliketruth.cfm*.

LeBaron, Michelle, "Culture-Based Negotiation Styles" in G. Burgess and H. Burgess (eds), *Beyond Intractability*. Conflict Research Consortium. U. of Colorado (2003).

Lederach, John Paul, *Preparing for Peace: Conflict Transformation Across Cultures* (New York: Syracuse University Press, 1996).

—, *The Moral Imagination: The Art and Soul of Building Peace* (Oxford: Oxford University Press, 2005).

Liebmann M., "*Community and Neighbourhood Mediation*: A UK Perspective" in Julie Macfarlane, *Rethinking Disputes: The Mediation Alternative* (London: Cavendish Publishing, 1997).

—, *Community and Neighbourhood Mediation* (Oxford: Routledge Cavendish, 1998).

Lesnick, Michael T. and John R. Ehrmann, "Selected Strategies for Managing Multiparty Disputes" (Summer 1987) 16 *Mediation Quarterly*.

Levine, David I., "Early neutral evaluation: a follow-up report" (1987) 70(4) *Judicature*.

—, "Early Neutral Evaluation: The Second Phase" (1989) *Journal of Dispute Resolution* 1.

Levine, Stuart, *Getting to Resolution: Turning conflict into collaboration,* 2nd edn (San Francisco: Berrett-Koehler Publishers, 2009).

Lewis, Richard. D., *When Cultures Collide,* 3rd edn (London: Nicholas Brearley Publishing, 2005).

Lide, E. Casey, "The Role of Alternative Dispute Resolution in Online Commerce, Intellectual Property and Defamation" [1998] A.D.R.L.J. 31 (and (1996) Ohio S.L.J).

Liebmann, Marian, *Community and Neighbour Mediation* (London: Cavendish Publishing, 1998).

Limbury, Alan, "'Why judges shouldn't be mediators' and 'mandatory mediation'—an Australian perspective" (2006) 11(1) *The Expert & Dispute Resolver*.

Lovenheim P. and Guerin L., *Mediate Don't Litigate* (California: Nolo, 2004).

Lyon, C.M., E. Surrey and J.E. Timms, *Effective Support Services for children and young people when parental relationships break down—a child-centred approach* (University of Liverpool, 1998).

MacFarlane, Julie, *Rethinking Disputes: the Mediation Alternative* (London: Cavendish Publishing, 1997).

Mackie, Karl J., *A Handbook of Dispute Resolution: ADR in Action* (London: Routledge, 1991).

—, *ADR Route Map* (London: Centre for Dispute Resolution, 1991).

—, "The Future for ADR Clauses After *Cable & Wireless v. IBM*" (2003) 19(3) *Arbitration International*.

—, & David Miles, William Marsh and Tony Allen, *The ADR Practice Guide,* 3rd edn (Haywards Heath: Bloomsbury Professional (previously Tottel Publishing), 2007).

BIBLIOGRAPHY

Maddux, Robert B., *Successful Negotiation* (London: Kogan Page, 1998).

Malcolm, Ewan & Fiona O'Donnell, *A Guide to Mediating in Scotland* (Dundee: Dundee University Press, 2009).

Marks, Jonathan, "Evaluative Mediation—Oxymoron or Essential Tool" AMN Lawyer May 1996.

Marlow, Lenard, "Is Divorce Mediation a Form of Dispute Resolution?" (Spring 2011) *Family Mediation News*.

Marriott, Arthur, QC, "Freshfields Lecture 1995" (1996) 12 (1) *Arbitration International*.

Marshall, Tony, *Reparation, Conciliation and Mediation* (London: Home Office Research & Planning Unit, 1984), Paper 27.

—, & Martin Walpole, *Bringing People Together: Mediation & Reparation Projects in Great Britain* (London: Home Office Research & Planning Unit, 1985), Paper 33.

—, "Power of Mediation" (1990) 8(2) *Mediation Quarterly* 115.

—, *Restorative Justice: An overview* (Home Office Research Development and Statistics Directorate, 1999).

Massie, Graham, "Deal mediation – Neutral chairing for contract negotiation", at *https://www.cedr.com/blog/deal-mediation/*.

Mathis, Richard D., "Couples from Hell: Undifferentiated Spouses in Divorce Mediation" (1998) 16(1) *Mediation Quarterly* (MQ) 37.

Mayer, Bernard, *Staying With Conflict—A Strategic Approach to Ongoing Disputes* (San Francisco: Jossey-Bass, 2009).

—, *The Dynamics of Conflict: A Guide to Engagement and Intervention*, 2nd edn (San Francisco: Jossey-Bass, 2012).

McDonough, Ian, "A Guide to Neighbour/Community Mediation" in Malcolm and O'Donnell, *A Guide to Mediating in Scotland* (Dundee: Dundee University Press, 2009).

McCold, Paul and Ted Wachtel, "In Pursuit of Paradigm: A Theory of Restorative Justice", Paper presented at the XIII World Congress of Criminology, 10–15 August 2003, Rio de Janeiro, Brazil.

McIntosh, Jennifer E., Caroline M. Long and Yvonne D. Wells, *Children beyond dispute: A four-year follow-up study of outcomes from Child Focused and Child Inclusive post-separation family dispute resolution* (Australian Attorney-General's Department, with Family Transitions, Relationships Australia and La Trobe University, 2009).

McIntyre, Douglas H., "Gay Parents and Child Custody: A Struggle Under the Legal System" (1994) 12(2) *Mediation Quarterly*.

McCrory, John P., "Confidentiality in Mediation of Matrimonial Disputes" (1988) 51 M.L.R. 442.

Menkel-Meadow, C., and H. Abramson, "Mediating Muliculturally: Culture and the Ethical Mediator" in E. Waldman (ed.) *Mediation Ethics: Cases and Commentaries* (Jossey Bass San Francisco 2011).

—, "The History and Development of 'A'DR" (Volkerrechtsblog 20 July 2016), at: *http://voelkerrechtsblog.org/the-history-and-development-of-a-dr-alternativeappropriate-dispute-resolution/*.

BIBLIOGRAPHY

Merry, Sally Engle, "Myth and practice in the mediation process" in M. Wright and Burt Galaway, *Mediation and Criminal Justice: Victims, Offenders and Community* (London: Sage Publications Limited, 1989).

Millar, Helen D., "Resolving Parental Abduction: Child Find of America's Mediation Program" (1996) 13(3) *Mediation Quarterly*.

Ministry of Justice, Consultation Paper CP6/2011, *Solving disputes in the county courts: creating a simpler, quicker and more proportionate system – A consultation on reforming civil justice in England and Wales* (London: HMSO, 2011), CM.8045.

—, The Admiralty & Commercial Courts Guide, 9th edn (2011).

Mnookin, Robert and Lewis Kornhauser, "Bargaining in the Shadow of the Law, The Case of Divorce" (1979) 88 *Yale Law Journal* 950.

—, Peppett, S. R., and A.S. Tulumello, *Beyond Winning: Negotiating to Create Value in Deals and Disputes* (Boston: Harvard University Press, 2004).

—, *Bargaining with the Devil: When to Negotiate, When to Fight* (New York: Simon & Schuster, 2010).

Moffitt, M. L., and R.C. Bordone, *The Handbook of Dispute Resolution* (San Francisco: Jossey-Bass 2005).

Moore, Christopher W., *The Mediation Process: Practical Strategies for Resolving Conflict*, 2nd Rubino-Sammartano, Mauro, International Arbitration 2014).

—, "The Caucus: Private Meetings That Promote Settlement" (1987) *Mediation Quarterly* 16.

Moore, Tim, "Ombudsman—Gender Neutral?", Briefing Paper for the Northern Ireland Assembly, June 2015, available at: http://www.niassembly.gov.uk/globalassets/documents/raise/publications/2015/ofmdfm/8115.pdf.

Morris, D., *Peoplewatching: The Desmond Morris Guide to Body Language* (United Kingdom: Vintage Books, 2002).

Mulcahy L., "The Possibilities and Desirability of Mediator Neutrality: Towards an Ethic of Partiality" (2001) 10(4) *Social and Legal Studies* 505–527.

Murray, John S., Alan Scott Rau and Edward F. Sherman, *Processes of Dispute Resolution: The Role of Lawyers*, 2nd edn (New York: Foundation Press, 1996; 3rd edn, 2002).

Murray, John, "Understanding Competing Theories of Negotiation" (1986) 2 *Negotiation Journal* 179.

Mustill, Sir Michael J., Stewart C. Boyd and Neil Andrews, *Commercial Arbitration*, 3rd edn (London: Butterworths, 2008).

Mutter, R., D. Shemmings, P. Dugmore, and M. Hyare, "Family group conferences in youth justice" (2008) 16(3) *Health and Social Care in the Community*Rubino-Sammartano, Mauro, International Arbitration 262.

Myers, David G., *Intuition: Its powers and perils* (Yale University Press, 2002).

Naughton, Philip QC, "Mega mediation—a case history" [1996] A.D.R.L.J. 215.

Ndekugri, Issaka and Victoria Russell, "Disputing the existence of a dispute as a strategy for avoiding construction adjudication" (2006) 13(4) *Engineering, Construction and Architectural Management* 380.

Neill P., QC, "Confidentiality in Arbitration" (1996) 12 *Arbitration International* 287.

Newmark, Chris and Anthony Monaghan, Butterworths *Mediators on Mediation: Leading mediator perspectives on the practice of commercial mediation* (Haywards Heath: Bloomsbury (previously Tottel Publishing), 2005).

New South Wales, Attorney General's Department, *ADR Blueprint: Discussion Paper: Framework for the delivery of alternative dispute resolution (ADR) services in NSW* (Sydney: NSW Attorney General's Department, 2009).

O'Brien, Nick and Mary Seneviratne, *Ombudsmen at the Crossroads: The Legal Services Ombudsman, Dispute Resolution and Democratic Accountability* (Palgrave Macmillan, 2017).

Olson, R., "An Alternative for Large Case Dispute Resolution" (Winter 1980) 6 *Litigation* 22.

Otis, Louise and Eric H. Reiter, "Mediation by Judges: A New Phenomenon in the Transformation of Justice" (2006) 6(3) *Pepperdine Dispute Resolution Law Journal*.

Palmer, Michael & Simon Roberts, *Dispute Processes: ADR and the Primary Forms of Decision Making* (London: Butterworths, 1998; 2nd edn Cambridge: Cambridge University Press, 2005).

Parkinson, Lisa, *Conciliation in Separation and Divorce: Finding Common Ground* (London, Sydney: Croom Helm, 1986).

—, *Family Mediation* (London: Sweet & Maxwell, 1997; 2nd edn, Family Law, 2011; 3rd edn, Jordan Publishing, 2014).

Parsons, Luke, "Independence, Impartiality and Conflicts of Interest in Arbitration" paper given at the 2nd IPBA (The Inter-Pacific Bar Association) Asia-PAC Arbitration Day, Kuala Lumpur in September 2016 at *http://www.quadrantchambers.com/images/uploads/documents/Luke_Parsons_QC_-_IPBA_paper.pdf*.

Patrick J.C., "The Mediation Process" in Liebmann, *Community and Neighbour Mediation*, 1998.

Peachey, Dean E., "The Kitchener Experiment" in Martin Wright and Burt Galaway, *Mediation and Criminal Justice: Victims, Offenders and Community* (London: Sage Publications Limited, 1989).

Pease, Allan, *Body Language: How to Read Others' Thoughts by Their Gestures* (London: Sheldon Press, 1984).

—, and Barbara Pease, *The Definitive Book of Body Language: How to Read Others' Attitudes by Their Gestures* (London: Orion, 2005).

Peppet, Scott R., "Contract Formation in Imperfect Markets: Should We Use Mediators in Deals?" (2004) 19(2) *Ohio State Law Journal*.

Pereira, I., C. Perry, H. Greevy, and H. Shrimpton, "The Varying Paths to Justice" (Ipsos Mori Research Institute, Ministry of Justice Analytical Research Series, 2015).

Phillipson, Gavin, "Transforming Breach of Confidence? Towards a Common Law Right of Privacy under the Human Rights Act" (2003) 66 M.L.R.

Podro, Sarah and Rachel Suff, "Mediation: An Approach to Resolving Workplace Issues—A guide February 2013" (Acas and the Chartered Institute of Personnel and Development (CIPD)).

BIBLIOGRAPHY

Prince, Sue, *Court-based Mediation: A preliminary analysis of the small claims mediation scheme at Exeter County Court* (Civil Justice Council, 2004).

Pruitt, Dean G., *Negotiation Behavior* (New York: Academic Press, 1981).

—, "Trends in the Scientific Study of Negotiation and Mediation" (1986) 2 *Negotiation Journal* 237.

Pynchon, Victoria, "Mediating? Bring Your Toothbrush." Joe Francis and "Girls Gone Wild" at Negotiation Law Blog *http://www.negotiationlawblog.com/conflict-resolution/mediating-bring-your-toothbrush-joe-francis-and-girls-gone-wild/*.

Quill, Deidre & Jean Wynne, *Victim & Offender: Mediation Handbook* (London: Save the Children and West Yorkshire Probation Service, 1993).

Rabinovich O. and E. Katsh "Digital Justice: Reshaping Boundaries in an Online Dispute Resolution Environment" (2014) 1(1) *International Journal of Online Dispute Resolution*.

Rack C., *Latino Anglo Bargaining: Culture, Structure and Choice in Court Mediation* (New York and London: Routledge, 2006).

Raiffa, Howard, *The Art and Science of Negotiation* (Massachusetts: Harvard University Press, 1982).

—, *Negotiation Analysis: The Science and Art of Collaborative Decision Making* (Massachusetts: Harvard University Press, 2007).

Ramsbotham, O., T. Woodhouse and H. Miall, *Contemporary Conflict Resolution*, 4th edn (Polity Press, 2016).

Reeves, Helen, "The Victim Support Perspective" in M. Wright and Burt Galaway, *Mediation and Criminal Justice: Victims, Offenders and Community* (London: Sage Publications Limited, 1989).

Regina, W.F., *Applying Family Systems Theory to Mediation* (University Press of America 2011).

Reid, Angus and Robert C.T. Ellis, "Common sense applied to the definition of a dispute" in (2007) 25(3/4) *Structural Survey* 239.

Restorative Justice Consortium, *Statement of Restorative Justice Principles—As applied in a school setting*, 2nd edn (London: Restorative Justice Consortium, 2005).

Richbell, David, "Mediating multi-party disputes", Ch.13 in C. Newmark and Anthony Monaghan, *Butterworths Mediators on Mediation: Leading mediator perspectives on the practice of commercial mediation* (Haywards Heath: Bloomsbury (previously Tottel Publishing), 2005).

—, *Construction Mediation* (London: Wiley-Blackwell, 2008).

Riskin, Leonard L., "Understanding Mediator's Orientations, Strategies and Techniques: A Grid for the Perplexed" (1996) 1 *Harvard Negotiation Law Review* 7.

Roberts, Marian, *Developing the Craft of Mediation: Reflections on Theory and Practice* (Jessica Kingsley Publishers, 2007).

—, *Mediation in Family Disputes: Principles of Practice*, 3rd edn (Surrey: Ashgate Publishing, 2008).

Roberts, Simon, *Order and Dispute: An Introduction to Legal Anthropology* (Harmondsworth: Penguin Books, 1979).

—, "Toward a Minimal Form of Alternative Intervention" (1986) *Mediation Quarterly* 11.

BIBLIOGRAPHY

Robinson, Gwen, *Victim-Offender Mediation: Limitations and Potential* (Oxford: Centre for Criminological Research, University of Oxford, 1996).

Robinson, Margaret, *Family Transformation Through Divorce and Remarriage* (London: Routledge, 1991; and with postscript, 1993).

Roebuck, Derek, *Ancient Greek Arbitration* (Oxford: Holo Books, 2001).

— "The myth of modern mediation." (2007) 73.1 *Arbitration: the Journal of the Chartered Institute of Arbitrators*.

—, *Disputes and Differences: Comparisons in Law, Language and History* (Oxford: Holo Books, 2010).

Rozee, Leonora and Kay Powell, *Mediation in Planning: Report commissioned by the National Planning Forum and the Planning Inspectorate* (2010).

Rubin J. Z., and B.R. Brown, *The Social Psychology of Bargaining and Negotiation* (New York: Elsevier, 2013).

Rubino-Sammartano, Mauro, *International Arbitration Law*, 2nd edn (Netherlands: Kluwer Law International, 1990; 2nd edn 2001).

Sander, F.E.A. and S.B. Goldberg, "Fitting the Forum to the Fuss: A User-Friendly Guide to Selecting an ADR Procedure" (1994) 10 Neg. J. 49, 66 or (2005–2006) 7 Cardozo J. Conflict Resol. 83.

Saposnek, Donald T., "Aikido: A Systems Model for Maneuvering in Mediation" (Winter-Spring) 1987 (14–15)) *Conflict Resolution Quarterly* 119.

Scarlett, Sarah, "Use of ADR in Lloyd's R&R Plan" *Insurance Day*, 25 February 1997.

Schlosser, Peter, *Das Recht der internationalen privaten Schiedsgerichtsbarkeit* (Mohr Siebeck, 1989).

Schneider, Andrea Kupfer and C. Honeyman, *The Negotiator's Fieldbook: The Desk Reference for the Experienced Negotiator* (Washington DC: American Bar Association, 2006).

Schneider, Michael E., and Paolo Michele Patocchi, "The New Swiss Law on International Arbitration" (1989) 55 *Arbitration* 268, 279.

Schornstein, Sherri L., *Domestic Violence and Health Care: What Every Professional Needs to Know* (California: Sage Publications, 1997).

Schuman, Sandy, *Creating a Culture of Collaboration: The International Association of Facilitators Handbook* (San Francisco: Jossey-Bass, 2006).

Schwab, Karl Heinz, *Schiedsgerichtsbarkeit* (Munich, 1979).

Sciencewise ERC, *International Comparison of Public Dialogue on Science and Technology* (London: Department for Business Innovation and Skills, 2011).

Scottish Law Commission Discussion Paper No.92 of March 1991.

Scottish Law Commission, *Report on Evidence: Protection of Family Mediation* (Edinburgh: HMSO, 1992) Scot. Law Com. No.136.

Sexton, Thomas L., Gerald R. Weeks and Michael S. Robbins, *Handbook of Family Therapy: Theory, Practice and Research* (London: Psychology Press, 2003).

Shapiro, D.L., "Negotiation Emotions" (2002) (20) *Conflict Resolution Quarterly* 67.

Shapland, Joanna, Anne Atkinson, Helen Atkinson, James Dignan, Lucy Edwards, Jeremy Hibbert, Marie Howes, Jennifer Johnstone, Gwen Robinson and

BIBLIOGRAPHY

Angela Sorsby, *Does restorative justice affect reconviction? The fourth report from the evaluation of three schemes* (Ministry of Justice Research Series 10/08, June 2008).

Sharp, I. G., *Industrial Conciliation and Arbitration in Great Britain* (London: Allen and Unwin, 1949).

Shipman, S, "Court Approaches to ADR" (2006) (25) *Civil Justice Quarterly* 181.

—, "Compulsory Mediation: the Elephant in the Room" (2011) 30 CJQ 163.

—, McGregor L. and R. Murray, Human Rights Claims, Process Standards and Agreement-Based ADR, *Human Rights Quarterly* (forthcoming).

Sime, S., *A Practical Approach to Civil Procedure*, 20th edn (Oxford: OUP, 2017).

Singer, Linda, "The Quiet Revolution in Dispute Settlement" (1989) 7(2) *Mediation Quarterly*.

Singer, Peter, "Arbitration in Family Financial Proceedings: the IFLA Scheme: Part 1" [2012] Fam Law 1353, and "Part 2" [2012] Fam Law 1496.

Skynner, Robin and John Cleese, *Families and how to survive them* (London: Methuen, 1983).

Steffek, L., and H. Unberath, *Regulating Dispute Resolution: ADR and Access to Justice at the Crossroad* (Oxford: Hart 2014).

Sternlight, J.R., C.J. Menkel-Meadow, L. Porter Loveand A. Kupfer Schneider, *Dispute Resolution: Beyond the Adversarial Model* (New York: Aspen Press 2010).

Stewart, Susan, *Conflict Resolution: A Foundation Guide* (Hampshire: Waterside Press, 1998).

Stolberg, J.B., "Must a Mediator be Neutral? You'd Better Believe It" (2012) (95) *Marquette Law Review* 829.

Strasser, Freddie and Paul Randolph, *Mediation: A Psychological Insight into Conflict Resolution* (New York/London: Continuum, 2004).

Street, The Hon. Sir Laurence, "Mediation and the judicial institution" (1997) *Arbitration and Dispute Resolution Law Journal* 88.

Susskind, Lawrence and Jeffrey Cruikshank, *Breaking the Impasse: Consensual Approaches to Resolving Public Disputes,* (New York: Basic Books, 1987) 358, 359–360.

—, "Multi-Party Public Policy Mediation: A Separate Breed" (Fall 1997) *Dispute Resolution Magazine*.

—, "Consensus Building and ADR: Why They are Not the Same Thing" in M.L. Moffatt and R.C. Bordone, *The Handbook of Dispute Resolution* (San Francisco: Jossey Bass, 2005).

—, *Tomorrow's Lawyers: An Introduction to Your Future* (Oxford: Oxford University Press, 2013).

Taleb, Nassim Nicholas, *The Black Swan: The Impact of the Highly Improbable* (Penguin, 2007).

Tan, N-T., "Community Mediation in Singapore: Principles for Community Conflict Resolution" (2002) 19(3) *Conflict Resolution Quarterly*.

Tapper, C., *Cross and Tapper on Evidence*, 8th edn (London: Butterworths, 1995); 12th edn (OUP Oxford, 2010).

BIBLIOGRAPHY

Telford, Megan Elizabeth, *Med-Arb: A Viable Dispute Resolution Alternative* (Canada: IRC Press, 2000).

Thompson F. and P. Smith, *The Use And Effectiveness of Anti-Bullying Strategies in Schools* (Goldsmiths report for the University of London, April 2011).

Thompson, Leigh L., *The Truth About Negotiations,* 2nd edn (Pearson, 2013).

Tomm, Karl, "Interventive Interviewing: Intending to Ask Lineal, Circular, Strategic, or Reflexive Questions" (1988) 27(1) *Family Process.*

Trakman, L.E., "The ICSID Under Siege" (2012) 45 Cornell Int'l L.J. 603 at *http://www.lawschool.cornell.edu/research/ILJ/upload/Trakman-final.pdf.*

Tyrrell, Jerry, *Peer Mediation: A Process For Primary Schools* (London: Souvenir Press, 2002).

Umbreit, Mark S., "Humanistic Mediation: A Transformative Journey of Peacemaking" (Spring 1997) 14(3) *Conflict Resolution Quarterly.*

—, and Jean Greenwood, "National Survey of Victim-Offender Mediation Programs in the United States" (1999) 16(3) *Mediation Quarterly* 235.

Ury, William, J. M. Brett and S. B. Goldberg, *Getting Disputes Resolved: Designing Systems to Cut the Costs of Conflict* (San Francisco: Jossey-Bass, 1989).

—, *Getting Past No: Negotiating with Difficult People* (London: Business Books Limited, 1991).

—, *The Power of a Positive No: How to say No and Still Get to Yes* (London: Hodder & Stoughton, 2007).

Vandersluis C., *"Poor Planning Can Sabotage Implementation"* Computing Canada, 25 May 1994.

Vindeløv, Vibeke, *Mediation: A Non-Model* (Copenhagen: DJÒF Publishing, 2007).

Vogiatzis, Nikos, *The European Ombudsman and Good Administration in the European Union* (Palgrave Macmillan, 2018).

Wade, John H., "Don't Waste My Time on Negotiation and Mediation: This Dispute Needs a Judge" (2001) 18(3) *Conflict Resolution Quarterly* 259–280.

—, "Liability of Mediators for Pressure, Drafting and Advice: Tapoohi v Lewenberg" (2004) 16 *Bond Dispute Resolution News.*

—, "Crossing the Last Gap" in Schneider, Andrea Kupfer and Honeyman, Christoper, *The Negotiator's Fieldbook: The Desk Reference for the Experienced Negotiator* (Washington D.C.: American Bar Association, Section of Dispute Resolution, 2006).

Wahrhaftig, Paul, "Nonprofessional Conflict Resolution" in J.E. Palenski and H.M. Launer, *Mediation Contexts and Challenges* (Illinois: Charles C. Thomas Pub Ltd, 1986).

Waldman, E., "The Evaluative-Facilitative Debate in Mediation: Applying the Lens of Therapeutic Jurisprudence" (1998) 82 *Marquette Law Review* 155.

—, (ed.), *Mediation Ethics: Cases and Commentaries* (San Francisco: Jossey Bass, 2011).

Walker, Janet, "Family Mediation" in Dr Julie Macfarlane, *Rethinking Disputes: The Mediation Alternative* (London: Cavendish, 1997).

BIBLIOGRAPHY

—, "Introduction to Family Mediation in Europe" Report to the Fourth European Conference on Family Law (Cambridge: University of Cambridge, 1998).

—, and Judy Corlyon, *Family Mediation: In Pursuit of Co-operative Relationships* (Surrey: Ashgate Publishing, 2008).

Walker S., *Mediation Advocacy; Representing Clients in Mediation* (London: Bloomsbury Professional, 2015).

Walsh, Elizabeth, *Working in the Family Justice System,* 2nd edn (Jordan Publishing, 2006).

Walter, Betsy J., "Lesbian Mediation: Resolving custody and visitation disputes when couples end their relationships" (2003) 41(1) AFCC *Family Court Review*.

Waters, B.D., "The Importance of Teaching Dispute Resolution in a Twenty-First-Century Law School" (2017) 51(2) *The Law Teacher* 227–246.

Watson C., "An Examination of the Impact of Gender and Power on Managers' Negotiation Behavior and Outcomes: Implications for ADR Practitioners." In Beyond Borders: 19th Annual International Conference, San Diego, CA, October 17–20, 1991. Washington, D.C.: Society of Professionals in Dispute Resolution (SPIDR), 1992.

Webb, J., J. Ching, P. Maharg, and A. Sherr, *Setting Standards: The Future of Legal Services Education and Training Regulation in England and Wales* (London, Legal Education and Training Review, 2013) (LETR Report) Available at: *http://letr.org.uk/the-report/index.html*.

Webne-Behrman, Harry, *The Practice of Facilitation: Managing Group Process and Solving Problems* (Westport: Quorum Books, Greenwood Publishing, 1998).

Whetten, David, Kim Cameron and Mike Woods, *Effective Conflict Management* (London: HarperCollins, 1996).

White, James J., "Machiavelli and the Bar: Ethical Limitations on Lying in Negotiation" (1980) 5.4 *Law & Social Inquiry* 926–938.

—, "The Pros and Cons of Getting to Yes" (1984) 34 *Journal of Legal Education* 115.

White Book Service 2017, edited by Lord Justice Jackson, 2017 edn (London: Sweet & Maxwell, 2017).

Whitehouse, M., "Regulating Civil Mediation in England and Wales: Towards a Win-Win Outcome" (2017) (2) *Mediation Theory and Practice*.

Wilburn, Kay O. and Mary Lynn Bates, "Conflict Resolution in America's Schools" (January 1997) *American Arbitration Association: Dispute Resolution Journal*.

Wilkinson, John H., (editor), *Donovan Leisure Newton & Irvine ADR Practice Book* (New York: Wiley Law Publications, 1990, and cumulative supplements 1992–1998).

—, "A Primer on Mini-trials" in the *Donovan Leisure Newton & Irvine ADR Practice Book* (New York: Wiley Law Publications, 1990).

Williams G. R., "Effective Negotiation" in J.H. Wilkinson, *Donovan Leisure Newton and Irvine ADR Practice Book* (New York: Wiley Law Publications, 1990).

—, *Legal Negotiation and Settlement* 18–40 (1983) in R. Korobkin, A Positive Theory of Legal Negotiation, 88 *Geo. L.J.* 1789 (1999–2000).

Williams, Michael, *Mediation: Why People Fight and How to Help Them to Stop* (Dublin: Poolbeg Press, 1998).

Williams, Rowland "Concilio-Arbitration: A New Proposal for the Quick and Inexpensive Resolution of Disputes" *Law Society Gazette,* 23 November 1983.

—, *Saving Litigation* (Rowland Williams, 1999).

Wing L., "Mediation and Inequality Reconsidered: Bringing the Discussion to the Table" (2009) 26(4) *Conflict Resolution Quarterly* 383–404.

Winslade W. and G.D. Monk, *Narrative Mediation: A New Approach to Conflict Resolution* (San Francisco: Jossey-Bass, 2000).

Wright, Martin and Burt Galaway, *Mediation and Criminal Justice: Victims, Offenders and Community* (London: Sage Publications Limited, 1989).

—, *Justice for Victims and Offenders: A Restorative Response to Crime* (Milton Keynes: Open University Press, 1991).

—, "Designing the future of criminal justice" (Summer 1997) 13(3) *Mediation.*

—, "Implications of the Crime and Disorder Act 1998 for mediation" (Spring 1999) 15(2) *Mediation.*

Wulff, Randall W., "A Mediation Primer" in J.H. Wilkinson, Donovan Leisure Newton and Irvine *ADR Practice Book*, (New York: Wiley Law Publications, 1990).

—, and Alan E. Harris, "Tips for a successful construction mediation" (Spring 1995) 18(1) *The Punch List.*

York, Stephen, *Practical ADR Handbook*, 2nd edn (London: Sweet & Maxwell, 2007).

Zariski, A, "A Theory Matrix for Mediators" (2010) (26) *Negotiation Journal* 203 *http://www.mediate.com/articles/metaphor.cfm.*

Zehr, Howard, *Little Book of Restorative Justice* (Pennsylvania: Good Books, 2002).

Zimmerman S., "Judges Gone Wild: Why Breaking The Mediation Confidentiality Privilege For Acting In 'Bad Faith' Should Be Re-evaluated In Court-Ordered Mandatory Mediation" [2009] 11 *Cardozo Journal of Conflict Resolution* 353.

INDEX

This index has been prepared using Sweet and Maxwell's Legal Taxonomy. Main index entries conform to keywords provided by the Legal Taxonomy except where references to specific documents or non-standard terms (denoted by quotation marks) have been included. These keywords provide a means of identifying similar concepts in other Sweet and Maxwell publications and online services to which keywords from the Legal Taxonomy have been applied. Readers may find some minor differences between terms used in the text and those which appear in the index. Suggestions to *sweetandmaxwell.taxonomy@tr.com*.

All references are to paragraph number

Acas
see also **Trade disputes**
arbitration, 13–014
collective conciliation, 13–010, 13–028—13–031
collective mediation
   meaning, 13–062
   mediation, 13–034
   operation of process, 13–063
conciliation
   collective conciliation, 13–010, 13–028—13–031
   compromise agreements, 13–032—13–033
   definition, 8–015
   early conciliation, 13–011
   employment arbitration, 13–064—13–066
   establishment, 13–005
   impartiality, 13–006
   independence, 13–006
   individual conciliation, 13–009, 13–023—13–027
mediation
   collective mediation, 13–012, 13–034
   conciliation distinguished, 13–012
services offered, 13–006
Adjudication
see also **Dispute boards; Statutory adjudication**
costs, 7–011
preparation, 10–173, 10–174
Administration of justice
see also **Family Procedure Rules**
case management, 5–004
Civil Procedure Rules
   conduct, 5–005
   overriding objective, 5–003, 5–006
   pre-action protocols, 5–009—5–011
   provisions, 5–001
   reform of procedure, 5–001
   rules affecting ADR, 5–003—5–005
   settlement, encouragement of, 5–003
   tracks, 5–004
courts adopting ADR processes, 5–001
pre-action protocols
   Civil Procedure Rules, 5–009—5–011
   Family Procedure Rules, 5–012
ADR organisations
see **Professional bodies**
ADR practitioners
see **Professionals**
Agendas
civil and commercial mediation, 10–080—10–082
family mediation, 11–087—11–096
mediation, 9–066—9–067
neighbourhood and community mediation, 12–049—12–055
trade dispute mediation, 13–042, 13–043
trade disputes, 13–042, 13–043
Alternative dispute resolution
see also **Court-annexed ADR; Professional bodies; Professionals**
academic developments, 22–016—22–021
adoption, 1–003
alternative
   appropriate, 1–009, 1–012
   criticism of term, 1–007
   effective dispute resolution, 1–010
   litigation as alternative, 1–008
   meaning, 1–006—1–012

non-adjudicatory processes, 1–007
professional culture, 1–007
proportionate dispute resolution, 1–011
use of term, 1–006—1–012
applicable law, 21–043—21–046
beneficial outcome sought, 3–039, 3–040
bespoke processes
  advantages, 2–041
  design, 2–043—2–046
  examples, 2–041
  high conflict cases, 2–041
  mediation, 2–043
  novel processes, 2–046
  ongoing conflicts, 2–041
  outline, 2–038
  preliminary meetings, 2–044—2–046
Brexit, 22–005—22–012
change, facilitation of, 3–012—3–014
Civil Courts Structure Review, 22–022—22–024
Civil Justice Council Working Party, 2–047—2–050
combination of processes, 2–008
compulsion, 2–048
consensual processes, 19–001
creativity, 3–020—3–025
decision-making, 3–015—3–019
development, 1–001, 2–001—2–009, 2–047—2–050
digital access, 2–050
educational developments, 22–016—22–021
empowerment, 3–015—3–019
encouragement for, 3–064
ethics
  values, 3–030—3–033
ethos, 3–065
facilitation of change, 3–012—3–014
flexibility, 2–002, 3–020—3–025
future directions
  academic developments, 22–016—22–021
  Brexit, 22–005—22–012
  compulsion, 22–025—22–026
  educational developments, 22–016—22–021
  General Data Protection Regulation, 22–027—22–031
  generally, 22–001—22–004, 22–032—22–034
  regulation, 22–013—22–015
  review of civil justice, 22–022—22–024
hybrid processes, 2–008
judicial support, 2–005
momentum towards, 3–062—3–067
outline of processes, 2–017—2–037
personal empowerment, 3–015—3–019
philosophies
  attributes of practitioners, 3–036—3–038
  beliefs, 3–002
  beneficial outcome sought, 3–039, 3–040
  broad church, 3–001—3–003

confidentiality, 3–034—3–035
costs, 3–041, 3–044
creativity, 3–020—3–025
decision-making, 3–015—3–019
delays, 3–041, 3–042
"design idiom", 3–025
differences, 3–043—3–057
directiveness, 3–055—3–057
ethics, 3–030—3–033
evaluative approach, 3–048, 3–049
facilitation of change, 3–012—3–014
facilitative approach, 3–048, 3–049
fields of activity, 3–044
flexibility, 3–020—3–025
fundamental shared principles, 3–003
healing potential, 3–026—3–029
intervention, 3–055—3–057
justice, 3–009
models of practice, 3–045—3–047
negotiated agreement, 3–006—3–011
outline, 3–001
personal empowerment, 3–015—3–019
problem solving, 3–050—3–051
public policy, 3–008
relationship preservation, 3–026—3–029
security, 3–034—3–035
sensitivity of practitioners, 3–036—3–038
settlement-geared mediation, 3–050—3–051
shared values, 3–004—3–042
skills of practitioners, 3–036—3–038
stuck positions, changing, 3–012—3–014
transformation, 3–052, 3–053
physical security, 3–035
public policy, 3–008
reformulation of terminology, 1–053
resolution
  meaning, 1–033—1–052
spectrum of processes, 2–015—2–017
standard processes
  outline, 2–038
summary of process, 3–068—3–069
support for process, 1–001
transformation, 3–052, 3–053
Amiable composition
concept, 3–022, 6–045
UNCITRAL Model Law, 6–045
use, 6–046, 6–047
use of concept, 3–022
"Amicable dispute resolution"
use of term, 1–009
Appeals
litigation, 2–012
mediation, 5–039—5–042
Applicable law
ADR, 21–043—21–046
agreement, 21–045
international disputes, 21–046
procedural, 21–044

INDEX

"Appropriate dispute resolution"
  meaning, 1–009
  use of term, 1–009, 1–012
Arbitration
  see also **Commercial arbitration;**
    International commercial arbitration
  Acas, 13–014
  use, 6–001
Arbitration agreements
  enforcement, 6–015
Arbitration awards
  court-annexed arbitration, 5–079
Arbitrators
  appointment
    impartiality, 6–022—6–025
    parties, 6–033
    procedure, 6–021
  due process, 6–003
  natural justice, 6–003
  procedural control, 6–028—6–034
Arb-med
  abbreviated arbitration, 19–099
  advantages, 19–100
  arbitration
    procedure held first, 2–027
  conclusion of arbitration, 19–097
  different person as mediator, 19–096
  experience of use, 19–101—19–102
  length of arbitration, 19–099
  meaning, 19–094
  med-arb-med, 2–027
  mini-trials, 19–097
  outline, 2–027
  procedure, 19–094
  research, 19–101
  same person as arbitrator and mediator, 19–095, 19–096
  settlement, 19–098
Association of British Travel Agents
  consumer dispute resolution, 6–059
Australia
  court-annexed ADR, 5–090—5–091
  court-annexed arbitration, 5–077
  med-arb, 19–091
Bar Council
  civil and commercial mediation
    pre-mediation phase, 10–024
  ethics, 16–020
  professional bodies, 16–020
"BATNA"
  civil and commercial mediation, 10–152—10–153
  examples, 4–010
  family mediation, 11–149—11–152
  negotiations, 4–008, 4–010
  trade disputes, 13–057
Best alternative to a negotiated agreement
  see **"BATNA"**

Bias
  expert determination, 7–039, 7–040, 7–042
Boundary disputes
  mediation
    generally, 10–003
    neighbourhood and community mediation, 12–012
Breach of confidence
  see also **Confidentiality**
  causes of action, 15–014
  duty of confidentiality, 15–015
Brexit
  cross-border disputes, 22–009—22–012
  future of alternative dispute resolution, 22–005—22–011
  jurisdiction, 22–008—22–011
  mediation, 22–006
Bundles
  civil and commercial mediation, 10–091—10–094
Canada
  court-annexed ADR, 5–089
  growth of ADR, 3–067
  judges as mediators, 5–024, 5–025
Case evaluation
  see **Evaluation in mediation**
"Caucuses"
  confidentiality, 15–032—15–032
  deadlock, 11–153
  family mediation, 11–128—11–130
  mediation, 9–077
Centre for Effective Dispute Resolution
  effective dispute resolution, 1–010
Chancery Division
  guidelines, 5–053
Child abuse
  family mediation, 11–058—11–060
China
  court-annexed ADR, 5–099
Chinese walls
  conflict of interest, 16–057
Civil justice system
  see **Administration of justice; Civil Procedure Rules; Family Procedure Rules**
Civil Mediation Council
  establishment, 10–014
  membership, 10–014
  objectives, 10–014
  role, 10–014
Civil partnerships
  family mediation, 11–009
Civil Procedure Rules
  conduct, 5–005
  overriding objective, 5–003, 5–006
  pre-action protocols, 5–009—5–011
  privilege, 15–075—15–078
  reform of procedure, 5–001
  rules affecting ADR, 5–003—5–005
  settlement, encouragement of, 5–003

single joint experts, 7–044
tracks, 5–004
Claims handling
agreements as ADR, 2–004
CMC
see **Civil Mediation Council**
Codes of conduct
confidentiality, 16–074—078
conflict of interest, 16–055
domestic violence, 11–050
ethics, 16–002, 16–021—025
mediators, 8–027, 8–028
neighbourhood and community mediation, 12–005
online dispute resolution, 20–009
trade associations, 10–043
Coercion
mediation, 8–038—8–043
Cohabitation
family mediation, 11–065, 11–066
Co-mediation
development, 11–006
family mediation, 11–028—030
multi-party disputes, 9–123
specialist information, 10–099
triangulation, 14–091
viable option, 17–028
Commercial arbitration
agreement to arbitrate, 6–014—6–019
Arbitration Act 1996
   assessment of Act, 6–013
   background, 6–012
   procedural freedom, 6–028—6–034
   reform proposals, 6–013
   scope, 6–011
availability, 6–001
confidentiality, 15–025—15–030
consumer disputes, 6–058—6–060
costs, 6–040—6–044
definition, 6–005
dispute requiring existence of, 1–013, 1–015—1–021
essential features
   agreement, 6–014—6–019
   binding award, 6–035—6–039
   costs, 6–040—6–044
   procedural freedom, 6–028—6–034
   expert determination distinguished, 7–046—7–050
interim relief, 6–015
jurisdiction of courts, 6–015
objective, 6–010
outline, 2–021
party autonomy, 6–021
private nature, 6–002
procedure
   freedom, 6–028—6–034
   overview, 6–004
rights-based, 3–022

settlement
   statistics, 6–048
   use, 6–051
statutory support, 6–010
Commercial Court
directing ADR processes, 5–049, 5–082
Communication
civil and commercial mediation, 10–136—138
family mediation, 11–113
learned skills, 3–037, 4–056, 10–076, 14–020, 14–042—101
mediators, 8–025, 9–085, 9–086
negotiations, 9–085, 9–086
Community mediation
see **Neighbourhood and community mediation**
Community relations
boundary disputes, 10–003
Complaints
review panel as ADR, 2–005
Compromise agreements
employment disputes, 13–032—13–033
Conciliation
see also **Trade disputes**
Acas, 8–015
family issues
   court-based conciliation, 11–012—11–014
informal resolution of complaints, 8–016
meaning, 8–013, 8–014
mediation, 8–012—8–019
mediation, and, 8–002
NHS, 8–016
outline, 2–036
process, 8–013
UNCITRAL Rules, 8–013
"Concilio-arbitration"
meaning, 5–084
Confidentiality
alternative dispute resolution
   arbitration, 15–025—15–030
   conclusions, 15–031
   generally, 15–022
   mediation, 15–023, 15–024
   not applicable, where confidentiality, 15–036
   process, 15–023
   separate meetings or caucuses, 15–032—15–035
   United States, 15–024
arbitration, 15–025—15–030
breach of confidence
   causes of action, 15–014
   duty of confidentiality, 15–015
   framework, 15–012
caucuses, 15–032—15–354
children, 15–072—15–074
codes of practice, 16–074—16–078
contracts, 15–114—15–117
court settlement process, 5–017

INDEX

cross-border disputes, 15–118—15–122
duty, 15–015, 16–074
ethics
  ADR, 16–071—16–092
  generally, 16–007, 16–072
  issues, 16–071—16–092
  private meetings, 16–079—16–092
EU Directive on Cross-Border Mediation, 15–010
exclusion by court
  determining existence of agreement, 15–080—15–093
  interpretation of agreement, 15–097—15–102
  mediation stipulated by court, 15–080—15–093
  negligence, 15–097—15–102
freedom of expression, 15–017, 15–018
general principles, 15–012—15–021
human rights, 15–017—15–021
inadvertent breaches, 15–034
legal issues, 15–001
legal obligation to maintain, 16–074
legal representation, 17–066
med-arb, 16–086
mediation, 8–044—8–046, 15–023, 15–024
mediation information and assessment meetings, 16–091
mini-trials, 19–041
money laundering, 15–106—15–113
obligation to breach, 16–074
online dispute resolution, 20–009
personal information, 15–017
philosophy of ADR, 3–034, 3–034—3–035
private meetings
  agreement to maintain confidentiality, 16–085—16–089
  caucusing, 16–079
  family mediation, 16–090
  joint meeting, disclosure from separate meeting to, 16–081—16–084
  material misapprehension, 16–087
  med-arb, 16–086
  mediation information and assessment meetings, 16–091
  separate, 16–080, 16–090—16–093
  settlement terms, 16–088
  shuttle diplomacy, 16–079
  special terms, 16–090—16–092
privilege distinguished, 15–002
proceeds of crime, 15–106—15–113
public information, 15–016
Republic of Ireland, 15–008
research, 5–018
Scotland, 15–006
settlement, 16–088
UNCITRAL Model Law, 15–007
United States, 15–007, 15–024
widely known information, 15–016

Conflict of interest
actual
  meaning, 16–053
bars to mediation
  absolute, 16–062—16–064, 16–066
  conflicting relationship, 16–062
  financial interest, 16–062
  freedom of choice, 16–066
  generally, 16–060
  impartiality, absence of, 16–063
  qualified, 16–065—16–066
  rules applying, 16–061
Chinese walls, 16–057
codes of conduct, 16–055
conclusion of mediation, after, 16–069, 16–070
ethics, 16–006
firm, service or consortium, 16–059
informed consent, 16–054
mediators
  requirements, 16–052
members of law firm or partnership, 16–057
perceived
  meaning, 16–053
  scope of rules, 16–057
post-commencement of mediation, 16–067, 16–068
potential
  meaning, 16–053
professional bodies, 16–056
regulation, 16–054—16–056
scope of regulation, 16–057—16–059
types, 16–053
working relationships, 16–057, 16–058
"Conflicts"
approaches, 1–026
avoidance, 1–050
clash of opposing principles, 1–027
conflict management
  intractable conflicts, 1–052
  purpose, 1–052
  values, 1–052
decision-making, 1–024
definitions, 1–023
differences, as manifestation of, 1–023
dispute distinguished, 1–022—1–028
emotional issues, 1–031
fact of life, 1–025
healthy and positive function, 1–026
intensity, 1–031
intervention required, 1–028
meaning, 1–022, 1–023
objective, 1–034
potential violence, 1–024
prevention, 1–050, 1–051
transformation, 1–043—1–047, 1–051
underlying issues aggravating conflict, 1–030
Construction industry
see also **Dispute boards**; **Statutory adjudication**

dispute resolution
   major projects, 2–007
   Scheme for Construction Contracts, 7–007

Consumers
   disputes
      arbitration, 6–058—6–060
      Independent Consumer Arbitrations Service, 6–060
      schemes, 6–060

Continuing professional development
   professional practice consultancy, 11–062, 11–063

Contractual adjudication
   see **Statutory adjudication**

Control
   litigation, 2–018
   ombudsman, 2–026

Costs
   commercial arbitration, 6–040—6–044
   court-annexed arbitration, 5–079
   dispute boards, 7–016
   jurisdiction, 5–079
   mini-trials, 19–041, 19–056
   private judging, 2–019
   sanctions
      Halsey principles, 5–061—066, 17–012—017
      where ADR not attempted, 5–061—066
   settlement, 5–080
   statutory adjudication, 7–011

Counselling
   see also **Psychotherapy**
   family mediation
      background, 11–022
      couples, 11–025
      resources, 11–026
      theory, 11–024—11–026
   meaning, 11–024
   psychotherapy distinguished, 11–024

Court of Appeal
   mediation, 5–039—5–042

Court settlement process
   confidentiality, 5–017
   evaluative mediation, 5–017
   non-binding settlement, 5–016
   outline, 5–015
   procedure, 5–015
   Technology and Construction Court, 5–015—5–018, 19–079

Court-annexed ADR
   see also **Court-annexed arbitration; Court-annexed mediation**
   assessment, 5–104—109
   Australia, 5–090—5–091
   Canada, 5–089
   China, 5–099
   Court of Appeal, 5–039—5–042
   Denmark, 5–095
   development, 5–001
   generally, 5–013, 5–086

   Germany, 5–092—5–094
   India, 5–102, 5–103
   Japan, 5–096—5–098
   judges as mediators, 5–024—5–031
   Singapore, 5–100—5–101
   Small Claims Mediation Service, 5–021—5–023
   Technology and Construction Court, 5–014—5–018
   United States, 5–087—5–088

Court-annexed arbitration
   adaption of procedures, 5–084, 5–085
   assessment of process, 5–083
   Australia, 5–077
   automatic referral to mediation, 5–035
   awards, 5–079
   costs, 5–079
   England, 5–078
   hearings, 5–082
   jurisdiction, 21–004
   meaning, 5–077
   non-binding, 5–077—5–083
   outline, 2–022
   rehearings, 5–079
   subject matter, 5–081
   terminology, 5–077
   United States, 5–087—5–088

Court-annexed mediation
   county courts, 5–034—5–035
   independent mediators, 5–032
   meaning, 5–032
   mediators, 5–033
   neutral role of judge or court official, 5–033

Court-attached ADR
   see **Court-annexed ADR; Court-annexed arbitration; Court-annexed mediation**

Courts
   see also **Litigation**
   directing ADR process, 5–048—5–060
   recommending ADR processes, 5–048—5–060
   sanctions where ADR not attempted, 5–061—5–066

Cross-border disputes
   confidentiality, 15–118—15–122
   privilege, 15–118—15–122

Culture
   family mediation, 11–002
   gangs, 12–025
   negotiations
      approach, 4–075
      aspects, 4–073
      community, 4–073
      diversity, 4–074, 4–075
      flexibility, 4–075
      geographical, 4–073
      industrial, 4–073
      sensitivity, 4–074
   professional, 1–007

INDEX

Data protection
General Data Protection Regulation, 22–027—22–031
Deadlock
caucuses, 11–153
cause of impasse, 9–097
civil and commercial mediation
adjournment, 10–162, 10–163
adjudication, preparation for, 10–173, 10–174
analyses, 10–161
BATNA, 10–152—10–153
creative options, 10–156—10–157
"crossing the last gap", 10–172
fairness, 10–169
leaving proposals open, 10–171
need for strategy, 10–142
non-binding settlement proposals, 10–164—10–168
reflection, 10–170
risk assessment, 10–143—10–151
self-examination, 10–170
summaries, 10–161
symbolism, 10–158, 10–159
underlying issues, examination of, 10–154, 10–155
WATNA, 10–152—10–153
written notes, 10–161
conflicting legal or technical advice, 9–108, 9–109
emotional blocks, 9–105—9–107
fairness, differences in perception of, 9–103
family mediation
adjudication, preparing for, 11–155
allowing parties to absorb process, 11–133
BATNA, 11–149—11–152
caucuses, 11–153
cyclical patterns of behaviour, dealing with, 11–139
draft summaries, 11–147, 11–148
generally, 11–131
legal perception, managing differences of, 11–146
pausing and reflecting, 11–132
perceptions of fairness, differing, 11–140, 11–141
powers of words and symbolism, recognising, 11–142—11–144
risk assessment, 11–149—11–152
short-term experiments, 11–145
underlying fears and concerns, addressing, 11–134, 11–135
unresolved emotional blocks, addressing, 11–136—11–138
WATNA, 11–149—11–152
"ginger jar" factor, 9–100
meaning, 9–095
neighbourhood and community mediation, 12–063—12–065

non-binding evaluation processes, 19–025—19–028
perceptions, differences of, 9–103, 9–104
purpose, 9–096
risk assessment, 9–110—9–112
role of mediator, 9–098
settlement or litigation, choice of, 9–114
simpler approach to, 9–113
strong positions, adoption of, 9–102
symbolism, 9–099—9–102, 10–158, 10–159, 11–142—11–144
termination of mediation, 9–115
terminology, problems of, 9–099—9–102
trade disputes, 13–052—13–057
Denmark
court-annexed ADR, 5–095
Diplomatic immunity
privilege, 15–041
Disclosure
litigation, 2–011
Dispute Adjudication Board
see **Dispute boards**
Dispute Avoidance Panel
see **Dispute boards**
Dispute boards
advantages, 2–007, 7–016
aims, 7–015
background, 7–015
communications, 7–023
composition, 7–018
concept, 7–017—7–021
costs, 7–016
duration, 7–019
establishment, 7–014, 7–019
examples, 7–024
expertise, 7–020
formal capacity, 7–021
informal capacity, 7–020
informality, 7–016
interim binding decisions, 7–023
membership, 7–018
non-binding recommendations, 7–022
origins, 7–014
outline, 2–025
powers, 2–007
projects, 7–024
recommendations, 7–022
site visits, 7–019
suggestions, 7–020
terminology, 7–017
uses, 2–007, 7–015
Dispute resolution
adjudicatory, 19–001
co-existence, 1–052
consensual, 19–001
creative methods, 2–007
early neutral evaluation, 1–041
essence, 3–069

marriage and cohabitation breakdown, 1–048
objective, 1–034
other interventions, 1–048—1–052
settlement, 1–035—1–039
skilled negotiators, 2–003
transformation, 1–043—1–047
underlying conflict, resolution of, 1–033
values, 1–052
Dispute Resolution Board
see **Dispute boards**
Dispute Review Board
see **Dispute boards**
Disputes
actual dispute, 1–015
arbitration clause, construction of, 1–016
arbitration referred to, 1–013, 1–014
attitudes of parties, factors affecting, 1–027
classification, 1–015
conflict distinguished, 1–022—1–028
construction adjudication, 1–021
existence, question of, 1–013
expert determination, 1–020
family disputes, 1–030
iceberg factor, 1–029
issues
 submerged, 1–029—1–031
meaning, 1–013—1–021, 1–022
ordinary meaning, 1–015
partnerships, 1–029
potential, 1–016
proper understanding required, 1–021
stay of proceedings, 1–018
types of, 1–013—1–021
Divorce
see also **Family mediation**
change in process, 11–002
generally, 11–001—11–003
Domain names
online dispute resolution, 20–010, 20–011
Domestic violence
codes of practice, 11–050
family mediation
 child abuse, 11–058—11–060
 codes of practice, 11–050
 couple, abuse between, 11–050—11–057
 independent advice, 11–056
 safety issues, 11–057
 screening, 11–054, 11–055
 separate meetings, 11–054
 signs, looking for, 11–055
 suitability for mediation, 11–055
 suspicion of violence, 11–055
 types of abuse, 11–052, 11–053
 vulnerable, protection of interests of, 11–051
separate meetings, 11–055
Early neutral evaluation
adoption in UK, 19–066
agreement, 19–071

case summaries, 19–071
Commercial Court, 19–070
continuing process, 19–071
court evaluation, 19–066—19–070
dispute resolution, 19–075
evaluator, 19–065
experts, 19–071
follow-up, 19–071
Lloyds insurance policies, 19–074
oral submissions, 19–071
origins, 19–062
outline, 2–029, 19–062—19–065
procedure, 19–071
process, 2–022
purpose, 19–064, 19–073
risk assessment, 19–072
settlement, 19–064
Technology and Construction Court, 5–014
timetable, 19–071
venue, 19–071
"Effective dispute resolution"
Centre for Effective Dispute Resolution, 1–010
Elder mediation
see **Mediation**
Emotional sensitivity
mediators, 14–023—030, 14–082
Employment disputes
see **Acas; Employment tribunals; Trade disputes**
Employment mediation and conciliation
see **Trade disputes**
Employment tribunals
early conciliation, 13–011
generally, 7–056
industrial tribunals, renaming of, 13–007
jurisdiction, 13–007
ENE
see **Early neutral evaluation**
Environmental mediation
see also **Public policy**
meaning, 14–001
multi-party disputes, 9–122
neighbourhood and community mediation, 12–013
Ethics
ADR, 16–002
codes of practice, 16–003, 16–021—16–025
confidentiality
 ADR, 16–071—16–092
 generally, 16–007
 issues, 16–071—16–092
conflicts of interest, 16–006
cornerstone of ADR practice, 16–024
fairness, 16–001—16–070, 16–005
generally, 16–001
mediation, 3–033
mediators, 14–011—14–018, 16–009
philosophy of ADR, 3–030—3–033

INDEX

power imbalances, 16–008
practitioner's values, attitudes and beliefs
    assumptions, 16–036—16–038
    conflict, attitude to, 16–030—16–031
    neutrality, 16–026—16–027
    personal, 16–028—16–038
    rationality/emotionality, 16–032—16–035
professional bodies, 16–003, 16–010—16–020
sources of standards, 16–022

European Convention on Human Rights
civil litigation, effect on conduct of, 5–072—5–076
confidentiality, 15–017—15–021
ombudsman, 2–006
right to fair and public hearing, 5–086—092

European Union
growth of ADR, 3–067

Evaluation in mediation
see **Non-binding evaluation processes**

"Executive Tribunal"
see **Mini-trials**

Expert determination
see also **Experts**
adaption of process, 7–029
appointment of expert, 7–026, 7–030
approach, 7–034
arbitration distinguished, 7–046—7–050
areas of application, 7–027—7–030
availability, 7–027
banking, 7–029
bias, 7–039, 7–040, 7–042
boundary disputes, 7–029
broadcasting, 7–029
challenging determinations, 7–036
commodity supply contracts, 7–029
companies, 7–027
discretion of expert, 7–030, 7–032, 7–037, 7–038
disputes, 1–20
finality of determination, 7–036—7–042
finance, 7–029
freedom of expert, 7–031
information technology, 7–029
joint ventures, 7–027
meetings, 7–034, 7–035
natural justice, 7–034, 7–040
oil and gas industry, 7–028
outline, 2–023
parties' experts, meetings with, 7–035
powers of expert, 7–030
preliminary meetings, 7–033
principles, 7–026
process, 7–026
property valuation, 7–027
regulation of process, 7–032
single joint experts distinguished, 7–043—7–045
standard form contract, 7–028

stay of proceedings, 1–018
summary of procedure, 7–031—7–035
uses, 7–025, 7–026

Experts
admissibility of opinion, 19–106
advice, 19–106
court procedures, 19–106
Experts Protocol, 19–103
non-binding opinion, 19–104
outline, 2–030
parties, involvement of, 19–105
selection, 19–105
single expert, 19–103
specialised issues, 19–103
United Kingdom, 19–104
United States, 19–104
Woolf reforms, 19–103

Facilitation
approach, 3–048, 3–049
civil and commercial mediation, 10–019
family mediation, 11–122—125
mediation, 8–033—037, 9–009—011, 9–075—076
mediators, 8–033—037, 14–106
non-binding evaluation processes, 19–015—017

Fairness
considerations, 16–050
ethics, 16–005
fundamental principle, 16–040
legal principles, 16–046, 16–047
legal representation, 16–049
manifest unfairness, 16–051
outcome, 16–039—16–043
parties' views, 16–044, 16–045, 16–051
process
    establishment, 16–042
    requirements, 16–043, 16–044
workability, 16–048

Families
see also **Family mediation**
range of processes, 11–003

Family law
see also **Financial dispute resolution appointments**
Family Law Arbitration Scheme, 6–061—6–066

Family mediation
agendas, 11–087—11–096
agreement to mediate, 11–079, 11–080
anchor mediation, 11–030
approaches, 1–048
caucuses, 11–128—11–130
child abuse, 11–058—11–060
children, involving, 11–040—11–049
civil and commercial mediation compared, 17–004—17–006
civil partnerships, 11–009
co-mediation, 11–028—11–030
communication skills, 11–113

conciliation
   court-based, 11–012—11–014
conclusion, 11–156—11–159, 11–156—11–168
consultant, supervision by, 11–061—11–064
counselling
   availability, 11–023
   background, 11–022
   couples, 11–025
   psychotherapy distinguished, 11–024
   resources, 11–026
   theory, 11–024—11–026
deadlock
   adjudication, preparing for, 11–152
   allowing parties to absorb process, 11–133
   BATNA, 11–149—11–152
   caucuses, 11–153
   cyclical patterns of behaviour, dealing with, 11–139
   draft summaries, 11–147, 11–148
   generally, 11–131
   legal perception, managing differences of, 11–146
   pausing and reflecting, 11–132
   perceptions of fairness, differing, 11–140, 11–141
   powers of words and symbolism, recognising, 11–142—11–144
   risk assessment, 11–149—11–152
   short-term experiments, 11–145
   underlying fears and concerns, addressing, 11–134, 11–135
   unresolved emotional blocks, addressing, 11–136—11–138
   WATNA, 11–149—11–152
decision-making, 11–122—11–125
different culture, 11–002
domestic violence or abuse
   child abuse, 11–058—11–060
   codes of practice, 11–050
   couple, abuse between, 11–050—11–057
   independent advice, 11–056
   safety issues, 11–057
   screening, 11–054, 11–055
   separate meetings, 11–055
   signs, looking for, 11–055
   suitability for mediation, 11–055
   suspicion of, 11–055
   types of abuse, 11–052, 11–053
   vulnerable, protection of interests of, 11–051
emotional sensitivity, 11–114—11–117
family arbitration, 11–154
Family Law Act 1996, 11–008
Family Mediation Council, 11–017, 11–018
Family Mediators Association, 11–006
financial dispute resolution appointments, 11–015, 11–016
funding
   encouragement to mediate, 9–035
future developments, 22–025—22–026

history, 11–004—11–011
holistic view, 11–003
information gathering
   continuing, 11–103
   financial, 11–097, 11–100—11–102
   full disclosure, 11–097, 11–098
   policy, 11–097
   sufficient, 11–104
   types of information, 11–099
intake sessions, 11–074—11–076
issues, establishment of, 11–087—11–096
lawyers as mediators, 11–038—11–039
legal advice, opportunity for, 11–091
legal aid, 11–008
legal history, 11–004—11–011
legal representation, 11–082, 17–005, 17–071—17–074
mediation information and assessment meetings, 5–043—5–045, 11–011, 11–020, 11–021, 11–074—11–076
mediators
   experts, 17–025—17–029
   ground rules, explaining, 11–090
   involvement after conclusion, 11–170
   summaries, 11–160—11–165
memoranda, 11–160—11–165
National Family Mediation, 11–005
negotiations
   caucuses, 11–128—11–130
   children's issues, 11–126—11–127
   communication skills, 11–113
   decision-making, 11–122—11–125
   emotional sensitivity, 11–114—11–117
   facilitation, 11–122—11–125
   hybrid processes, 11–128—11–130
   joint sessions, 11–105
   option development, 11–107—11–109
   parenting plans, 11–126—11–127
   process management, 11–118, 11–119
   reality-testing, 11–120—11–121
   separate meetings, 11–128—11–130
objectives, 8–053
opening the meeting, 11–087—11–096
operation with other systems, 11–003
options available, 11–003
organisations, 11–005, 11–006
overview, 11–004—11–021
parenting plans, 11–126—11–127
pilot schemes, 11–006
post-termination stage, 11–169, 11–170
preliminary communications and preparation, 11–081—11–086
preliminary meetings, 11–077, 11–078
pre-mediation stage
   agreement to mediate, 11–079, 11–080
   generally, 11–070—11–073
   intake sessions, 11–074—11–076
   mediation information and assessment meetings, 11–074—11–076

INDEX

meetings with lawyers, 11–077, 11–078
preliminary meetings, 11–077, 11–078
preparation, 17–048—17–049, 17–053—17–054
presentation of case, 17–061—17–062
process management, 11–118, 11–119
Professional Practice Consultant, 11–062, 11–063
psychotherapy
　availability, 11–023
　background, 11–022
　counselling distinguished, 11–024
　theory, 11–024—11–026
reception arrangements, 11–086
relationship crisis or breakdown, dealing with, 11–002
rights, 11–031—11–037
separation and divorce, issues other than, 11–067—11–068
sole mediation, 11–028—11–030
stages
　agenda setting, 11–087—11–096
　conclusion of mediation, 11–156—11–168
　deadlock, 11–131—11–155
　establishing the issues, 11–087—11–096
　information gathering, 11–097—11–104
　negotiations, 11–105—11–130
　opening the meeting, 11–087—11–096
　post-mediation, 11–169, 11–170
　preliminary communications, 11–081—11–086
　pre-mediation, 11–070—11–080
　preparation, 11–081—11–086
　recording the outcome, 11–160—11–165
symbolism, 11–142—11–144
United States, 11–064
unmarried cohabiting couples, 11–010, 11–065, 11–066
venue
　equipment and material, 11–089
　initial meeting, 11–085
　nature of, 11–085
　reception arrangements, 11–086
　seating arrangements, 11–088
　written submissions, 11–083
Family Mediation Council
co-operation, 11–018
establishment, 11–017
family mediation, 11–017, 11–018
membership, 11–017
Family Procedure Rules
adjournments, 5–007
encouragement to use ADR, 5–007
overriding objective, 5–006
Practice Direction, 5–008
pre-action protocols, 5–012
Financial dispute resolution appointments
assessment of procedure, 5–020
Chancery Division, 19–077—19–078
conduct, 5–019, 5–020

evaluation, 5–020
facts and issues, judge having grasp of, 5–019
family mediation, 11–015, 11–016
model, 19–066
origins, 19–076
privilege, 5–019, 15–078
process, 11–015
FMC
see **Family Mediation Council**
Freedom of expression
confidentiality, 15–017, 15–018
Funding
family mediation
　encouragement to mediate, 9–035
neighbourhood and community mediation, 12–034
Gangs
Aasha Gang Mediation Project, 12–030
Capital Conflict Management, 12–028
Centre for Conflict Transformation, 12–027
culture, 12–025
"Leap" Confronting Conflict, 12–029
mediation, 12–024—12–031
mediators, 12–031
summits, 12–026
United Kingdom, 12–037—12–031
Germany
court-annexed ADR, 5–092—5–094
Good faith
alternative dispute resolution, 4–096—4–099
common law and civil law systems distinguished, 4–086
culpa in contrahendo, 4–091—4–095
duties
　good faith, 4–091—4–095
　negotiation, 4–086—4–095
　not to break off negotiations, 4–095
　performance, 4–091—4–095
English law, 4–087, 4–091
European law, 4–091—4–195
failure to negotiate, 4–095
misrepresentation, 4–094
negotiation
　duties, 4–086—4–095
　United States, 4–088
performance in good faith, 4–091—4–095
promissory estoppel, 4–094
United States, 4–088
Harassment
neighbourhood and community mediation, 12–009
Hearings
court-annexed arbitration, 5–082
Human rights
confidentiality, 15–017—15–021
mandatory ADR, 5–072—5–076
ombudsman, 2–006
right to fair and public hearing, 5–072—5–076

Hybrid dispute resolution
  see also **Arb-med**; **Med-arb**; **Neutral fact-finding experts**; **Ombudsman**
  development, 19–080
  mediation, 9–022
  overview, 19–080—19–081
  processes, 2–008
ICSID
  investor protection, 6–052—6–057
Impartiality
  Acas, 13–006
  med-arb, 19–085
  mediators, 8–027—8–032
  non-binding evaluation processes, 19–013
Impasse strategies
  see **Deadlock**
India
  court-annexed ADR, 5–102, 5–103
Industrial disputes
  see **Trade disputes**
Industrial tribunals
  employment tribunals, renaming as, 13–007
Information gathering
  civil and commercial mediation
    bundles, 10–091—10–094
    disputed issues, 10–084
    information required, 10–083
    missing documents, 10–094
    parties' positions, 10–084
    pending litigation or arbitration, 10–098
    prior settlement negotiations, 10–098
    relationship between parties, 10–098
    sources, 10–084
    specialist information, 10–099
    third party views, 10–098
  family mediation
    continuing, 11–103
    financial, 11–097, 11–100—11–102
    full disclosure, 11–097, 11–098
    policy, 11–097
    sufficient, 11–104
    types of information, 11–099
  med-arb, 19–086
  mediation
    amount, 9–070—9–071
    displaying information, 9–069
    flip-charts, 9–069
    importance, 9–068
    multiple sessions, 9–068
    sources, 9–068
    substantive mediation, before, 9–068
    sufficiency, 9–070—9–071
    technical information, 9–068
    types, 9–068
  mediators, 14–105
  mini-trials, 19–041
  neighbourhood and community mediation, 12–056, 12–057

trade disputes, 13–044—13–046
Informed consent
  conflict of interest, 16–054
Insurance
  Lloyds insurance policies, 19–074
Intake sessions
  see **Family mediation**
Interim relief
  arbitration
    court orders, 6–015
International Chamber of Commerce
  arbitration, 6–009
International commercial arbitration
  International Centre for Settlement of Investment Disputes, 6–052—6–057
  International Chamber of Commerce, 6–009
  New York Convention, 6–007
  UNCITRAL Arbitration Rules, 6–008
  UNCITRAL Model law, 6–008
Investor protection
  ICSID, 6–052—057
Japan
  court-annexed ADR, 5–096—5–098
Judges
  see also **"Private judging"**
  mediators, 5–024—5–031
Jurisdiction
  adjudication, 21–002
  agreement
    arbitration clauses, 21–012, 21–013
    contract, 21–007—21–011
    generally, 21–005, 21–006
    non-adjudicatory ADR, 21–014—21–019
    post-dispute, 21–020—21–024
  arbitration, 21–002, 21–004
  contract clauses, 21–007—21–011
  court-annexed arbitration, 21–004
  enforcement of contract clauses, 21–025—21–038
  litigation, 21–001
  mediation, 21–002, 21–004
  private judging, 21–004
  statutory
    adjudication, 21–002, 21–003
    arbitration, 21–002, 21–004
    Arbitration Act 1996, 21–002, 21–004
    categories of ADR, 21–004
    court-annexed arbitration, 21–004
    mandatory mediation, 21–004
    mediation, 21–002, 21–004
    private judging, 21–004
Justice
  mediation, 3–009
Labour disputes
  see **Trade disputes**
Law Society
  civil and commercial mediation, 10–007
  ethics, 16–012—16–019

INDEX

mediation panels, 16–019
mediation rules, 16–019
pre-mediation phase, 10–024
Lawyers
see **Legal representation**
Legal history
alternative dispute resolution, 3–007
family mediation, 11–004—11–011
tribunals, 7–051—7–053
Legal profession
trends towards ADR, 3–065
Legal professional privilege
rules, 15–048—15–052
Legal representation
agreement to mediate, 17–040
basic duty, 17–002
best interests of client, 17–002
civil and commercial mediation, 10–069, 10–070
civil/commercial and family mediation compared, 17–004—17–006
client's best interests, 17–023
competing requirements, balancing, 17–003
conduct of negotiations, 17–066
confidentiality, 17–066
documentation
  commercial and civil disputes, 17–043—17–047
  family issues, 17–048—17–049
engaging other party in mediation, 17–030, 17–031
experts
  commercial and civil disputes, 17–022—17–024
  family issues, 17–025—17–029
  requirement, 17–020—17–029
formalising settlement terms, 17–075—17–079
forum
  court orders, 17–011
  decisions, 17–009
  experts, 17–020—17–029
  Halsey principles, 17–012—17–017
  relationship breakdown, 17–016
  strategic decisions, 17–015
  suitability of disputes, 17–010—17–017
  type of mediation required, 17–018, 17–019
generally, 17–001—17–003
information provision, 17–063
negotiations
  approaches, 17–064—17–068
  bottom lines, 17–066
  conduct, 17–066
  confidentiality, 17–066
  courtesy, 17–066
  experience, using, 17–068
  final offers, 17–066
  realistic assessment, 17–067
  settlement proposals, 17–066
  support for client, 17–066

post-mediation phase, 17–085—17–088
preliminary meetings, 17–035, 17–036
pre-mediation phase, 17–034—17–039
preparation
  commercial and civil disputes, 17–043—17–047, 17–050—17–052
  family cases, 17–053—17–054
presentation of case
  commercial and civil disputes, 17–057—17–060
  family cases, 17–061—17–062
selection of mediator, 17–037—17–039
settlement
  implementation, 17–086
  terms, drafting, 17–075—17–079
specialists, 17–007, 17–008
Standing Conference of Mediation Advocates (SCMA), 17–007, 17–008
strategies, 17–069, 17–070
substantive meeting, 17–055—17–062
understanding mediation process, 17–032, 17–033
Litigation
alternative, view that, 1–008
appeals, 2–012
case management
see **Administration of justice**
control, 2–018
costs
  discretion, 5–005
disclosure, 2–011
essence of, 2–012
judgment, 2–011
jurisdiction, 21–001
limitations, 3–020, 3–021
meaning, 2–011
mediation
  support, 2–014
negotiations, 2–010—2–014
outline of process, 2–018
power, 2–018
power imbalances, 16–097
preliminary stages, 2–011
procedures, 2–011
process of, 2–013
rights, based, 3–021
role, 1–003
significance, 1–003
State support, 2–012
symbiotic relationship with ADR, 2–014
trial, 2–011
witness statements, 2–011
Med-arb
agreements to arbitrate distinguished, 19–093
Australia, 19–091
concerns, 19–088—19–093
confidentiality, 16–086
decision to move to arbitration, 19–083
disadvantages, 19–084

531

experience of use, 19–101—19–102
generally, 2–008
impartiality, 19–085
information received during mediation phase, 19–086
issues, 19–082—19–087
med-arb-med, 2–027
mediation procedure comes first, 2–028
mediator-adviser, 19–092
mediators
  impartiality, 19–085
  role, 19–082
outline, 2–028, 19–082—19–087
role of mediator, 19–082
same person as mediator and arbitrator, 19–087

Mediation
see also **Family mediation**; **Med-arb**; **Mediation (civil and commercial)**; **Public policy**; **Trade disputes**
adoption, 1–003
advantages, 3–023
agendas, 9–066—9–067
anthropological background, 8–002
binding agreement, 9–119
caucuses, 9–077
commencement, 9–044—9–047
communications, 3–054
conciliation, 8–012—8–019
confidentiality, 15–023, 15–024
consensual decision-making, 8–048, 8–049
consistency, 2–039, 2–040
deal mediation, 1–032
  civil and commercial cases, 10–188—189
  uses, 1–032
definition, 3–059, 8–005—007
development, 8–010
disadvantages of one size fits all approach, 2–041
elder mediation, 12–023
engaging other party, 17–030, 17–031
escalation, containment of, 8–054—8–058
ethics, 3–033
evaluation, 9–009—9–011
expectations, 2–039
facilitation, 8–033—8–037, 9–009—9–011, 9–075—9–076
facilitative
  outline, 2–035
fields of activity, 9–127, 9–128
format, 2–039, 2–040
fundamentalist approach, 3–060, 3–061
helplines, 3–066
hybrid models, 9–022
impartiality, 8–027—8–032
information gathering
  amount, 9–070—9–071
  displaying information, 9–069
  flip-charts, 9–069
  importance, 9–068
  multiple sessions, 9–068
  sources, 9–068
  substantive mediation, before, 9–068
  sufficiency, 9–070—9–071
  technical information, 9–068
  types, 9–068
interest-based approach, 9–004—9–011
issues
  agenda, 9–062, 9–066—9–067
  crystallisation, 9–060
  establishing, 9–058—9–067
  neutrality, 9–061
  presentation, 9–059—9–062
  series of meetings, 9–062
  underlying issues, 9–063—9–067
joint or separate meetings, 9–077
judges as mediators, 5–024—5–031
justice, 3–009
Law Society rules, 16–012—16–019
litigation
  support, 2–014
meaning, 8–001—8–008
models
  evaluation, 9–009—9–011
  facilitation, 9–009—9–011
  humanistic, 9–021
  hybrid models, 9–022
  interest-based mediation, 9–004—9–008
  narrative model, 9–020
  non-model, 9–023
  overview, 9–001—003
  rights-based mediation, 9–004—9–008
  settlement, 9–012, 9–013
  therapeutic model, 9–014—9–015
  transformative, 9–016—9–019
multi-party disputes
  co-mediation, 9–123
  draft statements, 9–123
  effect, 9–120, 9–121
  environmental mediation, 9–122
  examples, 9–120
  length of meetings, 9–123
  oral presentation, 9–123
  planning, 9–123
  practical issues, 9–123—9–126
  preliminary meetings, 9–123
  public law, 9–122
  sequence of presentations, 9–123
  settlement, 9–120
  time between meetings, 9–123
  written statements, 9–123
narrative model, 9–020
negotiations
  communication skills, 9–085, 9–086
  emotional sensitivity, 9–091—9–093
  evaluation, 9–094
  facilitation, 9–075, 9–076
  joint meetings, 9–077
  management of process, 9–073, 9–074

INDEX

options, generation and development of, 9–078, 9–079
perceptions, positions and proposals, testing, 9–087—9–090
separate meetings, 9–077
skills, 9–085, 9–086
trust and understanding, building, 9–083—9–084
neutrality, 8–027—8–032
non-binding opinions, 8–004
opening the meeting, 9–057
options
   brainstorming, 9–080—9–082
   generation and development of, 9–078, 9–079
   mediator, role of, 9–079
oral presentation, 9–123
parties, empowerment of, 3–015—3–019, 8–059—8–063
party self-determination, 8–038—8–043
peer mediation, 12–016—12–022
perceptions
   differences of, 9–103, 9–104
   testing, 9–087—9–090
physical environment, 8–045, 8–046
popularity, 1–002
post-mediation
   overview, 9–031
post-termination stage, 9–119
practical preparation, 9–056
predominance, 2–002
preliminary communications and preparation
   accountants, 9–049
   attendance, 9–049
   authority, 9–049
   coaching, 9–056
   communications, 9–049—9–051
   costs, 9–055
   expert liaison, 9–049
   generally, 9–030
   hosting arrangements, 9–056
   importance, 9–050
   legal issues, 9–049
   legal representatives, 9–049
   practical preparation, 9–056
   preliminary meeting, 9–052—9–055
   pre-mediation phase distinguished, 9–052, 9–053
   procedure, 9–049
   reading, 9–056
   research, 9–056
   technology, 9–055
   timing, 9–057, 9–058
   venue, 9–056
preliminary meeting, 9–052—9–055
principles
   authority derived from parties, 8–047
   confidentiality, 8–044—8–046
   conflict resolution, 8–050—8–053
   consensual decision-making, 8–048, 8–049
   containing escalation, 8–054—8–058
   dispute management, 8–050—8–053
   empowerment of parties, 3–015—3–019, 8–059—8–063
   facilitation, 8–033—8–037
   impartiality, 8–027—8–032
   mediators, 8–021—8–026
   neutrality, 8–027—8–032
   overview, 8–020
   party self-determination, 8–038—8–043
   privilege, 8–044—8–046
privilege, 8–044—8–046, 15–123—15–144
project mediation, 1–032
purpose, 9–048
reading in preparation, 9–056
"real" mediation, 3–058—3–061, 8–009—8–011
research, preparation, 9–056
resolution objective, 8–050—8–053
rights-based approach, 9–004—9–011
schools, 12–016—12–022
schools of thought, 3–054
secure negotiating environment, provision of, 8–015
settlement, 8–050, 8–051, 9–012, 9–013
stages
   formulation, 9–025
   non-sequential models, 9–026
   number, 9–025
   overview, 9–024, 9–029—9–031
   phases, 9–027
   purpose, 9–024
   uses, 9–027
standard models of working, 2–039
strategies, 8–003, 8–008
subject matter, 3–023
submerged issues, 1–029—1–031
termination
   agreements and summaries, 9–119
   circumstances of, 9–116
   confirmation by mediator, 9–119
   deadlock, 9–115
   freedom, 8–047
   inappropriate to continue, where, 9–116
   settlement terms, 9–117
   without settlement, 9–118
terms of settlement, 3–024
test of success, 3–061
therapeutic model, 3–054
timing, 9–057, 9–058
transformation, 1–044—1–046, 9–016—9–019
venue
   choice of, 9–056
   reception arrangements, 9–056
   seating arrangements, 9–056

Mediation (civil and commercial)
agendas, 10–080—10–082
agreement to mediate, 10–044—10–048
assessment of suitability, 10–034—10–036
brackets, 10–160—10–161

bundles, 10–091—10–094
Civil Mediation Council, 10–014
conclusion, 10–176—10–183
contract clauses, 10–025—10–030
corporate representatives, 10–071—10–072
deadlock
  adjournments, 10–162, 10–163
  adjudication, preparation for, 10–173, 10–174
  analyses, 10–161
  BATNA, 10–152—10–153
  creative options, 10–156, 10–157
  "crossing the last gap", 10–172
  fairness, 10–169
  leaving proposals open, 10–171
  non-binding settlement proposals, 10–164—10–168
  reflection, 10–170
  risk assessment, 10–143—10–151
  self-examination, 10–170
  summaries, 10–161
  symbolism, 10–158, 10–159
  underlying issues, examination of, 10–154, 10–155
  WATNA, 10–152—10–153
  written notes, 10–161
deal mediation, 10–188—10–189
definition, 8–007
emotions, dealing with, 10–127—10–134
evaluation, 10–019, 10–139—10–141
examples of use, 10–004
facilitative basis, 10–019
facilities at venue, 10–067, 10–068
family disputes, 10–002
family mediation compared, 17–004—17–006
fields of activity, 10–001
HM Courts and Tribunal Service, 10–010
implementation of settlement, 10–184
importance of distinguishing, 10–001
information gathering
  bundles, 10–091—10–094
  disputed issues, 10–084
  information required, 10–083
  missing documents, 10–094
  parties' positions, 10–084
  pending litigation or arbitration, 10–098
  prior settlement negotiations, 10–098
  relationship between parties, 10–098
  sources, 10–084
  specialist information, 10–099
  third party views, 10–098
  written case summaries, 10–086—10–090
information provision, 10–037—10–042
issues
  establishing, 10–077—10–079
  oral presentation, 10–078—10–079
  underlying, 10–082, 10–095—10–097
Law Society, 10–007
legal aid, 10–010
legal profession, 10–015—10–019

legal representation, 10–069, 10–070
low cost mediations, 10–009, 10–010
meaning, 10–002
mediators
  background, 10–018
  experts, 17–022—17–024
  implementation of settlement, assisting, 10–184
  opening address, 10–073
  preliminary meeting with, 10–032—10–033
national helpline, 10–010
negotiations
  alternative methods, 10–135
  approaches, 10–107—10–109
  communication skills, 10–136—10–138
  emotions, dealing with, 10–127—10–134
  evaluative mode, 10–139—10–141
  first separate meetings, 10–104—10–106
  initiation, 10–107—10–109
  option development, 10–110—10–114
  professional representatives and advisers working with, 10–118—10–122
  purpose, 10–101
  reality testing, 10–110—10–114
  series of meetings arranged, 10–123—10–126
  shuttle mediation, 10–115—10–117
  substantive, 10–100—10–141
  terms, formulation of, 10–107—10–109
opening the meeting
  establishing the issues, 10–077—10–079
  opening address, 10–073
  opening the session, 10–075, 10–076
  oral submissions, 10–078—10–079
option development, 10–110—10–114
oral submissions, 10–078—10–079
parties
  relationships between, 10–098
personal disputes, 10–017
pledges, ADR, 10–025—10–030
post-termination stage, 10–184—10–187
preliminary communications
  adjournments, 10–058
  administrative preparation, 10–053
  advance information requirements, 10–054
  after-hours arrangements, 10–060
  bespoke processes, 10–057, 10–058
  case summaries, 10–060
  deal strategy, 10–052
  economy considerations, 10–061
  facilities at venue, 10–067, 10–068
  fixing a block of time, 10–056—10–059
  oral submissions, 10–060
  parties, 10–050
  practical arrangements, 10–056
  purpose, 10–050
  requirement, 10–049
  specialists, availability of, 10–060
  technical issues, 10–055
  technological resources, 10–061

INDEX

timetable, 10–056—10–059
timing, 10–050
venue, 10–062—10–066
viability, 10–061
waiting periods, 10–060
pre-mediation phase
   agreement to mediate, 10–044—10–048
   assessment of suitability, 10–034—10–036
   associations, 10–043
   Bar Council, 10–024
   contract clauses, 10–025—10–030
   impetus for mediation, 10–022
   information provision, 10–022, 10–037—10–042
   judicial support, 10–031
   Law Society, 10–024
   pledges, ADR, 10–025—10–030
   preliminary meeting with mediator, 10–032—10–033
   procedural rules, 10–047
   raising public and professional awareness, 10–023, 10–024
   reasons for mediation, 10–022
   trade associations, 10–043
preparation, 17–043—17–047, 17–050—17–052
presentation of case, 17–057—17–060
pro bono work, 10–009
professional bodies
   models, 10–005
   private sector, 10–005—10–008
   role post-termination, 10–185
publicly funded, 10–009, 10–010
range of cases, 10–003, 10–004
rationality, myth of, 10–127
recording outcome, 10–176—10–183
rights, influence of, 10–015, 10–016
session, opening, 10–075, 10–076
settlement
   implementation, 10–184
   non-binding proposals, 10–164—10–168
   written memorandum, 10–176—10–183
shuttle mediation, 10–115—10–117
specialist information, 10–099
specialist mediators, 10–011—10–013
stages
   concluding mediation, 10–176—10–183
   deadlock, 10–142—10–175
   information gathering, 10–083—10–099
   negotiations, 10–100—10–141
   opening meeting, 10–075—10–079
   post-mediation, 10–184—10–187
   preliminary communications and preparation, 10–049—10–072
   pre-mediation stage, 10–022—10–048
   setting agenda, 10–080—10–082
symbolism, 10–158, 10–159
trade associations, 10–043
training, 10–001

venue
   establishing, 10–062—10–066
   facilities, 10–067, 10–068
   location of rooms, 10–065
   number of rooms, 10–063, 10–064
   seating arrangements, 10–166
written memorandum of terms, 10–178

Mediation information and assessment meetings
assessment of suitability for mediation, 9–038
civil proceedings, 5–046—5–047
confidentiality, 16–091
exemptions, 11–021
extension of scheme, 11–020
family mediation, 11–074—11–076
family proceedings, 5–043—5–045, 11–011, 11–020, 11–021
future developments, 22–025, 22–026
generally, 5–012
objectives, 11–021
pre-mediation phase, 9–038

Mediators
advantages of third party involvement, 8–022
agendas, 9–066—9–067
alliances, avoiding, 14–085—14–091
attributes
   meaning, 14–042, 16–005
   types, 14–042
balance, 14–039—14–041
civil and commercial mediation
   background, 10–018
   code of practice, 10–018
   specialists, 10–011—10–013
codes of conduct, 8–027, 8–028
coercion, 8–038—8–043
communication skills, 8–025, 9–085, 9–086
compulsion to enter, 8–043
confidentiality, 8–044—8–046
conflict resolution skills, 8–025
constructive facilitation, 14–098—14–101
court-annexed mediation, 5–033
creativity, 14–033—14–035
determination, no authority to make, 8–038—8–043
emotional sensitivity, 9–091—9–093, 14–082
ethics, 14–011—14–018
evaluation, 9–094, 14–107—14–111
existing attributes and qualities, 14–002
experts
   civil and commercial mediation, 17–022—17–024
   family mediation, 17–025—17–029
facilitation, 8–033—8–037, 14–106
flexibility, 14–036—14–038
fundamental qualities, 14–008—14–018
gang mediation, 12–031
generally, 14–001—14–006
helping parties to hear, 14–056—14–059
host role, 14–112—14–116
impartiality, 8–027—8–032

535

information gathering, 14–105
interests in outcome, 8–031
judges, 5–024—5–031
language skills, 14–064—14–068
lateral thinking, 8–022
links to parties, 8–029, 8–030
listening skills, 14–043—14–045
med-arb, 19–082
mediation construct
    concept of, 14–007—14–041
metaphors, use of, 14–069—14–072
model code, 8–028
negotiation
    facilitating, 8–033—8–037
    skills, 8–026
neutrality, 8–027—8–032
new approach needed, 14–002
normalising, 14–073—14–074
parties
    authority derived from, 8–047
    personal empathy, 14–025—14–029
post-termination functions, 9–119
practical skills, 14–009—14–010
presence, 8–021
process management, 14–103, 14–104
qualities
    balance, 14–039—14–041
    creativity, 14–033—14–035
    emotional sensitivity, 14–023—14–030
    ethical awareness, 14–011—14–018
    flexibility, 14–036—14–038
    fundamental, 14–008—14–018
    personal empathy, 14–025—14–029
    practical skills, 14–009—14–010
    sound judgment, 14–020—14–022
    substantial knowledge, 14–012—14–018
    theoretical understanding, 14–008
questioning, 14–052—14–054
reality testing, 9–088—9–090, 9–111, 14–107—14–111
role
    evaluation, 14–107—14–111
    facilitation, 14–106
    generally, 8–002, 14–102
    host, 14–112—14–116
    information gathering, 14–105
    philosophy, 3–023
    process management, 14–103, 14–104
    reality testing, 14–107—14–111
    scribe, 14–117
    settlement supervisor, 14–118
scribe, as, 14–117
settlement supervisor, 14–118
silence, 14–095—14–097
skills
    acknowledging, 14–057—14–060
    alliances, avoiding, 14–085—14–091
    conflict management, 14–075—14–082
    constructive facilitation, 14–098—14–101

expression of emotions, managing, 14–075—14–082
generally, 9–085, 9–086
helping parties to hear, 14–049—14–051
language, 14–064—14–068
lateral thinking, 14–083, 14–084
learned or intuitive, 14–042
listening, 14–043—14–045
meaning, 14–005
metaphors, use of, 14–069—14–072
mutualising, 14–061—14–063
non-verbal communication, observing, 14–046—14–048
normalising, 14–073—14–074
problem-solving mode, encouraging, 14–092—14–094
questioning, 14–052—14–054
reframing, 14–064—14–068
silence, 14–095—14–097
summarising, 14–055, 14–056
triangulation, understanding, 14–085—14–091
sound judgment, 14–020—14–022
specialists
    civil and commercial mediation, 10–011—10–013
substantial knowledge, having, 14–012—14–018
theoretical understanding, 14–008
third party role, 8–022, 8–023
training, 14–119
    generally, 3–066
triangulation, understanding, 14–085—14–091
use, 8–021—8–026
values, attitudes and beliefs
    assumptions, 16–036—16–038
    conflict, attitude to, 16–030—16–031
    ethics, 16–004
    neutrality, 16–026—16–027
    personal, 16–028—16–038
    rationality/emotionality, 16–041—16–045
withdrawal of power from, 8–047
working principles, 9–066—9–067
MIAMs
    see **Mediation information and assessment meetings**
Mini-trials
appointment of neutral adviser, 19–037—19–039
assessment, 19–060
assessment of success, 19–055
cases suitable for, 19–050, 19–051
cases unsuitable for, 19–052
concept, 19–032—19–036, 19–039
conduct, 19–042
confidentiality, 19–041
costs, 19–041, 19–056
cross-examination, absence of, 19–057
disadvantages, 19–056

INDEX

early stage of dispute, at, 19–054
Executive Tribunal, 19–035
hearings, 19–034
information gathering, 19–041
meaning, 19–059
mock jury, 19–059
negotiations, 19–033
origins, 19–032
outline, 2–031
pleadings, after closing of, 19–053
preparation, 19–040—19–041
privilege, 19–041
procedure
    appointment of neutral adviser, 19–037—19–039
    conduct, 19–042
    preparation, 19–040—19–041
    subject matter, 19–041
purpose, 19–033—19–036
representation, 19–041, 19–042
role of neutral adviser, 19–041, 19–043—19–046
settlement
    negotiations, 19–047—19–049
    recording, 19–048
settlement following, 19–041
structure, 19–036, 19–042
subject matter, 19–041
suspension of litigation, 19–041
timetable, 19–041
timing, 19–053—19–054
United Kingdom, 19–061
United States, 19–059
use of term, 19–032
uses, 19–058
venue, 19–041
witnesses, 19–041, 19–042

Misrepresentation
remedies, 4–094

Money laundering
confidentiality, 15–106—15–113

Multi-door courthouse
assessment of concept, 5–071
courts as gateway to ADR, 5–067—071
implementation, 5–070
influence of concept, 5–071
intake officers, 5–069
meaning, 5–001
Nigeria, 5–071
origins, 5–067—069
role, 5–071
Singapore, 5–071

Multi-party disputes
co-mediation, 9–123
draft statements, 9–123
effect, 9–120, 9–121
environmental mediation, 9–122
examples, 9–120
generally, 9–120
length of meetings, 9–123
oral presentation, 9–123
planning, 9–123
practical issues, 9–123—9–126
public issue mediation, 9–123
settlement, 9–120
time between meetings, 9–123
written statements, 9–123

Natural justice
arbitrators, 6–003
expert determination, 7–034, 7–040

Negotiation
anchoring principle, 4–051, 4–054, 4–055
approaches, 4–004
BATNA, 4–008, 4–010
breaking off, 4–095
changing frame of reference, 4–054
communication skills, 9–085, 9–086
competitive theory
    distributional, 4–026
    distributive, 4–026
    goodwill, 4–027
    interest-based approaches, 4–031, 4–032, 4–033
    positional, 4–026
    power-based negotiation, 4–026
    problem-solving approach, 4–029
    responses, 4–029
    strategies, 4–028
continuation, 4–057—062
culture
    approach, 4–075
    aspects, 4–073
    community, 4–073
    diversity, 4–074, 4–075
    flexibility, 4–075
    geographical, 4–073
    industrial, 4–073
    sensitivity, 4–074
emotions, 4–059, 4–082—085
extreme demands, 4–053
fair divisions, creating, 4–036
false choices, 4–032
family mediation
    caucuses, 11–128—130
    children's issues, 11–126—127
    communication skills, 11–113
    decision-making, 11–122—125
    emotional sensitivity, 11–115—117
    facilitation, 11–122—125
    hybrid processes, 11–128—130
    joint sessions, 11–105
    option development, 11–107—109
    parenting plans, 11–126—127
    process management, 11–118, 11–119
    reality-testing, 11–120—121
    separate meetings, 11–128—130
framing, 4–059
fundamental attribution error, 4–059

game theory, 4–035
gender
  effectiveness, 4–080
  parties, 4–076
  perceptions, 4–077, 4–078, 4–079
  relevant factors, 4–077
  stereotypes, 4–077
good faith
  duties, 4–086—095
  United States, 4–088
information release and exchange, 4–060
integrative negotiation, 4–006
learning, 4–002, 4–005
legal history, 3–007
legal representation
  approaches, 17–064—068
  bottom lines, 17–066
  conduct, 17–066
  confidentiality, 17–066
  courtesy, 17–066
  experience, using, 17–068
  final offers, 17–066
  realistic assessment, 17–067
  respect, 17–066
  settlement proposals, 17–066
  support for client, 17–066
litigation, 2–010—014
meaning, 4–001
mediation
  communication skills, 9–085, 9–086
  emotional sensitivity, 9–091—093
  evaluation, 9–094
  facilitation, 9–075, 9–076
  joint meetings, 9–077
  management of process, 9–073, 9–074
  options, generation and development of, 9–078, 9–079
  perceptions, positions and proposals, testing, 9–087—090
  separate meetings, 9–077
  skills, 8–026, 9–085, 9–086
  trust and understanding, building, 9–083—084
mini-trials, 19–033
"negotiation dance", 4–045—047, 4–056
neighbourhood and community mediation, 12–058—062
neutral role
  communication, 4–102
  experience and skills, conversion of, 4–101
  functions, 4–102
  relevant principles, 4–100
opening negotiations, 4–048—051
parties, by
  outline, 2–037
perceptions
  gender, 4–078, 4–079
  negotiators, 4–082
  negotiators, about, 4–078

preconceptions, 4–077
psychology, 4–082—085
power
  blurred, 4–069
  both sides, 4–067, 4–070
  existence, 4–067
  forms, 4–067, 4–068
  irrationality, 4–068
  realities, understanding of, 4–072
  use, 4–070
practical aspects
  anchoring principle, 4–051, 4–054, 4–055
  changing frame of reference, 4–054
  continuation of negotiation, 4–057—063
  momentum, 4–061
  "negotiation dance", 4–045—047
  opening negotiations, 4–048—051
  overview, 4–038
  preparation, 4–042—044
  responses to proposals, 4–052—056
  set-up, 4–042—044
  symbolism, 4–062
  unrealistic demands, 4–053
  zone of possible agreement, 4–045—047
preparation, 4–042—044
principles, 4–007
problem-solving approach
  best alternative to a negotiated agreement (BATNA), 4–008
  competitive approach, 4–029
  creative solutions, 4–025
  illustration, 4–010, 4–017, 4–018
  integrative negotiation, 4–006
  joint gains, creating, 4–016
  positive no's, 4–019—024
  principled rejection, 4–019—024
  principles, 4–006—025
  relationships, building, 4–013
  transaction barriers, 4–011
  underlying needs, 4–014
  value, creating, 4–015—018
  worst alternative to a negotiated agreement (WATNA), 4–009
psychological and emotional factors, 4–082—085
representatives
  outline, 2–032
responses to proposals, 4–052—056
rights-based arbitration, 4–033
risk aversion, 4–059
risk intuition, 4–059
ritualisation, 4–034
set-up, 4–042—044
shared values, 3–006—011
skills
  meaning, 4–064
socio-anthropology, 4–034
strategies
  factors affecting, 4–066

INDEX

meaning, 4–064
  style and theory, 4–065
style
  meaning, 4–064
  strategy and theory, 4–065
symbolism, 4–062
theories
  competitive approach, 4–026—030
  game theory, 4–035
  interest-based problem solving, 4–006—025
  overview, 4–005
  rights-based negotiation, 4–033
  socio-anthropology, 4–034
trade disputes, 13–047—051
training, 4–004
unrealistic demands, 4–053
value creators and value claimers, 4–031
values, 4–081
zone of agreement, 4–045—047

Neighbourhood and community mediation
adaption of concept, 12–002, 12–003
agendas, 12–049—12–055, 12–055
assessment of suitability, 12–040—12–044
background, 12–005
boundary disputes, 12–012
charities, 12–034
codes of practice, 12–005
co-mediators, 12–038
commitment to mediate, 12–040—12–044
community mediation
  meaning, 12–004
conclusion, 12–066—12–068
conduct of mediation, 12–051
costs, 12–033
deadlock, 12–063—12–065
development, 12–001—12–006
disputes
  boundary issues, 12–012
  children's behaviour, 12–010
  environmental issues, 12–013
  eyesores, 12–013
  generally, 12–015
  harassment, 12–009
  inter-group disputes, 12–015
  neighbours, 12–007—12–015
  noise problems, 12–008
  parking, 12–014
  pets and other animals, 12–011
  rights of way, 12–014
  scope, 12–007, 12–032
  social conflicts, 12–015
elder mediation, 12–023
emotional sensitivity, 12–037
England, 12–005
extrinsic factors, 12–070
flexibility and informality, need for, 12–073
funding, 12–034
future-focus, 12–060
gangs, 12–024—12–031

information gathering, 12–056, 12–057
inter-group disputes, 12–015
issues, establishing, 12–049—12–055
Mediation UK, 12–005
mediators, 12–050
models, 12–034
negotiations, 12–058—12–062
noisy neighbours, 12–008
opening the meetings, 12–049—12–055
origins, 12–035
other parties, involvement of, 12–072
outcome, recording, 12–068
overseas use, 12–002
peer mediation, 12–016—12–022
post-mediation stage, 12–069
power imbalances, 12–071
practical solutions, 12–061
preliminary communications and preparation, 12–045—12–048
pre-mediation phase, 12–049—12–053
problem-solving, 12–058, 12–059
process, 12–037—12–039
resolution services, 12–033—12–036
schools, 12–016—12–022
scope, 12–004
Scotland, 12–006
services, 12–033—12–036
social conflicts, 12–015
terminology, 12–004
traditional concept, adaptation of, 12–003
umbrella body, 12–005
venue, 12–049

Neutral fact-finding experts
see **Experts**

Neutral non-binding evaluation
see **Non-binding evaluation processes**

Neutrality
mediators, 8–027—032

NHS trusts
Halsey v Milton Keynes General NHS Trust, 5–061—5–066, 17–012—17–017

Nigeria
multi-door courthouses, 5–071

Noise
neighbourhood and community mediation, 12–008

Non-binding evaluation processes
aim, 19–018
challenging assessment of merits, 19–014
comprehensive opinions, 19–014
considerations, 19–018
deadlock, 19–025—028
definition, 19–011—017
devil's advocate, 19–014
facilitation, 19–015—017
family mediation, 19–027
formal, 19–014
impartiality, 19–013

informality, 19–014
opposition, 19–029—031
outline, 2–034
parameters for negotiation, 19–022—024
private reservations, 19–014
realism, 19–019—021
reasons, 19–005—010
training, 19–029
"Non-binding evaluative processes"
see **Early neutral evaluation; Mediation; Mini-trials**
adjudication, conversion to, 19–003
expression of a view, 19–011—19–017
neutral evaluation, 19–011—19–017
off-the-record discussions, 19–011
overview, 19–001—19–004
reasons for evaluating, 19–006—19–010
Ombudsman
assessment of procedure, 18–020
background, 18–001—18–003
challenges, 18–035—18–040
complaints adjudication, 18–041—18–042
control, 2–026
developments, 18–035—18–040
EU Directive on alternative dispute resolution for consumers, 18–030—18–034
examples, 18–005, 18–007—18–011
exclusions, 18–014
Financial Ombudsman Service, 18–017—18–018
formal complaints, 18–012
functions, 18–004—18–006
human rights, 2–006
internet, 20–009
investigations, 18–015
Legal Ombudsman, 18–007, 18–016
meaning, 18–004
online ombudsmen, 18–023—18–029
operation, 18–012—18–020
origins, 18–006
  examples, 18–006
outline, 2–026
Parliamentary and Health Service Ombudsman, 18–006
Parliamentary Commissioner, 18–006
powers, 18–004
pre-complaint opportunities, 18–013
range of institutions, 18–007—18–011
remedies, 18–021—18–022
role, 18–004—18–006
Online dispute resolution
background, 20–001—20–004
codes of practice, 20–009
communications, 20–002
confidentiality, 20–032, 20–033
cross-border disputes, 20–031
development, 2–050
disputes
  arbitration, 20–017, 20–018

arising online, 20–005—20–011
domain names, 20–010, 20–011
double-blind bidding, 20–015
real world disputes, 20–012—20–021
visual blind bidding, 20–016
double-blind bidding, 20–015
eBay, 20–007
enforcement, 20–034—20–037
EU Alternative/ODR platform, 20–027—20–030
future developments, 22–033
harmonisation, 20–024—20–031
implementation, 20–025
Internet Ombudsman, 20–009
jurisdiction, 20–038—20–039
Money Claims Online, 20–040—20–042, 22–033
Online Ombuds Office, 20–005, 20–006
opportunities, 20–003
real world disputes, 20–012—20–021
resources, 20–022
retail customers, 20–008
scope, 20–004
traditional ADR, support for, 20–019—20–021
UNCITRAL, 20–026
uses of information technology, 20–022, 20–036
visual blind bidding, 20–016
Oral submissions
civil and commercial mediation, 10–078—079
early neutral evaluation, 19–071
mediation, 9–123
multi-party disputes, 9–123
Part 36 offers
without prejudice communications, 15–075—15–078
Pilot schemes
county court mediation, 5–034—035
family mediation, 11–006
Pledges
civil and commercial mediation
  pre-mediation phase, 10–025—10–030
Power imbalances
caution, mediation to proceed with, 16–119, 16–120
ethics, 16–008
husband and wife, between, 16–097
litigation, 16–096
mediators
  assumption of role, 16–102—104
  employment disputes, 16–101
  empowerment, 16–107, 16–108
  inappropriate use of mediation, 16–118
  redressing balance, 16–101—116
  role, 16–099—116
  steps taken to redress balance, 16–109—116
  transformation, 16–106
power
  analysis of dispute, 16–095
  covert, 16–098
  equality, 16–100

INDEX

exercise, 16–094
forms, 16–093—116
overt, 16–098
perceptions, 16–094
shifting, 16–094
Pre-action protocols
conduct, 5–009
examples, 5–010
Family Procedure Rules, 5–012
fundamental principle, 5–011
purpose, 3–063
support for ADR, 3–063
Pre-mediation phase
advice centres, 9–033
agreement to mediate, 9–041—043
assessment of suitability of mediation, 9–037—038
civil and commercial mediation
  agreement to mediate, 10–044—048
  assessment of suitability of mediation, 10–034—036
  associations, 10–043
  Bar Council, 10–024
  contract clauses, 10–025—030
  information provision, 10–022, 10–027—042
  judicial support, 10–031
  Law Society, 10–024
  pledges, ADR, 10–025—030
  procedural rules, 10–047
  raising public and professional awareness, 10–023, 10–024
  reasons for mediation, 10–022
  trade associations, 10–043
codes of practice, 9–042
commencement of mediation, 9–044—047
commitment to mediate, 9–039—043
contracts, 9–041
costs sanctions, 9–035
decision to mediate, 9–034—036
encouragement to mediate, 9–035
generally, 9–029
helplines, 9–033
information provision, 9–033
intake session, 9–033
legal representation, 17–034—039
meaning, 9–032
mediation information and assessment meetings, 9–038
neighbourhood and community mediation, 12–040—046
preparation
  commercial and civil disputes, 17–043—047, 17–050—052
  family cases, 17–048—049, 17–053—054
  trade disputes, 13–036
"Private judging"
costs, 2–019
enforcement of judgment, 7–060
jurisdiction, 21–004

legal principles, 7–060
meaning, 7–059
outline, 2–019
procedure, 7–060
process, 7–059
standard of proof, 7–060
United Kingdom, 7–061
United States, 7–061
Privilege
see also **Confidentiality; Without prejudice communications**
children, mediation concerning, 15–072—15–074
Civil Procedure Rules, 15–075—15–078
classes, 15–043, 15–044
compellability of witnesses, 15–038
competence of witnesses, 15–038—15–041
confidentiality distinguished, 15–002
contracts, 15–114—15–117
contractual obligations, 15–047
criminal proceedings, 15–040
cross-border disputes, 15–118—15–122
developments, 15–004—15–011
diplomatic immunity, 15–041
EU Directive on Cross-Border Mediation, 15–010
exclusion by court
  determining existence of agreement, 15–094—15–096
  interpretation of agreement, 15–103—15–105
  mediation stipulated by court, 15–080—15–093
  negligence, 15–097—15–102
financial dispute resolution appointments, 5–019, 15–078
general rule of evidence, 15–038
incompetent witnesses, 15–039
legal issues, 15–002
legal professional privilege, 15–048—15–052
mediation, 8–044—8–046, 15–123—15–144
mini-trials, 19–041
moral obligations, 15–047
professional obligations, 15–047
professional privilege, 15–048—15–052
public interest immunity, 15–045
qualified right, 15–009
reconciliation, 15–068—15–071
withholding information, ground for, 15–037
Privilege against self-incrimination
meaning, 15–046
Procurement
project mediation, 1–032
Professional bodies
see also **Law Society; Professionals**
Bar Council, 16–020
civil and commercial mediation
  models, 10–005
  private sector, 10–005—10–008
conflict of interest, 16–056

541

current position, 3–066
ethics, 16–010—16–020
legal profession
  Bar, 16–020
  Law Society, 16–012—16–019
scope, 3–066
Professional organisations
civil and commercial mediation
  regional groups, 10–008
"Professional practice consultancy"
consultancy rather than supervision,
  11–061—064
Professionals
see also **Ethics; Mediators; Professional bodies**
attributes, 3–036, 3–036—3–038
personality, 3–038
sensitivity, 3–038
skills, 3–036—3–038
Promissory estoppel
remedies, 4–094
"Proportionate dispute resolution"
terminology, 1–011
Psychotherapy
counselling distinguished, 11–024
family mediation
  availability, 11–023
  background, 11–023
  resources, 11–026
  theory, 11–024—11–026
meaning, 11–024
Public interest immunity
privilege, 15–045
Public policy
alternative dispute resolution, 3–008
without prejudice communications, 15–054
Rehearings
court-annexed arbitration, 5–079
Republic of Ireland
confidentiality, 15–008
Restorative justice
aims, 12–086
alternative approaches, 12–074
cautioning, 12–091, 12–092
circles, 12–108
conferences, 12–103, 12–104
development, 12–080
emotional sensitivity, 12–097, 12–098
Fife scheme, 12–107
forms, 12–075
meaning, 12–085
offences, 12–095—12–101
origins of concept, 12–074
policing, 12–095
principles, 12–086, 12–087
process, 12–078
programmes
  circles, 12–108
  family group conferencing, 12–103—12–107

victim/offender mediation, 12–088—12–090
young offenders projects, 12–093, 12–094
rationale, 12–076—12–079, 12–082, 12–083—12–087
schools, 12–109—12–111
service providers, 12–079
street justice, 12–095
Thames Valley Police scheme, 12–105
victim-offender mediation
  discussion opportunity, 12–081
  establishment, 12–081
  family group conferencing, 12–103—12–107
  programmes, 12–088—12–090
  reparation schemes, 12–081
  terminology, 12–082
  United States, 12–081
  young offenders, 12–093, 12–094
youth offenders, 12–103—12–107
Right to fair and public hearing
mandatory ADR, 5–072—5–076
Rights-based arbitration
see **Negotiation**
Rights-based mediation
see **Mediation**
Risk assessment
civil and commercial mediation, 10–143—151
Sanctions
court imposition where ADR not attempted, 5–061—5–066
Schools
mediation, 12–016—12–022
restorative justice, 12–109—12–111
Scotland
confidentiality, 15–006
Seat of arbitration
agreement, 21–039, 21–042
Brussels I Convention, 21–040
competing claims, 21–040
importance, 21–039
international disputes, 21–041
Settlement
arbitration
  statistics, 6–048
  use, 6–051
arb-med, 19–098
civil and commercial mediation
  implementation, 10–184
  non-binding proposals, 10–164—10–168
  written memorandum, 10–178—10–183
Civil Procedure Rules, 5–003
confidentiality, 16–088
costs, 5–080
deadlock, 9–114
dispute resolution, 1–035—1–039
early neutral evaluation, 19–064
legal representation
  implementation, 17–086
  terms, drafting, 17–075—17–079

INDEX

vetting proposals, 17–080—17–084
mediation, 8–050, 8–051, 9–012, 9–013
mini-trials
    negotiations, 19–047—19–049
    recording, 19–048
supervision, 14–118
terms
    examples, 3–024
    mediation, 3–024
without prejudice communications, 15–059, 15–064

Shuttle mediation
see **"Caucuses"**

Singapore
court-annexed ADR, 5–100—5–101
multi-door courthouses, 5–071

Single joint experts
Civil Procedure Rules, 7–044
expert determination distinguished, 7–043—7–045

Small Claims Mediation Service
assessment of scheme, 5–021
costs, 5–021
financial limits, 5–022
pilot schemes, 5–022
satisfaction levels, 5–022
timescale, 5–022

Solicitors
see **Law Society; Legal representation**

Statutory adjudication
adjudicators, 7–003
adversarial approach, 7–012
appointment of adjudicator, 7–009
arbitration, 7–011
Arbitration Act 1996, 7–006
authority, 7–003
binding, 7–003
commencement of proceedings, 7–009
common threads, 7–003
context, 7–012—7–013
costs, 7–011
decisions, 7–011
enforcement, 7–011
Housing Grants, Construction and Regeneration Act 1996, 7–004—7–007
impartiality, 7–008
information, 7–010
interest, 7–011
interim nature, 7–013
mandatory adjudication, 7–005
nature of procedure, 7–003
notice, 7–008, 7–009
objective, 7–005
outline, 2–024
outline of process, 7–008—7–011
provisions, 7–004—7–007
rationale, 7–002
referral notice, 7–009
Scheme for Construction Contracts, 7–007

terms of reference, 7–003
time limits, 7–008
timing of adjudication, 7–003

Stay of proceedings
disputes, 1–018
expert determinations, 1–018

Summary jury trial
see **Mini-trials**

Technology and Construction Court
Court Settlement Process, 5–015—5–018, 19–079
directing ADR processes, 5–051, 5–052
early neutral evaluation, 5–014
mediation, 5–014

Trade associations
codes of practice, 10–043

Trade disputes
see also **Acas**
agendas, 13–042, 13–043
arbitration, 13–014
background, 13–001—13–004
BATNA, 13–057
collective conciliation
    deadlock, 13–031
    meaning, 13–028
    process, 13–029, 13–030
compromise agreements, 13–032—13–033
conciliation
    collective conciliation, 13–028—13–031
    individual conciliation, 13–023—13–027
    meaning, 13–008
    practice, 13–022—13–033
    procedure, 13–022—13–033
deadlock, 13–052—13–057
employment and workplace issues distinguished, 13–015—13–016
history, 13–001—13–004
information gathering, 13–044—13–046
legislative history, 13–001—13–004
mediation
    agendas, 13–042, 13–043
    agreement to mediate, 13–036
    case summaries, 13–041
    conclusion of mediation, 13–058, 13–059
    deadlock, 13–052—13–057
    establishing the issues, 13–042, 13–043
    information gathering, 13–044—13–046
    meaning, 13–008
    negotiations, 13–047—13–051
    opening the meeting, 13–042, 13–043
    post-mediation, 13–060, 13–061
    preliminary communications, 13–038—13–041
    pre-mediation phase, 13–036
    preparation, 13–038—13–041
    recording outcome, 13–058, 13–059
    representation, 13–040
    timetable, 13–039
    uses, 13–035

negotiations, 13–047—13–051
pre-mediation phase, 13–036
processes, 13–007—13–014
rationale of use of ADR, 13–017—13–02421
risk assessment, 13–057
Training
civil and commercial mediation, 10–001
negotiations, 4–004
Triangulation
co-mediation, 14–091
understanding, 14–085—091
Tribunals
Administrative Justice and Tribunals Council, 7–058
examples, 7–056
Franks Report, 7–051
HM Courts and Tribunals Service, 7–058
legal history, 7–051—7–053
outline, 2–020
process, 7–055
range of administrative tribunals, 7–056, 7–057, 7–058
summary of law, 7–054
Tribunals, Courts and Enforcement Act 2007, 7–053, 7–054
UNCITRAL
Model Law
amiable composition, 6–045
international arbitration, 6–008
online dispute resolution, 20–026
United States
confidentiality, 15–007, 15–024
court-annexed ADR, 5–087—5–088
court-annexed arbitration, 5–087—5–088
family mediation, 11–064
good faith, 4–088
growth of ADR, 3–067
neutral fact-finding experts, 19–104
private judging, 7–061

summary jury trial, 19–059
victim/offender mediation, 12–081
"WATNA"
civil and commercial mediation, 10–152—10–153
examples, 4–010
family mediation, 11–149—11–152
trade disputes, 13–057
Without prejudice communications
ADR context, 15–065
blackmail, 15–063
compromise agreements, 15–063
costs, 15–075—15–078
delay, 15–063
estoppel, 15–063
express offer made subject to, 15–063
fraud, 15–063
general rule, 15–060
matrimonial conciliation, 15–063
meaning, 15–053
misrepresentation, 15–063
nature of rule, 15–058
Part 36 offers, 15–075—15–078
parties, privilege of, 15–066, 15–067
perjury, 15–063
preliminary meetings, 10–033
public policy, 15–054
scope of protection, 15–061
settlements, 15–059, 15–064
undue influence, 15–063
use of term, 15–055
waiver, 15–060
Witness statements
litigation, 2–011
Worst alternative to a negotiated agreement
see **"WATNA"**
Zone of agreement
see **Negotiation**